Media Effects

Advances in Theory and Research

LEA'S COMMUNICATION SERIES
Jennings Bryant/Dolf Zillmann, General Editors

Selected titles in Communication Theory and Methodology subseries
(Jennings Bryant, series advisor) include:

Berger • Planning Strategic Interaction: Attaining Goals Through
Communicative Action

Dennis/Wartella • American Communication Research: The
Remembered History

Ellis • Crafting Society: Ethnicity, Class, and Communication Theory

Greene • Message Production: Advances in Communication Theory

Heath/Bryant • Human Communication Theory and Research:
Concepts, Contexts, and Challenges, Second Edition

Olson • Hollywood Planet: Global Media and the Competitive
Advantage of Narrative Transparency

Perry • American Pragmatism and Communication Research

Riffe/Lacy/Fico • Analyzing Media Messages: Using Quantitative
Content Analysis in Research

Salwen/Stacks • An Integrated Approach to Communication Theory
and Research

For a complete list of titles in LEA's Communication Series, please
contact Lawrence Erlbaum Associates, Publishers, at www.erlbaum.com.

Media Effects

Advances in Theory and Research

Second Edition

Edited by

Jennings Bryant
Dolf Zillmann
University of Alabama

2002

LAWRENCE ERLBAUM ASSOCIATES, PUBLISHERS
Mahwah, New Jersey   London

Acquisitions Editor: Linda Bathgate
Editorial Assistant: Karin Bates
Cover Design: Kathryn Houghtaling Lacey
Textbook Production Manager: Paul Smolenski
Full Service & Composition: Black Dot Group/An AGT Company
Text and Cover Printer: Hamilton Printing Company

This book was typeset in 10/12 pt. Palatino, Bold, and Italic.
The heads were typeset in Palatino Bold and Palatino Bold Italic.

Lawrence Erlbaum Associates, Inc., Publishers
10 Industrial Avenue
Mahwah, New Jersey 07430

Library of Congress Cataloging-in-Publication Data

Media effects : advances in theory and research / Jennings Bryant & Dolf Zillmann,
   editors—2nd ed.
      p. cm. — (LEA's communication series)
   Includes bibliographical references and index.
      ISBN 0-8058-3863-5 (case : alk. paper) — ISBN 0-8058-3864-3 (pbk.: alk. paper)
      1. Mass media—United States—Psychological aspects. 2. Mass media—Social
aspects—United States. 3. Mass media—Political aspects—United States. 4. Mass
media—United States—Influence. I. Bryant, Jennings. II. Zillmann, Dolf. III. Series.
HN90.M3 M415 2002
302.12—dc21   2001055656

Contents

Preface

We hope that your responses to the chapters that make up the second edition of *Media Effects: Advances in Theory and Research* are similar to ours when we initially read the material as draft chapters. Obviously, an editor's evaluation of any foot-tall stack of chapter manuscripts is iterative and cumulative. In this instance, as the pile of unread, unedited drafts shrank, and the stack of edited manuscripts grew, we became happier and happier—and not entirely because the end of the arduous editing task was at hand. The bulk of our euphoria can more accurately be attributed to our convergent appraisals of the chapters: "This is undoubtedly the finest set of chapters we have ever had the opportunity to edit!"

To our wonderful contributors, who individually and collectively went the extra mile to ensure that each chapter is a work of art, we are exceedingly grateful. To our book adopters and readers, let us assure you that the contributors have presented not only the state of the art in their respective areas of expertise in media effects but also the art of the state.

Depending on how you count it, this is either the second or third edition of *Media Effects.* First there was *Perspectives on Media Effects* (1986), the progenitor of the clan. Designed primarily as a scholarly volume and reference text, the 16-chapter *Perspectives* received rather widespread adoption as a textbook. Therefore, when we updated the volume, we revised it considerably to better accommodate classroom use, and the offspring was renamed *Media Effects: Advances in Theory and Research* (1994). But, despite the name change, *Media Effects* owed much to its direct ancestor, including its 16-chapter format.

Eight years later, when it was time (or, as some adopters have suggested, long beyond time) to edit a new edition, we found it impossible to limit *Media Effects* to 16 chapters; in fact, we found it incredibly difficult to limit the volume to the 22 chapters you hold in your hands. Why? Media effects is a burgeoning field. Moreover, as new research domains have emerged and their traditions have matured, few have withered and died. It's an editor's and publisher's nightmare! On the other hand, the bounty of research certainly qualifies as marked progress in this important area of inquiry. But we certainly hope that the growth in size of this volume does not lead to carpel tunnel syndrome, "law school elbow," or the like.

What's new in this edition of media effects? First, all 16 chapters carried forward from the previous edition have been extensively revised and updated, some with the original authors, others with a new cast of contributors. Second, we have added several chapters on important topics that have received new or renewed attention of late from the media effects community of scholars: media consumption and its underlying reception processes, intermedia processes, educational and prosocial effects, individual differences in media effects, news effects on issue perception, and third-person effects.

Several things have remained the same from edition to edition. First is our respect for and appreciation of the contributors for their superlative work. Thank you, one and all. Second is our admiration for the good folk at Lawrence Erlbaum Associates, who have remained steadfast in their commitment to publishing quality scholarship in communication. Thank you, Larry, Linda, Joe, Art, and many, many others. You have become good friends as well as valued professional associates.

Finally, both *Perspectives on Media Effects* and the first edition of *Media Effects* were dedicated to our mutual best friends, Jennings Bryant, Sr., and Elvira Bryant. In the two decades that have elapsed since we began this series of volumes on media effects, our love for and devotion to these two special people have continued to flourish. We thus also dedicate the second edition of *Media Effects: Advances in Theory and Research* to our two best friends.

—*Jennings Bryant*
—*Dolf Zillmann*

Chapter 1

News Influence on Our Pictures of the World

MAXWELL McCOMBS
University of Texas at Austin

AMY REYNOLDS
Indiana University at Bloomington

Millions of Americans spent weeks using the media to keep track of the unique events surrounding the 2000 presidential contest between George W. Bush and Al Gore. Not only did they watch and read to find out the latest events and changes surrounding the vote count and the ensuing legal battles after Election Day, they also looked to the media for some direction on what issues to think about prior to election day. Through their day-to-day selection and display of the news, journalists, editors, and news directors focused our attention and influenced our perceptions of what were the most important issues in this contentious election. This ability to influence the salience of topics on the public agenda has come to be called the agenda-setting role of the news media.

Establishing this salience among the public so that an issue becomes the focus of public attention, thought, and perhaps even action is the initial stage in the formation of public opinion. Although many issues compete for public attention, only a few are successful in reaching the public agenda. The news media exert significant influence on our perceptions of what are the most salient issues of the day. Bernard Cohen says it best with his observation that the news media may not be successful in telling people what to think, but they are stunningly successful in telling them what to think about (Cohen, 1963). The news media can set the agenda for public thought and discussion.

Because so many people use the media to help them sort through important political issues before they vote, scholars have spent nearly 60 years studying the effect of mass communication on voters. In a benchmark study during the 1940 U.S. presidential election, Paul Lazarsfeld and his colleagues at Columbia University collaborated with pollster

1

Elmo Roper to conduct seven rounds of interviews with voters in Erie County, Ohio (Lazarsfeld, Berelson, & Gaudet, 1944). Those surveys and many subsequent investigations in other settings over the next 20 years found little evidence of major mass communication effects on attitudes and opinions. Many scholars have argued that the reason little evidence was found is because these early studies focused on the news media and mass communication's ability to persuade voters and change their attitudes. Traditional journalism and its notion of objectivity would suggest that the media are trying to inform, not persuade. These studies did support that notion, demonstrating that people acquired information from the mass media, even if they didn't change their opinions.

A limited-effects model for mass communication emerged from these early election studies. Summarized in the law of minimal consequences (Klapper, 1960), this notion ran counter to the ideas that Walter Lippmann (1922), the intellectual father of agenda-setting, proposed back in the early 1920s. Lippmann's opening chapter in *Public Opinion*, which is titled "The World Outside and the Pictures in Our Heads," summarized the agenda-setting idea even though he did not use that phrase. His thesis was that the news media, our windows to the vast world beyond our direct experience, determine our cognitive maps of that world. Public opinion, argued Lippmann, responds not to the environment, but to the pseudoenvironment constructed by the news media.

After decades of exploring the cognitive, long-term implications of daily journalism, researchers have discovered that media audiences not only learn factual information from exposure to news, but that people also learn about the importance of topics in the news based on how the news media emphasize those topics. This shift in perspective away from the law of minimal consequences took hold in the 1960s. During the 1968 presidential campaign, McCombs and Shaw (1972) launched the first study that would support Lippmann's notion that the information provided by the news media plays a key role in the construction of our pictures of reality. Their central hypothesis was that the mass media set the agenda of issues for a political campaign by influencing the salience of issues among voters. Those issues emphasized in the news come to be regarded over time as important by members of the public. McCombs and Shaw called this influence agenda-setting.

To test this hypothesis that the media agenda can set the public agenda, McCombs and Shaw conducted a survey among a sample of randomly selected undecided voters in Chapel Hill, North Carolina. In the survey, these undecided voters were asked what they thought were the key issues of the day, regardless of what the candidates might say. The issues named in the survey were ranked according to the percentage of voters naming each one to yield a description of the public agenda.

Concurrent with this survey of voters, the nine major news sources used by these voters—five local and national newspapers, two television networks, and two newsmagazines—were collected and content analyzed. The rank order of issues on the media agenda was determined by the number of news stories devoted to each issue. The high degree of correspondence between these two agendas of political and social issues established a central link in what has become a substantial chain of evidence for an agenda-setting role of the press.

Seeking additional support for Lippmann's perspective and their concept, McCombs and Shaw juxtaposed agenda-setting and the concept of selective perception, which often had been cited as the explanation for minimal media effects. This perspective assumes that individuals minimize their exposure to nonsupportive information and maximize their exposure to supportive information. If the correlation between the voters' agenda and the total news agenda were the highest, it would be evidence of agenda-setting. If the correlation with the voters' preferred party's agenda in the news coverage were higher, it would be evidence of selective perception. The vast majority of the Chapel Hill evidence favored an agenda-setting effect.

ACCUMULATED EVIDENCE

Since the Chapel Hill study, more than 350 empirical studies have been conducted on the agenda-setting influence of the news media (Dearing & Rogers, 1996). The accumulated evidence about the agenda-setting influence of the news media on the general public comes from many different geographic and historical settings worldwide and covers numerous types of news media and a wide variety of public issues. The evidence also provides greater detail about the time-order and causal links between the media and public agendas.

Shaw and McCombs' (1977) follow-up to the Chapel Hill study examined a representative sample of all voters in Charlotte, North Carolina, during the summer and fall of the 1972 presidential election and found that the salience of all seven issues on the public agenda was influenced by the pattern of news coverage in the *Charlotte Observer* and network television news.

During the 1976 presidential election, voters in three very different settings—Lebanon, New Hampshire; Indianapolis, Indiana; and Evanston, Illinois—were interviewed nine times between February and December (Weaver, Graber, McCombs, & Eyal, 1981). Simultaneously, election coverage by the three national networks and local newspapers in the three cities were content analyzed. In all three communities, the agenda-setting influence of both television and newspapers was greatest during the spring primaries. Using the correlation statistic, which summarizes the degree of correspondence between the ranking of issues on the media agenda and the ranking of those same issues on the public agenda, the correlation during the spring primaries was +.63. The possible range of scores for the correlation statistic is from +1.0, a perfect correspondence, to 0, no relationship, to −1.0, which represents a perfect inverse relationship. Agenda-setting theory predicts a high positive correlation between the media and public agendas.

Although election settings provide a natural laboratory in which to study agenda-setting effects, the evidence that supports the theory is not limited to elections. Winter and Eyal (1981) took a historical look at the civil rights issue between 1954 and 1976 using 27 Gallup polls. Comparison of the trends in public opinion with the results of a content analysis of the *New York Times'* coverage of civil rights in the weeks immediately prior to each poll yielded a correlation of +.71. Similar findings about the impact of news coverage on trends in public opinion come from an analysis of 11 different issues during a 41-month period in the 1980s (Eaton, 1989). In each of these analyses, the media agenda is based on a mix of television, newspapers, and newsmagazines, whereas the public agenda is based on 13 Gallup polls. All but one of the correlations (the issue of morality) was positive, although a pattern of considerable variability in the strength of the correlations was visible. This calls attention to factors other than media coverage that influence the public's perception and emphasizes that the public mind is not a blank slate waiting to be written on by the mass media. Significant psychological and social factors that impact the public's daily transactions with the mass media will be discussed later in this chapter.

Agenda-setting effects have also been found outside of the United States. In Pamplona, Spain, during the spring of 1995, comparisons of six major concerns on the public agenda with local news coverage showed a high degree of correspondence. The match with the dominant local daily newspaper was +.90. The correlation with the second Pamplona daily was +.72 and +.66 with television news (Canel, Llamas, & Rey, 1996).

In Germany, a look at national public opinion patterns during 1986 through weekly comparisons of the public and media agendas showed that television news coverage had a significant impact on public concern about five issues, including the country's energy supply (Brosius & Kepplinger, 1990). Early in 1986, the energy supply issue had little salience on either the news agenda or the public agenda. But a rapid rise in May on the news agenda was followed within a week by a similar rise on the public agenda. Public concern, which earlier hovered at around 15% of the population, suddenly moved into the 25 to 30% range. When news coverage subsequently declined, so did the size of the constituency expressing concern about Germany's energy supply.

Agenda-setting at the local level occurred in the October 1997 legislative elections in the Buenos Aires metropolitan area (Lennon, 1998). Corruption was prominent on both the public and media agendas throughout the fall, always ranking first or second. In September, the public agenda and the combined issue agenda of five major Buenos Aires newspapers only modestly agreed (+.43). As election day approached in October, the correspondence between the agendas soared to +.80, an increase that suggests considerable learning from the news media in the closing weeks of the election campaign (Weaver, 1996).

These real-world examples of agenda-setting effects are compelling but are not the best evidence for the core, causal proposition of agenda-setting. The best evidence that the news media are the cause of these kinds of effects comes from controlled laboratory experiments, a setting where the theorized cause can be systematically manipulated, subjects are randomly assigned to various versions of the manipulation, and systematic comparisons are made among the outcomes.

Changes in the salience of defense preparedness, pollution, arms control, civil rights, unemployment, and a number of other issues were produced in the laboratory among subjects who viewed TV news programs edited to emphasize a particular issue (Iyengar & Kinder, 1987). A variety of controls were used to show that changes in the salience of the manipulated issue were actually due to exposure to the news agenda. For example, in one experiment, control subjects viewed TV news programs that did not include the issue of defense preparedness. The change in salience of this issue was significantly higher for the test subjects than for the subjects in the control group. In contrast, there were no significant differences between the two groups from before to after viewing the newscasts for seven other issues.

A recent experiment documented the agenda-setting effects of an online newspaper. The salience of racism as a public issue was significantly higher among subjects exposed to various versions of an online newspaper that discussed racism than among those subjects whose online newspaper did not contain a news report on racism (Wang, 2000).

These studies are far from all of the accumulated evidence that supports the theory of agenda-setting. A meta-analysis of 90 empirical agenda-setting studies found a mean correlation of +.53, with most about six points above or below the mean (Wanta & Ghanem, forthcoming). There are, of course, a number of significant influences that shape individual attitudes and public opinion. How a person feels about a particular issue may be rooted in his or her personal experience or in the general culture or exposure to the mass media (Gamson 1992). But the general proposition supported by this accumulation of evidence on agenda-setting is that journalists' daily decisions do significantly influence their audience's picture of the world.

Many events and stories compete for journalists' attention. Because the news media have neither the capacity to gather all information nor the capacity to inform the audience about every single occurrence, they rely on a traditional set of professional norms to guide their daily sampling of the environment. The result is a limited view of the larger environment, something like the highly limited view of the outside world available through a small window.

Three portraits of public opinion—the major issues of the 1960s, the drug issue in the 1980s, and crime in the 1990s—tell us a great deal about the discretion of journalists and the discrepancies that are sometimes found in mass media portrayals of reality. In Funkhouser's (1973) study of public opinion trends during the 1960s, there was no correlation at all between the trends in news coverage of major issues and the reality of these issues. But there was a substantial correlation (+.78) between the patterns of news coverage and the public's perception of what were the most important issues. In the 1980s, there was an increasing trend in news coverage of drugs at a time when there was no change at all in the reality of the drug problem (Reese & Danielian, 1989). And, in the 1990s, there was an increase in the news coverage of crime at a time when there was a decreasing trend in the reality of crime (Ghanem, 1996).

THE ACAPULCO TYPOLOGY

Explorations of agenda-setting effects around the world have observed this mass communication phenomenon from a variety of perspectives. A four-part typology describing these perspectives is frequently referred to as the Acapulco typology because McCombs initially presented it in Acapulco, Mexico, at the invitation of International Communication Association president Everett Rogers. The Acapulco typology contains two dichotomous dimensions. The first dimension distinguishes between two ways of looking at agendas. The focus of attention can be on the entire set of items that define the agenda, or the focus of attention can be narrowed to a single, particular item on the agenda. The second dimension distinguishes between two ways of measuring the salience of items on the agenda, either aggregate measures describing an entire group or population or measures that describe individual responses.

One perspective includes the entire agenda and uses aggregate measures of the population to establish the salience of these items. The original Chapel Hill study took this perspective. For the media agenda, the salience of the issues was determined by the total number of news articles about each issue, whereas the public agenda was determined by the percentage of voters who thought the government should do something about each issue. This *competition* perspective examines an array of issues competing for positions on the agenda.

A second perspective is similar to the early agenda-setting studies with their focus on the entire agenda of items, but shifts its attention to the agenda of each individual. When individuals are asked to rank order a series of issues, there is little evidence of any correspondence at all between those individual rankings and the rank order of those same issues in the news media. This *automaton* perspective is an unflattering view of human behavior. For agenda-setting to occur, there must be individuals who are susceptible to being programmed by the mass media. An individual seldom reproduces to any significant degree the entire agenda of the media.

A third perspective narrows the focus to a single item on the agenda but, like the competition perspective, uses aggregate measures to establish salience. Commonly, the measures are the total number of news stories about the item and the percentage of the public citing an issue as the most important problem facing the country. This perspective is named *natural history* because the focus typically is on the degree of correspondence between the media agenda and the public agenda in the rise and fall of a single item over time. Winter and Eyal's (1981) study of the civil rights issue over a 23-year period is an example of this perspective.

Finally, a fourth perspective, *cognitive portrait*, like the automaton perspective, focuses on the individual, but narrows its observations to the salience of a single agenda item. This perspective is illustrated by the experimental studies of agenda-setting in which the salience of a single issue for an individual is measured before and after viewing news programs where the amount of exposure to various issues is controlled.

The existence of these varied perspectives on the agenda-setting phenomenon, especially an abundance of evidence based on the competition and natural history perspectives, strengthens the degree of confidence about this media effect. The competition perspective provides useful, comprehensive descriptions of the rich, ever-changing mix of mass media content and public opinion at particular points in time. This perspective strives to describe the world as it is. The natural history perspective provides useful descriptions of a single issue, but at the expense of the larger social context. Despite this, knowledge about the dynamics of a single issue over an extended time period is useful for understanding how the process of agenda-setting works. The cognitive portrait perspective also makes a valuable contribution to understanding the dynamics of agenda-setting. From a scholarly viewpoint, evidence generated by both the natural history and cognitive portrait perspectives are absolutely necessary for a detailed how and why explanation of agenda-setting. But the ultimate goal of agenda-setting theory returns us to the competition perspective, which provides a comprehensive view of mass communication and public opinion in communities and nations.

NEED FOR ORIENTATION

The news media are not the only source of information or orientation to issues of public concern. Issues can be arrayed along a continuum ranging from obtrusive (those issues that we experience personally) to unobtrusive (those issues that we know about only through the media).

For example, people do not need the mass media to alert them to many aspects of the economy. Personal experience usually informs people about pricing patterns at Christmas or about rising gas prices. These are obtrusive features of the economy. Other economic issues, however, are not experienced personally. Typically, the mass media inform us about national trade deficits or balancing the national budget. These are unobtrusive issues, which we encounter only in the news and not in our daily lives. Some issues can be both obtrusive and unobtrusive, depending on individual circumstances. Unemployment is a good example. People who have never faced unemployment as a reality would view the issue as unobtrusive. But for workers who have been laid off or for anyone who has filed an unemployment claim, the issue is obtrusive. Their understanding of unemployment is firsthand.

Broad portraits of the agenda-setting role of the media reveal strong effects for unobtrusive issues and no effects for obtrusive issues (Weaver et al., 1981; Winter & Eyal 1981; Zucker, 1978). More narrowly focused studies based on precise measures of where an issue falls on the continuum for each individual show similar results (Blood, 1981).

The concept of need for orientation provides an even richer theoretical explanation for variability in the agenda-setting process than simply classifying issues along the obtrusive/unobtrusive continuum. Need for orientation is based on psychologist Edward Tolman's general theory of cognitive mapping (McGuire, 1974; Tolman, 1932, 1948), which suggests that we form maps in our minds to help us navigate our external environment. His notion is similar to Lippmann's concept of the pseudoenvironment. The need for orientation concept further suggests that there are individual differences in the need for orienting cues about an issue and in the need for detailed background information about an issue.

Conceptually, an individual's need for orientation is defined in terms of two lower-order concepts, relevance and uncertainty, whose roles occur sequentially. Relevance is the initial defining condition. Most of us feel no discomfort or need for orientation to any number of situations, especially in the realm of public affairs, because we do not see those issues as personally relevant. In the 2000 presidential election, most citizens showed little interest in the issue of U.S. and Russian relations, for example. People were much more concerned with Social Security and continuing the growth of the American economy. In situations where the relevance of the issue to the individual is low, the need for orientation is low.

Among individuals who perceive a topic to be highly relevant, their level of uncertainty also must be considered. If a person already has all the information he or she needs about an issue, uncertainty is low. Under conditions of high relevance and low uncertainty, the need for orientation is moderate. When relevance and uncertainty are high, however, need for orientation is high. This is often the situation during primary elections, when many unfamiliar candidates clutter the political landscape. As one might guess, the greater a person's need for orientation, the more likely he or she will attend to the mass media agenda. During an election, voters frequently learn about the candidates and their issue positions from the news media and political advertisements.

Need for orientation provides an explanation for the near-perfect match—a correlation of +.97—between the media agenda and the public agenda in the original Chapel Hill study. Although need for orientation was not initially provided as an explanation for that early study, it seems clear in retrospect that the original Chapel Hill findings regarding undecided voters was evidence of agenda-setting effects based exclusively on people with a high need for orientation. There is additional evidence from the next presidential election in the finding that the importance voters attached to knowing the presidential candidates' issue positions increased as need for orientation increased (Weaver & McCombs, 1978). The consistently higher levels of interest in Jimmy Carter's issue positions, as he was the unknown challenger in that election, compared to the issue positions of incumbent Gerald Ford further validates the need for orientation concept.

On occasion, personal experience with an issue, rather than satisfying a need for orientation, triggers an increased need for more information and the validation that comes from the mass media (Noelle-Neumann, 1985). Sensitized to an issue, these individuals may become particularly adept at studying the media agenda. Need for orientation—the cognitive version of the principle that "nature abhors a vacuum"—clarifies the circumstances under which people are more likely to acquire the agenda of the mass media.

SECOND-LEVEL EFFECTS AND FRAMING

In most discussions of the agenda-setting role of the mass media, the unit of analysis on each agenda is an *object*, usually a public issue. But public issues are not the only objects that can be analyzed from the agenda-setting perspective. In the party primaries, the objects of interest are the candidates vying for the presidential nomination of their political party. Many other objects can define an agenda as well. Communication is a process, which can be about any object or set of objects competing for attention. In all these instances, the term *object* is used in the same sense that social psychologists use the term *attitude object*. We direct our attention to an object, or we have an attitude or opinion about an object.

Beyond the agenda of objects, there is another level of agenda-setting. Each of the objects on an agenda has numerous attributes—characteristics and properties. Just as objects vary in salience, so do their attributes. Both the selection of objects for attention and the selection of attributes for picturing those objects are powerful agenda-setting roles. An important part of the news agenda and its set of objects are the attributes that journalists and, subsequently, members of the public have in mind when they think about and talk about each object. How these news agendas of attributes influence the public agenda is the second level of agenda-setting. Explicit attention to the second level of agenda-setting further suggests that the media not only tell us what to think about (Cohen, 1963), but they can also tell us *how* to think about some objects.

The theoretical distinction between agendas of objects and agendas of attributes, which is diagrammed in Fig. 1.1, is especially clear in an election setting. The slate of candidates vying for an office are the agenda of objects. The descriptions of each candidate in the news media and the images of the candidates in voters' minds are the agendas of attributes. The second level of agenda-setting, attribute agenda-setting, is the influence of these media presentations on the public. Voters' perceptions of the presidential candidates in 1976 illustrate the second level of agenda-setting. The Republicans had incumbent Gerald Ford, whereas the Democrats had 11 potential candidates competing for the nomination. Comparisons of upstate New York Democrats' descriptions of this large group of candidates with *Newsweek*'s attribute agenda in its early sketches of the candidates showed significant evidence of media influence (Becker & McCombs, 1978). Similar media effects on voters' images of political candidates have been found in such diverse settings as the 1994 mayoral election in Taipei, Taiwan (King, 1997), the 1995 local elections in Pamplona, Spain (McCombs, Llamas, Lopez-Escobar, & Rey, 1997), and the 1996 Spanish general election (McCombs, Lopez-Escobar, & Llamas, 2000). Attribute agenda-setting effects on candidate images

FIG. 1.1.   The Agenda-Setting Process

also have been produced in laboratory experiments (Kiousis, Banti-maroudis, & Ban, 1999).

This influence of the mass media on the public's images of political candidates is a very straightforward instance of attribute agenda-setting. Most of our knowledge about the attributes of political candidates, from their personal ideology to their personalities, comes from the news stories and the advertising content of the mass media. Issue salience, which has been the central focus of agenda-setting theory, also can be examined at the second level. Public issues, like all other objects, have attributes. Different aspects of issues—their attributes—are emphasized to varying degrees in the news and in how people think and talk about issues.

Again demonstrating the validity of agenda-setting theory across cultures, analysis of the 1993 Japanese general election found effects at both the first and second levels for the issue of political reform (Takeshita & Mikami, 1995). The more people used the news media, the greater the overall salience of the issue of political reform and, in particular, the greater the salience of system-related aspects of political reform, the aspect of the issue emphasized in the news.

Outside an election setting, in Minneapolis the correspondence between the local newspaper's presentation of the national economic situation and the salience of specific economic problems, causes, and proposed solutions among the public was +.81 (Benton & Frazier, 1976). For an environmental issue in Indiana, the degree of correspondence was +.71 between the local newspaper's presentation and the public's views on the development of a large man-made lake (Cohen, 1975). In Japan, the correspondence between Tokyo residents' concerns and the coverage of two major dailies in the months leading up to the United Nations' 1992 Rio de Janeiro conference on global environmental problems reached a peak of +.78 just prior to the conference (Mikami, Takeshita, Nakada, & Kawabata, 1994).

Explication of attribute agenda-setting links the theory with the contemporaneous concept of framing (McCombs & Bell, 1996; McCombs & Evatt, 1995; McCombs & Ghanem, 2001). Both framing and attribute agenda-setting call attention to the perspectives used by communicators and their audiences to picture topics in the daily news. Recent research has identified two types of frames: central themes and aspects. McLeod and Detenber's (1999) experiment produced a variety of framing effects with news stories whose central theme was civil protest. In other framing research, the focus is on the relative salience of numerous aspects of the topic rather than the dominant attributes defining the central theme of the news stories. To catalog the variety of attributes of four GOP presidential candidates, Miller, Andsager, and Reichert (1998) used computerized content analysis to identify 28 frames defined by words that frequently co-occurred in 245 press releases and 296 news stories. Their research illustrates the convergence of framing and attribute agenda-setting. Although the study focused exclusively on identification of the frames defining the attribute agendas of the campaign press releases and news stories, subsequent analysis (McCombs, forthcoming) documented substantial agenda-setting effects of the press releases on the news stories. How the media frame an issue or political candidate—which attributes are selected either as the central organizing idea or as the aspects of the topic presented to the audience—is a powerful agenda-setting role.

WHO SETS THE MEDIA AGENDA?

As evidence accumulated about the agenda-setting influence of the mass media on the public, scholars in the early 1980s began to ask who set the media agenda. In this new line of inquiry, researchers began to explore the various factors that shape the media agenda. The media agenda became the dependent variable whereas in traditional agenda-setting research, the media agenda was the independent variable, the key causal factor shaping the public agenda.

The metaphor of "peeling an onion" is useful for understanding the relationships between these various factors and the agenda of the mass media. The concentric layers of the onion represent the numerous influences that shape the media agenda, which is at the core of the onion. Like an onion, the influence of an outer layer is, in turn, affected by layers closer to the core of the onion. A highly detailed elaboration of this metaphoric onion contains many layers, ranging from the prevailing social ideology to the beliefs and psychology of an individual journalist (Shoemaker & Reese, 1991).

At the surface of our theoretical onion, what Shoemaker and Reese call the extramedia level, are key external news sources. They include politicians, public officials, public relations practitioners, and any individual, like the president of the United States, who influences media content. For example, a study of Richard Nixon's State of the Union address in 1970 found that the agenda of 15 issues in that address did influence the subsequent month's news coverage in the *New York Times*, the *Washington Post*, and two of the three national television networks (McCombs, Gilbert, & Eyal, 1982). No evidence was found to suggest the media had an influence on the president. Sigal's (1973) examination of the *New York Times* and the *Washington Post* across a 20-year period found that nearly half of their news stories were based substantially on press releases and other direct information subsidies. About 17.5% of the total number of news stories were based, at least in part, on press releases, and press conferences and background briefings accounted for another 32%.

Deep inside the onion are the interactions and influence of various mass media on each other, a phenomenon commonly called intermedia agenda-setting. To a considerable degree, these interactions reinforce and validate the social norms and traditions of journalism. Those professional values and practices are the layer of the onion surrounding the core, the layer that defines the ground rules for the ultimate shaping of the media agenda.

The *New York Times* frequently plays the role of primary intermedia agenda-setter because an appearance on the front page of the *Times* can legitimize a topic as newsworthy. The contamination of Love Canal in New York State and the radon threat in Pennsylvania did not gain national prominence, despite intensive local media coverage, until these issues appeared on the *Times'* agenda (Mazur, 1987; Ploughman, 1984). The previous mention of the *Times'* coverage of the drug problem in the 1980s (Reese & Danielian, 1989) also supports this finding. That study showed that when the *New York Times* "discovered" the country's drug problem in late 1985, network news coverage and major newspaper coverage of the issue soon followed.

Finally, in a laboratory experiment that explored the agenda-setting function of the Associated Press, researchers found a high degree of correspondence (+.62) among topics between the proportion of news stories in a large wire file and the small sample selected by the subjects. The subjects were experienced newspaper and television wire editors (Whitney & Becker, 1982). This study, and others, connects agenda-setting theory to research about gatekeeping (Becker, McCombs, & McLeod, 1975; McCombs & Shaw, 1976).

PRIMING

The link between agenda-setting effects and the subsequent expression of opinions about public figures or other objects is called priming. This consequence of agenda-setting is diagrammed on the right side of Fig. 1.1. The psychological basis of priming is the selective attention of the public. People do not and cannot pay attention to everything. Rather than engaging in a comprehensive analysis based on their total store of information, citizens routinely draw on those bits of information that are particularly salient at the time they must make a judgment.

Strong causal evidence of priming was found during the 1986 Iran-Contra scandal (Krosnick & Kinder, 1990). On November 25, 1986, the U.S. Attorney General announced that funds obtained by the U.S. government from the secret sale of weapons to Iran had been improperly diverted to the Contras, a group attempting to overthrow the Sandinista government in Nicaragua. The story received major news coverage. By coincidence, the National Election Study's post-1986 presidential survey was in the field at the time of these announcements, creating a natural before-and-after comparison of the specific elements that influenced Americans' assessment of President Reagan's overall performance. The study showed that two elements, the public's opinion about the importance of providing assistance to the Contras and about U.S. intervention in Central America, played substantially increased roles in overall assessment of the president after the Attorney General's announcement.

Evidence of priming also exists in the public's assessments of President Clinton's job performance in the early months of the Monica Lewinsky sex scandal. A survey of Oregon residents found significant links between the frequency of media use, the formation of attribute agendas among the public, and assessments of Clinton's job performance (Wanta & Chang, 1999). Frequent newspaper readers and infrequent television viewers were more likely to describe Clinton in terms of public issues. There was no relationship between the frequency of media exposure and descriptions of Clinton in terms of the scandal, perhaps because of the saturation coverage in all media. In turn, there was a substantial link between the salience of issue positions as the president's dominant attribute and positive opinions about his overall job performance. Among people who believed that the president's involvement in the scandal was the most salient attribute, opinions about the president were negative.

An even more basic form of priming is the link between the salience of objects and their attributes in the mass media and the very existence of opinions among the audience. Media salience primes the creation and expression of opinions. Extensive analysis of election-year news about U.S. presidential candidates in all five elections between 1980 and 1996 found strong negative correlations between the pattern of media salience across these elections and the number of people who expressed completely ambivalent opinions about the candidates by checking the midpoint of various rating scales used by the National Election Study (Kiousis, 2000). Twenty of the 24 comparisons between the prominence of the presidential candidates in the total news coverage—media salience— and the proportion of the public without opinions were significant. Their median value was −.90. Similar results were found for the attribute agenda, where 17 of 24 comparisons for the attribute of morality were significant, and the median correlation between the pattern of salience in the media for this attribute across the elections and the number of people with ambivalent opinions was −.80.

Mass communication effects can result from the sheer volume of exposure, as we see in first-level agenda-setting. But, as both attribute agenda-setting and priming show, closer attention to the specific content of mass media provides a more detailed understanding of the pictures in our heads and of subsequent attitudes and opinions grounded in those pictures.

SUMMING UP

More than 50 years ago, Harold Lasswell (1948) observed that mass communication had three broad social roles—surveillance of the larger environment, achieving consensus among segments of society, and transmission of the culture. Agenda-setting is a significant part of the surveillance role because it contributes substantial portions of our pictures about the larger environment. But the agenda-setting process also has implications for social consensus and transmission of the social culture.

Evidence linking agenda-setting and social consensus was found by the North Carolina Poll among demographic groups that are commonly cited in public opinion polls as sources of differences rather than similarities (Shaw & Martin, 1992). Comparison of the issue agendas for men and women who infrequently read a daily newspaper was +.55. But for men and women who read a newspaper occasionally, the degree of correspondence rose to +.80. And, among men and women who read a newspaper regularly, the issue agendas were identical (+1.0). Similar patterns of increased consensus about the most important issues facing the country as a result of greater media exposure also were found in comparisons of young and old and black and white and were true for both newspaper and television use. These patterns of increased social consensus among demographic groups as a result of media exposure also have been found in Taiwan and Spain (Chiang, 1995; Lopez-Escobar, Llamas, & McCombs, 1998).

The transmission of culture is also linked to the agenda-setting process. Media and public agendas of issues, political candidates, and their attributes all rest on the foundations of democracy, the larger political culture defined by a basic civic agenda of beliefs about politics and elections. Exploration of yet other cultural agendas is moving agenda-setting theory far beyond its traditional realm of public affairs. These new lines of cultural inquiry extend from the historical agenda defining a society's collective memory of the past to the contemporary agenda of attributes defining the ideal physical appearance of young women and men. The imprint of the mass media that begins with its agenda-setting influence is found on many aspects of public opinion and behavior.

REFERENCES

Becker, L., & McCombs, M. E. (1978). The role of the press in determining voter reaction to presidential primaries. *Human Communication Research, 4*, 301–307.

Becker, L., McCombs, M. E., & McLeod, J. (1975). The development of political congnitions. In S. Chaffee (Ed.), *Political communication: Issues and strategies for research* (pp. 21–64). Beverly Hills, CA: Sage.

Benton, M., & Frazier, P. J. (1976). The agenda-setting function of the mass media at three levels of information-holding. *Communication Research, 3*, 261–274.

Blood, R. W. (1981). *Unobtrusive issues in the agenda-setting role of the press.* Unpublished doctoral dissertation, Syracuse University, Syracuse, NY.

Brosius, H. B., & Kepplinger, H. M. (1990). The agenda-setting function of television news: Static and dynamic views. *Communication Research, 17*, 183–211.

Canel, M. J., Llamas, J. P., & Rey, F. (1996). El primer nivel del efecto agenda setting en la informacion local: Los "problemas mas importantes" de la ciudad de Pamplona [The first level agenda setting effect on local information: The "most important problems" of the city of Pamplona]. *Communicacion y Sociedad, 9*, 17–38.

Chiang, C. (1995). *Bridging and closing the gap of our society: Social function of media agenda setting.* Unpublished master's thesis, University of Texas, Austin.

Cohen, B. C. (1963). *The press and foreign policy.* Princeton, NJ: Princeton University Press.

Cohen, D. (1975). *A report on a non-election agenda-setting study.* Paper presented to the Association for Education in Journalism, Ottawa, Canada.

Dearing, J., & Rogers, E. (1996). *Agenda setting.* Thousand Oaks, CA: Sage.

Eaton, H., Jr. (1989). Agenda setting with bi-weekly data on content of three national media. *Journalism Quarterly, 66*, 942–948.

Funkhouser, G. R. (1973). The issues of the sixties. *Public Opinion Quarterly, 37*, 62–75.

Gamson, W. (1992). *Talking politics.* New York: Cambridge University Press.

Ghanem, S. (1996). *Media coverage of crime and public opinion: An exploration of the second level of agenda setting.* Unpublished doctoral dissertation, University of Texas, Austin.

Iyengar, S., & Kinder, D. R. (1987). *News that matters: Television and American opinion.* Chicago: University of Chicago Press.

King, P. (1997). The press, candidate images and voter perceptions. In M. E. McCombs, D. L. Shaw, and D. Weaver (Eds.), *Communication and democracy: Exploring the intellectual frontiers in agenda setting* (pp. 29–40). Mahwah, NJ: Lawrence Erlbaum Associates.

Kiousis, S. (2000). *Beyond salience: Exploring the linkages between the agenda setting role of mass media and mass persuasion.* Unpublished doctoral dissertation, University of Texas, Austin.

Kiousis, S., Bantimaroudis, P., & Ban, H. (1999). Candidate image attributes: Experiments on the substantive dimension of second-level agenda setting. *Communication Research, 26*, 414–428.

Klapper, J. (1960). The effects of mass communication. Glencoe, IL: Free Press.

Krosnick, J., & Kinder D. R. (1990). Altering the foundations of support for the president through priming. *American Political Science Review, 84*, 497–512.

Lasswell, H. (1948). The structure and function of communication in society. In L. Bryson (Ed.), *The communication of ideas*. New York: Institute for Religious and Social Studies.

Lazarsfeld, P., Berelson, B., & Gaudet, H. (1944). *The people's choice*. New York: Columbia University Press.

Lennon, F. R. (1998). Argentina: 1997 elecciones. Los diarios nacionales y la campana electoral [The 1997 Argentina election. The national dailies and the electoral campaign]. Report by The Freedom Forum and Austral University.

Lippmann, W. (1922). *Public opinion*. New York: Macmillan.

Lopez-Escobar, E., Llamas, J. P., & McCombs, M. E. (1998). Agenda setting and community consensus: First and second level effects. *International Journal of Public Opinion Research, 10*, 335–348.

Mazur, A. (1987). Putting radon on the public risk agenda. *Science, Technology and Human Values, 12*, 86–93.

McCombs, M. E. (forthcoming). *Setting the agenda: The mass media and public opinion*. Cambridge, England: Blackwell Polity Press.

McCombs, M. E., & Bell, T. (1996). The agenda-setting role of mass communication. In M. Salwen & D. Stacks (Eds.), *An integrated approach to communication theory and research* (pp. 93–110). Mahwah, NJ: Lawrence Erlbaum Associates.

McCombs, M. E., & Evatt, D. S. (1995). Los temas y los aspectos: Explorando una nueva dimension de la agenda setting [Objects and attributes: Exploring a new dimension of agenda setting]. *Communicacion y Sociedad, 8*, 7–32.

McCombs, M. E., & Ghanem, S. (2001). The convergence of agenda setting and framing. In S. D. Reese, O. Gandy, & A. Grant (Eds.), *Framing in the new media landscape*. Mahwah, NJ: Lawrence Erlbaum Associates.

McCombs, M. E., Gilbert, S., & Eyal, C. H. (1982). *The State of the Union address and the press agenda: A replication*. Paper presented to the International Communication Association, Boston, MA.

McCombs, M. E., Llamas, J. P., Lopez-Escobar, E., & Rey, F. (1997). Candidate images in Spanish elections: Second-level agenda-setting effects. *Journalism & Mass Communication Quarterly, 74*, 703–717.

McCombs, M. E., Lopez-Escobar, E., & Llamas, J. P. (2000). Setting the agenda of attributes in the 1996 Spanish general election. *Journal of Communication, 50*, 77–92.

McCombs, M. E., & Shaw, D. L. (1972). The agenda-setting function of mass media. *Public Opinion Quarterly, 36*, 176–187.

McCombs, M. E., & Shaw, D. L. (1976). Structuring the unseen environment. *Journal of Communication, 26*, 18–22.

McGuire, W. J. (1974). Psychological motives and communication gratification. In J. G. Blumler & E. Katz (Eds.), *The uses of mass communication: Current perspectives on gratifications research* (pp. 167–196). Beverly Hills, CA: Sage.

McLeod, D., & Detenber, B. (1999). Framing effects of television news coverage of social protest. *Journal of Communication, 49*(3), 3–23.

Mikami, S., Takeshita, T., Nakada, M., & Kawataba, M. (1994). *The media coverage and public awareness of environmental issues in Japan*. Paper presented to the International Association for Mass Communication Research, Seoul, Korea.

Miller, M., Andsager, J., & Riechert, B. (1998). Framing the candidates in presidential primaries: Issues and images in press releases and news coverage. *Journalism & Mass Communication Quarterly, 75*, 312–324.

Noelle-Neumann, E. (1985). The sprial of silence: A response. In K. Sanders, L. L. Kaid, & D. Nimmo (Eds.), *Political Communication Yearbook 1984* (pp. 66–94). Carbondale: Southern Illinois University Press.

Ploughman, P. (1984). *The creation of newsworthy events: An analysis of newspaper coverage of the man-made disaster at Love Canal.* Unpublished doctoral dissertation, State University of New York at Buffalo.

Reese, S. D., & Danielian, L. (1989). Intermedia influence and the drug issue: Converging on cocaine. In P. Shoemaker (Ed.), *Communication campaigns about drugs* (pp. 29–46). Hillsdale, NJ: Lawrence Erlbaum Associates.

Shaw, D. L., & Martin, S. (1992). The function of mass media agenda setting. *Journalism Quarterly, 69,* 902–920.

Shaw, D. L., & McCombs, M. E. (Eds.). (1977). *The emergence of American political issues.* St. Paul, MN: West.

Shoemaker, P., & Reese, S. D. (1991). *Mediating the message: Theories of influences on mass media content.* New York: Longman.

Sigal, L. (1973). *Reporters and officials: The organization and politics of newsmaking.* Lexington, MA: D. C. Heath.

Takeshita, T., & Mikami, S. (1995). How did mass media influence the voters' choice in the 1993 general election in Japan? *Keio Communication Review, 17,* 27–41.

Tolman, E. C. (1932). *Purposive behavior in animals and men.* New York: Appleton-Century-Crofts.

Tolman, E. C. (1948). Cognitive maps in rats and men. *Psychological Review, 55,* 189–208.

Wang, T. L. (2000). Agenda-setting online: An experiment testing the effects of hyperlinks in online newspapers. *Southwestern Mass Communication Journal, 15*(2), 59–70.

Wanta, W., & Chang, K. (1999). *Priming and the second level of agenda setting: Merging two theoretical approaches.* Paper presented to the International Communication Association, San Francisco, CA.

Wanta, W., & Ghanem, S. (forthcoming). Effects of agenda-setting. In J. Bryant & R. Carveth (Eds.), *Meta-Analyses of Media Effects.* Mahwah, NJ: Lawrence Erlbaum Associates.

Weaver, D. (1996). What voters learn from the media. *Annals of the American Academy of Political and Social Science, 546,* 34–47.

Weaver, D., Graber, D. A., McCombs, M. E., & Eyal, C. H. (1981). *Media agenda-setting in a presidential election: Issues, images, and interests.* New York: Praeger.

Weaver, D., & McCombs, M. E. (1978). *Voters' need for orientation and choice of candidate: Mass media and electoral decision making.* Paper presented to the American Association for Public Opinion Research, Roanoke, VA.

Whitney, D. C., & Becker, L. (1982). "Keeping the gates" for gatekeepers: The effects of wire news. *Journalism Quarterly, 59,* 60–65.

Winter, J. P., & Eyal, C. H. (1981). Agenda-setting for the civil rights issue. *Public Opinion Quarterly, 45,* 376–383.

Zucker, H. G. (1978). The variable nature of news media influence. In B. D. Ruben (Ed.), *Communication yearbook 2* (pp. 225–240). New Brunswick, NJ: Transaction Books.

Chapter 2

Exemplification Theory of Media Influence

DOLF ZILLMANN
University of Alabama

This chapter provides an overview of the essentials of exemplification theory and research. After tracing the evolutionary roots of the exemplification process and considering its ecological ramifications in contemporary society, the theory and pertinent implications are elaborated. The focus is on the representational accuracy of reports of relevant social phenomena and on the heuristic processing of exemplar aggregations in forming assessments of these phenomena. Finally, drawing from research on the influence of news reporting, a sampling of experimental investigations is presented to support the theory.

EVOLUTIONARY CONSIDERATIONS

The wisdom of antiquity, the teachings of the Greek philosopher Heraclitus in particular, related to us that no two events are ever exactly the same. Indeed, the contention that reality expresses itself as a continual stream of events that never repeat themselves, at least not in all their manifestations, is rather compelling intuitively.

On the other hand, it would appear that no organism capable of learning ever honored such wisdom. Essentially for reasons of cognitive economy, organisms had to find ways of extracting experiential chunks from the continual flow of information about their environments. In so doing, they had to focus on vital events, that is, on events that furthered their welfare or that placed it at risk. They also had to get a sense of the prevalence of vital events under given circumstances. Irrelevant events, in contrast, could be ignored without loss. The selective retention of information about vital events thus served the welfare of individuals and secured their survival. The retention of information about the entire undifferentiated flow of events, inconceivable as it is, could not have such adaptive value.

19

Implicit in this contention is that if relevant events were deemed alike, they were lumped together in one category. Not that the events were necessarily considered to be identical. But they were considered alike for their sharing of essential features. The existence of concomitant irrelevant differences did not deter from the practical merit of such event categorization (Burns, 1992; Hayes-Roth & Hayes-Roth, 1977; Mervis & Rosch, 1981; Rosch & Lloyd, 1978).

The categorization of events allowed the aggregation of limited numbers of individual cases. This sampling of cases could be used to extrapolate information about other events within the same category, potentially about all other such events. Stored in memory, the aggregated segments of pertinent experience defined compounded knowledge about past occurrences that could guide future behavior. It fostered dispositions and ultimately directed actions toward similar occurrences on later encounter. A comparatively small number of experiences thus served as the basis for the perception of a larger body of like occurrences. The implicit generalization amounts to a spontaneously executed inductive inference. Inferences of this kind are made by all species capable of adaptation through learning. Humans, no doubt, have made these inferences through the millennia. They are still making them, routinely so, and nonconsciously for the most part.

The reliance on categorized events of primary experience has not appreciably changed for nonhuman species. For humans, in contrast, the experience base has been vastly expanded. With the refinement of communication skills, especially with the emergence of linguistic competencies, the pertinent experiences of others became communicable, and phenomena had to be judged by integrating primary experiences with communicated ones. However, communicated experiences were not necessarily others' primary ones. They could be accounts from third parties and amount to unreliable hearsay.

The indicated broadening of the experiential base is obviously advantageous in enabling individuals to judge phenomena lying outside the bounds of their own limited experience. It came at a cost, however. Experiences related by others could be self-serving, inadvertently erroneous, or deliberately deceptive. It thus became prudent to be on guard about others' communicative intentions. The apparent need for caution became imperative, in fact, for direct interpersonal communication generally, and for any mediated extension thereof in particular.

ECOLOGY OF MEDIATION

Considering the dissemination of information by media institutions, a call for caution is especially warranted. This is because such dissemination reaches large numbers of people, often the citizenry at large. The provision of information of consequence to the public is undoubtedly an essential civic service rendered by the media. However, the capacity to reach large audiences carries with it the risk of misleading the public in case the disseminated information proves to be distorted and inaccurate or simply in error. Conceivably, such misleading can result from featuring inappropriate selections of cases in efforts to illustrate an issue of interest. Media institutions committed to providing veridical accounts of phenomena of consequence thus should take some responsibility for their case aggregations, ensuring that the reported cases yield correct rather than distorted perceptions of the phenomena. Of central importance are the news media, whether in print, broadcast, or computer format, along with newslike educational efforts, also irrespective of means of delivery. Some media institutions, however, the entertainment industry in particular, claim poetic license and refuse to accept any responsibility for distorted perceptions of relevant social phenomena that their dissemination of selected cases is likely to create.

In the news, case reports are characteristically featured to justify statements about issues of which they are a part. Notwithstanding contentions such as that a handful of "carefully chosen" cases can entirely *define* issues, the cases certainly *exemplify* them. This renders the cases *exemplars* that exemplify the *exemplified*, namely the population of exemplars (i.e., all exemplars of the kind under consideration). *Exemplification* is not an all-or-nothing concept, however. The degree to which a selection of exemplars reliably exemplifies the exemplified phenomenon is subject to empirical determination. Some exemplifications may adequately represent the population from which they were drawn. Others may not. Exemplification by completely arbitrary selection of exemplars, for instance, is notoriously poor and might be more appropriately labeled *misexemplification*.

Such common sense has not prevented an obtrusive partiality by the media for extraordinary and atypical cases in the exemplification of phenomena. It can hardly be considered a revelation that fictional narrative favors the exceptional over the ordinary. Somewhat surprising should be that the news media often follow the lead of fiction in aggregating less-than-typical exemplars, mostly in efforts to enhance the so-called entertainment value of reports. The news is laden with exemplars, and often enough their selection seems more inspired by dramatic and ideological slants than by a commitment to impartial, balanced reporting (Zillmann & Brosius, 2000). The featured exemplars are almost always arbitrarily selected; their choice left to the writer's idiosyncrasies. The resulting exemplar samples are, at best, somewhat representative of their population and, at worst, entirely nonrepresentative. The projection of the exemplified issue accordingly varies from adequate to inadequate. Inadequate exemplification is, of course, bound to foster misperceptions of the phenomena under consideration.

The exemplification of phenomena is often supplemented by more general descriptions. Specifications may include measured and quantified assessments, such as incidence proportions and rates of change of occurrences. They may convey data that are collected in adherence to the principles of science. Information of this kind has been labeled *base-rate information*. It is generally considered to be less partial and hence more veridical than the information provided by selective exemplar aggregations. On occasion, such information gives impetus to news reports. On other occasions, it is furnished to correct likely misperceptions presumed to result from biased exemplification. More often than not, however, base-rate information is simply not reported, often because it is not known. In such cases, the perception of phenomena hinges entirely on the provision of exemplars.

Irrespective of the reasons for including base-rate information in the projection of phenomena, the issue of misperception from exposure to admixtures of selective exemplification and potentially more reliable base-rate information is defined by the reception of these messages. How will recipients process the information? Will they base their perception of issues primarily on the display of exemplars? This can be expected on grounds of the built-in heuristics that ensured the survival of the species. Or will recipients absorb the comparatively abstract base-rate information, process it carefully, and use it to correct false impressions invited by inappropriate exemplar aggregations? Those who believe in the careful digestion of news reports may expect that base-rate information does have this power to put exemplars in their place as mere illustrations, thereby depriving them of undue influence. On the other hand, the processing of less concrete, more abstract information may be considered evolutionarily too vernal to be capable of overpowering the impressions based on the deep-rooted mechanisms of extrapolating tacit knowledge about a population of events from a handful of actually known ones. Of particular interest are the delayed consequences of the provision of concrete versus abstract information. Are incidence rates and the like as well retained as concrete events, especially concrete events associated with strong emotions? If not, should it not be expected that the influence of base-rate information on the perception of issues will diminish more rapidly than that of exemplification, ultimately allowing the exemplar influence to become increasingly dominant?

These are some of the questions that exemplification theory addresses and that the reported experimental work seeks to answer.

DEFINITIONAL CLARIFICATION

Exemplars describe events. Not all events are exemplars, however. A singular event that does not share any features with other events is, by definition, not a member of a population of like events. Unique events, therefore, stand for themselves only and do not exemplify anything.

In order to function as exemplars, events must share attributes with others to a degree that makes them classifiable as members of the same population of events. They must share a number of primary, defining attributes. However, because the events are not likely to be identical in every other regard, they may differ on any number of secondary attributes. These secondary attributes define potentially significant variation within the population. This variation often justifies the specification of subpopulations. In such cases, the initially secondary attributes become primary ones, and variation in the subpopulation is defined by the secondary attributes specific to the events of this subpopulation. Finally, there may exist lower-order variation in attributes of minimal relevance. Such attributes, if inconsequential for all practical purposes, may be disregarded.

Events manifest in exemplars can be abstracted in specifications of entities that have certain properties, that perform certain actions, or that cause certain consequences. Conditions under which the indicated events occur may be stipulated in addition.

These conceptional considerations, as well as those concerning representation by exemplar displays that are discussed in the following section, are further elaborated in the initial presentation of exemplification theory (Zillmann, 1999).

EXEMPLAR DISPLAYS AND REPRESENTATION

Phenomena are exemplified under two distinct sets of conditions. In the first, essential parameters of the distribution of events in an event population of interest are known. These parameters can derive from assessments on all events in a population. More likely, however, the parameters are estimates based on the assessment of a representative sample of the event population. Representativeness is achieved by adherence to selection procedures that ensure that every event of the population has the same chance for inclusion in the sample. In the second set of conditions, a population of events is presumed to exist, but parameters of the event distribution are not known.

In case population parameters are known, the degree to which selected exemplars *represent* the variation of secondary event attributes can be ascertained. A high degree of representation is achieved by honoring the condition of equiprobability for the inclusion of exemplars in a sample. Random selection of exemplars is impartial to secondary attributes and thus prevents the inappropriate aggregation of specific event groups at the expense of others. The greater the violation of random exemplar extraction by the arbitrary selection of cases that are deemed "of particular interest" according to idiosyncratic criteria, the lower the degree of representation by the resulting exemplar sample.

In case population parameters are not known, the degree of representation is not discernible. Presumptions about variation in the event population might be used as a guide for exemplification. However, to the degree that such presumptions are erroneous, exemplar samples can only misrepresent the event population.

The representation of event populations by media exemplifications has been a prominent domain of inquiry for some time. In a groundbreaking investigation, Berelson and Salter (1946) introduced the comparative assessment of exemplar ratios and ratios of the exemplified events. Specifically, these investigators demonstrated bias in the representation of majority and minority Americans in magazine fiction by relating the proportions of ethnically identified protagonists to the proportions of the respective ethnic groups in the general population. Minorities were found to be grossly underrepresented as heroes, the majority grossly overrepresented.

Gerbner and his collaborators (e.g., Gerbner, Gross, Morgan, & Signorielli, 1986) have applied this technique to exemplifications in prime-time television and recorded a host of misrepresentations. For instance, in the cast of characters, men were vastly overexemplified, women vastly underexemplified. In fact, the portrayal of men outnumbered that of women by a factor of three. Teens and the elderly were severely underexemplified. The exemplification of minorities was found to be similarly nonrepresentative, with Blacks reaching only three-fourths and Hispanic Americans only one-third of their presence in the population. Regarding the overrepresentation of crime and its curtailment in fiction, the law enforcement personnel alone outnumbered all blue-collar and service workers by a far margin.

Greenberg, Simmons, Hogan, and Atkin (1980) analogously assessed television characters by a set of their features and then compared the characters' prevalence to census data. Among other things, these investigators reported an underrepresentation of women, children, older people, craftspersons, and clericals, as well as an overrepresentation of managers and persons ages 20 to 50.

The assessment of representation is not limited, however, to comparisons with segments of the populace. Exemplifications can be related to all situations for which reliable parameters exist. For instance, Dominick (1973) compared the portrayal of crime on prime-time television with crime statistics and observed a gross overrepresentation of violent crime, of assault and murder in particular. Comparisons also can be made against conceptually compelling standards. Stocking, Sapolsky, and Zillmann (1977), for example, ascertained the frequency of intergender putdowns in prime-time comedy and observed, counter to prevalent beliefs at the time, that men were as much the butt of jokes delivered by women as women were of jokes delivered by men. Moreover, comparisons have been made between exemplifications at different times (e.g., Seggar, 1977) or between different program genres, as well as between occurrences within genres (e.g., Brosius, Weaver, & Staab, 1993; Sapolsky & Molitor, 1996; Zillmann & Weaver, 1997).

Regarding the entertainment media, the less-than-perfect representation of known realities may be obtrusive, but its documentation is, by itself, largely inconsequential. The situation is different for the news and educational media. The news media, in particular, are ostensibly committed to correct representation. Given that events of interest usually vary along known parameters, one might assume that reports would involve exemplars in accordance with these parameters. For both practical and principal reasons this is often not possible, however (cf. Zillmann & Brosius, 2000). Correct representation should nonetheless be the objective that is to be pursued as best as the circumstances allow. If violations are unavoidable, corrective base-rate information may be added. In the presumably infrequent situations in which the parameters of variation within groups of events are not known, such objectives cannot be constructed, and representation is simply rendered unachievable.

It should be noted that demonstrations of misexemplification that are based on the comparison of manifest media content with existing parameters do not provide evidence of the creation of misperceptions of the misrepresented phenomena. Misrepresentation does not necessarily foster misperceptions. Skeptics are quick to argue that "people know better" than to let themselves be mislead by a few atypical exemplars. The burden of proof thus rests on the empirical demonstration of perceptual and dispositional effects of exposure to sets of exemplars that vary in the degree to which they represent or misrepresent issues of consequence.

Such proof shall be provided. First, however, we must delineate the theoretical framework that projects specific perceptual and dispositional consequences of exemplifications.

PREDICTION OF EXEMPLAR EFFECTS ON ISSUE PERCEPTION

In keeping with the evolutionary considerations outlined earlier, exemplification theory is based on three basic assumptions.

1. Comprehension, storage, and retrieval of elemental, concrete events are generally superior to those of complex, abstract events.

This is because concrete, usually observable occurrences place fewer demands on cognitive processing than do abstract events that require construction and generalization.

2. Events of consequence attract more attention and are more vigorously processed than irrelevant events. Accordingly, storage and retrieval of vital events are superior to those of inconsequential events.

This assumption pertains to emotional reactivity and is well founded in biological and neuroendocrine theory. Kety (1970), for instance, based a survival theory on it, arguing that retaining and recalling information about the encounter of emotion-arousing conditions, as these processes serve the preparation of effective coping behavior, had great adaptive value in the course of evolution. Retaining and recalling information about events that failed to evoke emotions, in contrast, did not have such value. It should be expected, therefore, that the vigilance of environmental screening is elevated during emotions, with more intense coding of information into memory as a result (Heuer & Reisberg, 1990). It may be considered firmly established, in fact, that informational displays that evoke emotions are better recalled than those that do not (Christianson, 1992; Spear & Riccio, 1994).

Research focusing on retention and retrieval of emotional events has actually led to clearly articulated mechanisms for the mediation of superior access to the information about these events. A structure within the limbic system, the amygdala, has emerged as the moderator that determines the significance of events at the onset and during acute emotions (LeDoux, 1992). Essentially, this structure serves self-preservation by continually monitoring the environment for threats and dangers of any kind, as well as for opportunities toward gratification, and on encounter of such vital situations signals the magnitude of the condition. The behavior-energizing emergency reaction (Cannon, 1929; Zillmann, 1996) unfolds alongside these emotional developments. An essential part of this reaction is the systemic release of adrenal catecholamines. In turn, part of this release is the central diffusion of epinephrine. The excitatory effect of these hormones persists during emotion and lingers for several minutes after the cessation of emotion. Superior conditions for information coding prevail throughout the entire emotional episode (Bower, 1992). The mechanism for the superior coding of emotion-arousing exemplars thus can be stated as follows: Amygdaloid monitoring prompts the discernment of exemplar salience that manifests itself, in part, in the activation of central norepinephrine receptors, and the enhanced sensitivity of these receptors creates the conditions for superior coding of emotional exemplars into indelible memory (Cahill, Prins, Weber, & McGaugh, 1994; McGaugh, 1992; McGaugh & Gold, 1989).

3. The incidence of events of the same kind is coded, and basal quantitative assessments are made on grounds of this coding.

It is assumed that exemplar groupings, whether directly perceived or retrieved from memory, are screened to discern the magnitude of the groupings. As a rule, such screening is nonconsciously performed, but on occasion, it may become conscious and deliberate. Irrespective of the level of awareness involved, however, the screening is assumed to yield incident assessments in at least ordinal terms (e.g., few, many, a lot of cases). Moreover, comparative assessments may be conducted, yielding a sense of relative incidence rates (e.g., one grouping is larger than another) and changes in incidence rates over time (e.g., a grouping is larger than before). The degree of difference or change again can be at least ordinally structured. Essentially, then, it is assumed that an archaic *quantification heuristic* exists that continually monitors the prevalence of exemplars as well as their relative distributions.

Exemplification theory further relies on two additional cognitive mechanisms: the representativeness and availability heuristics (Kahneman & Tversky, 1973; Tversky & Kahneman, 1973). Both mechanisms can be considered well established by compelling research demonstrations (cf. Fiske & Taylor, 1984; Sherman, Judd, & Park, 1989; Zillmann & Brosius, 2000).

The *representativeness heuristic* essentially projects that judgments about event populations are extrapolations based on the scrutiny of exemplar groupings, and that in this extrapolation the provision of abstract quantitative information about exemplar distributions is immaterial. The implicit devaluation of base-rate information for the assessment of event populations is also known as the *base-rate fallacy* (Bar-Hillel, 1980). This fallacy, it should be recognized, is entailed in the earlier-stated information-processing assumption that expresses the coding dominance of concrete over abstract displays.

A secondary projection of the representativeness heuristic is that the generalization from samples of events to populations of events is independent of the size of the samples. Although generalizations from larger samples are, of course, known to be more reliable than generalizations from smaller samples, a comparatively small exemplar group is thus expected to have the same inferential power as all larger exemplar groups.

The *availability heuristic* projects that judgments about event populations are greatly dependent on exemplars that, at the time judgments are rendered, are available in the sense of being cognitively manifest. This availability, in turn, is considered to be a function of the ease with which exemplars are accessed in memory and retrieved from it. In this context, retrieval is thought to be mostly involuntary and spontaneous. Ready retrieval thus may be characterized as a nondeliberate process by which exemplars impose themselves from memory, thereby exerting disproportional influence on the contemplation and ultimately on the evaluation of the exemplified event population.

Access to exemplars is primarily controlled by two variables (Higgins, 1996; Kahneman, Slovic, & Tversky, 1982; Nisbett & Ross, 1980). First, the likelihood of spontaneous availability of exemplars is known to increase with the recency of their activation. Recently activated exemplars, therefore, may be expected to exert greater influence on the perception of issues than exemplars whose activation occurred at a more distant time. Consideration of the recency of exemplar activation thus provides an explanation of the priming of numerous phenomena (Bargh, 1996; Jo & Berkowitz, 1994).

Second, the likelihood of spontaneous availability of exemplars is known to increase with the frequency of their activation. Frequently activated exemplars, then, are bound to exert greater influence on issue perception than rarely activated ones. In contrast to the recency of exemplar activation, which creates only a short-lived accessibility enhancement because of the continual supersedure by more recent activations of alternative concepts, the frequency of exemplification is thought capable of fostering enduring and stable influence on the perception of phenomena. Accessibility from frequent and consistent exposure to exemplars, in particular, is not considered to be transitory but chronic (Bargh, 1984; Bargh, Lombardi, & Higgins, 1988; Higgins, 1996). Such *chronic accessibility* is pivotal, as its effects are likely to dominate those of the recency of activation in most situations, barring only those of immediately preceding activation. Consideration of the frequency of exemplar activation therefore explains many cultivation phenomena (cf. Gerbner et al., 1986). Most significant media effects are, after all, thought to be built on frequent and consistent exposure to largely redundant concepts, most of which fall well within the conceptual range of exemplification.

We are now in a position to articulate predictions concerning media influence. In making these predictions, we shall adjust our nomenclature to the language of media effects. Specifically, we shall abandon the nomenclature of sampling and speak of *issues* and their perception. It is implied that issues are not defined by singular events, but by a multitude of events, and that all individual events of a multitude function as its exemplars.

1. A series of exemplars of concrete events influences issue perception more strongly than an abstract account of the issue. In relative terms, the superior influence of such exemplars increases with time.

This prediction addresses the dominant influence of the display of concrete situations over potentially more reliable, available quantitative base-rate information. It follows from Assumption 1 in connection with both the representativeness and availability heuristics. The prediction of the growing superior influence, over time, of exemplars of concrete situations also follows from these assumptions. Specifically, because retention of concrete events extends for longer periods than retention of complex, abstract information, it becomes increasingly likely that exemplars rather than quantifications impose themselves from memory and eventually exert unopposed influence on judgment. The effect under consideration is known as a *relative sleeper effect* (cf. Gruder et al., 1978). The influence of both exemplars and base-rate information is presumed to diminish over time, but that of exemplars is expected to fade less rapidly, thereby creating the predicted sleeper effect.

2. A series of exemplars of concrete events influences issue perception more strongly than a series of exemplars of abstract events, especially when the concrete events are iconically rather than symbolically displayed. In relative terms, the superior influence of concreteness increases with time.

This prediction, including the projected dominance of exemplification by images of concrete situations, derives from Assumptions 1 and 2 as well as from the availability heuristic. Imagery can be considered a basal form of representation that is partial to concreteness. As such, it places fewer demands on information processing than alternative forms of representation that require the ideation of concrete situations.

3. A series of exemplars of events that arouse emotions influences issue perception more strongly than a series of exemplars of events that are emotionally inconsequential, especially when the emotion-arousing events are iconically rather than symbolically displayed. In relative terms, the superior influence of emotional exemplification increases with time.

These predictions derive from Assumption 2 along with the availability heuristic.

4. A series of exemplars of events that differ in relevant characteristics fosters issue perception in which the proportions of the distribution of relevant characteristics are approximately correctly represented.

Assumption 3, the quantification heuristic, is the basis of this prediction. On condition that all exemplars entail similarly engaging situations and do not appreciably differ in presentational features that affect attention and retention, the predicted perception of the distribution of characteristics is expected to be stable over time. Retention of the distribution should simply fade along with that of the exemplars. The indicated condition is rarely met, however, and predictions of shifts in the perceived distribution of events become necessary. The following predictions address such over-time shifts.

> 5. A series of exemplars of emotion-arousing and nonarousing events fosters issue perception in which the incidence of emotion-arousing events is overestimated. The degree of this overestimation increases with time.

This prediction extends Prediction 3 to the perception of the distribution of relevant characteristics of events in a set of events. The prediction is based on Assumptions 2 and 3 as well as on the availability heuristic.

> 6. A series of exemplars of events with features that give the events different amounts of attention fosters issue perception in which the incidence of particular events is overestimated to the extent that these events are attentionally favored. The degree of this overestimation increases with time.

Prediction 5 focuses on emotional reactions to exemplars in projecting the perception of the relative incidence of subsets of events. The present prediction expands this focus by giving consideration to any aspect of exemplars that would give them increased attention, this at the expense of attention to other exemplars in a given set. Prediction 6 thus applies to attention that is drawn by presentational features and to attention that derives from the recipients' interest. Presentational features involve variables such as the vividness of displays. The recipients' interest entails elements of both epistemic curiosity and hedonistic inclinations. However, the degree to which aspects of exemplars are motivationally salient to the recipients, for whatever vital or idiosyncratic reasons, is likely to be the strongest interest-generating factor.

Prediction 6 derives from Assumption 3 in connection with the availability heuristic.

DEMONSTRATION OF EXEMPLAR EFFECTS
ON ISSUE PERCEPTION

An exhaustive review of the pertinent research on exemplification in the media, especially on the effects of various forms of exemplification on the perception of social issues, has been presented by Zillmann and Brosius

(2000). The purpose of the overview here cannot be to duplicate such coverage. It is, instead, to exhibit principal exemplification strategies and to relate the findings of representative research demonstrations to the predictions articulated in the previous section.

The Base-Rate Issue

Research on the effects of news reports in which arrays of exemplars are supplemented or juxtaposed by base-rate information shows with great consistency that recipients form their assessments of the presented issues on the basis of the exemplar sets rather than on abstract, quantitative information.

Research by Brosius and Bathelt (1994) demonstrates that recipients who learn about people's likes and dislikes of particular products, or about people's support for and opposition to various civic issues, tend to base their perception of the proportion of favorably disposed people on the relative frequency of exemplars presenting favorably disposed people, irrespective of the ratios that are explicitly stated in the base-rate information. In these investigations, the ineffectiveness of presented base rates was extreme in that, when ratios apparent from exemplar distributions were contradictory to those explicitly stated, recipients formed their judgments nonetheless on the exemplars and totally ignored the stated base rates. In later research (Brosius, 1995), base rates were especially highlighted to force attention on them. Even such efforts proved inconsequential, however, and recipients continued to base their perceptions of incidence rates on sets of exemplars rather than on provided ratios.

Corroborating evidence was obtained by Gibson and Zillmann (1994); Zillmann, Gibson, Sundar, and Perkins (1996); and Zillmann, Perkins, and Sundar (1992). In these investigations, the provided base-rate information was either precise (i.e., expressed as a ratio) or vague (i.e., expressed linguistically in comparisons like "most people"). Irrespective of the mode of expression, the base rates proved inconsequential, with recipients forming perceptions on the basis of relative exemplar frequencies.

These findings lend strong support to the initial part of Prediction 1. However, the growing relative influence of exemplars over time, predicted in the subsequent part, was not in evidence in any of the cited investigations. Instead, the exemplification effects proved stable over time. Delayed effects were observed one and two weeks after exposure to news reports. These findings suggest that base-rate information never received the careful attention that it would seem to deserve. Exemplars thus could exert their overpowering influence immediately after exposure, and growing influence could not materialize.

It would be premature, however, to conclude that base-rate information is always inconsequential. Krupat, Smith, Leach, and Jackson (1997), for instance, explored the influence of reliable quantitative information in situations that gave it great diagnostic significance for a purchasing decision (specifically, the choice of a car), whereas a competing single exemplar seemed anecdotal. Under these conditions, the abstract, quantitative information exerted dominant influence on judgment.

Base-rate information, then, can have *informational utility* (cf. Zillmann, 2000) that fosters attention and careful processing, ultimately giving such information due influence on judgment. In principal terms, information that relates to individuals' immediate and prospective encounter of predicaments or opportunities is thought to have utility for these individuals, the degree of utility increasing with (a) the perceived magnitude of threats or incentives, (b) the perceived likelihood of their materialization, and (c) their perceived proximity in time. The reported findings suggest that, in these terms, informational utility is rather high for purchasing decisions and comparatively low for most issues presented in the news.

Effects of Exemplar Distributions

Effects of distributions of exemplars that differ in relevant characteristics have been examined for series in which some exemplars are supportive of a given issue, whereas others are opposed to it.

Brosius and Bathelt (1994), for instance, explored the perception of public opinion concerning, among other things, the quality of a locally produced wine. A radio broadcast featured interviews of wine drinkers who either derogated or praised the wine. The ratio of negative and positive evaluations was systematically varied, however, ranging from no unfavorable versus four favorable evaluations to the inverse situation. Intermediate ratios were created as well (i.e., 1 vs. 3, 2 vs. 2, and 3 vs. 1). In addition, the interviewer provided survey data on public opinion that were either consistent or inconsistent with the distribution apparent from the exemplars. The findings show that the respondents based their estimates of the public's liking and disliking of the wine on the exemplar distribution, even when the apparent distribution was contradicted by the survey data. Fig. 2.1 displays the findings of this experiment.

An investigation by Daschmann (1999) in the realm of political communication yielded essentially the same results. The distribution of interviews of voters presented in a print-news report was analogously manipulated (i.e., the ratios of voters for candidate A vs. candidate B) and supplemented or not with consistent or inconsistent survey projections of the upcoming election. Respondents' estimates of the vote were again a function of the exemplar distributions, not of provided base-rate information.

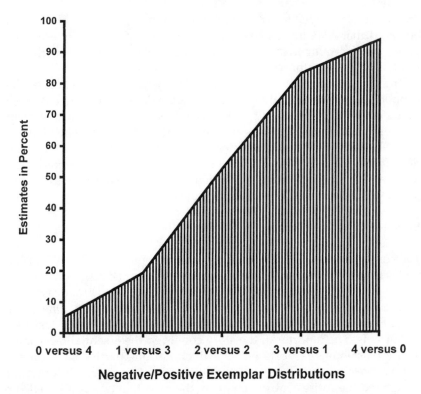

FIG. 2.1.   Perception of the public's evaluation of locally produced wine as a function of radio interviews of four wine drinkers who confessed to either like or dislike the wine of the last harvest. The ratio of likers to dislikers varied from 0:4 through 4:0. The shaded area indicates the respondents' estimates of the proportion of wine drinkers liking the wine. The close correspondence between exemplification ratio and population estimates was not affected by the revelation that in a survey only a dwindling number of wine drinkers had given the wine a favorable rating. From *Exemplification in communication* (p. 71), by D. Zillmann and H.-B. Brosius, 2000, Mahwah, NJ: Lawrence Erlbaum Associates. Copyright 2000 by Lawrence Erlbaum Associates. Adapted with permission.

Working with print-news reports, Zillmann et al. (1992) manipulated a series of interviews of dieters who either had managed to keep their weight down or failed to do so. Perceptions of the effectiveness of keeping weight under control were in line with the distribution of exemplars (i.e., 9 vs. 0, 6 vs. 3, and 3 vs. 6), the provision of base-rate information proving inconsequential again.

Zillmann et al. (1996), moreover, explored the effects of such exemplar distributions in print-news reports on family farming. Interviews with successful, rich farmers and interviews with poor farmers fearing bankruptcy were arranged in the indicated ratios. Base-rate information was presented alongside. In two similar experiments, it was once again observed that respondents base their perception of issues, the economic prospects of farming in this case, on exemplar distributions rather than on abstract base-rate information.

The findings of these investigations, in aggregate, give considerable support to Prediction 4, along with Prediction 1, and they are obviously consistent with Assumption 3, the basis of Prediction 4. Specifically, recipients of exemplar distributions apparently assess the relative incidence of exemplars with particular characteristics and retain a record of this quantification in memory. The implicit sensitivity to frequencies accords with the quantification heuristic, and the longevity of the consequences is evident from the observed effect duration of one and two weeks.

Effects of Emotional Exemplars

The consequences of audiovisually presented emotion-laden exemplars for issue perception, for the assessment of danger and risk in particular, have been examined by Aust and Zillmann (1996). Two broadcast-news reports were especially created and similarly manipulated. One of the stories concerned the risk of contracting food poisoning in fast-food restaurants. The reporter of the story conveyed the essential facts about a case of salmonella poisoning in which various parties had come to harm. Focus was on a retired couple that had died. This information comprised the entire control version of the report. In two additional versions, interviews with the retirees' adult daughter, along with the testimony of other victims, were incorporated. These interviews, although verbally identical, were given either in a nonemotional, calm and collected manner or in highly emotional fashion, with speech disrupted by choking and weeping.

The findings of the investigation reveal that emotional exemplars indeed convey threats of harm more effectively than exemplars devoid of emotion. In this particular case, the perception of risk to others and to self of contracting food poisoning in fast-food establishments, compared against the control condition, increased markedly after exposure to emotional exemplars, but not appreciably after exposure to nonemotional ones.

The effects of danger-conveying visual exemplars of a health broadcast were investigated by Zillmann and Gan (1996). The program was designed to apprise sunbathers of the danger of contracting skin cancer. After exhibiting beach lovers' habits of excessive sunbathing, it featured dermatologists who explained the etiology of melanoma and showed incidents of the cancer. The program ended with a summary of the threat of melanoma and a call for using sunblock lotion to minimize risk. The original program employed sanitized imagery of melanoma (i.e., a dime-sized affliction). This footage was replaced by more graphic, shocking, emotion-arousing images of tumors spread across arm and shoulder.

Embedded in an ostensibly unrelated survey of health-related behaviors such as smoking, excessive drinking, and sexual practices, the risk to others and self of contracting melanoma from extended sunbathing, as well as the willingness to use sunblock lotions for protection, was ascertained either shortly after exposure to the program or after a 2-week delay. The findings, summarized in Fig. 2.2, show that shortly after exposure the effect of threatening imagery was not appreciably different from that of sanitized imagery. Presumably, the message as a whole was potent enough to prevent an enhancement of concerns by the more ominous display of

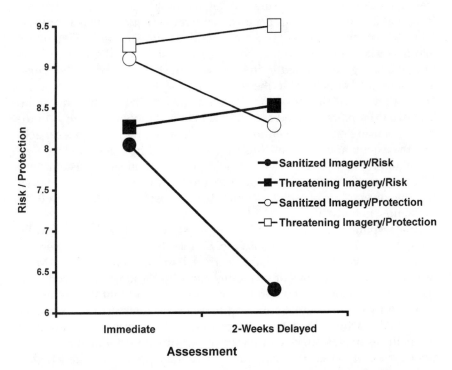

FIG. 2.2. Personal risk of contracting skin cancer from excessive sunbathing, and acceptance of preventive measures, as a function of exposure to a health broadcast featuring either sanitized or scary, threatening images of tumors. Effects were ascertained either shortly after exposure or after a 2-week delay. Relative sleeper effects of exposure are evident in the diverging gradients. Specifically, the effects of the threatening broadcast proved stable over time, whereas those of the sanitized broadcast deteriorated markedly. From *Exemplification in communication* (p. 102), by D. Zillmann and H.-B. Brosius, 2000, Mahwah, NJ: Lawrence Erlbaum Associates. Copyright 2000 by Lawrence Erlbaum Associates. Adapted with permission.

tumors. After the passage of time, however, the threatening imagery asserted itself by either elevating or sustaining the created concerns. After exposure to the sanitized imagery, the concerns clearly dissipated with time. More specifically, the influence of the program featuring sanitized images diminished over time, whereas the influence of the program featuring graphic, threatening images held steady and tended to grow.

Instead of using visual displays to evoke emotional reactions, Gibson and Zillmann (1994) employed vivid verbal descriptions of emotional happenings. A newsmagazine report about the crime of carjacking was created and manipulated. All versions presented base-rate information along with two detailed exemplars of carjackings. Base rates were given as percentages of the severity of injury incurred during such crimes, or they were suggested verbally in comparative terms. A survey was cited, stating that 75% of all carjackings do not involve physical injury to the victims, that 21% of the victims get away with minor injuries such as bruises, that 3.8% of the victims suffer severe bodily injury such as broken bones and major lacerations, and that only an exceedingly small number of victims, 0.2%, is getting killed in the course of the commission of the crime. The vague verbal parallel to these conditions stated that "most," "some," "only a few," or "almost nobody" would come to the harm in question. The two exemplars detailed carjackings in one of these four injury conditions. Focusing on the perception of the risk of getting killed in a carjacking, the exemplar conditions thus can be arranged from minimal misrepresentation (i.e., two exemplars of no injury, being most consistent with 75% or "most") through minor and severe to extreme misrepresentation (i.e., two exemplars of fatal outcomes, being most inconsistent with 0.2% or "almost nobody").

The respondents' fatality estimates are shown in Fig. 2.3. As can be seen, the presence of only two exemplars readily influenced risk perception, overpowering the available correct base-rate information. More important here, estimates of fatal outcomes of carjackings increased with the severity of exemplified bodily harm. To the extent that the exemplars that vividly detailed great suffering from severe injury elicited stronger emotional reactions than the exemplars describing minor and minimal harm, the estimates can be considered to accord with emotional reactivity. Stronger exemplar-elicited empathic distress apparently fostered higher estimates of severe harm from carjacking.

The investigation's most significant findings concern the perception of risk after the passage of time. Surely, the inappropriate exemplification of fatal outcomes resulted in a substantial misassessment of fatality-producing carjackings shortly after exposure to the report. With the passage of time, however, this misassessment grew to yet greater extremes. The divergent interaction apparent in the figure suggests, in fact, that the overestimation of risk increases with the degree of misrepresentation by

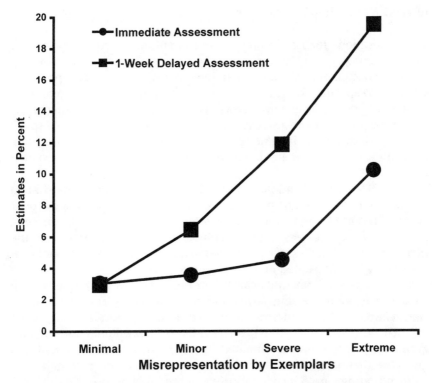

FIG. 2.3.   Perception of the relative frequency of victim fatality in carjackings as a function of exemplar usage in news reports. Under "extreme" misrepresentation, rare fatal victimizations were vividly detailed. Toward "minimal" misrepresentation, the victimizations involved successively less bodily injury but were more frequent, even typical. Despite abstract information to the contrary, fatality estimates increased with the severity of exemplified injury. This differentiation was observed shortly after exposure to the report. It was markedly stronger, however, 1 week after exposure. The divergence of the gradients indicates an absolute sleeper effect on issue perception as the result of gross misexemplification. From *Exemplification in communication* (p. 92), by D. Zillmann and H.-B. Brosius, 2000, Mahwah, NJ: Lawrence Erlbaum Associates. Copyright 2000 by Lawrence Erlbaum Associates. Adapted with permission.

exemplars. It further suggests that the indicated overestimation of risk grows with the distress-evoking capacity of exemplars.

Taken together, the reported evidence concerning the effects of emotion-evoking exemplars on the perception of issues, especially the evidence concerning substantially delayed effects of this kind, lends considerable support to all facets of Prediction 3 and its underlying components, that is, Assumption 2 and the representativeness and availability heuristics. It appears that, exactly as predicted, emotional experience fostered superior conditions for information coding and that, as a result, superior retention and ready accessibility mediated the reported effects, the delayed ones in particular.

Effects of Attentional Enhancement

The implications for issue perception of attentional focus on particular
exemplars of an exemplar series have been explored for printed news by
Gibson and Zillmann (1993, 1998). In their investigations, disproportional
attention to specific exemplars of a series, and thereby more careful processing of the specific exemplars, was accomplished by presenting assertions as personal utterances. Attention was drawn by letting people speak
for themselves, simply by placing their statements in quotation marks. In
the control condition, their statements were paraphrased and presented
as a third-person report.

In the 1998 experiment, poor and rich farmers were interviewed in an
article about the economic prospects of farming. In one version, the poor
farmers reported their plight in quotes, whereas the rich farmers'
accounts of their success were paraphrased. In the counterversion, the
rich farmers related their good fortunes in quotes, whereas the poor farmers' demise was presented in third-person format.

The results were unequivocal. When poor farmers were quoted, the
incidence of money-losing farms and of farms going into bankruptcy
was, relative to the countercondition, overestimated. Analogously, when
the rich farmers were quoted, the incidence of profitable and wealth-
generating farms was overestimated. The exemplified condition that was
given the attentional advantage, then, was consistently overestimated.

Such findings are clearly supportive of the initial part of Prediction 6
as based on Assumption 3 and the representativeness heuristic. The latter part, concerning effect shifts over time, cannot be evaluated at present, however, as the reported research did not involve delayed effect
assessments.

EPILOGUE

Exemplification theory of media influence has, no doubt, garnered a considerable amount of evidence in its support. The theory and the research it
generated, counter to likely impressions from the sampling of explorations reported here, are by no means limited to the influence of the
news, however. Much research has been conducted on the influence of
exemplification in media entertainment, and numerous findings in this
domain of media influence are also consistent with exemplification theory
(cf. Zillmann & Brosius, 2000; Zillmann & Vorderer, 2000). Exemplification
theory thus may be considered a media-influence theory of broad scope.

However, although exemplification research is burgeoning, many
aspects of the theory remain untested. Predictions 2 and 5, for instance,

have not yet been adequately examined, and the merits of others have been determined in part only. Moreover, some of the evidence is specific to particular domains of media influence, and demonstrations bridging gaps and spanning various facets of influence are yet to emanate.

Closer examination of the projected longitudinal influence of specific exemplification formats seems especially important. At present, demonstrations of over-time consequences are limited to periods of one to two weeks. Many effects, particularly those concerning the competition between image- versus text-conveyed information, might not materialize in such comparatively short periods of time. Months and perhaps years might be more appropriate units of time for compelling images to overwhelm textual specifics and to impose, if not dictate, the perception of issues. Examination of these possibilities would seem to be imperative at a time when the digital revolution of information transmission has laid the grounds for an increasingly analogue, iconic representation of all phenomena of personal consequence and civic relevance.

REFERENCES

Aust, C. F., & Zillmann, D. (1996). Effects of victim exemplification in television news on viewer perception of social issues. *Journalism & Mass Communication Quarterly, 73*(4), 787–803.

Bargh, J. A. (1984). Automatic and conscious processing of social information. In R. S. Wyer & T. K. Srull (Eds.), *Handbook of social cognition* (Vol. 3, pp. 1–43). Hillsdale, NJ: Lawrence Erlbaum Associates.

Bargh, J. A. (1996). Automaticity in social psychology. In E. T. Higgins & A. W. Kruglanski (Eds.), *Social psychology: Handbook of basic principles* (pp. 169–183). New York: Guilford.

Bargh, J. A., Lombardi, W. J., & Higgins, E. T. (1988). Automaticity of chronically accessible constructs in person X situation effects on person perception: It's just a matter of time. *Journal of Personality and Social Psychology, 55,* 599–605.

Bar-Hillel, M. (1980). The base-rate fallacy in probability judgements. *Acta Psychologica, 44,* 211–233.

Berelson, B., & Salter, P. (1946). Majority and minority Americans: An analysis of magazine fiction. *Public Opinion Quarterly, 10,* 168–190.

Bower, G. H. (1992). How might emotions affect learning? In S.-Å. Christianson (Ed.), *The handbook of emotion and memory: Research and theory* (pp. 3–31). Hillsdale, NJ: Lawrence Erlbaum Associates.

Brosius, H.-B. (1995). *Alltagsrationalität in der Nachrichtenrezeption: Ein Modell der Wahrnehmung und Verarbeitung von Nachrichteninhalten* [Everyday rationality in news reception: A model for the perception and the processing of news content]. Opladen: Westdeutscher Verlag.

Brosius, H.-B., & Bathelt, A. (1994). The utility of exemplars in persuasive communications. *Communication Research, 21*(1), 48–78.

Brosius, H.-B., Weaver, J. B., & Staab, J. F. (1993). Exploring the social and sexual "reality" of contemporary pornography. *Journal of Sex Research, 30*(2), 161–170.

Burns, B. (Ed.). (1992). *Percepts, concepts and categories: The representation and processing of information*. Amsterdam: Elsevier Science Publishers.

Cahill, L., Prins, B., Weber, M., & McGaugh, J. L. (1994). β-adrenergic activation and memory for emotional events. *Nature, 371,* 702–704.

Cannon, W. B. (1929). *Bodily changes in pain, hunger, fear and rage: An account of researches into the function of emotional excitement* (2nd ed.). New York: Appleton-Century-Crofts.

Christianson, S.-Å. (Ed.). (1992). *The handbook of emotion and memory: Research and theory*. Hillsdale, NJ: Lawrence Erlbaum Associates.

Daschmann, G. (1999, May). *Vox pop & polls: The impact of poll results and voter statements on voter judgment*. Paper presented to the Political Communication Division at the Annual Conference of the International Communication Association, San Francisco, CA.

Dominick, J. R. (1973). Crime and law enforcement on prime-time television. *Public Opinion Quarterly, 37,* 241–250.

Fiske, S. T., & Taylor, S. E. (1984). *Social cognition*. New York: Random House.

Gerbner, G., Gross, L., Morgan, M., & Signorielli, N. (1986). Living with television: The dynamics of the cultivation process. In J. Bryant & D. Zillmann (Eds.), *Perspectives on media effects* (pp. 17–40). Hillsdale, NJ: Lawrence Erlbaum Associates.

Gibson, R., & Zillmann, D. (1993). The impact of quotation in news reports on issue perception. *Journalism Quarterly, 70*(4), 793–800.

Gibson, R., & Zillmann, D. (1994). Exaggerated versus representative exemplification in news reports: Perception of issues and personal consequences. *Communication Research, 21*(5), 603–624.

Gibson, R., & Zillmann, D. (1998). Effects of citation in exemplifying testimony on issue perception. *Journalism & Mass Communication Quarterly, 75*(1), 167–176.

Greenberg, B. S., Simmons, K. W., Hogan, L., & Atkin, C. (1980). Three seasons of television characters: A demographic analysis. *Journal of Broadcasting, 24*(1), 49–60.

Gruder, C. L., Cook, T. D., Hennigan, K. M., Flay, B. R., Alessis, C., & Halamaj, J. (1978). Empirical tests of the absolute sleeper effect predicted from the discounting cue hypothesis. *Journal of Personality and Social Psychology, 36,* 1061–1074.

Hayes-Roth, B., & Hayes-Roth, F. (1977). Concept learning and the recognition and classification of exemplars. *Journal of Verbal Learning and Verbal Behavior, 16,* 321–338.

Heuer, F., & Reisberg, D. (1990). Vivid memories of emotional events: The accuracy of remembered minutiae. *Memory and Cognition, 18*(5), 496–506.

Higgins, E. T. (1996). Knowledge activation: Accessibility, applicability, and salience. In E. T. Higgins & A. W. Kruglanski (Eds.), *Social psychology: Handbook of basic principles* (pp. 133–168). New York: Guilford Press.

Jo, E., & Berkowitz, L. (1994). A priming effect analysis of media influences: An update. In J. Bryant & D. Zillmann (Eds.), *Media effects: Advances in theory and research* (pp. 43–60). Hillsdale, NJ: Lawrence Erlbaum Associates.

Kahneman, D., Slovic, P., & Tversky, A. (1982). *Judgment under uncertainty: Heuristics and biases*. Cambridge: Cambridge University Press.

Kahneman, D., & Tversky, A. (1973). On the psychology of prediction. *Psychological Review, 80,* 237–251.

Kety, S. S. (1970). The biogenic amines in the central nervous system: Their possible roles in arousal, emotion and learning. In F. O. Schmitt (Ed.), *The neurosciences: Second study program* (pp. 324–336). New York: Rockefeller University Press.

Krupat, E., Smith, R. H., Leach, C. W., & Jackson, M. A. (1997). Generalizing from atypical cases: How general a tendency? *Basic and Applied Social Psychology, 19*(3), 345–361.

LeDoux, J. E. (1992). Emotion as memory: Anatomical systems underlying indelible neural traces. In S.-Å. Christianson (Ed.), *The handbook of emotion and memory: Research and theory* (pp. 269–288). Hillsdale, NJ: Lawrence Erlbaum Associates.

McGaugh, J. L. (1992). Affect, neuromodulatory systems, and memory storage. In S.-Å. Christianson (Ed.), *The handbook of emotion and memory: Research and theory* (pp. 247–268). Hillsdale, NJ: Lawrence Erlbaum Associates.

McGaugh, J. L., & Gold, P. E. (1989). Hormonal modulation of memory. In R. B. Brush & S. Levine (Eds.), *Psychoendocrinology* (pp. 305–339). New York: Academic Press.

Mervis, C. G., & Rosch, E. (1981). Categorization of natural objects. *Annual Review of Psychology, 32,* 89–116.

Nisbett, R. E., & Ross, L. (1980). *Human inference: Strategies and shortcomings of social judgment.* Upper Saddle River, NJ: Prentice Hall.

Rosch, E., & Lloyd, B. (Eds.). (1978). *Cognition and categorization.* Hillsdale, NJ: Lawrence Erlbaum Associates.

Sapolsky, B. S., & Molitor, F. (1996). Content trends in contemporary horror films. In J. Weaver & R. Tamborini (Eds.), *Horror films: Current research on audience preferences and reactions* (pp. 33–48). Mahwah, NJ: Lawrence Erlbaum Associates.

Seggar, J. F. (1977). Television's portrayal of minorities and women, 1971–75. *Journal of Broadcasting, 21,* 435–446.

Sherman, S. J., Judd, J. M., & Park, B. (1989). Social cognition. *Annual Review of Psychology, 40,* 281–336.

Spear, N. E., & Riccio, D. C. (1994). *Memory: Phenomena and principles.* Boston: Allyn and Bacon.

Stocking, S. H., Sapolsky, B. S., & Zillmann, D. (1977). Sex discrimination in prime time humor. *Journal of Broadcasting, 21,* 447–457.

Tversky, A., & Kahneman, D. (1973). Availability: A heuristic for judging frequency and probability. *Cognitive Psychology, 5,* 207–232.

Zillmann, D. (1996). Sequential dependencies in emotional experience and behavior. In R. D. Kavanaugh, B. Zimmerberg, & S. Fein (Eds.), *Emotion: Interdisciplinary perspectives* (pp. 243–272). Mahwah, NJ: Lawrence Erlbaum Associates.

Zillmann, D. (1999). Exemplification theory: Judging the whole by some of its parts. *Media Psychology, 1,* 69–94.

Zillmann, D. (2000). Mood management in the context of selective exposure theory. In M. E. Roloff (Ed.), *Communication yearbook 23* (pp. 103–123). Thousand Oaks, CA: Sage.

Zillmann, D., & Brosius, H.-B. (2000). *Exemplification in communication: The influence of case reports on the perception of issues.* Mahwah, NJ: Lawrence Erlbaum Associates.

Zillmann, D., & Gan, S. (1996). Effects of threatening images in news programs on the perception of risk to others and self. *Medienpsychologie: Zeitschrift für Individual- und Massenkommunikation, 8*(4), 288–305, 317–318.

Zillmann, D., Gibson, R., Sundar, S. S., & Perkins, J. W. (1996). Effects of exemplification in news reports on the perception of social issues. *Journalism & Mass Communication Quarterly, 73*(2), 427–444.

Zillmann, D., Perkins, J. W., & Sundar, S. S. (1992). Impression-formation effects of printed news varying in descriptive precision and exemplifications. *Medienpsychologie: Zeitschrift für Individual- und Massenkommunikation, 4*(3), 168–185, 239–240.

Zillmann, D., & Vorderer, P. (Eds.). (2000). *Media entertainment: The psychology of its appeal.* Mahwah, NJ: Lawrence Erlbaum Associates.

Zillmann, D., & Weaver, J. B. (1997). Psychoticism in the effect of prolonged exposure to gratuitous media violence on the acceptance of violence as a preferred means of conflict resolution. *Personality and Individual Differences, 22*(5), 613–627.

Chapter 3

Growing Up with Television: Cultivation Processes

GEORGE GERBNER
Annenberg School of Communications, University of Pennsylvania

LARRY GROSS
University of Pennsylvania

MICHAEL MORGAN
University of Massachusetts–Amherst

NANCY SIGNORIELLI
University of Delaware

JAMES SHANAHAN
Cornell University

Television is the source of the most broadly shared images and messages in history. It is the mainstream of the common symbolic environment into which our children are born and in which we all live out our lives. Even though new forms of media seem to sprout up weekly, television's mass ritual shows no signs of weakening, as its consequences are increasingly felt around the globe.

Our research project, Cultural Indicators, is designed to study television policies, programs, and impacts. Begun in 1967, Cultural Indicators research tracks the central streams of television's prime-time and weekend-daytime dramatic content and explores the consequences of growing up and living in a cultural environment dominated by television. The project has accumulated a large database that we have used to develop and refine the theoretical approach and the research strategy we call Cultivation Analysis, which focuses specifically on television's contributions to viewers' conceptions of social reality. In this chapter, we summarize and illustrate our theory of the dynamics of the cultivation process, both in the United States and around the world. This chapter updates and expands material presented in earlier editions of this book (Gerbner, Gross, Morgan, & Signorielli, 1986; 1994; for more detailed treatments, see Signorielli & Morgan, 1990; Shanahan & Morgan, 1999).

TELEVISION IN SOCIETY

Television is a centralized system of storytelling. Its drama, commercials, news, and other programs bring a relatively coherent system of images and messages into every home. That system cultivates from infancy the predispositions and preferences that used to be acquired from other "primary" sources and that are so important in research on other media.

Transcending historic barriers of literacy and mobility, television has become the primary common source of socialization and everyday information (usually cloaked in the form of entertainment) of otherwise heterogeneous populations. We have now reached an unprecedented juncture at which television brings virtually everyone into a shared national culture. Television provides, perhaps for the first time since preindustrial religion, a daily ritual that elites share with many other publics. As with religion, the social function of television lies in the continual repetition of stories (myths, "facts," lessons, and so on) that serve to define the world and legitimize a particular social order.

Television is different from earlier media in its ever-centralizing mass production of a coherent set of images and messages produced for large and diverse populations and in its relatively nonselective, almost ritualistic, use by most viewers. Programs that seem to be intended for very different market segments are cut from the same mold; when surface-level differences are wiped away, what remains are often surprisingly similar and complementary visions of life and society, consistent ideologies, and stable accounts of the "facts" of life. Exposure to the total pattern rather than to specific genres or programs is therefore what accounts for the historically distinct consequences of living with television: the cultivation of shared conceptions of reality among otherwise diverse publics.

In saying this, we do not minimize the importance of specific programs, selective attention and perception, specifically targeted communications, individual and group differences, and research on individual attitude and behavior change. But giving primary attention to those aspects and terms of traditional media effects research risks losing sight of what is most distinctive and significant about television as the common storyteller of our age.

Compared to other media, television provides a relatively restricted set of choices for a virtually unrestricted variety of interests and publics. Even with the expansion of cable and satellite channels serving ever-narrower *niche* audiences, most television programs are by commercial necessity designed to be watched by large and heterogeneous audiences in a relatively nonselective fashion. Moreover, the general amount of viewing follows the lifestyle of the viewer. The audience is always the group available at a certain time of the day, week, and season. Viewing decisions depend more on the clock than on the program. The number and variety of choices available to view when most viewers are available to watch is also limited by the fact that many programs designed for the same broad audience tend to be similar in their basic makeup and appeal (Signorielli, 1986).

In the typical U.S. home, the television set is in use for about seven hours a day. The more people watch, the less selective they can be (Sun, 1989). The most frequently recurring features of television cut across all types of programming and are inescapable for the regular viewer (Signorielli, 1986). Researchers who attribute findings to news viewing or preference for action programs and so forth overlook the fact that most of those who watch more news or action programs watch more of all types of programs, and that, in any case, many different types of programs, including news, share similar important features of storytelling.

What is most likely to cultivate stable and common conceptions of reality is, therefore, the overall pattern of programming to which total communities are regularly exposed over long periods of time. That is the pattern of settings, casting, social typing, actions, and related outcomes that cuts across program types and viewing modes and defines the world of television. Viewers are born into that symbolic world and cannot avoid exposure to its recurrent patterns, usually many times a day. This is not to claim that any individual program, type of program, or channel (e.g., family programs, talk shows, sports networks, cooking channels, news channels, violent films, and so on) might not have some "effects" of some kind or another; rather, it is to emphasize that what we call "cultivation analysis" focuses on the consequences of long-term exposure to the entire *system* of messages, in the aggregate.

CULTURAL INDICATORS

The Cultural Indicators project is historically grounded, theoretically guided, and empirically supported (Gerbner, 1969, 1970, 1972a). Although most early studies focused on the nature and functions of television violence, the project was broadly conceived from the outset. Even violence was found to be primarily a demonstration of power in the world of television, with serious implications for social control and for the confirmation and perpetuation of minority status (Gerbner, Gross, Signorielli, Morgan, & Jackson-Beeck, 1979; Morgan, 1983). As it developed, the project continued to take into account a wider range of topics, issues, and concerns (Gerbner & Gross, 1976). We have investigated the extent to which television viewing contributes to audience conceptions and actions in areas such as gender, minority and age-role stereotypes, health, science, the family, educational achievement and aspirations, politics, religion, the environment, and numerous other topics, many of which have also been examined in a variety of cross-cultural comparative contexts.[1]

The Cultural Indicators approach involves a three-pronged research strategy. (For a more detailed description see Gerbner, 1973.) The first prong, called "institutional process analysis," is designed to investigate the formation and systematization of policies directing the massive flow of media messages. (For some examples see Gerbner, 1972b, 1988.) More directly relevant to our present focus are the other two prongs we call "message system analysis" and "cultivation analysis."

Message system analysis involves the systematic examination of week-long annual samples of network television drama, in order to reliably delineate selected features and trends in the world that television presents to its viewers. These analyses began in 1967 and have continued under various auspices until today.[2] In recent years, cable programming and additional genres have been added into the analysis. We believe that the most pervasive patterns common to many different types of programs but characteristic of the system of programming as a whole hold the potential lessons television cultivates.

In cultivation analysis, we examine the responses given to questions about social reality among those with varying amounts of exposure to the

---

[1]The Cultural Indicators Project began in 1967–1968 with a study for the National Commission on the Causes and Prevention of Violence. It has continued under the sponsorships of the U.S. Surgeon General's Scientific Advisory Committee on Television and Social Behavior, the National Institute of Mental Health, the White House Office of Telecommunications Policy, the American Medical Association, the U.S. Administration on Aging, the National Science Foundation, the W. Alton Jones Foundation, the International Research and Exchanges Board (IREX), the Carter Center of Emory University, the Hoso Bunka Foundation of Japan, the Finnish Broadcasting Company, the Hungarian Institute for Public Opinion Research, Moscow State University, the National Center for Public Opinion Research of the USSR, the Robert Wood Johnson Foundation, the Screen Actors Guild, Cornell University, and the Universities of Pennsylvania, Massachusetts, and Delaware.

[2]The most recent sample is from November 2000. To date, the message system database has accumulated detailed coded observations of over 46,000 major and minor characters and over 2,400 programs. A complementary database at the University of Delaware began in 1993 and contains observations for 1,200 programs and 4,600 major and supporting characters.

world of television. We want to determine whether those who spend more time with television are more likely to perceive social reality in ways that reflect the potential lessons of the television world (the "television answer") than are those who watch less television but are otherwise comparable (in terms of important demographic characteristics) to the heavy viewers.

We use the concept of "cultivation" to describe the independent contributions television viewing makes to viewer conceptions of social reality. The most general hypothesis of cultivation analysis is that those who spend more time "living" in the world of television are more likely to see the "real world" in terms of the images, values, portrayals, and ideologies that emerge through the lens of television. The "cultivation differential" is the margin of difference in conceptions of reality between light and heavy viewers in the same demographic subgroups. It represents the difference television viewing makes to some outlook or belief, in dynamic interaction with other factors and processes. Recent research has established the stability of the cultivation differential across different variables and populations, showing a remarkable consistency in the direction predicted by theory over many dozens of studies (Shanahan & Morgan, 1999).

THE SHIFT FROM "EFFECTS" TO "CULTIVATION" RESEARCH

The bulk of scientific inquiry (and most public discourse) about television's social impact follows theoretical models and methodological procedures of marketing and persuasion research. Much time, energy, and money have been invested in efforts to change people's attitudes and behaviors. By and large, however, the conceptualization of "effect" as short-run individual change has not produced research that helps us understand the distinctive features of television we have noted earlier. These features include massive, long-term, and common exposure of large and heterogeneous publics to centrally produced, mass-distributed, and repetitive systems of stories. But research traditions and ideological inhibitions both tend to produce resistance to the "cultivation perspective."

Traditional-effects research is based on evaluating specific informational, educational, political, or marketing efforts in terms of selective exposure and measurable before/after differences between those exposed to some message and others not exposed. Scholars steeped in those traditions find it difficult to accept the emphasis of cultivation analysis on total immersion rather than selective viewing and on the spread of stable similarities of outlook rather than on the remaining sources of cultural differentiation and change.

Similarly, we are still imbued with the ideology of print culture and its ideals of freedom, diversity, and an active electorate. This ideal also assumes the production and selection of information and entertainment from the point of view of a variety of competing and conflicting interests. That is why many also resist what they assume to be the emphasis of cultivation analysis on the "passive" viewer and the dissolution of authentic publics that this emphasis implies. They point to what they see as serious differences between cultivation theory and more recent excursions into reception models of mass communication (see McQuail, 2000). From the reception perspective, it seems logical to argue that other circumstances do intervene and can neutralize the cultivation process, that viewers do watch selectively, that program selections make a difference, and that how viewers construct meaning from texts is more important than how much they watch.

We do not dispute these contentions. The polysemy of mediated texts is well established. From the cultivation perspective, though, to say that audiences' interactions with media texts can produce enormous diversity and complexity does not negate that there can be important commonalities and consistencies as well across large bodies of media output. To explore those commonalities, as cultivation does, is not to deny that there are indeed differences; similarly, the examination of differences need not (and, arguably, *can*not) deny the possibility of shared meanings in a culture.

Polysemy is not limitless, and preferred readings can have great power. To glorify or privilege only the fact of polysemy is to risk removing any vestige of articulatory or determinational power from the text—and thereby to render culture impotent as well. Equally, concentrating on individual differences and immediate change misses the profound historical challenge television poses not only for research strategies but also for traditional theories of democratic government. That challenge is the absorption of diverse conceptions and attitudes into a stable and common mainstream. Thus, although individual viewers will certainly differ (and differ substantially) in their "reading" of any given television program, cultivation does not ask people what they think *about television texts,* much less any individual text. Rather, cultivation looks at exposure to massive flows of messages over long periods of time. The cultivation process takes place in the *interaction* of the viewer with the message; neither the message nor the viewer are all-powerful. In a sense, cultivation looks at the "master text" composed of the enduring, resilient, and residual core that is left over when all the particular individual and program-specific differences cancel each other out.

Thus, cultivation does not see television's contribution to conceptions of social reality as a one-way, monolithic "push" process. The influences of a pervasive medium on the composition and structure of the symbolic environment are subtle, complex, and intermingled with other influences. Moreover, the question of "which comes first" is misleading and irrelevant, as is the presumed dichotomy between an "active" or "passive" audience (see Shanahan & Morgan, 1999). People are born into a symbolic environment with television as its mainstream; viewing both shapes and is a stable part of lifestyles and outlooks. Many of those with certain social and psychological characteristics, dispositions, and worldviews, as well as those who have fewer alternatives, use television as their major vehicle of cultural participation. To the extent that television dominates their sources of entertainment and information, continued exposure to its messages is likely to reiterate, confirm, and nourish—that is, cultivate—its own values and perspectives (see Gerbner, 1990; Morgan & Signorielli, 1990).

The point is that cultivation is not conceived as a unidirectional but rather more like a gravitational process. The angle and direction of the "pull" depends on where groups of viewers and their styles of life are with reference to the line of gravity, the mainstream of the world of television. Each group may strain in a different direction, but all groups are affected by the same central current. Cultivation is thus a continual, dynamic, ongoing process of interaction among messages, audiences, and contexts.

METHODS OF CULTIVATION ANALYSIS

Cultivation analysis begins with message system analysis identifying the most recurrent, stable, and overarching patterns of television content. These are the consistent images, portrayals, and values that cut across most types of programs and are virtually inescapable for regular (and especially the heavy) viewers. They are the aggregate messages embedded in television as a system rather than in specific programs, types, channels, or genres.

There are many critical discrepancies between the world and the "world as portrayed on television." Findings from systematic analyses of television's message systems are used to formulate questions about the potential "lessons" viewing may hold for people's conceptions of social reality. Some of the questions are semiprojective, some use a forced-choice or forced-error format, and others simply measure beliefs, opinions, attitudes, or behaviors. (None ask respondents of their views about television itself or about any specific program or message.)

Using standard techniques of survey methodology, the questions are posed to samples (national probability, regional, convenience) of adults, adolescents, or children. Secondary analyses of large-scale national surveys (for example, the National Opinion Research Center's General Social Surveys) have often been used when they include questions that relate to potential "lessons" of the television world and when viewing data are available for the respondents.

Television viewing is usually assessed by asking about the amount of time respondents watch television on an "average day." Multiple measures are used when available. Because these measures of amount of viewing are assumed to provide relative, not absolute, indicators, the determination of what constitutes "light," "medium," and "heavy" viewing is made on a sample-by-sample basis, using as close to an even three-way split of hours of daily television viewing as possible. What is important is that there should be significant relative differences in viewing levels, not the actual or specific amount of viewing. The heaviest viewers of any sample of respondents form the population on which cultivation can be tested.[3] The analysis of simple patterns across light, medium, and heavy viewing groups (overall and in key subgroups) is useful to illuminate the general nature of the cultivation relationship, but it is normally followed up with more stringent multivariate analysis using continuous data.

The observable evidence of cultivation is likely to be modest in terms of absolute size. Even "light" viewers may be watching several hours of television a day and, of course, live in the same general culture as heavy viewers. Therefore, the discovery of a consistent pattern of even small but pervasive differences between light and heavy viewers may be of far-reaching consequence. Extensive and systematic reexamination of hundreds of cultivation studies carried out over more than two decades (using the statistical techniques of meta-analysis; Shanahan & Morgan, 1999) has shown that cultivation relationships typically manifest a strength of about .10 using a common metric, the Pearson correlation coefficient.

What some critics belittle as "small effects" may have significant repercussions. It takes but a few degrees shift in the average temperature to have an ice age or global warming. The 2000 U.S. presidential elections showed the havoc that could be wreaked by a miniscule percentage of votes. A range of 5 to 15% margins (typical of our "cultivation differentials") in a large and otherwise stable field often signals a landslide, a market takeover, or an epidemic, and it overwhelmingly tips the scale of any closely balanced choice, vote, or other decision. A single percentage point ratings difference is worth many millions of dollars in advertising revenue—as the media know only too well. Thus, a slight but pervasive (e.g., generational) shift in the cultivation of common perspectives may alter the cultural climate and upset the balance of social and political decision making.

---

[3]In all analyses we use a number of demographic variables as controls. These are applied both separately and simultaneously. Included are gender, age, race, education, income, and political self-designation (liberal, moderate, conservative). Where applicable, other controls, such as urban-rural residence, newspaper reading, and party affiliation, are also used.

MAINSTREAMING

Most modern cultures consist of many diverse currents but in the context of a dominant structure of attitudes, beliefs, values, and practices. This dominant current is not simply the sum total of all the crosscurrents and subcurrents. Rather, it is the most general, functional and stable mainstream, representing the broadest dimensions of shared meanings and assumptions. It is that which ultimately defines all the other crosscurrents and subcurrents, including what Williams (1977) called "residual and emergent strains." Television's central role in our society makes it the primary channel of the mainstream of our culture.

This mainstream can be thought of as a relative commonality of outlooks and values that heavy exposure to the television world tends to cultivate. "Mainstreaming" means that heavy viewing may absorb or override differences in perspectives and behavior that ordinarily stem from other factors and influences. In other words, differences found in the responses of different groups of viewers, differences that usually are associated with the varied cultural, social, and political characteristics of these groups, are diminished in the responses of heavy viewers in these same groups. For example, regional differences, political ideology, and socioeconomic differences are much less influential on the attitudes and beliefs of heavy viewers (Gerbner, Gross, Morgan, & Signorielli, 1980; Morgan, 1986).

As a process, mainstreaming represents the theoretical elaboration and empirical verification of television's cultivation of common perspectives. It represents a relative homogenization, an absorption of divergent views, and an apparent convergence of disparate outlooks on the overarching patterns of the television world. Former and traditional distinctions (which flourished, in part, through the relative diversity provided by print) become blurred as successive generations and groups are enculturated into television's version of the world. Through the process of mainstreaming, television may have become the true "melting pot" of the American people—and increasingly of other countries around the globe.

THE FINDINGS OF CULTIVATION ANALYSIS

Clear-cut divergences between symbolic reality and independently observable ("objective") reality provide convenient tests of the extent to which television's versions of "the facts" are incorporated or absorbed into what heavy viewers take for granted about the world. For example, we found in an early study that television drama tends to sharply underrepresent older people. Although those over 65 constitute a rapidly growing segment of the U.S. population, heavy viewers were more likely to feel that the elderly are a "vanishing breed"—that "compared to 20 years ago," there are fewer of them, that they are in worse health, and that they don't live as long—all contrary to fact (Gerbner, Gross, Signorielli, & Morgan, 1980).

As another example, consider how likely people on television are to encounter violence compared to the rest of us. Three decades of message system analyses show that half or more of television characters are involved each week in some kind of violent action. Although FBI statistics have clear limitations, they indicate that in any one year fewer than 1% of people in the United States are victims of criminal violence. We have found considerable support for the proposition that heavy exposure to the world of television cultivates exaggerated perceptions of the number of people involved in violence in any given week (Gerbner et al., 1979, 1980; Shanahan & Morgan, 1999), as well as numerous other inaccurate beliefs about crime and law enforcement.

The "facts" of the television world are evidently learned quite well, whether or not viewers profess a belief in what they see on television or claim to be able to distinguish between factual and fictional presentations. Indeed, most of what we know, or think we know, is a mixture of all the stories and images we have absorbed. The labels of "factual," which may be highly selective, and "fictional," which may be highly realistic, are more questions of style than function within a total framework of knowledge. But in any case, the investigation is not limited to the lessons of television "facts" compared to real-world (or even imaginary but different) statistics. The repetitive "lessons" we learn from television, beginning with infancy, are likely to become the basis for a broader worldview, making television a significant source of general values, ideologies, and perspectives as well as specific assumptions, beliefs, and images. Some of the most interesting and important issues for cultivation analysis involve the symbolic transformation of message system data into hypotheses about more general issues and assumptions (see also Hawkins & Pingree, 1982, 1990).

One example of this is what we have called the "mean world" syndrome. Our message data say little directly about either the selfishness or altruism of people, and there are certainly no real-world statistics about the extent to which people can be trusted. Yet, we have found that long-term exposure to television, in which frequent violence is virtually inescapable, tends to cultivate the image of a relatively mean and dangerous world. Responses of heavier compared to matching groups of lighter viewers suggest the conception of reality in which greater protection is needed, most people "cannot be trusted," and most people are "just looking out for themselves" (Gerbner et al., 1980; Signorielli, 1990).

The Mean World Index, composed of violence-related items, also illustrates the mainstreaming implications of viewing (Signorielli, 1990). For example, combining data from the 1980, 1983, and 1986 General Social Surveys, heavy and light viewers who had not been to college were equally likely to score high on the Mean World Index: 53% of both the heavy and light viewers agreed with two or three of the items. However, among those who had some college education, television viewing made a considerable difference: 28% of the light viewers compared to 43% of the heavy viewers in this subgroup had a high score on the Mean World Index. There is thus a 25-percentage point difference between the two subgroups of light viewers but only a 10-point spread between the two subgroups of heavy viewers. The heavy viewers of otherwise different groups are both in the "television mainstream."

Another example of extrapolated assumptions concerns the image of women. Our message system analyses in the 1970s and 1980s consistently showed that men outnumbered women on television by a factor of three to one; throughout the 1990s, despite all the changes taking place in the role of women in the real world, the population of the television world remained between 60 and 65% male (Signorielli & Kahlenberg, in press). Yet, the dominant majority status of men on television does not mean that heavy viewers ignore daily experience and underestimate the number of women in society. Rather, underrepresentation in the world of television means a relatively narrow (and thus more stereotyped) range of roles and activities. Most groups of heavy viewers—with other characteristics held constant—score higher on a "sexism scale" using data from the NORC General Social Surveys (Signorielli, 1989).

Several other studies have examined assumptions relating to gender roles in samples of children and adolescents. Morgan (1982) found that television cultivated such notions as "women are happiest at home raising children" and "men are born with more ambition than women." Rothschild (1984) found that third- and fifth-grade children who watched more television were more likely to stereotype both gender-related activities (e.g., cooking, playing sports) and gender-related qualities (e.g., warmth, independence) along traditional gender-role lines. Although viewing seems to cultivate adolescents' and children's attitudes about gender-related chores, viewing was not related to actually doing these chores (Morgan, 1987; Signorielli & Lears, 1992).

Other studies have dealt with assumptions about marriage and work. Signorielli (1993) found that television cultivates realistic views about marriage but contradictory views about work. Heavy viewing adolescents were more likely to want high-status jobs that would give them a chance to earn a lot of money but also wanted to have their jobs be relatively easy with long vacations and time to do other things. Signorielli (1991) found that television viewing cultivates conceptions that reflect the ambivalent presentation of marriage on television. Adolescents who watched more television were more likely to say they wanted to get married, to stay married to the same person for life, and to have children. Nevertheless, there was a positive relationship between amount of viewing and expressing the opinion that one sees so few good or happy marriages that one could question marriage as a way of life.

Many of television's families do not fit the "traditional nuclear" model, and single-parent families are overrepresented. Morgan, Leggett, and Shanahan (1999) found that, beyond all controls, heavy viewers were more likely than light viewers to accept single parenthood and out-of-wedlock childbirth. Nevertheless, the single parent on TV bears little resemblance to single-parent households in reality. On television, the single parent typically is a well-off male with full-time, live-in, domestic help. Heavy viewers may thus be more accepting of a highly fantasized and luxurious notion of single-parenthood.

Other studies have looked at issues of the cultivation of attitudes toward science or the environment. For instance, Shanahan, Morgan, and Stenbjerre (1997) found that heavy viewers are less likely to be knowledgeable about the environment, less likely to be active on environmental issues, and more likely to be fearful about specific environmental problems or issues. A cultivated fearful withdrawal from science issues was adduced, echoing earlier work (Gerbner, Gross, Morgan, & Signorielli, 1981) on the cultivation of images of science (also see Shanahan & McComas, 1999, for a more general treatment of TV and the environment).

Other extrapolations from content patterns have involved political views. For example, we have argued that as television seeks large and heterogeneous audiences, its messages are designed to disturb as few as possible. Therefore they tend to "balance" opposing perspectives, and to steer a "middle course" along the supposedly nonideological mainstream. We have found that heavy viewers are substantially more likely to label themselves as being "moderate" rather than either "liberal" or "conservative" (see Gerbner et al., 1982; Gerbner, Gross, Morgan, & Signorielli, 1984).

We have observed this finding in over two decades of the General Social Survey data. GSS data from 1994 through 1998 reveal this pattern once again, as shown in Table 3.1. Heavy viewers in all subgroups tend to see themselves as "moderate" and avoid saying they are either "liberal" or "conservative." Fig. 3.1 shows the patterns for Democrats, Independents, and Republicans. The percentage choosing the "moderate" label is again substantially higher among heavy viewers, regardless of party; heavy viewing Democrats are less likely to say they are "liberal," whereas heavy viewing Republicans are less likely to call themselves "conservative." The general pattern shown in these data has appeared every year since 1975.

TABLE 3.1

Television Viewing and Political Self-Designation, in the 1994, 1996, and 1998 General Social Surveys (N's in parentheses)

Percent who call themselves:

TV Viewing:	Liberal				Moderate				Conservative			
	L	M	H	Gamma	L	M	H	Gamma	L	M	H	Gamma
Overall (5972)	30	27	26	-.05	32	37	41	.13***	39	36	33	-.08***
Men (2594)	27	26	24	-.05	31	35	42	.15***	42	40	34	-.10**
Women (3378)	31	28	28	-.06	32	38	41	.11***	36	33	32	-.06*
Young (1250)	41	32	29	-.17***	28	37	43	.20***	30	31	28	-.04
Middle (3742)	27	27	28	.00	33	36	39	.08**	40	37	34	-.08**
Older (968)	20	20	21	.02	32	38	44	.15**	47	42	35	-.17**
Low Educ. (2737)	19	24	25	.07*	40	41	43	.03	40	34	32	-.09**
High Educ. (3221)	34	30	29	-.08*	28	33	38	.14***	38	38	33	-.06
Low Income (2793)	34	31	28	-.08*	31	38	41	.11***	35	31	31	.03
High Income (2518)	29	25	25	-.09*	30	34	39	.10**	40	41	37	-.03
Democrat (2083)	48	41	36	-.15***	34	38	40	.08*	18	21	24	.11*
Independent (2102)	31	27	24	-.12**	38	42	45	.08*	30	32	32	.02
Republican (1662)	9	12	13	.14*	21	29	36	.22***	70	59	50	-.25***

* p<.05   ** p<.01   *** p<.001

Notes: TV viewing: Light = 1 hour or less daily (N = 1586); Medium = 2 or 3 hours daily (N = 2860); Heavy = 4 or more hours daily (N = 1803). Age: Younger = 18 to 30 years old; Middle = 31 to 64 years old; Older = 65 years or older. Education: Low = 12 or fewer years; High = 13 or more years (at least some college). Income: Low = less than $35,000 yearly; High = $35,000 or more yearly.

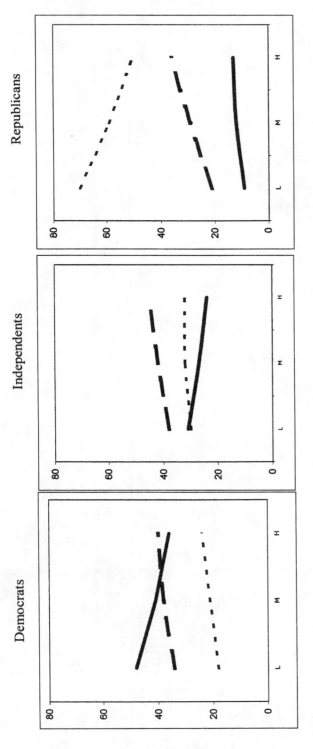

FIG. 3.1. Comparisons of political self-designation by amount of viewing within parties.

Liberals
Moderates
Conservatives

Yet, looking at the actual positions taken on a number of political issues shows that the mainstream does not mean the "middle of the road." When we analyzed responses to questions in the NORC General Social Surveys about attitudes and opinions on such topics as racial segregation, homosexuality, abortion, minority rights, and other issues that have traditionally divided liberals and conservatives, we found such division mostly among those who watch little television. Overall, self-styled moderates are much closer to conservatives than they are to liberals. Among heavy viewers, liberals and conservatives are closer to each other than among light viewers. We have also noted (Gerbner et al., 1982, 1984) that although mainstreaming bends toward the right on political issues, it leans toward a populist stance on economic issues (e.g., demanding more social services but lower taxes), reflecting the influence of a marketing orientation and setting up potential conflicts of demands and expectations.

Implications of cultivation for foreign policy were reflected in a study of attitudes toward the war in the Persian Gulf (Lewis, Jhally, & Morgan, 1991). Heavy television viewers were more familiar with the military terminology used and more supportive of the war but less informed about issues and the Middle East in general. Overall amount of viewing was far more important than specific exposure to news.

Also, the 1990s saw a great deal of progress on research seeking to uncover cognitive explanations for the mechanics of cultivation: how does it "work"? A model first offered by Hawkins and Pingree (1982) focused on how television contributes to conceptions of social reality "within the heads" of individuals by breaking down the process into two discrete steps, delineated as "learning" and "construction." Yet, no support for this model was generated. Similarly, studies that attempted to shed light on black-box cognitive processes by highlighting the concept of the "perceived reality" did not produce any firm conclusions (Slater & Elliott, 1982; Potter, 1986).

Shapiro and Lang (1991) hypothesized that television can affect reality perceptions because people simply forget that what they see on TV is not real. Mares (1996) tested this hypothesis and found that those who tended to confuse fiction programs for reality saw the world as a meaner, more violent place, and also gave "TV answers" to questions about social class estimates. But Shrum (1997) argued that people do not consider the source of their information when making social reality judgments, and he offered a different explanation of Mares' data.

Shrum's basic idea is that, because TV images are "heuristically" available to heavy viewers, they tend to use them more readily in making mental judgments, in a kind of cognitive shortcut. Most of Shrum's studies (see, e.g., Shrum 1995, 1999) find that heavy viewers give faster responses to questions about dependent variables, in directions consistent with what cultivation predicts. A speedy response to a question implies that an answer is more readily accessible, that the general issue is more salient, that the respondent does not have to dig very deeply to come up with an answer. Shrum's cognitive account is highly supportive of cultivation. It also suggests that television does not necessarily *change* attitudes, but that it makes them *stronger*.

INTERNATIONAL CULTIVATION ANALYSIS

Cultivation analysis is ideally suited to multinational and cross-cultural comparative study (Gerbner, 1977, 1989; Morgan, 1990). In fact, such a study is the best test of systemwide similarities and differences across national boundaries and of the actual significance of national cultural policies.

Every country's television system reflects the historical, political, social, economic, and cultural contexts within which it has developed (Gerbner, 1958, 1969). Although U.S. films and television are a significant presence on the screens of most countries, they combine with local and other productions to compose synthetic "worlds" that are culture specific. Other media systems and policies may or may not project images and portrayals that are as stable, coherent, and homogeneous as those of U.S. media (as we note later, we found this, surprisingly, to be the case in the former Soviet Union). Therefore, they may or may not lend themselves to the type of cultivation and mainstreaming we find in the United States (see Gerbner, 1990; Morgan, 1990; Morgan & Shanahan, 1995; Tamborini & Choi, 1990).

Pingree and Hawkins (1981) found that exposure to U.S. programs (especially crime and adventure) was significantly related to Australian students' scores on "Mean World" and "Violence in Society" indices concerning Australia, but not the United States. Viewing Australian programs was unrelated to these conceptions, but those who watched more U.S. programs were more likely to see Australia as dangerous and mean. Weimann's (1984) study of high school and college students in Israel found that heavy viewers had an idealized, "rosier" image of the standard of living in the United States.

In England, Wober (1978) found little support for cultivation in terms of images of violence. (See also Wober, 1984, 1990; Wober & Gunter, 1988.) But there was little violence in British programs, and U.S. programs only made up about 15% of British screen time (see also Shanahan & Morgan, 1999). Piepe, Charlton, and Morey (1990) found evidence of political "homogenization" (mainstreaming) in Britain that was highly congruent with U.S. findings (Gerbner, Gross, Morgan, & Signorielli, 1982), as did Morgan and Shanahan (1995) in Argentina.

In the Netherlands, Bouwman (1984) found weak associations between the amount of viewing and perceptions of violence, victimization, and mistrust. But the findings reveal the importance of cultural context in comparative cultivation research. Content analyses showed a good deal of similarity between U.S. and Dutch television (Bouwman & Signorielli, 1985; Bouwman & Stappers, 1984), and much programming was imported from the United States. Yet, it was found that both light and heavy viewers see about equal amounts of fictional entertainment, but heavy viewers see more "informational" programs, a situation quite different from that in the United States (see also Bouwman, 1987; Stappers, 1984).

Cultivation analyses about conceptions of violence, sex roles, political orientations, "traditional" values, social stereotypes, and other topics have been conducted in numerous other countries, including Sweden (Hedinsson & Windahl, 1984; Reimer & Rosengren, 1990), Argentina (Morgan & Shanahan, 1995), the Philippines (Tan, Tan, & Tan, 1987), Taiwan and Mexico (Tan, Li, & Simpson, 1986), Japan (Saito, 1991), and Thailand (Tan & Suarchavarat, 1988). These studies show the complex ways in which the viewing of local or imported programming can interact with distinct cultural contexts. For example, in Korea, Kang and Morgan (1988) found that exposure to U.S. television was associated with more "liberal" perspectives about gender roles and family values among females. At the same time, more viewing of U.S. television among Korean male students correlated with greater hostility toward the U.S. and protectiveness toward Korean culture, suggesting a "backlash" of nationalism among the more politicized college students.

Most of these studies examined single countries. Nevertheless, other studies have explored the comparative aspects of cultivation analysis. Morgan and Shanahan (1992) analyzed adolescents in Taiwan and Argentina. In Argentina, where television is supported by commercials and features many U.S. programs, heavy viewing cultivates traditional gender roles and authoritarianism. In Taiwan, where media are more state controlled, with fewer U.S. imports, and where overall viewing is much lighter, cultivation was much less apparent. Also, Morgan (1990) compared the cultivation of sex-role stereotypes in five different countries.

A study of U.S. and (what was then) Soviet television conducted in 1989 and 1990 found that television played a different role in the two countries. In the United States, but not in the former Soviet Union, television was associated with heightened anxieties about neighborhood safety, perhaps as a result of the much lower frequency of violence on Soviet television. In both countries, but especially in the former Soviet Union, the more people watched television the more likely they were to say that housework is primarily the responsibility of the woman. General satisfaction with life was consistently lower among heavy than among light television viewers in the United States, but not in the former Soviet Union (where it was relatively low for everyone).

Lacking regular prime-time dramatic series and relying more on movies, theater, documentaries, and the classics, Soviet television did, in fact, present more diversified dramatic fare than U.S. television. Perhaps due to this, television viewing seemed to have far greater mainstreaming consequences in the United States than was the case in the Soviet Union. The availability of different cultural and language programming in the different former Soviet republics may also have contributed to the relative diversity of their television—and to the centrifugal forces that eventually tore the Soviet Union apart.

In sum, in countries in which television's portrayals are less repetitive and homogeneous than in the United States, the results of cultivation analysis also tend to be less predictable and consistent. The extent to which cultivation will occur in a given country will also depend on various structural factors, such as the number of channels available, overall amount of broadcasting time, and amount of time audiences spend viewing. But it will especially depend on the amount of diversity in the available content, which is not necessarily related to the number of channels. A few channels with a diverse and balanced program structure can foster (and, in fact, compel) more diversified viewing than many channels competing for the same audience by using similar appeals and lending themselves to viewer selection of the same "preferences" most of the time.

Different media systems differ along all these dimensions, and complex interactions among these elements may account for substantial cross-cultural variations in cultivation. Imported U.S. programs can augment, diminish, or be irrelevant to these dynamics. The key questions are: (a) How important is television in the culture? and (b) How consistent and coherent is the total system of its messages? The more important, consistent, and coherent the more cultivation can be expected. The privatization of former public service broadcast systems around the world and the march toward globalization in programming, distribution, and marketing together make the need for international cultivation analysis more critical than ever.

CULTIVATION IN THE 21ST CENTURY

The theory of cultivation was developed when "television" in the United States was synonymous with three national broadcast networks, plus a small handful of independent and public/educational stations. The three major networks attracted well over 90% of the viewing audience, night after night. Fledgling cable systems simply extended the reach of the networks, providing little if any competitive programming.

Those days of network dominance are long gone. Technological developments such as cable and satellite networks, VCRs, and the Internet have brought a significant erosion in audience share (and revenue) for the old "Big Three" broadcasting networks and have altered the marketing and distribution of movies. Yet, there is little evidence that proliferation of channels has led to any substantially greater diversity of content. Indeed, the mere availability of more channels does not fundamentally change the socioeconomic dynamics that drive the production and distribution of programs. On the contrary, that dynamic is intensified by increased concentration of ownership and control and by the dissolution of the traditional barriers between and among networks, station owners, production studios, syndicators, MSOs, cable networks, and advertisers.

Viewers may feel a new sense of power and control derived from the ability to freeze a frame, review a scene, and zip through commercials (or zap them entirely), or interact with them. The easy availability of prerecorded cassettes and increasing choices offered via pay-per-view (PPV) may also give viewers an unprecedented range of potential choices. Digital videodiscs (DVD) may offer superior visual resolution and multichannel sound. But again, there is no evidence that any of this has changed viewing habits—or that the content that regular and heavy television viewers consume most presents worldviews, values, and stereotypes fundamentally different from most network-type programs (Morgan, Shanahan, & Harris, 1990). Digital signal compression will soon flood viewers with even more channels, but with what programming? In fact, as channels proliferate, sources of original dramatic programming and perspectives decline. One reflection of the monopoly of market orientation is the absence of poor (i.e., low-income) characters and of diverse ideological (i.e., political, religious) orientations.

In particular, computers and the Internet seem to threaten the stability of the traditional media landscape. But at the end of 2000, Nielsen/ Netratings reports that average Web usage amounts to just about 3 hours per week, a fraction of the time most people spend watching television (Nielsen, 2000). AOL Web sites reach nearly half of all Internet users, who visit for an average of 13 minutes per session. Figuring prominently among top sites are those with strong connections to dominant television networks and services, including Disney (owner of ABC) and Time Warner (owner of Turner's media empire, and merging with AOL). Clearly, the rise of the Web—though of great significance—represents not only a relatively small amount of audience time but also an ever-greater role for dominant media corporations.

A May 1999 Nielsen report noted that although people in Internet homes watch less television, "analyses of the same homes before they had Internet access revealed that they were lighter TV viewers to begin with. There is currently almost no indication that Internet access cannibalizes television usage; instead, it offers a targeted vehicle to supplement advertising reach among these lighter television viewers" (Nielsen, 1999). Moreover, a great deal of Web usage takes place at *work*—nearly 23 hours a month at the end of 2000—extending the reach of advertisers to the workplace as well (Nielsen, 2000). This shows quite clearly that although the Internet may provide access to alternative channels of information, it can also deepen and sharpen the reach of dominant media corporations.

Still, only a tiny minority uses the Internet for viewing video or listening to audio programs as an alternative to dominant message providers. Even when the Internet provides new delivery systems that threaten dominant interests, as in the case of Napster, it is quickly swallowed up within the existing institutional structure. Despite widespread hopes (and fears) that the Internet will make possible a new information highway that may replace standard mass media, there are no popular Internet or Web-based programs that yet threaten the network-cable alliance; on the contrary, networks and cable channels are working feverishly to drive their viewers to their Web sites, to allow them to obtain more personal information from viewers, and to create another platform for advertising exposures. At most, the most popular online services such as AOL gain audience share at any given time comparable to that of CNN or MTV, which is a rather small and specialized audience. Also, the dot-com frenzy of 1999 gave way to a much more sober atmosphere for Web entertainment, with many start-ups closing, having failed to make a single penny of profit. Moreover, a November 2000 study by Burke, Inc., found that viewers with home Internet access spend 4 hours a week watching television while online ("Individuals with Internet Access," 2000). The report noted that although "some have suggested that the Internet is killing TV," the results "show that Internet use not only coexists with TV viewing, it can encourage and enhance the viewing experience." Thus, cultivation theorists continue to proceed under the assumption that TV is "the dominant feature of Americans' free time" (Robinson & Godbey, 1997).

Channels will continue to proliferate, by cable, satellite, and digital transmission. New developments such as digital video recorders will become more common, allowing viewers to more easily indulge their own personal programming tastes (and, maybe, to ignore commercials). Digital technologies for storing and manipulating personal video libraries will continue to emerge, as will options for direct, on-demand delivery of special programs through more versatile set-top boxes (which may also include DVRs and high-speed Internet connections). The broadcast network audience share will continue to shrivel (despite the occasional blockbuster series) and be divided among an ever-increasing number of competing channels. Developments such as interactive TV that will allow advertisers to reach finely targeted groups—and even *individual* viewers—will be vigorously pursued.

Yet, all this is being accompanied by massive and unprecedented concentrations of ownership of media industries and program sources. Whether the most successful entertainment is delivered through television networks or in the form of video-on-demand through fiber-optic cable, satellites, or some other medium may make little difference if the messages don't change. Given that, there is little evidence to date that the dominant patterns of image cultivation will show any corresponding fragmentation. For most viewers, extended delivery systems signal even deeper penetration and integration of the dominant patterns of images and messages into everyday life. Nevertheless, the empirical investigation of these developments, and their implications for cultivation analysis in general and for mainstreaming in particular, represents a major challenge for the new century.

REFERENCES

Bouwman, H. (1984). Cultivation analysis: The Dutch case. In G. Melischek, K. E. Rosengren, & J. Stapper (Eds.), *Cultural indicators: An international symposium* (pp. 407–422). Vienna: Verlag der Osterreichischen Akademie der Wissenschaften.

Bouwman, H. (1987). *Televisie als cultuur-schepper*. Amsterdam: VU Uitgeverij.

Bouwman, H., & Signorielli, N. (1985). A comparison of American and Dutch programming. *Gazette, 35*, 93–108.

Bouwman, H., & Stappers, J. (1984). The Dutch violence profile: A replication of Gerbner's message system analysis. In G. Melischek, K. E. Rosengren, & J. Stappers (Eds.), *Cultural indicators: An international symposium* (pp. 113–128). Vienna: Verlag der Osterreichische Akademie der Wissenschaften.

Gerbner, G. (1958). On content analysis and critical research in mass communication. *AV Communication Review, 6*(2), 85–108.

Gerbner, G. (1969). Toward "Cultural Indicators": The analysis of mass mediated message systems. *AV Communication Review, 17*(2), 137–148.

Gerbner, G. (1970). Cultural indicators: The case of violence in television drama. *Annals of the American Academy of Political and Social Science, 388*, 69–81.

Gerbner, G. (1972a). Communication and social environment. *Scientific American, 227*(3), 152–160.

Gerbner, G. (1972b). The structure and process of television program content regulation in the U.S. In G. A. Comstock & E. Rubinstein (Eds.), *Television and social behavior, Vol. 1: Content and control* (pp. 386–414). Washington, DC: U.S. Government Printing Office.

Gerbner, G. (1973). Cultural indicators: The third voice. In G. Gerbner, L. Gross, & W. H. Melody (Eds.), *Communications technology and social policy* (pp. 555–573). New York: Wiley.

Gerbner, G. (1977). Comparative cultural indicators. In G. Gerbner (Ed.), *Mass media policies in changing cultures* (pp. 199–205). New York: Wiley.

Gerbner, G. (1988). Violence and terror in the mass media. In *Reports and papers in mass communication* (No. 102). Paris: Unesco.

Gerbner, G. (1989). Cross-cultural communications research in the age of telecommunications. In The Christian Academy (Eds.), *Continuity and change in communications in post-industrial society* (Vol. 2). Seoul, Korea: Wooseok.

Gerbner, G. (1990). Epilogue: Advancing on the path of righteousness (maybe). In N. Signorielli & M. Morgan (Eds.), *Cultivation analysis: New directions in media effects research* (pp. 249–262). Newbury Park, CA: Sage.

Gerbner, G., & Gross, L. (1976). Living with television: The violence profile. *Journal of Communication, 26*(2), 173–199.

Gerbner, G., Gross, L., Morgan, M., & Signorielli, N. (1980). The "mainstreaming" of America: Violence profile no. 11. *Journal of Communication, 30*(3), 10–29.

Gerbner, G., Gross, L., Morgan, M., & Signorielli, N. (1981). Scientists on the TV screen. *Society,* May/June, 41–44.

Gerbner, G., Gross, L., Morgan, M., & Signorielli, N. (1982). Charting the mainstream: Television's contributions to political orientations. *Journal of Communication, 32*(2), 100–127.

Gerbner, G., Gross, L., Morgan, M., & Signorielli, N. (1984). Political correlates of television viewing. *Public Opinion Quarterly, 48*(1), 283–300.

Gerbner, G., Gross, L., Morgan, M., & Signorielli, N. (1986). Living with television: The dynamics of the cultivation process. In J. Bryant & D. Zillman (Eds.), *Perspectives on media effects* (pp. 17–40). Hillsdale, NJ: Lawrence Erlbaum Associates.

Gerbner, G., Gross, L., Morgan, M., & Signorielli, N. (1994). Growing up with television: The cultivation perspective. In J. Bryant & D. Zillman (Eds.), *Media effects* (pp. 17–40). Hillsdale, NJ: Lawrence Erlbaum Associates.

Gerbner, G., Gross, L., Signorielli, N., & Morgan, M. (1980). Aging with television: Images on television drama and conceptions of social reality. *Journal of Communication, 30*(1), 37–47.

Gerbner, G., Gross, L., Signorielli, N., Morgan, M., & Jackson-Beeck, M. (1979). The demonstration of power: Violence profile no. 10. *Journal of Communication, 29*(3), 177–196.

Hawkins, R. P., & Pingree, S. (1982). Television's influence on social reality. In D. Pearl, L. Bouthilet, & J. Lazar (Eds.), *Television and behavior: Ten years of scientific progress and implications for the 80's, Vol. II, Technical reviews* (pp. 224–247). Rockville, MD: National Institute of Mental Health.

Hawkins, R. P., & Pingree, S. (1990). Divergent psychological processes in constructing social reality from mass media content. In N. Signorielli & M. Morgan (Eds.), *Cultivation analysis: New directions in media effects research* (pp. 35–50). Newbury Park, CA: Sage.

Hedinsson, E., & Windahl, S. (1984). Cultivation analysis: A Swedish illustration. In G. Melischek, K. E. Rosengren, & J. Stappers (Eds.), *Cultural indicators: An international symposium* (pp. 389–406). Vienna: Verlag der Osterreichischen Akademie der Wissenschaften.

"Individuals with Internet access spend almost four hours per week watching TV while online." (2000, November 20). [online press release]: retrieved 11/21/00 from http://biz.yahoo.com/bw/001120/oh_burke_n.html.

Kang, J. G., & Morgan, M. (1988). Culture clash: U.S. television programs in Korea. *Journalism Quarterly, 65*(2), 431–438.

Lewis, J., Jhally, S., & Morgan, M. (1991). *The Gulf War: A study of the media, public opinion, and public knowledge.* [Unpublished research report]. The Center for the Study of Communication, Department of Communication, University of Massachusetts/Amherst. Online at http://www.umass.edu/communication/Resources/gulfwar.html.

Mares, M. (1996). The role of source confusions in television's cultivation of social reality judgments. *Human Communication Research, 23*(2), 278–297.

McQuail, D. (2000). *Mass communication theory.* Thousand Oaks, CA: Sage.

Morgan, M. (1982). Television and adolescents' sex-role stereotypes: A longitudinal study. *Journal of Personality and Social Psychology, 43*(5), 947–955.

Morgan, M. (1983). Symbolic victimization and real-world fear. *Human Communication Research, 9*(2), 146–157.

Morgan, M. (1986). Television and the erosion of regional diversity. *Journal of Broadcasting & Electronic Media, 30*(2), 123–139.

Morgan, M. (1987). Television, sex-role attitudes, and sex role behavior. *Journal of Early Adolescence, 7*(3), 269–282.

Morgan, M. (1990). International cultivation analysis. In N. Signorielli & M. Morgan (Eds.), *Cultivation analysis: New directions in media effects research* (pp. 225–248). Newbury Park, CA: Sage.

Morgan, M., Leggett, S., & Shanahan, J. (1999). Television and "family values": Was Dan Quayle right? *Mass Communication and Society, 2*(1/2): 47–63.

Morgan, M., & Rothschild, N. (1983). Impact of the new television technology: Cable TV, peers, and sex-role cultivation in the electronic environment. *Youth and Society, 15*(1), 33–50.

Morgan, M., & Shanahan, J. (1992). Comparative cultivation analysis: Television and adolescents in Argentina and Taiwan. In F. Korzenny & S. Ting-Toomey (Eds.), *Mass media effects across cultures: International and intercultural communication annual* (Vol. 16, pp. 173–197). Newbury Park, CA: Sage.

Morgan, M., & Shanahan, J. (1995). *Democracy tango: Television, adolescents, and authoritarian tensions in Argentina.* Cresskill, NJ: Hampton Press.

Morgan, M., Shanahan, J., & Harris, C. (1990). VCRs and the effects of television: New diversity or more of the same? In J. Dobrow (Ed.), *Social and cultural aspects of VCR use* (pp. 107–123). Hillsdale, NJ: Lawrence Erlbaum Associates.

Morgan, M., & Signorielli, N. (1990). Cultivation analysis: Conceptualization and methodology. In N. Signorielli & M. Morgan (Eds.), *Cultivation analysis: New directions in media effects research* (pp. 13–34). Newbury Park, CA: Sage.

Nielsen/Netratings (1999). "TV in Internet homes." Retrieved 11/19/00 from http://www.nielsenmedia.com/reports/TV%20in%20Interent%20Homes/TV%20In %20Internet%20Homes.doc.

Nielsen/Netratings. (2000). "Hot off the Net." Retrieved 12/5/00 from http://209.249.142.27/nnpm/owa/NRpublicreports.usageweekly; http://209.249.142.27/nnpm/owa/NRpublicreports.topropertiesweekly; and http://209.249.142.27/nnpm/owa/NRPublicReports.Usages.

Piepe, A., Charlton, P., & Morey, J. (1990). Politics and television viewing in England: Hegemony or pluralism? *Journal of Communication, 40*(1), 24–35.

Pingree, S., & Hawkins, R. P. (1981). U.S. programs on Australian television: The cultivation effect. *Journal of Communication, 31*(1), 97–105.

Potter, W. J. (1986). Perceived reality and the cultivation hypothesis. *Journal of Broadcasting & Electronic Media, 30*(2), 159–174.

Reimer, B., & Rosengren, K. E. (1990). Cultivated viewers and readers: A life-style perspective. In N. Signorielli & M. Morgan (Eds.), *Cultivation Analysis: New directions in media effects research* (pp. 181–206). Newbury Park, CA: Sage.

Robinson, J., & Godbey, G. (1997). *Time for life: The surprising ways Americans use their time.* University Park: Pennsylvania State University Press.

Rothschild, N. (1984). Small group affiliation as a mediating factor in the cultivation process. In G. Melischek, K. E. Rosengren, & J. Stappers (Eds.), *Cultural indicators: An international symposium* (pp. 377–387). Vienna: Verlag der Osterreichischen Akademie der Wissenschaften.

Saito, S. (1991). *Does cultivation occur in Japan? Testing the applicability of the cultivation hypothesis on Japanese television viewers.* Unpublished master's thesis, The Annenberg School for Communication, University of Pennsylvania, Philadelphia.

Shanahan, J., & McComas, K. (1999). *Nature stories.* Cresskill, NJ: Hampton Press.

Shanahan, J., & Morgan M. (1999). *Television and its viewers: Cultivation theory and research.* Cambridge: Cambridge University Press.

Shanahan, J., Morgan, M., & Stenbjerre, M. (1997). Green or brown? Television's cultivation of environmental concern. *Journal of Broadcasting & Electronic Media, 41*(3): 305–323.

Shapiro, M., & Lang, A. (1991). Making television reality: Unconscious processes in the construction of social reality. *Communication Research, 18*(5), 685–705.

Shrum, L. J. (1995). Assessing the social influence of television: A social cognition perspective on cultivation effects. *Communication Research, 22*(4), 402–429.

Shrum, L. J. (1997). The role of source confusion in cultivation effects may depend on processing strategy: A comment on Mares. *Human Communication Research, 24*(2), 349–358.

Shrum, L. J. (1999). The relationship of television viewing with attitude strength and extremity: Implications for the cultivation effect. *Media Psychology, 1*, 3–25.

Signorielli, N. (1986). Selective television viewing: A limited possibility. *Journal of Communication, 36*(3), 64–75.

Signorielli, N. (1989). Television and conceptions about sex roles: Maintaining conventionality and the status quo. *Sex Roles, 21*(5/6), 337–356.

Signorielli, N. (1990). Television's mean and dangerous world: A continuation of the cultural indicators perspective. In N. Signorielli and M. Morgan (Eds.), *Cultivation analysis: New directions in media effects research* (pp. 85–106). Newbury Park, CA: Sage.

Signorielli, N. (1991). Adolescents and ambivalence towards marriage: A cultivation analysis. *Youth & Society, 23*(1), 121–149.

Signorielli, N. (1993). "Television and adolescents' perceptions about work." *Youth & Society, 24*(3), 314–341.

Signorielli, N., & Kahlenberg, N. (In press). The world of work in the nineties. *Journal of Broadcasting & Electronic Media.*

Signorielli, N., & Lears, M. (1992). Children, television and conceptions about chores: Attitudes and behaviors. *Sex Roles, 27*, 157–170.

Signorielli, N., & Morgan, M. (Eds) (1990). *Cultivation analysis: New directions in media effects research.* Newbury Park, CA: Sage.

Slater, D., & Elliott, W. R. (1982). Television's influence on social reality. *Quarterly Journal of Speech, 68*(1), 69–79.

Stappers, J. G. (1984). De eigen aard van televisie; tien stellingen over cultivatie en culturele indicatoren. *Massacommunicatie, XII*(5/6), 249–258.

Sun, L. (1989). *Limits of selective viewing: An analysis of "diversity" in dramatic programming.* Unpublished master's thesis, The Annenberg School for Communication, University of Pennsylvania, Philadelphia.

Tamborini, R., & Choi, J. (1990). The role of cultural diversity in cultivation research. In N. Signorielli & M. Morgan (Eds.), *Cultivation analysis: New directions in media effects research* (pp. 157–180). Newbury Park, CA: Sage.

Tan, A. S., Li, S., & Simpson, C. (1986). American television and social stereotypes of Americans in Taiwan and Mexico. *Journalism Quarterly, 63*, 809–814.

Tan, A. S., & Suarchavarat, K. (1988). American TV and social stereotypes of Americans in Thailand. *Journalism Quarterly, 65*(4), 648–654.

Tan, A. S., Tan, G. K. & Tan, A. S. (1987). American TV in the Philippines: A test of cultural impact. *Journalism Quarterly, 64*(1), 65–72.

Weimann, G. (1984). Images of life in America: The impact of American TV in Israel. *International Journal of Intercultural Relations, 8*(2), 185–197.

Williams, R. (1977). *Marxism and literature.* Oxford: Oxford University Press.

Wober, J. M. (1978). Televised violence and paranoid perception: The view from Great Britain. *Public Opinion Quarterly, 42*(3), 315–321.

Wober, J. M. (1984). Prophecy and prophylaxis: Predicted harms and their absence in a regulated television system. In G. Melischek, K. E. Rosengren, & J. Stappers (Eds.), *Cultural indicators: An international symposium.* Vienna: Verlag der Osterreichischen Akademie der Wissenschaften.

Wober, J. M. (1990). Does television cultivate the British? Late 80s evidence. In N. Signorielli & M. Morgan (Eds.), *Cultivation analysis: New directions in media effects research* (pp. 207–224). Newbury Park, CA: Sage.

Wober, J. M., & Gunter, B. (1988). *Television and social control.* New York: St. Martin's Press.

Chapter 4

Media Consumption and Perceptions of Social Reality: Effects and Underlying Processes

L. J. SHRUM
Rutgers University

*Don't come to television for the truth. TV's a goddamned amusement park.
We'll tell you the good guys always win. We'll tell you nobody ever gets cancer at Archie Bunker's house. We'll tell you any shit you want to hear.*
Paraphrasing Howard Beale, Paddy Chayefsky's
character in *Network* (Chayefsky, 1976)

Although in the movie it was unclear whether his words were those of a
madman or a sage, hardly anyone nowadays seems to question Howard
Beale's claim that television presents a distorted view of reality. What
people—whether they be researchers, media critics, television executives,
or the local bartender—do question is if the distortion has any effect, and
if so, why and how.

These interrelated questions about the whether and how of media
effects lie at the heart of scholarly debates and critiques of media effects
research. Over the past few decades, there have been two persistent criticisms. One is that the evidence accumulated to date has provided little
indication of sizable media effects on viewers' thoughts, feelings, or
actions, in spite of a generally held "myth of massive media impact" by
many researchers (McGuire, 1986). The second criticism of media effects
research is that it for the most part has lacked any focus on explanatory
mechanisms. That is, media effects research has been primarily concerned
with relations between input variables (e.g., media information and its
characteristics) and output variables (e.g., attitudes, beliefs, and behavior),
with little consideration of the cognitive processes that might mediate

these relations (Hawkins & Pingree, 1990; Reeves, Chaffee, & Tims, 1982; see Wyer, 1980, for a similar view on social psychological research).

Although the purpose of this chapter is to address the criticism pertaining to the lack of a cognitive process explanation for observed media effects, the two criticisms just noted are not independent. One of the useful features of process explanations is that ideally models are developed that can specify both moderating and mediating variables. McGuire (1986) notes in his fairly exhaustive review that even though research to date has shown remarkably small media effects, there are a number of possibilities that may ultimately allow for the "salvaging" of the massive effects notion. In particular, he notes that small main effects may be obscured by messages having different effects on different groups or as a function of different situations (moderators) and by focusing on direct effects at the expense of indirect ones (mediators). Thus, the development of cognitive process models for media effects has the potential to uncover new relations as well as to make sense out of old ones.

The development of cognitive process models that can explain media effects has other advantages as well. For one, it has the potential to increase internal validity, or the extent to which we are confident that we are observing a true causal effect and not one that is spurious (Hawkins & Pingree, 1990), another common criticism of many media effects studies (see Hirsch, 1980; Hughes, 1980; McGuire, 1986). A process model should provide clear links between the stimulus (e.g., media consumption) and the response (e.g., beliefs, behavior), and each link in the model should represent a testable proposition to be empirically verified. If these links stand on solid theoretical foundations and are empirically verified, then threats to internal validity such as spuriousness and reverse causality are rendered less plausible, as the threats would presumably have to occur at each stage. Another advantage is that process models may potentially address conflicting findings in previous research. A process model should provide boundary conditions for the effect; that is, a specification of the conditions under which the effect does *not* hold. To the extent that these boundary conditions are related to aspects of inconsistencies in previous research, disparate findings may be reconciled.

Given these advantages of a focus on process, the goals for this chapter are twofold: (1) to discuss some of the general underlying principles that have emerged in social cognition research that have particular implications for media effects, with reference to relevant media effects research that exemplify these principles, and (2) to demonstrate the advantages of a process focus just discussed by outlining a cognitive process model that can explain a particular media effect, the cultivation effect (see chapter 3).

SOCIAL COGNITION AND MEDIA EFFECTS

Social cognition can best be described as an orientation toward the cognitive processes that occur in social situations (Reeves, Chaffee, & Tims, 1982). To be more specific, social cognition research attempts to open the "black box" that operates between a stimulus (e.g., information) and a response (e.g., a judgment) (Wyer, 1980) and, as such, has its focus on the cognitive processes that mediate the relations between social information and judgment (Wyer & Srull, 1989).

Social cognition research has not only had a profound effect on the field of social psychology, but on numerous other fields as well (e.g., marketing communications, political communications, cross-cultural psychology, and organizational behavior, just to name a few). Given the maturity of the field, there are a number of theories and models that have been developed to account for how people acquire, store, and use social information, the most complete of which is that provided by Wyer and Srull (1989; but also see Wyer & Radvansky, 1999, for revisions of this model).[1] Even though the various theories differ in important ways, they all share some basic underlying principles (Carlston & Smith, 1996; Wyer, 1980).

For the purposes of this discussion, there are two important and inter-related principles underlying social cognition research.[2] *Principle 1* (Heuristic/Sufficiency Principle) concerns what information is retrieved in the course of constructing a judgment. This principle states that when people construct judgments, they typically do not search memory for all information that is relevant to the judgment, but instead retrieve only a small subset of the information available. Moreover, the criterion for what is retrieved is "sufficiency." That is, only the information that is sufficient to construct the judgment is retrieved, and the determinants of sufficiency are related to concepts such as motivation and ability to process information (Wyer & Srull, 1989; see also Chaiken, Liberman, & Eagly, 1989, for a similar perspective on attitude judgments).

---

[1]The comprehensive aspect of the Wyer and Srull (1989) model is that it specifies precise mechanisms for all stages in the information processing system (i.e., from input to output), and not necessarily that it is superior or more valid than other models. Most other models tend to focus on only selected aspects of the processing system (e.g., comprehension, storage, retrieval, response).

[2]These two principles are discussed at more length by Carlston and Smith (1996) and Wyer (1980), who each use slightly different names for the principles. I have taken the liberty of renaming the principles to provide a better fit with the definitions and context of the discussions.

Principle 2 (Accessibility Principle) concerns the role of the accessibility of information in the construction of judgments. In its simplest form, the principle states that the information that comes most readily to mind will be the information that comprises the "small subset"of available information that is retrieved and, in turn, is the information that is most likely to be used in constructing a judgment (Carlston & Smith, 1996; Higgins, 1996; Wyer, 1980).

Taken together, these two principles have important implications for explaining media effects. These implications revolve around the determinants and consequences of accessibility.

Determinants of Accessibility

There are a number of factors that may influence the ease with which something is recalled. Although a detailed discussion of these factors is beyond the scope of this chapter (for more extensive reviews, see Higgins, 1996; Higgins & King, 1981), certain ones have implications for media effects (Shrum, 1995). These factors are the frequency of construct activation, recency of construct activation, vividness of a construct, and relations with accessible constructs.

Frequency and Recency of Activation. Constructs that are frequently activated tend to be easily recalled (Higgins & King, 1981). This general finding has been shown both in studies of word recall and recognition (Paivio, 1971) as well as of trait concepts (Wyer & Srull, 1980). Moreover, if activated frequently enough, particular constructs may become "chronically accessible" (for a review, see Higgins, 1996) such that they are spontaneously activated under many different situations. The same general relation holds for recency of activation: The more recently a construct has been activated, the easier it is to recall (Higgins, Rholes, & Jones, 1977; Wyer & Srull, 1980). However, research suggests that the effect of recency of activation on accessibility is relatively transitory, with frequency effects tending to dominate after a short period of time (Higgins, Bargh, & Lombardi, 1985; Wyer & Radvansky, 1999).

This general relation of frequency and recency with accessibility has implications for potential media effects. For example, cultivation theory (see chapter 3) rests on the premise that the frequency of television viewing has effects on the beliefs of viewers. In terms of frequency of activation, heavier viewers should more frequently activate constructs portrayed on television than light viewers, particularly if those constructs tend to be portrayed more heavily on television than in real-world situations. Moreover, given that heavy viewers have a higher probability of having viewed recently than light viewers, accessibility may be enhanced for heavy viewers through the recency of viewing as well (although these effects may be relatively short term).

Vividness. Vividness relates to the extent to which something is "emotionally interesting, concrete and imagery provoking, and proximate in a sensory, temporal, or spatial way" (Nisbett & Ross, 1980, p. 45), and constructs that tend to be more vivid are more easily activated from memory (Higgins & King, 1981; Nisbett & Ross, 1980; Paivio, 1971). Like frequency and recency, vividness has particular applicability to media effects. It seems reasonable to think that television portrayals of particular actions or events may be more vivid than real-world experiences, given the drama-enhancing goal of entertainment. Examples might include a fistfight, an execution, family conflict, a natural disaster, military conflict, and so forth.

Vividness may also play a role in news reports. As Zillmann and colleagues have noted (see chapter 2; Zillmann & Brosius, 2000), news reports often convey information in the form of case studies or extreme examples. Such a bias in favor of vivid examples over precise but pallid statistical information may make those examples relatively easy to remember.

Relations with Accessible Constructs. As the accessibility of a particular construct increases, so does the accessibility of a closely related construct. This concept is consistent with the associative network/spreading activation model of memory made popular in cognitive psychology as a means of explaining the interconnectedness of knowledge (Collins & Loftus, 1975). This model holds that constructs are stored in memory in the form of nodes, and links are formed between the nodes. When a particular node (stored construct) is activated, other constructs will also be activated to the extent that they are related to that node.

It seems likely that the relation between accessible constructs may have implications for media effects. One of the attributes of media portrayals, particularly on television programs and films, is the relatively consistent and formulaic way in which particular concepts (e.g., anger and aggression, particular classes of people) are portrayed. These portrayals may provide "scripts" (Schank & Abelson, 1977) or "situation models" (Wyer & Radvansky, 1999) for what represents a construct and how to react to it. Given the relations between accessible constructs, the activation of a particular construct (e.g., aggression, anger) may similarly activate scripts for behavior that are closely related to these constructs (e.g., crime, violence).

In summary, it seems reasonable to think that media consumption—whether it be the frequency, recency, or the content features of viewing—may serve to enhance the accessibility of particular constructs. This "media effect" is an example of the interrelatedness of the Heuristic/Sufficiency Principle and the Accessibility Principle: Media consumption enhances accessibility, which influences the information that becomes a part of that small subset of available information.

Consequences of Accessibility

Simply demonstrating that media information may play a role in enhancing the accessibility of particular constructs is not sufficient to provide an explanation of media effects. It is also necessary to show that enhanced accessibility in turn produces effects that are consistent with the media effects literature.

The consequences of accessibility are directly related to Principle 2: The information that is most accessible is that which is most likely to be used to construct a judgment. Moreover, the way in which the most accessible information is used is a function of the type of judgment that is made.

Judgments about Persons.   One of the more consistent findings in the social cognition literature is that when people make judgments about other persons, they tend to use the constructs that are most readily accessible from memory (Accessibility Principle). In the now-classic priming studies (e.g., Higgins et al., 1977; Srull & Wyer, 1979, 1980), when participants were required to form trait judgments based on the ambiguous behaviors of a target person, they tended to use the trait concepts that had been "primed" (i.e., made more accessible) to interpret those ambiguous behaviors (for a review, see Higgins, 1996). The interpretations influenced participants' judgments about the target's behaviors (e.g., reckless, persistent) as well as judgments about how much they liked the target. These results have been replicated numerous times, even under conditions of subliminal presentation of the prime (Bargh & Pietromonaco, 1982).

Attitude and Belief Judgments.   Evaluations of an object may be constructed from beliefs that are most accessible (Fishbein & Ajzen, 1975). In the Fishbein and Ajzen model, attitude construction is a function of particular beliefs and the evaluations of those beliefs. It follows, then, that *which* beliefs are put into the attitude construction equation may be a function of which beliefs are most accessible at the moment. In a series of experiments, Wyer and colleagues (Henninger & Wyer, 1976; Wyer & Hartwick, 1984) examined the relation between accessible beliefs and evaluative judgments. In those experiments, which tested aspects of the *Socratic effect* (thinking about logically related beliefs makes those beliefs more consistent; McGuire, 1960), they showed that the accessibility of beliefs relating to premises increased the consistency between the beliefs in the premises and beliefs in the conclusions.

Judgments of Set Size and Probability.   Set-size judgments pertain to judgments of the extent to which a particular category occurs within a larger, superordinate category (e.g., the percentage of women [subordinate category] in the U.S. population [superordinate category]; Manis, Shedler, Jonides, & Nelson, 1993). Probability judgments pertain to estimates of likelihood. A finding that has been documented consistently is the relation between the accessibility of a construct and judgments of set size and probability (Sherman & Corty, 1984). In their seminal work on the *availability heuristic*, Tversky and Kahneman (1973) demonstrated that people tend to infer the frequency of a class or the probability of occurrence on the ease with which a relevant example can be recalled. For example, participants in one experiment estimated that words beginning with *k* occur more frequently in the English language than words having *k* as the third letter, even though the opposite is true. Presumably, words beginning with *k* are easier to recall because of how words tend to be organized in memory (by initial letters).

Media Effects and Accessibility Consequences

The three types of judgments just discussed, and their relation to accessibility, by no means exhaust the discussion of the types of judgments that have been shown to be influenced by the accessibility of information (for a review, see Higgins & King, 1981). Rather, those judgments are singled out because of their relevance to the types of judgments that are typically used in media effects studies.

Effects of News Reports on Issue Perceptions.   One domain in which information accessibility has been implicated is that of how information about particular issues presented in news reports (e.g., television, newspapers) affects judgments about those issues (e.g., attitudes, likelihood estimates). For example, research by Zillmann and colleagues has shown that information presented in the form of exemplars (e.g., case studies, vivid examples) tends to influence judgments to a greater degree than does more accurate but pallid base-rate information (for a review, see chapter 2). This general finding has been replicated for a variety of exemplar conditions, including manipulating the proportion of exemplars that are consistent with a story's focus (Zillmann, Gibson, Sundar, &

Perkins, 1996; Zillmann, Perkins, & Sundar, 1992), the degree of exaggeration of the exemplars (Gibson & Zillmann, 1994), and the emotionality of the exemplars (Aust & Zillmann, 1996). Other research has produced similar findings, with Iyengar (1990) reporting effects of the presence (vs. absence) of exemplars and Brosius and Bathelt (1994) finding an effect of number of exemplars on issue perceptions. Most of this research has conceptualized the results in terms of accessibility and the use of heuristics: The more vivid or frequent examples are easier to remember than less vivid or infrequent examples, and thus tend to be used to construct judgments.

Findings reported by Lichtenstein, Slovic, Fischhoff, Layman, and Combs (1978) have also been conceptualized in terms of accessibility and the application of the availability heuristic. They observed that roughly 80% of study participants estimated that death due to an accident is more likely to occur than death due to a stroke, even though strokes cause about 85% more deaths than accidents. Lichtenstein et al. suggest that examples of accidental deaths are easier to recall than examples of death by stroke, and at least partially because the former tend to be reported more than the latter in the media.

Effects of Television Viewing on Social Perceptions.   Another media effects domain in which accessibility has been used as an explanatory variable is in the relationship between television viewing and perceptions of social reality. This domain differs from news reports in that it considers all types of television viewing (e.g., fictional portrayals such as soap operas, action/adventure, dramas, situation comedies) rather than just news programs.

The results of a number of studies can be conceptualized in terms of the enhanced accessibility afforded by heavy television viewing and the subsequent application of judgmental heuristics, particularly when the dependent variables involve estimates of frequency of a class or likelihood of occurrence. For example, Bryant, Carveth, and Brown (1981) exposed participants, over a 6-week period, to either heavy or light viewing of films depicting crime, and those in the heavy exposure condition saw crime portrayals that featured either just or unjust resolutions. They found that those in the heavy exposure condition indicated a greater likelihood of being a victim of violence and more fear of victimization than those in the light exposure condition, regardless of whether the resolutions were just or unjust. As with the other studies just discussed, these results are consistent with predictions made by the availability heuristic: The heavy viewing conditions made examples of crime more accessible than the light viewing conditions, and this accessibility, or ease of recall, influenced judgments of prevalence and likelihood of occurrence. Other studies have made this same connection between accessibility as a function of viewing and judgments (cf. Ogles & Hoffner, 1987; Tamborini, Zillmann, & Bryant, 1984).

The applications of concepts such as accessibility and the use of heuristics is not confined only to studies of crime and violence. Zillmann and Bryant (1982; for a review, see chapter 12) found that participants who viewed portrayals of explicit sex scenes gave higher estimates of the prevalence of unusual sex practices among the general population, were less likely to object to public display of pornography, and recommended shorter jail sentences for a convicted rapist than did participants who viewed films that were not sexually explicit.

Effects of Media Portrayals on Aggression. Although the research just reviewed has focused predominantly on cognitive measures as dependent variables, the concept of accessibility has also been useful in explaining the effects of exposure to media violence on behavior. Berkowitz's *cognitive-neoassociationistic perspective* (1984; see also chapter 5) on the effects of violent media consumption posits that frequent viewing of violent media portrayals primes particular constructs (e.g., aggression, hostility) and thus makes these constructs more likely to be used in behavioral decisions (i.e., actions) as well as judgments about others. Note that this notion is very similar to the original trait priming studies of Higgins and colleagues and Wyer and Srull that were discussed earlier: A particular trait concept is made accessible and thus is used disproportionately as a basis for subsequent judgments.

The relation between the activation of a construct such as aggression through media portrayals and the accessibility of aggression-related constructs has been demonstrated in several studies. For example, Bushman and Geen (1990) showed that viewing violent films elicited more aggressive thoughts than viewing nonviolent films. Berkowitz, Parker, and West (cited in Berkowitz, 1973) produced similar findings, showing that children who read a war comic book were more likely to select words with aggressive meanings than children who read a neutral comic book. Other studies have made the connection between activation (and presumed enhanced accessibility) of aggression constructs and subsequent judgments. Carver, Ganellen, Froming, and Chambers (1983) found that people who viewed a brief film portraying a hostile interaction between a business executive and his secretary perceived more hostility in an ambiguous target person than did people who viewed a nonhostile portrayal, and Berkowitz (1970) showed that similar effects of aggressive portrayals on judgments can be observed even when the aggressive behavior is in the form of comedy.

It is also worth noting that what is primed does not necessarily have to be directly related to an eminent judgment, but may only have to share similar features to a judgment situation. Recall that one of the antecedents of a construct's accessibility is its relation to other accessible constructs. This notion is useful in explaining possible media effects in which the type of aggressive action viewers observe in media content is only tangentially related to the type of aggressive action taken by viewers, a pattern of results that theories of learning, imitation, or "modeling" (for a review, see chapter 6) have difficulty addressing (Berkowitz, 1984). In fact, as Berkowitz notes, the behavioral aggression measures that are used in studies are often quite different from the aggression observed in the media portrayals (whether they be experiments or field studies). For example, Phillips (1983) presented correlational data that showed that heavy media coverage of heavyweight championship boxing matches tended to be followed by an increase in homicides in the United States on certain days within a 10-day period following the fight (but see Freedman, 1984, for a criticism of this study). Similar aggression-related effects of viewing boxing matches have been reported in experimental studies as well (Turner & Berkowitz, 1972).

Indirect vs. Direct Investigations of Cognitive Processes

The research just presented is suggestive of the role of accessibility as a cognitive mediator of media effects. However, much of the evidence is still indirect in that many of the studies fall short of actually investigating the processes themselves, but rather offer process explanations for the obtained results. Exceptions to this generalization include Zillmann's work on excitation-transfer theory (Zillmann, 1983; Zillmann & Zillmann, 1996) and Berkowitz's cognitive-neoassociationistic perspective (Berkowitz, 1984).

The following section discusses a series of studies that directly investigate such potential cognitive processes. The results of these studies are then used as the basis for the development of a detailed cognitive processing model that can account for a particular media effect, the cultivation effect. This model builds on the general principles discussed earlier (heuristic/sufficiency and accessibility) that underlie social cognition research.

HEURISTIC PROCESSING MODEL OF CULTIVATION EFFECTS

One area of media effects research that has generated considerable controversy is the research on the cultivation effect (see chapter 2). For the purposes of this discussion, a cultivation effect is defined as a positive relation between frequency of television viewing and social perceptions that are congruent with the world as it is portrayed on television, with the presumption that television viewing is the causal factor. Although considerable evidence has accumulated that supports the existence of at least a small-sized cultivation effect (Morgan & Shanahan, 1996), other researchers have challenged the validity of this effect. Some research suggests that the relationship between viewing and perceptions is not causal, but rather a spurious one resulting from third-variable influences (e.g., direct experience, education, available time to view, personality) on both television viewing and social perceptions (Doob & Macdonald, 1979; Hirsch, 1980; Hughes, 1980; Wober & Gunter, 1988). Other research suggests that the causal relation between viewing and social perceptions may be reversed; that is, aspects of the individual (including preexisting social perceptions) may influence the amount and content of viewing (Zillmann, 1980).

As noted earlier, one of the advantages of developing a cognitive process model of media effects is that it has the potential to render implausible certain alternative explanations for the effect (e.g., spuriousness, reverse causality). Two caveats should be noted, however. First, rendering a particular alternative explanation implausible in a study merely means that the explanation cannot *completely* account for a particular pattern of results; it does not mean that the alternative explanation may not be operating simultaneously but independent of other effects. Second, the power of a process model is in the cumulative effect of a *pattern* of results, not a focus on a single study. Thus, even though alternative explanations may be possible for any one study, in the interest of parsimony, the alternative explanations should address the entire pattern of results to be an effective challenge.

General Propositions of the Model

Two very simple and general propositions that are based on the principles of heuristic/sufficiency and accessibility form the basis of the model. The first general proposition is that television viewing enhances construct accessibility. As discussed earlier, aspects of television viewing may plausibly be related to the accessibility of constructs encountered in typical television fare. The second general proposition is that the social perceptions that serve as indicators of a cultivation effect are constructed through heuristic processing. Specifically, rather than constructing judgments through an extensive search of memory for all available relevant information (systematic processing), only a subset of relevant information is retrieved, and specifically, the information retrieved is that which is most accessible from memory. A corollary of this second general proposition is that, at least for cases in which the judgments pertain to perceptions of frequency of a class (set size) or likelihood of occurrence, judgments are constructed through the application of the availability heuristic; that is, the magnitude of the judgments is positively related to the ease with which an example can be brought to mind (Tversky & Kahneman, 1973).

Testable Propositions

These general propositions can themselves be used to generate testable propositions regarding the relation between television viewing and social perceptions and the cognitive mechanisms that may mediate this relation.

Proposition 1: Television Viewing Influences Accessibility. Proposition 1 is a necessary condition for testing whether the availability heuristic can explain cultivation effects. This proposition was tested by operationalizing accessibility as the speed with which judgments could be constructed. Shrum and O'Guinn (1993) had participants provide prevalence and likelihood estimates of constructs frequently portrayed on television (e.g., crime, prostitution) and measured the time it took participants to answer each question. If television information was more accessible for heavy viewers than for light viewers, heavy viewers should not only provide higher estimates than light viewers (a cultivation effect), but should also construct their judgments faster (an accessibility effect). The results of the study confirmed these hypotheses, even when controlling for individual baseline latencies, grade point average, and use of other media. These same general relations have been replicated using a variety of dependent variables, different operationalizations of television viewing, and multiple control variables (cf. O'Guinn & Shrum, 1997; Shrum, 1996; Shrum, O'Guinn, Seminik, & Faber, 1991).

Other studies have attempted to operationalize accessibility in a more direct way. Busselle (2001) asked participants to recall an example of particular constructs, some of which were constructs frequently portrayed on television (shooting, affair, doctor) and measured the time it took participants to recall the example. Busselle and Shrum (2000) used a similar methodology, but also asked participants to indicate how easy it was to recall the example. Heavy viewers were expected to be able to recall a television-related example faster and easier than light viewers. The results from both studies indicated no differences between viewers in speed of recalling the examples, but subjective ease of recall was easier for heavy viewers than for light viewers (Busselle & Shrum, 2000). The fact that level of viewing was related to subjective ease but not to speed of recall suggests that the conscious act of recalling an example may not be the mechanism that is employed in the application of the availability heuristic. Rather, the perception of ease may be the causal mechanism, which may or may not be adequately captured by response time (see also Schwarz et al., 1991, regarding issues of ease of recall).

Proposition 2: Accessibility Mediates the Cultivation Effect. Proposition 1 (viewing influences accessibility) is a necessary but not sufficient condition to implicate the availability heuristic as an explanation for cultivation effects. It is also necessary to demonstrate that accessibility *mediates* the relation between level of viewing and magnitude of judgments (Manis et al., 1993); that is, it is also necessary to demonstrate that the enhanced accessibility leads to higher estimates. Otherwise, it could be argued that television viewing impacts accessibility and the magnitude of the judgments independently.

Some indirect evidence of the mediating role of accessibility was provided by Shrum and O'Guinn (1993). When accessibility (speed of response) was controlled, the cultivation effect was, for the most part, reduced to nonsignificance. More direct evidence of mediation was provided by Shrum (1996). Following the procedure used by Manis et al. (1993), path analyses were used to demonstrate that the level of television viewing was related to accessibility (again, operationalized as response latencies), which in turn was related to the magnitude of the estimates. However, the path analyses also revealed that the mediation was only a partial one: Television viewing still had a direct effect on the magnitude of the estimates, even when the influence of accessibility was controlled.

Busselle (2001) also provided evidence of the mediating role of accessibility by manipulating the conditions under which the prevalence estimates for particular constructs (e.g., a shooting) were constructed. Some participants provided their prevalence estimates before recalling an example of the construct (judgment-first condition) whereas other participants recalled an example before providing their estimates (recall-first condition). Level of television viewing was expected to make an example easier to recall in the judgment-first condition, whereas recalling an example before judgment was expected to make an example equally accessible for all participants, regardless of television viewing level. The results confirmed these expectations.

Proposition 3: Television Exemplars Are Not Discounted. An implicit assumption in the notion that the availability heuristic can explain cultivation effects is that the examples that are retrieved and used as a basis for judgment are considered relevant or applicable to the judgment. This is an important assumption because research has shown that accessibility effects typically obtain only when this condition is met (Higgins, 1996).

Moreover, the judged applicability of the construct is a function of the overlap between its attended features and the features of the judgment.

In terms of the cultivation effect, the recalled construct would presumably be a television example. However, it is counterintuitive that people would perceive a television example (e.g., doctor, lawyer) as applicable to a judgment about its real-world prevalence. If they do not perceive the example as relevant, alternative information would be retrieved and used as a basis for judgment (Higgins, 1996; Higgins & Brendl, 1995; Shapiro & Lang, 1991).

One way in which a television example could be perceived as relevant to a real-world judgment is if people generally do not consider the source of the example they retrieve in the course of judgment construction. Note that perceived applicability is a function of the overlap between the *attended* features of the recalled construct and the features of the judgment. It may well be that the source characteristics of the retrieved construct may not be a salient feature that is attended to, particularly when judgments are made automatically and with little effort. This may be a function of either lack of motivation to attend to source features (consistent with low involvement processing; Petty & Cacioppo, 1986, 1990) or lack of ability to recall source information (consistent with research on errors in source monitoring; Johnson, Hashtroudi, & Lindsay, 1993; Mares, 1996; Shrum, 1997).

To test Proposition 3, Shrum, Wyer, and O'Guinn (1998) conducted two experiments in which source characteristics were primed prior to judgments. In the first experiment, the priming events consisted of a source-priming condition, in which participants provided information regarding their television viewing habits prior to providing prevalence and likelihood judgments of crime and occupations, and a relation-priming condition, in which participants were told that the constructs they would be estimating appeared more often on television than in real life. In a third, no-priming condition, participants provided their estimates prior to providing television viewing information. Analyses revealed that when participants provided estimates under no-priming conditions, a cultivation effect was noted, but when they provided estimates under either source- or relation-priming conditions, the cultivation effect was eliminated. Follow-up analyses indicated that the estimates of light viewers did not differ as a function of priming conditions, but the priming conditions served to bring the estimates of heavy viewers more in line with those of light viewers. This pattern of results can be seen in Fig. 4.1.[3] A second study replicated this pattern of results, and further suggested that the

---

[3]The graph shown in Fig. 4.1 is merely a general representation of the effects across dependent variables and is for illustration purposes only. For details of the actual effects for each dependent variable, see Shrum et al. (1998).

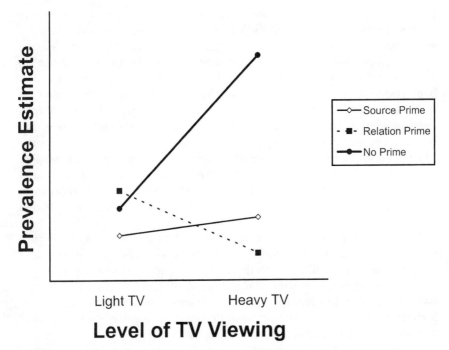

FIG. 4.1. Prevalence estimates as a function of priming condition and level of TV viewing. Represents pattern of results across dependent variables (see Shrum et al., 1998).

priming conditions induced a source-discounting process (heavy viewers discounted television information to a greater degree than light viewers) rather than an automatic adjustment process (heavy viewers adjusted their estimates downward because they were aware they were heavy viewers, but light viewers saw no need to adjust).

Proposition 4: Motivation to Process Information Moderates the Cultivation Effect. Proposition 4 is based on research showing that there are certain conditions under which heuristic processing (as opposed to systematic processing) is expected to occur (Chaiken et al., 1989; Petty & Cacioppo, 1986; Sherman & Corty, 1984). If so, then manipulating the types of processing in which people engage should have implications for whether a cultivation effect is obtained. To be specific, if people generally process heuristically in the course of constructing their judgments of prevalence or likelihood of occurrence, then inducing people to process heuristically should produce a cultivation effect that does not differ in magnitude from the cultivation effect obtained when people receive no such manipulation. But suppose people are induced to process systematically when constructing their judgments. Compared to heuristic processing, systematic processing is associated with the consideration of more information and greater scrutiny of the information that is considered. Systematic processing is used when it is important to determine the validity of information (Petty & Cacioppo, 1986) and has been shown to attenuate the effects of heuristics (Chaiken et al., 1989).

Under systematic conditions, it seems likely that the relation between level of viewing and social perceptions would be weakened or eliminated entirely. When people process systematically, they should be more likely to retrieve examples other than simply the first ones that come to mind, should be more likely to scrutinize the retrieved information, and thus should be more likely to ascertain and discount information from unreliable sources such as television programs, than when they process heuristically.

One condition that is related to whether heuristic or systematic processing strategies are adopted is the motivation to process information (Sherman & Corty, 1984): When motivation is high, systematic processing predominates; when motivation is low, heuristic processing predominates. Moreover, motivation is itself determined by a number of factors, including level of issue involvement (Petty & Cacioppo, 1990) and level of task involvement (Chaiken & Maheswaran, 1994).

To test Proposition 4, Shrum (2001) manipulated the processing strategies that participants used to construct their estimates of the prevalence of crime, marital discord, affluence, and certain occupations. Some participants were induced to process systematically via an accuracy motivation/task importance manipulation (Chaiken & Maheswaran, 1994), others were induced to process heuristically by asking them to give the first answer that came to mind, and a third (control) group received no manipulation, but were simply instructed to provide their estimates. Television viewing was then measured after the judgments were made. The results were consistent and as expected. Both the control group and the heuristic group produced cultivation effects that did not differ in magnitude from each other. However, the systematic group showed no cultivation effect. Moreover, the pattern of results was remarkably similar to those obtained by Shrum et al. (1998, Study 1): The estimates of light viewers did not differ as a function of condition, but the systematic condition affected only heavy viewers, bringing their estimates more in line with those of all light viewers, regardless of processing condition. This pattern of results can be seen in Fig. 4.2.[4]

---

[4]As with Fig. 4.1, the graph shown in Fig. 4.2 represents the general pattern of results across dependent variables. For details of the actual effects for each dependent variable, see Shrum (2001).

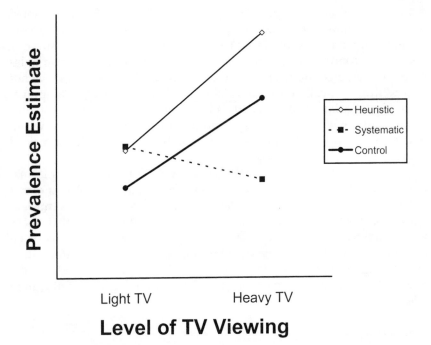

FIG. 4.2. Prevalence estimates as a function of processing condition and level of TV viewing. Represents pattern of results across dependent variables (see Shrum, 2001).

Proposition 5: Ability to Process Information Moderates the Cultivation Effect. Just as with Proposition 4, this proposition is based on the conditions that facilitate or inhibit whether people process information using systematic or heuristic strategies. In addition to motivation to process information, the ability to process information is also associated with processing strategies (Petty & Cacioppo, 1986; Chaiken et al., 1989). One factor that relates to the ability to process information is time pressure (Moore, Hausknecht, & Thamodaran, 1986; Ratneshwar & Chaiken, 1991): the more time pressure, the greater the likelihood of adopting a heuristic processing strategy.

To test Proposition 5, Shrum (1999a) used an experimental procedure that not only tested the proposition but also has implications for data collection methods. The experimental manipulation of time pressure was operationalized as either a mail survey (low time pressure) or a telephone survey (high time pressure) using a general population random sample. Pretests had indicated that the two data collection methods differed with respect to time pressure, but did not differ in terms of respondents' self-reported level of involvement. The reasoning and predictions for the experiment were similar to Shrum (2001). If the cultivation effect is a function of heuristic processing, then larger effects should be noted under conditions that favor more heuristic processing (phone survey) than under conditions that favor less heuristic processing (mail survey). The results confirmed this speculation. Across five composite variables representing perceptions of societal crime, societal vice (e.g., prevalence of prostitution, drug abuse), marital discord, affluence, and the prevalence of particular occupations, the magnitude of the effects was significantly larger in the phone survey condition than in the mail survey condition for four of the five measures (as with Shrum, 2001, all but marital discord).

Other evidence also supports the notion that ability to process information has implications for the cultivation effect. Mares (1996) found that people who tend to make particular kinds of source confusions (mistaking fiction for fact) tend to exhibit a larger cultivation effect than those who do not have a tendency toward those types of confusions. Thus, even in instances in which people may be motivated to process information (see Shrum, 1997), inability to properly process information (in this case, accurately ascertain source characteristics) may facilitate a cultivation effect.

Model Integration

The next step in model development is to integrate the testable propositions, and the implications of their supportive results, into a coherent conceptual framework. This conceptual framework, which is presented in the form of a flow chart in Fig. 4.3, specifies a series of links, or steps, which lead from television viewing to the production of a cultivation effect. For the most part, each link (designated by an arrow) represents a testable proposition that has been empirically verified. As the figure indicates, there are in fact a number of ways in which media exposure will not have an effect on judgments (no cultivation effect), but only one way (path) in which a cultivation effect will be produced.

In order to present as simple a model as possible, some misleading aspects arise that should be clarified. One of the misleading aspects of Fig. 4.3 is that the links (Yes/No) and the outcomes (Effect/No Effect) are portrayed as dichotomous variables. In fact, it is more accurate to think of each as a continuum, and movement along the continuum has implications for the size of the outcome. For example, rather than interpreting the figure as "high motivation to process results in no cultivation effect," it may be better interpreted as "the higher the motivation to process, the smaller the cultivation effect."

This notion of a continuum is similar to the elaboration continuum that forms the basis of the Elaboration Likelihood Model (ELM; Petty &

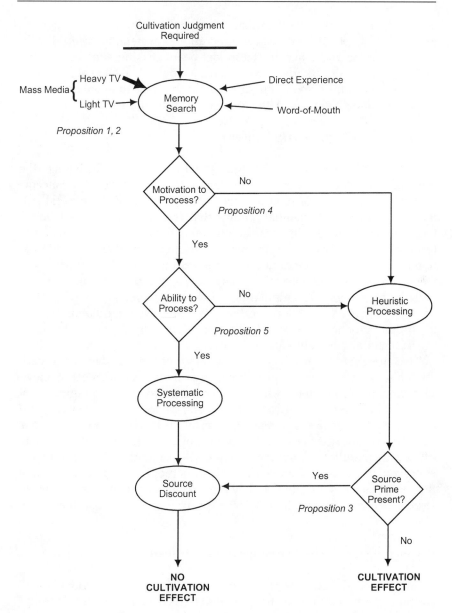

FIG. 4.3.   Flow diagram of the heuristic processing model of television effects. Circles represent mental processes. The thicker arrow from Heavy TV to Memory Search indicates a greater contribution to the search process.

Cacioppo, 1986). In fact, given that the model shown in Fig. 4.3 derives from the concepts of heuristic (peripheral) and systematic (central) processing, it is no accident that the model bears striking similarity to the ELM (as well as the Heuristic/Systematic Model, Chaiken et al., 1989). In general, the less the elaboration (due to such things as time pressure, mental ability, involvement, etc.), the greater the cultivation effect.

Implausible Alternative Hypotheses

Although some, if not all, of the studies that have formed the basis of the model have potential alternative explanations, it is difficult for concepts such as spuriousness or reverse causality to account for the general pattern. For example, the initial studies that tested Propositions 1 and 2 (accessibility) were strictly correlational and thus could be explained in terms of either spuriousness or reverse causality. However, these alternative explanations cannot account for the results of the experiments that tested Propositions 3 through 5, particularly the pattern showing that both the experimental manipulations of source priming and of processing strategy produced nearly identical results, with the manipulations reducing estimates of heavy viewers to the equivalent of light viewers, but leaving the estimates of light viewers unaffected.

The consistency of results across the different types of dependent variables also argues against explanations other than a causal effect of television viewing. Consistent results tended to be found for judgments of occupational prevalence (doctors, lawyers, police officers), crime, and affluence (and, to a lesser extent, marital discord). Although reverse causality or spuriousness explanations can be used (and often are) to explain the results for any one variable, it is difficult to account for the effects on all variables. Rather, the more parsimonious explanation is that the causal factor is the one that they most have in common: They are constructs overrepresented in television portrayals relative to their real-world incidence.

Reconciling Conflicting Findings in Past Research

As mentioned earlier, one of the useful features of a process model for cultivation effects is that it has the potential to reconcile conflicting findings that have been reported. The myriad of paths toward little or no cultivation effect that are shown in Fig. 4.3 has the potential to explain some of these conflicts.

Source-Priming Explanations. The source-priming manipulation used by Shrum et al. (1998) had participants provide information on how much television they watch prior to providing their prevalence and likelihood estimates. This order of data collection was sufficient to eliminate the cultivation effect. As Morgan and Shanahan (1996) note, a number of studies that have reported finding no evidence of a cultivation effect either measured television viewing prior to measuring social perceptions or introduced the study as one pertaining to television. Although Morgan and Shanahan's meta-analysis did not find support for such source-priming as a moderator, their results showed that the effect sizes for the non-source-primed studies tended to be slightly higher than the effect sizes for studies in which source was (inadvertently) primed. Thus, it seems possible that the inability to observe cultivation effects in previous studies may have been due to the inadvertent priming of source information.

Note also that it is not necessary to prime source characteristics through data collection. Priming simply refers to making a construct more accessible in memory. For some people, particular constructs may be chronically accessible (Higgins, 1996). So for whom might the construct of television, and its potential effects, be particularly accessible? One group may be communications majors, or for that matter, any student who might have had a course that deals with potential effects of television; in other words, people who may often comprise the subject pools that academics (and especially those in communications departments) use in their studies. Thus, it is plausible that null findings for cultivation effects in some studies may be due to the special characteristics of the sample.

Involvement Explanations. There are a number of factors that may relate to level of involvement with constructing judgments. For example, level of involvement may differ as a function of sample composition. College students may be less intimidated than older adults or younger people by the university setting that may be used to collect data (Shrum, 1997). Alternatively, individual differences may exist that relate to involvement, such as interest in the topic (e.g., crime by those with direct experience with it) or general interest in solving problems (e.g., those high on need for cognition; Cacioppo & Petty, 1982). Involvement may also vary as a function of data collection method. Data that are collected through anonymous questionnaires may induce less accuracy motivation than data collected in, say, personal interviews (Shrum, 1997, 2001).

Time Pressure Explanations. Shrum (1999a) showed that simple differences in data collection methods, presumably related to differences in time pressure, can have a significant impact on the magnitude of cultivation effects. In that study, the difference was whether the data were collected via a phone or mail survey. Other situations can contribute to time pressure, whether real or imagined. Although not entirely independent of involvement, it has been my experience that a majority of the college students that comprise subject pools seem to be in quite a hurry to finish their task and leave. Moreover, within any type of data collection method, some people will be in more of a hurry than others, whether because of individual (e.g., personality) or situational (e.g., family duties) factors.

All of the Above.   The point in discussing all of these explanations is that there are many factors that may contribute to reducing or eliminating the cultivation effect, and any or all may be at work at any time that a judgment is required. In fact, as one thinks of all the possibilities, it may seem surprising that we would *ever* observe a cultivation effect! Yet, that is one point of the model: Across studies, the cultivation effect tends to be rather small (McGuire, 1986; Morgan & Shanahan, 1996), and this may be largely explained by various conditions that may operate at the time of judgment.

When Cultivation?   Generally speaking, one would expect (larger) cultivation effects when people process heuristically rather than systematically. Put differently, cultivation effects are expected when people do not give much thought to their judgments. But does that make the cultivation effect trivial? We know that judgments made through heuristic processing tend to be less persistent, less resistant to change, and less predictive of behavior than those made via systematic processing (Chaiken et al., 1989; Petty & Cacioppo, 1986), and thus relatively inferior in terms of quality. Yet, people make heuristic judgments all the time. Examples might include providing opinions for pollsters, voting decisions when little is known about a candidate, whether to avoid someone on a street, or how to react in a dangerous situation. In fact, as research in social cognition accumulates, it is remarkable as to how little information is used in the course of constructing judgments and how often heuristics are employed (Wyer & Srull, 1989). Moreover, recent work suggests that much of this process is automatic rather than controlled (Bargh & Chartrand, 1999).

CONCLUSION

The purpose of this chapter was to make a case for the importance of investigating the cognitive processes underlying media effects. This was accomplished in two ways: first, by providing a discussion of some general principles that have emerged from social cognition research, and how the principles can be used to explain particular media effects, and second, by demonstrating how these general principles can be used to develop a cognitive process model to explain a particular media effect, the cultivation effect.

Some important shortcomings are worth noting briefly. First, the discussion of the application of process concepts to media effects other than the cultivation effect, which was provided in the first portion of the chapter, is necessarily impoverished. Not only do space limitations preclude a more thorough discussion, but much of this work is discussed in more illuminating detail in other chapters in this volume. Second, the model presented in the second portion of the chapter is very much incomplete. In arguing for the importance of this research perspective, I may have mistakenly given the impression that the model can successfully account for all, or even most, research on the cultivation effect. This is far from the case. The model is mute with respect to such things as so-called second-order cultivation judgments (e.g., attitude judgments; Hawkins & Pingree, 1990; Shrum, 1995). Similarly, it does not address in any detail such things as question wording (e.g., fear of victimization vs. likelihood of victimization, Sparks & Ogles, 1990; societal vs. personal judgments, Tyler, 1980) or the moderating influences of direct experience associated with mainstreaming and resonance (Gerbner, Gross, Morgan, & Signorielli, 1980). Although the social cognition principles of accessibility and heuristic/sufficiency have been applied to these areas of research as well (cf. Shrum, 1999b; Shrum & Darmanin Bischak, 2001), they are not included in the model.

Hopefully, the general theoretical perspective put forth in this chapter will serve as an incentive to further investigate process issues, with the aim of *reconciling* the corpus of research that has accumulated, rather than simply adding to it. In order to move an area of research forward, it would seem useful to develop general theories that can account for the majority of findings to date. Simple input/output models are typically insufficient in this regard. Rather, focusing on the mediating processes and understanding the conditions that both facilitate and inhibit a particular effect may provide a fruitful path.

REFERENCES

Aust, C. F., & Zillmann, D. (1996). Effects of victim exemplification in television news on viewer perception of social issues. *Journalism & Mass Communication Quarterly, 73,* 787–803.

Bargh, J. A., & Chartrand, T. L. (1999). The unbearable automaticity of being. *American Psychologist, 54,* 462–479.

Bargh, J. A., & Pietromonaco, P. (1982). Automatic information processing and social perception: The influence of trait information presented outside of conscious awareness on impression formation. *Journal of Personality and Social Psychology, 43,* 437–449.

Berkowitz, L. (1970). Aggressive humors as a stimulus to aggressive responses. *Journal of Personality and Social Psychology, 16,* 710–717.

Berkowitz, L. (1973). Words and symbols as stimuli to aggressive responses. In J. Knutson (Ed.), *Control of aggression: Implications from basic research* (pp. 113–143). Chicago: Aldine-Atherton.

Berkowitz, L. (1984). Some effects of thoughts on anti- and prosocial influences of media events: A cognitive-neoassociation analysis. *Psychological Bulletin, 95,* 410–427.

Brosius, H., & Bathelt, A. (1994). The utility of examples in persuasive communication. *Communication Research, 21,* 48–78.

Bryant, J., Carveth, R. A., & Brown, D. (1981). Television viewing and anxiety: An experimental investigation. *Journal of Communication, 31*(1), 106–119.

Bushman, B., & Geen, R. (1990). Role of cognitive-emotional mediators and individual differences in the effects of media violence on aggression. *Journal of Personality and Social Psychology, 58,* 156–163.

Busselle, R. W. (2001). The role of exemplar accessibility in social reality judgments. *Media Psychology, 3,* 43–67.

Busselle, R. W., & Shrum, L. J. (2000). *Media exposure and exemplar accessibility.* Unpublished manuscript.

Cacioppo, J. T., & Petty, R. E. (1982). The need for cognition. *Journal of Personality and Social Psychology, 42,* 116–131.

Carlston, D. E., & Smith, E. R. (1996). Principles of mental representation. In E. T. Higgins & A. W. Kruglanski (Eds.), *Social psychology: Handbook of basic principles* (pp. 184–210). New York: Guilford Press.

Carver, C., Ganellen, R., Froming, W., & Chambers, W. (1983). Modeling: An analysis in terms of category accessibility. *Journal of Experimental Social Psychology, 19,* 403–421.

Chaiken, S., Liberman, A., & Eagly, A. H. (1989). Heuristic and systematic processing within and beyond the persuasion context. In J. S. Uleman & J. A. Bargh (Eds.), *Unintended thought* (pp. 212–252). New York: Guilford Press.

Chaiken, S., & Maheswaran, D. (1994). Heuristic processing can bias systematic processing: Effects of source credibility, argument ambiguity, and task importance on attitude judgment. *Journal of Personality and Social Psychology, 66,* 460–473.

Chayefsky, P. (writer). (1976). *Network* [Film]. Metro-Goldwyn-Mayer, Inc.

Collins, A. M., & Loftus, E. F. (1975). A spreading-activation theory of semantic processing. *Psychological Review, 82,* 407–428.

Doob, A., & Macdonald, G. (1979). Television viewing and fear of victimization: Is the relationship causal? *Journal of Personality and Social Psychology, 37,* 170–179.

Fishbein, M., & Ajzen, I. (1975). *Belief, attitude, intention, and behavior: An introduction to theory and research.* Reading, MA: Addison-Wesley.

Freedman, J. L. (1984). Effect of television violence on aggressiveness. *Psychological Bulletin, 96,* 227–246.

Gerbner, G., Gross, L., Morgan, M., & Signorielli, N. (1980). The "mainstreaming" of America: Violence profile no. 11. *Journal of Communication, 30*(3), 10–29.

Gibson, R., & Zillmann, D. (1994). Exaggerated versus representative exemplification in news reports. *Communication Research, 21,* 603–624.

Hawkins, R. B., & Pingree, S. (1990). Divergent psychological processes in constructing social reality from mass media content. In N. Signorielli & M. Morgan (Eds.), *Cultivation analysis: New directions in media effects research* (pp. 33–50). Newbury Park, CA: Sage.

Henninger, M., & Wyer, R. S. (1976). The recognition and elimination of inconsistencies among syllogistically related beliefs: Some new light on the "Socratic effect." *Journal of Personality and Social Psychology, 34,* 680–693.

Higgins, E. T. (1996). Knowledge activation: Accessibility, applicability, and salience. In E. T. Higgins & A. W. Kruglanski (Eds.), *Social psychology: Handbook of basic principles* (pp. 133–168). New York: Guilford Press.

Higgins, E. T., Bargh, J. A., & Lombardi, W. (1985). The nature of priming effects on categorization. *Journal of Experimental Psychology: Learning, Memory, & Cognition, 11*, 59–69.

Higgins, E. T., & Brendl, C. M. (1995). Accessibility and applicability: Some "activation rules" influencing judgment. *Journal of Experimental Social Psychology, 31*, 218–243.

Higgins, E. T., & King, G. (1981). Accessibility of social constructs: Information processing consequences of individual and contextual variability. In N. Cantor & J. F. Kihlstrom (Eds.), *Personality, cognition and social interaction* (pp. 69–121). Hillsdale, NJ: Lawrence Erlbaum Associates.

Higgins, E. T., Rholes, W. S., & Jones, C. R. (1977). Category accessibility and impression formation. *Journal of Experimental Social Psychology, 13*, 141–154.

Hirsch, P. (1980). The scary world of the nonviewer and other anomalies: A reanalysis of Gerbner et al.'s findings on cultivation analysis. *Communication Research, 7*, 403–456.

Hughes, M. (1980). The fruits of cultivation analysis: A reexamination of some effects of television watching. *Public Opinion Quarterly, 44*, 287–302.

Iyengar, S. (1990). The accessibility bias in politics: Television news and public opinion. *International Journal of Public Opinion Research, 2*, 1–15.

Johnson, M. K., Hashtroudi, S., & Lindsay, D. S. (1993). Source monitoring. *Psychological Bulletin, 114*, 3–28.

Lichtenstein, S., Slovic, P., Fischhoff, G., Layman, M., & Combs, B. (1978). Judged frequency of lethal events. *Journal of Experimental Psychology: Human Learning and Memory, 6*, 551–578.

Manis, M., Shedler, J., Jonides, J., & Nelson, T. E. (1993). Availability heuristic in judgments of set size and frequency of occurrence. *Journal of Personality and Social Psychology, 65*, 448–457.

Mares, M. L. (1996). The role of source confusions in television's cultivation of social reality judgments. *Human Communication Research, 23*, 278–297.

McGuire, W. J. (1960). Cognitive consistency and attitude change. *Journal of Abnormal and Social Psychology, 60*, 345–353.

McGuire, W. J. (1986). The myth of massive media impact: Savagings and salvagings. In G. Comstock (Ed.), *Public communication and behavior* (Vol. 1, pp. 173–257). New York: Academic Press.

Moore, D. L., Hausknecht, D., & Thamodaran, K. (1986). Time compression, response opportunity, and persuasion. *Journal of Consumer Research, 13*, 85–99.

Morgan, M., & Shanahan, J. (1996). Two decades of cultivation research: An appraisal and meta-analysis. In B. R. Burleson (Ed.), *Communication yearbook 20* (pp. 1–45). Newbury Park, CA: Sage.

Nisbett, R., & Ross, L. (1980). *Human inferences: Strategies and shortcomings of human judgment*. Englewood Cliffs, NJ: Prentice Hall.

Ogles, R. M., & Hoffner, C. (1987). Film violence and perceptions of crime: The cultivation effect. In M. L. McLaughlin (Ed.), *Communication yearbook 10* (pp. 384–394). Newbury Park, CA: Sage.

O'Guinn, T. C., & Shrum, L. J. (1997). The role of television in the construction of consumer reality. *Journal of Consumer Research, 23*, 278–294.

Paivio, A. (1971). *Imagery and verbal processes*. New York: Holt, Rinehart & Winston.

Petty, R. E., & Cacioppo, J. T. (1986). *Communication and persuasion: Central and peripheral routes to attitude change*. New York: Springer-Verlag.

Petty, R. E., & Cacioppo, J. T. (1990). Involvement and persuasion: Tradition versus integration. *Psychological Bulletin, 107*, 367–374.

Phillips, D. (1983). The impact of mass media violence on U.S. homicides. *American Sociological Review, 48,* 560–568.

Ratneshwar, S., & Chaiken, S. (1991). Comprehension's role in persuasion: The case of its moderating effect on the persuasive impact of source cues. *Journal of Consumer Research, 18,* 52–62.

Reeves, B., Chaffee, S., & Tims, A. (1982). Social cognition and mass communication research. In M. E. Roloff & C. R. Berger (Eds.), *Social cognition and mass communication* (pp. 287–326). Newbury Park, CA: Sage.

Schank, R., & Abelson, R. P. (1977). *Scripts, plans, goals, and understanding.* Hillsdale, NJ: Lawrence Erlbaum Associates.

Schwarz, N., Bless, H., Strack, F., Klumpp, G., Rittenauer-Schatka, H., & Simons, A. (1991). Ease of retrieval as information: Another look at the availability heuristic. *Journal of Personality and Social Psychology, 61,* 195–202.

Shapiro, M. A., & Lang, A. (1991). Making television reality: Unconscious processes in the construction of social reality. *Communication Research, 18,* 685–705.

Sherman, S. J., & Corty, E. (1984). Cognitive heuristics. In R. S. Wyer & T. K. Srull (Eds.), *Handbook of social cognition* (Vol. 1, pp. 189–286). Hillsdale, NJ: Lawrence Erlbaum Associates.

Shrum, L. J. (1995). Assessing the social influence of television: A social cognition perspective on cultivation effects. *Communication Research, 22,* 402–429.

Shrum, L. J. (1996). Psychological processes underlying cultivation effects: Further tests of construct accessibility. *Human Communication Research, 22,* 482–509.

Shrum, L. J. (1997). The role of source confusion in cultivation effects may depend on processing strategy: A comment on Mares (1996). *Human Communication Research, 24,* 349–358.

Shrum, L. J. (1999a). *The effect of data-collection method on the cultivation effect: Implications for the heuristic processing model of cultivation effects.* Paper presented at the meeting of the International Communication Association, San Francisco, CA.

Shrum, L. J. (1999b). The relationship of television viewing with attitude strength and extremity: Implications for the cultivation effect. *Media Psychology, 1,* 3–25.

Shrum, L. J. (2001). Processing strategy moderates the cultivation effect. *Human Communication Research, 27,* 94–120.

Shrum, L. J., & Darmanin Bischak, V. (2001). Mainstreaming, resonance, and impersonal impact: Testing moderators of the cultivation effect for estimates of crime risk. *Human Communication Research, 27,* 187–215.

Shrum, L. J., & O'Guinn, T. C. (1993). Processes and effects in the construction of social reality: Construct accessibility as an explanatory variable. *Communication Research, 20,* 436–471.

Shrum, L. J., O'Guinn, T. C., Semenik, R. J., & Faber, R. J. (1991). Processes and effects in the construction of normative consumer beliefs: The role of television. In R. H. Holman & M. R. Solomon (Eds.), *Advances in consumer research* (Vol. 18, pp. 755–763). Provo, UT: Association for Consumer Research.

Shrum, L. J., Wyer, R. S., & O'Guinn, T. C. (1998). The effects of television consumption on social perceptions: The use of priming procedures to investigate psychological processes. *Journal of Consumer Research, 24,* 447–458.

Sparks, G. G., & Ogles, R. M. (1990). The difference between fear of victimization and the probability of being victimized: Implications for cultivation. *Journal of Broadcasting & Electronic Media, 34,* 351–358.

Srull, T. K., & Wyer, R. S. (1979). The role of category accessibility in the interpretation of information about persons: Some determinants and implications. *Journal of Personality and Social Psychology, 37,* 1660–1672.

Srull, T. K., & Wyer, R. S. (1980). Category accessibility and social perception: Some implications for the study of person memory and interpersonal judgment. *Journal of Personality and Social Psychology, 38*, 841–856.

Tamborini, R., Zillmann, D., & Bryant, J. (1984). Fear and victimization: Exposure to television and perceptions of crime and fear. In R. N. Bostrom (Ed.), *Communication Yearbook 8* (pp. 492–518). Beverly Hills, CA: Sage.

Turner, C., & Berkowitz, L. (1972). Identification with film aggressor (covert role taking) and reactions to film violence. *Journal of Personality and Social Psychology, 21*, 256–264.

Tversky, A., & Kahneman, D. (1973). Availability: A heuristic for judging frequency and probability. *Cognitive Psychology, 5*, 207–232.

Tyler, T. R. (1980). Impact of directly and indirectly experienced events: The origin of crime-related judgments and behaviors. *Journal of Personality and Social Psychology, 39*, 13–28.

Wober, M., & Gunter, B. (1988). *Television and social control.* Aldershot, England: Avebury.

Wyer, R. S. (1980). The acquisition and use of social knowledge: Basic postulates and representative research. *Personality and Social Psychology Bulletin, 6*, 558–573.

Wyer, R. S., & Hartwick, J. (1984). The recall and use of belief statements as bases for judgments: Some determinants and implications. *Journal of Experimental Social Psychology, 20*, 65–85.

Wyer, R. S., & Radvansky, G. A. (1999). The comprehension and validation of social information. *Psychological Review, 106*, 89–118.

Wyer, R. S., & Srull, T. K. (1980). The processing of social stimulus information: A conceptual integration. In R. Hastie, E. B. Ebbessen, T. M. Ostrom, R. S. Wyer, D. L. Hamilton, & D. E. Carlston (Eds.), *Person memory: The cognitive basis of social perception* (pp. 227–300). Hillsdale, NJ: Erlbaum.

Wyer, R. S., & Srull, T. K. (1989). *Memory and cognition in its social context.* Hillsdale, NJ: Lawrence Erlbaum Associates.

Zillmann, D. (1980). Anatomy of suspense. In P. H. Tannenbaum (Ed.), *The entertainment functions of television.* Hillsdale, NJ: Lawrence Erlbaum Associates.

Zillmann, D. (1983). Transfer of excitation in emotional behavior. In J. T. Cacioppo & R. E. Petty (Eds.), *Social psychophysiology: A sourcebook* (pp. 215–242). New York: Guilford.

Zillmann, D., & Brosius, H. (2000). *Exemplification in communication: The influence of case reports on the perception of issues.* Mahwah, NJ: Lawrence Erlbaum Associates.

Zillmann, D., & Bryant, J. (1982). Pornography, sexual callousness, and the trivialization of rape. *Journal of Communication, 32*(4), 10–21.

Zillmann, D., Gibson, R., Sundar, S. S., & Perkins, J. W. (1996). Effects of exemplification in news reports on the perception of social issues. *Journalism & Mass Communication Quarterly, 73*, 427–444.

Zillmann, D., Perkins, J. W., & Sundar, S. S. (1992). Impression-formation effects of printed news varying in descriptive precision and exemplification. *Medienpsychologie, 4*, 168–185.

Zillmann, D., & Zillmann, M. (1996). Psychoneuroendocrinology of social behavior. In E. T. Higgins & A. W. Kruglanski (Eds.), *Social psychology: Handbook of basic principles* (pp. 39–71). New York: Guilford Press.

Chapter 5

Media Priming: A Synthesis

DAVID R. ROSKOS-EWOLDSEN
University of Alabama

BEVERLY ROSKOS-EWOLDSEN
University of Alabama

FRANCESCA R. DILLMAN CARPENTIER
University of Alabama

The focus of research on media priming has shifted. Twenty years ago, research addressed the straightforward study of the influence of media content on people's thoughts, beliefs, judgments, and behavior. During the last 20 years, the emphasis among media scholars has moved toward the development of theories that specify the psychological mechanisms by which the media exert their influence. In other words, research has shifted from whether media priming exists to how media priming works. In this chapter we discuss the few empirical tests of media priming. We also consider explanations of media priming from the standpoints of mass communication and psychology. We conclude by arguing that using traditional psychological explanations of priming (i.e., priming within network models of memory) has limited our progress toward understanding media priming. Instead, we argue that a mental models approach provides a better explanation for media priming.

MEDIA PRIMING RESEARCH

Priming refers to the effect of some preceding stimulus or event on how we react, broadly defined, to some subsequent stimulus. As applied to the media, priming refers to the effects of the content of the media on people's later behavior or judgments related to the content. The ubiquitous nature of the media in our lives makes it a powerful tool for priming how we think and behave. Perhaps because of its nature, few media scholars have questioned whether media priming exists. However, there are few direct, empirical studies of its existence or of the conditions under which it occurs.

For a study to be a direct test of media priming, a control condition must be included in the design. A control condition could be as simple as a condition in which no media prime is presented before measuring relevant thoughts or behaviors. A recent meta-analysis of the media priming literature, using a loose definition of media, found only 42 published studies with sufficient control conditions (Roskos-Ewoldsen, Klinger, & Roskos-Ewoldsen, in press). Representative studies from these domains are described below to verify the existence of media priming and to highlight the kinds of results that need to be explained by theories of media priming.

Media Violence and Priming

Josephson (1987) investigated the priming effects of violent media on children's behavior. In this study, Josephson gathered measures of young boys' trait aggression from their teachers. The boys saw either a violent or a nonviolent television program, each of comparable excitement, likeability, and enjoyment value. The violent segment contained recurring images of walkie-talkies, whereas the nonviolent program contained no walkie-talkies. The walkie-talkies served as a cue for the violent television program, but not for the nonviolent program. Either before or after the television program, half the boys saw a 30-second nonviolent cartoon segment that had been edited to become increasingly static-ridden, eventually worsening to "snow." This cartoon segment was meant to frustrate the young viewers with its apparent technical malfunction.

After viewing their assigned programs, the boys were mock interviewed and then sent to the school gymnasium to play floor hockey. For the mock interview, either a walkie-talkie or a microphone was used. In this way, half of the boys were exposed to the violence-related cue and half were not. The boys then took turns playing hockey and were observed both on and off the court for signs of aggressive behavior, such as pushing other boys down, hitting other players with the hockey stick, or calling other boys abusive names. After three periods, each for 3 minutes of play, the boys were returned to the teachers.

Josephson (1987) found that violent television viewing primed boys who were high in trait aggressiveness to act more violently during initial sports activity (i.e., during the first period of play). This effect was heightened both when violent programming was coupled with the violence-related cue and when violent programming was followed by frustration.

However, this priming effect appeared to lessen with time, because violent programming and cues did not influence aggression in the later periods of play as strongly as in the initial period of play.

In another study, Anderson (1997) investigated the influence of violent media on the accessibility of aggression-related concepts. Undergraduate students were randomly assigned to view either movie clips containing violent scenes or movie clips featuring nonviolent content. After viewing their assigned clips, the undergraduate participants completed a questionnaire assessing their state hostility level (Experiment 1) or their trait and state hostility levels (Experiment 2).

Once the questionnaire was completed, participants were escorted to another room to perform a task in which they read aloud 192 words that appeared on a computer screen. These words were designed to elicit feelings of aggression, anxiety, escape, or control. For example, *attack* would be associated with aggression, whereas *flight* would be associated with escape. Unbeknownst to the participants, the time it took them to pronounce each word was recorded. Anderson (1997) hypothesized that participants who had viewed the violent clips would be primed, such that words associated with aggression (i.e., *attack*) would be more accessible, and thus more quickly pronounced, than words not associated with aggression (i.e., *flight*). In both experiments, participants who watched the violent clip rated themselves as higher in state hostility than participants who watched the nonviolent clips, but there were no differences in the aggressive word reading times between the violent and nonviolent conditions. This initial result suggested that, although participants' aggressive feelings were more accessible after the violent clip, their aggressive thoughts did not appear to be more accessible. However, in the second experiment, Anderson (1997) found that participants low in trait hostility who had seen the violent clip reacted faster to aggressive words than did low-hostility participants who had seen only the nonviolent clip. Participants high in trait hostility were not affected by the content of the film clips, in terms of their reading times for aggressive words. In sum, Anderson showed across two studies that violent media can prime both aggressive feelings (i.e., trait hostility) and aggressive thoughts (i.e., accessibility of aggression-related words). The latter is true primarily for persons low in trait hostility.

Consistent with Josephson's (1987) and Anderson's (1997) studies, the meta-analysis by Roskos-Ewoldsen et al. (in press) found that depictions of violence or violence-related concepts (e.g., weapons) prime violence and aggression-related concepts. The study of boys' aggression (Josephson, 1987) also suggested that priming may dissipate over time. Addressed next is the media priming literature regarding political news coverage.

Political News Coverage and Priming

As in the media violence literature, tests of political priming require an appropriate control group. Two representative studies that fit the criteria are discussed; their results need to be explained by theories of media priming.

Krosnick and Kinder (1990) measured the priming effect of Iran–Contra media coverage on public evaluations of President Reagan's overall performance, using data from the 1986 National Election Study. In 1986, the Center for Political Studies at the University of Michigan conducted lengthy face-to-face interviews with adult respondents who were chosen randomly from the national population. Included in the interview of 1,086 citizens was a survey asking for evaluations of President Reagan, both overall and regarding his performance on foreign affairs, domestic policy, and other publicized issues. The interviews were conducted both before and after November 25, 1986, the date on which the Attorney General publicly confirmed the sale of arms to Iran and the subsequent distribution of the sale profits to the Contras.

The study focused on people's opinions regarding Reagan (i.e., overall performance, competence, and integrity) and his handling of foreign affairs (i.e., the Contras and Central America, isolationism, and U.S. strength in foreign affairs) and domestic affairs (i.e., the national economy and aid to Blacks). Krosnick and Kinder (1990) compared responses obtained before and after the priming event—the Iran–Contra announcement—to see which foreign or domestic affairs issues contributed most to the respondents' overall performance evaluations of President Reagan. Before the priming event, domestic issues predicted their overall evaluations of Reagan more than foreign affairs issues. After the priming event, the opposite was true; foreign affairs issues, especially those issues involving Central America, predicted the respondents' overall evaluations of Reagan more than domestic issues. This study shows that media coverage of political events can prime people's thoughts and judgments.

Iyengar, Peters, and Kinder (1982) addressed the priming issue across two experiments. In their first experiment, Iyengar et al. exposed participants to four newscasts over four days. For half of the participants, each newscast contained a story about the inadequacies of U.S. defense preparedness. For the other half, the control group, the four newscasts were devoid of defense stories. In the second experiment, there were three groups, each viewing five newscasts across five days. Embedded in each newscast was a topical story that differed for each group. The topics were defense preparedness, pollution, and inflation. Each group received only one of these topics, and each group served as a control group for the other groups.

Participants in both experiments completed a questionnaire both before and after viewing the newscasts. The questionnaire asked participants to rate eight national problems in terms of national importance, personal concern, the need for more government action regarding each problem, and their estimated amount of interpersonal discussion with friends about the problem. In addition, participants rated then-President Carter's overall performance either in tackling defense (Experiment 1) or in tackling defense, pollution, and inflation (Experiment 2), as well as Carter's competence and integrity.

Results showed that participants in the experimental conditions became more concerned with their inserted issue (i.e., defense preparedness for Experiment 1; defense, pollution, or inflation for Experiment 2) compared with their concern before the newscasts and compared with the control groups. No other issue demonstrated an increase in importance. The second experiment also provided evidence that persistent coverage of an issue results in a stronger correlation between evaluations of Carter's performance concerning that issue and Carter's overall performance as president. These two experiments, in addition to Krosnick and Kinder's (1990) study, demonstrate that media coverage of a topic serves as a prime in influencing how the public formulates political opinions, including how they evaluate the effectiveness of the country's leader. Next, we discuss priming in other areas of the media.

Media Priming in Other Domains

Media priming has been studied within other contexts besides media violence and the political domain (Malamuth & Check, 1985; Schleuder, White, & Cameron, 1993; Wyer, Bodenhausen, & Gorman, 1985; Yi, 1990a, 1990b). One area that has received a fair amount of research concerns the potential for the media to prime various stereotypes (Hansen & Hansen, 1988; Hansen & Krygowski, 1994; Power, Murphy, & Coover, 1996). For example, exposure to rock music videos that portrays stereotypical images of men and women results in more stereotypical impressions of a man and a woman interacting in another videotape (Hansen & Hansen, 1988). In particular, participants perceived the woman as less dominant after exposure to these rock videos than after exposure to rock videos that included no stereotypical portrayals. Likewise, Power et al. (1996) found that reading stereotypical information in a newsletter about either African-Americans or women influenced judgments of later unrelated media events concerning the target group. For example, counterstereotypical depictions of women resulted in higher ratings in Anita Hill's credibility in the Clarence Thomas sexual harassment hearings, whereas stereotypical depictions lowered ratings of Hill's credibility. Finally, several studies found that the media primes rape myths, such as women enjoy being raped, which can influence later perceptions of the plaintiff and defendant in a rape trial (Intons-Peterson, B. Roskos-Ewoldsen, Thomas, Shirley, & Blut, 1989; Malamuth & Check, 1985; Wyer et al., 1985).

In the health domain, several studies have shown that commercials can prime stereotypes. For example, Pechmann and Ratneshwar (1994) exposed adolescents to either antismoking advertisements that focused on how unattractive smoking was (e.g., smelly), cigarette advertisements, or control advertisements, all embedded within an age-appropriate magazine. After looking through the magazine, the adolescents read about a teenager who either smoked or did not smoke. Exposure to the antismoking advertisements resulted in more negative judgments of the teenager who smoked, compared with exposure to the other advertisements. Furthermore, the prime influenced judgments of the smoking teenager that were consistent with the participants' stereotypes of smokers (e.g., lacking common sense and being immature) (see also Pechmann & Knight, 2000).

As in the other domains, research in the stereotype domain indicates that the media can prime stereotypes, and these primed stereotypes do influence how people are later perceived. The research on media priming of stereotypes increases our confidence in the generality of the media as a prime because this research provides validation that the media can act as a prime in a unique research domain and that a variety of media (e.g., advertisements, rock music videos, newsletters) can act as primes. Unfortunately, no research in this area has focused on behavioral manifestations of the media's priming of stereotypes, though the research by Pechmann (2001) suggests that these primed stereotypes do influence adolescents' intentions to smoke. Regrettably, as with the research on media violence and priming and political priming, there has been no research within this domain on the nature of media primes. Do more-intense or extreme portrayals of stereotypes result in stronger priming effects? Does the effect of the media prime of a stereotype fade with time? Currently, we cannot answer these questions because no research has addressed these issues.

Conclusions

The research on media priming currently is disjointed. Clearly, the media act as a prime: a number of studies have demonstrated, and a meta-analysis has confirmed, that the media influences later judgments and behavior. In particular, the research on media priming demonstrates that the media can prime aggressive thoughts and feelings (Anderson, 1997; Anderson, Anderson, & Deuser, 1996; Bushman & Geen, 1990), aggressive behaviors (Bushman, 1995; Josephson, 1987), the information and criteria that we use in making judgments of the president (Iyengar & Kinder, 1987; Iyengar, Kinder, Peters, & Krosnick, 1984; Iyengar et al., 1982; Iyengar & Simon, 1993; Krosnick & Brannon, 1993; Krosnick & Kinder, 1990; Pan & Kosicki, 1997), and various stereotypes that influence how we make judgments of people from the stereotyped group (Hansen & Hansen, 1988; Hansen & Krygowski, 1994; Malamuth & Check, 1985; Pechmann, 2001; Power et al., 1996; Wyer et al., 1985).

Unfortunately, there has been little focus on understanding the nature of the media priming phenomenon. Further, the few explanations of the mechanism by which the media acts as a prime vary from one domain to another. There have been no attempts to integrate the research on media priming across the different areas, let alone the models of how media priming work. However, as we shall see, what these models have in common is a reliance on the priming research from psychology. In the next section, we provide a brief background of the psychological research on priming and then discuss the current models of media priming within each domain.

MODELS OF PRIMING

Priming procedures were first used in cognitive psychology to explore the structure and representation of information within network models of memory (e.g., Anderson, 1983). Network models of memory assume that information is stored in memory in the form of nodes and that each node represents a concept (e.g., there is a "doctor" node in memory). Furthermore, these nodes are connected to related nodes in memory by associative pathways (e.g., "doctor" is linked to "nurse" but not to "butter"). An additional assumption of network models of memory is that each node has an activation threshold. If the node's level of activation exceeds its threshold, the node fires. When a node fires, it can influence the activation levels of other, associatively connected nodes. For example, if the "nurse" node fires, activation spreads from the "nurse" node to related nodes, such as "doctor." One consequence of spreading activation is that the related node now requires less additional activation for it to fire. The additional activation may accrue as a result of spreading activation from other related nodes, or it may result from environmental input (i.e., reading the word *doctor*). A typical behavioral outcome of spreading activation is that a judgment about or pronunciation of a word (e.g., *doctor*) is faster when it is preceded by a related word (*nurse*) than an unrelated word (*butter*). A final assumption of network models of memory is that the activation level of a node will dissipate over time if no additional source of activation is present. Eventually, given no more activation, the activation level of the node returns to its resting state and is no longer considered to be activated.

Social psychologists began using priming procedures in the late 1970s to study person perception, stereotyping, and attitude activation. The general priming procedure in social psychological experiments involves exposing participants to some priming event and then measuring whether the priming event biased their interpretation of later ambiguous information. For example, Srull and Wyer (1979) gave participants four words (e.g., *he, Sally, hit, kicked*), and their task was to use three of the words to construct a sentence. Unbeknownst to the participants, there are only two sentences that can be constructed from these four words: "He hit Sally" and "He kicked Sally." In either case, according to network models of memory, negative attitudes are activated, and the activation spreads to the negative attitudes of other concepts (Fazio, 1986). When participants next are asked to make various judgments of an ambiguously described person or event, the negative aspects of the person or event fire sooner than the positive aspects and subsequently influence the judgment more. Consistent with the predictions of network models, the research in this area typically finds that the ambiguous information is biased toward the primes so that, if the primes are negative, the ambiguously described person will be judged more harshly than if the primes are positive (Higgins, Rholes & Jones, 1977; Srull & Wyer, 1979, 1980).

Research by both cognitive and social psychologists has demonstrated two important characteristics of priming. First, the extent of a prime's effect on a target behavior or thought is a dual function of the *intensity* and the *recency* of the prime (see the synapse model of priming, Higgins, Bargh, & Lombardi, 1985). The intensity of a prime refers to either the frequency of the prime (e.g., a single exposure vs. five exposures in quick succession) or the duration of the prime. Higher-intensity primes produce larger priming effects, and these effects dissipate more slowly than lower-intensity primes (see Higgins et al., 1985). Recency simply refers to the time lag between the prime and the target. Recent primes produce larger priming effects than temporally distant primes.

A second important characteristic of priming is that the effects of a prime fade with time. In lexical decision tasks (i.e., deciding whether the target is a word or a nonword) and other related judgment tasks that use reaction time as the dependent variable, the effect of the prime usually fades within 700 milliseconds (Fazio, Sanbonmatsu, Powell, & Kardes, 1986; Neely, 1977). In tasks that involve judgments or evaluations of a social stimulus, the effect of the prime also fades with time, though the effect appears to fade more slowly (Srull & Wyer, 1979, 1980). In these experiments, the priming effect can last up to 15 or 20 minutes, and possibly up to one hour (Srull & Wyer, 1979). Srull and Wyer (1979, 1980) found evidence of priming effects influencing judgments after 24 hours. However, we are aware of no replications of this latter effect. Most research on the influence of priming on subsequent judgments involves a maximum delay of 15 to 20 minutes. As mentioned previously, priming effects are consistent at these time delays.

Along these lines, it is important to differentiate priming effects, which temporarily increase the accessibility of a concept from memory, from chronic accessibility. Chronic accessibility refers to concepts that are always highly accessible from memory (see research by Bargh, Bond, Lombardi, & Tota, 1986; Fazio et al., 1986; Higgins, King, & Mavin, 1982). In the attitudinal domain, someone's attitude toward cockroaches is probably chronically accessible from memory. On the other hand, someone's attitude toward Tibetan food is probably not chronically accessible. As one would expect, chronically accessible concepts have more persistent effects on people's judgments and behavior than do other concepts that are not chronically accessible. However, chronically accessible concepts can be primed so that they are temporarily even more accessible from memory (Bargh et al., 1986; Roskos-Ewoldsen et al., in press). Nevertheless, without some form of reinforcement, even chronically accessible concepts eventually become less accessible across time (Grant & Logan, 1993).

Returning to the characteristics of priming, Roskos-Ewoldsen et al. (in press) addressed the two main characteristics in their meta-analysis of the media priming literature. In particular, they investigated whether more-intense primes produce larger priming effects, and whether the priming effect fades across time. First, none of the studies included in the meta-analysis directly tested the time course of priming effects. As already discussed, Josephson (1987) found that when boys had been primed with aggressive media and then played field hockey, most of the boys' aggressive behavior occurred within the first three minutes of play. Although this finding has been interpreted as consistent with the time course of priming (Geen, 1990), no study has manipulated the time between the media violence prime and aggressive behavior to determine if aggressive behavior decreases at longer intervals from the media prime. Nevertheless, in Roskos-Ewoldsen et al.'s (in press) meta-analysis, they found that, across all media priming studies, media priming effects appear to fade with time. However, the decrease in media priming effects was not statistically significant. Second, none of the studies directly tested the effect of prime intensity on later aggression. The meta-analysis provided mixed support for the supposition that media primes should become stronger when they are of greater intensity. For example, media primes that lasted 5 to 20 minutes in length had stronger effects than did media primes that were less than 5 minutes in length. On the other hand, media priming effects that resulted from media campaigns (e.g., coverage of the Gulf

War), which were of the longest duration (highest intensity), were significantly smaller than the priming effects from shorter-duration (less-intense) media primes. However, these apparently contradictory results are confounded by the lag between the priming event and the measurement of the prime's effect. The lag between the priming event and the measure of the prime's effect was substantially longer in the campaign studies than in the other media priming studies.

Despite the lack of direct evidence for the two characteristics of priming, the meta-analysis has provided evidence that media priming has these two characteristics. Therefore, for models of media priming to be adequate, they must incorporate the two characteristics of priming. Of course, they must also be able to explain existing media priming results. For example, political priming effects last considerably longer than the typical priming effects found in psychological experiments (Iyengar & Simon, 1993; Krosnick & Brannon, 1993; Pan & Kosicki, 1997; Roskos-Ewoldsen et al., in press). In the next section, we discuss the current models in each domain, with a focus on their ability to incorporate the two characteristics of media priming and to explain the media priming results.

Models of Media Violence Priming

One of the most prominent explanations of the consequences of media violence is Berkowitz's (1984, 1990, 1994, 1997) neo-associationistic model. Berkowitz's model draws heavily from network models of priming. The model hypothesizes that depictions of violence in the media activate hostility- and aggression-related concepts in memory. The activation of these concepts in memory increases the likelihood that a person will engage in aggressive behaviors and that others' behavior will be interpreted as aggressive or hostile. Without further activation, however, the activation levels of these hostile and aggressive concepts, and their associated likelihood of influencing aggressive behavior, fades with time.

Anderson, Deuser, and DeNeve (1995) proposed as an extension of Berkowitz's (1984) neo-associationistic model the affective aggression model. This model incorporates affect and arousal into the network framework and introduces a three-stage process by which situations influence aggressive behavior and affect. In the first stage, situational variables such as pain, frustration, or depictions of violence prime aggressive cognitions (e.g., hostile thoughts and memories) and affect (e.g., hostility, anger), which results in increased arousal. In the second stage, the primed cognitions and affect, in conjunction with the increased arousal, influence *primary appraisal*. Primary appraisal involves the automatic interpretation of the situation (Fazio & Williams, 1986; Houston & Fazio, 1989) and of one's arousal in that situation (Fazio, Zanna, & Cooper, 1979; Schachter & Singer,

1962; Zanna & Cooper, 1974). The final stage of the model involves *secondary appraisals,* which are more effortful, controlled appraisals of the situation and a more thoughtful consideration of various behavioral alternatives to the situation. This final stage can correct or override the primary appraisal (Gilbert, 1991; Gilbert, Tafarodi, & Malone, 1993).

Berkowitz's (1984, 1990, 1994, 1997) neo-associationistic model and Anderson et al.'s (1995) affective aggression model explain many of the findings of the research on priming and media violence. Both models predict that media violence will temporarily increase aggressive thoughts ' (Anderson, 1997; Anderson et al., 1996; Bushman, 1998; Bushman & Geen, 1990) and aggressive behaviors (Bushman, 1995; Josephson, 1987). In addition, the affective aggression model predicts that hot temperatures, the presence of weapons, and competition will increase aggressive thoughts and affect (Anderson et al., 1995; Anderson et al., 1996; Anderson & Morrow, 1995). Furthermore, consistent with both models, individuals who are high in trait aggressiveness have more complex aggression-related associative networks in memory than do individuals who are low in trait aggressiveness (Bushman, 1996). Finally, both models specifically predict that the effects of media priming will fade with time. In addition, both models can predict that more intense primes will result in stronger media priming effects.

Models of Political Priming

Until recently, the theoretical mechanisms by which the media prime evaluations of the president have been largely unspecified. The first attempt used Tversky and Kahneman's (1973) availability heuristic to explain the effects of media coverage on political priming effects (Iyengar & Simon, 1993). According to this explanation, media coverage of an issue influences which exemplars are accessed from memory when people make judgments of the president (Iyengar & Simon, 1993). This process occurs in a manner similar to the process outlined by Shrum (1999; Shrum & O'Guinn, 1993) to explain cultivation effects (see chapter 4). However, this availability/cultivation explanation has not been well developed within the political priming domain and has not been subjected to any empirical tests within this domain.

Only one model of political priming has been developed sufficiently to explain the political priming results (Price & Tewksbury, 1997). Similar to Berkowitz's (1984) neo-associationistic model, Price and Tewksbury's model of political priming is based on network models of memory. As discussed earlier, network models maintain that both chronic and temporary accessibility of constructs influences their likelihood of firing. In addition, Price and Tewksbury incorporate the *applicability* of information into their model of political priming. Applicability refers to deliberate judgments of the relevance of information to the current situation. They maintain that information (e.g., constructs that are activated by the media) that is judged as applicable is actively thought about in working memory. To digress for a moment, short-term memory refers to that information that is currently activated within the memory system. Working memory is a subset of short-term memory and involves that information that is consciously available. Within Price and Tewksbury's model, constructs that are activated by the media and judged as applicable to the current situation are brought into working memory and subsequently influence how the message is framed or interpreted. On the other hand, those constructs that are activated by the media and judged as not applicable to the current situation are not brought into working memory, but the activation of these constructs by the media means that they may act as a prime.

Price and Tewksbury's model treats message framing (e.g., how the message is thought about) as resulting from more conscious judgments of information relevance and political priming as operating in a more automatic fashion as a consequence of temporary increases in the activation of various constructs by the media. Unfortunately, the priming component of that model has not been subjected to empirical test. In many of the media priming studies, the prime is presented at least 24 hours prior to the measure of the prime's effect (Iyengar et al., 1982; Iyengar & Kinder, 1987; Krosnick & Kinder, 1990), and in some instances, the media coverage that acts as a prime may have occurred weeks earlier (Iyengar & Simon, 1993; Krosnick & Brannon, 1993; Pan & Kosicki, 1997). Consequently, the time span involved in political priming makes it unlikely that priming, in the sense used by cognitive and social psychologists, is influencing the evaluations of the president. In the original sense, priming results in a temporary increase in the accessibility of a node (i.e., concept) that dissipates relatively quickly. It is perhaps unfortunate that the cognitive/social priming research is cited as support in the political realm, because the phenomenon does not fit the characteristics of priming. It is more likely that the frequent and repeated stories on a particular issue (e.g., the Gulf War) increases the *chronic* accessibility of the information (see Lau, 1989; Roskos-Ewoldsen, 1997; Roskos-Ewoldsen et al., in press; Shrum, 1999; Shrum & O'Guinn, 1993). Rather than calling this phenomenon political priming, perhaps it would be better if we referred to it as political cultivation.

Models of Media Priming in Other Media Domains

The only model in this area focuses on health appeals. Recently, Pechmann (2001) proposed her stereotype priming model in which the media act as a prime in public health campaigns. Past research on media health campaigns focused on rational health appeals. These rational appeals highlight the aversive consequences of a particular disease (e.g., AIDS or breast cancer) or behavior (e.g., binge drinking) and the risk of the aversive consequence occurring unless a particular course of action is taken, such as practicing safe sex, performing breast self-exams, or stopping binge drinking (see Floyd, Prentice-Dunn, & Rogers, 2000; Rogers, 1983; Witte, 1994, 1995). They focus on our ability to think and make decisions about the issues rationally. The stereotype priming model shifts away from this approach by maintaining that the media can also influence behavior by priming preexisting negative stereotypes of people who engage in the risky behavior or positive stereotypes of people who engage in the desired behavior. For example, a commercial might prime negative stereotypes of people who drink and drive (e.g., they are irresponsible or reckless with other people's lives). The model further maintains that the activation of these negative stereotypes in turn leads to impression management behaviors (e.g., if I drink and drive, I'm irresponsible).

Although the stereotype priming model incorporates media priming, it was not intended to explain media priming per se. Rather, it was intended to demonstrate how the phenomenon of priming can be used to elucidate how health appeals in the media can more effectively be used to effect adaptive behaviors (e.g., quitting smoking). As a result, it is vague in terms of the exact mechanisms of priming.

Summary and Conclusions

At one level, the theoretical development that has occurred in the area of media priming is impressive. There are currently five models that have been proposed to explain the cognitive processes that result in media priming: Berkowitz's (1984) neo-associationistic model; Anderson et al.'s (1995) affective aggression model; the availability heuristic explanation of political media priming; Price and Tewksbury's (1997) network model of political priming; and Pechmann's (2001) stereotype priming model (but see comments in the previous section). Three of these models (Berkowitz's, Anderson et al.'s, and Price and Tewksbury's) rely directly on network models of memory to explain media priming. All three of the network models of media priming predict that the intensity and recency of the priming event should influence the magnitude of the prime on subsequent behavior. However, there have been no empirical tests of these assumptions within the domain of media priming (Roskos-Ewoldsen et al., in press). In reading the literature on media priming, one gets the impression that media scholars identified the concept of priming in cognitive and social psychology and used it to explain their media effects metaphorically, but were not particularly interested in testing whether media priming is, in fact, a result of priming in a network model.

Furthermore, despite the commonalities across these theories, their domains differ too much to afford a single theory of media priming. For example, the affective aggression model's (Anderson et al., 1995) reliance on network models for explaining affective priming is problematic because recent research has seriously questioned the ability of network models to explain affective priming (Franks, Roskos-Ewoldsen, Bilbrey, & Roskos-Ewoldsen, 1999; Klinger, Burton, & Pitts, 2000). In addition, a unique feature of this model is that it incorporates secondary appraisals that can override the effect of the priming events on subsequent behavior. Clearly, this is a necessary addition to the model because it allows the model to explain how the priming of aggressive cognitions and affect does not always result in aggressive behavior. However, it is unclear how this component of the model would apply to political priming. Conversely, in Price and Tewksbury's (1997) model, judgments of applicability play a central role in determining whether activated nodes serve as primes or whether they influence how a media story is framed. Recall that judgments of applicability involve whether the particular construct that is activated by the media is applicable to what is being watched/read. When an activated construct is judged as applicable, it is then used to frame what is being watched/read and does not act as a prime. When it is judged as not applicable, then it can serve as a prime. In the context of media violence, the violence, although often not necessary, is typically applicable to the show. As a consequence, the violence would *trigger* a judgment of applicability, which should afford no aggressive priming by the media. Obviously, this is not the case. Ultimately, the difficulty in combining the different models of media priming into a coherent model that covers all the domains is that the current models were specifically crafted to explain the findings relevant to only that domain of study.

In our view, network models of media priming provide a starting point for understanding the effects of the media on subsequent judgments and behavior. However, we believe that network models need to be subsumed within a larger theoretical framework to explain adequately the phenomena that these models are attempting to explain. Following, we propose such a theoretical framework, a mental models approach.

A NEW FRAMEWORK FOR UNDERSTANDING MEDIA PRIMING: THE MENTAL MODELS APPROACH

The mental models approach reflects the observation that thinking typically occurs within and about situations (Garnham, 1997). Mental models are the cognitive representations of situations in real or imaginary worlds (including space and time), the entities found in the situation (and the states those entities are in), the interrelationships between the various entities and the situation (including causality and intentionality), and events that occur in that situation (Garnham, 1997; Johnson-Laird, 1983; Radvansky & Zacks, 1997; Wyer & Radvansky, 1999; Zwaan & Radvansky, 1998). Mental models are distinct from network models of memory, but the entities and events within a mental model are hypothesized to be linked to relevant representations in a network (Radvansky & Zacks, 1997; Wyer & Radvansky, 1999). In other words, mental models are hypothesized to exist alongside and coupled with the semantic networks that are hypothesized by network models of memory.

vanDijk (1998) argues that mental models involve the merger of semantic memory (knowledge of the world) and episodic memory (memory for our past experiences). However, this argument can be misleading. In particular, it might give the impression that mental models involve only the representation of past situations we have personally experienced (what vanDijk refers to as *experience mental models*). However, when defining mental models as cognitive representations of situations, the term *situation* is used very broadly. For example, we can have mental models of ownership and the interrelationships of owners and the objects that are owned (Radvansky & Zacks, 1997). Likewise, mental models can be used in reasoning to represent possible worlds in which the premises of an argument are true and to manipulate the possible worlds to discover what occurs (Johnson-Laird, 1983).

Mental models have been used to understand a number of different phenomena, including reasoning and problem solving (Greeno, 1984; Johnson-Laird, 1983), language processing (Garnham, 1997), children's understanding of the world (Halford, 1993), text comprehension and discourse (Graesser, Singer, & Trabasso, 1994; Morrow, Greenspan, & Bower, 1987; vanDijk & Kintsch, 1983; Zwaan & Radvansky, 1998), children's implicit theories of physics (Gentner & Gentner, 1984), spatial cognition (Radvansky, Spieler, & Zacks, 1993), message effects (Capella & Street, 1989), political commercials (Biocca, 1991), and ideology (vanDijk, 1998). We believe that they also can be used to understand media priming.

We want to be clear that we are not arguing that priming, as conceptualized by network models of memory, does not occur with the media. Commercials clearly prime various concepts, and this priming can influence the interpretation of other commercials or the show that the commercials were placed within (Yi, 1990a, 1990b). Likewise, watching a violent movie clip speeds the time it takes participants to pronounce aggression-related words, compared to participants who watched a violence-free movie clip (Anderson, 1997). Both of these findings are consistent with network models of priming.

However, the phenomena of interest to media scholars studying priming (e.g., violent media influencing aggressive behavior, political coverage influencing what information is used to make judgments of the president) cannot easily be explained by network-based theories of media priming. At a basic level, the priming effect that network models of memory address dissipates too quickly to explain many of the media priming effects. Of course, the time course issue can be addressed by assuming, as Price and Tewksbury (1997) do, that media portrayals increase the chronic accessibility of constructs, and it is the chronic accessibility of the constructs that results in the media effects that are being studied (see also Roskos-Ewoldsen et al., in press; Shrum, 1999; Shrum & O'Guinn, 1993). Although we believe that chronic accessibility is important (e.g., Roskos-Ewoldsen, 1997; Roskos-Ewoldsen, Arpan-Ralstin, & St. Pierre, in press; Roskos-Ewoldsen & Fazio, 1992a, 1992b, 1997), we propose that the phenomena of priming and of chronic accessibility should be incorporated into a larger theoretical frame that involves mental models of memory.

As one example of how the mental models approach works, we can look at the process model of the attitude–behavior relationship (Fazio, 1986, 1990; Fazio & Roskos-Ewoldsen, 1994; Roskos-Ewoldsen, 1997). In this model, accessible attitudes influence behavior by influencing how the current situation is defined. In other words, accessible attitudes influence behavior by influencing the mental model that is constructed of the situation. We argue that many priming effects can be similarly reinterpreted to operate in this manner. In brief, the prime influences how later information is interpreted by influencing the type of mental model that is constructed to understand the situation.

Mental models can relate to media priming in two ways. First, when dealing with a novel situation, there is the option of forming a new mental model or accessing an existing mental model from memory. Obviously, people have myriad mental models stored in long-term memory. If an existing mental model is accessed from memory, the issue becomes which mental models are accessed and used to understand/interpret a particular situation. Although the match between the mental models stored in memory and the existing situation will influence which model(s) are accessed, we argue further that, as with other constructs in memory, mental models will vary in their accessibility from memory (Radvansky & Zacks, 1997; Wyer & Radvansky, 1999). Consequently, mental models can be primed by the media, increasing the likelihood that they will be accessed. For example, when the media focused on the pending war over Kuwait during the Bush presidency, this coverage could result either in the creation of a new mental model of President Bush and the Kuwait crisis or the modification of an existing mental model of President Bush. In either case, the frequent coverage of the issue would increase the accessibility of the mental model (or that component of the mental model of President Bush that dealt with the crisis). Consequently, when asked to judge the effectiveness of President Bush, the recently constructed model should be relatively more accessible and exert more influence on judgments of President Bush's performance. Likewise, when the downturn in the economy became a major issue in late 1991 and 1992, the extensive media coverage resulted in the further development of mental models relevant to President Bush. In this way, mental models can explain the long-term consequences of political priming. Josephson's (1987) study of the influence of exposure to a violent TV program on young boys' level of aggression provides another example of this process. We argue that viewing the violent TV program activated a mental model that included violence as one of the relationships between the entities in the model. Consequently, when the boys were first put into a situation in which they were interacting with other boys, the mental model from the TV program was still active and influenced how the boys viewed the situation (i.e., they were more likely to view relationships with others as involving violence). In addition, when the boys were interviewed with a cue from the violent TV program (a walkie-talkie), the cue would further activate the mental model, because the walkie-talkie would be part of the model. This further activation would increase the likelihood that the boys used the mental model to guide their behavior.

A second way that mental models can relate to media priming involves the ability to prime specific information within a mental model. Research has demonstrated that the accessibility of particular information in mental models can vary, depending on the immediate task that a person is performing (Morrow, Bower, & Greenspan, 1989; Morrow et al., 1987; Radvansky & Zacks, 1997; cf. Wilson, Rinck, McNamara, Bower, & Morrow, 1993). In other words, the media could prime specific information within a particular mental model, making that information more accessible, in addition to priming mental models. However, the focus of the mental model will influence the ease with which information can be primed and retrieved from memory. For example, when watching the movie *Blue Velvet*, one could create a mental model concerning the story of the movie (e.g., an idyllic town where a number of bizarre and disturbing events occur) or the main character, Frank (played by Dennis Hopper), a psychotic drug dealer. If the mental model is structured around Frank, seeing Dennis Hopper in any other situation would activate the mental model of Frank. Indeed, such a occurrence happened to one of the authors who had seen *Blue Velvet* and then, less than a week later, the movie *Hoosiers*. In Dennis Hopper's first scene in *Hoosiers*, the author had an extreme reaction because Hopper's appearance activated the mental model of Frank from to *Blue Velvet*, and there was concern about what he was going to do to the boys on the high school basketball team in *Hoosiers*. However, if the mental model had been organized around the story of *Blue Velvet*, viewing Dennis Hopper in a different context would be much less likely to activate that mental model.

At a more general level, the mental models approach provides a flexible framework for an academic understanding of the media. In particular it has three useful characteristics. First, mental models exist at many levels of abstraction. If you are a reader of mysteries, you might have a mental model for Agatha Christie novels, more specific mental models for her Poirot and Miss Marple mysteries, and maybe more specific mental models for specific stories from the Poirot or Miss Marple series. A second characteristic is that new information can be integrated into existing mental models. A person's mental model of Shrewsbury, the setting for Ellis Peters' Brother Cadfael mysteries, could be updated as more information is provided about Shrewsbury and the abbey where Brother Cadfael lives (Wyer & Radvansky, 1999). Similarly, rumination about the content of a mental model would result in updating the mental model (Zwaan & Radvansky, 1998). A third characteristic is that mental models can represent both static situations, such as the mental model of the town of Shrewsbury (what Radvansky & Zacks (1997) refer to as *states-of-affairs models*), and dynamics situations that are evolving, such as the mental model of a specific mystery that is occurring at the abbey (what Radvansky & Zacks refer to as *course-of-event models*).

Several lines of research on mental models corroborate their usefulness for understanding the media in general. Research has found that the mix of linguistic and pictorial information improves the construction of mental models (Glenberg & Langston, 1992; Wyer & Radvansky, 1999). For this reason, the media should be particularly effective at influencing the construction of mental models. In addition, research has shown that previously created mental models will influence how new information is interpreted, and that they will influence the mental model that is constructed to understand the current event (Radvansky & Zacks, 1997; Wyer & Radvansky, 1999). Finally, as already discussed, mental models can vary in their degree of abstraction, so frequent viewers of a particular genre should have richer abstract mental models that are appropriate for understanding the nuances of that genre. Indeed, research has found that the mental models that people construct are dependent on the genre of the story they are reading (Zwann, 1994). Thus, genre differences that are found in media studies may well reflect the types of mental models that people construct of the media event.

The mental models approach also provides a framework for explaining how individuals understand the media. In particular, the mental models that we construct play an integral role in how we understand the media. Understanding interpersonal discourse, the media, or the world in general requires constructing a mental model to represent the event. To the extent that a person can construct such a model, the person is said to understand the event (Halford, 1993; Wyer & Radvansky, 1999). Furthermore, mental models aid in understanding information across scenes of the program and even across episodes of a series (Zwaan & Radvanski, 1998). Likewise, the mental model that one constructs of a show will drive the type of inferences that will be drawn about the show (Graesser et al., 1994).

Finally, the mental models approach provides a framework for understanding the effects of media on our perceptions and behavior. For example, Seigrin and Nabi (in press) recently found that people who watch more romantic TV programming have more idealistic expectations about marriage. We argue that viewing this genre of TV results in the creation of mental models that reflected the idealistic images of marriage reflect in the media. In other words, we argue that their expectations concerning marriage are a result of their mental models of marriage, which are influenced, at least in part, by the genre of TV that they watch. Wyer and Radvansky (1999) provided another example when they argued that the influence of the media on perceptions of a "mean world" (see Gerbner et al., 1977) may result from the use of mental models that are constructed from watching violent media to understand the social world. Given the amount of violence on TV, it is likely that heavy viewers of TV would construct abstract mental models to aid in comprehending these programs. However, the abstractness of the mental model could also increase the likelihood that it would be used to understand situations beyond the media. Thus, mental models can be used to explain media effects such as cultivation and the influence of the media on perceptions of reality.

In conclusion, we believe that the mental models approach has great potential for aiding our understanding of the media. A mental models approach can explain both short-term media priming (e.g., the priming of aggression-related thoughts) and long-term media priming (e.g., priming of the criteria used to judge the president across several weeks). In addition, a mental models approach offers the advantage of also being able to explain other media-related phenomenon, such as cultivation effects. Furthermore, although the mental models approach can explain media effects, it also explains how we understand and interpret the media. Consequently, we think that the mental models approach will provide a fruitful avenue both for explaining how the media influence us and for aiding our understanding of how people understand the media.

REFERENCES

Anderson, C. A. (1997). Effects of violent movies and trait hostility on hostile feelings and aggressive thoughts. *Aggressive Behavior, 23,* 161–178.

Anderson, C. A., Anderson, K. B., & Deuser, W. E. (1996). Examining an affective aggression framework: Weapon and temperature effects on aggressive thoughts, affect, and attitudes. *Personality and Social Psychology Bulletin, 22,* 366–376.

Anderson, C. A., Deuser, W. E., & DeNeve, K. M. (1995). Hot temperatures, hostile affect, hostile cognition, and arousal: Tests of a general model of affective aggression. *Personality and Social Psychology Bulletin, 21,* 434–448.

Anderson, C. A., & Morrow, M. (1995). Competitive aggression without interaction: Effects of competitive versus coppoerative instructions on aggressive behavior in video games. *Personality and Social Psychology Bulletin, 21,* 1020–1030.

Anderson, J. (1983). *The architecture of cognition.* Cambridge, MA: Harvard University Press.

Bargh, J. A., Bond, R. N., Lombardi, W. J., & Tota, M. E. (1986). The additive nature of chronic and temporary sources of construct accessibility. *Journal of Personality and Social Psychology, 50,* 869–878.

Berkowitz, L. (1984). Some effects of thoughts on anti- and prosocial influences of media events: A cognitive-neoassociationistic analysis. *Psychological Bulletin, 95,* 410–427.

Berkowitz, L. (1990). On the formation and regulation of anger and aggression: A cognitive-neoassociationistic analysis. *American Psychologist, 45,* 494–503.

Berkowitz, L. (1994). Is something missing? Some observations prompted by the cognitive-neoassociationist view of anger and emotional aggression. In L. R. Huesmann (Ed.), *Aggressive behavior: Current perspectives* (pp. 35–57). New York: Plenum Press.

Berkowitz, L. (1997). Some thoughts extending Bargh's argument. In R. S. Wyer (Ed.), *The automaticity of everyday life: Advances in social cognition* (Vol. 10, pp. 83–92). Mahwah, NJ: Lawrence Erlbaum Associates.

Biocca, F. (1991). Viewer's mental models of political ads: Toward a theory of semantic processing of television. In F. Biocca (Ed.), *Television and political advertising: Vol. 1. Psychological processes* (pp. 27–91). Hillsdale, NJ: Lawrence Erlbaum Associates.

Bushman, B. J. (1995). Moderating role of trait aggressiveness in the effects of violent media on aggression. *Journal of Personality and Social Psychology, 69,* 950–960.

Bushman, B. J. (1996). Individual differences in the extent and development of aggressive cognitive-associative networks. *Personality and Social Psychology Bulletin, 22,* 811–820.

Bushman, B. J. (1998). Priming effects of media violence on the accessibility of aggressive constructs in memory. *Personality and Social Psychology Bulletin, 24,* 537–545.

Bushman, B. J., & Geen, R. G. (1990). Role of cognitive-emotional mediators and individual differences in the effects of media violence on aggression. *Journal of Personality and Social Psychology, 58,* 156–163.

Capella, J. N., & Street, R. L., Jr. (1989). Message effects: Theory and research on mental models of messages. In J. J. Bradac (Ed.), *Message effects in communication science* (pp. 24–51). Newbury Park, CA: Sage.

Fazio, R. H. (1986). How do attitudes guide behavior? In R. H. Sorrentino & E. T. Higgins (Eds.), *The handbook of motivation and cognition: Foundations of social behavior* (pp. 204–243). New York: Guilford Press.

Fazio, R. H. (1990). Multiple processes by which attitudes guide behavior: The MODE model as an integrative framework. In M. Zanna (Ed.), *Advances in experimental social psychology* (Vol. 23, pp. 75–109). Orlando, FL: Academic Press.

Fazio, R. H., & Roskos-Ewoldsen, D. R. (1994). Acting as we feel: When and how attitudes guide behavior. In T. C. Brock & S. Shavitt (Eds.), *Psychology of persuasion* (pp. 71–94). Boston: Allyn & Bacon.

Fazio, R. H., Sanbonmatsu, D. M., Powell, M. C., & Kardes, F. F. (1986). On the automatic activation of attitudes. *Journal of Personality and Social Psychology, 50,* 229–238.

Fazio, R. H., & Williams, C. J. (1986). Attitude accessibility as a moderator of the attitude-perception and attitude behavior relations: An investigation of the 1984 presidential election. *Journal of Personality and Social Psychology, 51,* 505–514.

Fazio, R. H., Zanna, M. P., & Cooper, J. (1979). Dissonance and self-perception: An integrative view of each theory's proper domain of application. *Journal of Experimental Social Psychology, 13,* 464–479.

Floyd, D. L., Prentice-Dunn, S., & Rogers, R. W. (2000). A meta-analysis of research on protection motivation theory. *Journal of Applied Social Psychology, 30,* 407–429.

Franks, J. J., Roskos-Ewoldsen, D. R., Bilbrey, C. W., & Roskos-Ewoldsen, B. (1999). *Is attitude priming an artifact?* Manuscript under review.

Garnham, A. (1997). Representing information in mental models. In M. A. Conway (Ed.), *Cognitive models of memory* (pp. 149–172). Cambridge, MA: MIT Press.

Geen, R. G. (1990). *Human aggression.* Milton Keynes: Open University Press.

Gentner, D., & Gentner, D. R. (1984). Flowing waters or teeming crowds: Mental models of electricity. In D. Gentner & A. L. Stevens (Eds.), *Mental models* (pp. 99–129). Hillsdale, NJ: Lawrence Erlbaum Associates.

Gerbner, G., Gross, L., Eleey, M. F., Jackson-Beeck, M., Jeffries-Fox, S., & Signorielli, N. (1977). TV violence profile no. 8: The highlights. *Journal of Communication, 27*(2), 171–180.

Gilbert, D. T. (1991). How mental systems believe. *American Psychologist, 46,* 107–119.

Gilbert, D. T., Tafarodi, R. W., & Malone, P. S. (1993). You can't not believe everything you read. *Journal of Personality and Social Psychology, 65,* 221–233.

Glenberg, A. M., & Langston, W. E. (1992). Comprehension of illustrated text: Pictures help to build mental models. *Journal of Memory and Language, 31,* 129–151.

Grant, S. C., & Logan, G. D. (1993). The loss of repetition priming and automaticity over time as a function of degree of initial learning. *Memory & Cognition, 21,* 611–618.

Graesser, A. C., Singer, M., & Trabasso, T. (1994). Constructing inferences during narrative text comprehension. *Psychological Review, 101,* 371–395.

Greeno, J. G. (1984). Conceptual entities. In D. Gentner & A. L. Stevens (Eds.), *Mental models* (pp. 227–252). Hillsdale, NJ: Lawrence Erlbaum Associates.

Halford, G. S. (1993). *Children's understanding: The development of mental models.* Hillsdale, NJ: Lawrence Erlbaum Associates.

Hansen, C. H., & Hansen, R. D. (1988). How rock music videos can change what is seen when boy meets girl: Priming stereotypic appraisal of social interaction. *Sex Roles, 19,* 287–316.

Hansen, C. H., & Krygowski, W. (1994). Arousal-augmented priming effects: Rock music videos and sex object schemas. *Communication Research, 21,* 24–47.

Higgins, E. T., Bargh, J. A., & Lombardi, W. (1985). Nature of priming effects on categorization. *Journal of Experimental Psychology: Learning, Memory, & Cognition, 11,* 59–69.

Higgins, E. T., King, G. A., & Mavin, G. H. (1982). Individual construct accessibility and subjective impressions and recall. *Journal of Personality and Social Psychology, 43,* 35–47.

Higgins, E. T., Rholes, W. S., & Jones, C. R. (1977). Category accessibility and impression formation. *Journal of Experimental Social Psychology, 13,* 141–154.

Houston, D. A., & Fazio, R. H. (1989). Biased processing as a function of attitude accessibility: Making objective judgments subjectively. *Social Cognition, 7,* 51–66.

Intons-Peterson, M. J., Roskos-Ewoldsen, B., Thomas, L., Shirley, M., & Blut, D. (1989). Will educational materials reduce negative effects of exposure to sexual violence? *Journal of Social and Clinical Psychology, 8,* 256–275.

Iyengar, S., & Kinder, D. R. (1987). *News that matters: Television and American opinion.* Chicago: University of Chicago Press.

Iyengar, S., Kinder, D. R., Peters, M. D., & Krosnick, J. A. (1984). The evening news and presidential evaluations. *Journal of Personality and Social Psychology, 46*, 778–787.

Iyengar, S., Peters, M. D., & Kinder, D. R. (1982). Experimental demonstrations of the "not-so-minimal" consequences of television news programs. *American Political Science Review, 76*, 848–858.

Iyengar, S., & Simon, A. (1993). News coverage of the Gulf crisis and public opinion: A study of agenda-setting, priming, and framing. *Communication Research, 20*, 365–383.

Johnson-Laird, P. N. (1983). *Mental models.* Cambridge, MA: Harvard University Press.

Josephson, W. L. (1987). Television violence and children's aggression: Testing the priming, social script, and disinhibition predictions. *Journal of Personality and Social Psychology, 53*, 882–890.

Klinger, M. R., Burton, P. C., & Pitts, S. (2000). Mechanisms of unconscious priming: I. Response competition, not spreading activation. *Journal of Experimental Psychology: Learning, Memory, and Cognition, 26*, 441–455.

Krosnick, J. A., & Brannon, L. A. (1993). The impact of the Gulf War on the ingredients of presidential evaluations: Multidimensional effects of political involvement. *American Political Science Review, 87*, 963–975.

Krosnick, J. A., & Kinder, D. R. (1990). Altering the foundations of support for the president through priming. *American Political Science Review, 84*, 497–512.

Lau, R. R. (1989), Construct accessibility and electoral choice. *Political Behavior, 11*, 5–32.

Malamuth, N. M., & Check, J. V. P. (1985). The effects of aggressive pornography on beliefs in rape myths: Individual differences. *Journal of Research in Personality, 19*, 299–320.

Morrow, D. G., Bower, G. H., & Greenspan, S. L. (1989). Updating situation models during narrative comprehension. *Journal of Memory and Language, 28*, 292–312.

Morrow, D. G., Greenspan, S. L., & Bower, G. H. (1987). Accessibility and situation models in narrative comprehension. *Journal of Memory and Language, 26*, 165–187.

Neeley, J. H. (1977). Semantic priming and retrieval from lexical memory: Roles of inhibitionless spreading activation and limited-capactiy attention. *Journal of Experiemntal Psychology: General, 106*, 225–254.

Pan, Z., & Kosicki, G. M. (1997). Priming and media impact on the evaluations of president's performance. *Communication Research, 24*, 3–30.

Pechmann, C. (2001). A comparison of health communication models: Risk learning versus stereotype priming. *Media Psychology, 3*, 189–210.

Pechmann, C., & Knight, S. J. (2000). Cigarette and antismoking advertising and peer smoking: Interdependent influences on adolescents' smoking-related social cognitions and behavioral intentions. University of California, Irvine, Graduate School of Management, working paper.

Pechmann, C., & Ratneshwar, S. (1994). The effects of anti-smoking and cigarette advertising on young adolescents' perceptions of peers who smoke. *Journal of Consumer Research, 21*, 236–251.

Power, J. G., Murphy, S. T., & Coover, G. (1996). Priming prejudice: How stereotypes and counter-stereotypes influence attribution of responsibility and credibility among ingroups and outgroups. *Human Communication Research, 23*, 36–58.

Price, V., & Tewksbury, D. (1997). New values and public opinion: A theoretical account of media priming and framing. In G. A. Barnett & F. J. Boster (Eds.), *Progress in communication sciences: Advances in persuasion* (Vol. 13, pp. 173–212). Greenwich, CT: Ablex Publishing.

Radvansky, G. A., Spieler, R. T., & Zacks, R. T. (1993). Mental model organization. *Journal of Experimental Psychology: Learning, Memory, and Cognition, 19*, 95–114.

Radvansky, G. A., & Zacks, R. T. (1997). The retrieval of situation-specific information. In M. A. Conway (Ed.), *Cognitive models of memory* (pp. 173–213). Cambridge, MA: MIT Press.

Rogers, R. W. (1983). Cognitive and physiological processes in fear appeals and attitude change: A revised theory of protection motivation. In J. T. Cacioppo & R. E. Petty (Eds.), *Social psychophysiology: A sourcebook* (pp. 153–176). New York: Guilford Press.

Roskos-Ewoldsen, D. R. (1997). Attitude accessibility and persuasion: Review and a transactive model. In B. Burleson (Ed.), *Communication Yearbook 20* (pp. 185–225). Beverly Hills, CA: Sage.

Roskos-Ewoldsen, D. R., Arpan-Ralstin, L. A., & St. Pierre, J. (in press). The quick and the strong: Implications of attitude accessibility for persuasion. In J. P. Dillard & M. Pfau (Eds.), *The persuasion handbook: Developments in theory and practice*. Thousand Oaks, CA: Sage.

Roskos-Ewoldsen, D. R., & Fazio, R. H. (1992a). The accessibility of source likability as a determinant of persuasion. *Personality and Social Psychology Bulletin, 18,* 19–25.

Roskos-Ewoldsen, D. R., & Fazio, R. H. (1992b). On the orienting value of attitudes: Attitude accessibility as a determinant of an object's attraction of visual attention. *Journal of Personality and Social Psychology, 63,* 198–211.

Roskos-Ewoldsen, D. R., & Fazio, R. H. (1997). The role of belief accessibility in attitude formation. *Southern Communication Journal, 62,* 107–116.

Roskos-Ewoldsen, D. R., Klinger, M., & Roskos-Ewoldsen, B. (in press). Media priming. In J. B. Bryant & R. A. Carveth (Eds.), *Meta-analysis of media effects*. Mahwah, NJ: Lawrence Erlbaum Associates.

Schachter, S., & Singer, S. (1962). Cognitive, social, and physiological determinants of the emotional state. *Psychological Review, 69,* 379–399.

Schleuder, J. D., White, A. V., & Cameron, G. T. (1993). Priming effects of television news bumpers and teasers on attention and memory. *Journal of Broadcasting and Electronic Media, 37,* 437–452.

Segrin, C., & Nabi, R. L. (in press). Does television viewing cultivate unrealistic expectations about marriage? *Journal of Communication.*

Shrum, L.J. (1999). The relationship of television viewing with attitude strength and extremity: Implications for the cultivation effect. *Media Psychology, 1,* 3–26.

Shrum, L. J., & O'Guinn, T. C. (1993). Processes and effects in the construction of social reality. *Communication Research, 20,* 436–471.

Srull, T. K., & Wyer, R. S. (1979). The role of category accessibility in the interpretation of information about persons: Some determinants and implications. *Journal of Personality and Social Psychology, 37,* 1660–1672.

Srull, T. K., & Wyer, R. S. (1980). Category accessibility and social perception: Some implications for the study of person memory and interpersonal judgment. *Journal of Personality and Social Psychology, 38,* 841–856.

Tversky, A., & Kahneman, D. (1973). Availability: A heuristic for judging frequency and probability. *Cognitive Psychology, 5,* 207–232.

vanDijk, T. A. (1998). *Ideology: A multidisciplinary approach*. London: Sage.

vanDijk, T. A., & Kintsch, W. (1983). *Strategies of discourse comprehension*. New York: Academic Press.

Wilson, S. G., Rinck, M., McNamara, T. P., Bower, G. H., & Morrow, D. G. (1993). Mental models and narrative comprehension: Some qualifications. *Journal of Memory and Language, 32,* 141–154.

Witte, K. (1994). Fear control and danger control: A test of the extended parallel process model (EPPM). *Communication Monographs, 61,* 113–134.

Witte, K. (1995). Generating effective risk messages: How scary should your risk communication be? In B. R. Burleson (Eds.), *Communication Yearbook 18* (pp. 229–254). Thousand Oaks, CA: Sage.

Wyer, R. S., Jr., Bodenhausen, G. V., & Gorman, T. F. (1985). Cognitive mediators of reactions to rape. *Journal of Personality and Social Psychology, 48,* 324–338.

Wyer, R. S., Jr., & Radvansky, G. A. (1999). The comprehension and validation of social information. *Psychological Review, 106,* 89–118.

Yi, Y. (1990a). Cognitive and affective priming effects of the context for print advertisements. *Journal of Advertising, 19,* 40–48.

Yi, Y. (1990b). The effects of contextual priming in print advertisements. *Journal of Consumer Research, 17,* 215–222.

Zanna, M. P., & Cooper, J. (1974). Dissonance and the pill: An attribution approach to studying the arousal properties of dissonance. *Journal of Personality and Social Psychology, 29,* 703–709.

Zwaan, R. A. (1994). Effect of genre expectations on text comprehension. *Journal of Experimental Psychology: Learning, Memory, and Cognition, 20,* 920–933.

Zwaan, R. A., & Radvansky, G. A. (1998). Situation models in language comprehension and memory. *Psychological Bulletin, 123,* 162–185.

Chapter 6

Social Cognitive Theory of Mass Communication

ALBERT BANDURA
Stanford University

Because of the influential role the mass media play in society, understanding the psychosocial mechanisms through which symbolic communication influences human thought, affect, and action is of considerable import. Social cognitive theory provides an agentic conceptual framework within which to examine the determinants and mechanisms of such effects. Human behavior has often been explained in terms of unidirectional causation, in which behavior is shaped and controlled either by environmental influences or by internal dispositions. Social cognitive theory explains psychosocial functioning in terms of triadic reciprocal causation (Bandura, 1986). In this transactional view of self and society, personal factors in the form of cognitive, affective, and biological events; behavioral patterns; and environmental events all operate as interacting determinants that influence each other bidirectionally (Fig. 6.1).

Social cognitive theory is founded in an agentic perspective (Bandura, 1986, 2001a). People are self-organizing, proactive, self-reflecting, and self-regulating, not just reactive organisms shaped and shepherded by environmental events or inner forces. Human self-development, adaptation, and change are embedded in social systems. Therefore, personal agency operates within a broad network of sociostructural influences. In these agentic transactions, people are producers as well as products of social systems. Personal agency and social structure operate as codeterminants in an integrated causal structure rather than as a disembodied duality.

Seen from the sociocognitive perspective, human nature is a vast potentiality that can be fashioned by direct and observational experience into a variety of forms within biological limits. To say that a major distinguishing mark of humans is their endowed plasticity is not to say that they have no nature or that they come structureless (Midgley, 1978). The

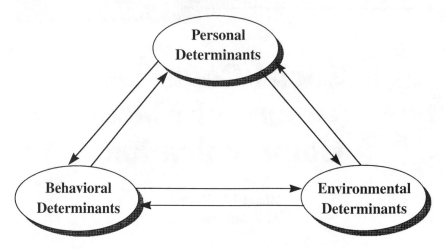

FIG. 6.1. Schematization of triadic reciprocal causation in the causal model of social cognitive theory.

plasticity, which is intrinsic to the nature of humans, depends on neuro-physiological mechanisms and structures that have evolved over time. These advanced neural systems specialized for processing, retaining, and using coded information provide the capacity for the very capabilities that are distinctly human—generative symbolization, forethought, evaluative self-regulation, reflective self-consciousness, and symbolic communication. These capabilities are addressed in the sections that follow.

SYMBOLIZING CAPABILITY

Social cognitive theory accords a central role to cognitive, vicarious, self-regulatory, and self-reflective processes. An extraordinary capacity for symbolization provides humans with a powerful tool for comprehending their environment and creating and regulating environmental events that touch virtually every aspect of their lives. Most external influences affect behavior through cognitive processes rather than directly. Cognitive factors partly determine which environmental events will be observed, what meaning will be conferred on them, whether they leave any lasting effects, what emotional impact and motivating power they will have, and how the information they convey will be organized for future use. It is with symbols that people process and transform transient experiences into cognitive models that serve as guides for judgment and action. Through symbols, people give meaning, form, and continuity to their experiences.

People gain understanding of causal relationships and expand their knowledge by operating symbolically on the wealth of information derived from personal and vicarious experiences. They generate solutions to problems, evaluate their likely outcomes, and pick suitable options without having to go through a laborious behavioral search. Through the medium of symbols, people can communicate with others at any distance in time and space. However, in keeping with the interactional perspective, social cognitive theory devotes much attention to the social origins of thought and the mechanisms through which social factors exert their influence on cognitive functioning. The other distinctive human capabilities are founded on this advanced capacity for symbolization.

SELF-REGULATORY CAPABILITY

People are not only knowers and performers. They are also self-reactors with a capacity for self-direction. Effective functioning requires the substitution of self-regulation for external sanctions and demands. The self-regulation of motivation, affect, and action operates partly through internal standards and evaluative reactions to one's own behavior (Bandura, 1991a). The anticipated self-satisfaction gained from fulfilling valued standards and discontent with substandard performances serve as incentive motivators for action. The motivational effects do not stem from the standards themselves but from the evaluative self-investment in activities and positive and negative reactions to one's performances.

Most theories of self-regulation are founded on a negative feedback system in which people strive to reduce disparities between their perceived performance and an adopted standard. But self-regulation by negative discrepancy tells only half the story and not necessarily the more interesting half. In fact, people are proactive, aspiring organisms. Human self-regulation relies on *discrepancy production* as well as on *discrepancy reduction*. People motivate and guide their actions through proactive control by setting themselves challenging goals and then mobilizing their resources, skills, and effort to fulfill them. After people attain the goal they have been pursuing, those with a strong sense of efficacy set higher goals for themselves. Adopting further challenges creates new motivating discrepancies to be mastered. Self-regulation of motivation and action thus involves a dual-control process of disequilibrating discrepancy production (proactive control) followed by equilibrating discrepancy reduction (reactive control).

In areas of functioning involving achievement strivings and cultivation of competencies, the internal standards that are selected as a mark of adequacy are progressively altered as knowledge and skills are acquired and challenges are met. In many areas of social and moral behavior the internal standards that serve as the basis for regulating one's conduct have greater stability. People do not change from week to week what they regard as right or wrong or good or bad. After they adopt a standard of morality, their self-sanctions for actions that match or violate their personal standards serve as the regulatory influencers (Bandura, 1991b). The exercise of moral agency has dual aspects—inhibitive and proactive. The *inhibitive* form is manifested in the power to refrain from behaving inhumanely. The *proactive* form of morality is expressed in the power to behave humanely (Bandura, 1999b).

The capability of forethought adds another dimension to the temporal extension of personal agency. Most human behavior is directed by forethought toward events and outcomes projected into the future. The future time perspective manifests itself in many different ways. People set goals for themselves, anticipate the likely consequences of their prospective actions, and otherwise plan courses of action that are likely to produce desired outcomes and to avoid undesired ones. Because future events have no actual existence, they cannot be causes of current motivation and action. However, by being represented cognitively in the present, conceived futures can operate anticipatorily as motivators and regulators of current behavior. When projected over a long time course on matters of value, a forethoughtful perspective provides direction, coherence, and meaning to one's life.

SELF-REFLECTIVE CAPABILITY

The capability to reflect on oneself and the adequacy of one's thoughts and actions is another distinctly human attribute that figures prominently in social cognitive theory. People are not only agents of action but self-examiners of their functioning. Effective cognitive functioning requires reliable ways of distinguishing between accurate and faulty thinking. In verifying thought by self-reflective means, people generate ideas, act on them, or predict occurrences from them. They then judge from the results the adequacy of their thoughts and change them accordingly. The validity and functional value of one's thoughts are evaluated by comparing how well thoughts match some indicant of reality. Four different modes of thought verification can be distinguished. They include enactive, vicarious, social, and logical forms.

Enactive verification relies on the adequacy of the fit between one's thoughts and the results of the actions they spawn. Good matches corroborate thoughts; mismatches tend to refute them. In *vicarious verification*, observing other people's transactions with the environment and the effects they produce provides a check on the correctness of one's own thinking. Vicarious thought verification is not simply a supplement to enactive experience. Symbolic modeling greatly expands the range of verification experiences that cannot otherwise be attained by personal action. When experiential verification is difficult or unfeasible, *social verification* is used, with people evaluating the soundness of their views by checking them against what others believe. In *logical verification* people can check for fallacies in their thinking by deducing from knowledge that is known what necessarily follows from it.

Such metacognitive activities usually foster veridical thought, but they can produce faulty thinking as well. Forceful actions arising from erroneous beliefs often create social environments that confirm the misbeliefs (Snyder, 1980). We are all acquainted with problem-prone individuals who, through offensive behavior, predictively breed negative social climates wherever they go. Verification of thought by comparison with distorted media versions of social reality can foster shared misconceptions of people, places, and things (Hawkins & Pingree, 1982). Social verification can foster bizarre views of reality if the shared beliefs of the reference group with which one affiliates are peculiar and the group is encapsulated from outside social ties and influences (Bandura, 1982; Hall, 1987). Deductive reasoning can lead one astray if the propositional knowledge on which it is based is faulty or biases intrude on logical reasoning processes (Falmagne, 1975).

Among the self-referent thought, none is more central or pervasive than people's belief in their efficacy to exert control over their level of functioning and events that affect their lives. This core belief is the foundation of human agency (Bandura, 1997; 2001a). Unless people believe that they can produce desired effects and forestall undesired ones by their actions, they have little incentive to act. Efficacy beliefs influence whether people think self-enhancingly or self-debilitatingly, optimistically or pessimistically; what courses of action they choose to pursue; the goals they set for themselves and their commitment to them; how much effort they put forth in given endeavors; the outcomes they expect their efforts to produce; how long they persevere in the face of obstacles; their resilience to adversity; how much stress and depression they experience in coping with taxing environmental demands; and the accomplishments they realize.

People do not live their lives in individual autonomy. They have to work together to secure what they cannot accomplish on their own. Social cognitive theory extends the conception of human agency to collective agency (Bandura, 1999a, 2000b). The more efficacious groups judge themselves to be, the higher their collective aspirations, the greater their motivational investment in their undertakings, the stronger their staying power in the face of impediments, the more robust their resilience to adversity, and the higher their performance accomplishments.

VICARIOUS CAPABILITY

Psychological theories have traditionally emphasized learning by the effects of one's actions. If knowledge and skills could be acquired only by response consequences, human development would be greatly retarded, not to mention exceedingly tedious and hazardous. A culture could never transmit its language, mores, social practices, and requisite competencies if they had to be shaped tediously in each new member by response consequences without the benefit of models to exemplify the cultural patterns. Shortening the acquisition process is vital for survival as well as for self-development because natural endowment provides few inborn skills, hazards are ever present, and errors can be perilous. Moreover, the constraints of time, resources, and mobility impose severe limits on the places and activities that can be directly explored for the acquisition of new knowledge and competencies.

Humans have evolved an advanced capacity for observational learning that enables them to expand their knowledge and skills rapidly through information conveyed by the rich variety of models. Indeed, virtually all behavioral, cognitive, and affective learning from direct experience can be achieved vicariously by observing people's actions and its consequences for them (Bandura, 1986; Rosenthal & Zimmerman, 1978). Much social learning occurs either designedly or unintentionally from models in one's immediate environment. However, a vast amount of information about human values, styles of thinking, and behavior patterns is gained from the extensive modeling in the symbolic environment of the mass media.

A major significance of symbolic modeling lies in its tremendous reach and psychosocial impact. Unlike learning by doing, which requires altering the actions of each individual through repeated trial-and-error experiences, in observational learning a single model can transmit new ways of thinking and behaving simultaneously to countless people in widely dispersed locales. There is another aspect of symbolic modeling that magnifies its psychological and social impact. During the course of their daily lives, people have direct contact with only a small sector of the physical and social environment. They work in the same setting, travel the same routes, visit the same places, and see the same set of friends and associates. Consequently, their conceptions of social reality are greatly influenced by vicarious experiences—by what they see, hear, and read—without direct experiential correctives. To a large extent, people act on their images of reality. The more people's images of reality depend on the media's symbolic environment, the greater is its social impact (Ball-Rokeach & DeFleur, 1976).

Most psychological theories were cast long before the advent of extraordinary advances in the technology of communication. As a result, they give insufficient attention to the increasingly powerful role that the symbolic environment plays in present-day human lives. Whereas previously, modeling influences were largely confined to the behavior patterns exhibited in one's immediate environment, the accelerated growth of video delivery technologies has vastly expanded the range of models to which members of society are exposed day in and day out. By drawing on these modeled patterns of thought and behavior, observers can transcend the bounds of their immediate environment. New ideas, values, behavior patterns, and social practices are now being rapidly diffused by symbolic modeling worldwide in ways that foster a globally distributed consciousness (Bandura, 1986, 2000d). Because the symbolic environment occupies a major part of people's everyday lives, much of the social construction of reality and shaping of public consciousness occurs through electronic acculturation. At the societal level, the electronic modes of influence are transforming how social systems operate and serving as a major vehicle for sociopolitical change. The study of acculturation in the present electronic age must be broadened to include electronic acculturation.

Mechanisms Governing Observational Learning

Because symbolic modeling is central to full understanding of the effects of mass communication, the modeling aspect of social cognitive theory is discussed in somewhat greater detail. Observational learning is governed by four subfunctions, which are summarized in Fig. 6.2.

Attentional processes determine what is selectively observed in the profusion of modeling influences and what information is extracted from ongoing modeled events. A number of factors influence the exploration and construal of what is modeled. Some of these determinants concern the cognitive skills, preconceptions, and value preferences of the observers. Others are related to the salience, attractiveness, and functional value of the modeled activities themselves. Still other factors are the structural arrangements of human interactions and associational networks, which largely determine the types of models to which people have ready access.

People cannot be much influenced by observed events if they do not symbolically code and remember them. A second major subfunction governing observational learning concerns the construction of cognitive representations. In social cognitive theory, observers construct generative conceptions of styles of behavior from modeled exemplars rather than merely scripts of habitual routines. Retention involves an active process of transforming and restructuring information conveyed by modeled events into rules and conceptions for memory representation. Retention is greatly aided by symbolic transformations of modeled information into

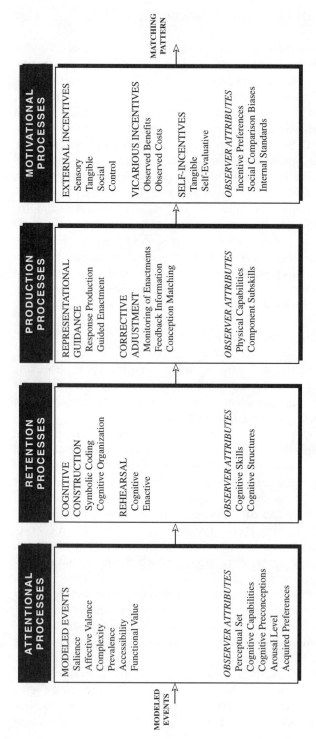

FIG. 6.2.   The four major subfunctions governing observational learning and the influential factors operating within each subfunction.

memory codes and cognitive rehearsal of the coded information. Preconceptions and affective states exert biasing influences on these representational activities. Similarly, recall involves a process of reconstruction rather than simply retrieval of registered events.

In the third subfunction in modeling—the behavioral production process—symbolic conceptions are translated into appropriate courses of action. This is achieved through a conception-matching process in which conceptions guide the construction and execution of behavior patterns, which are then compared against the conceptual model for adequateness. The behavior is modified on the basis of the comparative information to achieve close correspondence between conception and action. The mechanism for translating cognition into action involves both transformational and generative operations. Execution of a skill must be constantly varied to suit changing circumstances. Adaptive performance, therefore, requires a generative conception rather than a one-to-one mapping between cognitive representation and action. By applying an abstract specification of the activity, people can produce many variants of the behavioral style under differing conditions. Conceptions are rarely transformed into masterful performance on the first attempt. Monitored enactments serve as the vehicle for transforming knowledge into skilled action. Performances are perfected by corrective adjustments during behavior production. The more extensive the subskills that people possess, the easier it is to integrate them to produce new behavior patterns. When deficits exist, the subskills required for complex performances must first be developed by modeling and guided enactment.

The fourth subfunction in modeling concerns motivational processes. Social cognitive theory distinguishes between acquisition and performance because people do not perform everything they learn. Performance of observationally learned behavior is influenced by three major types of incentive motivators—direct, vicarious, and self-produced. People are more likely to exhibit modeled behavior if it results in valued outcomes than if it has unrewarding or punishing effects. The observed detriments and benefits experienced by others influence the performance of modeled patterns in much the same way as do directly experienced consequences. People are motivated by the successes of others who are similar to themselves, but are discouraged from pursuing courses of behavior that they have seen often result in adverse consequences. Personal standards of conduct provide a further source of incentive motivation. The self-approving and self-censuring reactions people generate to their own behavior regulate which observationally learned activities they are most likely to pursue. They pursue activities they find self-satisfying and give them a sense of worth but reject those they personally disapprove.

The different sources of consequences may operate as complimentary or opposing influences on behavior (Bandura, 1986). Behavior patterns are most firmly established when social and self-sanctions are compatible. Under such conditions, socially approvable behavior is a source of self-pride and socially disapprovable behavior is self-censured. Behavior is especially susceptible to external influences in the absence of countervailing self-sanctions. People who are not much committed to personal standards adopt a pragmatic orientation, tailoring their behavior to fit whatever the situation seems to call for (Snyder & Campbell, 1982). They become adept at reading social situations and guiding their actions by expediency.

One type of conflict between social and self-produced sanctions arises when individuals are socially punished for behavior they highly value. Principled dissenters and nonconformists often find themselves in this predicament. Here, the relative strength of self-approval and social censure determine whether the behavior will be restrained or expressed. Should the threatened social consequences be severe, people hold in check self-praiseworthy acts in risky situations but perform them readily in relatively safe settings. There are individuals, however, whose sense of self-worth is so strongly invested in certain convictions that they will submit to prolonged maltreatment rather than accede to what they regard as unjust or immoral.

People commonly experience conflicts in which they are socially pressured to engage in behavior that violates their moral standards. When self-devaluative consequences outweigh the benefits for socially accommodating behavior, the social influences do not have much sway. However, the self-regulation of conduct operates through conditional application of moral standards. We shall see shortly that self-sanctions can be weakened or nullified by selective disengagement of internal control.

Abstract Modeling

Modeling is not merely a process of behavioral mimicry, as commonly misconstrued. The proven skills and established customs of a culture may be adopted in essentially the same form as they are exemplified because of their high functional value. However, in most activities, subskills must be improvised to suit varying circumstances. Modeling influences convey rules for generative and innovative behavior as well. This higher-level learning is achieved through abstract modeling. Rule-governed judgments and actions differ in specific content and other details while embodying the same underlying rule. For example, a model may confront moral conflicts that differ widely in content but apply the same moral standard to them. In this higher form of abstract modeling, observers extract the rule governing the specific judgments or actions exhibited by others. Once they learn the rule, they can use it to judge or generate new instances of behavior that go beyond what they have seen or heard.

Much human learning is aimed at developing cognitive skills on how to gain and use knowledge for future use. Observational learning of thinking skills is greatly facilitated by having models verbalize their thoughts aloud as they engage in problem-solving activities (Bandura, 1986, 1997; Meichenbaum, 1984). The thoughts guiding their decisions and action strategies are thus made observable for adoption.

Acquiring generative rules from modeled information involves at least three processes: (a) extracting the generic features from various social exemplars, (b) integrating the extracted information into composite rules, and (c) using the rules to produce new instances of behavior. Through abstract modeling, people acquire, among other things, standards for categorizing and judging events, linguistic rules of communication, thinking skills on how to gain and use knowledge, and personal standards for regulating one's motivation and conduct (Bandura, 1986; Rosenthal & Zimmerman, 1978). Evidence that generative rules of thought and conduct can be created through abstract modeling attests to the broad scope of observational learning.

Modeling also plays a prominent role in creativity. Creativeness rarely springs entirely from individual inventiveness. By refining preexisting innovations, synthesizing them into new procedures, and adding novel elements, something new is created (Bandura, 1986; Bolton, 1993; Fimrite, 1977). When exposed to models of differing styles of thinking and behaving, observers vary in what they adopt and thereby create new blends of personal characteristics that differ from the individual models. Modeling new perspectives and innovative styles of thinking also fosters creativity by weakening conventional mind-sets (Harris & Evans, 1973).

Motivational Effects

The discussion thus far has centered on the acquisition of knowledge, cognitive skills, and new styles of behavior through observational learning. Social cognitive theory distinguishes among several modeling functions, each governed by different determinants and underlying mechanisms. In addition to cultivating new competencies, modeling influences have strong motivational effects. Vicarious motivators are rooted in outcome expectations formed from information conveyed by the rewarding and punishing outcomes of modeled courses of action. Seeing others gain desired outcomes by their actions can create outcome expectancies that function as positive incentives; observed punishing outcomes can create negative outcome expectancies that function as disincentives.

These motivational effects are governed by observers' judgments of their ability to accomplish the modeled behavior, their perceptions of the modeled actions as producing favorable or adverse consequences, and their inferences that similar or unlike consequences would result if they, themselves, were to engage in similar activities.

Vicarious incentives take on added significance by their power to alter the valence and force of external incentives (Bandura, 1986). The value of a given outcome is largely determined by its relation to other outcomes rather than inherent in their intrinsic qualities. The same outcome can function as a reward or punishment depending on social comparison between observed and personally experienced outcomes. For example, the same pay raise has negative valence for persons who have seen similar performances by others compensated more generously, but positive valence when others have been compensated less generously. Equitable rewards foster a sense of well-being; inequitable ones breed discontent and resentment.

Vicariously created motivators have been studied most extensively in terms of the inhibitory and disinhibitory effects of modeled transgressive, aggressive, and sexual behavior with accompanying outcomes (Bandura, 1973; Berkowitz, 1984; Malamuth & Donnerstein, 1984; Paik & Comstock, 1994; Zillmann & Bryant, 1984).

Transgressive behavior is regulated by two major sources of sanctions— social sanctions and internalized self-sanctions. Both control mechanisms operate anticipatorily. In motivators arising from social sanctions, people refrain from transgressing because they anticipate that such conduct will bring them social censure and other adverse consequences. In motivators rooted in self-reactive control, people refrain from transgressing because such conduct will give rise to self-reproach. Media portrayals can alter perceived social sanctions by the way in which the consequences of different styles of conduct are portrayed. For example, televised aggression is often exemplified in ways that tend to weaken restraints over aggressive conduct (Goranson, 1970; Halloran & Croll, 1972; Larsen, 1968). In televised representations of human discord, physical aggression is a preferred solution to interpersonal conflicts; it is acceptable and relatively successful; and it is socially sanctioned by superheroes triumphing over evil by violent means. Such portrayals legitimize, glamorize, and trivialize human violence.

Inhibitory and disinhibitory effects stemming from self-sanctions are mediated largely through self-regulatory mechanisms. After standards have been internalized, they serve as guides and deterrents to conduct by the self-approving and self-reprimanding consequences people produce for themselves. However, moral standards do not function as fixed internal regulators of conduct. Self-regulatory mechanisms do not operate unless they are activated, and there are many processes by which moral reactions can be disengaged from inhumane conduct (Bandura, 1991b, 1999b). Selective activation and disengagement of internal control permits different types of conduct with the same moral standards. Fig. 6.3 shows the points in the self-regulatory process at which moral control can be disengaged from censurable conduct.

One set of disengagement practices operates on the construal of the behavior itself by *moral justification*. People do not ordinarily engage in reprehensible conduct until they have justified to themselves the morality of their actions. What is culpable is made personally and socially acceptable by portraying it in the service of moral purposes. Moral justification is widely used to support self-serving and otherwise culpable conduct. Moral judgments of conduct are also partly influenced by what it is compared against. Self-deplored acts can be made benign or honorable by contrasting them with more flagrant transgressions. Because examples of human culpability abound, they lend themselves readily to cognitive restructuring of transgressive conduct by such *advantageous comparison*. Activities can take on a very different appearance depending on what they are called. Sanitizing *euphemistic labeling* provides another convenient device for masking reprehensible activities or even conferring a respectable status on them. Through convoluted verbiage, reprehensible conduct is made benign and those who engage in it are relieved of a sense of personal agency.

Cognitive restructuring of behavior through moral justifications and palliative characterizations is the most effective psychological mechanism for promoting transgressive conduct. This is because moral restructuring not only eliminates self-deterrents but also engages self-approval in the service of transgressive exploits. What was once morally condemnable becomes a source of self-valuation.

Ball-Rokeach (1972) attaches special significance to evaluative reactions and social justifications presented in the media, particularly in conflicts of power. This is because relatively few viewers experience sufficient inducement to use the aggressive strategies they have seen, but the transmitted justifications and evaluations can help to mobilize public support for policy actions favoring either social control or social change. The justificatory changes can have widespread social and political ramifications.

The mass media, especially television, provide the best access to the public through its strong drawing power. For this reason, television is increasingly used as the principle vehicle of justification. Struggles to legitimize and gain support for one's values and causes and to discredit those of one's opponents are now waged more and more through the electronic media (Ball- Rokeach, 1972; Bandura, 1990; Bassiouni, 1981). Because of its potential influence, the communication system itself is subject to constant

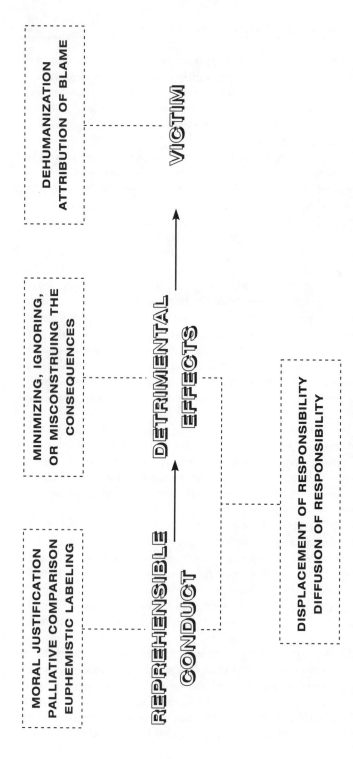

FIG. 6.3. Mechanisms through which self-sanctions are selectively activated and disengaged from detrimental conduct at critical points in the self-regulatory process.

pressures from different factions within society seeking to sway it to their ideology. Research on the role of the mass media in the social construction of reality carries important social implications.

Self-sanctions are activated most strongly when personal causation of detrimental effects is apparent. Another set of disengagement practices operates by obscuring or distorting the relationship between actions and the effects they cause. People will behave in ways they normally repudiate if a legitimate authority sanctions their conduct and accepts responsibility for its consequences (Milgram, 1974). Under conditions of *displacement of responsibility,* people view their actions as springing from the dictates of others rather than their being personally responsible for them. Because they are not the actual agent of their actions, they are spared self-prohibiting reactions. The deterrent power of self-sanctions is also weakened when the link between conduct and its consequences is obscured by *diffusion of responsibility* for culpable behavior. Through division of labor, diffusion of decision making, and group action, people can behave detrimentally without any one person feeling personally responsible (Kelman & Hamilton, 1989). People behave more injuriously under diffused responsibility than when they hold themselves personally accountable for what they do (Bandura, Underwood, & Fromson, 1975; Diener, 1977).

Additional ways of weakening self-deterring reactions operate through *disregard or distortion of the consequences of action.* When people pursue detrimental activities for personal gain or because of social inducements, they avoid facing the harm they cause or they minimize it. They readily recall the possible benefits of the behavior but are less able to remember its harmful effects (Brock & Buss, 1962, 1964). In addition to selective inattention and cognitive distortion of effects, the misrepresentation may involve active efforts to discredit evidence of the harm they cause. As long as the detrimental results of one's conduct are ignored, minimized, distorted, or disbelieved, there is little reason for self-censure to be activated.

The final set of disengagement practices operates at the point of recipients of detrimental acts. The strength of self-evaluative reactions to detrimental conduct partly depends on how the perpetrators view the people toward whom the behavior is directed. To perceive another as human enhances empathetic or vicarious reactions through perceived similarity (Bandura, 1992). As a result, it is difficult to mistreat humanized persons without risking self-condemnation. Self-sanctions against cruel conduct can be disengaged or blunted by *dehumanization,* which divests people of human qualities or invests them with bestial qualities. Whereas dehumanization weakens self-restraints against cruel conduct (Diener, 1977; Zimbardo, 1969), humanization fosters considerate, compassionate behavior (Bandura et al., 1975).

Attribution of blame to one's antagonists is still another expedient that can serve self-exonerative purposes. Deleterious interactions usually involve a series of reciprocally escalative actions, in which the antagonists are rarely faultless. One can always select from the chain of events an instance of the adversary's defensive behavior and view it as the original instigation. Injurious conduct thus becomes a justifiable defensive reaction to belligerent provocations. Others can, therefore, be blamed for bringing suffering on themselves. Self-exoneration is similarly achievable by viewing one's detrimental conduct as forced by circumstances rather than as a personal decision. By blaming others or circumstances, not only are one's own actions excusable but one can also even feel self-righteous in the process.

Because internalized controls can be selectively activated and disengaged, marked changes in moral conduct can be achieved without changing people's personality structures, moral principles, or self-evaluative systems. It is self-exonerative processes rather than character flaws that account for most inhumanities. The massive threats to human welfare stem mainly from deliberate acts of principle rather than from unrestrained acts of impulse.

The mechanisms of moral disengagement largely govern what is commonly labeled the "disinhibitory effect" of televised influences. Research in which the different disengagement factors are systematically varied in media portrayals of inhumanities attests to the disinhibitory power of mass media influences (Berkowitz & Geen, 1967; Donnerstein, 1984; Meyer, 1972). Viewers' punitiveness is enhanced by exposure to media productions that morally justify injurious conduct, blame and dehumanize victims, displace or diffuse personal responsibility, and sanitize destructive consequences. Research assessing self-reactive control provides evidence that sanctioning social conditions are linked to self-regulatory influences, which, in turn, are linked to injurious conduct (Bandura et al., 1975). The same disengagement mechanisms are enlisted heavily by members of the television industry in the production of programs that exploit human brutality for commercial purposes (Baldwin & Lewis, 1972; Bandura, 1973).

Acquisition and Modification of Affective Dispositions

People are easily aroused by the emotional expressions of others. Vicarious arousal operates mainly through an intervening self-arousal process (Bandura, 1992). That is, seeing others react emotionally to instigating conditions activates emotion-arousing thoughts and imagery in observers. As people develop their capacity for cognitive self-arousal, they can generate emotional reactions to cues that are only suggestive of a model's emotional experiences (Wilson & Cantor, 1985). Conversely, they can neutralize or attenuate the emotional impact of modeled distress by thoughts that transform threatening situations into nonthreatening ones (Bandura, 1986; Cantor & Wilson, 1988; Dysinger & Ruckmick, 1933).

If the affective reactions of models only aroused observers fleetingly, it would be of some interest as far as momentary communication is concerned, but of limited psychological import. What gives significance to vicarious influence is that observers can acquire lasting attitudes, emotional reactions, and behavioral proclivities toward persons, places, or things that have been associated with modeled emotional experiences. They learn to fear the things that frightened models, to dislike what repulsed them, and to like what gratified them (Bandura, 1986; Duncker, 1938). Fears and intractable phobias are ameliorated by modeling influences that convey information about coping strategies for exercising control over the things that are feared. The stronger the instilled sense of coping self-efficacy, the bolder the behavior (Bandura, 1997). Values can similarly be developed and altered vicariously by repeated exposure to modeled preferences.

SOCIAL CONSTRUCTION OF REALITY

Televised representations of social realities reflect ideological bents in their portrayal of human nature, social relations, and the norms and structure of society (Adoni & Mane, 1984; Gerbner, 1972). Heavy exposure to this symbolic world may eventually make the televised images appear to be the authentic state of human affairs. Some disputes about the vicarious cultivation of beliefs has arisen over findings from correlational studies using global indices based on amount of television viewing (Gerbner, Gross, Morgan & Signorielli, 1981; Hirsch, 1980). Televised influence is best defined in terms of the contents people watch rather than the sheer amount of television viewing. More particularized measures of exposure to the televised fare show that heavy television viewing shapes viewers' beliefs and conceptions of reality (Hawkins & Pingree, 1982). The relationship remains when other possible contributing factors are simultaneously controlled.

Vicarious cultivation of social conceptions is most clearly revealed in studies verifying the direction of causality by varying experimentally the nature and amount of exposure to media influences. Controlled laboratory studies provide converging evidence that television portrayals shape viewers' beliefs (Flerx, Fidler, & Rogers, 1976; O'Bryant & Corder-Bolz, 1978). Portrayals in the print media similarly shape conceptions of social reality (Heath, 1984; Siegel, 1958). To see the world as the televised messages portray it is to harbor some misconceptions. Indeed, many of the shared misconceptions about occupational pursuits, ethnic groups, minorities, the elderly, social and sex roles, and other aspects of life are at least partly cultivated through symbolic modeling of stereotypes (Bussey & Bandura, 1999; Buerkel-Rothfuss & Mayes, 1981; McGhee & Frueh, 1980). Verification of personal conceptions against televised versions of social reality can thus foster some collective illusions.

SOCIAL PROMPTING OF HUMAN BEHAVIOR

The actions of others can also serve as social prompts for previously learned behavior that observers can perform but have not done so because of insufficient inducements, rather than because of restraints. Social prompting effects are distinguished from observational learning and disinhibition because no new behavior has been acquired, and disinhibitory processes are not involved because the elicited behavior is socially acceptable and not encumbered by restraints.

The influence of models in activating, channeling, and supporting the behavior of others is abundantly documented in both laboratory and field studies (Bandura, 1986). By exemplification, one can get people to behave altruistically, to volunteer their services, to delay or seek gratification, to show affection, to select certain foods and drinks, to choose certain kinds of apparel, to converse on particular topics, to be inquisitive or passive, to think creatively or conventionally, or to engage in other permissible courses of action. Thus, the types of models who predominate within a social milieu partly determine which human qualities, from among many alternatives, are selectively activated. The actions of models acquire the power to activate and channel behavior when they are good predictors for observers that positive results can be gained by similar conduct.

The fashion and taste industries rely heavily on the social prompting power of modeling. Because the potency of vicarious influences can be enhanced by showing modeled acts bringing rewards, vicarious outcomes figure prominently in advertising campaigns. Thus, drinking a certain brand of wine or using a particular shampoo wins the loving admiration of beautiful people, enhances job performance, masculinizes self-conception, actualizes individualism and authenticity, tranquilizes irritable nerves, invites social recognition and amicable reactions from total strangers, and arouses affectionate overtures from spouses.

The types of vicarious outcomes, model characteristics, and modeling formats that are selected vary depending on what happens to be in vogue at the time. Model characteristics are varied to boost the persuasiveness of commercial messages. Prestigeful models are often enlisted to capitalize on the high regard in which they are held. The best social sellers depend on what happens to be popular at the moment. Drawing on evidence that similarity to the model enhances modeling, some advertisements portray common folk achieving wonders with the wares advertised. Because vicarious influence increases with multiplicity of modeling (Perry & Bussey, 1979), the beers, soft drinks, and snacks are being consumed with gusto in the advertised world by groups of wholesome, handsome, fun-loving models. Eroticism is another stimulant that never goes out of style. Therefore, erotic modeling does heavy duty in efforts to command attention and to make advertised products more attractive to potential buyers (Kanungo & Pang, 1973; Peterson & Kerin, 1979).

In sum, modeling influences serve diverse functions—as tutors, motivators, inhibitors, disinhibitors, social prompters, emotion arousers, and shapers of values and conceptions of reality. Although the different modeling functions can operate separately, in nature they often work in concert. Thus, for example, in the spread of new styles of aggression, models serve as both teachers and disinhibitors. When novel conduct is punished, observers learn the conduct that was punished as well as the restraints. A novel example can both teach and prompt similar acts.

DUAL-LINK VERSUS MULTIPATTERN FLOW OF INFLUENCE

It has been commonly assumed in theories of mass communication that modeling influences operate through a two-step diffusion process. Influential persons pick up new ideas from the media and pass them on to their followers through personal influence. Some communication researchers have claimed that the media can only reinforce preexisting styles of behavior but cannot create new ones (Klapper, 1960). Such a view is at variance with a vast body of evidence. Media influences create personal attributes as well as alter preexisting ones (Bandura, 1986; Williams, 1986).

The different modes of human influence are too diverse in nature to have a fixed path of influence or strengths. Most behavior is the product of multiple determinants operating in concert. Hence, the relative contribution of any given factor in a pattern of influences can change depending on the nature and strength of coexisting determinants. Even the same determinant operating within the same causal structure of factors can change in its causal contribution with further experience (Wood & Bandura, 1989). In the case of atypical behavior, it is usually produced by a unique constellation of the determinants, such that if any one of them were absent the behavior would not have occurred. Depending on their quality and coexistence of other determinants, media influences may be subordinate to, equal to, or outweigh nonmedia influences. Given the dynamic nature of multifaceted causal structures, efforts to affix an average strength to a given mode of influence calls to mind the nonswimming analyst who drowned while trying to cross a river that averaged three feet in depth.

The view that the path of media influence is exclusively a filter-down process is disputed by a wealth of knowledge regarding modeling influences. Human judgment, values, and conduct can be altered directly by televised modeling without having to wait for an influential intermediary to adopt what has been shown and then to serve as the diffuser to others. Watt and van den Berg (1978) tested several alternative theories about how media communications relate to public attitudes and behavior. The explanatory contenders included the conceptions that media influence people directly; media influence opinion leaders who then affect others; media have no independent effects; media set the public agenda for discussions by designating what is important but do not otherwise influence the public; and finally, media simply reflect public attitudes and behavior rather than shape them. The direct-flow model from media to the public received the best empirical support. In this study, the behavior was highly publicized and could bring benefits without risks. When the activities being advocated require the investment of time and resources, and failures can be costly, people are inclined to seek verification of functional value from other sources as well before they act.

Chaffee (1982) reviews substantial evidence that calls into question the prevailing view that interpersonal sources of information are necessarily more persuasive than media sources. People seek information that may be potentially useful to them from different sources. Neither informativeness, credibility, nor persuasiveness are uniquely tied to interpersonal sources or to media sources. How extensively different sources are used depends, in large part, on their accessibility and the likelihood that they will provide the kinds of information sought.

Modeling affects the adoption of new social practices and behavior patterns in several ways. It instructs people about new ways of thinking and behaving by informative demonstration or description. Learning about new things does not rely on a fixed hierarchy of sources. Efficacious modeling not only cultivates competencies but also enhances the sense of personal efficacy needed to transform knowledge and skills into successful courses of action (Bandura, 1997). The relative importance of interpersonal and media sources of information in initiating the adoption process varies for different activities and for the same activity at different stages in the adoption process (Pelz, 1983). Models motivate as well as inform and enable. People are initially reluctant to adopt new practices that involve costs and risks until they see the advantages that have been gained by early adopters. Modeled benefits accelerate social diffusion by weakening the restraints of the more cautious potential adopters. As acceptance spreads, the new ways gain further social support. Models also display preferences and evaluative reactions, which can alter observers' values and standards. Changes in evaluative standards affect receptivity to the activities being modeled. Models not only exemplify and legitimate new practices, they also serve as advocates for them by directly encouraging others to adopt them.

In effecting large-scale changes, communications systems operate through two pathways (Fig. 6.4). In the direct pathway, communications media promote changes by informing, enabling, motivating, and guiding participants. In the socially mediated pathway, media influences are used to link participants to social networks and community settings. These places provide continued personalized guidance, as well as natural incentives and social supports for desired changes (Bandura, 1997, 2001d). The major share of behavior changes is promoted within these social milieus. People are socially situated in interpersonal networks. When media influences lead viewers to discuss and negotiate matters of import with others in their lives, the media set in motion transactional experiences that further shape the course of change. This is another socially mediated process through which symbolic communications exert their effect.

The absence of individualized guidance limits the power of one-way mass communications. The revolutionary advances in interactive technologies provide the means to expand the reach and impact of communications media. On the input side, communications can now be personally tailored to factors that are causally related to the behavior of interest. Tailored communications are viewed as more relevant and credible, are better remembered, and are more effective in influencing behavior than general messages (Kreuter, Strecher, & Glassman, 1999). On the behavioral guidance side, interactive technologies provide a convenient means of individualizing the type and level of behavioral guidance needed to bring desired

Dual Paths of Influence

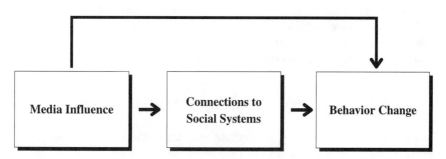

FIG. 6.4. Dual path of communication influences operating on behavior both directly and mediationally through connection to influential social systems.

changes to fruition (Bandura, 2000c). In the population-based approaches the communications are designed to inform, enable, motivate, and guide people to effect personal and social changes. In implementing the social linking function, communications media can connect people to interactive online self-management programs that provide intensive individualized guidance in their homes when they want it (Bandura, 2000d; Taylor, Winzelberg, & Celio, 2001).

In short, there is no single pattern of social influence. The media can implant ideas either directly or through adopters. Analyses of the role of mass media in social diffusion must distinguish between their effect on learning modeled activities and on their adoptive use and examine how media and interpersonal influences affect these separable processes. In some instances the media both teach new forms of behavior and create motivators for action by altering people's value preferences, efficacy beliefs, outcome expectations, and perception of opportunity structures. In other instances, the media teach but other adopters provide the incentive motivation to perform what has been learned observationally. In still other instances, the effect of the media may be entirely socially mediated. That is, people who have had no exposure to the media are influenced by adopters who have had the exposure and then, themselves, become the transmitters of the new ways. Within these different patterns of social influence, the media can serve as originating, as well as reinforcing, influences.

The hierarchical pattern is more likely to obtain for the print media, which has a more limited audience, than for the ubiquitous video media. Communication technologies and global interconnectedness provide people with ready direct access to information worldwide independent of time and place and unfettered by institutional and moneyed gatekeepers. The public is less dependent on a mediated filter-down system of persuasion and enlightenment. These vastly expanded opportunities for self-directedness underscore the growing primacy of agentic initiative in human adaptation and change in the electronic era (Bandura, 1997, 2000d). Ready access to communication technologies will not necessarily enlist active participation unless people believe that they can achieve desired results by this means. Perceived personal and collective efficacy partly determines the extent to which people use this resource and the purposes to which they put it.

SOCIAL DIFFUSION THROUGH SYMBOLIC MODELING

Much of the preceding discussion has been concerned mainly with modeling at the individual level. As previously noted, a unique property of modeling is that it can transmit information of virtually limitless variety to vast numbers of people simultaneously through the medium of symbolic modeling. Extraordinary advances in technology of communication are transforming the nature, reach, speed and loci of human influence (Bandura, 2001b). These technological developments have radically altered the social diffusion process. The video system feeding off telecommunications satellites has become the dominant vehicle for disseminating symbolic environments. Social practices are not only being widely diffused within societies, but ideas, values, and styles of conduct are also being modeled worldwide.

The electronic media are coming to play an increasingly influential role in transcultural change. Televised modeling is now being used to effect social change at community and societywide levels (Bandura, 1997; Sabido, 1981; Singhal & Rogers, 1999; Winett, Leckliter, Chinn, Stahl, & Love, 1985).

There are three major components of a sociocognitive communications model for social change. The first component is a *theoretical model* that specifies the determinants of psychosocial change and the mechanisms through which they produce their effects. This knowledge provides the guiding principles. The second component is a *translational and implementational model* that converts theoretical principles into an innovative operational model by specifying the content, strategies of change, and their mode of implementation. The third component is a social *diffusion model* on how to promote adoption of psychosocial programs in diverse cultural milieus. It does so by making functional adaptations of the programs to different sociostructural circumstances, providing incentives and enabling guidance, and enlisting the necessary resources to achieve success.

In applications to the most urgent global problems, this communications model uses long-running dramatic serials on television or radio as the vehicle of change. The story lines model family planning, women's equality, environmental conservation, AIDS prevention, and a variety of beneficial life skills. The dramatizations inform, enable, guide, and motivate people to effect personal lifestyle changes and to alter detrimental societal norms and practices. The dramatizations further assist people in their efforts at personal and social change by linking them to enabling and supportive subcommunities and beneficial human services. Over 80 worldwide applications of this creative format in Africa, Asia, and Latin America are enhancing people's efficacy to exercise control over their family lives, raising the status of women to have a say in their reproductive and social lives, promoting contraceptive methods, lowering the rates of childbearing, and fostering adoption of AIDS prevention practices (Bandura, in press; Rogers et al., 1999; Vaughan et al., 2000). The higher the exposure to the modeled values and lifestyles, the stronger the impact (Rogers et al., 1999; Westoff & Rodriquez, 1995).

Social cognitive theory analyzes social diffusion of new behavior patterns in terms of three constituent processes and the psychosocial factors that govern them. These include the acquisition of knowledge about innovative behaviors; the adoption of these behaviors in practice; and the social networks through which they spread and are supported. Diffusion of innovation follows a common pattern (Robertson, 1971; Rogers, 1995). New ideas and social practices are introduced by notable example. Initially, the rate of adoption is slow because new ways are unfamiliar, customs resist change and results are uncertain. As early adopters convey more information about how to apply the new practices and their potential benefits, the innovation is adopted at an accelerating rate. After a period in which the new practices spread rapidly, the rate of diffusion slows down. The use of the innovation then either stabilizes or declines, depending on its relative functional value.

Modeling Determinants of Diffusion

Symbolic modeling usually functions as the principal conveyer of innovations to widely dispersed areas. This is especially true in the early stages of diffusion. Newspapers, magazines, radio, and television inform people about new practices and their likely risks or benefits. The Internet provides instant communicative access worldwide. Early adopters, therefore, come from among those who have had greater access to media sources of information about innovations (Robertson, 1971). The psychosocial determinants and mechanisms of observational learning, which were reviewed earlier, govern the rate with which innovations are acquired.

Differences in the knowledge, skills, and resources particular innovations require produce variations in rate of acquisition. Innovations that are difficult to understand and use receive more reluctant consideration than simpler ones (Tornatzky & Klein, 1982). When television models new practices on the screens in virtually every household, people in widely dispersed locales can learn them. However, not all innovations are promoted through the mass media. Some rely on informal personal channels. In such instances, physical proximity determines which innovations will be repeatedly observed and thoroughly learned.

It is one thing to acquire skills; it is another thing to use them effectively under difficult circumstances. Human competency requires not only skills, but also self-belief in one's capabilities to use those skills well. Modeling influences must, therefore, be designed to build self-efficacy as well as to convey knowledge and rules of behavior. Perceived self-efficacy affects every phase of personal change (Bandura, 1997). It determines whether people even consider changing their behavior, whether they can enlist the motivation and perseverance needed to succeed should they choose to do so, and how well they maintain the changes they have achieved.

The influential role of people's beliefs in their personal efficacy in social diffusion is shown in their response to health communications aimed at altering health-impairing habits. Meyerowitz and Chaiken (1987) examined four alternative mechanisms through which health communications could alter health habits—by transmission of factual information, fear arousal, change in risk perception, and enhancement of perceived self-efficacy. They found that health communications fostered adoption of preventive health practices primarily by their effects on perceived self-efficacy. Beck and Lund (1981) have similarly shown that preventive health practices are better promoted by heightening self-efficacy than by elevating fear. Analyses of how communitywide media campaigns produce changes reveal that both the preexisting and induced level of perceived self-efficacy play an influential role in the adoption and social diffusion of health practices (Maibach, Flora, & Nass, 1991; Slater, 1989). The stronger the preexisting perceived self-efficacy and the more the media campaigns enhance people's beliefs in their self-regulative efficacy, the more likely they are to adopt the recommended practices. Health knowledge gets translated into healthful habits through the mediation of perceived self-efficacy (Rimal, 2000).

The findings just reviewed underscore the need to shift the emphasis from trying to scare people into healthy behavior to empowering them with the tools and self-beliefs for exercising personal control over their health habits. People must also experience sufficient success using what they have learned to become convinced of their efficacy and the functional value of what they have adopted. This is best achieved by combining modeling with guided mastery, in which newly acquired skills are first tried under conditions likely to produce good results and then extended to more unpredictable and difficult circumstances (Bandura, 1986, 2000a).

Adoption Determinants

The acquisition of knowledge and skills regarding innovations is necessary but not sufficient for their adoption in practice. A number of factors determine whether people will act on what they have learned. Environmental inducements serve as one set of regulators. Adoptive behavior is also highly susceptible to incentive influences, which may take the form of material, social, or self-evaluative outcomes. Some of the motivating incentives derive from the utility of the adoptive behavior. The greater the relative benefits provided by an innovation, the higher is the incentive to adopt it (Ostlund, 1974; Rogers & Shoemaker, 1971). However, benefits cannot be experienced until the new practices are tried. Promoters, therefore, strive to get people to adopt new practices by altering their preferences and beliefs about likely outcomes, mainly by enlisting vicarious incentives. Advocates of new technologies and ideologies create expectations that they offer better solutions than established ways do. Modeled benefits increase adoptive decisions. Modeling influences can, of course, impede as well as promote the diffusion process (Midgley, 1976). Modeling negative reactions to a particular innovation, as a result of having had disappointing experiences with it, dissuades others from trying it. Even modeled indifference to an innovation, in the absence of any personal experience with it, will dampen the interests of others.

Many innovations serve as a means of gaining social recognition and status. Indeed, status incentives are often the main motivators for adopting new styles and tastes. In many instances, the variant styles do not provide different natural benefits or, if anything, the most innovative styles are the most costly. Status is thus gained at a price. People who strive to distinguish themselves from the common and the ordinary adopt new styles in clothing, grooming, recreational activities, and conduct, thereby achieving distinctive social standing. As the popularity of the new behavior grows, it loses its status-conferring value until eventually it, too, becomes commonplace. It is then discarded for a new form.

Adoptive behavior is also partly governed by self-evaluative reactions to one's own behavior. People adopt what they value, but resist innovations that violate their social and moral standards or that conflict with their self-conception. The more compatible an innovation is with prevailing social norms and value systems, the greater its adoptability (Rogers & Shoemaker, 1971). However, we saw earlier that self-evaluative sanctions do not operate in isolation from the pressures of social influence. People are often led to behave in otherwise personally devalued ways by strategies that circumvent negative self-reactions. This is done by changing appearances and meanings of new practices to make them look compatible with people's values.

The amenability of an innovation to brief trial is another relevant characteristic that can affect the ease of adoption. Innovations that can be tried on a limited basis are more readily adoptable than those that have to be tried on a large scale with substantial effort and costs. The more weight given to potential risks and the costs of getting rid of new practices should they fail to live up to expectations, the weaker is the incentive to innovate. And finally, people will not adopt innovations even though they are favorably disposed toward them if they lack the money, the skills, or the accessory resources that may be needed. The more resources innovations require, the lower is their adoptability.

Analysis of the determinants and mechanisms of social diffusion should not becloud the fact that not all innovations are useful, nor is resistance to them necessarily dysfunctional (Zaltman & Wallendorf, 1979). In the continuous flow of innovations, the number of disadvantageous ones far exceeds those with truly beneficial possibilities. Both personal and societal well-being are well served by initial wariness to new practices promoted by unsubstantiated or exaggerated claims. The designations *venturesome* for early adopters and *laggards* for later adopters are fitting in the case of innovations that hold promise. However, when people are mesmerized by alluring appeals into trying innovations of questionable value, the more suitable designation is gullibility for early adopters and astuteness for resisters. Rogers (1995) has criticized the prevalent tendency to conceptualize the diffusion process from the perspective of the promoters. This tends to bias the search for explanations of nonadoptive behavior in negative attributes of nonadopters.

Social Networks and Flow of Diffusion

The third major factor that affects the diffusion process concerns social network structures. People are enmeshed in networks of relationships that include occupational colleagues, organizational members, kinships, and friendships, just to mention a few. They are linked not only directly by personal relationships. Because acquaintanceships overlap different network clusters, many people become linked to each other indirectly by interconnected ties. Social structures comprise clustered networks of people with various ties among them, as well as by persons who provide connections to other clusters through joint membership or a liaison role. Clusters vary in their internal structure, ranging from loosely knit ones to those that are densely interconnected. Networks also differ in the number and pattern of structural linkages between clusters. They may have many common ties or function with a high degree of separateness. In addition to their degree of interconnectedness, people vary in the positions and status they occupy in particular social networks, which can affect their impact on what spreads through their network. One is more apt to learn about new ideas and practices from brief contacts with causal acquaintances than from intensive contact in the same circle of close associates. This path of influence creates the seemingly paradoxical effect that innovations are extensively diffused to cohesive groups through weak social ties (Granovetter, 1983).

Information regarding new ideas and practices is often conveyed through multilinked relationships (Rogers & Kincaid, 1981). Traditionally, the communication process has been conceptualized as one of unidirectional persuasion flowing from a source to a recipient. Rogers emphasizes the mutuality of influence in interpersonal communication. People share information, give meaning by mutual feedback to the information they exchange, gain understanding of each other's views, and influence each other. Specifying the channels of influence through which innovations are dispersed provides greater understanding of the diffusion process than simply plotting the rate of adoptions over time.

There is no single social network in a community that serves all purposes. Different innovations engage different networks. For example, birth control practices and agricultural innovations diffuse through quite different networks within the same community (Marshall, 1971). To complicate matters further, the social networks that come into play in initial phases of diffusion may differ from those that spread the innovation in subsequent phases (Coleman, Katz, & Menzel, 1966). Adoption rates are better predicted from the network that subserves a particular innovation than from a more general communication network. This is not to say that there is no generality to the diffusion function of network structures. If a particular social structure subserves varied activities, it can help to spread the adoption of innovations in each of those activities.

People with many social ties are more apt to adopt innovations than those who have few ties to others (Rogers & Kincaid, 1981). Adoption rates increase as more and more people in one's personal network adopt an innovation. The effects of social connectedness on adoptive behavior may be mediated through several processes. Multilinked relations can foster adoption of innovations because they convey more factual information, they mobilize stronger social influences, or it may be that people with close ties are more receptive to new ideas than those who are socially estranged. Moreover, in social transactions, people see their associates adopt innovations as well as talk about them. Multiple modeling alone can increase adoptive behavior (Bandura, 1986; Perry & Bussey, 1979).

If innovations are highly conspicuous, they can be adopted directly without requiring interaction among adopters. Television is being increasingly used to forge large single-link structures, in which many people are linked directly to the media source, but they may have little or no direct relations with each other. For example, television evangelists attract loyal followers who adopt the transmitted precepts as guides for how to behave in situations involving moral, social, and political issues. Although they share a common bond to the media source, most members of an electronic community may never see each other. Political power structures are similarly being transformed by the creation of new constituencies tied to a single media source, but with little interconnectedness. Mass marketing techniques, using computer identification and mass mailings, create special-interest constituencies that bypass traditional political organizations in the exercise of political influence.

The evolving information technologies will increasingly serve as a vehicle for building social networks. Online transactions transcend the barriers of time and space (Hiltz & Turoff, 1978; Wellman, 1997). Through interactive electronic networking people link together in widely dispersed locals, exchange information, share new ideas, and transact any number of pursuits. Virtual networking provides a flexible means for creating diffusion structures to serve given purposes, expanding their membership, extending them geographically, and disbanding them when they have outlived their usefulness.

Although structural interconnectedness provides potential diffusion paths, psychosocial factors largely determine the fate of what diffuses through those paths. In other words, it is the transactions that occur within social relationships rather than the ties, themselves, that explain adoptive behavior. The course of diffusion is best understood by considering the interactions among psychosocial determinants of adoptive behavior, the properties of innovations that facilitate or impede adoption, and the network structures that provide the social pathways of influence. Sociostructural and psychological determinants of adoptive behavior should, therefore, be treated as complementary factors in an integrated comprehensive theory of social diffusion, rather than be cast as rival theories of diffusion.

REFERENCES

Adoni, H., & Mane, S. (1984). Media and the social construction of reality: Toward an integration of theory and research. *Communication Research, 11*, 323–340.

Baldwin, T. F., & Lewis, C. (1972). Violence in television: The industry looks at itself. In G. A. Comstock & E. A. Rubinstein (Eds.), *Television and social behavior: Vol. 1 Media content and control* (pp. 290–373). Washington, DC: U.S. Government Printing Office.

Ball-Rokeach, S. J. (1972). The legitimation of violence. In J. F. Short, Jr. & M. E. Wolfgang (Eds.), *Collective violence* (pp. 100–111). Chicago: Aldine-Atherton.

Ball-Rokeach, S., & DeFleur, M. (1976). A dependency model of mass media effects. *Communication Research, 3*, 3–21.

Bandura, A. (1973). *Aggression: A social learning analysis.* Upper Saddle River, NJ: Prentice Hall.

Bandura, A. (1982). The psychology of chance encounters and life paths. *American Psychologist, 37*, 747–755.

Bandura, A. (1986). *Social foundations of thought and action: A social cognitive theory.* Upper Saddle River, NJ: Prentice Hall.

Bandura, A. (1990). Mechanisms of moral disengagement. In W. Reich (Ed.), *Origins of terrorism: Psychologies, ideologies, theologies, states of mind* (pp. 162–191). Cambridge: Cambridge University Press.

Bandura, A. (1991a). Self-regulation of motivation through anticipatory and self-regulatory mechanisms. In R. A. Dienstbier (Ed.), *Perspectives on motivation: Nebraska symposium on motivation* (Vol. 38, pp. 69–164). Lincoln: University of Nebraska Press.

Bandura, A. (1991b). Social cognitive theory of moral thought and action. In W. M. Kurtines & J. L. Gewirtz (Eds.), *Handbook of moral behavior and development* (Vol. A, pp. 45–103). Hillsdale, NJ: Lawrence Erlbaum Associates.

Bandura, A. (1992). Social cognitive theory and social referencing. In S. Feinman (Ed.), *Social referencing and the social construction of reality in infancy* (pp. 175–208). New York: Plenum Press.

Marshall, J. F. (1971). Topics and networks in intravillage communiction. In S. Polgar (Ed.), *Culture and population: A collection of current studies* (pp. 160–166). Cambridge, MA: Schenkman.

McGhee, P. E., & Frueh, T. (1980). Television viewing and the learning of sex-role stereo-types. *Sex Roles, 6,* 179–188.

Meichenbaum, D. (1984). Teaching thinking: A cognitive-behavioral perspective. In R. Glaser, S. Chipman, & J. Segal (Eds.), *Thinking and learning skills (Vol. 2): Research and open questions* (pp. 407–426). Hillsdale, NJ: Lawrence Erlbaum Associates.

Meyer, T. P. (1972). Effects of viewing justified and unjustified real film violence on aggressive behavior. *Journal of Personality and Social Psychology, 23,* 21–29.

Meyerowitz, B. E., & Chaiken, S. (1987). The effect of message framing on breast self-examination attitudes, intentions, and behavior. *Journal of Personality and Social Psychology, 52,* 500–510.

Midgley, D. F. (1976). A simple mathematical theory of innovative behavior. *Journal of Consumer Research, 3,* 31–41.

Midgley, M. (1978). *Beast and man: The roots of human nature.* Ithaca, NY: Cornell University Press.

Milgram, S. (1974). *Obedience to authority: An experimental view.* New York: Harper & Row.

O'Bryant, S. L., & Corder-Bolz, C. R. (1978). The effects of television on children's stereo-typing of women's work roles. *Journal of Vocational Behavior, 12,* 233–244.

Ostlund, L. E. (1974). Perceived innovation attributes as predictors of innovativeness. *Journal of Consumer Research, 1,* 23–29.

Paik, H., & Comstock, G. (1994). The effects of television violence on antisocial behavior: A meta-analysis. *Communication Research, 21,* 516–546.

Pelz, D. C. (1983). Use of information channels in urban innovations. *Knowledge, 5,* 3–25.

Perry, D. G., & Bussey, K. (1979). The social learning theory of sex differences: Imitation is alive and well. *Journal of Personality and Social Psychology, 37,* 1699–1712.

Peterson, R. A., & Kerin, R. A. (1979). The female role in advertisements: Some experimental evidence. *Journal of Marketing, 41,* 59–63.

Rimal, R. N. (2000). Closing the knowledge-behavior gap in health promotion: The mediating role of self-efficacy. *Health Communication, 12,* 219–237.

Robertson, T. S. (1971). *Innovative behavior and communication.* New York: Holt, Rinehart & Winston.

Rogers, E. M. (1995). *Diffusion of innovations* (4th ed.). New York: Free Press.

Rogers, E. M. (1987). Progress, problems and prospects for network research: Investigating relationships in the age of electronic communication technologies. *Social Networks, 9,* 285–310.

Rogers, E. M., Vaughan, P. W., Swalehe, R. M. A., Rao, N., Svenkerud, P., & Sood, S. (1999). Effects of an entertainment-education radio soap opera on family planning behavior in Tanzania. *Studies in Family Planning, 30,* 192–211.

Rogers, E. M., & Kincaid, D. L. (1981). *Communication networks: Toward a new paradigm for research.* New York: Free Press.

Rogers, E. M., & Shoemaker, F. (1971). *Communication of innovations: A cross-cultural approach* (2nd ed.). New York: Free Press.

Rosenthal, T. L., & Zimmerman, B. J. (1978). *Social learning and cognition.* New York: Academic Press.

Sabido, M. (1981). *Towards the social use of soap operas. Mexico City, Mexico: Institute for Communication Research.*

Siegel, A. E. (1958). The influence of violence in the mass media upon children's role expectation. *Child Development, 29,* 35–56.

Singhal, A., & Rogers, E. M. (1999). *Entertainment-education: A communication strategy for social change.* Mahwah, NJ: Lawrence Erlbaum Associates.

Slater, M. D. (1989). Social influences and cognitive control as predictors of self-efficacy and eating behavior. *Cognitive Therapy and Research, 13,* 231–245.

Snyder, M. (1980). Seek, and ye shall find: Testing hypotheses about other people. In E. T. Higgins, C. P. Herman, & M. P. Zanna (Eds.), *Social cognition: The Ontario Symposium on Personality and Social Psychology* (Vol. 1, pp. 105–130). Hillsdale, NJ: Lawrence Erlbaum Associates.

Snyder, M., & Campbell, B. H. (1982). Self-monitoring: The self in action. In J. Suls (Ed.), *Psychological perspectives on the self* (pp. 185–207). Hillsdale, NJ: Lawrence Erlbaum Associates.

Taylor, C. B., Winzelberg, A., & Celio, A. (2001). Use of interactive media to prevent eating disorders. In R. Striegel-Moor & L. Smolak (Eds.), *Eating disorders: New direction for research and practice* (pp. 255–270). Washington, DC: American Psychological Association.

Tornatzky, L. G., & Klein, K. J. (1982). Innovation characteristics and innovation adoption-implementation: A meta-analysis of findings. *IEEE Transactions of Engineering and Management, EM-29,* 28–45.

Vaughan, P. W., Rogers, E. M., Singhal, A., & Swalehe, R. M. (2000). Entertainment-education and HIV/AIDS prevention: A field experiment in Tanzania. *Journal of Health Communication, 5,* 81–100.

Watt, J. G., Jr., & van den Berg, S. A. (1978). Time series analysis of alternative media effects theories. In R. D. Ruben (Ed.), *Communication Yearbook 2* (pp. 215–224). New Brunswick, NJ: Transaction Books.

Wellman, B. (1997). An electronic group is virtually a social network. In S. Kielser (Ed.), *Culture of the Internet* (pp. 179–205). Mahwah, NJ: Lawrence Erlbaum Associates.

Westoff, C. F., & Rodriguez, G. (1995). The mass media and family planning in Kenya. *International Family Planning Perspectives, 21,* 26–31.

Williams, T. M. (Ed.). (1986). *The impact of television: A natural experiment in three communities.* New York: Academic Press.

Wilson, B. J., & Cantor, J. (1985). Developmental differences in empathy with a television protagonist's fear. *Journal of Experimental Child Psychology, 39,* 284–299.

Winett, R. A., Leckliter, I. N., Chinn, D. E., Stahl, B. N., & Love, S. Q. (1985). The effects of television modeling on residential energy conservation. *Journal of Applied Behavior Analysis, 18,* 33–44.

Wood, R. E., & Bandura, A. (1989). Social cognitive theory of organizational management. *Academy of Management Review, 14,* 361–384.

Zaltman, G., & Wallendorf, M. (1979). *Consumer behavior: Basic findings and management implications.* New York: Wiley.

Zillmann, D., & Bryant, J. (1984). Effects of massive exposure to pornography. In N. M. Malamuth & E. Donnerstein (Eds.), *Pornography and sexual aggression* (pp. 115–138). New York: Academic Press.

Zimbardo, P. G. (1969). The human choice: Individuation, reason, and order versus deindividuation, impulse, and chaos. In W. J. Arnold & D. Levine (Eds.), *Nebraska Symposium on Motivation, 1969* (pp. 237–309). Lincoln: University of Nebraska Press.

Preparation of this chapter and some of the cited research were supported by grants from the Grant Foundation and the Spencer Foundation. Some sections of this chapter include revised, updated, and expanded material from the book *Social Foundations of Thought and Action: A Social Cognitive Theory,* Prentice Hall, 1986.

Chapter 7

Mass Media Attitude Change: Implications of the Elaboration Likelihood Model of Persuasion

RICHARD E. PETTY
Ohio State University

JOSEPH R. PRIESTER
University of Michigan

PABLO BRIÑOL
Universidad Autonoma de Madrid

It is conceivable that one persuasive person could, through the use of mass media, bend the world's population to his will.

(Cartwright, 1949, p. 253, in summarizing earlier views on the power of the media)

Undoubtedly, few social scientists today think that the mass media have the power to sway huge audiences to the extent once believed likely. Nevertheless, the technological advances of the last century—from the first primitive radio broadcasts to today's high-speed mobile Internet devices—have made it possible for individual communicators to have access to unprecedented numbers of potential message recipients. Millions of dollars are spent worldwide each year in attempts to change people's attitudes about political candidates, consumer products, health and safety practices, and charitable causes. In most of these instances, the ultimate goal is to influence people's behavior so that they will vote for certain politicians or referenda; purchase specific goods; engage in safer driving, eating, and sexual activities; and donate money to various religious, environmental, and educational organizations and institutions. To what extent are media persuasion attempts effective?

The success of media campaigns depends in part on: (a) whether the transmitted communications are effective in changing the attitudes of the recipients in the desired direction, and (b) whether these modified attitudes in turn influence people's behaviors. Our goal in this chapter is to present a brief overview of current psychological approaches to mass media influence and to outline in more detail a general framework that can be used to understand the processes responsible for mass media attitude change. This framework is called the elaboration likelihood model of persuasion (ELM; see Petty & Cacioppo, 1981, 1986b; Petty & Wegener, 1999). Before addressing the contemporary approaches, we provide a very brief historical overview of perspectives on mass media influence.

EARLY EXPLORATIONS OF MASS MEDIA PERSUASION

Direct Effects Model

The initial assumption about the effects of the mass media by social scientists in the 1920s and 1930s was that mass communication techniques were quite potent. For example, in an analysis of mass communication during World War I, Lasswell (1927) concluded that "propaganda is one of the most powerful instrumentalities in the modern world" (p. 220). During this period, there were several salient examples of seemingly effective mass communication effects. These included the panic following the 1929 stock market crash; the well-publicized mass hysteria following the radio broadcast of Orson Wells' *War of the Worlds* in 1938; and the rise in popularity of individuals such as Adolf Hitler in Germany, and the right wing Catholic priest, Father Coughlin, and Louisiana Senator Huey Long in the United States. The assumption of Lasswell and others was that transmission of information via mass communication produced direct effects on attitudes and behavior (e.g., Doob, 1935; Lippmann, 1922). In detailing the views about mass communication during this period, Sears and colleagues noted that it was assumed that "the audience was captive, attentive, and gullible . . . the citizenry sat glued to the radio, helpless victims" (Sears & Kosterman, 1994, p. 254), and that "propaganda could be made almost irresistible" (Sears & Whitney, 1973, p. 2).

Many analysts of the period based their startling assessments of the power of the media on informal and anecdotal evidence rather than on careful empirical research. For example, few attempts were made to measure the attitudes of message recipients prior to and following propaganda efforts. Thus, although it could be that the great propagandists of the time were changing the attitudes of their audience, it was also possible that the communicators were mostly attracting an audience that already agreed with them (called "selective exposure"; see Frey, 1986) or some combination of the two. Of course, not all analysts of the period were so optimistic about the prospects for the mass media to produce dramatic changes in opinion, but it was the dominant view (Wartella & Middlestadt, 1991).[1]

Although the direct effects model has been replaced by more sophisticated theoretical perspectives, there do remain echoes of this model within both popular and academic writings. The news media, for example, have been represented in the popular literature as directly influencing and shaping political attitudes (e.g., Adams, 1993), the development of racism (e.g., Suber, 1997), and consumer choices (e.g., Lohr, 1991). Traces of the direct effects model can also be discerned in current theoretical perspectives. Zaller (1991), for instance, argues that information presentation is the key to public opinion formation and shift. Specifically, he provides some evidence that one can predict opinion change (e.g., attitudes toward the Vietnam War) from the mere amount of information provided for a particular stance (e.g., pro- or counter-U.S. involvement in the war) in the media. As we will see shortly, most current analyses of attitude change hold that it is not the information per se that produces persuasion, but rather, people's idiosyncratic reactions to this information.

Indirect Effects Model

The direct effects model was tempered considerably in the next two decades, largely as a result of the subsequent empirical research conducted. For example, in analyzing survey information gathered by the National Opinion Research Center, Hyman and Sheatsley (1947) concluded that the effectiveness of mass communication campaigns could not be increased simply by increasing the number of messages. Rather, the specific psychological barriers to effective information dissemination must be considered and overcome (see also Cartwright, 1949). For example, they noted that people often distort incoming information to be consistent with prior attitudes, making change less likely. A similar conclusion was reached by Lazarsfeld, Berelson, and Gaudet (1948) in their

---

[1]In one of the relatively rare empirical efforts of the period, Peterson and Thurstone (1933) examined the power of movies such as D. W. Griffith's *Birth of a Nation*, controversial because of its depiction of Blacks, to modify the racial attitudes of adolescents. The conclusions of this research foreshadowed the modern period in that various moderators of effective influence were uncovered (e.g., greater influence for those with low knowledge rather than high issue-consistent knowledge; Wood, Rhodes, & Biek, 1995; see Wartella & Reeves, 1985).

influential study of the impact of the media in the 1940 presidential campaign. A major result from this study was that the media appeared to reinforce people's already existing attitudes rather than producing new ones
(see also Klapper, 1960; Lord, Ross, & Lepper, 1979). Some researchers
argued that when public attitude change was produced, it was only indirectly attributable to the media. That is, the media were more effective in
influencing various opinion leaders than the average person, and these
opinion leaders were responsible for changes in the mass public (i.e., a
"two-step" flow of communication; Katz & Lazarsfeld, 1955).

Studies conducted during World War II reinforced the "limited effects"
view of the media. Most notably, the wartime studies by Carl Hovland
and his colleagues showed that although various military training films
had an impact on the knowledge of the soldier recipients, the films were
relatively ineffective in producing mass changes in attitudes and behavior. Instead, the persuasive power of the films depended on a large number of moderating variables (Hovland, Lumsdaine, & Sheffield, 1949; see
also Shils & Janowitz, 1948). When World War II ended, Hovland returned
to Yale University, and the systematic examination of these moderating
variables was begun in earnest.

CONTEMPORARY APPROACHES TO MASS MEDIA PERSUASION

The Attitude Construct

Contemporary social psychologists concerned with the study of media
influence, like their predecessors (e.g., Peterson & Thurstone, 1933), have
focused on the concept of "attitudes," or people's general predispositions
to evaluate other people, objects, and issues favorably or unfavorably.
People are aware of most of their attitudes (explicit attitudes), but sometimes they come to have favorable or unfavorable predispositions of
which they are unaware (implicit attitudes). For example, people may
harbor implicit prejudices or stereotypes that they consciously reject
(Devine, 1989). In addition, sometimes people are aware of the causes of
their attitudes, and sometimes they are not (Greenwald & Banaji, 1995;
Wilson, Lindesy, & Schooler, 2000). The attitude construct achieved its
preeminent position in research on social influence because of the
assumption that a person's attitude—whether implicit or explicit—is an
important mediating variable between exposure to new information, on
the one hand, and behavioral change, on the other. For example, a television commercial might be based on the idea that giving people information about a candidate's issue positions will lead to favorable attitudes
toward the candidate and ultimately to contributing money to and voting

for the candidate. Or, mere repeated exposure to a product name in radio message might lead the listener to like the product name and therefore select it for purchase without much thought on the next shopping trip (Fazio, 1990).

Over the past 50 years, numerous theories of attitude change and models of knowledge–attitude–behavior relationships have been developed (see reviews by Eagly & Chaiken, 1993; Petty, Priester, & Wegener, 1994; Petty & Wegener, 1998a). Contemporary analyses of mass media persuasion have focused on the variables that determine when the media will be effective versus ineffective and what the underlying processes are by which the media induce change. Perhaps the most well-known psychological framework for categorizing and understanding mass media persuasion effects was popularized by Hovland and his colleagues (e.g., Hovland, 1954; Hovland, Janis, & Kelley, 1953) and elaborated considerably by William McGuire (McGuire, 1985, 1989; see McGuire, 1996, for a review of the Hovland approach). After describing this early influential model, we turn to more contemporary approaches.

The Communication/Persuasion Matrix Model of Media Effects

One of the most basic assumptions of initial theories of attitude change (e.g., Strong, 1925) that is also evident in contemporary approaches (e.g., McGuire, 1985) was that effective influence required a sequence of steps (Petty & Cacioppo, 1984b). For example, Fig. 7.1 presents McGuire's (1985, 1989) Communication/Persuasion Matrix model of persuasion. This model outlines the inputs (or independent variables) to the persuasion process that media persuaders can control along with the outputs (or dependent variables) that can be measured to see if any influence attempt is successful.

Matrix Inputs.   The inputs to the persuasion process in Fig. 7.1 are based in part on Lasswell's (1964) classic question: Who says what to whom, when, and how? First, a communication typically has some *source*. The source can be expert or not, attractive or not, male or female, an individual or group, and so on. This source provides some information, the *message*, and this message can be emotional or logical, long or short, organized or not, directed at a specific or a general belief, and so forth. The message is presented to a particular *recipient* who may be high or low in intelligence, knowledge, experience, in a good or bad mood, and so on. The message is presented via some *channel* of communication. Different media allow different types of input such as audio only (e.g., radio), audio plus moving visual (television, Internet), print only, or print plus static visual (e.g., magazines, newspapers). Some media allow presentation of

Communication Inputs:

Outputs:	SOURCE	MESSAGE	RECIPIENT	CHANNEL	CONTEXT
EXPOSURE					
ATTENTION					
INTEREST					
COMPREHENSION					
ACQUISITION					
YIELDING					
MEMORY					
RETRIEVAL					
DECISION					
ACTION					
REINFORCEMENT					
CONSOLIDATION					

FIG. 7.1. The Communication/Persuasion Process as an Input/Output Matrix. The figure depicts the primary independent and dependent variables in mass media persuasion research. (Adapted from McGuire, 1989.)

the message at the recipient's own pace (e.g., reading a magazine or browsing the Internet), whereas other media control the pace externally (e.g., radio and television). Finally, the message is presented to the recipient in some *context*. That is, the persuasion context may be one of group or individual exposure, noisy or quiet environment, and so forth.

Matrix Outputs.   Each of the inputs to the persuasion process can have an impact on one of the outputs depicted in Fig. 7.1. The Communication/Persuasion Matrix model contends that in order for effective influence to occur, a person first needs to be *exposed* to some new information. Media are often selected by potential persuaders after an estimation of the number and type of people the message is likely to reach. Also, by deciding what to present, those who control the mass media help define the range of issues to which the public is exposed (e.g., Iyengar, Kinder, Peters, & Krosnick, 1984).

Second, the person must *attend* to the information presented. Just because a person is sitting in front of the television doesn't mean that he or she knows what is going on. For example, in order to gain and attract attention, TV commercials often present attractive women and men in proximity to the attitude object. Even if the person does notice the information, this doesn't mean that the person's *interest* will be engaged. The next two stages involve *comprehension* and *acquisition,* or the question of what part of the information presented the person actually understands and learns. It is only at step 6 that attitude change or *yielding* occurs. Once the person accepts the information in the message, the next step in the sequence involves *memory* or storage of the new information and the attitude that it supports. The next three steps detail the processes involved in translating the new attitude into a behavioral response. That is, at some subsequent behavioral opportunity, the person must *retrieve* the new attitude from memory, *decide* to act on it, and perform the appropriate *action.* Finally, the model notes that if the attitude-consistent behavior is not *reinforced,* the new attitude might be undermined. For example, if you act on your attitude and become embarrassed, that attitude will not persist. If the behavior is rewarding, however, the attitude consistent behavior might lead to attitudinal *consolidation,* making the new attitude more likely to endure over time and guide future behavior.

Variants of this general information processing model were sometimes interpreted in theory and in practice as suggesting that a change early in the sequence (e.g., attention) would inevitably lead to a change later in the sequence (e.g., yielding). McGuire (1989) noted, however, that the likelihood that a message will evoke each of the steps in the sequence should be viewed as a conditional probability. Thus, even if the likelihood of achieving each of the first six steps in a mass media campaign was 60%, the maximum probability of achieving all six steps (exposure, attention, interest, comprehension, learning, and yielding), would be $.6^6$, or only 5%.

In addition, it is important to consider the fact that any one input variable can have different effects on the different output steps. For example, Hyman and Sheatsley (1947) noted that in the political domain, the knowledge and interest of a message recipient was positively related to exposure to political messages (i.e., the chronic "know-nothings" are more difficult to reach in a political campaign), but negatively related to attitude change (i.e., high interest and knowledge tends to produce assimilation of messages to one's original point of view). In a cogent analysis of this point, McGuire (1968) noted that several variables might have opposite effects on the steps involving *reception* of information (e.g., exposure, attention, comprehension, acquisition, memory) versus *acceptance* of (yielding to) the information. For example, the intelligence of the message recipient is related positively to reception processes, but negatively related to yielding. The joint action of reception and yielding processes implies that people of moderate intelligence should be easier to persuade than people of low or high intelligence, as this maximizes both reception and yielding (see also Rholes & Wood, 1992).

Additional Issues for the Communication/Persuasion Matrix Model. Although McGuire's input/output matrix model serves as a very useful way to think about the steps involved in producing attitude and behavior change via the mass media or other means, it is important to appreciate a number of things that the model does not address. First, it is now clear that some of the steps in the postulated information processing sequence may be completely independent of each other, rather than sequential. For example, although a person's ability to learn and recall new information (e.g., facts about a political candidate) was often thought to be an important causal determinant of and prerequisite to attitude and behavior change (e.g., favoring and voting for a candidate), little empirical evidence has accumulated to support the view that message learning is a *necessary* step for persuasion (Greenwald, 1968; McGuire, 1985; Petty & Cacioppo, 1981). Rather, the existing evidence shows that message comprehension and learning can occur in the absence of attitude change and that a person's attitudes can change without learning the specific information in the communication. That is, a person might be able to comprehend all of the intended information perfectly, but not be persuaded either because the information is counterargued or seen as personally irrelevant. On the other hand, a person might get the information all wrong (scoring zero on a knowledge or recall test), but think about it in a manner that produces the intended change. That is, misunderstanding the message can sometimes produce more change than correct understanding.

This analysis helps to explain why previous research on mass media effects has sometimes found that message learning and changes in knowledge occur in the absence of attitude change and vice versa (Petty, Gleicher, & Baker, 1991). For example, after an extensive review of the mass media programs commonly used by government agencies to educate and to reduce social problems involving drugs and alcohol, Kinder, Pape, and Walfish (1980) concluded that although these programs were typically successful in increasing participants' knowledge about drugs, there was very little evidence that they were successful in changing attitudes and behavior (see also Bruvold & Rundall, 1988).

Second, the model tells us little about the factors that produce yielding. Even though the initial steps in the information processing sequence are viewed as prerequisites to acceptance, McGuire did not mean to imply that people would invariably yield to all information they comprehended and learned. That is, the earlier steps were thought to be necessary but not sufficient for yielding. Rather, just as source and other variables determine the extent of attention, they also determine the extent of acceptance. As implied by the Communication/Persuasion matrix, current psychological research on influence focuses on how and why various features of a persuasion situation (i.e., aspects of the source, message, channel, recipient, and context) affect each of the steps in the communication sequence (e.g., How does the credibility of the source affect attention to the message?). The most research by far, however, focuses on the question of how variables affect the processes responsible for yielding to or resisting the communication.

Cognitive Response Approach.   Cognitive response theory (Greenwald, 1968; Petty, Ostrom, & Brock, 1981) was developed explicitly to address two key issues unaddressed by the communication/persuasion matrix. That is, cognitive response analysis attempted to account for the low correlation between message learning and persuasion observed in many studies and for the processes responsible for yielding. In contrast to the traditional view that acceptance of a message depended on learning the message content, the cognitive response approach contends that the impact of variables on persuasion depends on the extent to which individuals articulate and rehearse their own idiosyncratic thoughts to the information presented. The cognitive response perspective maintains that individuals are active participants in the persuasion process who attempt to relate message elements to their existing repertoires of information. The influence of cognitive responses—or one's own thoughts—on subsequent attitudes has been demonstrated in a variety of ways.

For example, in early research on "role playing," it was shown that asking people to self-generate arguments on an issue can lead to relatively enduring attitude change (e.g., Janis & King, 1956). When engaged in role playing (e.g., "generate a message to convince your friend to stop smoking"), people engage in a "biased scanning" of evidence on the issue and end up persuading themselves because the arguments they generate are seen as compelling (Greenwald & Albert, 1968). More recently, Tesser and his colleagues conducted a series of investigations of the effects of merely thinking about an attitude object without any external information presented. These studies have shown clearly that with mere thought, people's reactions and impressions to other people, objects, and issues can become more extreme, in either a positive or negative direction, depending on the valence of the initial thoughts generated (see Tesser, Martin, & Mendolia, 1995, for a review).

The cognitive response approach holds that even when external information is presented, people's thoughts or cognitive responses to this information, rather than learning the information per se, determine the extent of influence. Most studies of cognitive responses to messages focus on the valence and the extent of thinking. Valence refers to the favorableness or unfavorableness of the thoughts with respect to the message, and extent of thinking refers to the number of thoughts generated. In general, the more favorable thoughts people have to the message, the more persuasion that results, and the more unfavorable thoughts people have to a message, the less influence (or even change in a direction opposite to the advocacy) that occurs (Greenwald, 1968; Petty et al., 1981; Wright, 1973).

In addition to coding thoughts for valence and number, other categorization schemes have be used (e.g., coding for the origin of the thought, target, self-relevance, and so forth; see Cacioppo & Petty, 1981; Shavitt & Brock, 1986). One feature of thoughts that has proven to be useful is the confidence with which people hold their thoughts. That is, two people can have the same thought about the message (e.g., "the proposed tax increase should help our schools"), but one person might have considerably more confidence in the thought than another. According to *self-validation theory* (Petty & Briñol, 2000; Petty, Briñol, & Tormala, in press), the relationship between thoughts and attitudes should be greater when people have confidence rather than doubt in their thoughts, and many of the traditionally studied source, message, recipient, and channel variables can influence persuasion by influencing the extent to which people have confidence in the thoughts they have in response to a persuasive message. In a series of initial studies conducted to test the basic self-validation hypothesis, Petty, Briñol, and Tormala (in press) found that when the thoughts in response to a message were primarily favorable, increasing confidence in their validity increased persuasion, but increasing doubt about their validity decreased persuasion. When the thoughts about a message were mostly unfavorable, then increasing confidence reduced persuasion, but undermining confidence increased persuasion. These relationships held whether confidence in thoughts was measured or manipulated. Thus, research on cognitive responses suggest that generating favorable or unfavorable thoughts to a persuasive message is an important factor in producing attitude change, but it is not the only factor. Individuals also need to have confidence in the thoughts that they generate.

THE ELABORATION LIKELIHOOD MODEL OF PERSUASION

Although the cognitive response approach provided important insights into the persuasion process, it only focuses on those situations in which people are active processors of the information provided to them. The theory did not account very well for persuasion in situations where people were not actively thinking about the message content. To correct this deficit, the Elaboration Likelihood Model of persuasion (ELM) was proposed. The ELM holds that persuasion can occur when thinking is high or low, but the processes and consequences of persuasion are different in each situation (Petty & Cacioppo, 1981, 1986a; Petty & Wegener, 1999). More specifically, the ELM holds that the processes that occur during the "yielding" stage of influence can be thought of as emphasizing one of two relatively distinct "routes to persuasion" (see Fig. 7.2).[2]

Central and Peripheral Routes to Persuasion

Central Route. The first or *central route* to persuasion involves effortful cognitive activity whereby the person draws on prior experience and knowledge in order to carefully scrutinize all of the information relevant to determining the central merits of the position advocated (Petty, 1994; Petty & Cacioppo, 1986a). Consistent with the cognitive response approach to persuasion, the message recipient under the central route is actively generating favorable and/or unfavorable thoughts in response to

---

[2]Although the ELM has implications for the other stages in McGuire's information processing sequence described earlier (see Fig. 7.1), it does not attempt to provide a *general* theory of information exposure, memory, and so on. For example, even though the ELM would expect people to seek out and attend to messages of high personal relevance more so than messages of low personal relevance, the ELM provides an incomplete account of exposure, as variables unrelated to yielding processes could also determine message exposure. For example, people may seek messages for purposes of excitement or mood management (e.g., see chap. 2).

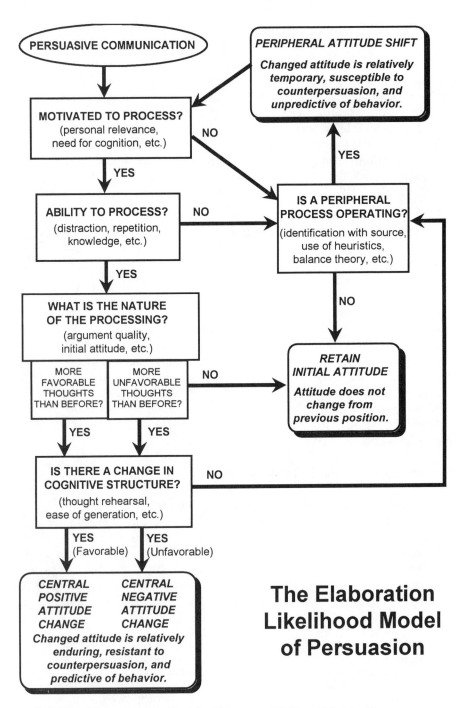

FIG. 7.2. Schematic depiction of the Elaboration Likelihood Model of Persuasion. The figure shows the possible endpoints after exposure to a persuasive communication for people following central and peripheral routes to attitude change. (Adapted from Petty & Cacioppo, 1986a.)

the persuasive communication. The goal of this cognitive effort is to determine if the position advocated has any merit. Not every message received from the media is sufficiently interesting or important to think about, and not every situation provides the time and opportunity for careful reflection. When people are motivated and able to take the central route, they carefully appraise the extent to which the communication provides information that is fundamental or central to the true merits of the position advocated.

Of course, the particular kind of information that is perceived central to the merits of any particular issue can vary from person to person and from situation to situation. For example, when some people think about social issues (e.g., capital punishment), religious considerations and arguments are particularly persuasive, but for others, legalistic arguments carry the most weight (Cacioppo, Petty, & Sidera, 1982). Likewise, research has shown that when some people evaluate ads for consumer products, they are primarily concerned about how usage of the product will affect the image that they project; for other people, this dimension is unimportant (DeBono & Packer, 1991; Snyder & DeBono, 1989). Dimensions that are most important will often receive the most scrutiny (Petty & Wegener, 1998b; Petty, Wheeler, & Bizer, 2000).

Research suggests that an important function of the media in the political domain is to make certain political and social issues more salient than others (see Iyengar & Kinder, 1987; see also chap. 1). For example, a study of magazine stories showed that from the 1960s to the 1990s, stories about drug abuse and nutrition increased dramatically, stories about communism and desegregation declined, and stories on pollution remained about the same (Paisley, 1989). If people come to believe that certain issues are more important due to extensive media coverage, it is reasonable that these dimensions of judgment will become more central in evaluating the merits of political candidates. By giving a problem great coverage (e.g., whether the oil crisis or a presidential sex scandal), newscasters make that problem readily accessible in the minds of recipients, making them more likely to think about that particular problem when they judge the "bottom line" on an attitude object (e.g., a president; see Sherman, Mackie, & Driscoll, 1990). So, by setting the agenda of what is important to evaluate, the media can have important "indirect" effects on attitude change.[3]

---

[3]Of course, much of the correlation between media coverage and ratings of issue-importance is due to the fact that the media cover issues people already think are important. Nevertheless, some research shows that the media coverage can precede public perceptions (e.g., MacKuen, 1981), and the mere accessibility of certain issues can cause people to give greater weight to them (Sherman et al., 1990).

In the central route, once people have had thoughts about the message, the final step involves integrating the new thoughts into one's overall cognitive structure. Such integration may be more likely to occur if one's thoughts are rehearsed and held with high confidence. It is important to note, however, that just because the attitude change process in the central route involves considerable cognitive work does not mean that the attitude formed will be a rational or "accurate" one. The extensive information processing activity might be highly biased by factors such as one's prior attitude and knowledge or one's current mood state. The important point is that sometimes attitudes are changed by a rather thoughtful process in which people attend carefully to the issue-relevant information presented, examine this information in light of their relevant experiences and knowledge, and evaluate the information along the dimensions they perceive central to the merits of the issue. People engaged in this effortful cognitive activity have been characterized as engaging in "systematic" (Chaiken, Liberman, & Eagly, 1989), "mindful" (Palmerino, Langer, & McGillis, 1984), and "piecemeal" (Fiske & Pavelchak, 1986) processing (see Chaiken & Trope, 1999, for a discussion of various "dual-route" models of social judgment). Attitudes changed by the central route have been shown to have a number of distinguishing characteristics. Because these attitudes are well articulated and integrated into a person's cognitive structure, these attitudes have been found to be relatively easy to access from memory, persistent over time, predictive of behavior, and resistant to change until they are challenged by cogent contrary information (Haugtvedt & Petty, 1992; Petty, Haugtvedt, & Smith, 1995; see Petty & Krosnick, 1995, for an extensive discussion of the determinants of attitude strength).

Peripheral Route. In stark contrast to the central route to persuasion, the ELM holds that attitude change does not always require effortful evaluation of the information presented by the mass media or other sources. Instead, when a person's motivation or ability to process the issue-relevant information is low, persuasion can occur by a *peripheral route* in which processes invoked by simple cues in the persuasion context influence attitudes. The peripheral route to persuasion recognizes that it is neither adaptive nor possible for people to exert considerable mental effort in thinking about all of the media communications to which they are exposed. In order to function in contemporary society, people must sometimes act as "lazy organisms" (McGuire, 1969) or "cognitive misers" (Taylor, 1981) and employ simpler means of evaluation (see also Bem, 1972). For example, various features of a communication (e.g., pleasant scenery in a TV commercial) can elicit an affective state (e.g., a good mood) that becomes associated with the advocated position (as in classical conditioning, Staats and Staats, 1958). Or, the source of a message can trigger a relatively simple inference or heuristic such as "experts are correct" (Chaiken 1987) that a person can use to judge the message. Similarly, the responses of other people who are exposed to the message can serve as a validity cue (e.g., "if so many agree, it must be true"; Axsom, Yates, & Chaiken, 1987). In the first half of the past century, the Institute for Propaganda Analysis, in a report on propaganda techniques, listed a number of "tricks" that speakers of the time used to persuade their audiences that relied on peripheral cues (e.g., the "bandwagon" effect was giving the sense that most other people already supported the speaker; see Lee & Lee, 1939).

We do not mean to suggest that peripheral approaches are necessarily ineffective. In fact, they can be quite powerful in the short term. The problem is that over time, moods dissipate, peoples' feelings about sources can change, and the cues can become dissociated from the message. These factors would then undermine the basis of the attitude. Laboratory research has shown that attitude changes based on peripheral cues tend to be less accessible, enduring, and resistant to subsequent attacking messages than attitudes based on careful processing of message arguments (see Petty et al., 1995). In sum, attitudes changed via the central route tend to be based on active thought processes resulting in a well-integrated cognitive structure, but attitudes changed via the peripheral route are based on more passive acceptance or rejection of simple cues and have a less well articulated foundation.[4]

The tendency for simple cue processes to dissipate over time along with the tendency for argument-based persuasion to persist can lead to interesting effects. For example, one such phenomena is the often cited but infrequently found (Gillig & Greenwald, 1978) "sleeper effect" (Gruder, Cook, Hennigan, Flay, Alessis, & Halamaj, 1978; Hovland, Lumsdaine, & Sheffield, 1949; Peterson & Thurstone, 1933). The sleeper effect can occur when a persuasive message is followed by a discounting cue (e.g., you learn that some information was reported in the *National Enquirer* after exposure). The effect is that although the discounting cue suppresses attitude change initially, over time the message can increase in effectiveness—opposite to the typical decay pattern found. The ELM predicts that such an effect should be most likely to occur under conditions in which the initial message is very strong, processed carefully, and then discounted. If the message was processed carefully and a simple cue follows message

---

[4]For expository purposes, we have emphasized the distinction between the central and the peripheral routes to persuasion. That is, we have focused on the prototypical processes at the endpoints of the elaboration likelihood continuum. In most persuasion situations (which fall somewhere along this continuum), some combination of central and peripheral processes are likely to have an impact on attitudes.

processing, what should happen is the following: Over time the impact of the peripheral discounting cue should fade, and people's attitudes should be governed by their initial (and more memorable) favorable thoughts to the strong arguments (see Priester, Wegener, Petty, & Fabrigar, 1999).

Persuasion Processes in the Elaboration Likelihood Model

Variables Affecting the Amount of Thinking.   Our discussion of the central and peripheral routes to persuasion has highlighted two basic processes of attitude change, but the depiction of the ELM in Fig. 7.2 outlines more-specific roles that variables can play in persuasion situations. First, some variables affect a person's general *motivation* to think about a message. Mendelsohn (1973) noted that placing potential media recipients "along a continuum ranging from those whose initial interest in a given subject area may be high to those who literally have no interest in what may be communicated becomes an essential step in developing effective public information campaigns" (p. 51). Several variables enhance interest in media messages. Perhaps the most important determinant of interest and motivation to process the message is the perceived personal relevance of the communication. In one study (Petty & Cacioppo, 1979b), for example, undergraduates were told that their own university (high personal relevance) or a distant university (low personal relevance) was considering implementing a policy requiring all seniors to pass an exam in their major as a prerequisite to graduation. The students then listened to a radio editorial that presented either strong or weak arguments in favor of the exam policy. As predicted by the ELM, when the speaker advocated that the exams should be instituted at the students' own campus, the quality of the arguments in the message had a greater impact on attitudes than when the speaker advocated that the exams should be instituted at a distant institution. That is, as the personal relevance of the message increased, strong arguments were more persuasive, but weak arguments were less persuasive than in the low-relevance conditions (see left panel of Fig. 7.3). In addition, an analysis of the thoughts that the students listed after the message suggested that the more extreme attitudes were accompanied by more extreme thoughts. When the arguments were strong, students exposed to the high-relevance message produced more than twice as many favorable thoughts as low-relevance students, and when the arguments were weak, high-relevance students generated almost twice as many unfavorable thoughts as students exposed to the low-relevance version.

In an interesting extension of this work, Burnkrant and Unnava (1989) have found that simply changing the pronouns in a message from the third person (e.g., *one* or *he and she*) to the second person (i.e., *you*) was

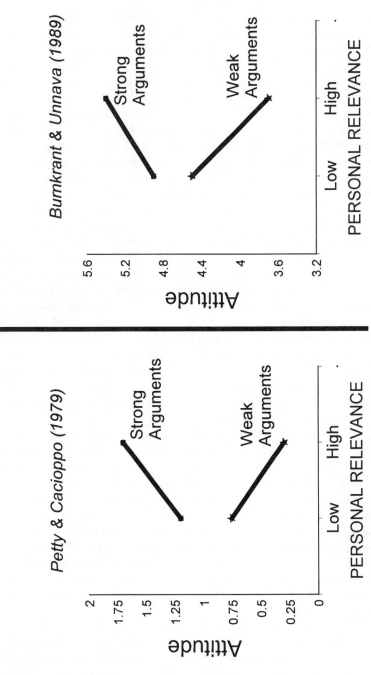

FIG. 7.3. Self-relevance increases message processing. In each panel, as self-relevance (involvement) increases, argument quality becomes a more important determinant of the attitudes expressed after exposure to a persuasive message. Data in the left panel are from an experiment by Petty and Cacioppo (1979b). Data in the right panel are from an experiment by Burnkrant and Unnava (1989). In each panel, higher numbers indicate more-favorable attitudes toward the position taken in the persuasive message.

sufficient to increase personal involvement and processing of the message arguments (see right panel of Fig. 7.3). That is, when the messages contained the self-relevant pronouns, strong arguments were more persuasive and weak arguments were less persuasive than when third-person pronouns were used. Yet another way to increase self-relevance is to frame a message to comport either with people's values or self-conceptions. For example, if a person is attuned to the image value of a product, framing the message as dealing with image can increase message processing (Petty & Wegener, 1998b; see Petty, Wheeler, & Bizer, 2000, for a review).

Although increasing the perceived personal relevance of a message is an important way to increase thinking (see Petty, Cacioppo, & Haugtvedt, 1992, for a review), it is hardly the only one. For example, the degree to which a source is perceived to be of questionable or low trustworthiness has also been found to increase the extent of elaboration (Priester & Petty, 1995). In this research, the extent to which a source could be trusted to convey accurate information was manipulated while keeping source expertise high. In one study, source trustworthiness was manipulated by either providing message recipients with background information that suggested that the speaker was honest and could be trusted or was dishonest and could not always be trusted to provide accurate information. In another study, trustworthiness was manipulated by having the source either advocate a self-serving position (relatively untrustworthy) or a position that violated the source's own self-interests (relatively trustworthy). Regardless of how source trustworthiness was manipulated, sources of questionable trustworthiness engendered greater elaboration than sources perceived to be trustworthy.

This increase in elaboration occurred primarily for individuals who are not intrinsically motivated to elaborate (i.e., low in need for cognition; Cacioppo & Petty, 1982), prompting them to elaborate when they would normally forgo such effortful processing. That is, an untrustworthy source increased elaboration under conditions when individuals would likely not normally have elaborated. In contrast, individuals who intrinsically enjoy elaboration (i.e., high need for cognition individuals) elaborated the messages equally regardless of source trustworthiness. Kaufman, Stasson, and Hart (1999) uncovered a similar pattern of results. Low need for cognition participants were more likely to elaborate the information presented by an untrustworthy (i.e., *National Enquirer*) than trustworthy (i.e., *Washington Post*) source.

Why does source trustworthiness influence elaboration? The ELM postulates both that (a) individuals are motivated to hold correct attitudes and that (b) although individuals are motivated to hold correct attitudes, the amount and nature of the elaboration on which these attitudes are based varies. In combination, these two postulates offer the explanation that source trustworthiness influences assurance of accuracy, and it is this assurance of accuracy that can influence elaboration. When a source is perceived to be expert and trustworthy (and hence likely to provide accurate information), individuals can be reasonably confident of the accuracy of their attitudes by merely accepting the position advocated. When a source is perceived to be an expert but of low trustworthiness, however, a message recipient cannot be assured of accuracy, and instead must scrutinize the information in order to be assured of an accurate attitude. As such, assuming the source has expertise (and is able to be accurate), perceived trustworthiness can influence the extent to which individuals engage in thinking.

Another source characteristic that has been found to affect message elaboration is the degree to which a source is stigmatized or not. Specifically, research has provided evidence that when the source of a message is a member of a stigmatized group (e.g., gay or African American), message recipients are more likely to elaborate than when the source is a member of a nonstigmatized group (White & Harkins, 1995). Interestingly, this influence of source stigma is apparent only for people who reject prejudicial beliefs (e.g., are low in modern racism or homophobia; Petty, Fleming, & White, 1999). Individuals low in prejudice might be chronically concerned that stigmatized individuals are treated unfairly by themselves or others. As such, they pay particular attention to (i.e., elaborate) information presented by stigmatized sources in order to assure that the sources are treated fairly.

Other variables that have been found to increase elaboration include whether the key arguments are presented as questions or assertions, the number of message sources, and the expectedness of a position. For example, several studies have shown that when a person is not normally motivated to think about the message arguments, more thinking can be provoked by summarizing the major arguments as *questions* rather than as *assertions* (Howard 1990; Petty, Cacioppo, & Heesacker, 1981; Swasy & Munch 1985). Thus, if an argument in a radio commercial was followed by a question (Isn't this candidate the best one?) rather than by an assertion (This candidate is the best one), greater processing of the argument presented would result. Greater thinking about a message can also be induced by having the individual arguments presented by multiple sources rather than just one (Harkins & Petty, 1981; Moore & Reardon, 1987). The multiple source effect is attenuated if people suspect that the multiple sources are not providing independent analyses of the issue (Harkins & Petty, 1987; Wilder, 1990).

When some feature of the message is unexpected, processing can be increased (e.g., Maheswaran & Chaiken, 1991). For example, if a newspaper headline implied that many people favored something that the message recipient disliked or that few people favored something the recipient liked, message scrutiny can be increased over cases in which the headline implied that few favored what the recipient disliked or many favored what the recipient liked (Baker & Petty, 1994). Of course, the enhanced thinking evoked by rhetorical questions, multiple sources, or surprising headlines will aid persuasion only if the arguments in the communication are subjectively cogent. The enhanced thinking will be detrimental to persuasion if the arguments are found to be specious.

As outlined in Fig. 7.2, having the necessary motivation to process a message is not sufficient for the central route to persuasion to occur. People must also have the ability to process the message. For example, a complex or long message might require more than one exposure for maximal processing, even if the recipient was highly motivated to think about it. The increased processing with multiple exposures should lead to more favorable thoughts and attitudes if the arguments are strong, but to more counterarguments and less-favorable attitudes if the arguments are weak (Cacioppo & Petty, 1989). Of course, repetition is just one variable that has an impact on a person's ability to think about a message. For example, if a message is accompanied by distraction (Petty, Wells, & Brock, 1976) or if the speaker talks too fast (Smith & Shaffer, 1991), thinking about the message will be disrupted. When strong arguments are presented, disrupting thinking should diminish persuasion, but when weak arguments are presented, disrupting thinking should enhance persuasion by reducing counterarguing (see Petty & Brock, 1981). Different media sources have an impact on people's ability to think about the message. Specifically, people are generally better able to process messages in media that allow self-pacing (magazines, Internet) than those that are controlled externally (e.g., radio and television; Chaiken & Eagly, 1976; Wright, 1981).

A consideration of motivational and ability variables together suggests some interesting effects. For example, research shows clearly that moderate repetition of a message can be beneficial if arguments and cues are positive, but repeating the same message over and over eventually leads to boredom and reduced effectiveness. This "wearout" effect occurs regardless of whether the message is on a topic of high or low interest (Sawyer, 1981). Because of this, a number of investigators have suggested that introducing some variation into the repeated ads should forestall the inevitable tedium effect (see Pechman & Stewart, 1989). The ELM suggests that different kinds of message variation should be attempted in a media campaign depending on the recipient's overall motivation to think about the issue of the campaign. In a test of this hypothesis, Schumann, Petty, and Clemons (1990) found that for highly motivated message recipients (those expecting to make an imminent decision about the issue discussed in the communications), repeated presentations on the same topic could be made more effective if the messages varied the substantive arguments that they presented. Variation in peripheral cues made no difference. On the other hand, for recipients low in motivation, variation in simple cues across repeated exposures enhanced the effectiveness of the campaign, but variation in arguments did not.

Objective Versus Biased Thinking.   In addition to influencing a person's general motivation or ability to think about a message, Fig. 7.2 indicates that variables can also have an impact on persuasion by influencing the *nature* of the thoughts that come to mind. That is, some features of the persuasion situation increase the likelihood of favorable thoughts being elicited, but others increase the likelihood of unfavorable thoughts coming to mind. Although the subjective cogency of the arguments used in a message is a prime determinant of whether favorable or unfavorable thoughts are elicited when message thinking is high, other variables can also be influential in determining whether favorable or unfavorable thoughts predominate (Petty & Cacioppo, 1990). For example, instilling "reactance" in message recipients by telling them that they have no choice but to be persuaded on an important issue *motivates* counterarguing, even when the arguments used are strong (Brehm, 1966; Petty & Cacioppo, 1979a). Thus, biased thinking often reduces the impact of message quality on persuasion (Manstead et al., 2001; Petty & Cacioppo, 1986a). Similarly, people who possess accessible attitudes bolstered by considerable attitude-congruent knowledge are better *able* to defend their attitudes than those who have inaccessible attitudes or attitudes with a minimal underlying foundation (Fazio & Williams, 1986; Wood 1982).

Sometimes variables bias people's thinking and influence their responses to a persuasive message without any awareness of the effect. At other times, however, people can become aware of some potentially contaminating influence on their thoughts and judgments. To the extent that people become aware of a possible bias and want to correct for it, they can take steps to debias their judgments. According to the Flexible Correction Model (FCM) of debiasing (Petty & Wegener, 1993; Wegener & Petty, 1997), to the extent that people become aware of a potential contaminating factor and are motivated and able to correct for it, they consult their intuitive theory of the direction and magnitude of the bias and adjust their judgment accordingly (see also Wilson & Brekke, 1994). Because people are not always aware of a biasing factor, as we noted previously, a high elaboration attitude is not necessarily bias free. Even attempts to correct for bias do not necessarily produce bias free judgments because people can be unaware of the actual magnitude or direction of bias and therefore make an inaccurate correction.

Arguments Versus Peripheral Cues.   As we noted before, when people have the motivation and ability to think about an issue, they scrutinize the issue-relevant information presented, such as the arguments provided in the communication. An argument is a piece of information that is relevant to determining the true merits of the position taken. Although we ordinarily think of arguments as features of the message content itself, source, recipient, and other factors can also serve as arguments. For example, if a spokesperson for a beauty product says that "if you use this product, you will look like me," the source's own physical attractiveness serves as relevant information for evaluating the effectiveness of the product (Petty & Cacioppo, 1984c). Or, a person might look to their own emotional state to provide evidence about the merits of something (e.g., "If I don't feel happy in your presence, I must not love you"). Just as source, recipient, and other factors can serve as persuasive arguments in the appropriate context, features of the persuasive message can serve as peripheral cues. A peripheral cue is a feature of the persuasion context that allows favorable or unfavorable attitude formation even in the absence of an effortful consideration of the true merits of the object or issue. Thus, just as source factors such as how expert or attractive the source is (Chaiken, 1980; Petty, Cacioppo, & Goldman, 1981; Petty, Cacioppo, & Schumann, 1983) can serve as peripheral cues when motivation or ability to think are low, so too can the mere number of arguments in the message (Aaker & Maheswaran, 1997; Alba & Marmorstein, 1987; Petty & Cacioppo, 1984a) and the length of the arguments used (Wood, Kallgren, & Priesler, 1985; see also Petty, Wheeler, & Bizer, 1999).

Summary.   The ELM holds that as the likelihood of elaboration is increased (as determined by factors such as the personal relevance of the message and the number of times it is repeated), the perceived quality of the issue-relevant information presented becomes a more important determinant of persuasion. Effortful evaluation of this information can proceed in a relatively objective or a relatively biased fashion, however. As the elaboration likelihood is decreased, peripheral cues become more important in determining any attitude change that occurs. That is, when the elaboration likelihood is high, the central route to persuasion dominates, but when the elaboration likelihood is low, the peripheral route takes precedence (see Petty, 1994; Petty & Wegener, 1999, for additional discussion of the operation of central and peripheral processes along the elaboration likelihood continuum).[5]

---

[5]As we have noted previously, the accumulated research on persuasion has pointed to many variables that can be used to either increase or decrease the amount of thinking about a persuasive message, and render that thinking relatively favorable or unfavorable. Although we have focused on motivational and ability variables that can be modified by external means (e.g., including rhetorical questions in a message to increase thinking about the arguments), other determinants of motivation and ability to process a message are dispositional (e.g., people high in "need for cognition" tend to chronically engage in and enjoy thinking, Cacioppo & Petty, 1982; Cacioppo, Petty, Feinstein, & Jarvis, 1996).

Multiple Roles for Variables in the Elaboration Likelihood Model

Now that we have explained the specific roles that variables can take on in persuasion settings, it is important to note that one of the most powerful features of the ELM is that it holds that any *one* variable can have an impact on persuasion by serving in different roles in different situations. That is, the same feature of a persuasive message can, depending on the context, serve as an issue-relevant argument or a peripheral cue, affect the motivation or ability to think about the message, bias the nature of the thoughts that come to mind, or affect structural properties of the thoughts such as how accessible they are or how much confidence people have in them.

If any one variable can influence persuasion by several means, it becomes critical to identify the general conditions under which the variable acts in each of the different roles or the ELM becomes descriptive rather than predictive (cf., Stiff, 1986). The ELM holds that when the elaboration likelihood is high (such as when perceived personal relevance and knowledge are high, the message is easy to understand, no distractions are present, and so on), people typically know that they want to and are able to evaluate the merits of the arguments presented, and they do so. Variables in the persuasion setting are likely to have little direct impact on evaluations by serving as simple peripheral cues in these situations. Instead, when the elaboration likelihood is high, a variable can serve as an argument if it is relevant to the merits of the issue, the variable can determine the nature of the ongoing information processing activity (e.g., it might bias the ongoing thinking), or the variable can influence structural properties of the cognitive responses that occur (e.g., the confidence with which they are held). On the other hand, when the elaboration likelihood is low (e.g., low personal relevance or knowledge, complex message, many distractions), people know that they do not want to or are not able to evaluate the merits of the arguments presented, or they do not even consider exerting effort to process the message. If any evaluation is formed under these conditions, it is likely to be the result of relatively simple associations or inferences based on salient cues. Finally, when the elaboration likelihood is moderate (e.g., uncertain personal relevance, moderate knowledge, moderate complexity), people may be uncertain as to whether or not the message warrants or needs scrutiny and whether or not they are capable of providing this analysis. In these situations they may examine the persuasion context for indications (e.g., Is the source trustworthy?) of whether or not they are interested in or should process the message. A few examples should help to clarify the multiple roles that a variable can have in different situations.

Multiple Roles for Source Factors. Consider first the multiple processes by which source factors, such as expertise or attractiveness, can have an impact on persuasion (see Petty & Cacioppo, 1984c). In various studies, source factors have been found to influence persuasion by serving as a peripheral cue when the likelihood of thinking was low. For example, when the personal relevance of a message was low, highly expert sources produced more persuasion than sources of low expertise regardless of the quality of the arguments they presented (Petty, Cacioppo, & Goldman, 1981; see also Chaiken, 1980).[6] On the other hand, in several studies in which the personal relevance of the message was not specified and nothing else was done to make the likelihood of thinking especially high or low (i.e., moderate elaboration likelihood), the source factors of expertise and attractiveness affected how much thinking people did about the message (Heesacker, Petty, & Cacioppo, 1983; Moore, Hausknecht, & Thamodaran, 1986; Puckett, Petty, Cacioppo, & Fisher, 1983). That is, attractive and expert sources led to more persuasion when the arguments were strong, but to less persuasion when the arguments were weak. The self-monitoring scale (see Snyder, 1987) has been used to distinguish people who tend to think more about what experts have to say (i.e., low self-monitors) from those who are more interested in what attractive sources have to say (i.e., high self-monitors; DeBono & Harnish, 1988).

When the likelihood of thinking is very high, source factors take on other roles. For example, if a source factor is relevant to the merits of a message, it can serve as a persuasive argument. Thus, as noted earlier, an attractive endorser might provide persuasive visual evidence for the effectiveness of a beauty product (Petty & Cacioppo, 1984c). In addition, Chaiken and Maheswaran (1994) demonstrated a biasing effect on information processing of source expertise. When recipients under high-elaboration conditions received an ambiguous message (i.e., not clearly strong or weak), expertise significantly affected the valence of the cognitive responses generated (i.e., expertise biased message processing). When the likelihood of thinking was low (i.e., the message was on an unimportant topic), expertise did not affect message-relevant thoughts and simply acted as a persuasion cue (see also Shavitt, Swan, Lowery, & Wanke, 1994).

Under high-elaboration conditions, source factors have also been found to influence persuasion by affecting the confidence people have in the validity of the thoughts they have in response to the message. In one study (Briñol, Tormala, & Petty, 2001), college students read a persuasive

---

[6]In studies varying expertise or attractiveness, source trustworthiness is assumed to be high.

message containing a set of strong arguments in favor of phosphate detergents. All participants were told to think about the message and to list the thoughts that came to mind. Because the message was composed of convincing arguments, recipients generated mostly favorable thoughts toward the proposal. After receiving the message, but just prior to reporting their attitudes, participants were led to believe that the message was written either by a government environmental agency (high credibility) or by the detergent manufacturer (low credibility source). The credibility of the source could not affect the nature of the thoughts elicited because this manipulation followed message processing. However, the manipulation affected the confidence that participants reported in the validity of their thoughts. That is, more confidence was reported when the message was said to have come from a high rather than a low credibility source. Because the arguments were strong and the thoughts mostly favorable, relying on these thoughts produced more favorable attitudes.

Under high-elaboration conditions, the role that source factors play depends on a number of factors. First, the source factor can serve as a message argument if it contains information central to the merits of the object. Otherwise, the source factor can either bias the direction of the thoughts or affect a person's confidence in the thoughts that are generated. The former role is more likely when the source information precedes the message where it can influence thought generation, but if the source information comes after the message, the latter role is more likely.

Finally, if people were made aware of the potentially biasing impact of source factors (either on information processing or on judgment), they might attempt to correct for this influence. For example, in one study Petty, Wegener, and White (1998) found that highly likable sources produced less persuasion than dislikable sources when participants tried to correct for this potential bias. This reversed effect of liking was a result of "overcorrection" (i.e., people overestimating the effect of source likability on their judgments; see also Wegener & Petty, 1995).

Multiple Roles for Message Factors. As we noted earlier, the mere number of arguments in a message can serve as a peripheral cue when people are either unmotivated or unable to think about the information. When motivation and ability are high, however, the informational items in a message are not simply counted as cues, but instead the information is processed for its cogency. When the number of items in a message serves as a cue (low-elaboration conditions), adding weak reasons in support of a position enhances persuasion, but when the items in a message serve as arguments, adding weak reasons reduces persuasion (Aaker & Maheswaran, 1997; Alba & Marmorstein, 1987; Friedrich, Fetherstonhaugh, Casey, & Gallagher, 1996; Petty & Cacioppo, 1984a).

One study examined multiple roles for message factors at three distinct levels of recipient elaboration. In this research, a regular advertisement for an unknown product was contrasted with an "upward comparison" ad that compared the new product to a well-established one (Pechmann & Estaban, 1993). Unlike a regular message that simply provides support for its position (e.g., You should vote for Candidate X because...), an upward comparison message suggests that the critical issue, product, or person is similar to one that is already seen as desirable (e.g., You should vote for Candidate X, who like Person Y, favors tax cuts). In order to examine the multiple roles for this message variable, regular and upward comparison ads containing either strong or weak arguments were presented following instructions and procedures designed to elicit either a relatively low, moderate, or high motivation to think about the critical ad.

Effectiveness of the ads was assessed by asking recipients to rate their intentions to purchase the product advertised. When the low-motivation instructions were used, the upward comparison ad produced more favorable intentions than the regular ad, but strong arguments did not produce more favorable intentions than weak ones. That is, under the low-elaboration likelihood conditions, the comparison with the well-known and liked product served as a simple peripheral cue, and argument processing was minimal. When the high-motivation conditions were examined, the opposite resulted. That is, under the high-elaboration instructions, the strong arguments produced more favorable intentions than the weak ones, but the upward comparison was completely ineffective as a cue for producing more favorable intentions. Finally, when the moderate motivation conditions were analyzed, the use of an upward comparison ad was found to enhance processing of the message arguments. Specifically, when the upward comparison ad used strong arguments, it led to more persuasion than the direct ad, but when the upward comparison ad used weak arguments, it produced less persuasion than the regular ad.

The mere number of arguments and the use of upward comparison are only some of the message factors that can influence persuasion by serving in different roles in different situations. To take one more example, consider the complexity of the message (e.g., difficult vocabulary, sentence structure). Such complexity could serve as a simple cue when the elaboration likelihood is low. For example, a person might use the heuristic, "the person doesn't seem to know what he is talking about, therefore I can't agree." Alternatively, the person might reason that "the person seems to know a lot about this, therefore the position is good." Whether one inference or the other is reached might depend on factors such as the person's self-esteem or perceived knowledge on the issue.

When the elaboration likelihood is not constrained to be high or low, complexity might affect the amount of thinking that occurs. That is, some people (e.g., those high in need for cognition; Cacioppo & Petty, 1982), might be challenged by a message that seems complex, but other individuals (e.g., those low in need for cognition) might eschew processing a message that is perceived as difficult (Evans & Petty, 1998). Finally, under high-elaboration conditions, other roles for message complexity are possible. In one study, for instance, it was shown that under high-elaboration conditions, complex information undermined people's confidence in their thoughts (Briñol & Petty, 2001).

Multiple Roles for Recipient Factors.   According to the ELM, recipient factors can serve in the same multiple roles as source and message factors. Consider the impact that a person's mood state has on persuasion. The mass medium of television has special power to present messages (commercials) in contexts in which people's moods vary (e.g., due to the television program they are watching). According to the ELM, when the likelihood of elaboration is relatively low, a person's mood should impact attitudes by a peripheral process. Consistent with this view, a number of studies have shown that the nonthoughtful "classical conditioning" of affect to an attitude object occurs more easily when the likelihood of thinking is low (e.g., Cacioppo, Marshall-Goodell, Tassinary, & Petty, 1992; Gorn, 1982; Priester, Cacioppo, & Petty, 1996). Also under low-elaboration conditions, affective states have been postulated to influence attitudes by a simple inference process in which misattribution of the cause of the mood state to the persuasive message or to the attitude object occurs (e.g., I must feel good because I like or agree with the message advocacy; see Petty & Cacioppo, 1983; Schwarz, 1990).

As the likelihood of elaboration increases, mood takes on different roles (see also Forgas, 1995). Specifically, when the elaboration likelihood is more moderate, mood has been shown to have an impact on the extent of argument elaboration. According to the hedonic contingency theory (Wegener & Petty, 1994, 1996), happy people tend to pay attention to the hedonic rewards of situations, and thus they are more likely than are sad people to process a message that is thought to be hedonically rewarding if processed (see Wegener, Petty, & Smith, 1995). On the other hand, if the message will not be rewarding to think about (e.g., because it is on a counterattitudinal or a depressing topic), then sad individuals will engage in greater message processing than will happy people because sadness tends to put people in a problem-solving mind-set (Schwarz, Bless, & Bohner, 1991).

When the elaboration likelihood is high, the ELM holds that affective states can influence attitudes by influencing the nature of the thoughts that come to mind. Memory research has demonstrated that material of a positive valence is more accessible in memory when people are in positive rather than in negative moods, whereas negatively valenced material is more accessible when they are in negative rather than positive moods (e.g., see Blaney, 1986; Bower, 1981; Isen, 1987). The increased accessibility of mood-congruent material in memory may lead to mood-congruent associations that may further influence the evaluation of the target. In other words, when the elaboration likelihood is high, mood can introduce a positive or negative bias to the thoughts generated in response to the persuasive message. Thus, positive mood can have a similar effect on attitudes under high- and low-elaboration conditions, but the process is different. In one examination of this, students watched a television commercial in the context of a program that induced either a happy or a neutral mood (Petty, Schumann, Richman, & Strathman, 1993). The likelihood of thinking about the critical ad was varied by telling some of the students that they would be allowed to select a free gift at the end of the experiment from a variety of brands of the target product (high involvement) or that they would be allowed to select a free gift from another product category (low involvement). Following exposure to the television program containing the ads, the students reported on their moods, rated their attitudes toward the target product, and listed the thoughts they had during the message. The results of this study revealed that the pleasant program led to a more positive mood and more positive evaluations of the product under both high- and low-elaboration conditions. Importantly, and consistent with the notion that a pleasant mood produces positive attitudes by different processes under high- and low-elaboration conditions, it was found that a pleasant mood was associated with more positive thoughts about the product when the elaboration likelihood was high, but not when it was low. Figure 7.4 presents the results from causal path analyses that simultaneously estimated the three paths between (a) manipulated mood and attitude toward the product, (b) manipulated mood and proportion of positive thoughts generated, and (c) proportion of positive thoughts and attitude toward the product. Under low-involvement (low-elaboration) conditions, mood had a direct effect on attitudes, but did not influence thoughts (see left panel). In contrast, under high- involvement (high-elaboration) conditions, mood had no direct effect on attitudes. Instead, mood influenced the production of positive thoughts, which in turn had an impact on attitudes (see right panel).

One way in which mood biases thoughts is by affecting how likely people think the consequences mentioned in the message are. Specifically, when in a good mood and thinking carefully, people believe that positive consequences mentioned in the communication are more likely, but negative consequences are less likely. The opposite occurs for a negative mood (e.g., Johnson & Tversky, 1983). Thus, positively framed arguments (e.g., if you stop smoking, you will live longer) are more effective when thoughtful people are in a positive rather than a negative mood because people overestimate the likelihood of the positive consequence, but negatively framed arguments (if you don't stop smoking, you'll die sooner) are

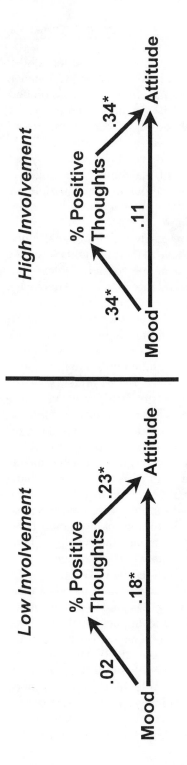

FIG. 7.4. Direct and indirect effects of positive mood on attitudes under high- and low-involvement conditions. Data in the left panel show that when involvement is low and people are not motivated to process the message, mood has a direct effect on attitudes. Data in the right panel show that when involvement is high and people are motivated to process the message, the effect of positive mood on attitudes is mediated by the generation of positive thoughts. (Figure adapted from Petty, Schumann, Richman, & Strathman, 1993.)

more effective in a negative than in a positive mood because thoughtful people overestimate the likelihood of the negative consequence (Wegener, Petty, & Klein, 1994). Research suggests that the effects of moods on perceived likelihoods are quite specific such that sad moods are especially effective in increasing the perceived likelihood of sad consequences and angering states are especially effective in increasing the perceived likelihood of angering consequences (DeSteno, Petty, Rucker, & Wegener, 2000). Because of this, more specific types of matching of messages to emotional states could prove effective in situations in which people are being thoughtful (e.g., presenting sad arguments to sad people but angering arguments to angry people).

In addition to biasing thoughts, recent research has shown that mood states can also affect the confidence people have in their thoughts when the elaboration likelihood is high. Research in nonpersuasion contexts has shown that a positive mood can enhance confidence in general knowledge structures (such as schemata, scripts, and stereotypes), and that happy individuals rely on these knowledge structures more than neutral or negative mood people (Bless, Clore, Schwarz, Golisano, Rabe, & Wolk, 1996; Krauth-Gruber & Ric, 2000). Similarly, in a series of studies, Briñol, Petty, and Barden (2001) found that high need for cognition individuals made to feel sad after message exposure came to have less confidence in the thoughts they generated during message exposure than people who were made to feel happy after message exposure. When the message was strong and elicited mostly favorable thoughts, causing doubt in these thoughts (via sad mood) led to reduced persuasion relative to causing confidence (via happy mood). But, when the message was weak and elicited mostly unfavorable thoughts, causing doubt in these thoughts led to more persuasion relative to causing confidence. In contrast, individuals low in motivation to elaborate (i.e., low need for cognition) simply showed more persuasion with happy than sad moods, regardless of argument quality. These low thoughtful individuals used their current mood state as a peripheral cue and generalized from their current mood state to the message.

Finally, it is important to note that the effects we have outlined for mood under different elaboration conditions assume that moods are not so salient that they are perceived as biasing. When moods are made salient and people perceive a possible biasing impact, they will often attempt to correct their judgments for the perceived contaminating impact of the emotional state (Schwarz & Clore, 1973). This can cause judgments to move in a direction opposite to people's intuitive theories of bias (Wegener & Petty, 1997, 2001). Thus, if people think a positive mood has a favorable impact on their judgments and they overestimate this bias, the corrected judgment in a positive mood can be more negative than the corrected judgment in a negative mood (e.g., Berkowitz, Jaffee, Jo, & Troccoli, 2000; Ottati & Isbell, 1996).

Consequences of Multiple Roles.   Although we have only provided illustrative examples of particular source, message, and recipient variables, the accumulated studies support the ELM notion that variables can serve in different roles in different situations (see Petty & Wegener, 1998a). That is, various source, message, and recipient variables have been shown to influence attitudes as: (a) a peripheral cue under low-elaboration likelihood conditions, (b) a determinant of the extent of thinking about the message under moderate elaboration conditions, (c) a message argument when the variable was relevant to the attitude object and elaboration was high, and finally, depending on whether the variable was introduced before or after the message to (d) bias message processing, or to (e) influence confidence in one's message-relevant cognitive responses.

Because any one variable can produce persuasion in multiple ways, it is important to understand the process by which the variable has influenced a person's attitude. For example, our discussion of the two routes to persuasion suggests that if a good mood has produced persuasion by serving as a simple cue under low-elaboration conditions, the attitude induced will be less accessible, less persistent, less resistant, and less predictive of behavior than if a good mood produced the same amount of persuasion, but worked by increasing positive thoughts to the message arguments under high-elaboration conditions. In empirical research on media campaigns in a variety of domains (see Rice & Atkin, 1989), many source, message, recipient, and contextual variables have been examined. Relatively little attention has been paid, however, to the processes by which these variables work. The ELM holds that the variables that determine persuasion can work by different processes in different situations, and that the process, central or peripheral, by which the variable induces change is critical for understanding the consequences of any attitude change that occurs (see Fig. 7.2).

Directions for Future Research

Thus far we have reviewed evidence that has supported the primary ELM postulates about the processes responsible for attitude change. Before addressing the links between attitude change and behavior change, it is useful to consider where some future basic research on persuasion processes might be directed. We explained that an important factor in the ELM is how much thinking a person is motivated or able to engage in regarding an attitude issue. Because of this, most of the research on the ELM to date has focused on variables that initiate message processing. Little attention has been paid to variables that determine when that processing will stop. Because most of the messages used in laboratory research are relatively short (e.g., 1–3 minutes; 1–2 pages of text), it is likely that once individuals embark on the central route, they will continue to think about the message until the message ends. On the other hand, the longer the message becomes, the less likely it seems that people will continue to diligently process every argument that is presented. At some point, the individual becomes tired, loses interest, or has considered enough information to come to a reasonable conclusion. Once this point is reached, the person becomes less attentive to the remaining message. As attention begins to wander, the person may become more aware of peripheral features of the persuasion context or may turn attention completely to noncommunication factors. In sum, future research might be directed profitably not only at additional variables and psychological conditions that initiate message processing ("start rules"), but also on those that determine when message processing will cease ("stop rules," Petty, Tormala, Hawkins, & Wegener, 2001) or shift processing from one mode to another ("shift rules," Mazursky & Schul, 2000).

ATTITUDE-BEHAVIOR LINKS

As we noted previously, the ELM provides a framework for understanding persuasion (yielding) processes. Once a person's attitude has changed, however, behavior change requires that the person's new attitude, rather than the old attitude or previous habits, guide action. Considerable research has addressed the links between attitudes and behavior, and a number of situational and dispositional factors have been shown to enhance attitude-behavior consistency (see Ajzen, 1988, for a comprehensive review).

Two general models of the process by which attitudes guide behavior have achieved widespread acceptance. One type is exemplified by Fishbein and Ajzen's (1975) "theory of reasoned action," which assumes that "people consider the implications of their actions before they decide to engage or not engage in a given behavior" (Fishbein & Ajzen, 1975, p. 5). In this model, people are hypothesized to form intentions to perform or not perform behaviors, and these intentions are based on the person's attitude toward the behavior as well as perceptions of the opinions of significant others (norms). The model focuses on the relatively thoughtful processing involved in considering the personal costs and benefits of engaging in a behavior. In particular, the model focuses on the perceived likelihood that certain benefits will be obtained or costs avoided and on the desirability or aversiveness of those benefits or costs. The model has accumulated considerable empirical support (Sheppard, Hartwick, & Warshaw, 1988). Ajzen (1991) has expanded the model into a "theory of planned behavior" and has shown that in addition to attitudes and norms, it is important to consider a person's perceptions of control over the behavior.

In contrast to the thoughtful processing highlighted by the theories of reasoned action and planned behavior, Fazio (1990, 1995) has proposed that much behavior is rather spontaneous and that attitudes guide behavior by a relatively automatic process. That is, if the relevant attitude comes to mind, consistent behavior is likely to follow. Fazio argued that attitudes can guide behavior without any deliberate reflection or reasoning if (a) the attitude is accessed spontaneously by the mere presence of the attitude object, and (b) the attitude colors perception of the object so that if the attitude is favorable (or unfavorable), the qualities of the object appear favorable (or unfavorable). Fazio (1990) further notes that motivational and ability factors are important in determining whether the reasoned action or the automatic activation process occurs. That is, for behavioral decisions that are high in perceived personal consequences, attitudes are likely to guide behavior by a deliberate reflection process, but when perceived consequences are low, spontaneous attitude activation should be more important as a determinant of behavior. Similarly, as the time allowed for a decision is reduced, the importance of spontaneous attitude activation processes should increase over more deliberative processes. When there is sufficient motivation and ability to think about one's behavior, a person may reflect on the costs and benefits of the anticipated action. Interestingly, depending on what costs and benefits are salient at the moment, this process could lead to a behavior that is consistent or inconsistent with the underlying attitude. For example, the underlying attitude might be based on a combination of both emotional and cognitive (e.g., belief-based) factors, but if reflection time is high, people might overweight cognitive over emotional considerations leading to later dissatisfaction with the decision (see Wilson, Dunn, Kraft, & Lisle, 1989). When motivation and ability to reflect are low, however, people's actions are determined by whichever attitudes are the most accessible.[7]

In some domains an accessible attitude is easily translated into behavior (e.g., I like candidate X, I will vote for this candidate). In other domains, however, translating new attitudes into new behaviors is rather complex, even if the person has the desire to act on the attitude (e.g., I want to consume a low-fat diet, but how do I do this?). Thus, for some media campaigns, attitude change, though an important first step, may still be insufficient to produce the desired behavioral responses, even if appropriate attitudes were formed by the central route. People may also need to rehearse the attitude sufficiently so that it overcomes and replaces past attitudes (Petty, Gleicher, & Jarvis, 1993; Wilson et al., 2000), or they may need to acquire new skills and self-perceptions of confidence that

---

[7]Because attitudes formed by the central route tend to be more accessible than attitudes formed by the peripheral route, peripheral cues in the behavioral environment are likely to have an impact on immediate actions only when the likelihood of reflection in the current situation is low and there are no accessible attitudes to guide behavior.

allow newly acquired attitudes and intentions to be translated into action. Bandura's (1977, 1986) social-cognitive theory provides a framework to understand these processes (see chap. 6).

SUMMARY AND CONCLUSIONS

Although considerable research on mass media effects has shown that it is possible for media messages to change the knowledge or facts that people have about some object, issue, or person, we have argued that knowledge reception does not invariably result in attitude and behavior change. Our brief review of the ELM and the research supporting it has emphasized that information will only be successful in producing enduring changes in attitudes and behavior if people are motivated and able to process the information and if this processing results in favorable thoughts and ideas that are integrated into the person's relatively enduring cognitive structure. Furthermore, once attitudes have changed, implementing changes in some behaviors may require overcoming past attitudes and learning new skills and perceptions of self-efficacy. Thus, current work on attitude and behavior change may help to account for some unsuccessful media campaigns in which knowledge acquisition failed to have attitudinal and/or behavioral consequences. First, the knowledge acquired may have been seen as irrelevant by the recipients or may have led to unfavorable rather than favorable reactions. Second, even if favorable reactions were produced, people may have lacked confidence in those favorable thoughts, attenuating their reliance on them and reducing the likelihood of change. Third, even if appropriate attitude changes were induced, the changes may have been based on simple peripheral cues rather than on elaborative processing of the message. Thus, whatever changes were produced would be unlikely to persist over time and guide behavior. Fourth, even if attitude changes were produced by the central route, the people influenced may have lacked the necessary skills or self-confidence to translate their new attitudes into action, or the impact of attitudes on behavior may have been undermined by competing norms.

Perhaps the three most important issues raised in our review are (1) although some attitudes are based on an effortful reasoning process in which externally provided information is related to oneself and integrated into a coherent belief structure (central route), other attitudes are formed as a result of relatively simple cues in the persuasion environment (peripheral route); (2) any one variable (e.g., source expertise, mood) can be capable of inducing persuasion by either the central or the peripheral route in different situations by serving in one or more roles (i.e., affecting motivation or ability to think, biasing thinking, affecting thought confidence, serving as an argument, or a peripheral cue); and (3) although both central and peripheral route processes can lead to attitudes similar in their valence (how favorable or unfavorable they are), there are important consequences of the manner of attitude change such that more thoughtful attitude changes tend to be more consequential than less thoughtful ones.

If the goal of a mass media influence attempt is to produce long-lasting changes in attitudes with behavioral consequences, the central route to persuasion appears to be the preferred persuasion strategy. If the goal is immediate formation of a new attitude, even if it is relatively ephemeral (e.g., attitudes toward the charity sponsoring a telethon), the peripheral route may prove acceptable. Influence via the central route requires that the recipient of the new information have the motivation and ability to process it. As noted previously, one of the most important determinants of motivation to think about a message is the perceived personal relevance of that message. Most of the media messages people receive are probably not perceived as directly relevant, and they have few immediate personal consequences. Thus, many of these messages will be ignored or processed primarily for peripheral cues. An important goal of any persuasion strategy aimed at enduring change will be to increase people's motivation to think about the messages by increasing the perceived personal relevance of the communications or employing other techniques to enhance processing (e.g., ending arguments with questions rather than statements; using multiple sources).

In conclusion, we note that research on mass media persuasion has come a long way from the early optimistic (and scary) notion that the mere presentation of information was sufficient to produce persuasion and the subsequent pessimistic view that media influence attempts were typically ineffective. We now know that media influence, like other forms of influence, is a complex, though explicable, process. We know that the extent and nature of a person's cognitive responses to external information may be more important than the information itself. We know that attitudes can be changed in different ways, such as central versus peripheral routes, and that some attitude changes are more accessible, stable, resistant, and predictive of behavior than others. We also know that even apparently simple variables such as how likable a source is or what mood a person is in can produce persuasion by very different processes in different situations.

REFERENCES

Aaker, J. L., & Maheswaran, D. (1997). The effect of cultural orientation on persuasion. *Journal of Consumer Research, 24,* 315–328.

Adams, C. (1993, April 7). The power of the media. *Michigan Chronicle,* p. A7.

Ajzen, I. (1988). *Attitudes, personality, and behavior.* Chicago: Dorsey Press.

Ajzen, I. (1991). The theory of planned behavior. *Organizational Behavior and Human Decision Processes, 50,* 179–210.

Alba, J. W., & Marmorstein, H. (1987). The effects of frequency knowledge on consumer decision making. *Journal of Consumer Research, 13,* 411–454.

Axsom, D., Yates, S., & Chaiken, S. (1987). Audience response as a heuristic cue in persuasion. *Journal of Personality and Social Psychology, 53,* 30–40.

Baker, S. M., & Petty, R. E. (1994). Majority and minority influence: Source advocacy as a determinant of message scrutiny. *Journal of Personality and Social Psychology, 67,* 5–19.

Bandura, A. (1977). *Social learning theory.* Upper Saddle River, NJ: Prentice Hall.

Bandura, A. (1986). *Social foundations of thought and action.* Upper Saddle River, NJ: Prentice Hall.

Bem, D. J. (1972). Self-perception theory. In L. Berkowitz (Ed.), *Advances in experimental social psychology* (Vol. 6, pp. 1–62). New York: Academic Press.

Berkowitz, L., Jaffee, S., Jo, E., & Troccoli, B. (2000). Some conditions affecting overcorrection of the judgment-distorting influence of one's feelings. In J. P. Forgas (Ed.), *Feeling and thinking: The role of affect in social cognition.* Cambridge: Cambridge University Press.

Blaney, P. H. (1986). Affect and memory: A review. *Psychological Bulletin, 99,* 229–246.

Bless, H., Clore, G. L., Schwarz, N., Golisano, V., Rabe, & Wolk. (1996). Mood and the use of scripts: Does a happy mood really lead to mindlessness? *Journal of Personality and Social Psychology, 71,* 665–679.

Bower, G. H. (1981). Mood and memory. *American Psychologist, 11,* 11–13.

Brehm, J. W. (1966). *A theory of psychological reactance.* New York: Academic Press.

Briñol, P., & Petty, R. E. (2001). *Multiples roles of message complexity.* (Working paper). Ohio State University, Columbus.

Briñol, P., Petty, R. E., & Barden, J. (2001). *Affect as a determinant of thought confidence.* (Working paper). Ohio State University, Columbus.

Briñol, P., Tormala, Z., & Petty, R. E. (2001). *Persuasive effects of source credibility: A multiple roles perspective.* (Working paper). Ohio State University, Columbus.

Bruvold, W. H., & Rundall, T. G. (1988). A meta-analysis and theoretical review of school based tobacco and alcohol intervention programs. *Psychology and Health, 2,* 53–78.

Burnkrant, R., & Unnava, R. (1989). Self-referencing: A strategy for increasing processing of message content. *Personality and Social Psychology Bulletin, 15,* 628–638.

Cacioppo, J. T., Marshall-Goodell, B. S., Tassinary, L. G., & Petty, R. E. (1992). Rudimentary determinants of attitudes: Classical conditioning is more effective when prior knowledge about the attitude stimulus is low than high. *Journal of Experimental Social Psychology, 28,* 207–233.

Cacioppo, J. T., & Petty, R. E. (1981). Social psychological procedures for cognitive response assessment: The thought listing technique. In T. Merluzzi, C. Glass, & M. Genest (Eds.), *Cognitive assessment* (pp. 309–342). New York: Guilford Press.

Cacioppo, J. T., & Petty, R. E. (1982). The need for cognition. *Journal of Personality and Social Psychology, 42,* 116–131.

Cacioppo, J. T., & Petty, R. E. (1989). Effects of message repetition on argument processing, recall, and persuasion. *Basic and Applied Social Psychology, 10,* 3–12.

Cacioppo, J. T., Petty, R. E., Feinstein, J., & Jarvis, W. B. G. (1996). Dispositional differences in cognitive motivation: The life and times of individuals varying in need for cognition. *Psychological Bulletin, 119,* 197–253.

Cacioppo, J. T., Petty, R. E., & Sidera, J. (1982). The effects of a salient self-schema on the evaluation of proattitudinal editorials: Top-down versus bottom-up message processing. *Journal of Experimental Social Psychology, 18,* 324–338.

Cartwright, D. (1949). Some principles of mass persuasion. *Human Relations, 2,* 253–267.

Chaiken, S. (1980). Heuristic versus systematic information processing and the use of source versus message cues in persuasion. *Journal of Personality and Social Psychology, 39,* 752–756.

Chaiken, S. (1987). The heuristic model of persuasion. In M. P. Zanna, J. Olson, & C. P. Herman (Eds.), *Social influence: The Ontario symposium* (Vol. 5, pp. 3–39). Hillsdale, NJ: Lawrence Erlbaum Associates.

Chaiken, S., & Eagly, A. H. (1976). Communication modality as a determinant of message persuasiveness and message comprehensibility. *Journal of Personality and Social Psychology, 34,* 605–614.

Chaiken, S., Liberman, A., & Eagly, A. H. (1989). Heuristic and systematic processing within and beyond the persuasion context. In J. Uleman & J. Bargh (Eds.), *Unintended thought* (pp. 212–252). New York: Guilford Press.

Chaiken, S., & Maheswaran, D. (1994). Heuristic processing can bias systematic processing: Effects of source credibility, argument ambiguity, and task importance on attitude judgment. *Journal of Personality and Social Psychology, 66,* 460–473.

Chaiken, S., & Trope, Y. (Eds.). (1999). *Dual-process theories in social psychology.* New York: Guilford Press.

DeBono, K., & Harnish, R. (1988). Source expertise, source attractiveness, and the processing of persuasive information: A functional approach. *Journal of Personality and Social Psychology, 55,* 541–546.

DeBono, K., & Packer, M. (1991). The effects of advertising appeal on perceptions of product quality. *Personality and Social Psychology Bulletin, 17,* 194–200.

DeSteno, D., Petty, R. E., Wegener, D. T., & Rucker, D. D. (2000). Beyond valence in the perception of likelihood: The role of emotion specificity. *Journal of Personality and Social Psychology, 78,* 397–416.

Devine, P. G. (1989). Stereotypes and prejudice: Their automatic and controlled components. *Journal of Personality and Social Psychology, 56,* 5–18.

Doob, L. (1935). *Propaganda, its psychology and technique.* New York: Holt.

Eagly, A. H., & Chaiken, S. (1993). *The psychology of attitudes.* Fort Worth, TX: Harcourt Brace Jovanovich.

Evans, L. M., & Petty, R. E. (1998, May). *The effect of expectations on knowledge use.* Presented at the annual meeting of the Midwestern Psychological Association, Chicago.

Fazio, R. H. (1990). Multiple processes by which attitudes guide behavior: The MODE model as an integrative framework. In M. Zanna (Ed.), *Advances in experimental social psychology* (Vol. 23, pp. 75–109). New York: Academic Press.

Fazio, R. (1995). Attitudes as object-evaluation associations: Determinants, consequences, and correlates of attitude accessibility. In R. E. Petty & J. A. Krosnick (Eds.), *Attitude strength: Antecedents and consequences* (pp. 247–282). Hillsdale, NJ: Lawrence Earlbaum Associates.

Fazio, R. H., & Williams, C. J. (1986). Attitude accessibility as a moderator of the attitude-perception and attitude-behavior relations: An investigation of the 1984 presidential election. *Journal of Personality and Social Psychology, 51,* 505–514.

Fishbein, M., & Ajzen, I. (1975). *Belief, attitude, intention, and behavior: An introduction to theory and research.* Reading, MA: Addison-Wesley.

Fiske, S. T., & Pavelchak, M. A. (1986). Category-based versus piecemeal-based affective responses: Developments in schema-triggered affect. In R. M. Sorrentino & E. T. Higgins (Eds.), *Handbook of motivation and cognition: Foundations of social behavior* (pp. 167–203). New York: Guilford Press.

Forgas, P. (1995). Mood and judgment: The affect infusion model (AIM). *Psychological Bulletin, 117,* 39–66.

Frey, D. (1986). Recent research on selective exposure to information. In L. Berkowitz (Ed.), *Advances in experimental social psychology* (Vol. 19, pp. 41–80). San Diego, CA: Academic Press.

Friedrich, J., Fetherstonhaugh, D., Casey, S., & Gallagher, D. (1996). Argument integration and attitude change: Suppression effects in the integration of one-sided arguments that vary in persuasiveness. *Personality and Social Psychology Bulletin, 22,* 179–191.

Gillig, P. M., & Greenwald, A. G. (1978). Is it time to lay the sleeper effect to rest? *Journal of Personality and Social Psychology, 29,* 132–139.

Gorn, G. J. (1982). The effects of music in advertising on choice behavior: A classical conditioning approach. *Journal of Marketing, 46,* 94–101.

Greenwald, A. G. (1968). Cognitive learning, cognitive response to persuasion, and attitude change. In A. Greenwald, T. Brock, & T. Ostrom (Eds.), *Psychological foundations of attitudes* (pp. 147–170). New York: Academic Press.

Greenwald, A. G., & Albert, S. M. (1968). Observational learning: A technique for elucidating S-R mediation processes. *Journal of Experimental Psychology, 76,* 273–278.

Greenwald, A. G., & Banaji, M. R. (1995). Implicit social cognition: Attitudes, self-esteem, and stereotypes. *Psychological Review, 102,* 4–27.

Gruder, C. L., Cook, T. D., Hennigan, K. M., Flay, B. R., Alessi, C., Halamaj, J. (1978). Empirical tests of the absolute sleeper effect predicted from the discounting cue hypothesis. *Journal of Personality and Social Psychology, 36,* 1061–1074.

Harkins, S. G., & Petty, R. E. (1981). The effects of source magnification cognitive effort on attitudes: An information processing view. *Journal of Personality and Social Psychology, 40,* 401–413.

Harkins, S. G., & Petty, R. E. (1987). Information utility and the multiple source effect in persuasion. *Journal of Personality and Social Psychology, 52,* 260–268.

Haugtvedt, C., & Petty, R. E. (1992). Personality and persuasion: Need for cognition moderates the persistance and resistance of attitude changes. *Journal of Personality and Social Psychology, 63,* 308–319.

Heesacker, M., Petty, R. E., & Cacioppo, J. T. (1983). Field dependence and attitude change: Source credibility can alter persuasion by affecting message-relevant thinking. *Journal of Personality, 51,* 653–666.

Hovland, C. I. (1954). Effects of the mass media of communication. In G. Lindzey (Ed.), *Handbook of social psychology* (Vol. 2, pp. 1062–1103). Cambridge, MA: Addison-Wesley.

Hovland, C. I., Janis, I., & Kelley, H. H. (1953). *Communication and persuasion.* New Haven, CT: Yale University Press.

Hovland, C. I., Lumsdaine, A., & Sheffield, F. (1949). *Experiments on mass communication.* Princeton, NJ: Princeton University Press.

Howard, D. J. (1990). Rhetorical question effects on message processing and persuasion: The role of information availability and the elicitation of judgment. *Journal of Experimental Social Psychology, 26,* 217–239.

Hyman, H., & Sheatsley, P. (1947). Some reasons why information campaigns fail. *Public Opinion Quarterly, 11,* 412–423.

Isen, A. (1987). Positive affect, cognitive processes, and social behavior. *Advances in Experimental Social Psychology, 20,* 203–253.

Iyengar, S., & Kinder, D. R. (1987). *News that matters: Television and American opinion.* Chicago: University of Chicago Press.

Iyengar, S., Kinder, D. R., Peters, M. D., & Krosnick, J. A. (1984). The evening news and presidential evaluations. *Journal of Personality and Social Psychology, 46,* 778–787.

Janis, I. L., & King, B. T. (1954). The influence of role-playing on opinion change. *Journal of Abnormal and Social Psychology, 49,* 211–218.

Johnson, E., & Tversy, A. (1983). Affect, generalization, and the perception of risk. *Journal of Personality and Social Psychology, 45,* 20–31.

Katz, D., & Lazarsfeld, P. R. (1955). *Personal influence.* New York: Free Press.

Kaufman, D., Stasson, M., & Hart, J. (1999). Are the tabloids always wrong or is that just what we think? Need for cognition and perceptions of articles in print media. *Journal of Applied Social Psychology, 29,* 1984–1997.

Kinder, B. N., Pape, N. E., & Walfish, S. (1980). Drug and alcohol education programs: A review of outcome studies. *International Journal of the Addictions, 15,* 1035–1054.

Klapper, J. T. (1960). *The effects of mass communication.* New York: Free Press.

Krauth-Gruber, S., & Ric, F. (2000). Affect and stereotypic thinking: A test of the mood-and-general-knowledge-model. *Personality and Social Psychology Bulletin, 26*, 1587–1597.

Lasswell, H. W. (1927). *Propaganda Techniques in the World War.* New York: Peter Smith.

Lasswell, H. W. (1964). The structure and function of communication in society. In L. Bryson (Ed.), *Communication of ideas* (pp. 37–51). New York: Cooper Square.

Lazarsfeld, P., Berelson, B., & Gaudet, H. (1948). *The people's choice.* New York: Columbia University Press.

Lee, A., & Lee, E. B. (1939). *The fine art of propaganda: A study of Father Coughlin's speeches.* New York: Harcourt, Brace.

Lippmann, W. (1922). *Public opinion.* New York: MacMillan.

Lohr, S. (1991, February 18). Troubled banks and the role of the press. *New York Times,* p. A33.

Lord, C. G., Ross, L., & Lepper, M. R. (1979). Biased assimilation and attitude polarization: The effects of prior theories on subsequently considered evidence. *Journal of Personality and Social Psychology, 37*, 2098–2109.

MacKuen, M. B. (1981). Social communication and the mass policy agenda. In M. B. MacKuen & S. L. Coombs (Eds.), *More than news: Media power in public affairs* (pp. 19–144). Beverly Hills, CA: Sage.

Maheswaran, D., & Chaiken, S. (1991). Promoting systematic processing in low motivation settings: Effect of incongruent information on processing and judgment. *Journal of Personality and Social Psychology, 61*, 13–25.

Mazursky, D., & Schul, Y. (2000). In the aftermath of invalidation: Shaping judgment rules on learning that previous information was invalid. *Journal of Consumer Psychology, 9*, 213–222.

McGuire, W. J. (1968). Personality and susceptibility to social influence. In E. F. Borgatta & W. W. Lambert (Eds.), *Handbook of personality theory and research* (pp. 1130–1187). Chicago: Rand McNally.

McGuire, W. J. (1969). The nature of attitudes and attitude change. In G. Lindzey & E. Aronson (Eds.), *Handbook of social psychology* (2nd ed., Vol. 3, pp. 136–314). Reading, MA: Addison-Wesley.

McGuire, W. J. (1985). Attitudes and attitude change. In G. Lindzey & E. Aronson (Eds.), *Handbook of social psychology* (3rd ed., Vol. 2, pp. 233–346). New York: Random House.

McGuire, W. J. (1989). Theoretical foundations of campaigns. In R. E. Rice & C. K. Atkin (Eds.), *Public communication campaigns* (2nd ed., pp. 43–65). Newbury Park, CA: Sage.

McGuire, W. J. (1996). The Yale communication and attitude change program in the 1950s. In E. E. Dennis & E. Wartella (Eds.), *American communication research: The remembered history* (pp. 39–59). Mahwah, NJ: Lawrence Erlbaum Associates.

Mendelsohn, H. (1973). Some reasons why information campaigns can succeed. *Public Opinion Quarterly, 11*, 412–423.

Moore, D. L., Hausknecht, D., & Thamodaran, K. (1986). Time pressure, response opportunity, and persuasion. *Journal of Consumer Research, 13*, 85–99,

Moore, D. L., & Reardon, R. (1987). Source magnification: The role of multiple sources in processing of advertising appeals. *Journal of Marketing Research, 24*, 412–417.

Ottati, V. C., & Isbell, L. M. (1996). Effects of mood during exposure to target information on subsequently reported judgments: An on-line model of misattribution and correction. *Journal of Personality and Social Psychology, 71*, 39–53.

Paisley, W. (1989). Public communication campaigns: The American experience. In R. E. Rice & C. K. Atkin (Eds.), *Public communication campaigns* (2nd ed., pp. 15–41). Newbury Park, CA: Sage.

Palmerino, M., Langer, E., & McGillis, D. (1984). Attitudes and attitude change: Mindlessness-mindfulness perspective. In J. R. Eiser (Ed.), *Attitudinal judgment* (pp. 179–195). New York: Springer-Verlag.

Pechmann, C., & Estaban, G. (1993). Persuasion processes associated with direct comparative and noncomparative advertising and implications for advertising effectiveness.
Journal of Consumer Psychology, 2, 403–432.

Pechman, C., & Stewart, D. W. (1989). Advertising repetition: A critical review of wearin
and wearout. *Current Issues and Research in Advertising, 11,* 285–330.

Peterson, R. E., & Thurstone, L. (1933). *Motion pictures and the social attitudes of children.*
New York: MacMillan.

Petty, R. E. (1994). Two routes to persuasion: State of the art. In G. d'Ydewalle, P. Eelen,
& P. Bertelson (Eds.), *International perspectives on psychological science* (Vol. 2,
pp. 229–247). Hillsdale, NJ: Lawrence Erlbaum Associates.

Petty, R. E., Baker, S. M., & Gleicher, F. (1991). Attitudes and drug abuse prevention:
Implications of the elaboration likelihood model of persuasion. In L. Donohew, H. E.
Sypher, & W. J. Bukoski (Eds.), *Persuasive communication and drug abuse prevention*
(pp. 71–90). Hillsdale, NJ: Lawrence Erlbaum Associates.

Petty, R. E., & Briñol, P. (2000, February). *Implications of self-validation theory for resistance to
persuasion.* Paper presented at the first annual meeting of the Society for Personality
and Social Psychology, Nashville, TN.

Petty, R. E., Briñol, P., & Tormala, Z. L. (in press). Thought confidence as a determinant of
persuasion: The self-validation hypothesis. *Journal of Personality and Social Psychology.*

Petty, R. E., & Brock, T. C. (1981). Thought disruption and persuasion: Assessing the
validity of attitude change experiments. In R. Petty, T. Ostrom, & T. Brock (Eds.), *Cognitive responses in persuasion* (pp. 55–79). Hillsdale, NJ: Lawrence Erlbaum Associates.

Petty, R. E., & Cacioppo, J. T. (1979a). Effects of forewarning of persuasive intent on cognitive responses and persuasion. *Personality and Social Psychology Bulletin, 5,* 173–176.

Petty, R. E., & Cacioppo, J. T. (1979b). Issue-involvement can increase or decrease persuasion by enhancing message-relevant cognitive responses. *Journal of Personality and
Social Psychology, 37,* 1915–1926.

Petty, R. E., & Cacioppo, J. T. (1981). *Attitudes and persuasion: Classic and contemporary
approaches.* Dubuque, IA: Wm. C. Brown.

Petty, R. E., & Cacioppo, J. T. (1983). Central and peripheral routes to persuasion: Application to advertising. In L. Percy & A. Woodside (Eds.), *Advertising and consumer psychology* (pp. 3–23). Lexington, MA: D. C. Heath.

Petty, R. E., & Cacioppo, J. T. (1984a). The effects of involvement on responses to argument quantity and quality: Central and peripheral routes to persuasion. *Journal of Personality and Social Psychology, 46,* 69–81.

Petty, R. E., & Cacioppo, J. T. (1984b). Motivational factors in consumer response
to advertisements. In W. Beatty, R. Geen, & R. Arkin (Eds.), *Human motivation*
(pp. 418–454). New York: Allyn & Bacon.

Petty, R. E., & Cacioppo, J. T. (1984c). Source factors and the elaboration likelihood model
of persuasion. *Advances in Consumer Research, 11,* 668–672.

Petty, R. E., & Cacioppo, J. T. (1986a). *Communication and persuasion: Central and peripheral
routes to attitude change.* New York: Springer-Verlag.

Petty, R. E., & Cacioppo, J. T. (1986b). The elaboration likelihood model of persuasion. In
L. Berkowitz (Ed.), *Advances in experimental social psychology* (Vol. 19, pp. 123–205)
New York: Academic Press.

Petty, R. E., & Cacioppo, J. T. (1990). Involvement and persuasion: Tradition versus integration. *Psychological Bulletin, 107,* 367–374.

Petty, R. E., Cacioppo, J. T., & Goldman, R. (1981). Personal involvement as a determinant of argument-based persuasion. *Journal of Personality and Social Psychology, 41,*
847–855.

Petty, R. E., Cacioppo, J. T., & Haugtvedt, C. (1992). Involvement and persuasion: An
appreciative look at the Sherifs' contribution to the study of self-relevance and atti-

tude change. In D. Granberg & G. Sarup (Eds.), *Social judgment and intergroup relations: Essays in honor of Muzafer Sherif* (pp. 147–174). New York: Springer-Verlag.

Petty, R. E., Cacioppo, J. T., & Heesacker, M. (1981). The use of rhetorical questions in persuasion: A cognitive response analysis. *Journal of Personality and Social Psychology, 40,* 432–440.

Petty, R. E., Cacioppo, J. T., & Schumann, D. (1983). Central and peripheral routes to advertising effectiveness: The moderating role of involvement. *Journal of Consumer Research, 10,* 134–148.

Petty, R. E., Fleming, M. A., & White, P. (1999). Stigmatized sources and persuasion: Prejudice as a determinant of argument scrutiny. *Journal of Personality and Social Psychology, 76,* 19–34.

Petty, R. E., Gleicher, F., & Baker, S. M. (1991). Multiple roles for affect in persuasion. In J. Forgas (Ed.), *Emotion and social judgments* (pp. 181–200). London: Pergamon.

Petty, R. E., Gleicher, F. H., & Jarvis, B. (1993). Persuasion theory and AIDS prevention. In J. B. Pryor & G. Reeder (Eds.), *The social psychology of HIV infection* (pp. 155–182). Hillsdale, NJ: Lawrence Erlbaum Associates.

Petty, R. E., Haugtvedt, C., & Smith, S. M. (1995). Elaboration as a determinant of attitude strength: Creating attitudes that are persistent, resistant, and predictive of behavior. In R. E. Petty & J. A. Krosnick (Eds.), *Attitude strength: Antecedents and consequences* (pp. 93–130). Mahwah, NJ: Lawrence Erlbaum Associates.

Petty, R. E., & Krosnick, J. A. (Eds.). (1995). *Attitude strength: Antecedents and consequences.* Hillsdale, NJ: Lawrence Erlbaum Associates.

Petty, R. E., Ostrom, T. M., & Brock, T. C. (Eds.). (1981). *Cognitive responses in persuasion.* Hillsdale, NJ: Lawrence Erlbaum Associates.

Petty, R. E., Priester, J. R., & Wegener, D. T. (1994). Cognitive processes in attitude change. In R. S. Wyer & T. K. Srull (Eds.), *Handbook of social cognition* (2nd ed., Vol. 2, pp. 69–142). Hillsdale, NJ: Lawrence Erlbaum Associates.

Petty, R. E., Schumann, D., Richman, S., & Strathman, A. (1993). Positive mood and persuasion: Different roles for affect under high and low elaboration conditions. *Journal of Personality and Social Psychology, 64,* 5–20.

Petty, R. E., Tormala, Z., Hawkins, C., & Wegener, D. T. (2001). Motivation to think and order effects in persuasion: The moderating role of chunking. *Personality and Social Psychology Bulletin, 27,* 332–344.

Petty, R. E., & Wegener, D. T. (1993). Flexible correction processes in social judgment: Correcting for context induced contrast. *Journal of Experimental Social Psychology, 29,* 137–165.

Petty, R. E., & Wegener, D. T. (1998a). Attitude change: Multiple roles for persuasion variables. In D. Gilbert, S. Fiske, & G. Lindzey (Eds.), *The handbook of social psychology* (4th ed., Vol. 1, pp. 323–390). New York: McGraw-Hill.

Petty, R. E., & Wegener, D. T. (1998b). Matching versus mismatching attitude functions: Implications for scrutiny of persuasive messages. *Personality and Social Psychology Bulletin, 24,* 227–240.

Petty, R. E., & Wegener, D. T. (1999). The elaboration likelihood model: Current status and controversies. In S. Chaiken & Y. Trope (Eds.), *Dual process theories in social psychology* (pp. 41–72). New York: Guilford Press.

Petty, R. E., Wegener, D. T., & White, P. H. (1998). Flexible correction processes in social judgment: Implications for persuasion. *Social Cognition, 16,* 93–113.

Petty, R. E., Wells, G. L., & Brock, T. C. (1976). Distraction can enhance or reduce yielding to propaganda. *Journal of Personality and Social Psychology, 34,* 874–884.

Petty, R. E., Wheeler, S. C., & Bizer, G. (1999). Is there one persuasion process or more? Lumping versus splitting in attitude change theories. *Psychological Inquiry, 10,* 156–153.

Petty, R. E., Wheeler, S. C., & Bizer, G. (2000). Matching effects in persuasion: An elaboration likelihood analysis. In G. Maio & J. Olson (Eds.), *Why we evaluate: Functions of attitudes* (pp. 133–162). Mahwah, NJ: Lawrence Erlbaum Associates.

Priester, J. M., Cacioppo, J. T., & Petty, R. E. (1996). The influence of motor processes on
attitudes toward novel versus familiar semantic stimuli. *Personality and Social Psychology Bulletin, 22,* 442–447.

Priester, J. R., & Petty, R. E. (1995). Source attribution and persuasion: Perceived honesty as
a determinant of message scrutiny. *Personality and Social Psychology Bulletin, 21,* 639–656.

Priester, J. R., Wegener, D. T., Petty, R. E., & Fabrigar, L. F. (1999). Examining the psychological processes underlying the sleeper effect: The elaboration likelihood model
explanation. *Media Psychology, 1,* 27–48.

Puckett, J., Petty, R. E., Cacioppo, J. T., & Fisher, D. (1983). The relative impact of age and
attractiveness stereotypes on persuasion. *Journal of Gerontology, 38,* 340–343.

Rholes, N., & Wood, W. (1992). Self-esteem and intelligence affect influenceability: The
mediating role of message reception. *Psychological Bulletin, 111,* 156–171.

Rice, R. E., & Atkin, C. K. (Eds.). (1989). *Public communication campaigns.* Newbury Park,
CA: Sage.

Sawyer, A. G. (1981). Repetition, cognitive responses and persuasion. In R. E. Petty, T. M.
Ostrom, & T. C. Brock (Eds.), *Cognitive responses in persuasion* (pp. 237–261). Hillsdale,
NJ: Lawrence Erlbaum Associates.

Schumann, D., Petty, R. E., & Clemons, S. (1990). Predicting the effectiveness of different
strategies of advertising variation: A test of the repetition-variation hypothesis. *Journal of Consumer Research, 17,* 192–202.

Schwarz, N. (1990). Feelings as information: Informational and motivational functions of
affective states. In E. T. Higgins & R. M. Sorrentino (Ed.), *Handbook of motivation and
cognition: Foundations of social behavior* (Vol. 2, pp. 527–561). New York: Guilford.

Schwarz, N., Bless, H., & Bohner, G. (1991). Mood and persuasion: Affective states influence the processing of persuasive communications. In M. P. Zanna (Ed.), *Advances in
experimental social psychology* (Vol. 24, pp. 161–201). San Diego, CA: Academic Press.

Schwarz, N., & Clore, G. (1983). Mood, misattribution, and judgments of well-being:
Informative and directive functions of affective states. *Journal of Personality and Social
Psychology, 45,* 513–523.

Sears, D. O., & Kosterman, R. (1994). Mass media and political persuasion. In T. C. Brock
& S. Shavitt (Eds.), *Persuasion: Psychological insights and perspective* (pp. 251–278).
Needham Heights, MA: Allyn & Bacon.

Sears, D. O., & Whitney, R. E. (1973). *Political persuasion.* Morristown, NJ: General Learning Press.

Shavitt, S., & Brock, T. C. (1986). Delayed recall of copytest responses: The temporal stability of listed thoughts. *Journal of Advertising, 19,* 6–17.

Shavitt, S., Swan, S., Lowrey, T. M., & Wanke, M. (1994). The interaction of endorser
attractiveness and involvement in persuasion depends on the goal that guides message processing. *Journal of Consumer Psychology, 3,* 137–162.

Sheppard, B. H., Hartwick, J., & Warshaw, P. (1988). The theory of reasoned action: A
meta-analysis of past research with recommendations for modifications and future
research. *Journal of Consumer Research, 15,* 325–343.

Sherman, S. J., Mackie, D. M., & Driscoll, D. M. (1990). Priming and the differential use of
dimensions in evaluation. *Personality and Social Psychology Bulletin, 16,* 405–418.

Shils, E. A., & Janowitz, M. (1948). Cohesion and disintegration in the Wehrmacht, *Public
Opinion Quarterly, 12,* 300–306; 308–315.

Smith, S. M., & Shaffer, D. R. (1991). Celebrity and cajolery: Rapid speech may promote or
inhibit persuasion via its impact on message elaboration. *Personality and Social Psychology Bulletin, 17,* 663–669.

Snyder, M. (1987). *Public appearances, private realities: The psychology of self-monitoring*. New York: Freeman.

Snyder, M., & DeBono, K. G. (1989). Understanding the functions of attitudes: Lessons from personality and social behavior. In A. Pratkanis, S. Breckler, & A. Greenwald (Eds.), *Attitude structure and function* (pp. 339–359). Hillsdale, NJ: Lawrence Erlbaum Associates.

Staats, A. W., & Staats, C. (1958). Attitudes established by classical conditioning. *Journal of Abnormal and Social Psychology, 67*, 159–167.

Stiff, J. B. (1986). Cognitive processing of persuasive message cues: A meta-analytic review of the effects of supporting information on attitudes. *Communication Monographs, 53*, 75–89.

Strong, E. K. (1925). *The psychology of selling and advertising*. New York: McGraw-Hill.

Suber, B. (1997, December 3). Talk radio can fuel racism. *St. Louis Post-Dispatch*, p. B7.

Swasy, J. L., & Munch, J. M. (1985). Examining the target of receiver elaborations: Rhetorical question effects on source processing and persuasion. *Journal of Consumer Research, 11*, 877–886.

Taylor, S. E. (1981). The interface of cognitive and social psychology. In J. H. Harvey (Ed.), *Cognition, social behavior, and the environment* (pp. 189–211). Hillsdale, NJ: Lawrence Erlbaum Associates.

Tesser, A., Martin, L., & Mendolia, M. (1995). The impact of thought on attitude extremity and attitude-behavior consistency. In R. E. Petty & J. A. Krosnick (Eds.), *Attitude strength: Antecedents and consequences* (pp. 73–92). Hillsdale, NJ: Lawrence Erlbaum Associates.

Wartella, E., & Middlestadt, S. (1991). Mass communication and persuasion: The evolution of direct effects, limited effects, information processing, and affect and arousal models. In L. Donohew, H. E. Sypher, & W. J. Bukoski (Eds.), *Persuasive communication and drug abuse prevention* (pp. 53–69). Hillsdale, NJ: Lawrence Erlbaum Associates.

Wartella, E., & Reeves, B. (1985). Historical trends in research on children and the media: 1900–1960. *Journal of Communications, 35*, 118–133.

Wegener, D. T., & Petty, R. E. (1994). Mood management across affective states: The hedonic contingency hypothesis. *Journal of Personality and Social Psychology, 66*, 1034–1048.

Wegener, D. T., & Petty, R. E. (1995). Flexible correction processes in social judgment: The role of naive theories in corrections for perceived bias. *Journal of Personality and Social Psychology, 68*, 36–51.

Wegener, D. T., & Petty, R. E. (1996). Effects of mood on persuasion processes: Enhancing, reducing, and biasing scrutiny of attitude-relevant information. In L. L. Martin & A. Tesser (Eds.), *Striving and feeling: Interactions between goals and affect* (pp. 329–362). Mahwah, NJ: Lawrence Erlbaum Associates.

Wegener, D. T., & Petty, R. E. (1997). The flexible correction model: The role of naive theories of bias in bias correction. In M. P. Zanna (Ed.), *Advances in experimental social psychology* (Vol. 29, pp. 141–208). San Diego, CA: Academic Press.

Wegener, D. T., & Petty, R. E. (2001). Understanding effects of mood through the elaboration likelihood and flexible correction models. In L. L. Martin, & G. L. Clore (Eds.), *Theories of mood and cognition: A user's guidebook* (pp. 177–210). Mahwah, NJ: Lawrence Erlbaum Associates.

Wegener, D. T., Petty, R. E., & Klein, D. J. (1994). Effects of mood on high elaboration attitude change: The mediating role of likelihood judgments. *European Journal of Social Psychology, 23*, 25–44.

Wegener, D. T., Petty, R. E., & Smith, S. M. (1995). Positive mood can increase or decrease message scrutiny: The hedonic contingency view of mood and message processing. *Journal of Personality and Social Psychology, 69*, 5–15.

White, P. H., & Harkins, S. G. (1994). Race of source effects in the elaboration likelihood model. *Journal of Personality and Social Psychology, 67*, 790–807.

Wilder, D. A. (1990). Some determinants of the persuasive power of ingroups and out-groups: Organization of information and attribution of independence. *Journal of Personality and Social Psychology, 59*, 1202–1213.

Wilson, T. D., & Brekke, N. (1994). Mental contamination and mental correction: Unwanted influences on judgments and evaluations. *Psychological Bulletin, 116*, 117–142.

Wilson, T. D., Dunn, D. S., Kraft, D., & Lisle, D. (1989). Introspection, attitude change, and attitude-behavior consistency: The disruptive effects of explaining why we feel the way we do. In L. Berkowitz (Ed.), *Advances in experimental social psychology* (Vol. 22, pp. 287–343). San Diego, CA: Academic Press.

Wilson, T. D., Lindsey, S. & Schooler, T. Y. (2000). A model of dual attitudes. *Psychological Review, 107*, 101–126.

Wood, W. (1982). Retrieval of attitude relevant information from memory: Effects on susceptibility to persuasion and on intrinsic motivation. *Journal of Personality and Social Psychology, 42*, 798–810.

Wood, W., Kallgren, C., & Priesler, R. (1985). Access to attitude relevant information in memory as a determinant of persuasion. *Journal of Experimental Social Psychology, 21*, 73–85.

Wood, W., Rhodes, N., & Biek, M. (1995). Working knowledge and attitude strength: An information processing analysis. In R. E. Petty & J. A. Krosnick (Eds.), *Attitude strength: Antecedents and consequences* (pp. 283–313). Hillsdale, NJ: Lawrence Erlbaum Associates.

Wright, P. L. (1973). The cognitive processes mediating acceptance of advertising. *Journal of Marketing Research, 10*, 53–62.

Wright, P. L. (1981). Cognitive responses to mass media advocacy. In R. E. Petty, T. M. Ostrom, & T. C. Brock (Eds.), *Cognitive responses in persuasion* (pp. 263–282). Hillsdale, NJ: Lawrence Erlbaum Associates.

Zaller, J. (1991). Information, values, and opinion. *American Political Science Review, 85*, 1215–1237.

Chapter 8

Intermedia Processes and Powerful Media Effects

EVERETT M. ROGERS
University of New Mexico

"Mass communication ordinarily does not serve as a necessary and sufficient cause of audience effects, but rather functions among and through a nexus of mediating factors and influences, [but] there are certain residual situations in which mass communication seems to produce direct effects. . . ."
Joseph T. Klapper, *The Effects of Mass Communication* (1960, p. 8)

The purpose of this chapter is to analyze several situations in which the mass media have strong effects. We seek to identify when and why such relatively rare but important situations occur. We argue that the finding of strong versus weak media effects may depend in part on the research designs and the research methods used in an investigation. Further, intermedia processes, when the mass media stimulate interpersonal communication about a topic, often considerably magnify the effects of direct exposure to media messages.

WHEN DO THE MEDIA HAVE STRONG EFFECTS?

Research on mass media effects has been the most popular single issue for mass communication researchers since this scholarly specialty got underway with the pioneering works of Harold D. Lasswell and Paul F. Lazarsfeld in the 1930s (Rogers, 1994). Lasswell studied the effects of propaganda, mainly through content analysis, whereas Lazarsfeld originally investigated the effects of the then-new medium of radio via survey research methods. As techniques for studying media effects gradually became more precise, in part due to the methodological advances pioneered by Lazarsfeld, mass communication investigators concluded that the media generally have minimal direct effects (the most-cited statement of the minimal effects of the media is Joseph Klapper's generalization, which appears at the top of the present chapter). On the relatively rare occasions when the media were found to have strong effects, they were thought to occur due to massive exposure to media messages by a particularly vulnerable audience (such as the effects of violent television programs on children).

The media often have strong *indirect* effects, such as the agenda-setting process through which the media tell their audience what news issues are most important (Dearing & Rogers, 1996). But communication researchers have generally found that the mass media have limited effects for most individuals under most circumstances. Even though the occasions in which the media have strong effects may be relatively rare, these instances can be quite important in illuminating the nature of media effects.

Background of Research on Media Effects

Several classic communication "milestones" (Lowery & DeFleur, 1995) are scholarly studies of the relatively unusual circumstances in which the media have strong effects. Two examples of noted early investigations of media effects are (1) the investigation by Hadley Cantril with others (1940) of the widespread panic resulting from Orson Welles' "War of the Worlds" radio broadcast in 1938, and (2) the study by Robert K. Merton with others (1946) of the 1943 Kate Smith radio marathon to sell War Bonds during World War II. These two media events had two characteristics:

1. Highly unusual radio messages whose effects were easily discernible from those of the regular content of radio programming. A dramatic end-of-the-world show and a patriotic marathon fund-raiser by a popular singer, respectively, served as "markers" for Cantril, Merton, and their fellow scholars who traced the effects of these two radio programs. These unique radio programs stood out starkly from the backcloth of other radio programming of the day.
2. A specific, measurable individual-level behavior resulting from the media event, which served as a distinctive indicator of the media's effects. For example, the effects of the Kate Smith

marathon were measured by individuals' purchases of, and pledges to buy, U.S. War Bonds, which totaled an amazing $39 million (two earlier radio marathons had raised only $1 million and $2 million, respectively). Merton and associates' (1946) dependent variable was whether or not their survey respondents made telephone pledges in response to the radio marathon. Orson Welles' "Invasion from Mars" radio broadcast panicked an estimated one million (16 %) of the approximately 6 million individuals who listened to the broadcast (Cantril, with others, 1940). As Lowery and DeFleur (1995, p. 45) stated: "What occurred that October night was one of the most remarkable media events of all time. If nothing else was proved that night, it was demonstrated to many people that radio could have a powerful impact on its audience."

These early, influential media effects studies of 60 years ago helped form the central elements in the initial paradigm (Kuhn, 1962/1970) for scholarly research investigating media effects: (a) select an unusual media event for study, (b) gather data from audience individuals about its behavioral effects (for example, buying War Bonds or panicking), and (c) analyze the message content in order to understand how the media effects occurred. For example, Merton et al. (1946, p. 142) concluded that the perceived genuineness of Kate Smith's patriotic appeals in the radio fund-raiser were actually a carefully engineered kind of "pseudo-*Gemeinschaft*," defined as the feigning of personal concern for another individual in order to manipulate the individual more effectively.[1] The paradigm for the early media effects research represented (a) a combination of audience survey methods and message content analysis, (b) both qualitative and quantitative data,[2] and (c) "firehouse

---

[1]This concept of pseudo-*Gemeinschaft* led to later research (1) by Beniger (1987) on psuedo-community and the mass media, and (2) by Horton and Wohl (1956), and many others, on *parasocial interaction*, defined as the degree to which an individual perceives a media personality as someone with whom they have an interpersonal relationship (Sood & Rogers, 2000). Carl Hovland, the founder of experimental research on persuasion, said that he became interested in investigating the attitude change effects of source credibility because of the Kate Smith radio marathon (Rogers, 1994, p. 375).

[2]For example, the Merton et al. (1946) investigation was based on 100 focused interviews with New York City respondents, 75 of whom had called in pledges to buy War Bonds, plus survey interviews with another sample of 978 respondents in New York City. A generally similar procedure was followed by Cantril with others (1940) in studying the effects of the "War of the Worlds" broadcast on panic behavior. So both studies used a combination of quantitative and qualitative data-gathering methods.

research," in which the data were gathered immediately after the media event of study.[3]

Both the Cantril et al. (1940) and the Merton et al. (1946) investigations were closely associated with Paul F. Lazarsfeld, a main founder of mass communication research (Rogers, 1994). Hadley Cantril, a Princeton University psychologist, was an Associate Director of the Rockefeller Foundation-supported Radio Research Project, which Lazarsfeld directed. Lazarsfeld played an influential role in designing the 1938 War of the Worlds study and in raising funds for its conduct. Robert K. Merton was Lazarsfeld's faculty colleague in the Columbia University Department of Sociology and also served as the Associate Director of Lazarsfeld's Office of Radio Research, the research institute through which the 1943 War Bond study was conducted. So the scholars who conducted the two early communication researches on strong media effects constituted a small network of like-minded individuals.

Shortly thereafter, Lazarsfeld designed the well-known Erie County voting study (Lazarsfeld, Berelson, & Gaudet, 1944) in order to test the strong media effects model. However, the research findings did not support this model and led instead to the limited effects paradigm that has dominated mass communication thinking to this day. *Later scholars discarded, along with the powerful media effects model, the special methodology utilized by Cantril, Merton, and their colleagues for investigating media effects.* Current scholars of media effects seldom concentrate on tracing the impacts on a specialized audience of a particular and spectacular media event or message. For instance, the body of communication research on the effects of exposure to violent television programs focuses on violent television shows *in general*, rather than on a particular television program or a specific television episode.

The present chapter suggests a return to a contemporary version of the earlier Lazarsfeld/Cantril/Merton approach to investigating media effects. Here we look at the effects on specialized audiences of specific media messages through a combination of quantitative and qualitative

---

[3]Paul F. Lazarsfeld, then Director of the Radio Research Project, telephoned Frank Stanton, Director of Research at the CBS radio network, on the morning after the "War of the Worlds" broadcast on CBS to request funding for a "firehouse research project" (Hyman, 1991, p. 193). Stanton also provided immediate funding for the Merton et al. (1946) study of the effects of the Kate Smith radio fund-raiser. Firehouse research is today referred to as "quick-response" research. The advantage of such immediate investigation of media effects is (1) that possible cause-effect relationships are less likely to be clouded by intervening factors, and (2) that respondents are able to report on their media effects more accurately.

data-gathering that is conducted rather immediately after the media event of study. This more disaggregated approach has seldom been used in most media effects studies.[4]

THE PRESENT METHODOLOGY

The author's interest in reconsidering mass communication research on media effects began when he read a brief research report by Gellert, Weismuller, Higgins, and Maxwell (1992) in the *New England Journal of Medicine*. These scholars traced the effects of five AIDS-related news events (for example, Rock Hudson's death in October 1985, Magic Johnson's announcement of his HIV-positive status in November 1991, and so forth) on the number of individuals getting AIDS blood tests in Orange County, California. These data suggested strong media effects.

Four distinctive aspects of the Gellert et al. (1992) research methodology can be identified:

1. The focus of study was on one or more important media events that occurred at a specific point in time.
2. Each event received major news coverage.
3. The media effects were measured by data available from an independent source (clinic records) about overt behavior changes on the part of individuals (obtaining an AIDS blood test).
4. The data on the overt behavioral effects of the media were obtained rather immediately after the media coverage and at a specific point in time, and thus it could be assumed that the effects were caused by the media messages about the media event (for example, Magic Johnson's announcement that he was HIV positive).

The methodology utilized by Gellert et al. (1992) is remarkably similar to that used by Cantril and Merton and their colleagues 50 years previously. Gellert and others are not communication scholars, nor did they know of the media effects research on the "Invasion from Mars" broadcast and the Kate Smith War Bond marathon. So they rather naively rediscovered powerful effects. A communication scholar, trained and experienced in the paradigm of mass communication effects research, might have missed this opportunity.

---

[4]This disaggregated research strategy has been useful in agenda-setting research, in longitudinal studies of a single issue (like AIDS in the 1980s) (Dearing & Rogers, 1996).

A search for other data sets or studies characterized by similar research methodologies to those used by Gellert et al. (1992) located four studies:

1. Data on the number of calls made to the National AIDS Telephone Hotline (provided by Dr. Fred Kroeger, Centers for Disease Control and Prevention) at the time of such specific media events as basketball player Magic Johnson's announcement that he was HIV positive on November 7, 1991. Some 118,124 telephone call attempts were made the day following Magic Johnson's announcement, then an all-time record for the hotline, up from an average of 7,372 call-attempts for the 90 previous days.
2. The January 26, 1986, *Challenger* disaster and its effects on the American public's participation in memorial events for the *Challenger's* crew, as measured in a national sample survey conducted by Dr. Jon D. Miller (1987) at Northern Illinois University's Public Opinion Laboratory.[5]
3. The diffusion of a highly unusual news event in New Delhi, India, on September 21, 1995: That stone and metal statues of Hindu deities were drinking milk (Singhal, Sood, & Rogers, 1999).
4. An investigation of the effects of an entertainment-education radio soap opera to promote family planning and HIV/AIDS prevention in Tanzania in 1993–1999 (Rogers et al., 1999; Vaughan, Rogers, Singhal, & Swalehe, 2000; Vaughan & Rogers, 2000).

Magic Johnson and Calls to the AIDS Hotline

The federal government established the National AIDS Hotline in 1983 through a contract by the Centers for Disease Control and Prevention (CDC) with the American Social Health Association to provide a toll-free telephone system 24 hours a day, 7 days a week. The hotline furnishes information on how HIV is spread and how its transmission can be prevented. Access is provided to the English-speaking population, the Spanish-speaking population, and to the deaf community (through TDD/TTY) by calling 1–800–342-AIDS. The CDC's National AIDS Hotline is by far the most important of numerous AIDS hotlines in the United States and is the only service provided to the entire nation.

---

[5]The *Challenger* accident caused a 20% drop in the price of Morton-Thiokol stock on the New York Stock Exchange within 30 minutes immediately following this event (the Morton-Thiokol Company manufactured the rocket boosters whose O-rings failed). Obviously, the investment community was immediately effected by media coverage of the *Challenger* disaster.

Earvin "Magic" Johnson, a professional basketball player for the Los Angeles Lakers, announced that he was seropositive and that he was retiring as an active player at a press conference on November 7, 1991. (The story had leaked to certain media on November 6th.) Magic Johnson was perhaps the most famous sports figure in America at the time of his announcement and was the first African-American celebrity to disclose seropositivity.[6] The media gave massive coverage to this news event: The *New York Times*, for example, devoted 300 column inches to the Magic Johnson story on November 8–10, 1991. As is the usual pattern for most news issues (Dearing & Rogers, 1996), however, media attention then fell off, with The *New York Times* devoting 140 column inches to Magic Johnson's disclosure the following week (November 11–17), 35 column inches in the week of November 18–24, and no coverage the following week. This rise and fall of a news issue occurs because newer issues push the earlier issue out of its high priority on the media agenda (Dearing & Rogers, 1996).

The National AIDS Hotline was immediately deluged with telephone calls following Magic Johnson's November 7 disclosure (Fig. 8.1). During the preceding 90 days, the National AIDS Hotline averaged 7,372 call attempts, about half of which could be answered. On November 7, 1991, when news of Johnson's HIV infection was carried by the media, the number of calls jumped by a factor of six times to 42,741. The following day, November 8th, when Magic Johnson's announcement was the major news item in the United States (in terms of the amount of news coverage), the number of call attempts to the National AIDS Hotline surged to 118,124, 19 times the average number of calls previously and a then-record for the hotline.[7] During the 60 days immediately following Magic Johnson's announcement, 1.7 million call attempts were made, an average of 28,333 per day, or four times the average number of call attempts for the preceding 90 days.[8] No other important HIV/AIDS-related events

---

[6]Movie actor Rock Hudson and schoolboy Ryan White played a major role in putting the issue of AIDS on the media agenda in the United States by disclosing their HIV/AIDS status. For the 3 years prior to their disclosures in October 1985, there were an average of 14 news stories about AIDS in six national media (like The *New York Times* and CBS News) per month. During the 4 years after their disclosures, the average number of news stories per month increased to 143 (Rogers, Dearing, & Chang, 1991).

[7]The slowly decreasing effects over time of the Magic Johnson disclosure on the number of call attempts to the National AIDS Hotline presumably is a function of the decreasing media coverage of this news event (as in the case of The *New York Times*, cited previously).

[8]As is evident in Fig. 8.1, this deluge of call attempts completely swamped the hotline's capacity to respond, with only about 3,000 of the 118,124 call attempts answered on November 8, 1991. A few months later, the National AIDS Hotline added staff, telephone lines, and call-intercept capacities so as to better address the enormous volume of call attempts that occurred due to celebrity disclosures and to other media events like Oprah Winfrey's television program on AIDS on April 8, 1992, in which she broadcast the telephone numbers for the National AIDS Hotline.

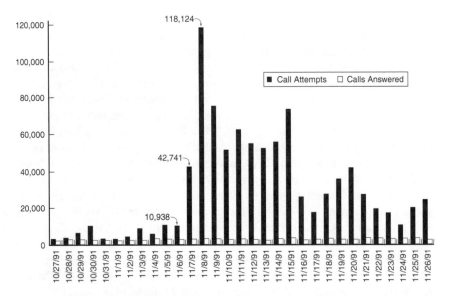

FIG. 8.1.   The effects of Magic Johnson's news conference on November 7, 1991, on the number of call attempts made to the National AIDS Hotline (only English-language calls are shown here).
Source: CDC National Aids Hotline.

occurred during this 5-month period, so it seems clear that *most of the increase in calls to the CDC's National AIDS Hotline was due to mass media reports of Magic Johnson's disclosure of seropositivity.*[9]

This conclusion is supported, and amplified, by several other investigations of the effects of Magic Johnson's disclosure of his HIV status:

1. A comparison of 186 patients at an STD (sexually transmitted disease) clinic in the Washington, D.C., suburbs during the 14 weeks prior to November 1, 1991, versus 97 patients at this clinic during the 14 weeks following Magic Johnson's announcement (Boekeloo et al., 1993). The patients were predominantly African American and male. The main impact of the Johnson disclosure was a decrease in the number of sexual partners and fewer "one-night stands," rather than in increased condom use. These effects fit

---

[9]A somewhat similar investigation of the effects of President Ronald Reagan's July 13, 1985, colon cancer operation by Brown and Potosky (1990) showed a fourfold increase in the number of telephone calls to the Cancer Information Service (CIS) of the National Cancer Institute, a major increase (more than doubling) in the number of examinations to detect colon cancer (reported to Medicare), and a decrease in the reported incidence of colorectal cancer in the several years following the president's operation, leading to an estimated saving of 5,163 lives.

with the message content of Magic Johnson's announcement, in which he told of his promiscuous sexual behavior, but said relatively little about practicing safe sex by using condoms.

2. Wanta and Elliott (1995) interviewed 366 Illinois respondents in March 1991, prior to Johnson's announcement, and 307 respondents 10 days after the November 7, 1991, disclosure. Correct knowledge that sneezing does not transmit the virus increased from 77% to 91%. Knowledge that using the same restroom as someone with AIDS could not transmit the virus increased from 80% to 93%. Further, the respondents reported a major increase in knowing the difference between HIV and AIDS, which is consistent with the content of the Johnson announcement (he disclosed that he had the virus but did not have AIDS). The difference between HIV and AIDS was stressed in news stories about Magic Johnson's disclosure.

3. Kalichman and Hunter (1992) gathered data from 361 men waiting for mass transportation in downtown Chicago, before and after the Magic Johnson announcement. A marked change occurred in perceptions of AIDS, with increased concern about AIDS, greater interest in AIDS-related information, and more-frequent interpersonal discussions about AIDS. All of the men heard about Magic Johnson's HIV infection, and 86% discussed his disclosure with their friends during the 3 days following his news conference (100% had talked about it by 10 days after November 7, 1991). The percentage of the respondents who reported they "often" talked with friends about AIDS increased from about 24% prior to the Johnson disclosure, to 37% three days after, and to 48% ten days after.

4. An investigation by Brown and Basil (1995), utilizing interviews with university students a few days after the event, found a high level of awareness of Magic Johnson's disclosure, increased knowledge of HIV/AIDS, and a higher level of discussion of the issue.

One of the important effects of mass media messages about Magic Johnson's HIV infection was to encourage interpersonal communication about the issue of AIDS (a crucial matter to which we shall return in our later discussion of intermedia processes).

The *Challenger* Disaster

Jon Miller (1987) conducted three sets of telephone interviews with samples of the U.S. adult population: (1) an initial telephone survey of 2,005 interviews about a week prior to the *Challenger* disaster on January 26,

1986, which fortunately included a battery of questions about the U.S. space program, (2) a news event diffusion survey of 1,557 respondents conducted 3 days after the disaster, and (3) a follow-up survey of 1,111 respondents conducted 6 months later, after the report of the Rogers Commission, which investigated the accident, was released. The 1986 news event attracted spectacular audience attention: 18 hours after the disaster (which occurred at 10:00 A.M. EST), 95% of U.S. adults had seen television pictures of the exploding shuttle. Such exposure had strong emotional effects:

1. Some 90% talked to family members about the accident, and 73% talked to friends or colleagues at work or at school about the accident.
2. Some 78% watched all or part of a televised memorial service for the eight astronauts broadcast from the Johnson Space Center in Houston.
3. About 6% (more than 10 million adults) attended a local memorial service for the deceased astronauts. In addition, many others attended regular religious services, which included a prayer for the *Challenger* astronauts and their families. Some 54% of the respondents said they cried or felt like crying.
4. Some 4% contacted their senator or congressman about the accident, and 1% wrote to NASA or to the U.S. president about the accident.[10]

Compared to the usual news event diffusion study, which only focuses on the dependent variable of awareness-knowledge of the news event (DeFleur, 1987; Rogers, 2000), media messages about the 1986 *Challenger* disaster had strong effects on the overt behavior of the U.S. public. Further, the impact of the *Challenger* disaster news coverage had a stronger, long-term effect on the attention of the American public than any of 480 other major news events (including the 1995 O. J. Simpson trial, the 1989 San Francisco earthquake, and the 1995 bombing of the Federal Building in Oklahoma City).[11]

---

[10]Note the evidence of a hierarchy-of-effects (McGuire, 1989) here, with 90% of the respondents talking to someone, 78% watching the televised memorial service, 6% attending a memorial service, and 1% writing a letter.

[11]According to the Times Mirror Center for the People and the Press (now the Pew Research Center for the People and the Press). Some 75,000 people in 54 national sample surveys were asked which news events they had paid most attention to (according to an AP press release dated December 29, 1995).

Feeding Milk to Hindu Dieties

Singhal and others (1999) gathered data by telephone interviews from a sample of 199 residents of Delhi, India, about a spectacular news event soon after it occurred in the very early morning of September 21, 1995: That statues of Hindu dieties were drinking milk! Some 87% of the respondents said that on hearing the news, they told an average of 21 others. Word-of-mouth channels were particularly important because the mystery surrounding this event led to a high degree of personal involvement with the event, and thus to a social construction of the meaning of the milk drinking.

Upon initially hearing the news that the Hindu gods were drinking milk, only 17% believed this divine miracle and 36% were unsure. The news set off an unprecedented devotional frenzy, with 74% of the 199 respondents trying to feed milk to the dieties, either at a Hindu temple or at an altar in their home. This experimental behavior convinced 68% of the individuals that the dieties had indeed consumed the milk.

By the late morning of September 21, milk supplies were exhausted in all major cities in India, and by midday, police had to intervene in order to maintain order as crowds at Hindu temples became unmanageable. Newspaper headlines proclaimed: "Dieties Drink Milk in Tonnes," "Divine Miracle Stuns the World," and "Miracles Claimed in Temples Abroad." Soon, Indians living abroad in the Indian diaspora in England and the United States were feeding milk to Hindu gods. Scientists and many others dismissed the milk drinking by the gods as a hoax "perpetrated on gullible and devout people of a deeply religious country" (*Hindustan Times*, p. 1). Some doubters explained the miraculous events as due to such processes in physics as surface tension or capillary action. The controversy over the milk drinking was reported in the mass media for several weeks after September 21, 1995.

As in the previous two media events of study, mass media coverage of an important event set off interpersonal discussions, which led to overt behavior change. The action in this case was feeding milk to the Hindu gods, reported by 74% of the respondents in India.

INTERMEDIA PROCESSES IN TANZANIA

Both theoretical models and empirical research (Rogers, 1995) suggest that the mass media often have effects in changing human behavior through stimulating interpersonal communication about a message topic. *Intermedia processes* occur when a mass media message leads to interpersonal communication among peers, which in turn influences behavior change.[12]

Rogers and others (1999) investigated the effects of a 5-year entertainment-education[13] radio soap opera in Tanzania that was designed to promote the adoption of family planning methods and HIV/AIDS prevention. The soap opera centered on a dozen main characters who represented positive and negative role models for family planning and HIV/AIDS prevention. For instance, Mkwaju (literally "walking stick") is a promiscuous truck driver and a male chauvinist, who displays strong son preference. A negative role model for the two educational issues, he is punished in the soap opera's story line; ultimately he becomes seropositive and suffers from AIDS.

Data were gathered via personal interviews from about 3,000 respondents in mid-1993, prior to broadcast of the twice-weekly episodes of the soap opera *Twende na Wakati (Let's Go with the Times)*. Annual samples of about 3,000 respondents were interviewed in 1994, 1995, 1996, and 1997. The radio program was not broadcast in 1993–1995 in the Dodoma region of Tanzania, which served as a control (or comparison) group, in order to remove the effects of contemporaneous changes on the main dependent variables of family planning and HIV/AIDS prevention.

Although the degree of exposure to the radio soap opera was highly related to its effects, *most individuals adopted family planning and HIV/AIDS prevention as the result of interpersonal communication stimulated by the entertainment-education radio soap opera* (Rogers et al., 1999; Vaughan et al., 2000; Vaughan & Rogers, 2000). The degree of listening to *Twende na Wakati* was related to spouse/partner discussions of family planning and HIV/AIDS prevention, which in turn was related to the adoption of family planning and HIV/AIDS prevention. Discussion of family planning with others increased from 17% of audience members in 1993–1994 (the first year of broadcasting the radio soap opera) to 53% in 1996–1997 (Vaughan, 2000). Married women who were both exposed to the radio soap opera and who talked about it with their spouse/part-

---

[12]Intermedia processes, a term coined by Gumpert and Cathcart (1986), were referred to as "mass media-generated interpersonal communication" by Valente, Poppe, and Merritt (1996).

[13]*Entertainment-education* is the strategy of placing educational content in entertainment messages in order to change the overt behavior of audience members concerning the educational issue. This entertainment-education strategy has been utilized to promote family planning, female equality, adult literacy, and HIV/AIDS prevention in over 100 different projects, mainly in developing countries of Latin America, Africa, and Asia (Singhal & Rogers, 1999).

ner were especially likely to adopt family planning.[14] Talking about family planning with one's spouse led to more accurate perceptions of the spouse's attitude toward family planning (Vaughan, 2000).

Direct exposure to Twende na Wakati *was less important in influencing the adoption of family planning and HIV/AIDS prevention than was interpersonal communication with a friend, or especially, a spouse or partner.*[15] Interpersonal communication with a spouse/partner stimulated by a media intervention is likely to be particularly important for family planning and HIV/AIDS prevention because negotiation with a spouse/partner is necessary for adoption.

CONCLUSIONS

The present chapter recommends returning to a research methodology pioneered 60 years ago by Paul Lazarsfeld and his colleagues at Columbia University's Bureau of Applied Social Research, in which data are gathered (a) about an important media event (b) by tracing its effects on the overt behavior of individuals exposed to the media messages, (c) whose contents are analyzed, and (d) whose effects are evaluated by means of data gathered rather immediately after the event occurs. Here, we summarized the results of four investigations: (a) Magic Johnson's 1991 disclosure of his HIV infection on calls to the National AIDS Hotline, (b) diffusion of news of the 1986 Challenger disaster, (c) diffusion of news of feeding milk to Hindu gods in India in 1995, and (d) the effects of an entertainment-education radio soap opera on the adoption of family planning and HIV/AIDS prevention in Tanzania in 1993–1997. These studies show that *the media can have strong effects, especially when the media messages stimulate interpersonal communication about a topic through intermedia processes.*

One distinctive aspect of the entertainment-education strategy is that the educational messages, because of their entertaining aspect, often cause people to engage in peer communication as they seek to make sense

---

[14]Another possible reason for the strong effects of *Twende na Wakati* may have been the high frequency of audience individual's exposure to the educational content, which occurred because of the popularity of the radio soap opera. As DeFleur and Dennis (1991, pp. 560–565) pointed out, strong media effects can occur due to the accumulation of minimal effects.

[15]Similar evidence for this statement is reported by Valente and others (1996) for family planning adoption in Peru.

out of what is happening.[16] For example, the Tanzanian respondents often discussed the characters in the radio soap opera with their friends and family members, relating the positive and negative role models' behavior to their own lives (Rogers et al., 1999). Further, entertainment-education messages are highly involving for audience individuals, as they develop parasocial relationships with media personalities (Sood & Rogers, 2000).

Our present analysis shows that intermedia processes (Gumpert & Cathcart, 1986) are a basic reason why the mass media sometimes have strong effects. The notion that media messages have their effects through peer communication raises basic questions about the dichotomy of inter-personal versus mass media communication that pervades communication study (Hawkins, Wiemann, & Pingree, 1988; Reardon & Rogers, 1988; Rogers, 1999). Past research has often "created a false competition between mass and interpersonal communication" (Chaffee, 1986, p. 62). Perhaps this false dichotomy is created because communication scholars in the academy divide themselves into two subdisciplines (Reardon & Rogers, 1988; Rogers, 1999). Then the world that they perceive consists of *either* mass media or interpersonal communication, rather than the two types of channels working together to have effects.

We conclude that *past mass communication effects research may have supported a minimal effects model, in part, because of the methodology with which it was conducted.* Tracing a specific and spectacular message content that is conveyed by the mass media to audience individuals and taking into account their interpersonal communication about the media message event represent fruitful approaches for media effects research in the future.

ACKNOWLEDGMENT

The data reported in the present paper were made available by Fred Kroeger of the Centers for Disease Control and Prevention, Atlanta; Dr. Arvind Singhal, Ohio University; and Dr. Peter Vaughan, Department of Biology, Macalester College. The present essay was originally presented as a paper at the 1995 National Communication Association session, *At the Helm in Mass Communication* and in a revised version as Rogers (1998).

---

[16]One evidence of the social construction process through which entertainment-education messages are given meaning by audience individuals is the oppositional readings that may take place. For example, some Tanzanian listeners to *Twende na Wakati* perceived Mkwaju as a *positive* role model; this oppositional reading, also called the "Archie Bunker effect" (Vidmar & Rokeach, 1974), occurred for only 1% of the male respondents and decreased with the degree of exposure to the radio program (Singhal & Rogers, 1999).

REFERENCES

Beniger, J. R. (1987). Personalization of mass media and the growth of pseudo-community. *Communication Research, 14*(3), 352–371.

Boekeloo, B., Schiavo, L., Rabin, D. Jordan, C., & Matthews, J. R. (1993). Sexual risk behaviors of STD clinic patients before and after Earvin "Magic" Johnson's HIV-infection announcement: Maryland, 1991–1992. *Morbidity and Mortality Weekly Report, 42*(3), 46–48.

Brown, M. L., & Potosky, A. L. (1990). The presidential effect: The public health response to media coverage about Ronald Reagan's colon cancer episode. *Public Opinion Quarterly, 54*(3), 317–329.

Brown, W. J., & Basil, M. D. (1995). Media celebrities and public health: Response to "Magic" Johnson's HIV disclosure and its impact on AIDS risk and high-risk behaviors. *Health Communication, 7*, 345–371.

Cantril, H., Gaudet, H., & Herzog, H. (1940/1966). *The invasion from Mars: A study in the psychology of panic.* Princeton, NJ: Princeton University Press/New York: Harper and Row.

Chaffee, S. H. (1986). Mass media and interpersonal channels: Competitive, convergent, or complementary? In G. Gumpert, & R. Cathcart (Eds.), *Inter/media: Interpersonal communication in a media world* (3rd ed., pp. 62–80). New York: Oxford University Press.

Dearing, J. W., & Rogers, E. M. (1996). *Agenda-setting.* Thousand Oaks, CA: Sage.

DeFleur, M. L. (1987). The growth and decline of research on the diffusion of news. *Communication Research, 14*, 109–130.

DeFleur, M. L., & Dennis, E. E. (1991). *Understanding mass communication* (4th ed.). Boston: Houghton Mifflin.

Gellert, G. A., Weismuller, P. C, Higgins, K. V., & Maxwell, R. M. (1992). Disclosure of AIDS in celebrities. *New England Journal of Medicine, 327*(19), 1389.

Gumpert, G., & Cathcart, R. (Eds.). (1986). *Inter/media: Interpersonal communication in a media world* (3rd ed.). New York: Oxford University Press.

Hawkins, R., Wiemann, J., & Pingree, S. (Eds.). (1988). *Advancing communication science: Merging mass and interpersonal processes.* Thousand Oaks, CA: Sage.

Horton, D., & Wohl, R. R. (1956). Mass communication and para-social interaction: Observations on intimacy at a distance. *Psychiatry, 19*(3), 215–229.

Hyman, H. H. (1991). *Taking society's measure: A personal history of survey research.* New York: Russell Sage Foundation.

Kalichman, S. C., & Hunter, T. L. (1992). The disclosure of celebrity HIV infection: Its effects on public attitudes. *American Journal of Public Health, 82*, 1374–1376.

Klapper, J. Y. (1960). *The effects of mass communication.* New York: Free Press.

Kuhn, T. S. (1962/1970). *The structure of scientific revolutions.* University of Chicago Press.

Lazarsfeld, P. F., Berelson, B., & Gaudet, G. (1944). *The people's choice: How the voter makes up his mind in a presidential campaign.* New York: Duell, Sloan and Pearce.

Lowery, S. A., & DeFleur, M. L. (1995). *Milestones in mass communication research* (3rd ed.). White Plains, NY: Longman.

McGuire, W. J. (1989). Theoretical foundations of campaigns. In R. E. Rice & C. A. Atkin (Eds.), *Public communication campaigns* (2nd ed., pp. 43–65). Thousand Oaks, CA: Sage.

Merton, R. K., Fiske, M., & Curtis, A. (1946/1958/1971). *Mass persuasion: The social psychology of a War Bond drive.* New York: Harper & Brothers.

Miller, J. D. (1987). *The impact of the Challenger accident on public attitudes toward the space program.* DeKalb, IL: Northern Illinois University, Public Opinion Laboratory, Report to the National Science Foundation.

Reardon, K. K., & Rogers, E. M. (1988). Interpersonal versus mass media communication: A false dichotomy. *Human Communication Research, 15*(2), 284–303.

Rogers, E. M. (1994). *A history of communication research: A biographical approach.* New York: Free Press.

Rogers, E. M. (1995). *Diffusion of innovations* (4th ed.). New York: Free Press.

Rogers, E. M. (1998). When the media have strong effects: Intermedia processes. In Judith S. Trent (Ed.). *Communication: Views from the helm for the 21st century* (pp. 276–285). Boston: Allyn and Bacon.

Rogers, E. M. (1999). Anatomy of the two sub-disciplines of communication study. *Human Communication Research, 25*(4), 618–631.

Rogers, E. M. (2000). Reflections on news event diffusion research. *Journalism & Mass Communication Quarterly, 77,* 561–576.

Rogers, E. M., Dearing, J. W., & Chang, S. (1991). *AIDS in the 1980s: The agenda-setting process for a public issue.* Journalism Monographs 126.

Rogers, E. M., Vaughan, P. W., Swalehe, R. M. A., Rao, N., Svenkerud, P., & Sood, S. (1999). Effects of an entertainment-education radio soap opera on family planning in Tanzania. *Studies in Family Planning, 30*(3), 193–211.

Singhal, S., & Rogers, E. M. (1999). *Entertainment-education: A communication strategy for social change.* Mahwah, NJ: Lawrence Erlbaum Associates.

Singhal, A., Sood, M., & Rogers, E. M. (1999). The Gods are drinking milk! Word-of-mouth diffusion of a major news event in India. *Asian Journal of Communication, 9*(1), 86–107.

Sood, S., & Rogers, E. M. (2000). Dimensions of parasocial interaction by letter-writers to a popular entertainment-education soap opera in India. *Journal of Broadcasting and Electronic Media, 44*(3), 386–414.

Valente, T. W., Poppe, P. R., & Merritt, A. P. (1996). Mass-media-generated interpersonal communication as sources of information about family planning. *Journal of Health Communication, 1,* 247–265.

Vaughan, P. W. (2000, September 18). The power of talk: Using entertainment-education to stimulate interpersonal communication as a step towards adoption of interpersonal behavior change. Paper presented at the Third International Conference on Entertainment-Education, Papindol, Netherlands.

Vaughan, P. W., & Rogers, E. M. (2000). A staged model of communication effects: Evidence from an entertainment-education radio soap opera in Tanzania. *Journal of Health Communication, 5*(3), 207–227.

Vidmar, N., & Rokeach, M. (1974). Archie Bunker's bigotry: A study in selective perception and selective exposure. *Journal of Communication, 24*(1), 36–47.

Vaughan, P. W., Rogers, E. M., Singhal, S., & Swalehe, R. M. A. (2000). Entertainment-education and HIV/AIDS prevention: A field experiment in Tanzania. *Journal of Health Communication, 25*(4), 81–100.

Wanta, W., & Elliott, W. R. (1995). Did the "Magic" work? Knowledge of HIV/AIDS and the knowledge gap hypothesis. *Journalism and Mass Communication Quarterly, 72*(2): 312–321.

Chapter 9

Resurveying the Boundaries of Political Communications Effects

DOUGLAS M. McLEOD
University of Wisconsin–Madison

GERALD M. KOSICKI
The Ohio State University

JACK M. McLEOD
University of Wisconsin–Madison

A decade ago, we contributed a chapter on political communication effects (McLeod, Kosicki, & McLeod, 1994) to Bryant and Zillman's (1994) collection of essays on media effects. In that chapter, we argued that recent developments in political communication research indicated a renewed concern for normative orientations about how social institutions "ought to" work, a concern that had been largely ignored by political communication researchers since the days of Walter Lippman (1922). Since this chapter was published, a flourish of interest in the concepts of social capital, the public sphere, social protest, and civic journalism indicate the implicit concern that many political communication researchers have for the importance of citizen participation in democratic societies. To reflect this expanded concern, the scope of this chapter has been broadened to include research on civic engagement, participation, and socialization. The value of participatory democracy, active and widespread popular participation informed by a free and responsible press, serves as an important impetus to political communication research. In reviewing political communication research, we broaden the scope beyond the individual level to macro-level concerns about the role of mass media in democratic systems. We also expand the traditional emphasis on voting research to encompass a broad conception of the antecedents and consequences of political communication.

OBJECTIVES, ASSUMPTIONS, AND ORGANIZATION

The purpose of this chapter is to convey a sense of the broadened scope of recent political communication research. The particular argument made here is that understanding political communication effects, because of their dependence on specific sociopolitical environments, requires examination in broader spatial and temporal contexts than that required by other types of media effects. This argument is based on five metatheoretical assumptions:

1. The connection between normative democratic standards for the media and empirical political communication research, which was severed for several decades, should be restored. In democratic societies, normative expectations can serve as useful criteria for evaluating the performance of media institutions and the workings of political communication more generally.

2. Evaluation of media performance requires specification of observable indicators of the adequacy of institutional performance, their formats and processes, and the products and output they produce.

3. Understanding of the performance by media institutions requires examination of their constraints and conventions, both induced and self-imposed. Attribution of effects to the media is dependent on evidence that the media production process was involved in shaping the message and not simply in acting as a conduit for other sources.

4. Examination of performance requires going beyond critiques of media content and other institutional outputs to study individual cognitive, affective, and behavioral effects of these products. It is important to examine effects not only on individual citizens but also on key political actors, such as political leaders, information strategists, and journalists.

5. Understanding political communication requires an examination of outcomes for the political system resulting from the collective reactions of individuals and the cumulative consequences of institutional performance.

We begin by conceptualizing the boundaries of political communication. This is followed by a brief historical overview of political communication research. A third section examines the context of changes in the social, political, and mass media environments. Media content is the focus of the fourth section. The fifth section reviews results of recent political communication research that fall into the traditional categories of affective, cognitive, perceptual, behavioral, and systemic effects. The sixth section considers recent work adopting more complex O-S-O-R effects models. A seventh section discusses possible media effects on politicians and policymakers. The next section looks at recent research concerned with improving the functioning of political processes. Finally, we extend the normative standards of Gurevitch and Blumler (1990) by integrating media effects research into a larger media performance model.

THE BOUNDARIES OF POLITICAL COMMUNICATION

Defining the boundaries of political communication has become an increasingly difficult task, as the contributions from a variety of disciplines and research traditions—including political science, psychology, sociology, linguistics, rhetoric, and mass communication—have broadened the focus of research. Whereas the study of political communication once was confined to the relationship between print media use and voting choices, it has been expanded to other political aspects of communication as researchers incorporated additional facets of the communication process. The theoretical fermentation has been accentuated by the development of new approaches to political communication research and the use of multiple methods. Indeed, it has led to the recognition that all facets of social behavior, including interpersonal relationships shown on entertainment television programming, could be conceived of as political.

For practical purposes, however, the boundaries of political communication must be narrowed. Generally speaking, political communication involves the exchange of symbols and messages between political actors and institutions, the general public, and news media that are the products of or have consequences for the political system (Meadow, 1980). The outcomes of these processes involve the stabilization or alteration of power. For this chapter, the definition can be further narrowed by focusing on symbols and messages exchanged via the mass media, particularly in their news content.

Political communication effects are phenomena that have consequences for the political system. Explanation of them involves attributing the effect to some personal or institutional source of influence (e.g., a political leader, advertising message, news media, or news story). Thus, political effects of mass media are a subset of a larger set of political communication effects. Effects can be manifested at the micro level of individual behavior, the intermediary level of political groups, or at the macro level of the system itself. There are also effects that involve cross-level relationships such as the impact of political institutions on individual behavior or the process by which individual political sentiments become translated into social policy. In addition, the term *effect* commonly implies some type of change, but it can also include processes that maintain stability (McLeod & Reeves, 1980). This review focuses on mass mediated political communication, considering factors that shape the content of mediated messages and the impact that these messages have on the audience, politicians and policymakers, and the journalists themselves.

THE DEVELOPMENT OF POLITICAL COMMUNICATION RESEARCH

Political communication research has traditionally played a central role in research on the effects of mass media. Klapper's (1960) conclusion that the effects of mass media are "limited" was based largely on studies of political election campaigns by researchers at Columbia University (Berelson, Lazarsfeld, & McPhee, 1954; Lazarsfeld, Berelson, & Gaudet, 1948). The "limited effects" perspective rests uneasily on several underlying assumptions, including the power of selectivity processes (exposure, attention, perception, and recall), reinforcement and crystallization, social predispositions, interpersonal mediation, and the stability of social systems. Despite its landmark status in the history of the field, sharp criticism has been leveled against the limited effects model (Blumler & McLeod, 1974; Chaffee & Hochheimer, 1985; Gitlin, 1978). At a minimum, the limited effects model presented an overly stable picture of the "functional" role of politics and the media.

The Rebirth of Political Communication Inquiry

For 20 years following the last Columbia study of the 1948 election, voting studies paid little attention to media influences in political campaigns and highlighted the effects of party affiliation. Lacking alternatives, the limited effects model held sway until the 1970s. The growth and changing nature of political communication inquiry starting in the 1970s was accompanied by marked shifts in the political and media environments. Four important historical influences fostered substantial recent growth in political communication research (McLeod, Kosicki, & Rucinski, 1988). First, important sociopolitical changes made voting a far less predictable behavior. Second, the development of new media, particularly television, produced concern over their potentially detrimental effects on the political system. Third, the field benefitted from the influx of European scholarship from a variety of theoretical perspectives. Finally, the "cognitive revolution" in social science also widened the focus of political communication research.

Trends in Political Communication Research

Several promising trends in political communication research can be noted. First, there has been some progress in connecting audience effects with other parts of the communication process: news sources, media organizations, and content. Second, investigation at the macrosocial level of analysis has been revitalized to complement the already extensive research at the individual level. Coinciding with the resurgence of macrolevel concern, research making comparisons between communities, nations, and historical periods has also emerged (Bennett, 2000; Blumler, 1983; Blumler, McLeod, & Rosengren, 1992; Tichenor, Donohue, & Olien, 1980). A fourth trend is a renewed interest in language, not only the language of media content, but also language as it relates to the production and interpretation of mediated information. Fifth, there has been an increase in the number of studies that combine methodologies and/or use multiple sources of data to provide more complete answers to research questions. Sixth, there has been a rebirth of interest in issues of civic socialization and community. The final trend is the development of more-complex models of political communication processes. Each of the trends has been stimulated by the increasing complexity of the political environment and has facilitated the growth of knowledge in the field.

THE CHANGING CONTEXT OF POLITICAL COMMUNICATION

Political communication is shaped by several layers of systemic context. For instance, the sociopolitical environment in a given society structures the form and content of political communication processes. More specifically, the media environment, both in terms of the context in which information is produced and in which it is disseminated to the public, is also an important determinant of the nature of political communication.

U.S. society in the post–World War II era has been rapidly evolving in ways driven by increased education, suburbanization, and immigration, as well as by increasing disparity between rich and poor. Ethnic and racial heterogeneity has been rapidly expanding. Results of these changing circumstances include increased tension in the political dialogue and a complication of political discourse. As society diversifies, the political system becomes less predictable. Party identification, along with voter turnout, is down, and split-ticket voting in a given election and party instability across elections are more common, leading to divided government at almost every level. Several prominent third party and independent candidates have exerted a visible effect on election outcomes (in some cases, such as Jesse Ventura, winning them). Social movements, protesters, and interest groups have been gaining visibility and impact. Accompanying these trends is a loss of confidence in institutions and leaders, including government, business, and journalism.

One of the most visible factors is the growth of special-interest groups. Adept at raising funds and at using public relations strategies, often in consort with other like-minded groups, interest groups have become increasingly powerful in their efforts to lobby politicians and shape political discourse. As part of their strategies, they attempt to influence policy making indirectly by targeting public opinion through the media. Organized interest groups permeate social discourse by getting their "experts" on news and talk shows, providing "background" information to reporters, and inducing the news media to adopt their "frames" on controversial issues (Gandy, 1982; Pertschuk & Schaetzel, 1989). Playing directly to these organized interest groups are candidates who raise special-interest money and build their own organizations largely independent of party influences. Once elected, these individuals are relatively free of party discipline and seem mainly concerned with preserving their own power bases. This new freedom can be translated into national political power on selected issues for those able to use their posts to become recurrent news sources.

Although the impact of organized interest groups with considerable resources has clearly continued to expand, so too has the presence of grassroots groups. There has been a growing activism from citizen groups extending beyond the local level, using the Internet to coordinate activities. Perhaps the most visible example has been the diverse coalition of "antiglobalism" protest activity, which has snowballed through a series of mass demonstrations in Seattle; Quebec; Washington, D.C.; Genoa; and elsewhere. These protests provide an example of how the Internet has helped groups organize to foster participation from geographically dispersed individuals, amplifying marginalized voices.

Some groups have organized to provide a watchdog on the media specifically. Such groups come from various locales on the political spectrum such as Accuracy in Media (AIM) and Fairness and Accuracy in Reporting (FAIR). These are but two examples of the many groups that organize to influence political processes. Often the media are at the center of their attempts to influence policy and public opinion. Such organizations (interest groups, protest groups, watchdog groups, etc.) are increasing in influence and diversity, and thus must be considered as players in the political environment.

The center of the new political system appears to be the media. Presidential candidates, for example, travel incessantly to generate opportunities to appear on the news and to raise campaign funds for advertising.

Candidates learn to speak in brief sound bites, and advertisements are increasingly limited in length. Neither affords the opportunity for any sustained political reasoning, even if the candidates were inclined to reason. Political ads make sophisticated use of music, symbols, and imagery, particularly to impute negative qualities to opponents. Fear of attacks increasingly dictates that political decisions of all kinds be directed by considerations of how easy a course of action is to explain.

From the demands of the new styles of campaigning, a new set of professional roles have emerged—image managers, spin doctors, photo opportunists, opinion poll readers, media pundits, and so on (Blumler, 1990). A large part of the communicator's job is to design visually compelling scenes that journalists will find irresistible (Altheide & Snow, 1991). Such factors contribute to the increasing complexity of the media environment.

Perhaps no other factor has contributed more to the growing complexity of the media environment than the Internet. Its impact has been far too profound to adequately address in this chapter. It provides access to an extremely wide array of information content. The user plays a much greater role in selecting information, and exposure is much more specialized and individualized. The flow of information in the system is much more difficult to trace than for previous media, as information passes through many hands. Consequently, the original source and the accuracy and credibility of the information are also more difficult to assess. Nevertheless, the benefits of the technology are marked, both in terms of access to information and in terms of the potential for individuals to contribute to the discourse. The Internet allows like-minded individuals to find each other and permits groups to organize for action.

However, as with most other forms of mass media, access and uses of the Internet are asymmetric across class, racial, and generational boundaries (Jung, Qiu, & Kim, 2001; Loges & Jung, 2001). Interestingly, heavier use of the Internet among younger adults may offset age-related differences in the opposite direction when it comes to newspapers. Although there are economic factors related to class, race, and age that constrain access to the Internet and other media (Roberts, 2000; Shah, Kwak, & Schmierbach, 2000), what is more important is the nature of the preferred content and the way that it is used. For instance, entertainment television viewing and playing computer games may be associated with lower levels of knowledge and participation (Niemi & Junn, 1998; Shah, 1998). Effects are very different when those media are used for accessing information about current affairs. In other words, the consequences of information versus recreational uses of any media are very different (Shah, McLeod, & Yoon, 2001). Sociocultural differences may in fact interact with differences in usage patterns, in part tied to differences in the perceived utility of various types of media content. For example, research has revealed differences in the way that computers are taught in schools; lower-income schools focus on rudimentary computer skills such as keyboarding, whereas affluent schools are more likely to teach complex technological and cognitive skills (Packard Foundation, 2001).

The Internet contributes to several important trends including the proliferation of media, the differentiation of information channels, content specialization, and the fragmentation of media audiences. Along with the expansion of other media such as cable and direct broadcast television, the Internet has scattered the mass audience in search of highly specialized forms of media content. The consequences, both positive and negative, are profound. On one hand, more people have access to more content that is more personally of interest. On the other, the fragmentation of the audience may reduce exposure to a diversity of viewpoints as individuals seek narrowly focused sources of information that is consistent with their own points of view. In addition, audience fragmentation has prompted media conglomerates to diversify their holdings to recapture the scattered audience.

There are content implications as well. For instance, cable expansion and channel specialization have led to declining audiences for the networks. The shrinking network audience threatens resources available for news production. This, in turn, may contribute to the "tabloidization" of news in an attempt to sustain ratings, a trend that may also be affecting the content of print media. Other potential consequences include a greater reliance on routine news sources, like press conferences and news releases, than on enterprise reporting. It may affect the format of news programming as networks look to produce relatively cheap forms of content such as talk shows. Many media critics argue that the pressure to put profits above public services is reflective of growing ownership concentration.

Although concentration of media ownership has been seen as a problem for more than half a century, recent corporate takeovers have added to the problem. News has increasingly come under the control of executives whose values are shaped by their experiences in financial or entertainment circles. This leads to attempts to make the news more appealing to broader audiences, prompting stronger demands for entertainment values in story selection and structure.

These social and political trends place considerable strain on the media. Performance expectations have increased as media replace political parties in the center of the political communication process. At the same time, social trends toward change and diversity, political instability, and the dispersion of power forces media to do more with less and do it in a more difficult environment.

MEDIA CONTENT

Prior to considering the state of research on political communication effects, we discuss research that seeks to understand the nature of media content and the antecedents that shape it. There are advantages to the usual scheme of studying content in terms of its most manifest features: reliability of measurement, face validity, comparability, and so on (e.g., Berelson, 1952; Stempel, 1989). But there are several reasons to consider alternatives. First, recent research examining more latent forms of political content has suggested ways in which more subtle use of language may shape audience understanding of public issues (Entman, 1993; Gamson & Modigliani, 1989; Glasgow Media Group, 1982; Hallin, 1992; Pan & Kosicki, 1993; van Dijk, 1988). Interest in deconstructing media content has produced a flurry of research (e.g., Akhavan-Majid & Ramaprasad, 1998; Durham, 1998; Lee, Chan, Pan, & So, 2000; McLeod & Hertog, 1992; Teo, 2000). Second, the results of skilled strategies that modern political practitioners use to influence news are not likely to be captured by gross manifest content categories. Finally, the usual categories of manifest content analysis are not readily connected with theoretical conceptions of media effects.

We can study latent aspects of media content by analyzing the frames used to shape the story (Gamson, 1992; Gamson & Lasch, 1983; McLeod, Kosicki, Pan, & Allen, 1987; Pan & Kosicki, 1993; Reese, Gandy, & Grant, 2001; Tuchman, 1978). According to Gamson and Lasch, a frame suggests a "central organizing idea for understanding events related to the issue in question" (p. 398). As part of the "package" containing the core frame, there are various framing devices (metaphors, exemplars, catchphrases, depictions, and visual images) and reasoning devices (causal attributions, consequences, and appeals to principles). Linsky (1986) distinguished five stages of the policy process: problem identification, solution formulation, policy adoption, implementation, and evaluation. At least early in the history of an issue, a reporter or editor may have considerable latitude to choose among several frame packages; later the options narrow as elites take positions and media content begins to show consensus in choosing particular frames. Frames are clearly important to the study of effects, as they influence how audiences understand issues and policy options.

Whereas framing refers to the organization of content contained in a given story, the term *bracketing* refers to the placement of evaluative information surrounding a story. This can be seen most clearly in instances of reporters "disdaining the news" by commentary that casts scorn or cynical comments on news they have just delivered (Levy, 1981). Disdaining is used when the news must be presented for competitive reasons, but the journalist feels used because the source controls the framing of the story.

Apart from the manifest or latent features of news content, we might consider variations in news format. This can refer to the parameters of story length or size, length of sound bites or quotes within stories, labels or other means of identifying the genre of the story, or congruency of audio and visual tracks. Features of form in entertainment television programs have been shown to have effects independent of content (Watt & Krull, 1977).

Considerable research has examined the factors that shape the construction of news content. Among the factors cited in the newswork literature are the values of individual journalists; their sources; organizational deadlines and routines; occupational ideologies; ownership; and legal, social, and ideological constraints (e.g., Bennett, 2001; Herman & Chomsky, 1988; Shoemaker & Mayfield, 1987; Shoemaker & Reese, 1996; Sparrow, 1999).

Media institutions and media workers have developed distinctive organizational procedures, values, and work routines to facilitate their tasks of producing the news on a regular basis. Given their proximity to East Coast government and financial centers, elite universities, and think tanks, there is a tendency to draw from sources with geographic and social proximity, thus restricting the range of sources and views (e.g., Gans, 1979; Herman & Chomsky, 1988; Lee & Solomon, 1990). Effects of this bias range from assessments of the relative importance of presidential primaries (Adams, 1987) to a general sense of conformity to establishment priorities and worldviews (Gitlin, 1980).

Sourcing the news has long been recognized as a central problem in journalism because of the role sources play as "primary definers" (Ericson, Baranek, & Chan, 1989; Hall, Critcher, Jefferson, Clarke, & Roberts, 1978; Soley, 1992). Although choices of sources are generally crucial, the influence of these decisions on what is actually printed or broadcast may be mediated by the overall context in which the story is embedded. For example, although political candidates often set the tone for campaigns by waging low-key or intense, negative campaigns (Jamieson, 1992), these actions by sources will influence decisions about the resources news organizations are willing to commit to coverage of any given race (Clarke & Evans, 1983; Westlye, 1991).

Much of this literature, however, grows out of sociological concerns and remains, with certain exceptions, rather uniformed by advances in cognitive and social psychology (Kennamer, 1988; Stocking & Gross, 1989). This arguably has led to an overemphasis on news production as a selection process and drawn attention away from the constructionist aspects that might link more readily with certain media effects traditions (Ryan, 1991). Nonetheless, Bennett and others such as Iyengar (1991) identified characteristics of news that are helpful in conceptualizing media effects. Iyengar based his experimental studies of framing on differences between episodic and thematic coverage. Episodic coverage, characterizing much of day-to-day journalism, grows out of standard news events and news values.

Bennett (2001) also examined episodic news routines and suggested several common flaws in news: *Personalization* is the focus on individuals and incorrectly seeing large social issues in terms of individual actors. *Fragmentation* is the presentation of information in ahistorical capsule summaries, disconnected from each other. *Dramatization* is using news values rather than importance as selection criteria, suggesting that many important but undramatic issues do not make the news unless they reach crisis proportions. Finally, *normalization* is the overlaying of problems with solutions emanating from the political system, thus reinforcing existing power structures.

Although the literature on the content of political communication continues to grow, there is much more work that needs to be done to connect content characteristics to effects consequences. For example, researchers might attempt to systematically investigate how the content characteristics identified by Bennett (2001), as described previously, might translate into specific audience effects. Perhaps the areas where the content-effects linkage has received the most recent attention are the assessments of priming and framing effects (Iyengar, 1991; McLeod & Detenber, 1999; Pan & Kosicki, 1997; Reese et al., 2001), both of which are described in the following section.

POLITICAL COMMUNICATION EFFECTS

Political communication effects research has continued to develop in ways that reflect (a) the increased complexity of effects models, (b) augmented conceptions of media messages, and (c) expanded emphasis on diverse types of effects. Cognitive aspects of political psychology continue to expand their influence in the field, providing new concepts and relationships for future study (Lodge & McGraw, 1995).

Complex models have been developed that go beyond the predispositional demographic forces in the Columbia model and the influences of partisanship in the Michigan model. These complicated models reflect the realities of voters using informational shortcuts and uncertainties of cognitive judgmental processes (Herstein, 1985; Lau & Erber, 1985). Although the early cognitive models did not explicitly include media variables, they did assume that the media are major sources of information for judgments included in the models. Recent work has tended to stress complex information environments (Rahn, 1995), motivated political reasoning and affect (Lodge & Taber, 2000), and expanded models of political choices and information reflecting a blend of rational choice and social-psychological models (Lupia, McCubbins, & Popkin, 2000). Although recognizing the complexity of voting decisions, scholars have begun to realize that these additional types of effects (e.g., learning, framing, perceptions of issue salience) are themselves worthy criteria of effects, not merely pathways to some ultimate political choice.

We distinguish four major classes of individual effects: opinion formation and change, cognitive, perceptual, and behavioral. We then turn from individual effects to collective outcomes for the political system.

Opinion Formation and Change

A substantial body of literature concerns the media's impact on the formation, change, and stabilization of opinions on political issues and candidates. Opinion change is likely to be what comes to mind when thinking of media effects. The early work of Lazarsfeld et al. (1948) failed to find persuasive media effects. The study of political opinion change was revitalized, however, by the application of the Elaboration Likelihood Model (ELM) of persuasion (Petty & Cacioppo, 1986) and the Reasoned Action Model (Fishbein & Ajzen, 1975) linking attitudes, perceived social norms, and behavior. At least some success has been noted in their application to campaign effects studies (Fazio & Williams, 1986; Granberg & Brown, 1989; Krosnick, 1988; O'Keefe, 1985; O'Keefe, Rosenbaum, Lavrakas, Reid, & Botta, 1996; Rice & Atkin, 2000). These models remain more applicable to political advertising than to the less intentionally persuasive content of news (Ansolabehere & Iyengar, 1996). Zaller (1992) proposed, based on cognitive principles, a general political attitude model called Receive-Accept-Sample that has become widely used in many topic domains. Examples of opinion change associated with media use are more frequently documented than are instances of its opposite, stabilization. However, debates and other forms of campaign information have been shown to increase the consistency of partisan attitudes (Katz & Feldman, 1962; Sears & Chaffee, 1979). In the context of political campaigns, it is increasingly recognized that time matters, in terms of who is attending to what kind of information and using it as the basis for decision making (Chaffee & Rimal, 1996).

Cognitive Effects

Here we summarize six types of cognitive effects that have received considerable attention in recent years: agenda setting, priming, knowledge gain, cognitive complexity, framing, and principled reasoning.

Agenda Setting. Once nearly synonymous with studying public issues, agenda setting is increasingly recognized as a limited special case of examining the importance of a broadly defined issue topic in the public domain. Agenda-setting research is based on two related propositions: (a) the media control the agenda by selecting certain broad issue topics for prominent coverage, and (b) prominence subsequently determines which issues are judged as important (McCombs & Shaw, 1972; McCombs, Shaw, & Weaver, 1997). Over three decades agenda setting has inspired a vast literature and contains substantial evidence supporting the second proposition that public judgments of the salience (importance) of issues follow the prominence of the media agenda. The early evidence took three distinct forms: time-series comparisons of the national news agenda with aggregated issue ratings from opinion polls (Funkhouser, 1973; MacKuen, 1981; McCombs & Shaw, 1972), panel studies examining the sequencing of changes in the media agenda with corresponding changes in the issue saliences of individual respondents (McCombs, 1977; Tipton, Haney, & Basehart, 1975), and cross-sectional surveys comparing contrasting media agendas with the issue saliences of their respective audiences (McLeod, Becker, & Brynes, 1974). An ingenious series of experiments manipulating the agenda of televised newscasts (Iyengar & Kinder, 1987) not only strengthened the evidence but also attempted to tie agenda-setting research to cognitive theories. A number of other investigators have begun investigating "attribute agenda setting," claiming that agenda setting is such a robust theoretical structure that it can encompass, in addition to issue or object salience, the specific attributes of a topic and how this influences public opinion (Ghanem, 1997).

Some additional words of caution are in order. Audience agenda-setting research has become so well recognized that it has become almost synonymous with powerful political effects of media. We should be careful to note that agenda-setting effects are not necessarily powerful, consequential, and universal. Real-world events such as wars and terrorist attacks are more likely to command the agenda than are fluctuations in media coverage. In terms of impact on audiences, news sources may be far more influential than are stories under media control (Iyengar & Kinder, 1987). Changes in issue salience, as cognitive effects, may not alter affect and behavior. In political campaigns, for example, advancement of an issue may not change voting preferences unless the issue is more favorable to one candidate than another. The power of the media to control issue salience was undoubtedly overstated as "stunningly successful" in its early formulation (Cohen, 1963) and, as discussed later, the agenda is likely to influence primarily certain sectors of the public.

More ambiguity surrounds the first agenda-setting proposition that the media determine the agenda. The news media certainly serve at least as carriers of the agenda to the public, and clearly selection is involved. Less certain is how the power to control the agenda is distributed between the media and sources and how the news agenda is struggled over. Agenda setting continues to be controversial on theoretical and methodological terms (Kosicki, 1993).

Priming. A venerable social science concept, priming was applied to media use in the 1980s (Iyengar & Kinder, 1987; Krosnick & Kinder, 1990). The key insight is that media use, exposure to a given type of content or message, activates a concept, which for a period of time increases the probability that the concept, and thoughts and memories connected with it, will come to mind again (Berkowitz & Rogers, 1986). As applied to politics, media priming suggests that focus on a political issue can encourage citizens to develop their overall evaluation of political leaders from their performance on that issue. Early experiments examined priming effects of television news and found that television news shaped the standards by which presidential performance is judged (Iyengar & Kinder, 1987). When primed by stories focusing on national defense, for example, respondents gave disproportionate weight to judgments of how well they thought the president had done on that issue in judging his overall performance. This held across six issues for presidents from each party and for good news as well as for bad. Additional experiments by the same authors showed priming influences may extend to vote choices. Additional work has used survey research and content analysis to examine the rise and fall of evaluative criteria in the press such as the Gulf War and the economy and evaluations of President George H. W. Bush (Pan & Kosicki, 1997). Recent work has shown additional effects of media trust (Miller & Krosnick, 2000) .

Knowledge Gain. Evidence of knowledge gain from news media use can be found as far back as the Columbia studies. Special forms of political communication, debates, and conventions, along with standard news coverage, convey discernible if modest amounts of information to their audiences (Gunter, 1987; McLeod, Bybee, & Durall, 1979; Neuman, 1976, 1986; Neuman, Just & Crigler, 1992). Still, citizens remain remarkably uninformed about public affairs. Despite a threefold increase in the proportion of Americans who have attended college, factual knowledge of politics has increased only marginally since the 1960s and has actually declined when education is controlled (Delli Carpini & Keeter, 1996). Yet, many voters feel the information they have is enough to make vote decisions by the time of the election (Dautrich & Hartley, 1999). Popkin (1991) argued that although increments of learning from news are small, they may be sufficient for the voter's purposes, for example, to connect issues to offices and to separate the candidates on the issues. Some of the revisionist work in the area (Mondak, 1995) used local communities and a natural experiment to examine the effect of newspapers on political learning and activation.

Many reasons have been offered for the relatively weak increments of political knowledge conveyed by the routine political news media. Most prominent is the charge that the "horse race" coverage of political campaigns, focusing on who is winning rather than on issues, deters learning (Patterson, 1980). News content considered more generally may also limit learning. Picking news for its entertainment value rather than for its political importance may prevent more-complex issues from reaching the public. Increasingly shorter sound bites on television news and presentation of "nuggetized factoids" devoid of historical or political context in all media may lead to processing information episodically rather than reflectively. For the most part, these charges emanate from critical observation of content alone without systematic tests as to their actual impact on the audience. Systematic efforts to connect psychological theorizing on memory and comprehension with research on news forms and content and their effects on the audience include Ferejohn and Kuklinski (1990), Gunter (1987), and Robinson and Levy (1986). Price and Zaller (1993) examined the role of media exposure in news story recall across a wide range of topics and found that prior knowledge was the best predictor. They also concluded that there is a general audience for political news, but note that the audience is sharply stratified by prior knowledge.

Substantial research has examined questions about differential rates of knowledge acquisition across different social strata and groups, as articulated by Tichenor, Donohue, and Olien's (1970) "Knowledge Gap Hypothesis." For instance, research has fairly consistently identified difference in knowledge between high and low SES groups (Viswanath & Finnegan, 1996). Some studies have tried to evaluate, theoretically and/or empirically, whether these knowledge gaps result from such factors as differences in cognitive complexity or processing abilities, disparities in media access and exposure, or differences in the perceived utility of being informed (McLeod & Perse, 1994; Ettema & Kline, 1977). Each of these factors may contribute to knowledge gaps. For instance, higher levels of education facilitate knowledge acquisition; income provides great access to information; social situations socialize people into different patterns of media use; and social circumstances reward different types of knowledge. Recently, the emergence of new information technologies and evidence of differences in the diffusion and use patterns across SES lines (Roberts, 2000; Shah et al., 2000) has furthered concern about knowledge gaps and the "digital divide" (Jung et al., 2001; Loges & Jung, 2001).

Cognitive Complexity. Traditional measures of factual knowledge may be too limited to capture the full range of what audience members take away from political communication. To evaluate learning from the media, researchers have gone beyond the recognition or recall of specific factual knowledge to examine audience understandings of news stories and events more broadly. Techniques of open-ended questions and recording of group discussion are used to measure the complexity and structure of audience thinking on a given issue or news story. The *cognitive complexity* of audience understanding can be measured reliably by counting such features of open-ended responses as the number of arguments, time frames, and causes and implications the person brings into the discussion (McLeod et al., 1987; McLeod, Pan, & Rucinski, 1989; Sotirovic, 2001a). Cognitive complexity so measured is moderately correlated with factual knowledge from closed-ended questions, but the two criteria have distinct sets of social structural and media use antecedents. Complexity of thinking about public issues appears to be a function both of personal characteristics and patterns of news media use.

Framing. Consideration of framing effects on audiences has become an important and lively research area. A key theoretical concern is that news reports can alter patterns of knowledge activation (Price & Tewksbury, 1997). Their formulation of framing suggests that news messages help determine what aspects of a problem are focused on by individuals. Although their knowledge activation model is primarily an organizing model rather than a precise set of hypotheses, it does involve both applicability effects and accessibility effects. Applicability involves first-order effects of media messages at the time of message processing. Once activated, ideas and feelings retain some potential for further use, making them likely to be drawn on in making subsequent evaluations. These secondary effects of messages are known as accessibility effects (Price, Tewksbury, & Powers, 1997).

For framing research to meet its full potential, audience research needs to be tied carefully to the work of journalists in meaningful ways beyond merely the simple dimensions of episodic versus thematic as specified by Iyengar (1991), denoting framing effects of event-oriented news stories versus stories embedded in considerable background information and issue context. Corresponding to the journalist's role in framing news stories discussed earlier (Tuchman, 1978), audiences also can be seen as framing (or perhaps reframing) the news that comes to their attention. Audience framing involves, according to Goffman (1974), invoking "schemata of interpretation" that allow individuals to "locate, perceive, identify, and label" information coming from the environment. News stories use standard forms such as the summary lead and the inverted pyramid style, but audience members assemble the data about a candidate or issue into a causal narrative or story that reflects their point of view or frame (Kinder & Mebane, 1983). This narrative serves as a framework for understanding other news stories.

Framing of media messages, in most instances, involves low levels of attention and the use of various cognitive shortcuts to make enough sense of a story or issue. Processing is likely to be of "low information rationality," sufficient only to satisfy whatever level of understanding the person considers "good enough" (Popkin, 1991). Information processing typical of most citizens can be categorized into three types of heuristic biases: categorization, selection, and integration of information about an issue or candidate. To analyze such biases, political communication research has borrowed heavily from cognitive psychology, using concepts such as availability (Krosnick, 1989), default values (Lau & Sears, 1986), schema (Graber, 1988), and causal attribution (Iyengar, 1991). Causal attribution, discussed in greater detail later, is particularly relevant in that it connects meaning at the individual level with potential for political action. Audience framing research has been influenced by constructivist perspectives (Gamson, 1996; Gamson & Modigliani, 1989).

Audience framing is a complex construct in that it refers both to the process of individual and interpersonal sense making and to the content or output of that process. Audience frames are both cognitive representations in an individual's memory and devices embedded in public discourse (Kinder & Sanders, 1990; Pan & Kosicki, 1993). They may be elicited in a number of ways: through experimental manipulation of news broadcasts (Iyengar, 1991), as reactions to actual news broadcasts to types of news stories, a set of public issues (Neuman, Just, & Crigler, 1992), or a major issue in the news (McLeod et al., 1987; McLeod et al., 1989). The unit of analysis may be the individual or a natural social grouping such as the family or work group.

One striking feature of the meanings given to news stories and to political issues by individuals is their polysemy—there seem to be almost as many interpretations as there are perceivers. But this overstates their variety. Audience frames can be coded in meaningful ways (e.g., cognitive complexity, personal vs. systemic causation), and the structure of news stories does affect how people think and talk about issues (Iyengar, 1991; Kinder & Sanders, 1996; McLeod et al., 1987).

The origins of audience frames are thus likely to be some combination of the news media "packages" (Gamson & Modigliani, 1989), the person's structural location and values, political beliefs and knowledge, and the political norms and discourse of social groups. The framing of any audience member may be consonant with the news package, it may be in active opposition to the media frame, or it might appear to be independent of the news form and content. Better identification of the influences on framing patterns and the effects of such patterns on subsequent behavior are high priorities for political communication research. Careful empirical content analysis work such as that of Huddie (1997) is valuable in identifying frames in news coverage. Tying audience frames to news content, however, may require considerable understanding of not only media content but also social movements and their role in the process of bringing issues to the fore in public life. McCarthy (1994) develops an extended empirical case of the interplay of social movement actors and public officials in the identification of drunk driving as a key issue. Case studies offer rich opportunities for examining the role of deliberation, framing, and a wide range of political and social actors (Pan & Kosicki, 2001) in complex issues such as health care reform.

Shah, Domke, and Wackman (1996) attempt to study the effects of framing issues in terms of ethical values such as morality, honesty, and compassion. Individuals who encounter such frames in public discourse are more likely to view not only that issue, but also other issues along similar lines. These results extend even to political tolerance issues (Nelson, Oxley, & Clawson, 1997) among others.

Principled Reasoning. Patterns of media use may affect how citizens arrive at their decisions about public policy. Coding of answers to open-ended questions revealed two distinctive reasons citizens gave for their decisions on First Amendment issues (McLeod, Sotirovic, Voakes, Guo, & Huang, 1998). Those with strong public affairs media use were more likely to invoke principles among the reasons they gave. Their principled reasoning, in turn, was associated with decisions supporting civil liberties. In contrast, those with customary patterns of high television entertainment viewing expressed more negative affect in their responses and were less supportive of rights. The effects of education on reasoning and support for rights worked entirely indirectly through patterns of media use and knowledge.

Perceptions of the Political System

Self-Interest and Systemic Perceptions. Making connections between the individual-cognitive and social systems levels is a problem common to all areas of social science (Price, Ritchie, & Eulau, 1991). The problem is particularly acute for political communication, however. Most political action and power relationships operate at the societal or other systemic levels, whereas the bulk of empirical theory and research concentrate on the behavior of the individual citizen. Although we think of voting as a private act (save for the probing of pollsters) based on narrow self-interest, this highly individualized account may be illusory. Citizens may have difficulty recognizing their own self-interest, and their perception of it may not be entirely selfish in that such judgments include concern for the welfare of others (Popkin, 1991). Further, although strength of the evidence is disputed (Kramer, 1983), voting decisions seem to be made less on the basis of perceived "pocketbook" self-interest than on "sociotropic" estimates of how well the country is doing economically (Fiorina, 1981; Kinder & Kiewiet, 1983). People clearly distinguish between their own economic situation and that of the nation. At levels between the nation and the individual lie a host of other entities and groups potentially consequential to individual voting and participation.

The implications of sociotropic conceptions for media effects are quite clear. Given that systemic perceptions are based largely on media inputs, the news media have responsibilities for presenting an accurate and comprehensive picture of governmental operations. Many have expressed doubt as to how well the press plays this role. Although the public is exposed to the moves of the president and prominent members of Congress, little emphasis is placed on how government actually works in terms of processes, compromises, and so on (Popkin, 1991). Sociotropic values such as worldviews (judgments of how the world works), materialism versus postmaterialism, and normative roles of media are all related to newspaper public affairs reading, entertainment television viewing, and likelihood of engaging in discussions of public issues (McLeod, Sotirovic, & Holbert, 1998).

Causal Attribution. Jones and Nisbett (1972) suggested that actors attribute causality or responsibility for their own behavior to situational factors, whereas observers attribute the actor's behavior to stable dispositions of the actor. Applied to political judgments, this can be seen in the tendency to ascribe weaknesses of public officials to their personal faults and in blaming the poor and the homeless for their condition. Iyengar (1989) showed that failure to link social problems with societal responsibility extends to poverty, racism, and crime. Media coverage may accentuate the attribution of personal causation. Television often portrays politics as conflict between individuals rather than as struggles between institutions and principles (Rubin, 1976; Weaver, 1972). A study of newspapers in congressional campaigns found that they generally focused on personal weaknesses of incumbents, not on the system (Miller, Goldenberg, & Erbring, 1979).

Iyengar (1991) provided important experimental evidence that television influences attribution of responsibility for both the creation of problems (causal) and their resolution (treatment). Adapting the psychologism conception of framing from Kahneman and Tversky (1984), Iyengar distinguished between episodic and thematic framing of news stories. Episodic framing uses case-study or event-oriented reports and concrete instances; thematic forms place the issue in a more general or abstract context. Although content analyses showed that few television news stories were exclusively one or the other, nearly 80% of a sample of CBS news stories were predominantly episodic.

Experimental variation of the two types of story frames showed that whereas thematic stories increased the attributions of responsibility to government and society, episodic treatments decreased system-level responsibility overall (Iyengar, 1991). The strength of framing effects varied across the five issues used. The consequences of episodic versus thematic framing have substantial implications for subsequent political behavior. Iyengar found that people who attribute the cause of a problem to systemic forces are more likely to bring that problem into their political judgments than are people citing dispositional causes.

The 30-year trend of increasing dominance of television as the primary news medium may have stimulated a concomitant trend toward nonsystemic attribution. Political stories in the print media are more likely to be thematic than those of television news, and print media use may enhance systemic attribution. McLeod, Sun, Chi and Pan (1990), in a survey of public reactions to the "war on drugs," found responses to open-ended questions about causes of the problem formed three distinct attributional dimensions, each having a dispositional (individual-family, interpersonal, drug supplier) and a systemic (foreign nations, economic conditions, social-legal) end. Frequent and attentive newspaper readers were more likely to invoke systemic causes and responsibilities on two of the three dimensions. Television news use was unrelated to any dimension.

A somewhat different pattern of attributional effects was shown in a 1972–1974 panel study during the Watergate era (McLeod, Brown, Becker, & Ziemke, 1977). During an interval when trust in government declined markedly, the most avid users of both newspaper and television news held relatively stable levels of trust. When rating different sources as to blame for Watergate, they tended to blame Nixon more and the political system less than did other respondents, even after partisanship was controlled. This may have been the result of the statements appearing frequently in the news of that period that "the system works." Singling out the "bad apple in the barrel" may be easier than considering the more fundamental problems of system storage. Recent work by Sotirovic (2001b) ties individualistic explanations for crime and welfare dependency to media and active processing of political information. Active processing of national television public affairs content increases likelihood of individualistic explanations, whereas active processing of newspaper public affairs content decreases individualistic explanations. Individualistic explanations for crime and welfare are also related to support for death penalty and opposition to public assistance programs.

Climate of Opinion.   A crucial assumption in Noelle-Neumann's (1984) *Spiral of Silence* is that people make "quasi-statistical" judgments about which side is ahead and gaining support on controversial issues. According to her theory, this diminishes expression of opinion by the losing side, starts a spiral of silence, and ultimately affects change of opinion and political behavior. Noelle-Neumann claimed that German television news affected electoral outcomes because of newscasters having portrayed the climate of opinion as being unfavorable to the Christian Democratic party.

Other System Perceptions.   Other systemic perceptions could be explored as criteria of media effects. There is a connection, for example, between use of public affairs media content and support for the various aspects of the political system—for authority and trust in government but also for the need for the press to criticize government. Attentive news users tend to be more tolerant of political diversity, to have more empathy with various parts of the society, and to hold distinctive perceptions of the legitimacy or marginality of various groups and of how the world works (Amor, McLeod, & Kosicki, 1987).

There is evidence that the horse race coverage of politics, instead of substantive matters, contributes to a "spiral of cynicism" that leads to decline of interest in politics (Cappella & Jamieson, 1997). Moy & Pfau (2000), using content analysis and audience surveys, find that news coverage varies in cynicism across years and across political institutions. Use of network news, entertainment talk shows, and political talk radio is associated with lower levels of confidence in institutions, whereas newspaper use is associated with positive evaluations.

Media portrayals are also linked to public attitudes toward racially charged attitudes such as citizens views on welfare policy. Gilens (1999) shows through content analysis and survey data that news organizations have racialized discussions of poverty over decades and that these racialized discussions are systematically related to public support for welfare policies. Gilliam, Iyengar, Simon, and Wright (1996) have used creative experiments manipulating the race of perpetrators on local news coverage and found that the presence of racial cues activated stereotypic beliefs about African Americans as antecedents of opinions about crime.

Political Participation

Media effects on voting preferences have long dominated the political communication agenda. Voting decisions remain the ultimate criterion in much of the research reviewed here; however, recent work no longer looks for direct media effects and instead sees voting as a complex behavior influenced indirectly through the various cognitive influences. Another change is that interpersonal communication has become part of the participation process rather than simply an antecedent of voting.

Voter Turnout. Turnout was once thought to be a rather uninteresting phenomenon simply explained and highly stable, but it seems less predictable and more interesting in recent years. Turnout continues to be predicted by education, partisanship, age, church attendance, community involvement, and marital status (Strate, Parrish, Elder, & Ford, 1989; Wolfinger & Rosenstone, 1980), but abstention from voting remains on the rise, and television is thought to contribute to the decline of participation (Ranney, 1983). In a panel study of the unusually high abstention rate in the 1970 British general election, media influences were found to be complex (Blumler & McLeod, 1974). Those mostly likely to abstain as a result of disenchantment with the televised image of the person's party leader, surprisingly, tended to be the more-educated and better-informed voters. Turnout studies in the United States suggest that exposure and attention to hard news in the print media are associated with turnout and with other forms of participation as well (McLeod, Bybee, Luetscher, & Garramone, 1981; McLeod & McDonald, 1985). Teixeira (1992) goes well beyond structural factors such as poverty and mobility to examine a range of motivational variables that are shown to affect turnout positively and negatively and suggests a number of campaign and media reforms designed to increase turnout.

Interpersonal Communication. The Columbia studies posed interpersonal communication as an alternative to mass media influence, noting that on an average day, 10% more discussed the election than read or heard about it through the media (Lazarsfeld et al., 1948). Other observers have come to see this as a "synthetic competition" (Chaffee, 1982), arguing that media and interpersonal channels may have convergent, complementary, or other relationships as well. There is substantial evidence that both customary patterns of exposure and attention to newspaper public affairs content and exposure to the media during the campaign stimulate interpersonal discussion (McLeod et al., 1979). Although not very efficient in conveying information about issues, the media do seem to stimulate interpersonal discussion and interest in the campaign (McLeod et al.,

1979). Interpersonal discussion helps people decide how to vote and may stimulate turnout except where the others in the conversational network are of the opposite party. Even discussion with strangers may affect voting. Noelle-Neumann (1984) reported that willingness to express a particular side of an issue in conversations with strangers ultimately led to change in opinion toward that side. Popkin (1990) found that in the early primary states where door-to-door canvassing is still possible, people contacted by one candidate's supporters subsequently paid more attention to all candidates in the news. This had the effect of increasing turnout on primary election day.

Systemic Effects

Two very different processes are implied by systemic effects. The first are media effects on individuals that have consequences for societal and community systems. The second involves the influence of the collective features of institutions on individual behavior. The two are examples of micro-to-macro and macro-to-micro processes (McLeod, Pan, & Rucinski, 1995; Pan & McLeod, 1991).

Connecting micro individual-level effects and macro institutional-level consequences poses several difficult problems. First, systemic consequences are manifested through institutional policies, practices, and laws and other outcomes that transcend individual judgments. Second, systemic consequences are not reducible to the simple aggregation of individual-level effects. The distribution of effects, for example, can be of great theoretical significance, as in knowledge gap issues (Tichenor et al., 1970). Quite different concepts and theories are appropriate to various micro and macro levels (McLeod & Blumler, 1987). Finally, democratic practices involve collective forms of action such as socal movements whose fate involves the connection of groups to information and power.

In lieu of formal attempts at cross-level theorizing, we can take current problems with the political system and work backward to possible ways in which the media might be responsible. The problems of the American political system are well documented. Despite substantial increases in educational attainment over several decades, there has been no corresponding increase in knowledge (Delli Carpini & Keeter, 1996) and a substantial decline in voter turnout and certain other indicators of participation have been noted with alarm (Putnam, 1995, 2000). Unfortunately, the search for causes of political system stagnation has been confined largely to the potential displacement effects of spending time with television.

More substantial progress over the past decade has been made in research on macro-systemic to micro-individual effects. The structure of the person's discussion network influences participation (Huckfeldt &

Sprague, 1995; McLeod, Daily, et al., 1996). Size of discussion networks influence traditional participation not only directly but also indirectly by stimulating public affairs media use, issue discussion and reflection about the content of news, and issue talk (McLeod et al., 2001). The diversity or heterogeneity of network composition also affects these communication processes and knowledge of local affairs (McLeod et al., 2001; Sotirovic & McLeod, 2001).

Beyond the effects of microsocial discussion networks, the contexts of the larger neighborhood and community may have consequences for individual citizens' media use and participation. The level of community stability, the contextual aggregation of residential stability (low likelihood and desire to move) across all individuals sampled in a community, was associated with higher levels of trust and participation after all individual level variables had been introduced (Shah, McLeod, & Yoon, 2001). Further, contextual community stability interacted with individuals' level of Internet information exchange use to bolster participation. Newspaper hard news reading interacted with two contextual variables, institutional confidence and connectedness, to foster participation. Media impact depends on where we live collectively as well as how we live individually.

Evidence of political stratification depicts a political world sharply divided into a small group of sophisticated, involved citizens and a much larger group of uninterested and relatively uninformed citizens (Neuman, 1986). This stratified model of the political system may need qualification. Popkin (1991) has argued that increases in education have not deepened but nonetheless have broadened the number of issues seen as relevant to citizens' lives. It is likely that television news deserves some credit for this (Blumler & McLeod, 1974). Broadening may have led to an increase in the number of issue publics, that is, relatively small groups with intense interest in a particular issue but with much less interest in most other issues. Issue specialization poses problems for political party mobilization and for coverage by news media increasingly constrained in resources.

MORE-COMPLEX MODELS OF POLITICAL EFFECTS

Recent political communication effects research provides ample evidence that media impact is likely to be conditional rather than universal. Effects depend on orientations of audiences as well as on exposure to media content stimuli. They take the form of O-S-O-R models (Markus & Zajonc, 1985). The first O represents the set of structural, cultural, cognitive, and motivational characteristics the audience brings to the reception situation that affect the impact of messages (S). They are often referred to as individual differences, although they are likely to be socially determined.

They represent the person's *subjective* reactions to the *objective* conditions of the community and world in which he or she lives. These subjective orientations may alter effects either by directing the extent of use (dosage) of the messages or though interactions with message content magnifying or diminishing the strength (potency) of effect. In the former case, media use may *mediate* the effects of the orientations on some dependent variable. In the latter case, the orientation is said to act as a *moderator* of media effects (Baron & Kenny, 1986).

The second O denotes various ways audiences may deal with media messages and indicates which is likely to happen between the reception of messages and the subsequent response (R) or outcome. Activity is the label given to various intervening orientations (Hawkins & Pingree, 1986). As is true for the first O, activities may be conceptualized at various levels ranging from short-term physiological responses to more enduring complex behaviors after the reception.

Prereception Orientations

Political Sophistication and Involvement. Educational and other status factors have produced large differences in how much citizens know and care about politics. Since the UN campaign study more than a half-century ago (Star & Hughes, 1950), evidence has consistently shown that those already informed are more likely to learn new information. Such sophistication also provides more-complex schema for interpretation of ambiguous political campaign events (Graber, 1988). Although enhancing learning, sophistication may moderate other campaign effects such as agenda setting (Iyengar & Kinder, 1987; McLeod et al., 1974; Weaver, Graber, McCombs, & Eyal, 1981). More-involved citizens may have already formed their own agendas.

Partisanship. Political partisanship serves as a moderator of media effects. Where supportive sources of information are available, say Rush Limbaugh's radio show attracting gun owners, de facto selectivity is likely (Katz, 1987). Partisanship may act to minimize the effects of the media agenda (Iyengar & Kinder, 1987; McLeod et al., 1974). Priming is reduced among partisans when the primed news story is inconsistent with their predispositions (Iyengar & Kinder, 1987).

Worldviews and Values. Basic beliefs that seem to have little to do directly with political behavior may nonetheless have important implications for citizen activity. Worldviews, for example, are persons' lay theories about the world around them. Those who believe the world is fair and just, as well as those who are fatalistic in outlook, are less active because they imply different values and expectations as to how the news media should operate (McLeod, Sotirovic, & Holbert, 1998). Worldviews can be thought of as personal beliefs or lay theories about the world as it *is* or appears to be (empirical) to them in contrast to values as normative theories of the world as it *ought* to be.

Values that people hold as goals for their society and community have strong implications for media use and political participation (Inglehart, 1977, 1990). Holding strong *postmaterial* values (freedom to express ideas, helping each other, etc.) is strongly related to higher levels of public affairs media use and discussion of issues and to reflection on how the content of news and discussion fits into their lives (McLeod, Sotirovic, Voakes, et al., 1998; McLeod et al., 2001; Sotirovic & McLeod, 2001). Holding of *material* values (order, control by defense and fighting crime, etc.) tends to have a dampening effect on citizen action through more soft entertainment media use and less-frequent discussions that deter political engagement. Communication thus mediates the effects of worldviews and values on informed participation. Values may also act as moderators interacting with messages. Strength of values held by audience members interact with the value framing of content to affect decision-making outcomes (Shah, 2001).

News Media Orientations. The images or "common-sense theories" that people hold about news affect how much they learn from news (Kosicki & McLeod, 1990). Those who are skeptical about news quality appear to process it more critically and thoughtfully and thereby learn more (McLeod, Kosicki, Amor, Allen, & Philps, 1986). Those seeing news as having underlying patterns also tend to learn more from news. Citizens also differ in their level of agreement with various normative roles of the news media. Those emphasizing the *pluralistic* functions of watchdog, providing a forum for ideas, and helping people play active roles are much more likely to attentively use the news media, thus indirectly stimulating their knowledge and participation (McLeod, Sotirovic, Voakes, et al., 1998; Sotirovic & McLeod, 2001). In contrast, those more strongly advocating *consensual* functions are less knowledgeable and active due to their higher levels of attending to soft news and entertainment television.

Gratifications Sought from News. Uses-and-gratifications research originally was seen as an alternative rather than a complement to media effects research. Evidence has mounted to support a more dynamic role. Strength of motivation acted as a moderator in enhancing information gain from party broadcasts in an early British study (Blumler & McQuail, 1969) and has been validated for effects in the United States (McLeod & Becker, 1974). Gratifications sought may weaken as well as strengthen media effects. Readers with the strongest motivation to gain information failed to shift their salience ratings of issues in accordance with the agenda of the newspaper they read (McLeod et al., 1974).

Reception Activity Orientations

Effects are also conditioned by orientations during exposure to news. These can be measured physiologically below the level of the person's awareness (Reeves, Thorson, & Schleuder, 1986) or by using self-report measures that suffer the weaknesses of other self-report measures but do reveal substantial variance between persons.

Attention. Attention is the conscious focusing of increased mental effort. As applied to news, it can be measured from closed-ended questions regarding various types of news content and separately or combined across media. Attention is particularly important for television, where exposure takes place under very different levels of attention. In contrast, the reading of a newspaper or Internet information site demand more attention. Learning from news is enhanced at higher levels of attention (Chaffee & Choe, 1980; Chaffee & Schleuder, 1986). Exposure to debates may convey only minimal knowledge, but it does stimulate campaign interest and discussion in formulating voting decisions (McLeod et al., 1979). Exposure and attention may have more than additive effects. Exposure to hard news interacted with attention to increase both knowledge about the economy and community participation (McLeod & McDonald, 1985).

Information-Processing Strategies. Audience activity includes strategies people employ to cope with the "flood of information" that threatens to overwhelm them (Graber, 1988). Surveys using a set of self-report items found three dimensions of audience news information-processing strategies (Kosicki & McLeod, 1990; Kosicki, McLeod, & Amor, 1987): *selective scanning*, skimming, and turning out items; *active processing*, going beyond or "reading through" a story to reinterpret it according to the person's needs; and *reflective integration*, replaying the story in the person's mind and using it as a topic of discussion. The extent of political learning, political interest, and participation were restricted by selective scanning and enhanced by reflective integration. Active processing had little effect on learning but did stimulate interest and participation. All three processing strategies were related to different conceptual frames that people use to interpret and understand public issues (McLeod et al., 1987).

More-recent research has tended to concentrate on reflective integration, particularly on its intrapersonal aspects often called simply *reflection*. Reflective integration in its more inclusive measurement mediates news use impact in its direct effects on political knowledge (Fredin & Kosicki, 1989; Kosicki, Becker, & Fredin, 1994; McLeod, Scheufele, & Moy, 1999; Sotirovic & McLeod, 2001). Reflection also mediates news in enhancing traditional forms of participation (McLeod, Scheufele, & Moy, 1999; McLeod et al. 2001; Sotirovic & McLeod, 2001) as well as participation in public forums (McLeod, Scheufele, Moy, Horowitz, et al., 1999; McLeod et al., 2001). Reflection acted as the strongest mediating variable in specifying the indirect effects of 11 antecedent variables on cognitive complexity, citizen efficacy, and three forms of participation (McLeod et al., 2001).

EFFECTS ON POLITICIANS AND POLICY MAKERS

Media also influence policy makers and the public policy process. But, as seen earlier, these effects too are unlikely to be simple and direct. We consider several types of effects on public institutions, on politicians, and on public policy processes.

Protess et al. (1991) considered the effects of investigative reporting on achieving various civic reforms in areas such as health care, crime, and housing. Their coalition model of agenda building focuses attention on the interactions of investigative journalism with government policy makers, citizens, and interest groups. The effects of investigative reporting are thus not seen as acting through a mobilization model in which journalists stir up the citizenry to press their elected officials to work for reforms. Instead, the coalition model focuses on the interactions of journalists with a variety of interest groups and public officials to garner public support for necessary reforms.

Kaniss (1991) examined a variety of press procedures and workways on reporting of major civic projects such as the $523 million Philadelphia Convention Center, the most expensive undertaking in the history of the city. Kaniss argued that fundamental media values—metropolitan pride, economic self-interest, and a variety of workways—drive the local media to support such mammoth civic spending projects.

In the legislative arena, the nomination of Judge Robert Bork to the U.S. Supreme Court provided an unusual focal point for the intersection of media, interest groups, and legislators. Bork's nomination was ultimately rejected by the Senate, but only after one of the most intense information campaigns in history, notable for its use of formative research (Pertschuk & Schaetzel, 1989). Regarding more typical legislative activity, Cook (1989) presented a variety of ways that media influence the legislative process. These range from structural changes in office procedures thereby accommodating the press to influencing the legislative strategies of individual members. Media publicity coupled with the chairmanship of an important committee or subcommittee can be a powerful tool for achieving policy goals (Smith, 1988) and raising large amounts of money to help ward off electoral challengers and wage reelection campaigns (Etzioni, 1988; Goldenberg & Traugott, 1984). The vast amount of money raised by politicians for their campaigns is now thought by some to represent a major antidemocratic force (e.g., Bennett, 1992; Drew, 1983; Etzioni, 1988). This conclusion is controversial, however (e.g., Sabato, 1987).

RETHINKING CITIZENSHIP AND EFFORTS
TO RECONSTRUCT CIVIC LIFE

Decline in Citizen Engagement?

Discrepancies between the high normative standards of democratic theory and empirical evidence of low levels of citizens' engagement have been noted repeatedly since the early Columbia voting studies (Berelson et al., 1954). Narrow concern with falling voting turnout rates turned to near panic with the popular acceptance of Robert Putnam's (1995) "bowling alone" thesis and evidence for a 30-year decline in a wide range of other political and civic participation indicators. Twelve political and communal activities declined an average of 27% from 1973–74 to 1993–94, for example (Putnam, 2000, p. 45). Trust in other people, a key indicator in Putnam's concept of social capital, slipped from 55% to 35% from 1960 to 1999 (Putnam, 2000, p. 140).

How serious are these problems? Putnam (2000) himself notes that volunteering is at a record high and adds that helping behavior is positively related to other activities and to low levels of cynicism. He finds some mixed evidence for an increase in small group and social movements activity. Others have noted that his trends may actually be cycles; the period of the 60s and early 70s was a high-water mark for electoral participation being preceded by a dormant period of the 20s equal to that of the 80s and 90s.

Michael Schudson (1998, 1999) attacks the criteria of Putnam's thesis, arguing that the outdated "rationalistic information-based" *informed citizen* model should be replaced by a *rights-based monitorial citizen* model better suited to the conditions of contemporary society. Assertion of rights by a diverse set of groups is a key feature of public life. This "revolution in due process" expands the political field and results in a growth of elite-challenging political action and a proliferation of nonparty political agencies, social movements often spinning off from one another. Rather than resting on a consensual base of shared knowledge and active participation, integration of society is based on "plural equality," acceptance of noninvidious social differences and on "fundamental civility and social connectedness" (Schudson, 1999, pp. 19–21).

What can we conclude from this debate and what implications does this have for the study of political communication? It appears many forms of participation have declined over the past 30 years, some forms are stable, and some may be increasing. One point of agreement is that participation rates have not kept up with the rising levels of education over recent decades. This same generalization holds for political knowledge as well (Delli Carpini & Keeter, 1996). Levels of knowledge have, overall, remained rather stable despite increased levels of educational attainment. Even if we downplay the allegations of democratic stagnation and accept Schudson's rights-based model, his monitorial citizen still requires some knowledge and willingness to act when threats to the public good arise and in various ways is more demanding of thought, skills, and activity than is the informed citizen role. It is important, however, that we rethink what forms of knowledge and skills citizens need to be effectively engaged in contemporary society. Citizens need media content that helps them to reflect on and connect whatever facts they acquire to their own lives and to larger issue frameworks.

What is most striking is the failure of Putnam and others involved in the debate over declining civic engagement to deal with news media use in any meaningful way. Putnam's concern is confined to the alleged effects of time spent with television displacing participation. The evidence for displacement is weak and reverse causation is likely—those who stay home rather than going out to participate may well turn to television for diversion. More surprising is their ignoring decades of mass communication showing positive effects of news media use (when adequately measured) on political knowledge and participation (e.g., Blumler & McLeod,1974; Chaffee & Schleuder, 1986; McLeod & McDonald, 1985; McLeod, Daily, et al., 1996; Smith, 1986; Wattenberg, 1984). Declining patterns of regular newspaper reading, along with lower levels of availability of a local daily paper in many local areas, have not been investigated as sources of stagnation in civic life.

Implications for Political Communication Research

Political communication research nonetheless has been greatly affected by increased concern over the health of American democracy. Two related trends are particularly important. First, the term *civic* has gradually replaced *political* as the label for the field, and second, the community has become an important context and unit of analysis for research. Citizens' active participation takes place primarily at the local level, and there is considerable carryover from the networks formed in apolitical contexts to activities traditionally thought of as political (Verba, Schlozman, & Brady, 1995).

Civic Participation. The civic turn has markedly broadened the criteria for communication effects through the examination of local issues and nontraditional forms of participation (McLeod, Daily, et al., 1999; McLeod, Guo, et al., 1996) and interpersonal trust as a mediator (Shah, 1998; Shah, Kwak, & Holbert, 2001; Shah, McLeod, & Yoon, 2001). It has redirected the study of participation toward the question of how civic engagement is stimulated conjointly by local media use, local issue discussion, and community ties (McLeod, Daily, et al., 1996; McLeod, Scheufele, & Moy, 1999; Stamm, Emig, & Hesse, 1997).

Community Focus. Community has been reconceptualized to meet changing urban environments as a communicatively integrated unit rapidly advancing to a networked form of social organization (Friedland, 2001a). Social networks, potentially facilitated by the new technology, are seen as the structural linkages between individuals, neighborhoods, associations, and the local media (Friedland & McLeod, 1999). Communities serve as the arenas for citizen action and provide the context for norms and expectations for such actions. In larger urban areas, neighborhoods take on these functions and potentially convey a sense of belonging to residents (Ball-Rokeach, Kim, & Matei, 2001).

Civic Socialization. That younger people participate less has been a consistent finding over a half-century of political behavior research. Citizen involvement increases with age. What is disturbing from research of the past decade is that a cohort phenomenon may be at work along with the maturational effect. For example, in the three presidential elections (1988 to 1996), voter turnout in the 18–24 age group averaged 37%, 21% lower than among all citizens (Casper & Bass, 1998). This compares unfavorably with three previous elections (1972 to 1980), when the 18–24 age group averaged 44% turnout, 17% below that of all citizens. Recent cohorts have contributed most to the decline in other aspects of electoral participation (Miller & Shanks, 1996) and in civic engagement (Putnam, 2000).

Also fueling concern are findings of cohort effects in the decline of newspaper reading in recent decades (Peiser, 2000). News use is a strong factor in stimulating youth participation (Chaffee, McLeod, & Wackman, 1973; Chaffee, Pan, & McLeod, 1995). The implication of the cohort effects findings is that the current pattern of low participation among the young is apt to translate into even lower rates of overall participation as they move through the life cycle.

Concern with declining youth participation has precipitated a reexamination of the political socialization research that was popular in the 1960s (Flanagan & Sherrod, 1998; Niemi, 1999). Political socialization work virtually disappeared after the 1970s, in large part because it was based on a flawed developmental transmission model. The developing adolescent was seen as a passive recipient in the learning process. Reflecting the stability bias of the historical period, what was to be learned was a fixed set of "norms, values, attitudes, and behaviors accepted and practiced by the ongoing system" (Sigel, 1965, p. 1). Diversity and conflict within the society were not considered. Today it seems appropriate to treat societies and communities not as unified wholes, but as arenas where many forces with differing interests are contending.

The new civic socialization research conceives of youth as potential participants actively engaged in the world around them, often trying out roles in anticipation of adulthood. Civic knowledge, interpersonal trust, and efficacious attitudes remain as criteria for socialization effects, but so are news media use, issue discussion, thoughtful processing of information, listening and turn-taking in discussions, and working out compromises (McLeod, 2000).

Programs for Improving Democractic Processes

Concern for the health of democratic practices has led to an unprecedented number of reform efforts during the past decade. Many of the reform programs addressed problems in the conduct of election campaigns. Reforms not limited to campaigns focus on the news media whereas others target youth as a crucial category for long-term change.

Adwatch. These efforts, which are now a staple of network and local news coverage of campaigns, represent a new level of activity by journalists. Jamieson (1992) promulgated a series of "visual grammar" principles to guide journalists toward effective efforts to combat the power of negative ads after noticing that previous efforts seemed to magnify the power of the ads they were designed to attack. This occurs largely through the need to quote the offending ad in order to then systematically attack it. Adwatch efforts have come under criticism (Ansolabehere & Iyengar, 1995; Pfau & Louden, 1994) as ineffective, largely because of journalistic timidity; that is, journalists too often quote an ad in a news program, thus giving it an audience it would never have on its own, and attack its principles in ineffective ways (Jamieson & Cappella, 1997). Various suggestions have been investigated to improve the power of journalism to fight advertising, including greater attention to the audiovisual narrative elements of ads, and focusing on larger patterns, not details (Richardson, 1998).

Deliberative Forums. The deliberative forms of democracy have been emphasized more in the past decade as a result of growing concern about erosion of the ability of average citizens to influence their own futures. Although the media may do much to raise consciousness of issues, the argument goes, they do little to help their audiences to *work through* issues to connect them to their own lives (Yankelovich, 1991). Forums and other means of bringing average citizens together to discuss issues have been used as a potential corrective. Deliberative polling, bringing a cross-section sample of citizens from across the country to Austin, Texas, in 1996 to discuss campaign issues was the most ambitious (and expensive) of these experiments (Fishkin, 1996).

Though the sponsors of this Deliberative Polling program claim very positive results, others view the evidence less favorably (Merkle, 1996). More common have been local issue forums, often sponsored by local media as part of their civic journalism efforts. Contrasting citizens attracted to these local forums with participants in more traditional political behavior reveals some marked differences. The effects of education, age, income, and home ownership are much stronger for traditional than for forum participation (McLeod, Daily, et al., 1996; Mcleod, Guo, et al., 1996, McLeod et al., 2001). Beyond social status, large discussion networks appear to recruit citizens for traditional behaviors also characterized by high levels of civic knowledge. In contrast, values, public affairs media use, reflection, and perceptions of citizen efficacy have stronger impact on forum attendance (McLeod et al., 2001). The lesser status influence on the composition of forums is an advantage by egalitarian democratic standards; however, their lack of selectivity in terms of knowledge may limit their utility for exchange of information between citizens.

Civic/Public Journalism. Civic journalism emerged in the 1990s as a broad-based grassroots movement, primarily within local news organizations. The approach is motivated by a critique of existing journalistic norms and workways promulgated by Mathews (1994), Merritt (1995), and Rosen (1999) and supported by foundations including the Kettering Foundation and Pew Charitable Trusts. A variety of typical practices have become associated with civic journalism, although no single civic journalism product has emerged. Typical practices involve ways to engage citizens such as civic forums, putting ordinary citizens in touch with powerful officeholders, and saturation coverage of social issues such as crime or substance abuse. Controversial elements of the civic journalism approach include the use of surveys and focus groups to guide selection of topics for news coverage of elections and the sponsoring of civic forums. Such practices give critics cause to say journalists are overstepping their bounds as neutral observers. Different media often work together cooperatively on large multimedia projects. These attempts to avoid characteristic biases of journalism are noteworthy and have provided numerous opportunities for scholars to examine local journalism in the context of communities (Friedland, Sotirovic, & Daily, 1998).

The variety in goals and strategies used in the dozens of local civic journalism efforts makes overall generalizations about success difficult. One key to their successes is that local media can facilitate the construction of local networks of deliberation and action that endure beyond the time frame of the program (Friedland, 2001a, 2001b). Denton and Thorson (1998) also found positive effects on political knowledge of a civic journalism intervention in a local community. Eksterowicz, Roberts, and Clark (1998) look to civic journalism as a recipe for improving levels of political knowledge. On the national level, Alvarez (1997) has examined several elections using national survey data and complex rational choice models to show, among other things, that voters are unlikely to vote for candidates about whom they know very little. Knowledge gain was also featured prominently in results of the National Issues Convention experiment in which a nationally representative random sample of people were assembled in Austin in 1996 to hear discussion and debate about the upcoming national election. People did learn from this exercise. The challenge is to draw lessons for the coverage of national politics.

Media-Based Youth Programs.   Concern with low levels of participation among the young led to the development in the 1990s of dozens of school-based intervention programs using media as sources of learning or media production by youth as a learning device (Sirianni & Friedland, 2001). The strong interest of adolescents in new media beyond television—videos, computers, and CDs (Roberts, 2000)—provides the basis for such programs. The low level of news media use among adolescents is partly compensated for by their use of new technologies. Young adults not only are more likely than older adults to use the Internet for information search and exchange, but also the strength of effect of such use on civic engagement is greater (Shah, Kwak, & Holbert, 2001; Shah, McLeod, & Yoon, 2001). Though various media-based programs have been successful, the complex processes by which they achieve their goals are seldom evaluated. A KidsVoting USA project was successful in stimulating adolescent civic engagement through strategically combining the strengths of teachers, parents, and local media (Chaffee et al., 1995; McDevitt & Chaffee, 1998; McLeod, Eveland, & Horowitz, 1998). Local media provided publicity for the program and content for classroom assignments. The program also reduced knowledge and participation gaps by gender (McLeod, Eveland, & Horowitz, 1998) and social class (McDevitt & Chaffee, 2000).

What lessons can be learned from the evaluation of these reform programs involving media? First, programs involving active and reflective learning have more lasting impact than do those confined to the passive learning of facts. Civics courses involving expressive activities were more effective in conveying knowledge (Niemi & Junn, 1998). Service learning in activities provide knowledge and skills lasting into adulthood (Youniss, McLellan, & Yates, 1997), particularly where the subject matter is tied to the field experience and where there is adequate reflection and evaluation (Niemi, Hepburn, & Chapman, 2000). Second, inducing change through media use is more likely to be effective when combined with the development of networks to discuss issues, support participation, and sustain change. Media use patterns and networks developed around one issue are apt to carry over and provide the social capital for citizen action on other issues (Friedland, 2001a). Finally, fundamental improvement in the quantity and quality of civic life requires not only change in individual citizens but also the involvement of local associations and institutions in the community.

EVALUATING DEMOCRATIC STANDARDS FOR NEWS MEDIA PERFORMANCE

As we mentioned at the outset of this chapter, political communication research, perhaps more than any other area, cannot ignore normative questions about how the media "ought" to work. Gurevitch and Blumler (1990) identified eight normative standards (discussed later) for mass media systems in democratic societies. As these authors note, the media often fall far short of these democratic standards. They suggested that four major obstacles hinder the attainment of these democratic goals. First, these expectations may themselves conflict, necessitating trade-offs and compromises. For example, the principle of editorial autonomy may conflict with providing platforms for advocacy. Second, the dialogue of elite political communicators is often distanced from the perspectives of ordinary people, thus limiting the latter's participation. Third, because political participation is voluntary in a democratic society, many citizens may choose to be politically apathetic. Finally, social, political, and economic environments may constrain the media's pursuit of these democratic ideals. These are problems that require closer examination.

It may be useful to extend Gurevitch and Blumler's (1990) eight democratic standards by using knowledge gained from political communication effects research to discuss problems of media performance and their
possible antecedents and consequences. We consider each standard in
turn, presenting some alleged news performance deficiencies and possible constraints accounting for these deficiencies. We then suggest possible
individual effects of the alleged deficiencies and what might be their consequences for the political system. In the process, we propose some new
directions for future research.

Surveillance of Relevant Events

Although surveillance of the environment has long been recognized as a
primary function of the press (Lasswell, 1948), the press is not only a simple conduit of events. News coverage involves selecting a few developments that are most likely to impinge on the welfare of citizens (Gurevitch
& Blumler, 1990). The many publics in a modern society attach themselves
to issues in quite different ways, and few stories are similarly relevant to
all citizens. Budgetary constraints, grown tighter in recent years, limit the
resources available for news coverage. This increases dependence on official sources and presentation as elite versions of events rather than as
problems confronting average citizens. The market structure of media not
only has limited, less "cost-efficient" coverage, but also has shifted news
style to short and entertaining "infotainment." Network television news
is constrained by shortened sound bites and its rigid "22-minute ration"
of time, with fixed placement of commercials (Gurevitch & Blumler, 1990).
    Political learning research seems to confirm the fear that the problems
of media coverage adversely affect audiences. The amount of learning
from television is slight. Large numbers of citizens see news as boring and
politics as disconnected from their lives. System consequences may
include not only a less-informed electorate and low voter turnout but also
campaigns that focus on pseudoevents and personalities rather than
issues (Jamieson, 1992).
    A case can be made in defense of media performance, however. The
media present a more-extensive diet of events than most citizens appear
willing to consume. Popkin (1991) argued that people learn from media as
much as they think they need to know, or perhaps as much as they think
they can comprehend. Research techniques may confuse the issue, to the
extent that research showing weak learning effects has used specific "factual" information as a criterion. This may paint too bleak a picture of citizen awareness and, by implicitly blaming the audience for its lack of
interest, may justify even further shortening and softening of news.
Research has recently broadened the criteria to examine how audiences

construct the news to fit their own experiences (McLeod et al., 1987; Morley, 1980; Philo, 1990). The resulting protocols are often impressive in their sense-making structure, if not their factual basis. Future research might test whether variations in characteristics of news (e.g., Bennett, 2000) restrict complexity of understanding.

Identification of Key Issues

The media have a responsibility not only to identify key issues but also to analyze the forces that have formed them and the possibilities for their resolution. Critics charge that the agenda set by the media is not broad, balanced, or meaningful. Rather, it is set from the agenda of dominant institutions. Decontextualized and ahistorical presentation of issues are said to lead to issues being understood as little more than labels without consequences. Abstract issues that are difficult to portray visually, and those requiring specialized knowledge seldom found among news staffs, may have difficulty getting onto the media agenda. Lack of meaningful agenda setting may have systemic consequences in restricting governmental decisions to immediate appearances and short-term payoffs. Adoption of the media agenda, being most common among those least attached to the political system, has implications for greater system instability.

The media agenda undoubtedly does affect audience judgments of the importance of issues. More research is needed, however, on the processes by which the agenda is set, including the struggles of contending powers to control language as well as priorities of the agenda. It matters a great deal, for example, whether an insurgent army is framed in the press as "brave freedom fighters" or as "hired guns," and perhaps even more whether the audience adopts that frame (McLeod et al., 1990).

Provision of Platforms for Advocacy

Democratic change depends on consideration of a wide range of views and proposals. The media thus could be judged on how well they provide for "intelligible and illuminating platforms" from which politicians and spokespersons of various causes can make appeals (Gurevitch & Blumler, 1990). Public access cable channels have very low viewership, and mainstream media are apt to grant access only if the group takes direct action whose illegality or unusual character makes it newsworthy. Even mainstream groups are forced to conform to media practices by "running the news value gauntlet" (Blumler, 1990). The ideologies of objectivity and press autonomy contribute to resist access; journalists tend to see advocacy as a threat to a free press and to control over their own jobs.

Media effects research barely touches on the issues of access, partly because access is so limited. If sufficient variation in access could be found, criteria might include how aware citizens are of nonmainstream groups and positions and their approval of political participation even in less-traditional forms. Systemic outcomes might include the popularity of public access programming and participation of lower-status groups in the political process.

Transmission of Diverse Political Discourse

Media can be judged by how well they facilitate dialogue between diverse views and two-way communication between power holders and mass publics. Critics charge that the media focus instead on "mainstream currents bounded politically by the two-party system, economically by the imperative of private enterprise capitalism, and culturally by the values of a consumer society" (Gurevitch & Blumler, 1990, p. 269). Nonmainstream political groups are marginalized as "deviant" (Gitlin, 1980; McLeod & Hertog, 1992), and little coverage is given to less-attractive audiences like the poor and the elderly. The result may be that citizens are lacking in awareness of political alternatives and unable even to articulate their own views. The implication for the political system is a narrowing of the boundaries of the "marketplace of ideas."

A combination of content analysis and audience research might be useful for evaluating media on this standard. Dialogue may be effective only if the media systematically compare diverse points of view and alternate frames. Media presentations might be expected to help citizens recognize and articulate their own feelings and connect them to larger political contexts. Attentive reading of hard news in the print media does seem to facilitate such connections and allows them to be discussed with others (McLeod et al., 1989).

Scrutiny of Institutions and Officials

The media standing as a watchdog over government is one of the cherished images of U.S. journalism. Investigative reporting is a key mechanism for holding officials accountable for their performance. Critics charge, however, that the growth of government and of economic organizations has far outstripped the ability of the press to engage in costly investigations of these institutions. The result is a general lack of government and corporate accountability. Investigative reporting that is done may aim too low in the chain of corruption, as in focusing on street pushers and users in drug coverage, and in many cases the blame is placed on individuals rather than on fundamental systemic causes.

Research on causal attribution is highly relevant to this standard. Coverage of government wrongdoing, unless placed in a larger structural and historical context, may nullify any beneficial effects the stories might have had on citizens. Future research might investigate whether sustained episodic coverage of government problems lessens interest in knowing how government works and/or increases cynicism about politics.

Activation of Informed Participation

News media may be evaluated by how well they provide incentives for citizens to learn about and become involved in politics. The news media do not appear to pay much attention to this standard, at least to the extent there is a lack of "mobilizing information" (Lemert, Mitzman, Seither, Cook, & Hackett, 1977). Citizen activation may require articulation of the feelings of less-involved citizens and transforming them into more-organized views. Although techniques of reaching mass voting publics have become more sophisticated, feedback from the public remains limited, indirect, and distorted. The political system pays a price in loss of potential "participatory energy the system might generate" (Gurevitch & Blumler, 1990).

The vast literature on political participation pays little attention to media influences (Verba & Nie, 1972; Verba et al., 1995). Media effects findings do have implications for participation, however. The failure to see systemic consequences, limited in part by the episodic and personalized media content of television news, may deter active participation. Political activation is also a matter of media treatment of protest groups. The social movement literature is highly relevant for evaluation of press performance on activation.

Maintenance of Media Autonomy

Protection of the press from governmental interference is a key element of the First Amendment. Without such protection, all other democratic standards are in jeopardy. Maintenance of media autonomy, however, is much more than the absence of governmental restraints envisioned by the founding fathers. Government growth and corporate power deserve close scrutiny by the press, but this is made difficult because major media have themselves become part of larger corporate conglomerates. Given the problems of media in the modern marketplace, the autonomy standard demands a "principled resistance to the efforts of forces outside the media to subvert their independence, integrity and ability to serve the audience" (Gurevitch & Blumler, 1990, p. 279). In cases where such resistance has been attempted, as in press attempts to forestall strict governmental controls in the Gulf War, efforts to assert autonomy have failed. At worst, the result is elite perspectives presenting a high proportion of news generated from official bureaucratic sources. Journalists may react to covering stories dominated by manipulative sources by inserting disdaining comments in the stories they cover. This may bolster the self-respect of the journalist, but its impact on learning and interest in politics among the viewers is a matter to be investigated.

Consideration of Audience Potential

Each of the first seven democratic standards concerns media performance highly constrained by relationships where individual journalists have limited room to maneuver. Consideration of audience potential is less constrained by production forces and more a matter of how journalists define their audiences. As Gurevitch and Blumler put it, consideration involves "a sense of respect for the audience member, as potentially concerned and able to make sense out of his or her environment" (p. 270). The complaint here is that journalists and media executives, faced with pressures to maximize their audiences and to produce news according to consumer-driven standards, have bought into the hierarchical view that there is only a small elite core of interested citizens and a very large uninterested mass. Existing preferences for light fare and the seemingly limited abilities of most citizens to comprehend news may be seen as being natural and immutable, rather than as functions of life experiences or as stemming from inadequacies in the construction of news. Journalists may use their own working theories that see the information-seeking citizen as a fiction to justify short sound bites, episodic stories, and the blurring of lines between news and entertainment.

Research indicates that most citizens are at least somewhat aware of important public issues, and many have greater interest and knowledge in a particular issue that is consequential to them (Krosnick, 1990). Despite low levels of specific knowledge, citizens often develop elaborate frameworks to make sense of the world. Unless news producers make efforts to develop alternatives to the increasingly homogeneous patterns of news construction, the trend toward lower interest in politics is likely to continue. The long-term consequences for the political system are to erode political discourse toward the simplistic and to increase the social status disparities in political participation.

SOME CONCLUDING REMARKS

We have presented various ways in which the boundaries of political communication effects research have expanded in recent years. Movement has been "horizontal," connecting individual effects with other parts of the mass communication process: potential problems of media content, institutional and professional forms and practices constraining media content, and consequences of individual effects for political system operation. Broadening of effects also necessitates "vertical" linkages of individual behavior with political system institutions and interpersonal processes. Expansion is also seen in the diversity of media effects considered and in alternative conceptualizations of media messages. Political effects are now more likely to be seen as having varying impact contingent on characteristics of particular segments of the audience and as operating in an indirect and delayed fashion. Finally, we have shown how very different methodological strategies have informed the body of political communication knowledge.

We have noted the particularly close connection of political research to normative assumptions of how societies ought to work. Rather than trying to separate normative assumptions from empirical research, we suggest such assumptions might operate as standards against which we can evaluate media performance. McQuail (1992) used a similar starting point to develop an elaborate system for media evaluation including appropriate empirical research strategies. To illustrate how such standards might help to separate often-conflated charges about media performance, we have used eight democratic standards developed by Gurevitch and Blumler (1990). Charges about deficiencies in media performance are often vague and lacking in evidence. It appears, however, that a considerable amount of empirical research on political effects is highly pertinent to particular standards. Many critical assertions about media performance have not been examined empirically, and these are appropriate subjects for research. More systematic connections, particularly those between production constraints and media content and those between individual effects and system consequences, will be needed before more comprehensive theories are possible. This will require searching for variance between systems where little is found within systems and using a variety of methods to search out connections.

In conclusion, we should like to point out that the news media are by no means the sole cause nor even a major cause of current problems in the political system. Responsibility must be shared with other social institutions: the family, schools, political parties, and political leaders who have "joint custody" of democracy. That makes systematic study of the media's political effects no less necessary.

REFERENCES

Adams, W. C. (1987). As New Hampshire goes. . . . In G. Orren & N. Polsby (Eds.), *Media and momentum: The New Hampshire primary and nomination politics* (pp. 42–59). Chatham, NJ: Chatham House.

Akhavan-Majid, R., & Ramaprasad, J. (1998). Framing and ideology: A comparative analysis of U.S. and Chinese newspaper coverage of the Fourth United Nations Conference on Women and the NGO Forum. *Mass Communication and Society, 1,* 131–152.

Altheide, D. L., & Snow, R. P. (1991). *Media worlds in the postjournalism era.* Hawthorn, NY: Aldine de Gruyter.

Alvarez, R. M. (1997). *Information and elections.* Ann Arbor: University of Michigan Press.

Amor, D. L., McLeod, J. M., & Kosicki, G. M. (1987, May). *Images of the mass media, orientation to the world: Where do public images of the mass media come from?* Paper presented at the meeting of the International Communication Association, Montreal, Quebec.

Ansolabehere, S., & Iyengar, S. (1995). *Going negative.* New York: Free Press.

Ansolabehere, S. & Iyengar, S. (1996). The craft of political advertising: A progress report. In D. C. Mutz, P. M. Sniderman, & R. A. Brody (Eds.), *Political persuasion and attitude change* (pp. 101–122). Ann Arbor: University of Michigan Press.

Ball-Rokeach, S. J., Kim, Y-C., & Matei, S. (2001). Storytelling neighborhood: Paths to belonging in diverse urban environments. *Communication Research, 28,* 392–428.

Baron, R. M., & Kenny, D. A. (1986). The moderator-mediator variable distinction in social psychological research: Conceptual, strategic, and statistical considerations. *Journal of Personality and Social Psychology, 51,* 1173–1182.

Bennett, W. L. (1992). *The governing crisis: Media, money and marketing in American elections.* New York: St. Martin's Press.

Bennett, W. L. (2000). Introduction: Communication and civic engagement in comparative perspective. *Political Communication, 17,* 307–312.

Bennett, W. L. (2001). *News: The politics of illusion* (4th ed.). New York: Longman.

Berelson, B. R. (1952). *Content analysis as a tool of communication research.* New York: Free Press.

Berelson, B. R., Lazarsfeld, P. F., & McPhee, W. N. (1954). *Voting: A study of opinion formation in a presidential campaign.* Chicago: University of Chicago Press.

Berkowitz, L., & Rogers, K. H. (1986). A priming effect analysis of media influences. In J. Bryant & D. Zillmann (Eds.), *Perspectives on media effects* (pp. 57–81). Hillsdale, NJ: Lawrence Erlbaum Associates.

Blumler, J. G. (Ed.). (1983). *Communicating to voters: Television in the first European parliamentary election.* London: Sage.

Blumler, J. G. (1990). Elections, media and the modem publicity process. In M. Ferguson (Ed.), *Public communication: The new imperatives: Future directions for media research* (pp. 101–113). London: Sage.

Blumler, J. G., & McLeod, J. M. (1974). Communication and voter turnout in Britain. In T. Legatt (Ed.), *Sociological theory and social research* (pp. 265–312). London, Beverly Hills, CA: Sage.

Blumler, J. G., McLeod, J. M., & Rosengren, K. E. (1992). An introduction to comparative communication research. In J. G. Blumler, J. M. McLeod, & K. E. Rosengren (Eds.), *Comparatively speaking: Communication and culture across space and time* (pp. 3–18). Newbury Park, CA: Sage.

Blumler, J. G., & McQuail, D. (1969). *Television in politics: Its uses and influence.* Chicago: University of Chicago Press.

Bryant, J., & Zillmann, D. (Eds.). (1994). *Media effects: Advances in theory and research.* Hillsdale, NJ: Lawrence Erlbaum Associates.

Cappella, J. N., & Jamieson, K. H. (1997). *Spiral of cynicism: The press and the public good.* New York: Oxford University Press.

Casper, L. M., & Bass, L. E. (1998). Voting and registration in the election of November, 1996. *Current Population Reports, 20,* 20–504. Washington, DC: U.S. Bureau of the Census.

Chaffee, S. H. (1982). Mass media and interpersonal channels: Competitive, convergent or complementary? In G. Gumpert & R. Cathcart (Eds.), *Intermedia: Interpersonal communication in a media world* (pp. 57–77). New York: Oxford University Press.

Chaffee, S. H., & Choe, S. Y. (1980). Time of decision and media use during the Ford-Carter campaign. *Public Opinion Quarterly, 44,* 53–59.

Chaffee, S. H., & Hochheimer, J. (1985). The beginnings of political communication research in the United States: Origins of the limited effects model. In M. Gurevitch & M. Levy (Eds.), *Mass communication review yearbook* (Vol. 5, pp. 75–104). Beverly Hills, CA: Sage.

Chaffee, S. H., McLeod, J. M., & Wackman, D. B. (1973). Family communication patterns and adolescent political socialization. In J. Dennis (Ed.). *Socialization to politics* (pp. 349–363). New York: Wiley.

Chaffee, S. H., Pan, Z., & McLeod, J. M. (1995). *Effects of kids voting in San Jose: A quasi-experimental evaluation.* Final Report. Policy Study Center. Program in Media and Democracy, Annenberg School for Communication, University of Pennsylvania.

Chaffee, S. H., and Rimal, R. N. (1996). Time of decision and openness to persuasion. In D. C. Mutz, P. M. Sniderman, & R. A. Brody, (Eds.). *Political persuasion and attitude change* (pp. 267–291). Ann Arbor: University of Michigan Press.

Chaffee, S. H., & Schleuder, J. (1986). Measurement and effects of attention to media news. *Human Communication Research, 13,* 76–107.

Clarke, P., & Evans, S. (1983). *Covering campaigns.* Stanford, CA: Stanford University Press.

Cohen, B. C. (1963). *The press and foreign policy.* Princeton, NJ: Princeton University Press.

Cook, T. E. (1989). *Making laws and making news: Media strategies in the U.S. House of Representatives.* Washington, DC: Brookings Institution.

Dautrich, K., & Hartley, T. H. (1999). *How the news media fail American voters.* New York: Columbia University Press.

Delli Carpini, M. X. & Keeter, S. (1996). *What Americans know about politics and why it matters.* New Haven, CT: Yale University Press.

Denton, F. & Thorson, E. (1998). Effects of public multimedia journalism project on political knowledge and attitudes. In E. B. Lambeth, P. E. Meyer, & E. Thorson (Eds.), *Assessing public journalism.* Columbia, MO: University of Missouri Press.

Drew, E. (1983). *Politics and money: The new road to corruption.* New York: Macmillan.

Durham, F. (1998). News frames as social narratives: TWA Flight 800. *Journal of Communication, 48,* 100–117.

Entman, R. M. (1993). Toward clarification of a fractured paradigm. *Journal of Communication, 43,* 41–53.

Eksterowicz, A. J., Roberts, R., and Clark, A. (1998). Public journalism and public knowledge. *Harvard International Journal of Press/Politics, 3,* 74–95.

Ericson, R. V., Baranek, P. M., & Chan, B. L. (1989). *Negotiating control: A study of news sources.* Toronto: University of Toronto Press.

Ettema, J. S., & Kline, F. G. (1977). Deficits, differences, and ceilings: Contingent conditions for understanding the knowledge gap. *Communication Research, 4,* 179–202.

Etzioni, A. (1988). *Capital corruption: The new attack on American democracy.* New Brunswick, NJ: Transaction Books.

Fazio, R. H., & Williams, C. J. (1986). Attitude accessibility as a moderator of the attitude-perception and attitude-behavior relations: An investigation of the 1984 presidential election. *Journal of Personality and Social Psychology, 51,* 505–514.

Ferejohn, J. A., & Kuklinski, J. H. (1990). *Information and democratic processes.* Urbana, IL: University of Illinois Press.

Fiorina, M. P. (1981). *Retrospective voting in American national elections.* New Haven, CT: Yale University Press.

Fishbein, M., & Ajzen, I. (1975). *Belief, attitude, intention and behavior: An introduction to theory and research*. Reading, MA: Addison-Wesley.

Fishkin, J. S. (1996). Bringing deliberation to democracy. *Public Perspective, 7*, 1–4.

Flanagan C. A., & Sherrod, L. R. (1998). Youth political development: An introduction. *Journal of Social Issues, 54*, 447–456.

Fredin, E. S., & Kosicki, G. M. (1989) Cognitions and attitudes about community: Compensating for media images, *Journalism Quarterly, 66*, 571–578.

Friedland, L. A. (2001a). Communication, community, and democracy: Toward a theory of the communicatively integrated community. *Communication Research, 28*, 358–391.

Friedland, L. A. (2001b). *Learning public journalism*. Dayton, OH: Kettering Foundation.

Friedland, L. A., & McLeod, J. M. (1999). Community integration and mass media: A reconsideration. In D. Demers & K. Viswanath (Eds.) *Mass media, social control, and social change* (pp. 197–226). Ames: Iowa State University Press.

Friedland, L., Sotirovic, M., & Daily, K. (1998). Public journalism and social capital. In E. B. Lambeth, P. E. Meyer, & E. Thorson (Eds.), *Assessing public journalism* (pp. 191–220). Columbia: University of Missouri Press.

Funkhouser, G. R. (1973). The issues of the sixties: An exploratory study in the dynamics of public opinion. *Public Opinion Quarterly, 37*, 62–75.

Gamson, W. A. (1992). *Talking politics*. Cambridge: Cambridge University Press.

Gamson, W. A. (1996). Media discourse as a framing resource. In A. N. Crigler (Ed.), *The psychology of political communication* (pp. 111–132). Ann Arbor: University of Michigan Press.

Gamson, W. A., & Lasch, K. E. (1983). The political culture of social welfare policy. In S. Spiro & E. Yuchtman-Yaar (Eds.), *Evaluating the welfare state: Social and political perspectives* (pp. 397–415). New York: Academic Press.

Gamson, W. A., & Modigliani, A. (1989). Media discourse and public opinion: A constructivist approach. *American Journal of Sociology, 95*, 1–37.

Gandy, O. H. (1982). *Beyond agenda setting: Information subsidies and public policy*. Norwood, NJ: Ablex.

Gans, H. J. (1979). *Deciding what's news: A study of the CBS Evening News, NBC Nightly News, Newsweek and Time*. New York: Vintage Books.

Ghanem, S. (1997). Filling in the tapestry: The second level of agenda setting. In M. McCombs, D. L. Shaw, & D. Weaver (Eds.), *Communication and Democracy: Exploring the intellectual frontiers in agenda-setting theory* (pp. 3–14). Mahwah, NJ: Lawrence Erlbaum Associates.

Gilens, M. (1999). *Why Americans hate welfare*. Chicago: University of Chicago Press.

Gilliam, F. D., Iyengar, S., Simon, A., & Wright, O. (1996). Crime in black and white: The violent, scary world of local news. *Harvard International Journal of Press/Politics, 1*, 6–23.

Gitlin, T. (1978). Media sociology: The dominant paradigm. *Theory and Society, 6*, 205–253. Reprinted in G. Wilhoit & H. de Bock (Eds.), (1980). *Mass communication review yearbook* (Vol. 2, pp. 73–121). Beverly Hills, CA: Sage.

Gitlin, T. (1980). *The whole world is watching: Mass media and the making and unmaking of the New Left*. Berkeley, CA: University of California Press.

Glasgow Media Group. (1982). *Really bad news*. London: Writers & Readers.

Goffman, E. (1974). *Frame analysis*. New York: Harper & Row.

Goldenberg. E., & Traugott, M. (1984). *Campaigning for Congress*. Washington, DC: CQ Press.

Graber, D. (1988). *Processing the news: How people tame the information tide* (2nd ed.). New York: Longman.

Granberg, D., & Brown, T. A. (1989). On affect and cognition in politics. *Social Psychology Quarterly, 52,* 171–182.

Gunter, B. (1987). *Poor reception: Misunderstanding and forgetting broadcast news.* Hillsdale, NJ: Lawrence Erlbaum Associates.

Gurevitch, M., & Blumler, J. G. (1990). Political communication systems and democratic values. In J. Lichtenberg (Ed.), *Democracy and the mass media* (pp. 269–289). Cambridge: Cambridge University Press.

Hall, S., Critcher, C., Jefferson, T., Clarke, J., & Roberts, B. (1978). *Policing the crisis.* New York: Holmes & Meier.

Hallin, D. C. (1992). Sound bite news: Television coverage of elections, 1968–1988. *Journal of Communication, 42,* 5–24.

Hawkins, R. P., & Pingree, S. (1986). Activity in the effects of television on children. In J. Bryant & D. Zillmann (Eds.), *Perspectives on media effects* (pp. 233–250). Hillsdale, NJ: Lawrence Erlbaum Associates.

Herman, E. S., & Chomsky, N. (1988). *Manufacturing consent: The political economy of the mass media.* New York: Pantheon Books.

Herstein, J. A. (1985). Voter thought processes and voting theory. In S. Kraus & R. Perloff (Eds.), *Mass media and political thought* (pp. 15–36). Beverly Hills, CA: Sage.

Huckfeldt, R., & Sprague, J. (1995). *Citizens, politics, and social communication.* Cambridge: Cambridge University Press.

Huddie, L. (1997). Feminists and feminism in the news. In P. Norris (Ed.), *Women, media and politics* (pp. 183–220). New York: Oxford University Press.

Inglehart, R. (1977). *The silent revolution: Changing values and political styles among Western publics.* Princeton, NJ: Princeton University Press.

Inglehart, R. (1990). *Cultural shift in advanced industrial societies.* Princeton, NJ: Princeton University Press.

Iyengar, S. (1989). How citizens think about national issues. *American Journal of Political Science, 33,* 878–897.

Iyengar, S. (1991). *Is anyone responsible? How television frames political issues.* Chicago: University of Chicago Press.

Iyengar, S., & Kinder, D. R. (1987). *News that matters.* Chicago: University of Chicago Press.

Jamieson, K. H. (1992). *Dirty politics: Deception, distraction and democracy.* New York: Oxford University Press.

Jamieson, K. H., & Cappella, J. N. (1997). Setting the record straight: Do ad watches help or hurt? *Harvard International Journal of Press/Politics, 2,* 13–22.

Jones, E. E., & Nisbett, R. E. (1972). The actor and the observer: Divergent perceptions of the causes of behavior. In E. Jones, D. Kanouse, H. Kelley, R. Nisbett, S. Valins, & R. Kidd (Eds.), *New directions in attribution research* (pp. 79–94). Morristown, NJ: General Learning Press.

Jung, J. Y., Qiu, J. L., & Kim, Y. C. (2001). Internet connectedness and inequality. *Communication Research, 28,* 507–535.

Kahneman, D., & Tversky, A. (1984). Choice, values and frames. *American Psychologist, 39,* 341–350.

Kaniss, P. (1991). *Making local news.* Chicago: University of Chicago Press.

Katz, E. (1987). On conceptualizing media effects: Another look. In S. Oskamp (Ed.), *Applied Social Psychology Annual* (Vol. 8, pp. 32–42). Beverly Hills, CA: Sage.

Katz, E., & Feldman, J. J. (1962). The debates in the light of research: A survey of surveys. In S. Kraus (Ed.), *The great debates* (pp. 173–223). Bloomington: Indiana University Press.

Kennamer, J. D. (1988). News values and the vividness of information. *Written Communication, 5,* 108–123.

Kinder, D. R., & Kiewiet, D. R. (1983). Sociotropic politics: The American case. *British Journal of Political Science, 11,* 129–161.

Kinder, D. R., & Mebane, W. R., Jr. (1983). Politics and economics in everyday life. In K. Monroe (Ed.), *The political process and economic change* (pp. 141–180). New York: Agathon.

Kinder, D. R., & Sanders, L. M. (1990). Mimicking political debate with survey questions: The case of white opinion on affirmative action for blacks. *Social Cognition, 8,* 73–103.

Kinder, D. R., & Sanders, L. M. (1996). *Divided by color: Racial politics and democratic ideals.* Chicago: University of Chicago Press.

Klapper, J. T. (1960). *The effects of mass communications.* Glencoe, IL: Free Press.

Kosicki, G. M. (1993). Problems and opportunities in agenda-setting research. *Journal of Communication, 43,* 100–127.

Kosicki, G. M., Becker, L. B., & Fredin, E. S. (1994). Buses and ballots: The role of media images in a local election. *Journalism Quarterly, 71,* 76–89.

Kosicki, G. M., & McLeod, J. M. (1990). Learning from political news: Effects of media images and information-processing strategies. In S. Kraus (Ed.), *Mass communication and political information processing* (pp. 69–83). Hillsdale, NJ: Lawrence Erlbaum Associates.

Kosicki, G. M., McLeod, J. M., & Amor, D. L. (1987, May). *Processing the news: Some individual strategies for selecting, sense-making and integrating.* Paper presented at the meeting of the International Communication Association, Montreal, Quebec.

Kramer, G. H. (1983). The ecological fallacy revisited: Aggregate versus individual level findings on economics and elections and sociotropic voting. *American Political Science Review, 77,* 77–111.

Krosnick, J. A. (1989). Attitude importance and attitude accessibility. *Personality and Psychology Bulletin, 15,* 297–308.

Krosnick, J. A. (1990). Government policy and citizen passion: A study of issue publics in contemporary America. *Political Behavior, 12,* 59–93.

Krosnick, J. A. (1988). The role of attitude importance in social evaluation: A study of policy preference, presidential candidate evaluations, and voting behavior. *Journal of Personality and Social Psychology, 55,* 196–210.

Krosnick, J. A., & Kinder, D. R. (1990). Altering support for the president through priming: The Iran-Contra affair. *American Political Science Review, 84,* 497–512.

Lasswell, H. (1948). The structure and function of communication in society. In L. Bryson (Ed.), *The communication of ideas* (pp. 37–51). New York: Institute of Religious and Social Studies.

Lau, R. R., & Erber, R. (1985). Political sophistication: An information-processing approach. In S. Kraus & R. Perloff (Eds.), *Mass media and political thought: An information-processing approach* (pp. 37–64). Newbury Park, CA: Sage.

Lau, R. R., & Sears, D. O. (1986). Social cognition and political cognition: The past, the present and the future. In R. Lau & D. Sears (Eds.), *Political cognition* (pp. 347–366). Hillsdale, NJ: Lawrence Erlbaum Associates.

Lazarsfeld, P. F., Berelson, B. R., & Gaudet, H. (1948). *The people's choice* (7th ed.). New York: Columbia University Press.

Lee, C. C., Chan, J. M., Pan, Z., & So, C. Y. K. (2000). National prisms of a global "media event." In J. Curran & M. Gurevitch (Eds.), *Mass Media and Society* (pp. 295–309). London: Arnold.

Lee, M. A., & Solomon, N. (1990). *Unreliable sources: A guide to bias in news media.* New York: Lyle Stuart.

Lemert, J. B., Mitzman, B. N., Seither, M. A., Cook, R. H., & Hackett, R. (1977). Journalists and mobilizing information. *Journalism Quarterly, 54,* 721–726.

Levy, M. R. (1981). Disdaining the news. *Journal of Communication, 31,* 24–31.

Linsky, M. (1986). *Impact: How the press affects federal policymaking.* New York: W. W. Norton.

Lippman, W. (1922). *Public opinion.* New York: MacMillan.

Lodge, M., & McGraw, K. M. (Eds.), (1995). *Political judgment: Structure and process.* Ann Arbor: University of Michigan Press.

Lodge, M., & Taber, C. (2000). Three steps toward a theory of motivated political reasoning. In A. Lupia, M. D. McCubbins, & S. L. Popkin (Eds.), *Elements of reason: Cognition, choice, and the bounds or rationality* (pp. 183–213). Cambridge: Cambridge University Press.

Loges, W. E., & Jung, J. Y. (2001). Exploring the digital divide: Internet connectedness and age. *Communication Research, 28,* 536–362.

Lupia, A., McCubbins, M. D., & Popkin, S. L. (2000). *Elements of reason: Cognition, choice, and the bounds of rationality.* Cambridge: Cambridge University Press.

MacKuen, M. (1981). Social communication and the mass policy agenda. In M. MacKuen & S. Coombs (Eds.), *More than news: Media power in public affairs* (pp. 19–144). Beverly Hills, CA: Sage.

Markus, H., & Zajonc, R. B. (1985). The cognitive perspective in social psychology. In G. Lindzey & E. Aronson (Eds.), *The handbook of social psychology* (3rd ed., pp. 137–230). New York: Random House.

Mathews, D. (1994). *Politics for people: Finding a responsible public voice.* Urbana: University of Illinois Press.

McCarthy, J. D. (1994). Activists, authorities and media framing of drunk driving. In E. Larana, H. Johnston, & J. R. Gusfield (Eds.), *New social movements: From ideology to identity* (pp. 133–167). Philadelphia: Temple University Press.

McCombs, M. E. (1977). Newspapers versus television: Mass communication effects across time. In D. Shaw & M. McCombs (Eds.), *The emergence of American political issues: The agenda-setting function of the press* (pp. 89–105). St. Paul, MN: West.

McCombs, M. E., & Shaw, D. L. (1972). The agenda-setting function of the mass media. *Public Opinion Quarterly, 36,* 176–187.

McCombs, M. E., Shaw, D. L., & Weaver, D. (1997). *Communication and democracy: Exploring the intellectual frontiers in agenda-setting theory.* Mahwah, NJ: Lawrence Erlbaum Associates.

McDevitt, M., & Chaffee, S. H. (1998). Second chance political socialization: Trickle-up effects of children on parents. In T. Johnson, C. Hays, & S. Hays (Eds.), *Engaging the public: How government and the media can reinvigorate American democracy* (pp. 57–74). New York: Rowan Littlefield.

McDevitt, M., & Chaffee, S. H. (2000). Closing gaps in political knowledge: Effects of a school intervention program via communication in the home. *Human Communication Research, 27,* 259–292.

McLeod, D. M., & Detenber, B. H. (1999). Framing effects of television news coverage of social protest. *Journal of Communication, 49,* 3–23.

McLeod, D. M., & Hertog, J. K. (1992). The manufacture of "public opinion" by reporters: Informal cues for public perceptions of protest groups. *Discourse & Society, 3,* 259–275.

McLeod, D. M., & Perse, E. M. (1994). Direct and indirect effects of socioeconomic status on public affairs knowledge. *Journalism Quarterly, 71,* 433–442.

McLeod, J. M. (2000). Media and civic socialization of youth. *Journal of Adolescent Health, 27S,* 45–51.

McLeod, J. M., & Becker, L. B. (1974). Testing the validity of gratification measures through political effects analysis. In J. G. Blumler & E. Katz (Eds.), *The uses of mass communication: Current perspectives on gratifications research* (pp. 137–164). Beverly Hills, CA: Sage.

McLeod, J. M., Becker, L. B., & Byrnes, J. E. (1974). Another look at the agenda-setting function of the press. *Communication Research, 1,* 131–165.

McLeod, J. M., & Blumler, J. G. (1987). The macrosocial level of communication science. In S. Chaffee & C. Berger (Eds.), *Handbook of communication science* (pp. 271–322). Beverly Hills, CA: Sage.

McLeod, J. M., Brown, J. D., Becker, L. B., & Ziemke, D. A. (1977). Decline and fall at the White House: A longitudinal analysis of communication effects. *Communication Research, 4,* 3–22.

McLeod, J. M., Bybee, C. R., & Durall, J. A. (1979). The 1976 presidential debates and the equivalence of informed political participation. *Communication Research, 6,* 463–487.

McLeod, J. M., Bybee, C. R., Luetscher, W., & Garramone, C. (1981). *Mass communication and voter volatility. Public Opinion Quarterly, 45,* 69–90.

McLeod, J. M., Daily, C., Guo, Z. , Eveland, W. P., Bayer, J., Yang, S., & Wang, H. (1996). Community integration, local media use, and democratic processes. *Communication Research, 23,* 179–209.

McLeod, J. M., Eveland, W. P., & Horowitz, E. M. (1998). Going beyond adults and voter turnout: Evaluations of a socialization program involving schools, family and the media. In T. Johnson, C. Hays, & S. Hays (Eds.), *Engaging the public: How government and the media can reinvigorate American democracy* (pp. 195–205). New York: Rowan Littlefield.

McLeod, J. M., Guo, S., Daily, C., Steele, C., Huang, H., Horowitz, E., & Chen, H. (1996). The impact of traditional and non-traditional media forms in the 1992 presidential election. *Journalism and Mass Communication Quarterly, 73,* 401–416.

McLeod, J. M., Kosicki, G. M., Amor, D. L., Allen, S. G., & Philps, D. M. (1986, August). *Public images of mass media news: What are they and does it matter?* Paper presented at the meeting of the Association for Education in Journalism and Mass Communication, Norman, OK.

McLeod, J. M., Kosicki, G. M., & McLeod, D. M. (1994). The expanding boundaries of political communication effects. In J. Bryant and D. Zillmann (Eds.) *Media effects: Advances in theory and research* (pp. 123–162). Hillsdale, NJ: Lawrence Erlbaum Associates.

McLeod, J. M., Kosicki, G. M., Pan, Z., & Allen, S. G. (1987, August). *Audience perspectives on the news: Assessing their complexity and conceptual frames.* Paper presented at the meeting of the Association for Education in Journalism and Mass Communication, San Antonio, TX.

McLeod, J. M., Kosicki, G. M., & Rucinski, D. M. (1988). Political communication research: An assessment of the field. *Mass Communication Review, 15,* 8–15, 30.

McLeod, J. M., & McDonald, D. G. (1985). Beyond simple exposure: Media orientations and their impact on political processes. *Communication Research, 12,* 3–33.

McLeod, J. M., Pan, Z., & Rucinski, D. (1989, May). *Framing a complex issue: A case of social construction of meaning.* Paper presented at the meeting of the International Communication Association, San Francisco, CA.

McLeod, J. M., Pan, Z., & Rucinski, D. (1995). Levels of analysis in public opinion research. In T. Glasser & C. Salmon (Eds.), *Public opinion and the communication of consent* (pp. 55–85). New York: Guilford Press.

McLeod, J. M., & Reeves, B. (1980). On the nature of mass media effects. In S. Withey & R. Abeles (Eds.), *Television and social behavior: Beyond violence and children* (pp. 17–54). Hillsdale, NJ: Lawrence Erlbaum Associates.

McLeod, J. M., Scheufele, D. A., & Moy, P. (1999). Community, communication, and participation: The role of mass media and interpersonal discussion in local participation in a public forum. *Political Communication, 16,* 315–336.

McLeod, J. M., Scheufele, D. A., Moy, P., Horowitz, E. M., Holbert, R. L., Zhang, W., Zubric, S., & Zubric, J. (1999). Understanding deliberation: The effects of discussion networks on participation in a public forum. *Communication Research, 26,* 743–774.

McLeod, J. M., Sotirovic, M., & Holbert, R. L. (1998). Values as sociotropic judgments influencing communication patterns. *Communication Research, 25,* 453–480.

McLeod, J. M., Sotirovic, M., Voakes, P. S., Guo, Z., & Huang, K. Y. (1998). A model of public support for First Amendment rights. *Communication Law and Policy, 3,* 479–514.

McLeod, J. M., Sun, S., Chi, A., & Pan, Z. (1990, August). *Metaphor and the media: What shapes public understanding of the "war" on drugs?* Paper presented at the meeting of the Association for Education in Journalism and Mass Communication, Minneapolis, MN.

McLeod, J. M., Zubric, J., Keum, H., Deshpande, S., Cho, J., Stein, S., & Heather, M. (2001, August). *Reflecting and connecting: Testing a communication mediation model of civic participation.* Paper presented at the meeting of the Association for Education in Journalism and Mass Communication, Washington, DC.

McQuail, D. (1992). *Media performance: Mass communication and the public interest.* London: Sage.

Meadow, R. B. (1980). *Politics as communication.* Norwood, NJ: Ablex.

Merkle, D. M. (1996). The National Issues Convention poll. *Public Opinion Quarterly, 60,* 588–619.

Merritt, D. (1995). Public journalism—defining a democratic art. *Media Studies Journal, 9,* 125–132.

Miller, A. H., Goldenberg, E. N., & Erbring, L. (1979). Type-set politics: Impact of newspapers on public confidence. *American Political Science Review, 73,* 67–84.

Miller, J. H., & Krosnick, J. A. (2000). News media impact on the ingredients of presidential evaluations: Politically knowledgeable citizens are guided by a trusted source. *American Journal of Political Science, 44,* 295–309.

Miller, W. E., & Shanks, J. (1996). *The new American voter.* Cambridge, MA: Harvard University Press.

Mondak, J. J. (1995). *Nothing to read: Newspapers and elections in a social experiment.* Ann Arbor: University of Michigan Press.

Morley, D. (1980). *The "nationwide" audience* (Television Monograph No. 11). London: British Film Institute.

Moy, P., & Pfau, M. W. (2000). *With malice towards all? The media and public confidence in democratic institutions.* Westport, CT: Greenwood.

Nelson, T. E., Oxley, Z. M., & Clawson, R. A. (1997). Media framing of a civil liberties conflict and its effect on tolerance. *American Political Science Review, 91,* 567–583.

Neuman, W. F. (1976). Patterns of recall among television news viewers. *Public Opinion Quarterly, 40,* 115–123.

Neuman, W. R. (1986). *The paradox of mass politics: Knowledge and opinion in the American electorate.* Cambridge, MA: Harvard University Press.

Neuman, W. R., Just, M. R., & Crigler, A. N. (1992). *Common knowledge: News and the construction of political meaning.* Chicago: University of Chicago Press.

Niemi, R. G. (1999). Editor's introduction. *Political Psychology, 20,* 471–476.

Niemi, R. G., Hepburn, M. A., & Chapman, C. (2000). Community service by high school students: A cure for civic ills? *Political Behavior, 22,* 45–69.

Niemi, R. G., & Junn, J. (1998). *Civic education: What makes people learn?* New Haven, CT: Yale University Press.

Noelle-Neumann, E. (1984). *The spiral of silence: Public opinion—our social skin.* Chicago: University of Chicago Press.

O'Keefe, G. J. (1985). "Taking a bite out of crime": The impact of a public information campaign. *Communication Research, 12,* 147–178.

O'Keefe, G. J., Rosenbaum, D. P., Lavrakas, P. J., Reid, K., & Botta, R. A. (1996). *Taking a bite out of crime: The impact of the National Citizens' Crime Prevention Media Campaign.* Thousand Oaks, CA: Sage.

Packard Foundation Report. (2001, January 22). Reported in *New York Times*, A11.

Pan, Z., & Kosicki, G. M. (1993). Framing analysis: An approach to news discourse. *Political Communication, 10,* 55–75.

Pan, Z., & Kosicki, G. M. (1997). Priming and media impact on the evaluations of the president's performance. *Communication Research, 24,* 3–30.

Pan, Z., & Kosicki, G. M. (2001). Framing as a strategic action in public deliberation. In S. D. Reese, O. H. Gandy, Jr., & A. E. Grant (Eds.), *Framing public life: Perspectives on media and our understanding of the social world* (pp. 35–65). Mahwah, NJ: Lawrence Erlbaum Associates.

Pan, Z., & McLeod, J. M. (1991). Multi-level analysis in mass communication research. *Communication Research, 18,* 140–173.

Patterson, T. E. (1980). *The mass media election: How Americans choose their president.* New York: Praeger.

Peiser, W. (2000). Cohort replacement and the downward trend in newspaper readership. *Newspaper Research Journal, 21,* 11–23.

Pertschuk, M., & Schaetzel, W. (1989). *The people rising: The campaign against the Bork nomination.* New York: Thunder's Mouth Press.

Petty, R. E., & Cacioppo, J. T. (1986). *Communication and persuasion: Central and peripheral routes to attitude change.* New York: Springer-Verlag.

Pfau, M. W., & Louden, A. (1994). Effectiveness of Adwatch formats in deflecting political attack ads. *Communication Research, 21,* 325–341.

Philo, G. (1990). *Seeing and believing: The influence of television.* London: Routledge.

Popkin, S. L. (1990, September). The Iowa and New Hampshire primaries: The interaction of wholesale and retail campaigning. Paper presented at the meeting of the American Political Science Association, Washington, DC.

Popkin, S. L. (1991). *The reasoning voter. Communication and persuasion in presidential campaigns.* Chicago: University of Chicago Press.

Price, V., Ritchie, L. D., & Eulau, H. (1991). Micro-macro issues in communication research (Special Issue). *Communication Research, 18,* 133–273.

Price, V. & Tewksbury, D. (1997). News values and public opinion: A theoretical account of media priming and framing. In G. Barnett and F. J. Boster (Eds.), *Progress in communication sciences* (pp. 173–212). Greenwich, CT: Ablex.

Price, V., Tewksbury, D., & Powers, E. (1997). Switching trains of thought: The impact of news frames on reader's cognitive responses. *Communication Research, 24,* 481–506.

Price, V., & Zaller, J. (1993). Who gets the news? Alternative measures of news reception and their implications for research. *Public Opinion Quarterly, 57,* 133–164.

Protess, D. L., Cook, F. L., Doppelt, J. C., Ettema, J. S., Gordon, M. T., Leff, D. R., & Miller, P. (1991). *The journalism of outrage: Investigating reporting and agenda building in America.* New York: Guilford Press.

Putnam, R. D. (1995). Bowling alone: America's declining social capital. *Journal of Democracy, 6,* 65–78.

Putnam, R. D. (2000). *Bowling alone: The collapse and revival of American community.* New York: Simon & Schuster.

Rahn, W. (1995). Candidate evaluation in a complex information environments: Cognitive organization and comparison process. In M. Lodge & K. M. McGraw (Eds.) *Political judgment: Structure and process* (pp. 43–64). Ann Arbor: University of Michigan Press.

Ranney, A. (1983). *Channels of power.* New York: Basic Books.

Reese, S. D., Gandy, O. H., Jr., & Grant, A. E. (Eds.). (2001). *Framing public life: Perspectives on media and our understanding of the social world.* Mahwah, NJ: Lawrence Erlbaum Associates.

Reeves, B., Thorson, E., & Schleuder, J. (1986). Attention to television: Psychological theories and chronometric measures. In J. Bryant & Zillmann (Eds.), *Perspectives on media effects* (pp. 251–279). Hillsdale, NJ: Lawrence Erlbaum Associates.

Rice, R. E., & Atkin, C. K. (2000). *Public communication campaigns* (3rd ed.) Thousand Oaks, CA: Sage Publications.

Richardson, G. W., Jr. (1998). Building a better ad watch: Talking patterns to the American voter. *Harvard International Journal of Press/Politics, 3,* 76–95.

Roberts, D. F. (2000). Media and youth: Access, exposure and privatization. *Journal of Adolescent Health, 27S,* 8–14.

Robinson, J. P., & Levy, M. R. (1986). *The main source: Learning from television news.* Beverly Hills, CA: Sage.

Rosen, J. (1999). *What are journalists for?* New Haven, CT: Yale University Press.

Rubin, R. (1976). *Party dynamics: The Democratic coalition and the politics of change.* New York: Oxford University Press.

Ryan, C. (1991). *Prime time activism: Media strategies for grassroots organizing.* Boston: South End Press.

Sabato, L. (1987). Real and imagined corruption in campaign financing. In J. Reichley (Ed.), *Election American style* (pp. 155–179). Washington, DC: Brookings Institute.

Schudson, M. (1998). *The good citizen: A history of American civic life.* Cambridge, MA: Harvard University Press.

Schudson, M. (1999). *Good citizens and bad history: Today's political ideals in historical perspective.* Murfreesboro, TN: John Seigenthaler Chair of Excellence, First Amendment Studies, College of Mass Communication, Middle Tennessee State University.

Sears, D. O., & Chaffee, S. H. (1979). Uses and effects of the 1976 debates: An overview of empirical studies. In S. Kraus (Ed.), *The great debates, 1976: Ford vs. Carter* (pp. 223–261). Bloomington, IN: Indiana University Press.

Shah, D. V. (1998). Civic engagement, interpersonal trust, and television use: An individual level assessment of social capital. *Political Psychology, 19,* 469–496.

Shah, D. V. (2001). The collision of convictions: Value framing and value judgments. In R. P. Hart & D. R. Shaw (Eds.), *Communication in U.S. elections* (pp. 55–74). Lanham, MD: Rowan & Littlefield.

Shah, D. V., Domke, D., & Wackman, D. B. (1996). "To thine own self be true": Values, framing, and voter decision-making strategies. *Communication Research, 23,* 509–561.

Shah, D. V, Kwak, N., & Holbert, R. L. (2001). "Connecting" and "disconnecting" with civic life: Patterns of Internet use and the production of social capital. *Political Communication, 8,* 141–162.

Shah, D. V., Kwak, N. & Schmierbach, M. (2000, November). *Digital media in America: Practices, preferences and policy implications.* Final report produced for the Digital Media Forum/Ford Foundation.

Shah, D. V., McLeod, J. M., & Yoon, S. H. (2001). Communication, context, and community: An exploration of print, broadcast, and Internet influences. *Communication Research, 28,* 464–506.

Shoemaker, P. J., & Mayfield, E. K. (1987). Building a theory of news content. *Journalism Monographs, 103,* 1–36.

Shoemaker, P. J., & Reese, S. D. (1996). *Mediating the message: Theories of influences on mass media content,* (2nd ed.). White Plains, NY: Longman.

Sigel, R. (1965). Assumptions about the learning of political values. *The Annals of the American Academy, 361,* 1–9.

Sirianni, C. J., & Friedland, L. A. (2001). *Civic innovation in America: Community, empower-*

ment, public policy, and the movement for civic renewal. Berkeley: University of California Press.

Smith, H. (1988). *The power game.* New York: Random House.

Smith, H. H., III. (1986). Newspaper readership as a determinant of political knowledge and activity. *Newspaper Research Journal, 7,* 47–54.

Soley, L. C. (1992). *The news shapers: The sources who explain the news.* New York: Praeger.

Sotirovic, M. (2001a). Affective and cognitive processes as mediators of media influence on crime policy preferences. *Mass Communication and Society, 3,* 269–296.

Sotirovic, M. (2001b). How individuals explain social problems: The influences of media use. *Journal of Communication, 53,* in press.

Sotirovic, M., & McLeod, J. M. (2001). Values, communication behavior, and political participation. *Political Communication, 18,* 273–300.

Sparrow, B. H. (1999). *Uncertain guardians: The news media as a political institution.* Baltimore: Johns Hopkins University Press.

Stamm, K. R., Emig, A. G., & Hesse, M. B. (1997). The contribution of local media to community involvement. *Journalism & Mass Communication Quarterly, 74,* 97–107.

Star, S. A., & Hughes, H. M. (1950). Report on an education campaign: The Cincinnati plan for the UN. *American Journal of Sociology, 55,* 389–400.

Stempel, G. H., III. (1989). Content analysis. In G. Stempel & B. Westley (Eds.), *Research methods in mass communication* (pp. 119–131). Upper Saddle River, NJ: Prentice Hall.

Stocking, S. H., & Gross, P. H. (1989). *How do journalists think? A proposal for the study of cognitive bias in newsmaking.* Bloomington, IN: ERIC Clearinghouse on Reading and Communication Skills.

Strate, J. M., Parrish, C. J., Elder, C. D., & Ford, C., III. (1989). Life span and civic development and voting participation. *American Political Science Review, 83,* 443–464.

Teixeira, R. A. (1992). *The disappearing American Voter.* Washington, DC: Brookings.

Teo, P. (2000). Racism in the news: A critical discourse analysis of news reporting in two Australian newspapers. *Discourse and Society, 11,* 7–49.

Tichenor, P. J., Donohue, G. A., & Olien, C. N. (1970). Mass media flow and differential growth of knowledge. *Public Opinion Quarterly, 34,* 159–170.

Tichenor, P. J., Donohue, C. A., & Olien, C. N. (1980). *Community conflict and the press.* Beverly Hills, CA: Sage.

Tipton, L. P., Haney, R. D., & Basehart, J. R. (1975). Media agenda-setting in city and state election campaigns. *Journalism Quarterly, 52,* 15–22.

Tuchman, G. (1978). *Making news.* New York: Free Press.

van Dijk, T. A. (1988). *News as discourse.* Hillsdale, NJ: Lawrence Erlbaum Associates.

Verba, S., & Nie, N. H. (1972). *Participation in America.* New York: Harper & Row.

Verba, S., Schlozman, K. L., & Brady, H. E. (1995). *Voice and equality: Civic voluntarism in American Politics.* Cambridge, MA: Harvard University Press.

Viswanath, K., & Finnegan, J. R. (1996). The knowledge gap hypothesis: Twenty-five years later. In B. Burleson (Ed.), *Communication Yearbook 19* (pp. 187–227). Thousand Oaks, CA: Sage.

Watt, J. H., & Krull, R. (1977). An examination of three models of television viewing and aggression. *Human Communication Review, 3,* 99–112.

Wattenberg, M. P. (1984). *The decline of American political parties, 1952–1980.* Cambridge, MA: Harvard University Press.

Weaver, D. H., Graber, D. A., McCombs, M. E., & Eyal, C. H. (1981). *Media agenda-setting in a presidential election: Issues, images and interests.* New York: Praeger.

Weaver, P. (1972, Winter). Is television news biased? *Public Interest, 57*–74.

Westlye, M. C. (1991). *Senate elections and campaign intensity.* Baltimore: Johns Hopkins University Press.

Wolfinger, R. E., & Rosenstone, S. J. (1980). *Who votes?* New Haven, CT: Yale University Press.

Yankelovich, D. (1991). *Coming to public judgment: Making democracy work in a complex world.* Syracuse, NY: Syracuse University Press.

Youniss, J., McLellan, J. A., & Yates, M. (1997). What we know about engendering civic identity. *American Behavioral Scientist, 40,* 620–631.

Zaller, J. R. (1992). *The nature and origins of mass opinion.* Cambridge: Cambridge University Press.

Chapter 10

Effects of Media Violence

GLENN G. SPARKS
CHERI W. SPARKS
Purdue University

In December 2000, government officials, officials from the entertainment industry, parents, and their children were busy playing out an all too familiar script. In this case, the setting for this latest episode of the media violence controversy was Japan. Movie director Kinji Fukasaku had released an incredibly popular movie, *Battle Royale*. The film deals with conflict between junior high school delinquents who are sent to an island and told to battle to their death with automatic weapons. One viewer, who reacted to the film by noting that it "makes you think," still declined to see it a second time because "it was just too grotesque" (Schaefer, 2000). Japan's education minister, Nobutaka Machimura, discouraged owners of theaters from showing the film at all and clearly implied that its contents were "of a harmful nature." The Motion Picture Code Committee restricted admission to children who were under 16 years old. However, this restriction did little to diminish the film's popularity. It made world headlines, partially due to the fact that young viewers camped out on sidewalks for 2 days in order to gain admission to the opening showing. Part of the controversy was fueled by an apparent "copycat" crime in 1998 that involved a Japanese TV show titled *Gift*. Characters on that show carried butterfly knives and were blamed by parents, educators, and government officials for inspiring a 13-year-old boy to stab his teacher to death—with a butterfly knife (Schaefer, 2000).

For scholars of media violence, the *Battle Royale* episode includes many of the elements that have been present in the media violence controversy in the United States since the rise in popularity of movies in the 1920s and, especially, since the rise of television in the 1950s. At the same time that a segment of the population finds electronic depictions of violence highly entertaining, other segments of society express concern about the potential harmful effects of such depictions. More recently, the controversy has extended to violent video games in the aftermath of the Columbine High School shootings, where authorities discovered that the perpetrators had an appetite for this sort of entertainment. To what extent does consumption of media violence lead directly to subsequent aggressive behavior? What does scientific research have to say about the relationship between exposure to media violence and various negative outcomes involving cognitions, emotions, or behaviors? What questions should scholars be attempting to answer in their future studies on the effects of media violence? These are the main questions that we take up in this chapter. The first task is to briefly outline the history of research on media violence. Unlike other areas of media effects, the violence controversy is not new, and it is important to have some historical context before examining the research in more detail.

A BRIEF HISTORY OF THE MEDIA VIOLENCE CONTROVERSY

Hoberman (1998) discussed one of the earliest cases of controversy surrounding media violence (1908) that is not unlike the modern-day case involving the Japanese film *Battle Royale*. In this case, Chicago police refused to issue the permit required to run the film *The James Boys in Missouri* in a public theater. As in the controversy over *Battle Royale* over 90 years later, the perceived problem with the film was the potential influence that its content might have on criminal behavior. Although the tradition of scientific research on the impact of media violence does not extend back quite as far as the public controversy, it does extend back nearly 75 years. Most scholars see the Payne Fund Studies as the formal beginning of scientific inquiry into media impact. These studies were carried out in response to growing public concern about the possible deleterious effects of sex and violence in the movies.

The Payne Fund Studies

The Payne Fund Studies were conducted as a result of private funding from a philanthropic foundation and the invitation to scholars issued by William Short, the Executive Director of the Motion Picture Research Council (a private educational group). Not all of the studies focused on media violence, but two in particular helped to reinforce the notion that violent media content might be a serious public concern. First, Dale (1935) conducted a content analysis of 1,500 movies that revealed a heavy emphasis on crime. Second, a survey of nearly 2,000 respondents conducted by Blumer (1933) revealed that many people were conscious of the fact that they had directly imitated acts of violence that they had witnessed in violent movies. In the aftermath of these studies, public concern about media violence was high. Those concerns were exacerbated in the 1950s when Wertham (1954) published his analysis of comic book content.

Part of Wertham's thesis was that a disproportionate amount of comic book content featured grotesque images of violence that contributed to juvenile delinquency on the part of young boys, many of whom tended to be heavy consumers of these images. Although Wertham's views gained exposure and forever changed the comic book industry by forcing self-censorship of content, scholars were reluctant to accept his strong claims of media impact. They were based on content studies that failed to meet scientific rigor in terms of sample selection and systematic coding techniques. Claims of impact on juvenile delinquency were similarly tainted by Wertham's reliance on anecdotes and testimony from boys who were being treated for a wide range of psychological problems. Sustained scholarly interest in the potential impact of media violence did not emerge until the latter part of the 1950s when the possible effects of television on the public began to attract attention from government officials, who saw it as a negative influence on children and a potential contributor to juvenile delinquency.

The Rise of TV

The proliferation of TV sets in the 1950s meant that by 1960, 90% of American homes could receive TV signals. This level of saturation set the stage for a new era of controversy about media violence. Schramm, Lyle, and Parker (1961) discussed a number of examples of imitative violence that news sources disseminated in the 1950s. These authors argued that the apparent connection between exposure to TV violence and imitations of violent crime was not coincidental.

The U.S. government began to express concern about the effects of televised violence as early as the 1950s. In their review of the early events surrounding the government's role in the media violence issue, Liebert, Sprafkin, and Davidson (1982) traced the role of Senator Estes Kefauver's Senate Subcommittee on Juvenile Delinquency (which questioned the need for violence on television) through the 1972 report of the Surgeon General, a collection of 23 different research projects that were funded by the National Institute of Mental Health. Although these studies certainly failed to establish any wide consensus on the effects of televised violence, they signaled the high priority that this topic would enjoy in the scholarly community for years to come. One major line of investigation launched during this period of time helped to elevate media violence to a high priority in the scholarly community—a series of content analyses by George Gerbner and his associates. Gerbner (1972) defined violence as "the overt expression of physical force against others or self, or the compelling of action against one's will on pain of being hurt or killed." Using this definition, he found that prime-time TV contained about eight instances of violence per hour, a rate that indicated little change from an earlier study that he had conducted for the National Commission on the Causes and Prevention of Violence. With the prevalence of violent content firmly established in a quantitative way, the stage was set for researchers to delve into the question of the impact of that content.

DOES VIEWING MEDIA VIOLENCE CAUSE AGGRESSIVE BEHAVIOR?

The central question that has framed the controversy over the effects of media violence over the last four decades is the question about how exposure to violent media images affects the tendency for viewers to behave aggressively. There is a wealth of research evidence to draw on for this question, and a comprehensive review of this literature is well beyond the scope of this chapter, especially because a number of recent reviews already exist (Comstock & Scharrer, 1999; Jason, Kennedy, & Brackshaw, 1999; Murray, 1998; Smith & Donnerstein, 1998). Despite the fact that studies abound on this central question, the literature has always been characterized by controversy that seems to mature in step with the methodological progress that is made over the years.

Early in the history of this controversy, Bandura, Ross, and Ross (1963a, 1963b) presented evidence in favor of the theory of social learning when they demonstrated that children were more likely to imitate the aggressive actions of a model when the model was rewarded instead of punished. These studies were criticized because the measure of aggression (hitting an inflatable doll) did not seem to be related necessarily to the construct of *human* aggression (see Liebert et al., 1982). The studies were also criticized for their reliance on programs that had little resemblance to programs that children were likely to view on television. As evidence has gathered over the years in favor of a causal relationship between exposure to media violence and aggressive behavior in the laboratory context, the nature of the controversy has shifted away from these types of methodological issues to a focus on whether laboratory results in general have any relevance to aggression outside the laboratory. This dimension of the controversy was featured by Barbara Walters on a segment of the October 20, 2000, ABC news program *20/20*. The segment focused on Jonathan Freedman (one of the few scholars who strongly dissents from the opinion that media violence increases aggressive behavior), Leonard Eron, L. Rowell Huesmann, and their ongoing argument about the extent to which research on the effects of media violence demonstrates a causal connection between exposure to violence and increased aggression outside the laboratory. These authors have all been prominent contributors to the media violence literature (see Freedman, 1984, 1988; Huesmann & Eron, 1986; Huesmann, Lagerspetz, & Eron, 1984), and their debate on the public airwaves left more questions than answers, even for viewers who considered themselves to be experts on the key issues. The ultimate message of this broadcast for the layperson was that the scientific community was completely unsettled about the real-world consequences of exposure to media violence. The published literature reveals that this message is hardly an accurate one. Numerous reviews by researchers, professional associations, and organizations all agree that exposure to media violence is causally related to aggressive behavior (see recent reviews by the American Psychological Association, 1993; Centers for Disease Control, 1991; Heath, Bresolin, & Rinaldi, 1989, and the National Academy of Science, 1993). Wilson et al. (1997), writing for the National Television Violence Study, also concluded that the evidence in favor of a causal connection between exposure to media violence and violence in society was clear. Several meta-analyses lend strong credence to this conclusion (e.g., Paik & Comstock, 1994; Wood, Wong, & Chachere, 1991).

Despite the fact that controversy still exists about the impact of media violence, the research results reveal a dominant and consistent pattern in favor of the notion that exposure to violent media images *does* increase the risk of aggressive behavior. It is important to note that even among studies that are not able to yield clear conclusions about causality, the most frequent result remains consistent with the hypothesis that viewing violence causes an increase in aggressive behavior. Briefly considered, what is the nature of the research evidence on this most central question? Following Gunter's (1994) review of the evidence on this question, we will examine the literature from different types of experiments and surveys, followed by a consideration of the theoretical mechanisms that might be responsible for the relationship between exposure to media violence and subsequent aggression.

Experiments

A number of early experiments with children provided evidence for the facilitation of aggressive behavior after viewing violent media. One of the most widely cited studies was conducted by Liebert and Baron (1971). Using children from 5 to 9 years old, the authors randomly assigned the subjects to view a brief clip from either a violent program (*The Untouchables*) or a nonviolent sports program. Following exposure to one of these programs, subjects were told that they could either "help" or "hurt" the progress of another child in an adjoining room who was trying to win a game. By pressing a "help" button the subjects were told that they could make it easier for the other child to turn a handle that was critical for success in the game. However, if they pressed the "hurt" button, they were told that the handle would become too hot to touch and, thus, would result in hurting the child's progress in the game. Those children who watched the violent film clip prior to being placed in this situation were more likely to press the "hurt" button and more likely to keep the button pressed for a long duration than were the children who watched the sports program. Stein and Friedrich (1972) conducted another experiment with children that randomly assigned subjects to view *Batman* and *Superman* cartoons (violent condition) or episodes of *Mister Rogers Neighborhood* (prosocial condition). During the two weeks of observation following this manipulation, the children who viewed the violent cartoons were more likely to be aggressive in their interactions with other children than were the children who viewed the prosocial programming. Both of these early experiments, along with the ones by Bandura mentioned earlier, helped to attract attention to the potential problem of media violence as a facilitator of aggression.

In contrast to these early experiments that used children as the research subjects, Leonard Berkowitz conducted a series of experiments that used college students as subjects (Berkowitz & Alioto, 1973; Berkowitz & Geen, 1966, 1967; Berkowitz & LePage, 1967; Berkowitz & Powers, 1979; Berkowitz & Rawlings, 1963). The typical paradigm employed in these investigations was to expose subjects who were either provoked or unprovoked by an experimenter to either violent media or nonviolent media. Following exposure, Berkowitz discovered that provoked subjects behaved more aggressively to the experimenter after viewing violence than after viewing nonviolence.

Laboratory experiments, although capable of providing unequivocal evidence for cause-effect relationships, are more equivocal in their application to various contexts that exist outside the laboratory. Scholars and critics who offer a dissenting view from the strong consensus that exists among social scientists on the effects of media violence usually feature some version of the argument that laboratory experiments lack ecological validity. As Zillmann and Weaver (1999) have recently noted, "It seems that critics of media-violence research could only be satisfied with longitudinal experimental studies in which, within gender and a multitude of personality variables, random assignment is honored and exposure to violent fare is rigorously controlled—that is, with research that in a free society simply cannot be conducted" (p. 147). In addition, it also seems that critics demand that researchers be able to set up real-world opportunities for aggression in order to settle the controversy about the generalizability of laboratory findings to settings outside the lab. Of course, even if it were possible to do so, researchers would never want to set up such opportunities for ethical reasons. Despite the limitations of experimentation, some researchers have attempted to employ this method outside the confines of the laboratory using methods appropriate for field research.

Berkowitz and his associates have conducted a number of field experiments in institutions for delinquent boys (Leyens, Parke, Camino, & Berkowitz, 1975; Parke, Berkowitz, Leyens, West, & Sebastian, 1977). These experiments assessed physical and verbal aggression in boys who had been assigned to watch media violence for several weeks and compared their levels of aggression with similar boys who did not watch violence. The findings of these studies converged with laboratory investigations; boys who watched media violence were more likely to engage in aggressive behavior.

The work of Williams (1986) is especially noteworthy in that she was able to study changes in aggression that occurred naturally over several years in a Canadian town that initially had no access to TV signals but, over the course of the natural experiment, gained TV access. The results of Williams' research converged with the findings of the laboratory studies: increases in exposure to media violence lead to increases in aggressive behavior. Unfortunately, because of the pervasiveness of TV signals today, the possibility of gathering more evidence of this type is steadily decreasing.

The experimental evidence on the causal impact of media violence has been so consistent in favor of the conclusion that exposure causes increased aggression that fewer experiments have been conducted in recent years. However, one recent experiment that was reported by Zillmann and Weaver (1999) exposed participants to either four consecutive days of gratuitous violence or nonviolence in the form of feature films. As in earlier experimental results, their findings showed that the participants who saw the violent films were more hostile in their behavior subsequent to exposure. Unlike prior experiments, which tended to show that participants would only show hostility toward a person who had provoked them earlier, Zillmann and Weaver's participants showed such hostility regardless of whether they had been provoked earlier or not.

Some researchers have attempted to study the possible facilitation of aggression through exposure to media violence by recourse to the natural experiment. Most notable among these attempts are studies by Phillips (1979, 1983, 1986) and Centerwall (1989). According to Centerwall, prior to television's emergence in the United States, the national homicide rate was 3 per 100,000. By 1974, the homicide rate had doubled. Centerwall argues that this increase is directly linked to massive exposure to television throughout the culture. He notes that essentially the same kind of increase in homicides occurred in Canada. Moreover, he argues that despite its similarities on nearly any variable of interest, homicides did not increase in South Africa from 1945 to 1974 while a ban existed on TV. However, as soon as this ban was lifted, homicides began to increase there as well—more than doubling in less than 20 years, just as it had in the United States and Canada. Centerwall concludes that the data he examined indicated that about half of all homicides in the United States are caused, in part, by exposure to TV.

Phillips has also analyzed naturally occuring data and reached conclusions that are similar to Centerwall's. With respect to homicides, Phillips argues that after widely publicized heavyweight prize fights, the homicide rate increased. Similarly, he notes that after news stories of widely publicized suicides, increases occurred in single-car fatalities and airplane crashes. Of course, unequivocal conclusions about causality are not possible based on the type of data presented by Centerwall and Phillips. However, other researchers have recently analyzed their own data and drawn conclusions that support the validity of the claims made about the link between media violence and subsequent homicides and suicides (Cantor, Sheehan, Alpers, & Mullen, 1999).

Surveys

As in natural experiments such as the ones reported by Phillips and Centerwall, surveys on the topic of media violence and aggression are designed to add data that are free from the constraints of the laboratory. In exchange for this freedom, researchers who use the survey methodology give up the ability to make conclusive claims about causality. Although a few surveys report little or no relationship between media violence and aggression (Milavsky, Kessler, Stipp, & Rubens, 1982; Singer & Singer, 1980), the most ambitious survey research that has examined the relationship over a period of decades (Huesmann & Eron, 1986) seems to draw the same general conclusion that emerges from experimental studies. These researchers collected data from children when they were 8 years old and followed these same children in a panel study until they were 30 years old. Those who watched the highest levels of TV violence as children were more likely to be involved in serious crime when they were adults. Huesmann (1986) summarized the basic conclusion from this work by stating: "Aggressive habits seem to be learned early in life, and once established, are resistant to change and predictive of serious adult antisocial behavior. If a child's observation of media violence promotes the learning of aggressive habits, it can have harmful lifelong consequences. Consistent with this theory, early television habits are in fact correlated with adult criminality" (pp. 129–130) (see also Huesmann, Moise, & Podolski, 1997).

Controversy About the Effects of Media Violence

If most scholars agree that the research evidence tends to converge on the conclusion that exposure to media violence causes aggressive behavior, then why has scholarly and public debate on this topic produced so much controversy? One important source of the dispute revolves around confusion, even among researchers, about the concepts of statistical significance, statistical importance, and social importance. When statistically significant results show that media violence is causally related to aggressive behavior, researchers can be confident that they have observed a relationship that is unlikely due to chance. Such a conclusion seems to point to a clear conclusion of a media effect.

However, statistical *significance* says little about the strength of the relationship. In order to gauge the strength of the relationship or its statistical *importance*, researchers usually appeal to some index of the statistical variance accounted for in aggressive behavior by knowing the level of exposure to media violence. Studies on media violence and aggression are no different than studies on other areas of human behavior in that they typically enable researchers to account for 10 to 15% of the variance in the dependent variable. There are two aspects to this state of affairs that lead some to minimize the overall magnitude of media violence effects on aggression. First, the effect appears to be quite modest in that 85 to 90% of aggressive behavior in most studies is left unaccounted for by media exposure. Second, the extent to which the variance accounted for in aggressive behavior in any given study can be used as a general guideline for the nature of the relationship between these variables in the real world is unclear. There is no easy way to map statistical indexes from isolated studies to a general statement about the strength of the relationship in the real world. Critics who minimize the relationship between media violence and aggression emphasize the large proportion of aggressive behavior that seems to derive from sources other than exposure to media violence. Alternatively, others emphasize that given the multiplicity of causes for any human behavior, to be able to account for 10 to 15% of the variance in aggressive behavior in a given study by knowing only about media exposure is quite impressive.

Added to the controversy about the magnitude of the effect size (statistical importance) is the notion of *social* importance. Because media audiences sometimes number in the millions, even very small statistical effects can translate into very important social problems. If just one person in several hundred thousand is influenced by a violent movie to commit a serious act of aggression, the social consequences of several million viewers watching that movie might be dramatic. On the other hand, such a small statistical effect might seem to some to be virtually unpreventable and nearly guaranteed by the vast diversity of people in any given audience. The difficulty in untangling these issues has tended to obscure the clear consensus that exists among scholars about the fact that exposure to media violence *is* causally related to aggressive behavior.

Theoretical Mechanisms

Catharsis.   One of the earliest theoretical formulations proposed to account for the relationship between exposure to media violence and aggressive behavior was symbolic catharsis (Feshbach, 1955). The idea formulated by Feshbach was one that pleased media producers because it predicted that exposure to media violence would permit angry or frustrated viewers to purge their feelings such that after viewing was completed, they would be *less* likely to behave aggressively. The idea was that viewing media violence would permit viewers to engage in fantasy aggression, thus discharging their pent up hostility in a satisfactory way and reducing the need to carry out aggression in the behavioral realm. One early study that tested this theory on nursery-school children failed to find any evidence (Siegel, 1956). The children in this study who viewed media violence (a *Woody Woodpecker* cartoon) behaved *more* aggressively following exposure, revealing a tendency that was completely opposite of the one predicted by the catharsis hypothesis, but in keeping with the findings of most of the studies that were completed in later years. These results notwithstanding, Feshbach and Singer (1971) carried out a field experiment that exposed institutionalized boys to a media diet of violent or nonviolent films and observed the extent to which the boys' subsequent behavior was either aggressive or nonaggressive. The results seemed encouraging to the catharsis hypothesis because, as predicted by the theory, the boys who watched the violent films behaved less aggressively than their counterparts who were exposed to nonviolent material. However, scholars came to understand these results in a context that was very different from the one that Feshbach and Singer suggested. The boys who watched the nonviolent films did not enjoy this type of media to the same extent as the boys assigned to watch violent films. Thus, the difference in likability, quite apart from the differences in violent content, may have been sufficient to produce higher levels of aggressive behavior among the boys assigned to watch nonviolence. Ultimately, the failure to find any solid confirmations of the catharsis hypothesis, combined with the relatively large number of studies that produced findings directly counter to this formulation, resulted in a virtual abandonment of this notion by the research community.

Social Learning. The theory of social learning was applied to media violence by Bandura (1965; also see chap. 6). This theory projected that media characters who serve as models for aggressive behavior may be attended to by viewers and, depending on whether the behaviors are rewarded or punished, would either disinhibit or inhibit imitation of the behavior respectively. As discussed earlier, Bandura's program of studies offered considerable support for social learning processes. Bandura's more recent statement of social cognitive theory (chap. 6) shows how the initial formulation has evolved over the years and currently stands as one of the major theoretical options for understanding the effects of media violence.

Priming. Chapter 5 deals with the idea of priming, so we do not extensively review the role of this process in explaining how media violence can cause aggressive behavior. Initially, Berkowitz focused attention on media violence by emphasizing the "aggressive cues" contained in this type of content. He thought that these cues could combine psychologically with a viewer's emotional state of anger or frustration and trigger subsequent aggression. Jo and Berkowitz (1994) revised this formulation to focus on the fact that media violence could prime thoughts of aggressive behavior and, consequently, make actual aggressive behavior more likely. The priming hypothesis has received extensive support in the context of media violence (Anderson, 1983; Bushman & Geen, 1990). Perhaps most significantly, Zillmann and Weaver (1999) discuss how Bargh and his associates have extended the priming idea so that it can account not just for short-term effects of aggression after media exposure, but long-term effects as well (Bargh, 1984; Bargh, Lombardi, & Higgins, 1988). Summarizing the notion of priming, Jo and Berkowitz (1994) commented on one result by stating that, "It is as if the thought of the particular action had, to some degree, activated the motor program linked to this action" (p. 48).

Arousal. In his theory of excitation transfer, Zillmann (1991) advanced the notion that the arousal-inducing properties of media violence were very important for understanding the intensity of emotional reactions that occur immediately after viewing. For example, when viewers became angry after exposure to a highly arousing violent depiction, this arousal could subsequently transfer to the anger and intensify it—making aggressive behavior more likely. Similarly, the arousal could also intensify a positive emotion that might occur subsequent to viewing. The theory of excitation transfer is well documented in the study of media effects, and the arousing properties of media violence must be taken seriously given the evidence from studies by Zillmann and his colleagues.

Desensitization. One way that media violence might increase aggressive behavior is through emotional desensitization. According to this notion, with repeated exposure to media violence, a psychological saturation or emotional adjustment takes place such that initial levels of tension, anxiety, or disgust diminish or weaken. These lower levels of negative emotion associated with exposure to media violence may reduce the urgency to respond to violence in real life. Some research with children supports this idea (Drabman & Thomas, 1976), and desensitization effects are commonly observed in studies that employ sexually violent stimulus materials (Dexter, Penrod, Linz, & Saunders, 1997; Krafka, Linz, Donnerstein, & Penrod, 1997). As people's sensitivities to violence become increasingly dull, violent behavior may increase, in part because it is simply not recognized any longer as behavior that should be curtailed.

Cultivation and Fear. Other chapters in this volume discuss the effects of media violence on the cultivation of attitudes (chap. 3) and on viewers' fright reactions (chap. 11). Suffice it to say here that in addition to the studies that document the effects of violence on aggressive behavior, other research programs have investigated the possibility that viewing violence over the long term cultivates a particular view of social reality (Gerbner, Gross, Morgan, & Signorielli, 1994) and induces high levels of fright that can linger on for days, months, and even years after initial exposure (Cantor, 1999).

THE FUTURE OF RESEARCH ON THE
EFFECTS OF MEDIA VIOLENCE

As the study of media effects continues into the new millennium, it is apparent that the research on certain types of media violence will be prevalent in the literature. Recently, scholars have become interested in the impact of violent video games on aggressive behavior. Dill and Dill's (1998) review of the literature on the effects of violent video games reveals that exposure to these games does increase aggressive behavior, a finding consistent with other recent research on the topic (Anderson & Dill, 2000; Sherry, 2001). However, it is also clear that the literature in this area is quite sparse compared with the volumes of material available on TV and filmed violence. As the video technology changes rapidly to permit more realistic depictions of violence and online contests between virtual strangers, researchers will undoubtedly take up the new gauntlet and begin to study the effects of media violence in this new, high-tech arena (see chap. 22).

We also anticipate that the future holds promise for more basic research on the reasons underlying viewers' attraction to media violence. As

Sparks and Sparks (2000) have recently noted, there is very little data to conclusively establish the fact that programs containing media violence are generally preferred over versions of the same programs that contain no violence. A complete understanding of the impact of media violence on viewers must include a much more comprehensive set of studies on the attractions of violent entertainment than is currently available in the literature.

One additional theme that holds promise to increase understanding about the impact of media violence is the role of individual differences (see chap. 19). Zillmann and Weaver (1997) demonstrated that males who were high on psychoticism were more likely to be affected by media violence than males who were low on this variable. Similarly, Aluja-Fabregat and Torrubia-Beltri (1998) found that variables such as sensation seeking, neuroticism, and psychoticism correlated positively with favorability ratings on violent cartoons.

Finally, we would note that there seem to be at least three assumptions held in academic and political circles about the effects of media violence. The first of these assumptions is that violent material is likely to produce an effect rather than no effect and that this effect is more likely to be negative than positive. A second assumption is that violent media is more likely to promote violent thinking and behavior than other kinds of media depictions. A final assumption is that violent media is more deserving of research concern and political and social action than are other types of media depictions.

The first assumption is one that has inspired a host of research studies, many of which are cited in this essay. It is an assumption that scholars have tested repeatedly under various conditions, and our conclusion is that the assumption is warranted. In contrast, the second two assumptions are ones that have inspired few studies and appear to us to be far less warranted. That is, little if any research has been done that actually compares the effects on aggressive behavior and thinking of other types of media depictions or content with the effects of violent depictions. Yet, there is certainly good reason to think that other types of media content might inspire aggression as well. What might be the effects of exposure to media depictions of hate speech or to successful people or other images that foster frustration and jealousy? How do viewers respond to political rhetoric that promotes "legalized violence" that might be encountered in depictions of war or in stories related to capital punishment? Does speech that promotes the appeal of guns or other weapons affect aggressive behavior in viewers? What about discussions that objectify others, demean others, or ridicule members of particular social or ethnic groups? Answers to these questions will only come with new lines of systematic research that are not evident in the current literature.

Although we certainly would underscore the importance of research on media violence in the new millennium, we would not welcome a situation where the resources of the scholarly community were nearly exhausted on this single type of media content. Even for aggressive behavior, and certainly for other types of behavior, it would appear that nonviolent media depictions may have direct implications.

REFERENCES

Aluja-Fabregat, A., & Torrubia-Beltri, R. (1998). Viewing of mass media violence, perception of violence, personality and academic achievement. *Personality & Individual Differences, 25*(5), 973–989.

American Psychological Association. (1993). *Violence and youth: Psychology's response.* Washington, DC: American Psychological Association.

Anderson, C. (1983). Imagination and expectation. The effect of imagining behavioral scripts on personal intentions. *Journal of Personality & Social Psychology, 45*, 293–305.

Anderson, C. A., & Dill, K. E. (2000). Video games and aggressive thoughts, feelings, and behavior in the laboratory and in life. *Journal of Personality & Social Psychology, 78*(4), 772–790.

Bandura, A. (1965). Influence of models' reinforcement contingencies on the acquisition of imitative responses. *Journal of Personality & Social Psychology, 1*, 589–595.

Bandura, A., Ross, D., & Ross, S. A. (1963a). Imitation of film-mediated aggressive models. *Journal of Abnormal and Social Psychology, 66*(1), 3–11.

Bandura, A., Ross, D., & Ross, S. A. (1963b). Vicarious reinforcement and imitative learning. *Journal of Abnormal and Social Psychology, 67*(6), 601–607.

Bargh, J. A. (1984). Automatic and conscious processing of social information. In R. S. Wyer & T. K. Srull (Eds.), *Handbook of social cognition* (Vol. 3, pp. 1–43). Hillsdale, NJ: Lawrence Erlbaum Associates.

Bargh, J. A., Lombardi, W. J., & Higgins, E. T. (1988). Automaticity of chronically accessible constructs in person x situation effects on person perception: It's just a matter of time. *Journal of Personality and Social Psychology, 55*, 599–605.

Berkowitz, L., & Alioto, J. T. (1973). The meaning of an observed event as a determinant of its aggressive consequences. *Journal of Personality and Social Psychology, 28*, 206–217.

Berkowitz, L., & Geen, R. G. (1966). Film violence and the cue properties of available targets. *Journal of Personality and Social Psychology, 3*, 525–530.

Berkowtiz, L., & Geen, R. G. (1967). Stimulus qualities of the target of aggression: A further study. *Journal of Personality and Social Psychology, 5*, 364–368.

Berkowitz, L., & LePage, A. (1967). Weapons as aggression-eliciting stimuli. *Journal of Personality and Social Psychology, 7*, 202–207.

Berkowitz, L., & Powers, P. C. (1979). Effects of timing and justification of witnessed aggression on the observers' punitiveness. *Journal of Research in Personality, 13*, 71–80.

Berkowitz, L., & Rawlings, E. (1963). Effects of film violence on inhibitions against subsequent aggression. *Journal of Abnormal and Social Psychology, 66*(5), 405–412.

Blumer, Herbert. (1933). *The Movies and Conduct.* New York: The Macmillan Company.

Bushman, B., & Geen, R. (1990). Role of cognitive-emotional mediators and individual differences in the effects of media violence on aggression. *Journal of Personality and Social Psychology, 58*, 56–163.

Cantor, C. H., Sheehan, P., Alpers, P., & Mullen, P. (1999). Media and mass homicides. *Archives of Suicide Research, 5*(4), 283–290.

Cantor, J. (1999). *"Mommy, I'm scared": How TV and movies frighten children and what we can do to protect them.* San Diego: Harcourt Brace.

Centers for Disease Control. (1991). *Position papers from the Third National Injury Conference: Setting the national agenda for injury control in the 1990s.* Washington, DC: Department of Health and Human Services.

Centerwall, B. S. (1989). Exposure to television as a cause of violence. In G. Comstock (Ed.), *Public communication and behavior* (Vol. 2, pp. 1–58). San Diego: Academic Press.

Comstock, G., & Scharrer, E. (1999). *What's on, who's watching, and what it means.* San Diego: Academic Press.

Dale, E. (1935). *The Content of Motion Pictures.* New York: The Macmillan Company.

Dexter, H. R., Penrod, S., Linz, D., & Saunders, D. (1997). Attributing responsibility to female victims after exposure to sexually violent films. *Journal of Applied Social Psychology, 27*(24), 2149–2171.

Dill, K. E., & Dill, J. C. (1998). Video game violence: A review of the empirical literature. *Aggression & Violent Behavior, 3*(4), 407–428.

Drabman, R. S., & Thomas, M. H. (1976). Does watching violence on television cause apathy? *Pediatrics, 57,* 329–331.

Feshbach, S. (1955). The drive-reducing function of fantasy behavior. *Journal of Abnormal and Social Psychology, 50,* 3–11.

Feshbach, S., & Singer, R. (1971). *Television and aggression.* San Francisco: Jossey-Bass.

Freedman, J. (1984). Effect of television violence on aggressiveness. *Psychological Bulletin, 96*(2), 227–246.

Freedman, J. (1988). Television violence and aggression: What the evidence shows. In S. Oskamp (Ed.), *Applied social psychology annual: Television as a social issue* (Vol. 8, pp. 144–162). Newbury Park, CA: Sage.

Gerbner, G. (1972). Violence in television drama: Trends in symbolic functions. In G. A. Comstock & E. A. Rubinstein (Eds.), *Television and social behavior: Vol. 1. Media content and control* (pp. 28–187). Washington, DC: United States Government Printing Office.

Gerbner, G., Gross, L., Morgan, M., & Signorielli, N. (1994). Growing up with television: The cultivation perspective. In J. Bryant & D. Zillmann (Eds.), *Media effects: Advances in theory and research* (pp. 17–41). Hillsdale, NJ: Lawrence Erlbaum Associates.

Gunter, B. (1994). The question of media violence. In J. Bryant & D. Zillmann (Eds.), *Media effects: Advances in theory and research* (pp. 163–211). Hillsdale, NJ: Lawrence Erlbaum Associates.

Heath, L., Bresolin, L., & Rinaldi, R. (1989). Effects of media violence on children: A review of the literature. *Archives of General Psychiatry, 46,* 376–379.

Hoberman, J. (1998). "A test for the individual viewer": Bonnie and Clyde's violent reception. In J. H. Goldstein (Ed.), *Why we watch: The attractions of violent entertainment* (pp. 116–143). New York: Oxford University Press.

Huesmann, L. R. (1986). Psychological processes promoting the relation between exposure to media violence and aggressive behavior by the viewer. *Journal of Social Issues, 42,* 125–139.

Huesmann, L. R., & Eron, L. D. (Eds.). (1986). *Television and the aggressive child: A cross-national comparison.* Hillsdale, NJ: Lawrence Erlbaum Associates.

Huesmann, L. R., Lagerspetz, K., & Eron, L. D. (1984). Intervening variables in the TV violence-aggression relation: Evidence from two countries. *Developmental Psychology, 20,* 746–775.

Huesmann, L. R., Moise, J. F., & Podolski, C. (1997). The effects of media violence on the development of antisocial behavior. In D. M. Stoff & J. Breiling (Eds.), *Handbook of antisocial behavior* (pp. 181–193). New York: John Wiley & Sons.

Jason, L. A., Kennedy, H. L., & Brackshaw, E. (1999). Television violence and children: Problems and solutions. In T. P. Gullotta & S. J. McElhaney (Eds.), *Violence in homes and communities: Prevention, intervention, and treatment: Vol. 11. Issues in children's and families' lives* (pp. 133–156). Thousand Oaks, CA: Sage.

Jo, E., & Berkowitz, L. (1994). A priming effect analysis of media influences: An update. In J. Bryant and D. Zillmann (Eds.), *Media effects: Advances in theory and research* (pp. 43–60). Hillsdale, NJ: Lawrence Erlbaum Associates.

Krafka, C., Linz, D., Donnerstein, E., & Penrod, S. (1997). Women's reactions to sexually aggressive mass media depictions. *Violence Against Women, 3*(2), 149–181.

Leyens, J. P., Parke, R. D., Camino, L., & Berkowitz, L. (1975). Effects of movie violence on aggression in a field setting as a function of group dominance and cohesion. *Journal of Personality and Social Psychology, 32,* 346–360.

Liebert, R. M., & Baron, R. A. (1971). Short-term effects of televised aggression on children's aggressive behavior. In J. P. Murray, E. A. Rubinstein, & G. A. Comstock (Eds.), *Television and social behavior: Vol. II. Television and social learning* (pp. 181–201). Washington, DC: U.S. Government Printing Office.

Liebert, R. M., Sprafkin, J. N., & Davidson, E. S. (1982). *The early window: Effects of television on children and youth.* New York: Pergamon Press.

Milavsky, J. R., Kesser, R. C., Stipp, H., & Rubens, W. S. (1982). *Television and aggression: A panel study.* New York: Academic Press.

Murray, J. P. (1998). Studying television violence: A research agenda for the 21st century. In J. K. Asamen & G. L. Berry (Eds.), *Research paradigms, television, and social behavior* (pp. 369–410). Thousand Oaks, CA: Sage.

National Academy of Science. (1993). *Understanding and preventing violence.* Washington, DC: National Academy Press.

Paik, H., & Comstock, G. (1994). The effects of television violence on anti-social behavior: A meta-analysis. *Communication Research, 21,* 516–546.

Parke, R. D., Berkowitz, L., Leyens, J. P., West, S. G., & Sebastian, R. J. (1977). The effects of repeated exposure to movie violence on aggressive behaviour in juvenile delinquent boys. Field experimental studies. In L. Berkowitz (Ed.), *Advances in Experimental Social Psychology* (Vol. 10, pp. 135–172). New York: Academic Press.

Phillips, D. P. (1979). Suicide, motor vehicle fatalities, and the mass media: Evidence toward a theory of suggestion. *American Journal of Sociology, 84,* 1150–1173.

Phillips, D. P. (1983). The impact of mass media violence on U.S. homicides. *American Sociological Review, 48,* 560–568.

Phillips, D. P. (1986). The found experiment: A new technique for assessing the impact of mass media violence in real world aggressive behaviour. In G. Comstock (Ed.), *Public communication and behavior* (Vol. 1, pp. 259–307). Orlando, FL: Academic Press.

Schaefer, G. (2000, December 17). Japan's teens ignore official's plea, line up to see violent film. *Journal and Courier,* p. A-9.

Schramm, W., Lyle, J., & Parker, E. (1961). *Television in the lives of our children.* Stanford, CA: Stanford University Press.

Sherry, J. (2001). The effects of violent video games on aggression: A meta-analysis. *Human Communication Research, 27,* 409–431.

Siegel, A. E. (1956). Film-mediated fantasy aggression and strength of aggressive drive. *Child Development, 27,* 365–378.

Singer, S. L., & Singer, D. G. (1980). *Television, imagination and aggression: A study of preschoolers' play.* Hillsdale, NJ: Lawrence Erlbaum Associates.

Smith, S. L., & Donnerstein, E. (1998). Harmful effects of exposure to media violence: Learning of aggression, emotional desensitization, and fear. In R. G. Geen & E. Donnerstein (Eds.), *Human aggression: Theories, research, and implications for social policy* (pp. 167–202). San Diego: Academic Press.

Sparks, G. G., & Sparks, C. W. (2000). Violence, mayhem, and horror. In D. Zillmann & P. Vorderer (Eds.), *Media entertainment: The psychology of its appeal* (pp. 73–91). Mahwah, NJ: Lawrence Erlbaum Associates.

Stein, A. H., & Friedrich, L. K. (1972). Television content and young children's behavior. In J. P. Murray, E. A. Rubinstein, & G. A. Comstock (Eds.), *Television and social behavior: Vol. II. Television and social learning* (pp. 202–317). Washington, DC: U.S. Government Printing Office.

Wertham, F. (1954). *Seduction of the innocent.* New York: Holt Rinehart.

Williams, T. M. (1986). *The impact of television.* New York: Academic Press.

Wilson, B. J., Kunkel, D., Linz, D., Potter, J., Donnerstein, E., Smith, S. L., Blumenthal, E., & Gray, T. (1997). The effects of exposure to media violence. In *National Television Violence Study* (Vol. 1, pp. 8–18). Thousand Oaks, CA: Sage.

Wood, W., Wong, F. Y., & Chachere, J. G. (1991). Effects of media violence on viewers' aggression in unconstrained social interaction. *Psychological Bulletin, 109,* 371–383.

Zillmann, D. (1991). Television viewing and physiological arousal. In J. Bryant & D. Zillmann (Eds.), *Responding to the screen: Reception and reaction processes* (pp. 103–133). Hillsdale, NJ: Lawrence Erlbaum Associates.

Zillmann, D., & Weaver, J. B., III. (1997). Psychoticism in the effect of prolonged exposure to gratuitous media violence on the acceptance of violence as a preferred means of conflict resolution. *Personality & Individual Differences, 22*(5), 613–627.

Zillmann, D., & Weaver, J. B., III. (1999). Effects of prolonged exposure to gratuitous media violence on provoked and unprovoked hostile behavior. *Journal of Applied Social Psychology, 29*(1), 145–165.

Chapter 11

Fright Reactions to Mass Media

JOANNE CANTOR
University of Wisconsin—Madison

The purpose of this chapter is to investigate fright reactions produced by mass media presentations. First, research findings related to the prevalence and intensity with which feelings of fear are experienced as a result of exposure to media drama are reviewed. Then the paradox that fright reactions to media fiction occur at all is discussed, and an explanation is proposed based on principles of stimulus generalization. The theory is then refined to include other factors that are needed to account for observed effects in response to both dramatic and nonfictional presentations. Developmental differences in the media stimuli that frighten children and in the effectiveness of coping strategies are then discussed. Finally, gender differences are explored.

FEELINGS OF FRIGHT IN REACTION TO THE SCREEN

Anyone who has ever been to a horror film or thriller appreciates the fact that exposure to television shows, films, and other mass media presentations depicting danger, injury, bizarre images, and terror-stricken protagonists can induce intense fright responses in an audience. Most of us seem to be able to remember at least one specific program or movie that terrified us when we were children and that made us nervous, remained in our thoughts, and affected other aspects of our behavior for some time afterward. And this happened to us even after we were old enough to know that what we were witnessing was not actually happening at the time and that the depicted dangers could not leave the screen and attack us directly. These reactions can also occur when we know that what is being portrayed did not actually happen; at times we may have such reactions even when we understand that there is no chance that the depicted events could ever occur.

The predominant interest in this chapter is fright as an immediate emotional response that is typically of relatively short duration, but that may endure, on occasion, for several hours, days, or even longer. The focus here is on emotional reactions involving components of anxiety, distress, and increased physiological arousal that are frequently engendered in viewers as a result of exposure to specific types of media productions.

Research interest in the phenomenon of fright reactions to mass media goes back as far as Herbert Blumer's (1933) studies of children's fright reactions to movies. Although sporadic attention was paid to the media as a source of children's fears in the succeeding several decades, research attention began to focus on this issue more prominently in the 1980s. One reason for this more recent focus on fright may have been the release of several blockbuster frightening films in the 1970s. As anecdotal reports of intense emotional responses to such popular films as *Jaws* and *The Exorcist* proliferated in the press, public attention became more focused on the phenomenon. Although many adults experience such reactions, the major share of public concern has been over children's responses. The furor over children's reactions to especially intense scenes in the 1984 movies *Indiana Jones and the Temple of Doom* and *Gremlins* prompted the Motion Picture Association of America to add "PG-13" to its rating system in an attempt to caution parents that, for whatever reason, a film might be inappropriate for children under the age of 13 (Zoglin, 1984). In addition, the rapid expansion in the number of cable channels has meant that most films produced for theatrical distribution, no matter how brutal or bizarre, eventually end up on television and thus become accessible to large numbers of children, often without their parents' knowledge. Finally, as television news became more graphically visual and sensational in the 1990s, observers began speculating about the effects of such images on children's psychological health. The September 2001 terrorist attacks on New York and Washington, DC, intensified these concerns.

Prevalence and Intensity of Media-Induced Fright Reactions

As early as the 1930s Blumer (1933) reported that 93% of the children he questioned said they had been frightened or horrified by a motion picture. More recently, about 75% of the respondents in two separate samples of preschool and elementary school children in Wisconsin said that they had been scared by something they had seen on television or in a movie (Wilson, Hoffner, & Cantor, 1987).

In other research, a survey of more than 2,000 third through eighth graders in Ohio public schools revealed that as the number of hours of television viewing per day increased, so did the prevalence of symptoms of psychological trauma, such as anxiety, depression, and posttraumatic stress (Singer, Slovak, Frierson, & York, 1998). Moreover, a survey of the parents of almost 500 public schoolchildren in kindergarten through fourth grade in Rhode Island revealed that the amount of children's television viewing (especially television viewing at bedtime) and having a television in their own bedroom were significantly related to sleep disturbances (Owens et al., 1999). Although these survey data cannot rule out the alternative explanation that children experiencing trauma or sleep difficulties are more likely to turn to television for distraction, they are consistent with the conclusion that exposure to frightening and disturbing images on television contributes to a child's level of stress and anxiety. Indeed, 9% of the parents in the study by Owens et al. (1999) reported that their child experienced TV-induced nightmares at least once a week.

An experimental study suggests that witnessing scary media presentations may also lead children to avoid engaging in activities related to the events depicted (Cantor & Omdahl, 1991). In this study, kindergarten through sixth-grade children who were exposed to dramatized depictions of a deadly house fire from *Little House on the Prairie* increased their self-reports of worry about similar events in their own lives. Moreover, they were also less interested in learning how to build a fire in a fireplace than were children who were not shown the episode. Similarly, children who saw a scene involving a drowning expressed more concerns about water accidents and were less willing to learn canoeing than were children who had not watched that scene. Although the duration of such effects was not measured, the effects were undoubtedly short lived, especially because debriefings were employed and safety guidelines were taught so that no child would experience long-term distress (Cantor & Omdahl, 1999).

There is an increasing body of evidence, in fact, that the fear induced by mass media exposure is often long lasting, with sometimes intense and debilitating effects (Cantor, 1998). In a study designed to assess the severity of enduring fright reactions to mass media, Johnson (1980) asked a random sample of adults whether they had ever seen a motion picture that had disturbed them "a great deal." Forty percent replied in the affirmative, and the median length of the reported disturbance was 3 days. Respondents also reported on the type, intensity, and duration of symptoms such as nervousness, depression, fear of specific things, and recurring thoughts and images. Based on these reports, Johnson judged that 48% of these respondents (19% of the total sample) had experienced, for at least 2 days, a "significant stress reaction" as the result of watching a movie.

Recent retrospective studies of adults' detailed memories of having been frightened by a television show or movie provide more evidence of the severity and duration of media-induced fear (Harrison & Cantor, 1999; Hoekstra, Harris, & Helmick, 1999). In these studies, involving samples of undergraduates from three universities, the presence of vivid memories of enduring media-induced fear was nearly universal. All of the participants in one study (Hoekstra et al., 1999) reported such an incident. In the other study (Harrison & Cantor, 1999), 90% of the participants reported an intense fear reaction to something in the media, in spite of the fact that the respondents could receive full extra credit for participating in the study if they simply said "no" (meaning "I never had such an experience"), and thereby avoid writing a paper and filling out a three-page questionnaire.

Both studies revealed a variety of intense reactions, including generalized anxieties, specific fears, unwanted recurring thoughts, and disturbances in eating and sleeping. Moreover, Harrison and Cantor (1999) reported these fears to be long lasting: One-third of those who reported having been frightened said that the fear effects had lasted more than a year. Indeed, more than one-fourth of the respondents said that the emotional impact of the program or movie (viewed an average of six years earlier) was still with them at the time of reporting.

The most extreme reactions reported in the literature come from psychiatric case studies in which acute and disabling anxiety states enduring several days to several weeks or more (some necessitating hospitalization) are said to have been precipitated by the viewing of horror movies such as *The Exorcist, Invasion of the Body Snatchers*, and *Ghostwatch* (Buzzuto, 1975; Mathai, 1983; Simons & Silveira, 1994). Most of the patients in the cases reported had not had previously diagnosed psychiatric problems, but the viewing of the film was seen as occurring in conjunction with other stressors in the patients' lives.

A STIMULUS GENERALIZATION APPROACH
TO MEDIA-INDUCED FEAR

As can be seen from the literature summarized here, there is a good deal of evidence regarding viewers' experiences of fear in response to mass media presentations. The next part of this chapter is devoted to speculations about why such fear reactions occur and the factors that promote or inhibit their occurrence.

Fear is generally conceived of as an emotional response of negative hedonic tone related to avoidance or escape, due to the perception of real or imagined threat (e.g., Izard, 1977). A classic fear-arousing situation is one in which the individual senses that he or she is in physical danger, such as on encountering a poisonous snake on a walk through the woods. Fear can be conceived of as a response involving cognitions, motor behavior, and excitatory reactions that, except under extreme conditions, prepare the individual to flee from the danger.

Using this definition of fear, it is not difficult to explain the public terror that was produced by perhaps the most infamous frightening media drama on record—the 1938 radio broadcast of H. G. Wells' *War of the Worlds*. Many people who tuned in late thought they were listening to a live news bulletin informing them that Martians were taking over the United States (Cantril, 1940). Thus, if they believed what they heard, they justifiably felt that their own lives and indeed the future of their society were in great peril.

But in typical situations in which people are exposed to mass media drama, the audience understands that what is being depicted is not actually happening; in many cases, they know that it never did happen; and in some cases, they know that it never could happen. Objectively speaking, then, the viewer is not in any immediate danger. Why, then, does the fright reaction occur? Although fright responses to media presentations are undoubtedly the result of the complex interaction of a variety of processes, a preliminary explanation for this phenomenon is proposed, based on the notion of stimulus generalization (see Pavlov, 1927). In conditioning terms, if a stimulus evokes either an unconditioned or conditioned emotional response, other stimuli that are similar to the eliciting stimulus will evoke similar, but less intense emotional responses. This principle implies that, because of similarities between the real and the mediated stimulus, a stimulus that would evoke a fright response if experienced firsthand will evoke a similar, but less intense response when encountered via the mass media. In order to explore the implications of this explanation, it should be instructive to identify major categories of stimuli and events that tend to induce fear in real-life situations and that are frequently depicted in frightening media productions, and, second, to delineate the factors that should promote or reduce the viewer's tendency to respond emotionally to the mediated stimulus.

Stimuli and Events that Generally Produce Fear

Based on a review of the literature on the sources of real-world fears and on the effects of frightening media, three categories of stimuli and events that tend to produce fear in real-life situations and that occur frequently in frightening presentations are proposed: (a) dangers and injuries, (b) distortions of natural forms, and (c) the experience of endangerment and fear by others. These categories are obviously not mutually exclusive: On the contrary, a frightening scene usually involves more than one of these categories.[1]

---

[1]These categories are also not considered exhaustive. Many theorists have proposed additional categories of stimuli that readily evoke fear, such as certain types of animals (especially snakes; see Jersild & Holmes, 1935; Yerkes & Yerkes, 1936) and loud noises, darkness, and stimuli related to loss of support (see Bowlby, 1973). These categories are not discussed separately here because it seems that in mass media productions, such stimuli tend to co-occur with danger or signal its imminence. For example, the snakes, bats, and spiders in horror films are usually depicted as poisonous as well as repulsive. Sudden loud noises, darkness, and the perception of rapid movement are often used to intensify the perceived dangerousness of situations.

Dangers and Injuries. Stimuli that are perceived as dangerous should, by definition, evoke fear. The depiction of events that either cause or threaten to cause great harm is the stock-in-trade of the frightening film. Natural disasters such as tornadoes, volcanoes, plagues, and earthquakes; violent encounters on an interpersonal, global, or even intergalactic level; attacks by vicious animals; and large-scale industrial and nuclear accidents are typical events in frightening media fare. If any of these events were witnessed directly, the onlooker would be in danger, and fear would be the expected response. In addition, because danger is often present when injuries are witnessed, the perception of injuries should come to evoke fear as a conditioned response, even in the absence of the danger that produced the injuries. Through stimulus generalization, one might thus expect mediated depictions of danger, violence, and injury to produce fright reactions as well. Reports of fright produced by depictions of dangerous stimuli in media drama abound in the survey and experimental literature (e.g., Cantor, 1998; Harrison & Cantor 1999).

Distortions of Natural Forms. In addition to dangerous stimuli and the outcomes of dangerous situations, a related set of stimuli that typically evoke fear might be referred to as deformities and distortions, or familiar organisms in unfamiliar and unnatural forms. Hebb (1946) observed fear responses to such "deviations from previously experienced patterns" in chimpanzees and argued that such responses are spontaneous, in that they do not require conditioning. Organisms that have been mutilated as a result of injury could be considered to fall into this category as well as the previous category. In addition, distortions that are not the result of injury are often encountered in thrillers in the form of realistic characters like dwarves, hunchbacks, and mutants. Moreover, monsters abound in thrillers. Monsters are unreal creatures that are similar to natural beings in many ways, but deviant from them in other ways, such as through distortions in size, shape, skin color, or facial configuration. In scary movies, monstrous and distorted characters are typically, but not universally, depicted as evil and dangerous. Monsters, ghosts, vampires, mummies, and other supernatural beings are frequently cited as sources of children's fear in both surveys and anecdotal reports (e.g., Cantor, 1998; Cantor & Sparks, 1984).

The Experience of Endangerment and Fear by Others. Although in some cases viewers seem to respond directly to depictions of fear-evoking stimuli such as dangers, injuries, and distortions, in most dramatic presentations these stimuli are shown to affect the emotional responses and outcomes of depicted characters. In many cases, the viewer can be said to respond indirectly to the stimuli through the experiences of the characters. One mechanism underlying such responses is empathy. Although there is controversy over the origins of empathic processes (see Berger, 1962; Feshbach, 1982; Hoffman, 1978), it is clear that under some circumstances, people experience fear as a direct response to the fear expressed by others. Many frightening films seem to stress characters' expressions of fear in response to dangers as much as the perceptual cues associated with the threat itself (see Wilson & Cantor, 1985).

Another indirect mechanism that may be proposed to account for emotional responses to the experiences of others derives from the fact that witnessing other people risk danger can produce the "vicarious" experience of fear, even when the persons at risk do not express fear. Zillmann and Cantor (1977) showed that people respond with dysphoria to the misfortunes of characters for whom they have affection or for whom they at least do not feel antipathy. Therefore, fear may be seen as deriving from the anticipation of empathy with the distress responses of liked characters. Both survey and experimental findings indicate that the threat of harm to human or animal protagonists is a common source of media-induced fear (e.g., Cantor, 1998; Cantor & Omdahl, 1991).

Factors Affecting the Tendency to Respond Emotionally to Mediated Stimuli

Three factors are proposed to have an impact on viewers' tendencies to respond emotionally to mediated fear-evoking stimuli: (a) the similarity of the depicted stimuli to real-life fear-evokers, (b) viewers' motivations for media exposure, and (c) factors affecting emotionality, generally.

Similarity of Depicted Stimuli to Real-Life Fear-Evokers. The notion of stimulus generalization implies that the greater the similarity between a conditioned or unconditioned stimulus and the substitute stimulus, the stronger the generalization response will be. Perceptually speaking, realistic depictions of threatening events are more similar to events occurring in the real world than are animated or stylized depictions of the same events. Thus, the stimulus generalization notion would predict more intense responses to live-action violence than to cartoon violence or violence between puppets, for example. Experimental findings are consistent with this expectation (e.g., Gunter & Furnham, 1984).

The similarity of depicted stimuli to those stimuli that provoke fear in a particular individual should also enhance stimulus generalization. Experiments have shown that an individual's fears (for example, of spiders and of death) and prior experiences with stressful events (such as childbirth) intensify the emotional effects of related media presentations (e.g., Sapolsky & Zillmann, 1978; Weiss, Katkin, & Rubin, 1968).

The theory of stimulus generalization, although helpful, cannot account for all situations in which viewers respond with fear to media presentations. The theory also includes the notion of stimulus discrimination, which implies that as viewers come to recognize the different reinforcement contingencies associated with viewing a frightening stimulus on screen as opposed to being exposed to it in real life, their emotional reactions should diminish greatly. Because even adolescents and adults, who understand the mediated nature of frightening images, often experience intense media-induced fright reactions, it is necessary to invoke additional factors to explain their responses.

Motivations for Media Exposure.   One set of factors that the stimulus generalization notion does not take into account are motivations for media exposure. In order to enhance the emotional impact of a drama, viewers may, for example, adopt the "willing suspension of disbelief" by cognitively minimizing the effect of knowledge that the events are mediated. In addition, mature viewers may enhance their emotional responses by generating their own emotion-evoking visual images or by cognitively elaborating on the implications of the portrayed events. Mature viewers who seek to avoid intense arousal may employ other appraisal processes to diminish fright reactions to media stimuli by using the "adult discount," for example (see Dysinger & Ruckmick, 1933), and concentrating on the fact that the stimuli are only mediated. Although such appraisal processes often operate, they are by no means universally effective. Moreover, such processes are especially limited in young children (Cantor & Wilson, 1984).

In addition to seeking entertainment, viewers may expose themselves to media for purposes of acquiring information. Because part of the emotional response to such stimuli might arise from viewers' anticipations of future consequences to themselves, depictions of real threats should evoke more fear than dramatic portrayals of events that could never happen. Moreover, depicted threatening agents that are considered to be proximate or imminent should evoke more fear than remote threats. Support for this notion comes from anecdotes regarding the especially intense reactions to *Jaws*, a movie about shark attacks, by people who saw the movie while vacationing at the seashore. Similarly, in an experiment (Cantor & Hoffner, 1990), children who thought that the threatening agent depicted in a movie existed in their environment were more frightened by the movie than were children who did not believe that the threat could be found in their local area.

Factors Affecting Emotionality Generally.   Because physiological arousal is an important component of fear, it is a critical element in viewers' reactions to frightening media. Experiments testing the role of excitation transfer (e.g., Zillmann, 1978) in responses to emotion-evoking films have demonstrated that excitatory residues from prior arousing experiences can combine with responses to unrelated, subsequently presented movie scenes and thereby intensify emotional reactions to the movie (e.g., Zillmann, Mody, & Cantor, 1974).

This reasoning leads to the expectation that factors within a frightening presentation that tend to produce arousal may combine with the depiction of fear-evoking stimuli to increase the viewer's arousal and thus the intensity of the fear experienced while viewing. Producers of frightening movies employ a variety of stylistic devices, including music and suspense, to intensify the audience's fright (see, e.g., Björkqvist & Lagerspetz, 1985; Cantor, Ziemke, & Sparks, 1984).

DEVELOPMENTAL DIFFERENCES AND MEDIA-INDUCED FEAR

A large body of research has examined two major developmental issues in fright reactions to media: (a) the types of mass media stimuli and events that frighten children at different ages, and (b) the strategies for preventing or reducing unwanted fear reactions that are most effective for different-aged children. Experiments and surveys have been conducted to test expectations based on theories and findings in cognitive development research. The experiments have had the advantage of testing rigorously controlled variations in program content and viewing conditions, using a combination of self-reports, physiological responses, the coding of facial expressions of emotion, and behavioral measures. For ethical reasons, only small excerpts from relatively mild stimuli are used in experiments. In contrast, the surveys have investigated the responses of children who were exposed to a particular mass media offering in their natural environment, without any researcher intervention. Although less tightly controlled, the surveys permit the study of responses to much more intensely frightening media fare.

Developmental Differences in the Media Stimuli That Produce Fright

One might expect that as children get older, they become less and less susceptible to all media-produced emotional disturbances. However, this is not the case. As children mature cognitively, some things become less likely to disturb them, whereas other things become potentially more upsetting. This generalization is consistent with developmental differences in children's fears in general. According to a variety of studies using diverse methodologies, children from approximately 3 to 8 years of age are frightened primarily by animals; the dark; supernatural beings, such as ghosts, monsters, and witches; and by anything that looks strange or moves suddenly. The fears of 9- to 12-year-olds are more often related to personal injury and physical destruction and the injury and death of family members. Adolescents continue to fear personal injury and physical destruction, but school fears and social fears arise at this age, as do fears regarding political, economic, and global issues (see Cantor, Wilson, & Hoffner, 1986, for a review). The findings regarding the media stimuli that frighten children at different ages are consistent with observed changes in children's fears in general.

Perceptual Dependence. The first generalization about fright-provoking stimuli is that the relative importance of the immediately perceptible components of a fear-inducing media stimulus decreases as a child's age increases. Research on cognitive development indicates that, in general, very young children react to stimuli predominantly in terms of their perceptible characteristics and that with increasing maturity, they respond more and more to the conceptual aspects of stimuli (see Flavell, 1963; Melkman, Tversky, & Baratz, 1981). Research findings support the generalization that preschool children (approximately 3 to 5 years old) are more likely to be frightened by something that looks scary but is actually harmless than by something that looks attractive but is actually harmful; for older elementary schoolchildren (approximately 9 to 11 years), appearance carries much less weight, relative to the behavior or destructive potential of a character, animal, or object.

One set of data that supports this generalization comes from a survey conducted in 1981 (Cantor & Sparks, 1984) asking parents to name the programs and films that had frightened their children the most. In this survey, parents of preschool children most often mentioned offerings with grotesque-looking, unreal characters, such as the television series *The Incredible Hulk* and the feature film *The Wizard of Oz*; parents of older elementary school children more often mentioned programs or movies (like *The Amityville Horror*) that involved threats without a strong visual component and that required a good deal of imagination to comprehend. Sparks (1986) replicated this study, using children's self-reports rather than parents' observations, and obtained similar findings. Both surveys included controls for possible differences in exposure patterns in the different age groups.

A second investigation that supports this generalization was a laboratory study involving an episode of *The Incredible Hulk* (Sparks & Cantor, 1986). In the 1981 survey of parents, this program had spontaneously been mentioned by 40% of the parents of preschoolers as a show that had scared their child (Cantor & Sparks, 1984). The laboratory study concluded that preschool children's unexpectedly intense reactions to this program were partially due to their overresponse to the visual image of the Hulk character. When participants were shown a shortened episode of the program and were asked how they had felt during different scenes, preschool children reported the most fear after the attractive, mild-mannered hero was transformed into the monstrous-looking Hulk. Older elementary schoolchildren, in contrast, reported the least fear at this time, because they understood that the Hulk was really the benevolent hero in another physical form and that he was using his superhuman powers to rescue a character who was in danger.

Another study (Hoffner & Cantor, 1985) tested the effect of appearance more directly by creating a story in four versions, so that a major character was either attractive and grandmotherly looking or ugly and grotesque. The character's appearance was factorially varied with her behavior—she was depicted as behaving either kindly or cruelly. In judging how nice or mean the character was and in predicting what she would do in the subsequent scene, preschool children were more influenced than older children (6–7 and 9–10 years) by the character's looks and less influenced than older children by her kind or cruel behavior. As the age of the child increased, the character's looks became less important and her behavior carried increasing weight. A follow-up experiment revealed that all age groups engaged in physical appearance stereotyping in the absence of information about the character's behavior.

Harrison and Cantor's (1999) retrospective study of fright responses also provided evidence in support of the diminishing influence of appearance. When descriptions of the program or movie that had frightened respondents were categorized as whether they involved immediately perceptible stimuli (e.g., monstrous-looking characters, eerie noises), the percentage of respondents whose described scene fell into this category declined as the respondent's age at exposure increased.

Fantasy vs. Reality as Fear Inducers. A second generalization that emerges from research is that as children mature, they become more responsive to realistic and less responsive to fantastic dangers depicted in the media. The data on trends in children's fears suggest that very young children are more likely than older children and adolescents to fear things that are not real, in the sense that their occurrence in the real world is impossible (e.g., monsters). The development of more "mature" fears seems to presuppose the acquisition of knowledge regarding the objective dangers posed by different situations. One important component of this knowledge includes an understanding of the distinction between reality and fantasy, a competence that develops only gradually throughout childhood (see Flavell, 1963; Morison & Gardner, 1978).

This generalization is supported by Cantor and Sparks' (1984) survey of parents. In general, the tendency to mention fantasy offerings, depicting events that could not possibly occur in the real world, as sources of fear decreased as the child's age increased, and the tendency to mention fictional offerings, depicting events that could possibly occur, increased. Again, Sparks (1986) replicated these findings using children's self-reports. Further support for this generalization comes from a study of children's fright responses to television news (Cantor & Nathanson, 1996). A random survey of parents of children in kindergarten, second, fourth, and sixth grades showed that fear produced by fantasy programs decreased as the child's grade increased, whereas fear induced by news stories increased with age. Valkenburg, Cantor, and Peeters (2000), in a random survey of Dutch children, also found a decrease between the ages of 7and 12 in fright responses to fantasy content.

Responses to Abstract Threats. The third generalization from research is that as children mature, they become frightened by media depictions involving increasingly abstract concepts. This generalization is clearly consistent with the general sources of children's fears, cited earlier. It is also consistent with theories of cognitive development (e.g., Flavell, 1963), which indicate that the ability to think abstractly emerges relatively late in cognitive development.

Data supporting this generalization come from a survey of children's responses to the television movie *The Day After,* which depicted the devastation of a Kansas community by a nuclear attack (Cantor et al., 1986). In a random telephone survey of parents, conducted the night after the broadcast of this movie, children under 12 were reportedly much less disturbed by the film than were teenagers, and parents were the most disturbed. The very youngest children seem to have been the least frightened. The findings seem to be due to the fact that the emotional impact of the film comes from the contemplation of the potential annihilation of the earth as we know it—a concept that is beyond the grasp of the young child. The visual depictions of injury in the movie were quite mild compared to what most children have become used to seeing on television.

A study of children's reactions to television coverage of the war in the Persian Gulf also supports the generalization that, as they mature, children are increasingly responsive to abstract as opposed to concrete aspects of frightening media (Cantor, Mares, & Oliver, 1993). In a random survey of parents of children in public school in Madison, Wisconsin, conducted shortly after the Gulf War, there were no significant differences between 1st, 4th, 7th, and 11th graders in the prevalence or intensity of negative emotional reactions to television coverage of the war. However, children in different grades were upset by different aspects of the coverage. Parents of younger children, but not of adolescents, stressed the visual aspects of the coverage and the direct, concrete consequences of combat (e.g., the missiles exploding) in their descriptions of the elements that had disturbed their child the most. As the child's age increased, the more abstract, conceptual aspects of the coverage (e.g., the possibility of the conflict spreading) were cited by parents as the most disturbing.

Developmental Differences in the Effectiveness of Coping Strategies

Research in cognitive development has also been used to determine the best ways to help children cope with fear-producing stimuli or to reduce their children's fear reactions once they occur (Cantor, 1998; Cantor & Wilson, 1988). Developmental differences in children's information-processing abilities yield differences in the effectiveness of strategies to prevent or reduce their media-induced fears. The findings of research on coping strategies can be summed up in the following generalization: In general, preschool children benefit more from "noncognitive" than from "cognitive" strategies; both cognitive and noncognitive strategies can be effective for older elementary schoolchildren, although this age group tends to prefer cognitive strategies.

Noncognitive Strategies. Noncognitive strategies are those that do not involve the processing of verbal information and that appear to be relatively automatic. The process of visual desensitization, or gradual exposure to threatening images in a nonthreatening context, is one such strategy that has been shown to be effective for both preschool and older elementary schoolchildren. In several experiments, prior exposure to filmed footage of snakes (Wilson & Cantor, 1987), still photographs of worms (Weiss, Imrich, & Wilson, 1993), rubber replicas of spiders (Wilson, 1987), and live lizards (Wilson, 1989a) reduced children's fear in response to movie scenes featuring similar creatures. Also, fear reactions to the Hulk character in *The Incredible Hulk* were reduced by exposure to footage of Lou Ferrigno, the actor who plays the character, having his makeup applied so that he gradually took on the menacing appearance of the character (Cantor, Sparks, & Hoffner, 1988). None of these experiments revealed developmental differences in the effectiveness of desensitization techniques.

Other noncognitive strategies involve physical activities, such as clinging to an attachment object or having something to eat or drink. Although these techniques are available to viewers of all ages, younger children consider them to be more effective and report using them more often than older children do. In a study of children's perceptions of the effectiveness of strategies for coping with media-induced fright, preschool children's evaluations of "holding onto a blanket or a toy" and "getting something to eat or drink" were significantly more positive than those of older elementary schoolchildren (Wilson et al., 1987). Harrison and Cantor's (1999) retrospective study also showed that the percent of respondents who reported having used a "behavioral" (noncognitive) coping strategy to deal with media-induced fear declined as age at exposure to the frightening fare increased.

Another noncognitive strategy that has been shown to have more appeal and more effectiveness for younger than for older children is covering one's eyes during frightening portions of a presentation. In an experiment by Wilson (1989b), when covering the eyes was suggested as an option, younger children used this strategy more often than older children did. Moreover, the suggestion of this option reduced the fear of younger children, but actually increased the fear of older children. Wilson noted that the older children recognized the limited effectiveness of covering their eyes (while still being exposed to the audio features of the program) and may have reacted by feeling less in control, and therefore more vulnerable, when this strategy was offered to them.

Cognitive Strategies. In contrast to noncognitive strategies, cognitive (or "verbal") strategies involve verbal information that is used to cast the threat in a different light. These strategies involve relatively complex cognitive operations, and research consistently finds such strategies to be more effective for older than for younger children.

When dealing with fantasy depictions, the most typical cognitive strategy seems to be to provide an explanation focusing on the unreality of the situation. This strategy should be especially difficult for preschool children, who do not have a full grasp of the implications of the fantasy-reality distinction. In an experiment by Cantor and Wilson (1984), older elementary schoolchildren who were told to remember that what they were seeing in *The Wizard of Oz* was not real showed less fear than their classmates who received no instructions. The same instructions did not help preschoolers, however. A study by Wilson and Weiss (1991) also showed developmental differences in the effectiveness of reality-related strategies.

Children's beliefs about the effectiveness of focusing on the unreality of the stimulus have been shown to be consistent with these experimental findings. In Wilson et al.'s (1987) study of perceptions of fear-reducing techniques, preschool children's ranking of the effectiveness of "tell yourself it's not real" was significantly lower than that of older elementary schoolchildren.

For media depictions involving realistic threats, the most prevalent cognitive strategy seems to be to provide an explanation that minimizes the perceived severity of the depicted danger. This type of strategy is not only more effective with older children than with younger children, in certain situations it has been shown to have a fear-enhancing rather than anxiety-reducing effect with younger children. In an experiment involving the snake-pit scene from *Raiders of the Lost Ark* (Wilson & Cantor, 1987), children were either exposed or not exposed to reassuring information about snakes (e.g., the statement that most snakes are not poisonous). Although this information tended to reduce the fear of older elementary schoolchildren, kindergarten and first-grade children seem to have only partially understood the information, responding to the word *poisonous* more intensely than to the word *not*. For them, negative emotional reactions were more prevalent if they had heard the supposedly reassuring information than if they had not heard it.

Data also indicate that older children use cognitive coping strategies more frequently than preschool children do. In the survey of reactions to *The Day After* (Cantor et al., 1986), parents' reports that their child had discussed the movie with them after viewing it increased with the age of the child. In a laboratory experiment involving exposure to a scary scene (Hoffner & Cantor, 1990), significantly more 9- to 11-year-olds than 5- to 7-year-olds reported spontaneously employing cognitive coping strategies (thinking about the expected happy outcome or thinking about the fact that what was happening was not real). Finally, Harrison and Cantor's (1999) retrospective study showed that the tendency to employ a cognitive strategy to cope with media-induced fear increased with the respondent's age at the time of the incident.

Studies have also shown that the effectiveness of cognitive strategies for young children can be improved by providing visual demonstrations of verbal explanations (Cantor et al., 1988) and by encouraging repeated rehearsal of simplified, reassuring information (Wilson, 1987).

GENDER ISSUES AND MEDIA-INDUCED FRIGHT

Gender Differences in Media-Induced Fear

There is a common stereotype that girls are more easily frightened than boys (Birnbaum & Croll, 1984), and indeed that females in general are more emotional than males (e.g., Fabes & Martin, 1991; Grossman & Wood, 1993). There is quite a bit of research that would seem to support this contention, although the gender differences may be less strong than they appear at first glance. Moreover, the observed gender differences seem to be partially attributable to socialization pressures on girls to express their fears and on boys to inhibit them.

Peck (1999) conducted a meta-analysis of the studies of media-induced fear that were produced between 1987 and 1996. Her analysis, which included 59 studies that permitted a comparison between males and females, reported a moderate gender-difference effect size (.41), with females exhibiting more fear than males. Females' responses were more intense than those of males for all dependent measures. However, the effect sizes were largest for self-report and behavioral measures (those that are under the most conscious control) and smallest for heart rate and facial expressions. In addition, the effect size for gender differences increased with age.

Peck (1999) also conducted an experiment in which male and female college students were exposed to two scenes from the *Nightmare on Elm Street* series of movies, one featuring a male victim and the other featuring a female victim. She found that women's self-reports of fear were more intense than those of males, especially when the victim was female. However, when the victim was male, certain of the responses (pulse amplitude and hemispheric asymmetry) suggested that men were experiencing more intense physiological reactions than women.

Although more research is needed to explore the extent of gender differences in media-induced fear and the factors that contribute to them, these findings suggest that the size of the gender difference may be partially a function of social pressures to conform to gender-appropriate behavior.

Gender Differences in Coping Strategies

There is some evidence of gender differences in the coping strategies used to counteract media-induced fear, and these gender differences may also reflect gender-role socialization pressures. Hoffner (1995) found that adolescent girls reported using more noncognitive coping strategies than boys did, but that there were no gender differences in the use of cognitive strategies. Similarly Valkenburg et al. (2000) found that among 7- to 12-year-old Dutch children, girls reported resorting to social support, physical intervention, and escape more often than boys did, but that there was no gender difference in the use of cognitive reassurance as a coping strategy.

Both of these findings are consistent with Hoffner's (1995) explanation that because boys are less willing than girls to show their emotions, they avoid noncognitive strategies, which are usually apparent to others. In contrast, the two genders employ cognitive strategies with equal frequency because these strategies are less readily observable.

SUMMARY AND CONCLUSIONS

In summary, research shows that children often experience anxiety and distress while watching mass media presentations and that these feelings, in varying intensities, often linger after exposure. Recent surveys demonstrate that media-induced fears often interfere with children's sleep, and retrospective reports suggest that the negative effects of scary media can endure for years, even into adulthood.

Research on the relationship between cognitive development and emotional responses to television has been very helpful in predicting the types of television programs and movies that are more or less likely to frighten children of different ages and in devising effective intervention and coping strategies for different age groups. In addition to providing empirical tests of the relationship between cognitive development and affective responses, these developmental findings can help parents and other caregivers make more sensible viewing choices for children (Cantor, 1998).

ACKNOWLEDGMENTS

Much of the research reported in this chapter was supported by Grant RO1 MH 35320 from the National Institute of Mental Health and by grants from the Graduate School of the University of Wisconsin.

REFERENCES

Birnbaum, D. W., & Croll, W. L. (1984). The etiology of children's stereotypes about sex differences in emotionality. *Sex Roles, 10,* 677–691.

Berger, S. M. (1962). Conditioning through vicarious instigation. *Psychological Review, 69,* 450–466.

Björkqvist, K., & Lagerspetz, K. (1985). Children's experience of three types of cartoon at two age levels. *International Journal of Psychology, 20,* 77–93.

Blumer, H. (1933). *Movies and conduct.* New York: Macmillan.

Bowlby, J. (1973). *Separation: Anxiety and anger.* New York: Basic Books.

Buzzuto, J. C. (1975). Cinematic neurosis following *The Exorcist. Journal of Nervous and Mental Disease, 161,* 43–48.

Cantor, J. (1998). *"Mommy, I'm scared": How TV and movies frighten children and what we can do to protect them.* San Diego, CA: Harvest/Harcourt.

Cantor, J., & Hoffner, C. (1990). Children's fear reactions to a televised film as a function of perceived immediacy of depicted threat. *Journal of Broadcasting & Electronic Media, 34,* 421–442.

Cantor, J., Mares, M. L., & Oliver, M. B. (1993). Parents' and children's emotional reactions to televised coverage of the Gulf War. In B. Greenberg & W. Gantz (Eds.), *Desert storm and the mass media* (pp. 325–340). Cresskill, NJ: Hampton Press.

Cantor, J., & Nathanson, A. (1996). Children's fright reactions to television news. *Journal of Communication, 46*(4), 139–152.

Cantor, J., & Omdahl, B. (1991). Effects of fictional media depictions of realistic threats on children's emotional responses, expectations, worries, and liking for related activities. *Communication Monographs, 58,* 384–401.

Cantor, J., & Omdahl, B. (1999). Children's acceptance of safety guidelines after exposure to televised dramas depicting accidents. *Western Journal of Communication, 63*(1), 1–15.

Cantor, J., & Sparks, G. G. (1984). Children's fear responses to mass media: Testing some Piagetian predictions. *Journal of Communication, 34*(2), 90–103.

Cantor, J., Sparks, G. G., & Hoffner, C. (1988). Calming children's television fears: Mr. Rogers vs. The Incredible Hulk. *Journal of Broadcasting & Electronic Media, 32,* 271–288.

Cantor, J., & Wilson, B. J. (1984). Modifying fear responses to mass media in preschool and elementary school children. *Journal of Broadcasting, 28,* 431–443.

Cantor, J., & Wilson, B. J. (1988). Helping children cope with frightening media presentations. *Current Psychology: Research & Reviews, 7,* 58–75.

Cantor, J., Wilson, B. J., & Hoffner, C. (1986). Emotional responses to a televised nuclear holocaust film. *Communication Research, 13,* 257–277.

Cantor, J., Ziemke, D., & Sparks, G. G. (1984). The effect of forewarning on emotional responses to a horror film. *Journal of Broadcasting, 28,* 21–31.

Cantril, H. (1940). *The invasion from Mars: A study in the psychology of panic.* Princeton, NJ: Princeton University Press.

Dysinger, W. S., & Ruckmick, C. A. (1933). *The emotional responses of children to the motion picture situation.* New York: Macmillan.

Fabes, R. A., & Martin, C. L. (1991). Gender and age stereotypes of emotionality. *Personality and Social Psychology Bulletin, 17,* 532–540.

Feshbach, N. D. (1982). Sex differences in empathy and social behavior in children. In N. Eisenberg (Ed.), *The development of prosocial behavior* (pp. 315–338). New York: Academic Press.

Flavell, J. (1963). *The developmental psychology of Jean Piaget.* New York: Van Nostrand.

Grossman, M., & Wood, W. (1993). Sex differences in the intensity of emotional experience: A social role interpretation. *Journal of Personality and Social Psychology, 65,* 1010–1022.

Gunter, B., & Furnham, A. (1984). Perceptions of television violence: Effects of programme genre and type of violence on viewers' judgements of violent portrayals. *British Journal of Social Psychology, 23,* 155–164.

Harrison, K., & Cantor, J. (1999). Tales from the screen: Enduring fright reactions to scary media. *Media Psychology, 1*(2), 97–116.

Hebb, D. O. (1946). On the nature of fear. *Psychological Review, 53,* 259–276.

Hoekstra, S. J., Harris, R. J., & Helmick, A. L. (1999). Autobiographical memories about the experience of seeing frightening movies in childhood. *Media Psychology, 1*(2), 117–140.

Hoffman, M. L. (1978). Toward a theory of empathic arousal and development. In M. Lewis & L. A. Rosenblum (Eds.), *The development of affect* (pp. 227–256). New York: Plenum.

Hoffner, C. (1995). Adolescents' coping with frightening mass media. *Communication Research, 22,* 325–346.

Hoffner, C., & Cantor, J. (1985). Developmental differences in responses to a television character's appearance and behavior. *Developmental Psychology, 21,* 1065–1074.

Hoffner, C., & Cantor, J. (1990). Forewarning of a threat and prior knowledge of outcome: Effects on children's emotional responses to a film sequence. *Human Communication Research, 16,* 323–354.

Izard, C. E. (1977). *Human emotions.* New York: Plenum Press.

Jersild, A. T., & Holmes, F. B. (1935). Methods of overcoming children's fears. *Journal of Psychology, 1,* 75–104.

Johnson, B. R. (1980). General occurrence of stressful reactions to commercial motion pictures and elements in films subjectively identified as stressors. *Psychological Reports, 47,* 775–786.

Mathai, J. (1983). An acute anxiety state in an adolescent precipitated by viewing a horror movie. *Journal of Adolescence, 6,* 197–200.

Melkman, R., Tversky, B., & Baratz, D. (1981). Developmental trends in the use of perceptual and conceptual attributes in grouping, clustering and retrieval. *Journal of Experimental Child Psychology, 31,* 470–486.

Morison, P., & Gardner, H. (1978). Dragons and dinosaurs: The child's capacity to differentiate fantasy from reality. *Child Development, 49,* 642–648.

Owens, J., Maxim, R., McGuinn, M., Nobile, C., Msall, M., & Alario, A. (1999). Television-viewing habits and sleep disturbance in school children. *Pediatrics, 104*(3), 552 (Abstract). Available at http://www.pediatrics.org/cgi/content/full/104/3/c27.

Pavlov, I. P. (1960). *Conditioned reflexes* (G. V. Anrep, Trans.). London: Oxford University Press. (Original work published 1927.)

Peck, E. Y. (1999). *Gender differences in film-induced fear as a function of type of emotion measure and stimulus content: A meta-analysis and a laboratory study.* Unpublished doctoral dissertation, University of Wisconsin–Madison.

Sapolsky, B. S., & Zillmann, D. (1978). Experience and empathy: Affective reactions to witnessing childbirth. *Journal of Social Psychology, 105,* 131–144.

Simons, D., & Silveira, W. R. (1994). Post-traumatic stress disorder in children after television programmes. *British Medical Journal, 308,* 389–390.

Singer, M. I., Slovak, K., Frierson, T., & York, P. (1998). Viewing preferences, symptoms of psychological trauma, and violent behaviors among children who watch television. *Journal of the American Academy of Child and Adolescent Psychiatry, 37*(10), 1041–1048.

Sparks, G. G. (1986). Developmental differences in children's reports of fear induced by the mass media. *Child Study Journal, 16,* 55–66.

Sparks, G. G., & Cantor, J. (1986). Developmental differences in fright responses to a television program depicting a character transformation. *Journal of Broadcasting & Electronic Media, 30,* 309–323.

Valkenburg, P. M., Cantor, J., & Peeters, A. L. (2000). Fright reactions to television: A child survey. *Communication Research, 27,* 82–99.

Weiss, B. W., Katkin, E. S., & Rubin, B. M. (1968). Relationship between a factor analytically derived measure of a specific fear and performance after related fear induction. *Journal of Abnormal Psychology, 73,* 461–463.

Weiss, A. J., Imrich, D. J., & Wilson, B. J. (1993). Prior exposure to creatures from a horror film: Live versus photographic representations. *Human Communication Research, 20,* 41–66.

Wilson, B. J. (1987). Reducing children's emotional reactions to mass media through rehearsed explanation and exposure to a replica of a fear object. *Human Communication Research, 14,* 3–26.

Wilson, B. J. (1989a). Desensitizing children's emotional reactions to the mass media. *Communication Research, 16,* 723–745.

Wilson, B. J. (1989b). The effects of two control strategies on children's emotional reactions to a frightening movie scene. *Journal of Broadcasting & Electronic Media, 33,* 397–418.

Wilson, B. J., & Cantor, J. (1985). Developmental differences in empathy with a television protagonist's fear. *Journal of Experimental Child Psychology, 39,* 284–299.

Wilson, B. J., & Cantor, J. (1987). Reducing children's fear reactions to mass media: Effects of visual exposure and verbal explanation. In M. McLaughlin (Ed.), *Communication Yearbook 10* (pp. 553–573). Beverly Hills, CA: Sage.

Wilson, B. J., Hoffner, C., & Cantor, J. (1987). Children's perceptions of the effectiveness of techniques to reduce fear from mass media. *Journal of Applied Developmental Psychology, 8,* 39–52.

Wilson, B. J., & Weiss, A. J. (1991). The effects of two reality explanations on children's reactions to a frightening movie scene. *Communication Monographs, 58,* 307–326.

Yerkes, R. M., & Yerkes, A. W. (1936). Nature and conditions of avoidance (fear) response in chimpanzee. *Journal of Comparative Psychology, 21,* 53–66.

Zillmann, D. (1978). Attribution and misattribution of excitatory reactions. In J. H. Harvey, W. Ickes, & R. F. Kidd (Eds.), *New directions in attribution research* (Vol. 2, pp. 335–368). Hillsdale, NJ: Lawrence Erlbaum Associates.

Zillmann, D., & Cantor, J. (1977). Affective responses to the emotions of a protagonist. *Journal of Experimental Social Psychology, 13,* 155–165.

Zillmann, D., Mody, B., & Cantor, J. (1974). Empathetic perception of emotional displays in films as a function of hedonic and excitatory state prior to exposure. *Journal of Research in Personality, 8,* 335–349.

Zoglin, R. (1984, June 25). Gremlins in the rating system. *Time,* p. 78.

Chapter 12

Effects of Sex in the Media

RICHARD JACKSON HARRIS
Kansas State University

CHRISTINA L. SCOTT
California State University–Chico

One recent hot afternoon in New York's Central Park, a group of men sexually assaulted several dozen women. Where did these men learn such sexually violent behavior? How did they come to think that it was acceptable? From where do any of us learn about sex, and what is the impact of those experiences? Throughout childhood, adolescence, and into adulthood we learn about sex, including sexual violence, from many sources, including parents, schools, friends, siblings, and media outlets such as movies, television, magazines, song lyrics, videos, and the Internet. For example, we may learn about French kissing from an older brother's stories, orgasms from a pornographic movie, oral sex from an erotic Web site, and rape from a television movie. However, recent research suggests that for young adults some sources of information about sex are more important than others.

According to a 1998 *Time*/CNN poll (Stodghill, 1998), 29% of U.S. teens identified TV as their most important source of information about sex, up from 11% in 1986. Although the most-mentioned source (45%) was "friends," only 7% cited parents, and 3% cited sex education. One study found that 90% of Toronto adolescent boys and 60% of the girls (mean age =14) had seen at least one pornographic movie (Check & Maxwell, 1992, in Russell, 1998). Also, 43% of American males saw at least one sex magazine in 1995 (Russell, 1998), and 29% of boys rated pornography as their *most-significant source* of sex education, higher than schools, parents, books, peers, or magazines (Check, 1995). Surveys of college men have shown that 35–55% report having consumed violent pornography in some form (Demare, Briere, & Lips, 1988; Garcia, 1986).

Throughout adolescence and early adulthood we continually learn more about sex, with media being a major source of information (Brown,

Steele, & Walsh-Childers, 2002; Dorr & Kunkel, 1990; Wartella, Heintz, Aidman, & Mazzarella, 1990). Relative to other sources, media are becoming increasingly important (Check, 1995; Greenberg, Brown, & Buerkel-Rothfuss, 1993; Gunter, 2001). The effects of this heavy consumption of sexually oriented media is the topic of this chapter. We begin by examining the nature of sex in the media, focusing on content analysis studies. The rest of the chapter presents a review of the research on how consuming sexually explicit media impacts sexual arousal, attitudes, and behavior.

THE NATURE OF SEX IN THE MEDIA

Taxonomy of Sexual Content

When people speak of sexually oriented media, they can be referring to a wide variety of sources. Some classes of materials in magazines, videos, films, and Internet Web sites have labels like *erotic, pornographic, X-rated,* or *sexually explicit.* Pornography is big business; about 10,000 pornographic videos were released in 1999 as part of what is an estimated $56 billion industry worldwide (Morais, 1999).

Most scholars distinguish between *violent sexual material,* which portrays rape, bondage, torture, sadomasochism, hitting, spanking, hair pulling, and genital mutilation, and *nonviolent sexual* material. Further classifying the nonviolent sexual material is more difficult. Some nonviolent sexual material is entirely mutually consenting and affectionate (sometimes called *erotica*), depicting vaginal or oral intercourse in a loving or at least noncoercive fashion. On the other hand, some of it is *sexually dehumanizing,* depicting *degradation, domination, subordination,* or *humiliation.* This nonviolent, but dehumanizing, material typically presents the woman with no human qualities other than body parts and sexual appetite. She often is verbally abused and degraded, but appears hysterically receptive and responsive to men's sexual demands. Also, the man appears in the sexually dominant position, and the woman is far more likely than the man to be more exposed or nude.

Sex in media is not limited to explicit portrayals of intercourse or nudity but rather may include any representation that portrays or implies sexual behavior, interest, or motivation. Sex also occurs in many other places besides these explicitly sexual materials. Sex is rampant in advertising, particularly for products like perfume, cologne, and aftershave but also for tires, automobiles, and kitchen sinks. For example, one automobile ad on network television featured two women discussing whether a man's choice of a car was related to the size of his penis ("I wonder what he's got under the hood") (Leo, in Strasburger, 1995).

Sex in Literature. Sexual themes in fiction have been around as long as fiction itself. Ancient Greek comedies were often highly sexual in content, such as Aristophanes' *Lysistrata,* an antiwar comedy about women who withhold sex from their husbands to coerce them to stop fighting. Literary classics like Chaucer's *Canterbury Tales* and Shakespeare's *The Taming of the Shrew* are filled with sexual double entendres and overtly sexual themes, some of which may be missed today due to the archaic language and the "classic" aura around such works. In contrast to what is normally thought of as pornography, sex in literature usually has some accepted literary purpose or merit, which makes it much more socially acceptable.

Electronic Media. Since the advent of broadcast media, standards have usually been more conservative for radio and television than for print media, because it is easier to shield children from sexually oriented print media than from X-rated radio or TV. With the advent of widespread cable and video technology, a sort of double standard has arisen, with greater acceptance of more sexual materials in video and premium cable channels than for network television. The logic appears to be that premium cable and rented movies are "invited" into the home, whereas network programming is there uninvited and accessible wherever a TV set is present. Even more controversial is the problem of availability of sexual materials on the Internet, which has virtually no restrictions. Although there is much interest in legally restricting children's access to sexually explicit sites, there is considerable disagreement about both how much sex is actually on the Internet (Elmer-Dewitt, 1995; Glassner, 1999; Wilkins, 1997) and what kinds of restrictions or blocking software would be both legal and effective, without blocking useful nonsexual sites like breast cancer information or art sites.

Turning to television specifically, content analyses have shown that the sex on network television is not explicit, but innuendoes are rampant, often occurring in a humorous context (Greenberg et al., 1993; Greenberg & Hofschire, 2000; Kunkel et al., 1999; Lowry & Towles, 1989). An extensive content analysis study found that 56% of TV shows on network and cable in 1997–98 contained sexual content, whereas 23% presented physical sexual behaviors (Kunkel et al., 1999). References to premarital and extramarital sexual encounters outnumbered references to sex between spouses by at least 6:1 (Greenberg & Hofschire, 2000) and were as high as 24:1 for unmarried versus married partners in soap operas (Lowry & Towles, 1989) or 32:1 in R-rated movies with teens (Greenberg et al., 1993)! The latter study also found that nudity occurred in all R-rated films in its sample, with female exceeding male nudity by a 4:1 margin.

Although content analyses of soap operas showed considerable sexual content in 1985, there was a 35% increase by 1994 (Greenberg & D'Alessio,

1985; Greenberg & Busselle, 1996; Greenberg & Hofschire, 2000). Also, in 1994, compared to 1985, there were more themes of (a) negative conse-quences of sex, (b) rejection of sexual advances, and (c) portrayals of rape. None of these three themes had been very common in the studies of the 1970s and 1980s. Not surprisingly, R-rated movies and sex magazines had more explicit sex than appeared on television (Greenberg et al., 1993).

The major focus of this article is on sexually explicit materials, includ-ing, though not limited to, what is generally called "pornography," both violent and nonviolent. The term *pornography* is highly value laden, how-ever, and as such is rather scientifically imprecise. Thus, we will most often refer to such materials as "sexually explicit" rather than "porno-graphic," although that term is so widely used that it cannot be com-pletely avoided. When we consider effects of sex in the media, we need to look more widely than at what is typically considered "pornography."

EFFECTS OF CONSUMING SEXUAL MEDIA

Although many people might wish it otherwise, sex apparently does sell, even very explicit sex. Sexually oriented print, video, broadcast, and Inter-net materials are highly profitable commercially, a condition that in itself assures their continued presence. Three major classes of effects of this expo-sure have been identified, namely arousal, attitudinal changes, and behav-ioral effects. See Gunter (2001); Linz and Malamuth (1993); Lyons, Ander-son, and Larson (1994); Malamuth (1993); Malamuth and Impett (in press); Pollard (1995); and the papers in Greenberg et al. (1993) and Brown et al. (2002) for more detailed reviews of various types of effects of sex in media.

Research on effects of sex in the media have been guided by a variety of theoretical perspectives. Although these theories are not the focus of this chapter, the reader is referred to other chapters in this volume for thorough explications and reviews of these different perspectives: Gerbner, Gross, Morgan, Shanahan, and Signorielli (cultivation theory, chap.3), Bandura (social cognitive theory, chap. 6), Petty (attitude change through the Elabo-ration Likelihood Model, chap. 7), and Rubin (uses-and-gratifications per-spective, chap. 20). Each of these perspectives has informed and guided certain areas of research on the effects of sexual media. These theoretical influences are alluded to in the following sections, although the focus of the rest of the chapter is on the effects of sexual media.

Arousal

One straightforward effect of consuming sexual media is sexual arousal, the heightened physiological state that energizes or intensifies sexual behavior. Arousal may be measured by a self-rating ("How aroused are you?"—7-point scale). It may also be measured more directly, albeit more obtrusively, through the physiological measures of penile tumescence (Eccles, Marshall, & Barbaree, 1988; Malamuth & Check, 1980; Schaefer & Colgan, 1977), vaginal changes (Sintchak & Geer, 1975), or thermography (Abramson, Perry, Seeley, Seeley, & Rothblatt, 1981).

Overall, by most measures men are typically more aroused than women are, especially in response to sexually violent or dehumanizing materials (Murnen & Stockton, 1997). Sexual violence may be particularly arousing to sex offenders and other violence-prone men and even to "normal" men if the victim is portrayed as being aroused by the assault; these findings are discussed later.

Sexual arousal in response to stimuli that would not typically be arousing may be learned through classical conditioning. For example, Rachman (1966) and Rachman and Hodgson (1968) classically conditioned heterosexual men to be sexually aroused by women's boots by pairing the boots with nude female photos, thus providing a model of how sexual "turnons" can be learned. This process could account for the vast individual differences in which specific stimuli arouse people sexually. Through different experiences, people have been conditioned to respond to different stimuli through their associations with those they love. Because of its association with a particular person, someone may be aroused by a certain perfume or cologne, type of clothing, or specific behaviors. Media provide many of the images and associations for such conditioning.

The degree of arousal is not highly correlated with the degree of explicitness of the media. Sometimes people are actually more aroused by a less sexually explicit story than a more explicit one (Bancroft & Mathews, 1971). A scene that cuts suddenly from a bedroom one night to the next morning may sometimes be more arousing than a more explicit version with the intervening night uncut! Censoring a sex scene may make a film more arousing because viewers can fill in their own script. Sexual arousal is enormously individual. When people are allowed to use their own imaginations to construct the ending of a romantic scene, they are more likely to construct a reality that is more arousing to them personally than if they view someone else's idea of what is arousing. There is some validity to the old truism that the most important sex organ is the brain.

The Gender Skew. Explicit sexual materials have traditionally been designed by men and for men. As such, they have a distinctly macho and hypermasculinized orientation. Although magazines and videos show all varieties of heterosexual intercourse, they place little emphasis on associated foreplay, afterplay, cuddling, or general tenderness. Women are seen eagerly desiring and participating in sex, often with insatiable euphoria. There is little concern with the consequences of sex or the relational matrix within which most people experience it. Men are much more active seekers and users of sexual material than are women, with an estimated 71% of sex videos viewed by men by themselves (Gettleman, 1999). However, this cannot be assumed to be due to greater intrinsic male interest in sex; it may merely reflect the pornography industry's extreme slant to the traditional male perspective. Indeed, a few studies have shown women to have more positive reactions to sexual videos written and directed by women and for women (Mosher & Maclan, 1994; Quackenbush, Strassberg, & Turner, 1995), although men appear to be more likely to seek out sexual media and be aroused by it, even after controlling for content (Malamuth, 1996).

This is consistent with an evolutionary psychological explanation for sex differences in sexual media consumption and effects (Buss, 1995; Malamuth, 1996, 1999). From this perspective, males are more interested in seeking a greater number of sexual partners, whereas females, for whom intercourse has potentially greater consequences, are more interested in a longer-term commitment from a mate to help raise the offspring. These ideas are consistent with observed findings that men seek out and use sexual media more than women and are generally more aroused than women by them, especially media that visually represent many different potential partners. Women, however, are less aroused than men by typical pornography, preferring more contextually based sexual expressions like romance novels.

The Catharsis Legend.   One often hears the argument that consuming sexually explicit material allows the expression of sexual urges and thus *decreases* the rate of arousal. This invokes the construct of **catharsis,** the emotional release that follows the expression of an impulse. This popular idea comes from psychodynamic models of personality, notably Freud. Applied to sex, the catharsis argument says that consuming sexual media relieves sexual urges, with the magazine or video acting (perhaps in conjunction with masturbation) as a sort of imperfect substitute for the real behavior. Although a catharsis argument has been used to support loosening restrictions on pornography (Kutchinsky, 1973) and has been reported by sex offenders as a strategy for reducing impulses for committing an offense (Carter, Prentky, Knight, Vanderveer, & Boucher, 1987; Langevin et al., 1988), the research support for catharsis is weak to nonexistent (Bushman, Baumeister, & Stack, 1999; Comstock, 1985; Final Report, 1986). As discussed earlier, viewing sexual material *increases*, not decreases, sexual arousal, and, after viewing, one is thus *more*, not *less*, motivated to engage in sexual behavior. Thus, consuming pornography as a means to reduce and satisfy sexual urges is likely to have the opposite effect. Nor is it going to reduce the rate of rape, which is energized by a power motive, not a lack of sexual fulfillment (Prentky & Knight, 1991).

Attitudinal Effects

Sex and Values.   Many concerns about sexually explicit media have to do with communicating attitudes and values. Repeated exposure to media with a more-or-less consistent set of messages may cultivate a worldview that increasingly reflects the perspective of the media (Gerbner et al., chap. 3). For example, watching numerous sitcoms and movies showing teenagers being sexually active may cultivate acceptance of such a position in the viewer and thus weaken family-taught values against premarital sex. Increasing numbers of ads using themes of coercion and sexual violence (e.g., a bikini-clad woman held in mock bondage by a giant shock absorber) may desensitize readers to violence toward women. A cartoon featuring a child molester may encourage readers to see that as a humorous subject. Such effects are especially likely to happen if the TV characters holding those values are respected characters with whom viewers identify. Sexual promiscuity by a prostitute is less likely to influence the values of a viewer than comparable behavior by a respected suburban mother.

One of the major social criticisms of pornography is that it is anti-women in an ideological sense (e.g., Buchwald, Fletcher, & Roth, 1993; Russell, 1998). It is usually women, not men, who are the playthings or victims of the opposite sex. This concern is particularly leveled at violent and nonviolent but dehumanizing pornography. For example, sex magazines have shown a picture of a jackhammer in a woman's vagina as the opening photo to a story "How to Cure Frigidity" or a photo spread of a gang rape turning into an orgy where the women appeared to be aroused by the assault. One article in a sex magazine aimed at male teenagers was entitled "Good Sex with Retarded Girls"; another sex video showed a woman's breast tied and squeezed for the entertainment of men who were watching.

Scientific Evidence.   A large body of research has shown effects on a variety of sexual attitudes and values after exposure to nonviolent sexually explicit materials. After seeing slides and movies of beautiful female nudes engaged in sexual activity, men in one study rated their own partners as being less physically endowed, although they reported undiminished sexual satisfaction (Weaver, Masland, & Zillmann, 1984). In another study, men reported that they loved their own partners less after seeing sexually explicit videos of highly attractive models (Kenrick, Gutierres, & Goldberg, 1989). Men who saw a pornographic video responded more sexually to a subsequent female interviewer than did men seeing a control video, although this result only held for men holding traditional gender schemas (McKenzie-Mohr & Zanna, 1990). It is as if the voluptuous model has become the "normal" anchor (Tversky & Kahneman, 1974) to which real people are compared.

Such effects are not limited to men. Relative to control groups, both men and women who watched weekly pornographic films later reported less satisfaction with the affection, physical appearance, sexual curiosity, and sexual performance of their real-life partners (Zillmann & Bryant, 1988a, 1988b). They also saw sex without emotional involvement as being relatively more important than did the control group, and they showed greater acceptance of premarital and extramarital sex and placed lesser value on marriage and monogamy. They also reported less desire to have children and greater acceptance of male dominance and female submission.

Using the same methodology of showing weekly films and questioning 1 to 3 weeks later, Zillmann and Bryant (1982, 1984) found that participants watching sexually explicit films overestimated the frequency of sexual practices like fellatio, cunnilingus, anal intercourse, sadomasochism, and bestiality in the general population, relative to perceptions of a control group seeing nonsexual films. This may reflect the cognitive heuristic of *availability*, whereby we judge the frequency of occurrence of various activities by the ease with which we can generate examples (Taylor, 1982; Tversky & Kahneman, 1973, 1974). Recent exposure to vivid media instances thus leads to an overestimation of such occurrences in the real world and a perceived reality substantially at odds with reality.

The sexual material need not even be explicit or graphic to help shape attitudes. Bryant and Rockwell (1994) found that, compared to controls, adolescents who watched a heavy diet of highly sexual prime-time programs were more lenient in their judgment about sexual impropriety and how much a victim had been wronged, although these effects were greatly attenuated by open family communication and active critical viewing.

One may not even need pictures. In one study all-verbal print descriptions of sex (e.g., the *Penthouse* Advisor column) were actually more conducive than photos to fantasizing about one's own partner (Dermer & Pyszczynski, 1978). Many issues require further study, and the effects of newer types of sexual media such as phone sex and Internet pornography are still largely unknown.

Behavioral Effects

Teaching New Behaviors.   Beyond arousal and attitude change, consuming sexual media also has effects on behavior. On the one hand, the media may actually teach new behaviors, including potentially some extremely violent and destructive ones. Although examples like men watching a movie depicting a gang rape on a pool table and soon afterward perpetrating a similar act are thankfully not commonplace, the juxtaposition of such events when they actually happen is compelling. Very violent and disturbing images are available, from extreme objectification like a naked woman as a hamburger smeared with condiments or women being tortured or even killed in a variety of ways (see Russell, 1998, for many gruesome examples). For obvious ethical reasons, there has been virtually no controlled scientific study of effects of viewing such extreme materials.

In a review of correlational research examining the role of pornography in the sexual development of sex offenders, including the possible role of pornography to incite sexual offenses, Bauserman (1996) concluded that such links have not been demonstrated as general trends, although they point out that sex offenders are a highly diverse group, and there may be a subset who use violent pornography in significant ways. Allen, D'Alessio, and Emmers-Sommer (2000) found that, although convicted sex offenders did not consume more pornography than did nonoffender controls, they were more aroused by it and were more likely to commit some form of sexual act afterward (masturbation, consensual, or coercive sex).

Disinhibition of Known Behaviors.   Aside from teaching new behaviors, sexual media may also disinhibit previously learned behavior. For example, watching a video with oral sex or bondage may disinhibit the viewer's prior existing inhibitions against engaging in such behavior. Watching a rape scene where a woman is portrayed as enjoying being assaulted may disinhibit the constraint against some men's secret urge to commit such a crime (see discussion in Sexual Violence section). Such a possibility is of particular concern given that between 25 and 57% of college men reported that they might rape if they were sure they would not be caught (Check, 1985; Malamuth, 1984; Malamuth, Haber, & Feshbach, 1980). The amount of violent pornography consumed significantly predicted self-rated likelihood to rape, although there was no effect of nonviolent pornography (Demare et al., 1988). We return to a detailed discussion of sexual violence later.

Relation to Rape and Other Crimes.   One of the main concerns about behavioral effects of viewing sexual explicit materials is their possible relationship with rape and other so-called sex crimes. Most Western nations have experienced a large increase both in the availability of sexually explicit media and in the rise in reported rapes since the 1960s. The relationship between the two, however, has been difficult to clarify. There have been many studies looking at correlations of rates of crimes like rape, exhibitionism, and child molestation, relative to sexual media consumption and changes in the availability of pornography within and across many different countries (see Bauserman, 1996, for a review of such studies).

Results have been inconsistent, sometimes showing that an increase in availability of sexual explicit media is associated with in increase in rape rates (e.g., Court, 1984; Jaffee & Straus, 1987), and other times suggested a decrease or no difference in rates of rape and other crimes (e.g., Kutchinsky, 1973, 1991). This inconsistency in the literature may be in part due to sampling and procedural differences across studies and in part due to cultural and national differences in social attitudes toward rape, rates of reporting, and likelihood and severity of punishment.

One of the most interesting examples of cultural factors is seen in the case of Japan, which has wide availability of sexually explicit materials (including high levels of sexual violence) but at the same time very low rape rates (Abramson & Hayashi, 1984; Diamond & Uchiyama, 1999). Sexual themes in Japanese art and society go back centuries and continue to be strong, without being associated with shame or guilt. Although Japan has specific legal restrictions against showing pictorial representations of pubic hair or adult genitalia, sexual depictions are not restricted to "X-rated" magazines, books, and films. Thus, nudity, bondage, sado-masochism, and rape occur regularly on commercial television, popular movies, magazines, and even in advertising. Films often portray very vivid scenes of rape and bondage. In recent years a market has surged for magazines featuring pictures of naked schoolgirls. It is legal in Japan for men to have sex with children over 12, and some schoolgirls earn extra money from prostitution or catering to men's sexual fantasies in Tokyo's "image clubs" ("Lolita in Japan," 1997).

Why, then, is the incidence of reported rapes in Japan less than one-tenth the rate in the United States and one-quarter the rate in western Europe? Some have suggested that rape in Japan is more likely to be group instigated, perpetrated by juveniles, and greatly underreported by victims (Goldstein & Ibaraki, 1983). These factors are unlikely to entirely explain the difference, however (Abramson & Hayashi, 1984). Japanese society emphasizes order, obligation, cooperation, and virtue, and one who violates social norms is the object of shame. This probably discourages victims from reporting rape but also greatly discourages and stigmatizes those who perpetrate it.

Firmly establishing a causal relationship between the availability of sexually explicit materials and the incidence of crimes like rape is extremely difficult, due to the many other relevant factors, including the different varieties of sexual material, cultural differences, changes in social consciousness about reporting sexual assaults, and changing norms sanctioning such behavior. Although there may be positive correlations between a specific measure like sex magazine circulation and reported rapes within a narrow geographical area (e.g., Court, 1984; Jaffee & Straus, 1987), a more general conclusion remains elusive.

What About the Context?

Responses to sexual materials are not entirely due to the nature of the material itself. They also depend on a variety of intangible and hard-to-study factors, which Eysenck and Nias (1978) collectively called the *prevailing tone*. A documentary on rape or a tasteful drama on incest may be considered perfectly acceptable and noncontroversial, whereas a comedy with the same theme, even one far less sexually explicit, may be considered highly offensive or even pornographic. We react very differently to a sexually explicit drawing by Picasso than we do to one in *Hustler* magazine. Because Shakespeare, Chaucer, *The Song of Solomon* in the Bible, and serious sex manuals are seen to have serious literary or didactic intentions, the sex therein is considered more acceptable and even healthy.

The context and expectations that are brought to the experience can greatly affect the experiencing of sex in the media. When watching an erotic film with one's parents, one's children, by oneself, in a group of close same-sex friends, or with one's spouse or significant other, the reaction to it may be very different because of who else is there. Taking a first date to an unexpectedly explicit erotic movie may be a much less pleasant experience than seeing the same move with a longtime companion. A photo of a nude women being fed through a meat grinder might be unsurprising in *Hustler* magazine but shocking if suddenly encountered in *Newsweek*. The stimulus may be the same, but the perceived experiential reality of the act of seeing is considerably different.

One interesting issue of prevailing tone is how to respond to something of clear artistic worth but written at a time when standards differed from today. For example, should Rhett Butler's forcing his attentions on Scarlett O'Hara in *Gone with the Wind* be seen as rape or as the noncontroversial romantic moment that it appeared to be in 1939? In many old Westerns of the 1940s and 1950s a man comes on sexually to a woman, she initially refuses, and finally she falls breathlessly into his arms. Ralph Kramden regularly threatened to punch his wife in the 1950s sitcom *The Honeymooners* (although he never did so), and Ricky Ricardo occasionally spanked his wife in *I Love Lucy*. Although such scenes were never sexually explicit, their effect on the modern viewer from a different world is unknown. Do these "safe" shows from an earlier "golden age" of television trivialize or even condone rape or spousal battering, or does the modern media scholar–critic need to "lighten up"?

The relation and integration of sex to the overall plot is another part of the prevailing tone. A sex scene, even a mild and nonexplicit one, may offend people if it appears to be added merely to spice up the story but has no connection to it. Something far more explicit may be accepted much better if it is seen as necessary and central to the plot. Sex scenes in a story about a prostitute may be much less gratuitous than similar scenes in a story about a female corporate executive. Few argued that the graphic pool table gang rape scene in *The Accused* was gratuitous in that story about the effects of rape on the victim. Sex, of course, is not the only common gratuitous factor; contemporary movies frequently contain car chases and rock music video segments at best marginally related to the plot.

The prevailing tone can be culturally specific, as noted in the earlier discussion of Japanese media. Some cultures do not consider female breasts to be particularly erotic or inappropriate for public display. Thus, most readers, at least over about age 13, do not consider topless women from some distant culture in *National Geographic* photos to be erotic, sexual, or pornographic. However, when *National Geographic* first began to publish such photographs in the early 20th century, it was a carefully reasoned, but risky, editorial decision (Lutz & Collins, 1993). Even within Western culture, standards have changed. In much of the 19th century, knees and calves were thought to be erotic, and the sight of a bare-kneed woman would be considered as scandalous as a topless woman would today. As societies go, North America overall is moderate in what is allowable sexual expression in dress, media, and behavior. Many Western European and Latin American cultures are far more permissive, whereas many Islamic and East Asian cultures are far more restrictive.

We now turn to examine in more detail that potent combination of sex and violence in the media—sexual violence.

SEXUAL VIOLENCE: WORSE THAN THE SUM OF ITS PARTS

Although neither sexual nor violent media are new, the integral combination has become far more prevalent and available in recent years. Many people unwilling or forbidden to visit theaters that show pornographic films now have the chance to view sexual material on cable, video, or the Internet safely and privately at home. Beyond the explicit sexuality of videos and pornographic Internet sites, there is increasing sexual violence in sex magazines, both in some particularly violent publications but also in more "established" publications like *Penthouse* and *Playboy*. Even the old genre of horror films has recently evolved into showing increasingly graphically violent scenes in a sexual context (Weaver & Tamborini, 1996). Not generally considered pornographic, these films are heavily marketed to teenagers, in spite of their R ratings. With all of these materials, the major concern is not with the sex or violence in and of itself, but with the way the two appear together. For an extensive review of the effects of sexual violence, see Pollard (1995). We turn now to examining some of the arousal, attitudinal, and behavioral effects of viewing sexual violence.

Sexual Materials as Trigger for Violent Behavior

Links between sex and aggression have long been speculated on, particularly in the sense of sexual arousal facilitating violent behavior. The research has been inconsistent, however, with some studies showing that erotic materials facilitate aggressive behavior, especially if the participant is angry (Baron, 1979; Donnerstein & Hallam, 1978), and others showing they inhibit it (Donnerstein, Donnerstein, & Evans, 1975; Ramirez, Bryant, & Zillmann, 1982). The resolution of this issue may lie in the precise character of the material. Sexual violence and dehumanizing themes typically facilitate aggression, whereas some loving and pleasant erotica may inhibit it (Zillmann, Bryant, Comisky, & Medoff, 1981). Also, sexual violence affects different people in different ways.

Impact Depends on How the Woman Is Portrayed

To understand the effects of sexual violence, the way that the woman is portrayed must be must be examined carefully. Neil Malamuth (1984) reported several studies in which men viewed scenes of violent pornography and afterward rated their attitudes on several topics. Men who saw those films showed a more callous attitude toward rape and women in general, especially if the women victims in the film were portrayed as coming to orgasm in the assault.

Individual Differences in Male Viewers. Some early studies examined convicted rapists and found them to be aroused by both rape and consenting sex, whereas normal men were aroused only by the consenting sex (Abel, Barlow, Blanchard, & Guild, 1977; Quinsey, Chaplin, & Upfold, 1984), although later studies did not find this consistent arousal effect in sex offenders (Baxter, Barbaree, & Marshall, 1986; Hall, 1989).

Going beyond convicted rapists, studies of "normal" college undergraduates found that these men could on occasion be aroused by scenes of sexual violence. For example, men, though not women, were equally or even more aroused by a rape scene than by a consenting sex scene, but only if the victim was portrayed as enjoying the rape and coming to orgasm (Malamuth, 1984; Malamuth, Heim, & Feshbach, 1980; Ohbuchi, Ikeda, & Takeuchi, 1994). The men were not aroused if the victim was shown to be terrorized.

In further examining this question in regard to individual differences in men, Malamuth and Check (1983; see also Malamuth, 1981) had men listen to a tape of a sexual encounter of (a) consenting sex, (b) nonconsenting sex where the woman showed arousal, or (c) nonconsenting sex where she showed disgust. Where the woman showed disgust, both force-oriented and non-force-oriented men were more aroused, in terms of both self-report and penile tumescence, by the consenting than by the nonconsenting (rape) scene. However, when the woman was portrayed as being aroused, the non-force-oriented (nonviolent) men were equally aroused by both consenting and nonconsenting versions, whereas the force-oriented men actually showed more arousal to the nonconsenting (rape) version.

Another variable that can interact with these factors is anger. Yates, Barbaree, and Marshall (1984) showed that normal men were equally aroused by depictions of rape and consenting sex, but only after they had been angered by a female confederate. Otherwise the consenting sex scene was more arousing. Alcohol consumption may enhance existing tendencies to either harshly judge or empathize with a female victim, although it generally decreased sensitivity to victim distress, especially so in "hypermasculine" men (Norris, George, Davis, Martell, & Leonesio, 1999).

Transfer to New Situations.   Can such effects carry over to new settings? The answer appears to be yes. Donnerstein and Berkowitz (1981) showed men a sexually violent film where a woman is attacked, stripped, tied up, and raped. In one version of the film the woman was portrayed as enjoying the rape. Afterward, participants were given a chance to administer electric shocks to a confederate of the experimenter, the same confederate who had earlier angered them in an ostensibly unrelated study. Men who had seen the film where the woman appeared to enjoy being raped administered more shocks to a female, though not to a male, confederate. This suggests that the sexual violence in the film led to violent behavior being transferred to the target confederate in a new situation. In a similar vein, Zillmann and Bryant (1984) found that participants with repeated exposure to sexually explicit media recommended shorter prison sentences for a rapist than did a control group.

In a meta-analysis of studies examining the relationship of the exposure to sexual media to the acceptance of rape myths, Allen, Emmers, Gebhardt, and Giery (1995) concluded that experimental studies show a consistent positive effect between pornography exposure and rape myth acceptance, whereas correlational and field studies show only a very small positive or nonexistent effect. The relationship was consistently stronger when the pornography was violent than when it was nonviolent, although some experimental studies obtained effects with both types.

Several conclusions emerge from the sexual violence research. The most consistently important factor is whether the woman is presented as enjoying and being aroused by the assault. Far more undesirable effects occur in normal men if the woman is seen to be aroused than if she is seen to be terrorized or tortured. This portrayal of women as being "turned on" by rape is a common type of portrayal in pornography but is at enormous odds with reality. A second important conclusion is that sexual violence may affect individual men very differently, depending on their own propensity to use force in their lives. Men more naturally prone to violence, or even those situationally angered or under the influence of alcohol, are more likely to be aroused or even incited to violence by sexually violent media, especially if the woman is shown as aroused by the assault.

Slasher Films

Sex + Violence in Mainstream Movies.   Although the studies discussed used sexually explicit materials, sexual violence is by no means confined to clearly pornographic materials. Hundreds of mainstream R-rated horror films are readily available to teenagers anywhere, in theaters and especially in video stores. There are the highly successful series such as *I Know What You Did Last Summer, Halloween, Child's Play, Friday the Thirteenth, Scream, Nightmare on Elm Street*, and many lesser-known films. Many are extremely violent with strong sexual overtones. Although some, such as the *Scream* series and *Scary Movie,* are billed as "satires" of the genre, it is not clear that they are received very differently by the youthful audiences than are the nonsatirical films.

Nor are violent sexual themes confined to horror or even R-rated movies. The 1995 PG-rated James Bond movie *Goldeneye* featured a villainess who seduces men to have sex with her and then crushes them to death. It also contains scenes of seduction with very violent mutual battering as a sort of foreplay. The major concern with such films is the juxtaposition of sex and violence. In countries like India and Japan, rape and other acts of violence against women are even more standard entertainment fare in action-adventure films.

Although many of these films have R ratings in the United States, others are released unrated or direct to video to avoid the "accompanied by parent" restriction of R-rated movies. Given that so many viewings of movies are in video format and are widespread among youth, the ratings are, at best, of limited use. Oliver (1993) found that punitive attitudes toward sexuality and traditional attitudes toward women's sexuality were associated with high school students' greater enjoyment of previews of slasher films. Although viewers have noted a trend to stronger, less-victimized, female characters in recent films such as *Urban Legend, I Know What You Did Last Summer,* and *Bride of Chucky,* effects of such portrayals remain untested.

Effects of Viewing Slasher Films.   Linz, Donnerstein, and Penrod (1984; see also Linz, Donnerstein, & Adams, 1989) examined the effects of slasher films. Their male college-student participants were initially screened to exclude those with prior hostile tendencies or psychological problems. The remaining men in the experimental group were shown one standard Hollywood-released R-rated film per day over one week. All of the films were very violent and showed multiple instances of women being killed in slow, lingering, painful deaths in situations associated with much erotic content (e.g., a woman masturbating in her bath is assaulted and killed by an intruder with a nail gun). Each day, the participants filled out some questionnaires evaluating that film and completed some personality measures.

Results showed that over the week the men became generally less depressed, less annoyed, and less anxious in response to the films. The films themselves were gradually rated over time as increasingly enjoyable, humorous, and socially meaningful, and progressively less violent, offensive, and degrading to women. Over the week's time, the violent episodes in general and rape episodes in particular were rated as less frequent. Although these data provide clear evidence of desensitization in men, there is still the question of generalization to other situations.

To answer this question, Linz et al. (1984) arranged to have the participants from the prior study later observe a rape trial at the law school and evaluate it in several ways. Compared to a control group, men who had seen the slasher films rated the rape victim as less physically and emotionally injured. These results are consistent with those of Zillmann and Bryant (1984), who found that massive exposure to sexually explicit media by juror participants resulted in shorter recommended prison sentences for a rapist. Using Linz et al.'s methodology of rating movies followed by evaluation of an "unrelated" rape trial, Weisz and Earls (1995) used both men and women and four types of films: man raped by a man—*Deliverance,* woman raped by a man—*Straw Dogs,* nonsexual male aggression toward both men and women—*Die Hard 2,* and nonaggressive action film—*Days of Thunder.* They found strong desensitizing effects of the two sexually aggressive films in men (though not in women). Interestingly enough, it did not matter whether a man (*Deliverance*) or a woman (*Straw Dogs*) was the victim; both films desensitized men to the female rape trial victim, though neither effect appeared in women. Such findings show that effects of seeing slasher films do indeed transfer to new situations.

There have been some methodological (Weaver, 1991) and content (Sapolsky & Molitor, 1996) criticisms of this research, and some effects have not been replicated in later work (Linz & Donnerstein, 1988). Some have questioned Donnerstein and Linz' conclusion of sharply different effects of viewing violent versus nonviolent sexual materials (Weaver, 1991; Zillmann & Bryant, 1988c). Check and Guloien (1989) found that men exposed to a steady diet of rape-myth sexual violence reported a higher likelihood of committing rape themselves, compared to a no-exposure control group, but the same result was also found for a group exposed to nonviolent erotica.

Press Coverage of Sexually Violent Crimes

use this info!!

Sexual violence can be a media issue beyond the realm of entertainment. The way that news media cover crimes like rape can subtly support rape myths (Benedict, 1992; Meyers, 1997). For example, even extreme violence may be described in terms of "passion" or "love." When a man killed his ex-wife and her boyfriend, the press once called this a "love triangle." When a man shot and killed several coworkers, including a woman that refused to date him, it was described as a "tragedy of spurned love." When a man kidnapped, raped, and strangled to death his estranged wife, the press reported that he "made love to this wife, and then choked her when he became overcome with jealous passion" (Jones, 1994). Does love really have anything to do with such crimes?

Benedict (1992) offered several critiques of news coverage of rapes and sexual assaults. To begin with, those writing such stories are most often the crime and police reporters, who are two or three times more likely to be male than female. There is also a gender bias of language, with women more likely than men to be described in terms of their physical appearance and sexuality. Some rape myths are subtly supported, for example, rape as being a sex crime perpetrated out of unfulfilled sexual need. Less often do we encounter rape presented as an act of torture, although that perspective is typically used in reporting of wartime rapes. For example, when mass raping of Bosnian women occurred in the civil war in the early 1990s, it was accurately reported as an act of war, as torture, and there was no description of the victims' attractiveness or dress or flirtatious behavior. Indeed, such a description in a reporting of wartime rapes would have appeared grotesquely inappropriate. However, it is all too common in reports of individual rapes.

In her content-analysis studies of numerous newspaper reports of several high-profile rape cases, Benedict (1992) identified two common rape narratives, both of which distort and trivialize the crime. The most common is the "vamp," a sexually aggressive woman who intentionally seduces and incites the lust of a man, who then cannot control himself and rapes her. A second narrative is the "virgin," the pure and innocent woman attacked by a vicious monster, who is often portrayed as crazed and who often has darker skin and lower status than the victim. Benedict identifies several factors that increase the likelihood that the press will use the vamp narrative, which blames the victim. These factors include (a) the victim knew the assailant, (b) no weapon was used, (c) she was young and pretty, (d) she showed deviation from traditional gender roles, and (e) she was of the same or lower-status race, class, and ethnicity as the rapist. The more of these conditions that hold, the more likely it is that the reporting will conform to the vamp narrative; the fewer of them that hold, the more likely it is that the case will be told as a virgin narrative.

Why does such bias occur? Benedict in part blames the habitual pressure of newspaper deadlines but also indicts our persistent emphasis on victims of crimes. Although this is in part a well-meaning sympathy for those who have been wronged, it also taps into a desire of reporters and all of us to reassure ourselves that such acts will not happen to *us* because *we* don't behave like that. Thus, the behaviors and attributes of the victim are highlighted. There is less emphasis on the rapist, especially in the vamp narrative, and not much examination of societal forces that drive some men to behave so violently. Such biases have consequences, as when a 1993 Texas grand jury refused to indict a man for rape because his quick-thinking victim had convinced him to wear a condom.

Mitigating the Effects of Sexual Violence

Even given some remaining questions to be answered, results from the sexual violence research are disturbing, especially given the widespread viewing of sexually violent films by children and young teens and the hugely increased availability through video and the Internet. Some studies have developed and evaluated extensive preexposure training procedures to attempt to lessen the desensitizing effects of sexual violence (Intons-Peterson & Roskos-Ewoldsen, 1989; Intons-Peterson, Roskos-Ewoldsen, Thomas, Shirley, & Blut, 1989; Linz, Donnerstein, Bross, & Chapin, 1986; Linz, Fuson, & Donnerstein, 1990). These studies have typically shown mitigating effects on some measures and not on others. Linz et al. (1990) found that men were most strongly positively affected by the information that women are not responsible for sexual assaults perpetrated on them. There is also some evidence that desensitization can be reduced by introducing pertinent information about rape myths and the inaccuracy of media portrayals *after* people have seen some of the sexually violent media. Participants were more impressed with such arguments after they had felt themselves excited and aroused by the film and had seen very specific examples to illustrate the point of the debriefing/mitigation information. In the context of having seen such a film, the specific points of the sensitization training have greater impact. Thus experimental participation may at least sometimes actually *decrease* rape myth acceptance.

Using a different approach, Wilson, Linz, Donnerstein, and Stipp (1992) measured the effect of seeing a prosocial TV movie about rape. Compared to a control group, people viewing the film generally showed more awareness and concern about rape. However, not all groups were so affected. Unlike women and young and middle-aged men, men over 50 had preexisting attitudes reinforced and actually blamed women more for rape *after* seeing the film. This suggests that ages, attitudes, and life experiences of the target audience of interventions must be carefully considered.

CONCLUSION

What may we conclude from the research on the effects of consuming sexual media? First, it is useful to reiterate the importance of the distinction between violent and nonviolent sexual media. Although there are some documented negative effects of nonviolent but dehumanizing pornography, especially on attitudes toward women, the research is particularly compelling in the case of violent pornography. Sexual violence is arousing to sex offenders, force-oriented men, and sometimes even to "normal" young men if the woman is portrayed as being aroused by the assault. For reviews and meta-analyses of results from numerous experimental studies on the effects of viewing pornography, see Allen, D'Alessio, and Brezgel (1995); Allen, Emmers, et al. (1995); Davis & Bauserman (1993); Lyons et al. (1994); Malamuth and Impett (2001); Pollard (1995); and Strasburger (1995).

Repeated exposure to sexual violence may lead to desensitization toward violence against women in general and greater acceptance of rape myths. Not only does this suggest that the combination of sex and violence together is considerably worse than either one by itself, but the nature of the portrayal also matters. If the woman being assaulted is portrayed as being terrorized and brutalized, desensitizing effects on normal men are much less than if she is portrayed as being aroused and/or achieving orgasm through being attacked. There is nothing arousing or exciting about being raped in real life, and messages to the contrary do not help teenage boys understand the reality of how to relate to girls and women.

One largely unexamined area of sexual media is the Internet. Although Internet surfing is rapidly becoming a leisure activity of choice (Ferguson & Perse, 2000), it is still largely unknown how many sexually explicit Internet sites exist, with estimates varying from less than one-half of one percent to 84% of all Internet sites being sexually explicit (Barak, Fisher, Belfry, & Lashambe, 1999)! To date, only two experimental studies of effects of Internet sex exposure have been published (Barak, & Fisher, 1997; Barak et al., 1999), and these both failed to find a consistent effect of amount of Internet sex exposure on any of several measures of misogynistic attitudes. Clearly, however, more research is needed about the uses and effects of this new medium, which allows unprecedented availability and privacy of viewing sexually explicit material.

Finally, most of us believe that *other people* are more influenced by advertising (Gunther & Thorson, 1992), media violence (Salwen & Dupagne, 2001), and news coverage (Gunther, 1991; Perloff, 1989) than we are; this is the *third-person effect* (Davison, 1983; Gunther, 1991). The same is true about the perceived effects of sexual media (Gunther, 1995); we believe it affects others more than it affects us. See Perloff (chap. 18) for a review of third-person media effects. As society accepts increasingly explicit sexual materials, no one is immune from their reach. The influence is much more far reaching than the adolescent boy's transient titillation from looking at a *Playboy* centerfold. What we learn about sexuality from the media forms a large part of what sexuality means to us.

ACKNOWLEDGMENTS

Thanks are expressed to Scott Hemenover, Jennifer Bonds-Raacke, and Fred Sanborn for comments on earlier drafts of this manuscript.

REFERENCES

Abel, G. G., Barlow, D. H., Blanchard, E. B., & Guild, D. (1977). The components of rapists' sexual arousal. *Archives of General Psychiatry, 34*, 895–903.

Abramson, P. R., & Hayashi, H. (1984). Pornography in Japan: Cross-cultural and theoretical considerations. In N. M. Malamuth & E. Donnerstein (Eds.), *Pornography and sexual aggression*. Orlando, FL: Academic Press.

Abramson, P. R., Perry, L., Seeley, T., Seeley, D., & Rothblatt, A. (1981). Thermographic measurement of sexual arousal: A discriminant validity analysis. *Archives of Sexual Behavior, 10*(2), 175–176.

Allen, M., D'Alessio, D., & Brezgel, K. (1995). A meta-analysis summarizing the effects of pornography II: Aggression after exposure. *Human Communication Research, 22*, 258–283.

Allen, M., D'Alessio, D., & Emmers-Sommer, T. M. (2000). Reactions of criminal sexual offenders to pornography: A meta-analytic summary. In M. Roloff (Ed.), *Communication Yearbook 22* (pp. 139–169). Thousand Oaks, CA: Sage.

Allen, M., Emmers, T., Gebhardt, L., & Giery, M. A. (1995). Exposure to pornography and acceptance of rape myths. *Journal of Communication, 45*(1), 5–26.

Bancroft, J., & Mathews, A. (1971). Autonomic correlates of penile erection. *Journal of Psychosomatic Research, 15*, 159–167.

Barak, A., & Fisher, W. A. (1997). Effects of interactive computer erotica on men's attitudes and behavior toward women: An experimental study. *Computers in Human Behavior, 13*, 353–369.

Barak, A., Fisher, W. A., Belfry, S., & Lashambe, D. R. (1999). Sex, guys, and cyberspace: Effects of Internet pornography and individual differences on men's attitudes toward women. *Journal of Psychology and Human Sexuality, 11*, 63–91.

Baron, R. A. (1979). Heightened sexual arousal and physical aggression: An extension to females. *Journal of Research in Personality, 13,* 91–102.

Bauserman, R. (1996). Sexual aggression and pornography: A review of correlational research. *Basic and Applied Social Psychology, 18,* 405–427.

Baxter, D. J., Barbaree, H. E., & Marshall, W. L. (1986). Sexual responses to consenting and forced sex in a large sample of rapists and nonrapists. *Behavior Research and Therapy, 24,* 513–520.

Benedict, H. (1992). *Virgin or vamp: How the press covers sex crimes.* New York: Oxford University Press.

Brown, J. D., Steele, J. R., & Walsh-Childers, K. (Eds.). (2002). *Sexual teens, sexual media.* Mahwah, NJ: Lawrence Erlbaum Associates.

Bryant, J., & Rockwell, S. C. (1994). Effects of massive exposure to sexually oriented prime time television programming on adolescents' moral judgment. In D. Zillmann, J. Bryant, and A. C. Huston (Eds.), *Media, children, and the family: Social scientific, psychodynamic, and clinical perspectives* (pp. 183–195). Hillsdale, NJ: Lawrence Erlbaum Associates.

Buchwald, E., Fletcher, P., & Roth, M. (Ed.). (1993). *Transforming a rape culture.* Minneapolis: Milkweed Eds.

Bushman, B. J., Baumeister, R. F., & Stack, A. D. (1999). Catharsis, aggression, and persuasive influences: Self-fulfilling or self-defeating prophecies? *Journal of Personality and Social Psychology, 76,* 367–376.

Buss, D. M. (1995). Evolutionary psychology: A new paradigm for psychological science. *Psychological Inquiry, 6,* 1–30.

Carter, D. L., Prentky, R. A., Knight, R. A., Vanderveer, P. L., & Boucher, R. J. (1987). Use of pornography in the criminal and developmental histories of sexual offenders. *Journal of Interpersonal Violence, 2,* 196–211.

Check, J. V. P. (1985). *The effects of violent and nonviolent pornography.* Ottawa: Dept. of Justice for Canada.

Check, J. V. P. (1995). Teenage training: The effects of pornography on adolescent males. In L. Lederer and R. Delgado (Eds.), *The price we pay: The case against racist speech, hate propaganda, and pornography* (pp. 89–91). New York: Hill and Wang.

Check, J. V. P., & Guloien, T. H. (1989). Reported proclivity for coercive sex following repeated exposure to sexually violent pornography, nonviolent pornography, and erotica. In D. Zillmann & J. Bryant (Eds.), *Pornography: Research advances and policy considerations* (pp. 159–184). Hillsdale, NJ: Lawrence Erlbaum Associates.

Comstock, G. (1985). Television and film violence. In S. J. Apter & A. P. Goldstein (Eds.), *Youth violence: Programs and prospects.* New York: Pergamon Press.

Court, J. H. (1984). Sex and violence: A ripple effect. In N. M. Malamuth & E. Donnerstein (Eds.), *Pornography and sexual aggression.* Orlando, FL: Academic Press.

Davis, C. M., & Bauserman, R. (1993). Exposure to sexually explicit materials: An attitude change perspective. In J. Bancroft (Ed.), *Annual Review of Sex Research* (Vol. 4, pp. 121–209). Mt. Vernon, IA: Society for the Scientific Study of Sex.

Davison, W. P. (1983). The third-person effect in communication. *Public Opinion Quarterly, 47,* 1–15.

Demare, D., Briere, J., & Lips, H. M. (1988). Violent pornography and self-reported likelihood of sexual aggression. *Journal of Research in Personality, 22,* 140–153.

Dermer, M., & Pyszczynski, T. A. (1978). Effects of erotica upon men's loving and liking responses. *Journal of Personality and Social Psychology, 36,* 1302–1309.

Diamond, M., & Uchiyama, A. (1999). Pornography, rape, and sex crimes in Japan. *International Journal of Law and Psychiatry, 22,* 1–11.

Donnerstein, E., & Berkowitz, L. (1981). Victim reactions in aggressive erotic films as a factor in violence against women. *Journal of Personality and Social Psychology, 41,* 710–724.

Donnerstein, E., Donnerstein, M., & Evans, R. (1975). Erotic stimuli and aggression: Facilitation or inhibition? *Journal of Personality and Social Psychology, 32,* 237–244.

Donnerstein, E., & Hallam, J. (1978). Facilitating effects of erotica on aggression against women. *Journal of Personality and Social Psychology, 36,* 1270–1277.

Dorr, A., & Kunkel, D. (1990). Children and the media environment: Change and constancy amid change. *Communication Research, 17,* 5–25.

Eccles, A., Marshall, W. L., & Barbaree, H. E. (1988). The vulnerability of erectile measures to repeated assessments. *Behavior Research and Therapy, 26,* 179–183.

Elmer-Dewitt, P. (1995, July 3). On a screen near you: Cyberporn. *Time,* 38–45.

Eysenck, H. J., & Nias, D. K. B. (1978). *Sex, violence, and the media.* New York: Harper.

Ferguson, D. A., & Perse, E. M. (2000). The World Wide Web as a functional alternative to television. *Journal of Broadcasting & Electronic Media, 44,* 155–174.

Final report of the attorney general's commission on pornography. (1986). Nashville, TN: Rutledge Hill Press.

Garcia, L.T. (1986). Exposure to pornography and attitudes about women and rape: A correlational study. *Journal of Sex Research, 22,* 378–385.

Gettleman, J. (1999, October 28). XXX = $$$, *Manhattan Mercury,* p. A6.

Glassner, B. (1999). *The culture of fear: Why Americans are afraid of the wrong things.* New York: Basic Books.

Goldstein, S., & Ibaraki, T. (1983). Japan: Aggression and aggression control in Japanese society. In A. Goldstein & M. Segall (Eds.), *Aggression in global perspective.* New York: Pergamon Press.

Greenberg, B. S., Brown, J. D., & Buerkel-Rothfuss, N. L. (Eds.). (1993). *Media, sex, and the adolescent.* Creskill, NJ: Hampton Press.

Greenberg, B. S., & Busselle, R. W. (1996). Soap operas and sexual activity: A decade later. *Journal of Communication, 46*(4), 153–160.

Greenberg, B. S., & D'Alessio, D. (1985). Quantity and quality of sex in the soaps. *Journal of Broadcast & Electronic Media, 29,* 309–321.

Greenberg, B. S., & Hofschire, L. (2000). Sex on entertainment television. In D. Zillmann & P. Vorderer (Eds.), *Media entertainment: The psychology of its appeal* (pp. 93–111). Mahwah, NJ: Lawrence Erlbaum Associates.

Gunter, B. (2001). *Media sex: What are the issues?* Mahwah, NJ: Lawrence Erlbaum Associates.

Gunther, A. C. (1991). What we think others think: Cause and consequence in the third-person effect. *Communication Research, 18,* 355–372.

Gunther, A. C. (1995). Overrating the X-rating: The third-person perception and support for censorship of pornography. *Journal of Communication, 45*(1), 27–38.

Gunther, A. C., & Thorson, E. (1992). Perceived persuasive effects of product commercials and public-service announcements: Third-person effects in new domains. *Communication Research, 19,* 574–596.

Hall, G. C. N. (1989). Self-reported hostility as a function of offense characteristics and response style in a sexual offender population. *Journal of Consulting and Clinical Psychology, 57,* 306–308.

Intons-Peterson, M. J., & Roskos-Ewoldson, B. (1989). Mitigating the effects of violent pornography. In S. Gubar & J. Hoff-Wilson (Eds.), *For adult users, only.* Bloomington: Indiana University Press.

Intons-Peterson, M. J., & Roskos-Ewoldson, B., Thomas, L., Shirley, M., & Blut, D. (1989). Will educational materials reduce negative effects of exposure to sexual violence? *Journal of Social and Clinical Psychology, 8,* 256–275.

Jaffee, D., & Straus, M. A. (1987). Sexual climate and reported rape: A state-level analysis. *Archives of Sexual Behavior, 16,* 107–123.

Jones, A. (1994, March 10). Crimes against women: Media part of problem for masking violence in the language of love. *USA Today.*

Kenrick, D. T., Gutierres, S. E., & Goldberg, L. L. (1989). Influence of popular erotica on judgments of strangers and mates. *Journal of Experimental Social Psychology, 25,* 159–167.

Kunkel, D., Cope, K. M., Farinola, W. J., Biely, E., Rollin, E., & Donnerstein, E. (1999). Sex on TV: Content and context. Menlo Park, CA: Kaiser Family Foundation.

Kutchinsky, B. (1973). The effect of easy availability of pornography on the incidence of sex crimes: The Danish experience. *Journal of Social Issues, 29*(3), 163–181.

Kutchinsky, B. (1991). Pornography and rape: Theory and practice? *International Journal of Law and Psychiatry, 14,* 47–64.

Langevin, R., Lang, R. A., Wright, P., Handy, L., Frenzel, F. R., & Black, E. L. (1988). Pornography and sexual offenses. *Annals of Sex Research, 1,* 335–362.

Linz, D., & Donnerstein, E. (1988). The methods and merits of pornography research. *Journal of Communication, 38*(2), 180–184.

Linz, D., Donnerstein, E., & Adams, S. M. (1989). Physiological desensitization and judgments about female victims of violence. *Human Communication Research, 15,* 509–522.

Linz, D., Donnerstein, E., Bross, M., & Chapin, M. (1986). Mitigating the influence of violence on television and sexual violence in the media. In R. Blanchard (Ed.), *Advances in the study of aggression* (Vol. 2, pp. 165–194). Orlando, FL: Academic Press.

Linz, D., Donnerstein, E., & Penrod, S. (1984). The effects of multiple exposures to filmed violence against women. *Journal of Communication, 34*(3), 130–147.

Linz, D., Fuson, I. A., & Donnerstein, E. (1990). Mitigating the negative effects of sexually violent mass communications through preexposure briefings. *Communication Research, 17,* 641–674.

Linz, D., & Malamuth, N. (1993). *Pornography.* Newbury Park, CA: Sage.

"Lolita in Japan" (1997, April 6). *Manhattan Mercury,* p. A7.

Lowry, D. T., & Towles, D. E. (1989). Soap opera portrayals of sex, contraception, and sexually transmitted diseases. *Journal of Communication, 39*(2), 76–83.

Lutz, C. A., & Collins, J. L. (1993). *Reading National Geographic.* Chicago: University of Chicago Press.

Lyons, J. S., Anderson, R. L., & Larson, D. B. (1994). A systematic review of the effects of aggressive and nonaggressive pornography. In D. Zillmann, J. Bryant, & A. C. Huston (Eds.), *Media, family, and children: Social, scientific, psychodynamic, and clinical perspectives.* Hillsdale, NJ: Lawrence Erlbaum Associates.

Malamuth, N. M. (1981). Rape fantasies as a function of exposure to violent sexual stimuli. *Archives of Sexual Behavior, 10,* 33–47.

Malamuth, N. M. (1984). Aggression against women: Cultural and individual causes. In N. M. Malamuth & E. Donnerstein (Eds.), *Pornography and sexual aggression.* Orlando, FL: Academic Press.

Malamuth, N. M. (1993). Pornography's impact on male adolescents. *Adolescent Medicine: State of the Art Reviews, 4,* 563–576.

Malamuth, N. M. (1996). Sexually explicit media, gender differences, and evolutionary theory. *Journal of Communication, 46*(3), 8–31.

Malamuth, N. M. (1999). Pornography. *Encyclopedia of Violence, Peace, and Conflict, 3,* 77–89.

Malamuth, N. M., & Check, J. V. P. (1980). Penile tumescence and perceptual responses to rape as a function of victim's perceived reactions. *Journal of Applied Social Psychology 10,* 528–547.

Malamuth, N. M., & Check, J. V. P. (1983). Sexual arousal to rape depictions: Individual differences. *Journal of Abnormal Psychology, 92,* 55–67.

Malamuth, N. M., Haber, S., & Feshbach, S. (1980). Testing hypotheses regarding rape: Exposure to sexual violence, sex differences, and the "normality" of rapists. *Journal of Research in Personality, 14,* 121–137.

Malamuth, N. M., Heim, M., & Feshbach, S. (1980). Sexual responsiveness of college students to rape depictions: Inhibitory and disinhibitory effects. *Journal of Personality and Social Psychology, 38,* 399–408.

Malamuth, N. M., & Impett, E. A. (2001). Research on sex in the media: What do we know about effects on children and adolescents? In D. Singer & J. Singer (Eds.), *Handbook of Children and the Media.* Newbury Park, CA: Sage.

McKenzie-Mohr, D., & Zanna, M. P. (1990). Treating women as sexual objects: Look to the (gender schematic) male who has viewed pornography. *Personality and Social Psychology Bulletin, 16,* 296–308.

Meyers, M. (1997). *News coverage of violence against women: Engendering blame.* Thousand Oaks, CA: Sage.

Morais, R. C. (1999, June 14). Porn goes public. *Forbes,* 214.

Mosher, D. L., & Maclan, P. (1994). College men and women respond to X-rated videos intended for male or female audiences: Gender and sexual scripts. *Journal of Sex Research, 31,* 99–113.

Murnen, S. K., & Stockton, M. (1997). Gender and self-reported sexual arousal in response to sexual stimuli: A meta-analytic review. *Sex Roles, 37,* 135–153.

Norris, J., George, W. H., Davis, K. C., Martell, J., & Leonesio, R. J. (1999). Alcohol and hypermasculinity as determinants of men's empathic responses to violent pornography. *Journal of Interpersonal Violence, 14,* 683–700.

Ohbuchi, K., Ikeda, T., & Takeuchi, G. (1994). Effects of violent pornography upon viewer's rape myth beliefs: A study of Japanese males. *Psychology, Crime, & Law, 1,* 71–81.

Oliver, M. B. (1993). Adolescents' enjoyment of graphic horror. *Communication Research, 20,* 30–50.

Perloff, R. M. (1989). Ego-involvement and the third person effect of television news coverage. *Communication Research, 16,* 236–262.

Pollard, P. (1995). Pornography and sexual aggression. *Current Psychology: Developmental, Learning, Personality, Social, 14*(3), 200–221.

Prentky, R. A., & Knight, R. A. (1991). Identifying critical dimensions for discriminating among rapists. *Journal of Consulting and Clinical Psychology, 59,* 643–661.

Quackenbush, D. M., Strassberg, D. S., & Turner, C. W. (1995). Gender effects of romantic themes in erotica. *Archives of Sexual Behavior, 24,* 21–35.

Quinsey, V. L., Chaplin, T. C., & Upfold, D. (1984). Sexual arousal to nonsexual violence and sadomasochistic themes among rapists and on sex offenders. *Journal of Consulting and Clinical Psychology, 52,* 651–657.

Rachman, S. (1966). Sexual fetishism: An experimental analogue. *Psychological Record, 16,* 293–296.

Rachman, S., & Hodgson, R. J. (1968). Experimentally-induced "sexual fetishism": Replication and development. *Psychological Record, 18,* 25–27.

Ramirez, J., Bryant, J., & Zillmann, D. (1982). Effects of erotica on retaliatory behavior as a function of level of prior provocation. *Journal of Personality and Social Psychology, 43,* 971–978.

Russell, D. E. H. (1998). *Dangerous relationships: Pornography, misogyny, and rape.* Thousand Oaks, CA: Sage.

Salwen, W. B., & Dupagne, M. (2001). Third-person perception of television violence: The role of self-perceived knowledge. *Media Psychology, 3,* 211–236.

Sapolsky, B. S., & Molitor, F. (1996). Content trends in contemporary horror films. In J. B. Weaver & R. Tamborini (Eds.), *Horror films: Current research on audience preferences and reactions* (pp. 33–48). Mahwah, NJ: Lawrence Erlbaum Associates.

Schaefer, H. H., & Colgan, A. H. (1977). The effect of pornography on penile tumescence as a function of reinforcement and novelty. *Behavior Therapy, 8,* 938–946.

Sintchak, G., & Geer, J. (1975). A vaginal plethysmograph system. *Psychophysiology, 12,* 113–115.

Stodghill, R. (1998, June 15). Where'd you learn that? *Time,* 52–59.

Strasburger, V. C. (1995). *Adolescents and the media: Medical and psychological impact.* Thousand Oaks, CA: Sage.

Taylor, S. (1982). The availability bias in social perception and interaction. In D. Kahneman, P. Slovic, & A. Tversky (Eds.), *Judgment under uncertainty: Heuristics and biases* (pp. 190–200). Cambridge: Cambridge University Press.

Tversky, A., & Kahneman, D. (1973). Availability: A heuristic for judging frequency and probability. *Cognitive Psychology, 5,* 207–232.

Tversky, A., & Kahneman, D. (1974). Judgment under uncertainty: Heuristics and biases. *Science, 185,* 1124–1131.

Wartella, E., Heintz, K. E., Aidman, A. J., & Mazzarella, S. R. (1990). Television and beyond: Children's video media in one community. *Communication Research, 17,* 45–64.

Weaver, J. B. (1991). Responding to erotica: Perceptual processes and dispositional implications. In J. Bryant & D. Zillmann (Eds.), *Responding to the screen.* Hillsdale, NJ: Lawrence Erlbaum Associates.

Weaver, J. B., Masland, J. L., & Zillmann, D. (1984). Effects of erotica on young men's aesthetic perception of their female sexual partners. *Perceptual and Motor Skills, 58,* 929–930.

Weaver, J. B., & Tamborini, R. (Eds.). (1996). *Horror films: Current research on audience preferences and reactions.* Mahwah, NJ: Lawrence Erlbaum Associates.

Weisz, M. G., & Earls, C. M. (1995). The effects of exposure to filmed sexual violence on attitudes toward rape. *Journal of Interpersonal Violence, 10,* 71–84.

Wilkins, J. (1997, September/October). Protecting our children from Internet smut: Moral duty or moral panic? *Humanist, 57,* 4–7.

Wilson, B. J., Linz, D., Donnerstein, E., & Stipp, H. (1992). The impact of social issue television programming on attitudes toward rape. *Human Communication Research, 19,* 179–208.

Yates, E., Barbaree, H. E., & Marshall, W. L. (1984). Anger and deviant sexual arousal. *Behavior Therapy, 15,* 287–294.

Zillmann, D., & Bryant, J. (1982). Pornography, sexual callousness, and the trivialization of rape. *Journal of Communication, 32*(4), 10–21.

Zillmann, D., & Bryant, J. (1984). Effects of massive exposure to pornography. In N. M. Malamuth & E. Donnerstein (Eds.), *Pornography and sexual aggression.* Orlando, FL: Academic Press.

Zillmann, D., & Bryant, J. (1988a). Pornography's impact on sexual satisfaction. *Journal of Applied Social Psychology, 18,* 438–453.

Zillmann, D., & Bryant, J. (1988b). Effects of prolonged consumption of pornography on family values. *Journal of Family Issues, 9,* 518–544.

Zillmann, D., & Bryant, J. (1988c). A response to Linz and Donnerstein. *Journal of Communication, 38*(2), 185–192.

Zillmann, D., Bryant, J., Comisky, P. W., & Medoff, N. J. (1981). Excitation and hedonic violence in the effect of erotica on motivated intermale aggression. *European Journal of Social Psychology, 11,* 233–252.

Chapter 13

Minorities and the Mass Media: Television Into the 21st Century

BRADLEY S. GREENBERG
Michigan State University

DANA MASTRO
Boston College

JEFFREY E. BRAND
Bond University, Queensland, Australia

In updating the status of social science examinations of racial/ethnic minorities and television, this chapter details current research efforts in three primary domains: (1) content analyses, (2) usage patterns, and (3) effects studies. Additionally, the 30 years of prior investigations of minorities and mass media are reviewed. In this manner, we can report systematically on the extent to which minority groups appear across time and genres of television programming, the types of portrayals of minorities that are found, as well as the potential for these depictions to influence perceptions of self and others. Within these assessments, particular emphasis is placed on the four largest U.S. racial/ethnic minority groups: Blacks, Latinos, Asian Americans, and Native Americans.

Earlier efforts have assiduously synopsized the research on minorities and television (see the following: Comstock & Cobbey, 1979; Greenberg, 1986; Greenberg & Atkin, 1982; Greenberg & Brand, 1994; Poindexter & Stroman, 1981; Signorielli, 1985, 1991). These studies suggest that although racial/ethnic diversity on television has improved, this process has been challenging and protracted. This can be evidenced by the recent controversy surrounding the dearth of new minority characters in the Fall

1999 prime-time television season. Outraged by the lack of minority characters across the 26 new programs for that season, prominent activist groups (including the National Association for the Advancement of Colored People [NAACP], the National Council of LaRaza [NCLR], and the Media Action Network for Asian-Americans [MANAA]), mandated a call for action in protest against the insufficiency of minority images (Daniels, 2000; Hanania, 1999).

NCLR responded with a "brownout" during the week of September 12–19, 1999, encouraging Latino viewers to boycott the four major broadcast networks (Hanania, 1999). MANAA held a news conference and released a petition to be sent to the networks. The NAACP launched a legal campaign demanding increased diversity on the air (Daniels, 2000). Ultimately, an agreement was reached with executives from four networks resulting in separate but overlapping commitments. Each included enhancement and outreach pertaining to four major areas: education and training, recruitment, procurement, and management and operations (Daniels, 2000).

As an independent validation of the legitimacy of these criticisms and the networks' response, the first author compared the distribution of Black and White characters, separately for men and women, in the photo sections of the Fall Preview editions of TV Guide for the 1999 and 2000 seasons. In 1999, 91% of the characters on the new shows were White and 9% were Black; in 2000, 80% were White and 20% were Black—a striking shift. Interesting as a sidelight is that the proportion of White males on new shows in both seasons did not change; the increase in minority roles came at the expense of White females.

As this recent controversy illustrates, the intervening 24 years after the U.S. Commission on Civil Rights (1977) reported on the invisibility and insensitivity of media depictions of racial minorities have failed to assuage media scholars, advocacy groups, and community leaders as to the quantity and quality of television images. This chapter accents the continuing research efforts to document these representations and their potential effects.

CONTENT ANALYSES

Here we provide a comprehensive account of the quantity and nature of portrayals of minorities found among the principal television genres and day-parts. The studies reported are classified into three major categories: prime-time, fictional programming; analyses of advertisements; and studies examining television news. Findings across categories include quantitative inquiries into the sheer volume of portrayals as well as assessments of the quality of these images.

Prime-Time Television

Early studies on the portrayals of minorities on prime-time television (see Greenberg & Brand, 1994, for summary) focused predominantly on the images of Blacks, inasmuch as depictions of Latinos, Asian Americans, and Native Americans were negligible, if at all present (Seggar, Hafen, & Hannonen-Gladden, 1981; Signorielli, 1983). Unlike Blacks, however, these remaining groups have yet to achieve parallel levels of parity in their relative presence on television (Gerbner, 1993; Mastro & Greenberg, 2000; Seggar et al., 1981). From the early days of television and into the 1990s, images of Latinos, Asian Americans, Native Americans, and other minority groups were effectively absent, altogether occupying about 3% to 5% of all prime-time roles during that period (Mastro & Greenberg, 2000; Seggar et al., 1981; U.S. Commission on Civil Rights, 1977).

A study of the prime-time series in the 2000–01 season found this racial distribution for primary recurring characters: 76% White, 18% African American, 2% Latino/Hispanic, 2% Asian Pacific American and 0.2% Native American. An additional finding was that the greatest prime-time diversity was from 10 to 11 p.m., and the least was from 8 to 9 p.m. (Children Now, 2001). Consequently, few studies of non-Black minorities yield adequate numbers of portrayals to permit comprehensive content analytic treatment.

Blacks. Concern regarding the paucity and nature of the depictions of Blacks on television prior to the Civil Rights movement resulted in a series of studies into the quality and regularity of these portrayals. These early content analyses found Blacks to be underrepresented compared to their numbers in the real world. Although the number of representations of Blacks on TV increased from approximately 6 to 9% of the prime-time population from the 1970s to the 1980s, Blacks made up roughly 11% of the actual U.S. population (Gerbner & Signorielli, 1979; Greenberg & Brand, 1994; Lichter, Lichter, Rothman, & Amundson, 1987; Poindexter & Stroman, 1981; Seggar et al., 1981). It was not until the early 1990s that Blacks began to constitute a proportion of the prime-time TV population (11%) that approximated their actual population of 12% (Gerbner, 1993). Weigel, Kim, and Frost (1995) found that Black appearance time had increased from the previous decade (up from 8% in 1978 to 17% in 1989). However, one-third of all Black appearances in their sample appeared in six sitcoms, constituting less than 6% of overall programming. Notably, this trend toward increased visibility for Black males failed to materialize for Black females (Gerbner, 1993).

A current examination of the prime-time, entertainment television landscape revealed modest improvements in the amount and types of images available for Blacks. In analysis of the 1996–1997 television season,

Blacks occupied 16% of the main and minor roles on prime-time, exceeding their population statistic (12%) (Mastro & Greenberg, 2000). These characters appeared most frequently in crime dramas (40%) and situation comedies (34%), which represents an overpresence in the former genre and underrepresentation in the latter.

As for the types of portrayals, in the beginning years of fictional entertainment television, Blacks were largely relegated to roles as supporting or minor characters (Berry, 1980; Cummings, 1988; Gerbner & Signorielli, 1979), disproportionately centralized in sitcoms (Roberts, 1971; Signorielli, 1983). The portrayals consistently reinforced many of the negative, stereotypical images developed in early films as well as radio serials (Atkin, 1992; Cummings, 1988; Fife, 1974). Throughout the 1950s and earlier, Blacks were shown on a repeated basis in pre-Civil Rights-era roles including servants and overweight mammies (e.g., *Beulah*) or as buffoons (such as in *The Amos 'n Andy Show*) (Atkin, 1992; Cummings, 1988; Wilson & Gutierrez, 1995). Subsequently, Blacks began to appear in more professional roles (e.g., *I Spy, Julia, Room 222*).

This notwithstanding, by the early 1970s, several situation comedies focusing on Black families marked a resurgence in oversimplified portrayals of Blacks. These caricatures could be seen on shows from *What's Happening* and *Good Times* to *The Jeffersons* and were maintained even into the 1980s with a revived mammy role in *Gimme a Break*. In some of these programs, the representations varied from images of Blacks as poor, lazy, and unemployable to depictions as servants or aggressive, ignorant clowns. Concurrently, a considerable number of Blacks appeared in such regulatory roles such as police officers (Atkin, 1992). By the early 1980s, entertainment TV began featuring more successful African-American professionals and authority figures (Cummings, 1988; Wilson & Gutierrez, 1995). This is most often attributed to the success of *The Cosby Show,* albeit several other programs with egalitarian roles also met with much success (e.g., *227, A Different World*).

Although analyses of entertainment programming in the 1990s suggest that Blacks have achieved equivalence with regard to the number of roles, the quality and variety remain debatable. Blacks were found to be more provocatively dressed and unprofessional than their White counterparts (Mastro & Greenberg, 2000). Other studies have found that Blacks in fictional programming related to the criminal justice system were overrepresented as police officers (Mastro & Robinson, 2000) and that characteristics of verbal and physical aggression in criminal justice roles were on par with Whites (Tamborini, Mastro, Chory-Assad, & Huang, 2000).

Latinos.   Extant studies examining the depiction of Latinos on television from the 1950s to the 1980s reported that Latinos commonly comprised between 1.5% and 2.5% of the TV population (Gerbner & Signorielli,

1979; Greenberg & Baptista-Fernandez, 1980). This marked a decline from 3% in the 1950s to around 1% in the 1980s (NCLR, 1994). Throughout the 1980s, the casting of Latinos converged in the area of law enforcement, maintaining roles as both officers and criminals (Greenberg, Heeter, Graef, et al., 1983). By the early 1990s, the occurrence of Latinos on TV (between 1.1% and 1.6%) remained underrepresentative of population demographics (then approximately 11% of the U.S. population) (Gerbner, 1993; Nardi, 1993). More recent examinations of the images of Latinos in prime-time fictional programming found that this group is still dramatically underrepresented (3%) compared to real-world statistics (12%) (Mastro & Greenberg, 2000).

The most recent study showed a decrease in Latino characters from 3% to 2% between the 1999–2000 and 2000–2001 seasons. Most of the characters found were in secondary or tertiary roles. It also noted that that Latino population is six times greater in real life than on television (Children Now, 2001). Moreover, roles continue to dominate in the arena of the criminal justice system, either as officers or criminals (Mastro & Greenberg, 2000).

Repeatedly, these scarce images of Latinos have focused on unfavorable and confining stereotypes that can be traced back to early film images (Barrera & Close, 1982; Garcia Berumen, 1995; NCLR 1994, 1996; Ramirez Berg, 1990; Subervi-Velez, 1994). Ramirez Berg (1990) classified these roles into six principal categories. The first is that of the Mexican bandit. This character is disheveled, untrustworthy, and dishonest—typified in representations such as the Latin American drug runner or the inner-city gangster found in many police crime dramas. Next is that of the harlot. This female figure is the embodiment of sex and sexuality whose entire existence revolves around physical pleasures. The third stereotype identified by Ramirez Berg is that of the male buffoon. This character is dim-witted and laughable, largely due to his inability to master the English language. Ricky Ricardo from *I Love Lucy* is synonymous with this stereotype. The female counterpart to this male buffoon is the clown. She is the object of derisive humor and is an incontestable contrast to the sexuality of the harlot. A current example of this character can be found in the role of Rosario on NBC's *Will & Grace*. The fifth stereotype, that of the Latin lover, traces back to the films of the 1920s. This image represents seduction, suavity, and passion. Last, Ramirez Berg notes the stereotype of the dark lady. This character is mysterious and alluring but aloof. Customarily, she is placed in contrast to her direct and straightforward White female counterparts.

Asian Americans.   Prior to the 1960s, the nearly nonexistent roles for Asians on TV seemed to parallel the notion of the "yellow peril" prevalent in the movies (Fung, 1994; Mok, 1998). The inference was that Asians were a threat to Western civilization and U.S. economic stability. On rare occasions, television viewers would encounter a Chinese character portrayed as a submissive laborer or a Japanese role as cruel soldier (Mok, 1998). As such, Asians were often characterized as scheming and mysterious. One example was the short-lived series *Flash Gordon* (1953–1954), which centered on the adventures of a White protagonist attempting to save the world from depraved Asian villains.

From 1968 to 1980, the popularity of the program *Hawaii 5-0* resulted in an increase in the absolute frequency of Asian Americans on TV (Signorielli, 1983). Yet, although it was set in the state with the greatest Asian-American population in the country, Asians were found often in background roles (Mok, 1998). Much the same was true for the series *Magnum PI* (1980–1988) and *Island Son* (1989–1990), both set in Hawaii. Still, a few notable portrayals of Asian Americans merit attention during this time, including *Star Trek* (1966–1969), *Barney Miller* (1975–1978), and *Quincy* (1977–1982), all of which depicted Asian Americans in prominent and respectable roles.

In the mid-1990s, Asian Americans held at only 1% of the TV population (Mastro & Greenberg, 2000). In the 2000–2001 season, it increased to 3% of all TV characters but was only 2% of primary recurring characters. A few programs during that time featured these scattered characters (Mok, 1998). For example, the controversial sitcom *All American Girl* (1994–1995) had an all Asian-American cast. In addition, two current series—*ER* and *Star Trek: Voyager*—present recurring Asian-American characters.

For Asian-American women, roles in television from the 1950s to the 1970s included the peasant, the prostitute/geisha, or the "Dragon Lady" (Mok, 1998). This imagery has not disappeared from the television landscape. In the character Ling, on the popular Fox dramedy *Ally McBeal*, one can see the reappearance of this formulaic role for Asian women.

Native Americans. For Native Americans, almost no images are available for analysis. In their analysis of the 1996–1997 season, Mastro and Greenberg (2000) found no Native Americans on prime-time television. The occasional roles that do exist typically are based in a historical context (Merskin, 1998). As such, Native Americans are not seen as part of contemporary U.S. society on television. The common TV characterizations of Native Americans identified by researchers include images as lazy, pensive simpletons who are tied to ancient, mystical religions. When westerns went out of favor in television, Native American depictions disappeared. The few recurring roles for Native Americans can be found in programs from the 1990s such as *Northern Exposure* and *Dr. Quinn: Medicine Woman* (Merskin, 1998).

Advertising

Historically, the portrayals of minorities in advertising have been scarce and even entirely absent for some groups (Coltrane & Messineo, 2000; Wilson & Gutierrez, 1995). As such, images in both print and television will be addressed. Content analyses suggest that when minorities do appear in advertising, only a few, narrowly defined roles tend to be prevalent (Wiegel, Lumis, & Soja, 1980; Wilson & Gutierrez, 1995). Rather than showing the diversity of cultures in the United States, advertising images oftentimes are constructed to accommodate the perceived values and norms of the White mainstream (Coltrane & Messineo, 2000). These include portrayals of subservience as well as depictions in crowds or in the background (Wilkes & Valencia, 1989).

Blacks. Both Greenberg and Brand (1994) and Wilson and Gutierrez (1995) have summarized the trends in advertising across several decades. Early studies from the 1940s to the middle 1960s indicated that between 0.06% and 3% of magazine advertisements contained portrayals of Blacks. When there were appearances, most often they were of entertainers, athletes, and servants. Research in the late 1960s found a rise in magazine ad appearances to about 5% (Cox, 1969–1970). This rise in the number of portrayals and the increase of more positive images has been attributed to pressure from Black civil rights groups (Wilson & Gutierrez, 1995). Although the actions of these groups did lead to positive changes for Blacks, the trend was not generalized to other racial groups. Further, by the late 1970s, the number of portrayals of Blacks in magazine ads had fallen to approximately 2% (Bush, Resnick, & Stern, 1980).

Conversely, a look at television revealed an increase in depictions of Blacks in commercials from 5 to 11% of all characters from the middle to late 1960s (Dominick & Greenberg, 1970). Bush, Solomon, and Hair (1977) as well as Culley and Bennett (1976) reported additional increases to approximately 10% to 13% by the mid-1970s. However, these images were centered in crowd scenes. By the late 1970s, Blacks were found in less than 2% of commercials (Weigel et al., 1980). In fact, animated commercials with no human occurrences occurred twice as frequently as commercials with Blacks. In an analysis of television commercials from 1978 and 1989 the frequency of Black appearances remained relatively unchanged at 8.5% and 9.1%, respectively (Weigel et al., 1995). During the same time period, Wilkes and Valencia (1989) reported that Blacks appeared most frequently in ads for food, cars, alcohol, electronics, and health care products and appeared at a rate approaching 17%. By 1994 Blacks were represented in 31.8% of all commercial advertisements that included models (Taylor & Stern, 1997).

Latinos.   Research on Latinos are sparse because Latinos are scarce in advertising. Early depictions of Latinos (1960s) were nearly nonexistent and revolved around negative and condescending roles (Wilson & Gutierrez, 1995). By the end of the 1970s, Latinos appeared in less than 2% of prime-time commercials and less than 1% of weekend commercials (Gerbner, Gross, Morgan, & Signorielli, 1981). Even in the mid-1980s, Latinos were featured in under 6% of all television commercials (Wilkes & Valencia, 1989). When they did appear, it was most often in background roles in commercials for entertainment, alcohol, and furniture. By the mid-1990s Latinos were found in 8.5% of prime-time commercials with human models.

Asian Americans.   In their analysis of Asian Americans in all prime-time television advertising, Taylor and Stern (1997) found that this group was represented in 8.4% of all commercials with models. This proportion exceeded their percentage in the population at the time (3.6%). Indeed, these figures are measurably greater than their representation in print ads, ranging from approximately 2% to 4%. These appearances are most often found in ads associated with wealth and work (e.g., technology, banks) and less often found in commercials for domestic products or socializing (e.g., food, household supplies).

Natives.   Images of Native Americans are nearly nonexistent in print ads and broadcast commercials (Wilson & Gutierrez, 1995). Research suggests that three main images of Native Americans appear in advertising: the noble savage, the civilized savage, and the bloodthirsty savage (Green, 1993; Merskin, 1998).

Television News

Analyses of television news suggest that portrayals of minorities are far more negative than in fictional programming (Dixon & Linz, 2000). Because consumers of news look to this source for accurate information and knowledge about the social world, the types of images of racial/ethnic minorities that are highlighted are consequential (Gilens, 1996). As such, television news provides a unique position from which to examine portrayals of racial/ethnic minorities.

News Depictions.   In 1979, the U.S. Commission on Civil Rights stated that among television news stories, fewer than 2% were allocated to coverage of minorities. When depicted, the images of minorities often were associated with issues of crime and deviance (Entman, 1990; Entman, 1992). Research on local television news programming in New Orleans indicated that Blacks accounted for over 80% of robbery suspects (Sheley & Ashkins, 1981). In a sample of 55 days of local news from Chicago, nearly half of all local TV news stories depicted Blacks involved in violent crime (Entman, 1990; Entman, 1992). Furthermore, over three-fourths of crimes reported on network news were associated with Blacks, measured against 42% of stories featuring White criminal suspects (Entman, 1994a).

Blacks have been found to be more often depicted as criminal suspects in TV news, compared to their White counterparts, and are more likely to be depicted as nameless, restrained, and disheveled (Entman, 1992). In a sample of national news from 1985 to 1989, Blacks appeared more frequently than Whites as criminal suspects and were more often depicted as menacing (Jamieson, 1992). Entman (1994b) has suggested that these news portrayals may encourage the promulgation of racial/ethnic stereotypes as well as induce fear in White viewers.

In a sample of late evening news (11 p.m.) from Philadelphia, Pennsylvania, researchers found that minorities were depicted at a frequency equal to that of Whites when the news story was not crime related (Romer, Jamieson, & DeCoteau, 1998). However, minorities were pictured at a rate of over twice that of Whites in crime-related reports. Within these stories, Whites were more likely to be shown as victims (60% to 65% of the time) rather than perpetrators of crimes. In contrast, minorities were more likely to be shown as perpetrators (62% to 64% percent of the time). Among reports with minority perpetrators, 42% of the victims were White.

Dixon and Linz (2000) asserted similar findings in their examination of 20 weeks of news programming from Southern California. Blacks were more likely than Whites to be depicted as perpetrators on TV news, and the disparity was found to increase when looking only at felonies. Additionally, Blacks were four times more likely to be depicted as suspects than police officers. In this study, the same patterns emerged for Latinos. However, when comparing these trends in coverage, the researchers noted that the number of Black perpetrators on TV news was an overrepresentation (37%) compared to actual Southern California crime reports (21%), whereas the number of Latino perpetrators on the news (29%) was underrepresentative of real-world figures (47%).

In representations of Native Americans in the news, Weston (1996) indicated that images of Natives are infrequent and confined to a few, stereotypic roles based on White, mainstream conventions. These images ignore the cultural diversity among Native Americans and emphasize poverty, alcohol-related illness, and educational failure.

News Employment. Greenberg and Brand (1998) noted that in the late 1980s approximately 64% of commercial television stations employed minorities. This marked an increase of a mere 1% since 1972 (Stone, 1988).

Specific examinations of employment placement revealed that among TV news reporters and editors, between 8% to 10% were Black, between 1% to 3% were Latinos, roughly 1% was Asian American, and less than 0.5% was Native American (Greenberg & Brand, 1998; Stone, 1988; Weaver, Drew, & Wilhoit, 1985).

The proportion of minority news anchors did not deviate considerably from this pattern. Seven percent were Black, 2% were Latino, 1% was Asian American, and approximately 0.5% was Native American. Among producers, 8% were Black, 4% were Latino, 2% were Asian American, and 0.5% was Native American. However, regional differences can be found with regard to employment patterns. In a study based in the Detroit, Michigan, market, Atkin and Fife (1993–1994) found that Black TV news anchors, reporters, and staffers were overrepresented when compared to their actual population frequencies, more so for men than for women.

USAGE PATTERNS

Decades of social science research attest to the relationship between exposure to television content and social learning (Berkowitz & Geen, 1967; Dominick & Greenberg, 1972; McLeod, Atkin, & Chaffee, 1972; Smith et al., 1998). Although the bulk of these studies address the learning of aggression from TV content, they also indicate that a number of factors, including usage rates, identification, liking, and preferences, are fundamental to the learning process. As such, these determinants are examined here.

In the main, research on usage patterns points to Blacks and Latinos as the heaviest consumers of television (Comstock & Cobbey, 1979; Nielsen 1988, 1998). At the household level, Blacks have been found to watch up to 23 more hours of television per week than Whites (Neilsen, 1988). Assessed on an individual level, Brown, Campbell, and Fischer (1986) estimated this to be approximately 4–7 more hours of television viewing per week for Black teens than White teens. This disparity in TV consumption is further corroborated by studies on daily viewing habits, which suggest that Blacks watch 1 to 2 more hours each day than Whites (Greenberg & Linsangan, 1993). Botta's (2000) results indicated that Black adolescent girls watched significantly more TV than their White counterparts.

Differences in television preferences also have been distinguished. Black audiences favor shows featuring Black characters or all Black casts (Nielsen, 1998) more so than Whites (Dates, 1980). This tendency was consistent across age groups for Black viewers (Eastman & Liss, 1980). Black children and teens reported partiality toward same-race characters (Dates, 1980; Liss, 1981), additionally declaring increased belief in the reality of television (Poindexter & Stroman, 1981) and stating greater levels of identification with Black characters (Greenberg & Atkin, 1982), particularly when highly culturally identified (Whittler, 1991).

Mixed findings have resulted from studies examining programming preferences among Latinos, due in part to the limited number of Latinos on prime-time U.S. television. The research notes a proclivity for Latino-associated content (Greenberg, Heeter, Burgoon, Burgoon, & Korzenny, 1983) and Latino characters (Eastman & Liss, 1980) alongside an average viewing rate of 29 hours per week (Subervi-Velez & Necochea, 1990). However, evaluations of the quality of these images vary. Greenberg, Heeter, Burgoon, et al., (1983) found that Latino youth believed in the realism and decency of Latino models on television. Conversely, Faber, O'Guinn, and Meyer (1987) reported that Latino adults were dissatisfied with both the quantity and quality of the images of Latinos on TV. Moreover, their findings suggest that race was a significant predictor of these perceptions. Heavy-viewing Whites were more likely to report that the quality of images of Latinos was fair, whereas heavy-viewing Latinos noted the opposite.

Among Latinos, a penchant for similar characters and content is further exemplified by the increased persuasive appeal of Spanish-language television commercials. Advertisements for the same brands were found to be significantly more persuasive in Spanish than in English among both bilingual and Spanish-dominant Latinos in the United States (Roslow & Nicholls, 1996).

No studies of general media use among representative groups of Asian Americans or Native Americans were found.

EFFECTS STUDIES

A small roster of studies examines the relationship between mass media depictions of racial/ethnic groups and their subsequent impact on social perceptions. The findings indicate that televised portrayals of racial/ethnic minorities influence majority group members' real-world perceptions about minority groups as well as minority group members' evaluations of self (Armstrong, Neuendorf, & Brentar, 1992; Botta, 2000; Faber, O'Guinn, & Meyer, 1987; Ford, 1997; McDermott & Greenberg, 1984). This research includes a diverse set of attributes, incorporating both content-based elements and individual viewer characteristics, that influence knowledge acquisition and belief systems among minority and majority groups (Bandura, 1994; Potter, 1994; Potter & Chang, 1990). More specifically, the factors facilitating this learning process include frequency of television exposure, characteristics of the content/message, realism of the portrayal, similarity to the model, identification with the model, and level of individual cognitive ability (Bandura, 1986; Potter, 1986). Taken together, these variables provide one framework for understanding the extent to which the content and number of portrayals of minorities on television may result in judgment formation.

Early survey research identified a modest association between White children's exposure to TV content and real-world perceptions about racial/ethnic minorities. Zuckerman, Singer, and Singer (1980) reported that increased exposure to violent television among Whites was significantly related to attributions of Blacks as less competent and less obedient than Whites. Additionally, Atkin, Greenberg, and McDermott (1983) linked White children's exposure to programming featuring Black characters to elevated estimates of Blacks in various real-world roles, noting no differences in physical or behavioral traits based on TV exposure. This relationship was not moderated by actual contact.

Correspondingly, Faber, O'Guinn, and Meyer (1987), in a random sample phone survey, found that White audience members with high rates of TV consumption were more likely to assert a belief in the equitable treatment of Latinos on television. The reverse was observed among Latinos, among whom heavy viewers were less likely to rate television depictions of Latinos as fair. In addition, Armstrong et al. (1992) reported a significant relationship between television content and racial perceptions. In their survey of White college students, the researchers found that increased exposure to TV news was associated with negative ratings of the socioeconomic status of Blacks. The reverse was true of exposure to entertainment programming. Heavy exposure to fictional TV shows resulted in more-favorable estimates of Black socioeconomic status relative to Whites.

Similarly, Ford (1997) found that when exposed to negative, stereotypic depictions of Blacks, Whites reported higher levels of negative evaluations of Blacks compared with nonstereotypical depictions. This pattern did not emerge when the depicted image was White. Ford conjectured that these findings may result from the use of humor in stereotypical depictions of Blacks, which, he suggests, increases tolerance for disparaging images of minority groups.

Additional experimental research corroborates this association between televised depictions of race and social stereotyping. When exposed to experimentally manipulated news broadcasts (varying only in the race of the suspect), White college students' judgments of guilt were significantly influenced by the visual image of the race of the suspect. As a result, Black suspects were evaluated as guilty more so than were White suspects. This finding was augmented by predispositions toward negative stereotyping among participants. Further, these respondents were more likely to perceive that the Black suspect would repeat the behavior (Peffley, Shields, & Williams, 1996).

With some inconsistencies, this association between exposure and belief systems also has been linked to minority group members' evaluations of self-esteem. McDermott and Greenberg (1984) revealed that, conjointly, parental communication and the regularity of watching programming with Black characters were positively related to self-esteem among Black fourth and fifth graders. Further, Stilling (1997) examined the way in which television viewing influenced acculturation among Latinos. Acculturation, defined as the extent to which an individual assumes the traits of a secondary culture, was significantly associated with exposure to television programming. More specifically, the findings of this study suggest that English-language TV exposure amplifies the level of acculturation among Latinos with low and medium durations of residence in the United States. However, Subervi-Velez and Necochea (1990) found no association between amount and type of television exposure and self-concept among Latino elementary schoolchildren.

DISCUSSION

When taken in aggregate, several conclusions can be submitted from the present review of research on television and minorities. Most strikingly, few improvements have materialized for groups other than Blacks, with these depictions also highly variant, depending on program type. For Latinos, an insubstantial rise in the number of portrayals is evidenced, but for Asian Americans and Native Americans no measure of progress exists. For all but Blacks, drawing generalizations concerning the quality of these depictions is not possible without a TV presence from which to sample. In essence, these studies attest to the fact that racial/ethnic minorities remain confined to a sparse and restricted assortment of roles.

Even among Black representations, it becomes questionable whether this numeric equality is truly enviable, particularly when considering their news portrayals. Instead, one might regard a lack of representation to be more desirable when the types of images are considered. The isolation of television programming into genres may provide a meaningful documentation of trends and fluctuations in portrayals. However, the entire range of images must be examined to fully understand the potential impact of TV exposure. When fictional content is juxtaposed with news shows, a contrasting picture emerges, which blurs the television landscape.

According to Clark (1969), there exists an evolutionary process in the portrayals of minorities on television. These stages of representation, though not discrete, mark a steady progression in the quality and types of roles available for racial/ethnic minorities. Starting with complete absence, the racial/ethnic group is without representation on television. Next, roles of ridicule develop, as the group becomes the humorous object of White contempt. In the third stage, or regulatory phase, the minority group appears on both sides of the law, as both officers of the court and criminals. Finally, images begin to emerge in the stage of egalitarianism wherein the minority group members can be seen in a variety of roles exhibiting the richness and diversity of the culture.

Using this framework, the images of Blacks have made inroads in their development in fictional, entertainment programming. The same cannot be said of their representations in the news. Moreover, for Latinos, the types of depictions may indicate stagnation in regulatory roles. Yet, based on the frequency of these images, it would be difficult to argue that Latinos have transcended absence on TV. Even clearer is the continued absence of Asian Americans, Native Americans, and other minority groups on television.

One attempt to rectify this ongoing struggle for representation has been the development of cable networks aimed at these underrepresented groups. Black cable channels, Spanish-language channels, and other minority channels are becoming increasingly accessible. Latino cable networks such as Univision and Telemundo reach 93% and 85% of U.S. Latino households, respectively (Tobenkin, 1997), and new networks are in development. For example, Azteca America, prelaunched in January 2001, has set out to capture part of the growing Latino market (McClellan, 2000).

Nevertheless, based on programming preferences, it would be easy for any viewer to miss the few shows that showcase minority characters. Their concentration of Blacks in a few genres during distinct time frames may result in a noticeable absence. Given this omission, mere frequencies are inadequate to describe the television landscape. As such, alternative content analysis strategies have been used to more explicitly capture the nature of these depictions. Intergroup comparisons have been used in order to examine distinctions between groups on television (e.g., Blacks and Whites). Certain features of the portrayals can then be used in evaluating equity in representation (Dixon & Linz, 2000). For example, "Are Blacks or Whites more likely to be depicted in a subservient role in situation comedies?"

Interrole comparisons provide another method of exploring televised depictions of minorities. This strategy involves comparing frequencies and types of roles within the same racial or cultural group. This technique responds to questions such as: "Are Latinos more likely to be depicted as aggressors or recipients of aggression in crime dramas?"

Interreality comparisons provide another promising approach to these depictions. This strategy focuses on comparing televised portrayals with real-world social indicators. One example of this method would be to examine the extent to which Blacks, Whites, Latinos, Asian Americans, and Native Americans are featured as criminals weighed against actual crime indices.

Used in conjunction, these three measures provide a highly informed account of the TV environment. Again, however, the absence and shortage of portrayals of several groups limits comprehensive attempts of this kind. Until then, research may be better served by isolating programming with recurring Latino, Asian-American, and Native American characters, if any, to assess their status and role development across time.

Although the content analyses lead to speculation about the impact of these images, behavioral research on the effects of these images is notably limited. Even usage data, save for Blacks, has not been available for intensive analysis. Also consequential, however, is the need to advance our understanding of how a near or complete absence of TV portrayals influences audience members. Do such absences equate with insignificance? For Whites (and Blacks), does this endorse a perception of superiority or prominence? Conversely, are Latinos, Asian Americans, and Native Americans to conclude that they are secondary or subordinate in U.S. society? How does this affect self-concept? Continued investigations of these issues remain acutely essential.

REFERENCES

Atkin, C., Greenberg, B., & McDermott, S. (1983). Television and race role socialization. *Journalism Quarterly, 60,* 407–414.

Atkin, D. (1992). An analysis of television series with minority-lead characters. *Critical Studies in Mass Communication, 9,* 337–349.

Atkin, D., & Fife, M. (1993–1994). The role of race and gender as determinants of local TV news coverage. *Howard Journal of Communications, 5,* 123–137.

Armstrong, G., Neuendorf, K., & Brentar, J. (1992). TV entertainment, news, and racial perceptions of college students. *Journal of Communication, 42,* 153–176.

Bandura, A. (1986). *Social foundations of thought and action: A social cognitive theory.* Upper Saddle River, NJ: Prentice Hall.

Bandura, A. (1994). Social cognitive theory of mass communication. In J. Bryant & D. Zillmann (Eds.), *Media Effects* (pp. 61–90). Hillsdale, NJ: Lawrence Erlbaum Associates.

Barrera, A., & Close, F. (1982). Minority role models. In M. Schwartz (Ed.), *TV and teens: Experts look at the issues* (pp. 88–95). Reading, MA: Addison-Wesley.

Berkowitz, L., & Geen, R. (1967). Stimulus qualities of the target of aggression: A further study. *Journal of Personality and Social Psychology, 5,* 364–368.

Berry, G. (1980). Television and Afro-Americans: Past legacy and present portrayals. In S. Withey & R. Ables (Eds.), *Television and social behavior* (pp. 3–32). Hillsdale, NJ: Lawrence Erlbaum Associates.

Botta, R. (2000). The mirror of television: A comparison of Black and White adolescents' body image. *Journal of Communication, 50,* 144–159.

Brown, J., Campbell, K., & Fischer, L. (1986). American adolescents and music videos— Why do they watch? *Gazette, 37,* 19–32.

Bush, R., Resnick, A., & Stern, B. (1980). A content analysis of the portrayal of Black models in magazine advertising. In R. Bagozzi (Ed.), *Marketing in the '80s: Changes and challenges* (pp. 484–487). Chicago: American Marketing Association.

Bush, R., Solomon, P., & Hair, J., Jr. (1977). There are more Blacks in TV commercials. *Journal of Advertising Research, 17,* 21–25.

Children Now. (2001, April). Fall Colors 2000–01. From www.childrenandmedia.org.

Clark, C. (1969). Television and social controls: Some observations on the portrayal of ethnic minorities. *Television Quarterly, 8,* 19.

Coltrane, S., & Messineo, M. (2000). The perpetuation of subtle prejudice: Race and gender imagery in 1990s television advertising. *Sex Roles, 42,* 363–389.

Comstock, G., & Cobbey, R. (1979). Television and the children of ethnic minorities. *Journal of Communication, 29,* 104–115.

Cox, K. (1969–1970). Changes in stereotyping of Negroes and whites in magazine advertisements. *Public Opinion Quarterly, 33,* 603–606.

Culley, J. D., & Bennett, R. (1976). Selling women, selling Blacks. *Journal of Communication, 26,* 160–174.

Cummings, M. (1988). The changing image of the Black family on television. *Journal of Popular Culture, 22,* 75–85.

Daniels, G. (August, 2000). *Television network diversity deals and citizen group action in 21st century broadcasting policy.* Paper presented at the National Communication Association Doctoral Honors Conference, Evanston, IL.

Dates, J. (1980). Race, racial attitudes and adolescent perceptions of Black television characters. *Journal of Broadcasting, 24,* 549–560.

Dixon, T., & Linz, D. (2000). Overrepresentation and underrepresentation of African Americans and Latinos as lawbreakers on television news. *Journal of Communication, 50,* 131–154.

Dominick, J., & Greenberg, B. S. (1970). Three seasons of Blacks on television. *Journal of Advertising Research, 10,* 21–27.

Dominick, J., & Greenberg, B. S. (1972). Attitudes toward violence: The interaction of television exposure, family attitudes, and social class. In G. A. Comstock & E. A. Rubinstein (Eds.), *Television and social behavior: Vol. 3. Television and adolescent aggressiveness* (pp. 314–335). Washington, DC: U.S. Government Printing Office.

Eastman, H., & Liss, M. (1980). Ethnicity and children's preferences. *Journalism Quarterly, 57,* 277–280.

Entman, R. (1990). Modern racism and the images of Blacks in local television news. *Critical Studies in Mass Communication, 7,* 332–345.

Entman, R. (1992). Blacks in the news: Television, modern racism and cultural change. *Journalism Quarterly, 69,* 341–361.

Entman, R. (1994a). Representation and reality in the portrayal of Blacks on network television news. *Journalism Quarterly, 71,* 509–520.

Entman, R. (1994b). African Americans according to TV news. *Media Studies Journal, 8,* 29–38.

Faber, R., O'Guinn, T., & Meyer, T. (1987). Televised portrayals of Hispanics. *International Journal of Intercultural Relations, 11,* 155–169.

Ford, T. (1997). Effects of stereotypical television portrayals of African-Americans on person perception. *Social Psychology Quarterly, 60,* 266–278.

Fife, M. (1974). Black images in American TV: The first two decades. *Black Scholar, 6,* 7–15.

Fung. R. (1994). Seeing yellow: Asian identities in film and video. In K. Aguilar-San Juan (Ed.), *The state of Asian America: Activism and resistance in the 1900s* (pp. 161–171). Boston, MA: South End Press.

Garcia Berumen, F. (1995). *The Chicano/Hispanic image in American film.* New York: Vantage Press.

Gerbner, G. (1993). *Women and minorities on television (a report to the Screen Actors Guild and the American Federation of Radio and Television Artists).* Philadelphia: Annenberg School of Communication, University of Pennsylvania.

Gerbner, G., Gross, L., Morgan, M., & Signorielli, N. (1981). *Aging with television commercials: Images on television commercials and dramatic programming, 1977–1979.* Philadelphia: Annenberg School of Communication, University of Pennsylvania.

Gerbner, G., & Signorielli, N. (1979). *Women and minorities in television drama 1969–1978.* Philadelphia: Annenberg School of Communication, University of Pennsylvania.

Gilens, M. (1996). Race and poverty in America: Public misperceptions and the American news media. *Public Opinion Quarterly, 60,* 515–541.

Green, M. (1993). Images of Native Americans in advertising: Some moral issues. *Journal of Business Ethics, 12,* 323–330.

Greenberg, B. S. (1986). Minorities and the mass media. In J. Bryant & D. Zillmann (Eds.), *Perspectives on media effects* (pp. 165–188). Hillsdale, NJ: Lawrence Erlbaum Associates.

Greenberg B. S., & Atkin, C. (1982). Learning about minorities from television: A research agenda. In G. Berry & C. Mitchell-Kernan (Eds.), *Television and the socialization of the minority child* (pp. 215–243). New York: Academic Press.

Greenberg, B. S., & Baptista-Fernandez, P. (1980). Hispanic-Americans: The new minority on television. In B. Greenberg (Ed.), *Life on television: Content analyses of U.S. TV drama* (pp. 3–13). Norwood, NJ: Ablex.

Greenberg, B. S., & Brand, J. (1998). U.S. minorities and the news. In Y. Kamalipour & T. Carilli (Eds.), *Cultural diversity and the U.S. media* (pp. 3–22). Albany: State University of New York Press.

Greenberg, B. S., & Brand, J. (1994). Minorities and the mass media: 1970s-1990s. In J. Bryant & D. Zillmann (Eds.), *Media effects: Advances in theory and research* (pp. 273–314). Hillsdale, NJ: Lawrence Erlbaum Associates.

Greenberg, B. S., Heeter, C., Graef, D., Doctor, K., Burgoon, J., & Korzenny, F. (1983). Mass communication and Mexican Americans. In B. Greenberg, M. Burgoon, J. Burgoon, & F. Korzenny (Eds.), *Mexican Americans and the mass media* (pp. 305–323). Norwood, NJ: Ablex.

Greenberg, B. S., Heeter, C., Burgoon, M., Burgoon, J., & Korzenny, F. (1983). Mass media use, preferences, and attitudes among young people. In B. Greenberg, M. Burgoon, J. Burgoon, & F. Korzenny (Eds.), *Mexican Americans and the mass media* (pp. 147–201). Norwood, NJ: Ablex.

Greenberg, B., & Linsangan, R. (1993). Gender differences in adolescents' media use, exposure to sexual content, parental mediation and self-perceptions. In B. S. Greenberg, J. Brown, & N. Boerkel-Rothfoss (Eds.), *Media, sex and the adolescent* (pp. 134–144). Cresskill, NJ: Hamilton Press.

Hanania, J. (1999). White out: Latinos on TV. *TV Guide, 47*(34), 31–39.

Jamieson, K. (1992). *Dirty Politics.* New York: Oxford University Press.

Lichter, S. R., Lichter, L. S., Rothman, S., & Amundson, D. (1987). Prime-time prejudice: TV's images of Blacks and Hispanics. *Public Opinion, 10,* 13–16.

Liss, M. (1981). Children's television selections: A study of indicators of same-race preferences. *Journal of Cross Cultural Psychology, 12,* 103–110.

Mastro, D., & Greenberg, B. S. (2000). The portrayal of racial minorities on prime-time television. *Journal of Broadcasting & Electronic Media, 44,* 690–703.

Mastro, D., & Robinson, A. (2000). Cops & crooks: Images of minorities on prime-time television. *Journal of Criminal Justice, 28,* 385–396.

McClellan, S. (2000). Room for *tres? Broadcasting & Cable, 130*, 26–32.

McDermott, S., & Greenberg, B. (1984). Parents, peers and television as determinants of Black children's esteem. In R. Bostrom (Ed.), *Communication Yearbook 8* (pp. 164–177). Beverly Hills, CA: Sage.

McLeod, J., Atkin, C., & Chaffee, S. (1972). Adolescents, parents, and television use: Adolescents self-report measures from Maryland and Wisconsin samples. In G. A. Comstock & E. A. Rubinstein (Eds.), *Television and social behavior: Vol. 3. Television and adolescent aggressiveness.* Washington, DC: U.S. Government Printing Office.

Merskin, D. (1998). Sending up signals: A survey of Native American media use and representation in the mass media. *Howard Journal of Communications, 9,* 333–345.

Mok, T. (1998). Getting the message: Media images and stereotypes and their effect on Asian Americans. *Cultural Diversity and Mental Health, 4,* 185–202.

Nardi, P. (1993). *The issue of diversity on prime-time television.* Claremont, CA: Pitzer College Press.

NCLR (1994). *Out of the picture: Hispanics in the media.* National Council of La Raza (pp. 1–30). Washington, DC.

NCLR (1996). *Don't Blink: Hispanics in television entertainment.* National Council of La Raza. Washington, DC.

Nielsen Media Research. (1998). *1998 Report on television.* New York: Nielson Research Inc.

Nielsen Media Research. (1988). *Television viewing among Blacks* (4th annual report). New York: Nielson Research Inc.

Peffley, M., Shields, T., & Williams, B. (1996). The intersection of race and crime in television news stories: An experimental study. *Political Communication, 13,* 309–327.

Poindexter, P. M., & Stroman, C. (1981). Blacks and television: A review of the research literature. *Journal of Broadcasting, 25,* 103–122.

Potter, W. (1994). Cultivation theory and research. *Journalism Monographs, 147,* 1–3.

Potter, W. (1986). Perceived reality and the cultivation hypothesis. *Journal of Broadcasting and Electronic Media, 30,* 159–174.

Potter, W., & Chang, I. (1990). Television exposure measures and the cultivation hypothesis. *Journal of Broadcasting and Electronic Media, 34,* 313–333.

Ramirez Berg, C. (1990). Stereotyping in films in general and of the Hispanic in particular. *Howard Journal of Communication, 2,* 286–300.

Roberts, C. (1971). The protrayal of Blacks on network television. *Journal of Broadcasting, 15,* 45–53.

Romer, D., Jamieson, K., & DeCoteau, N. (1998). The treatment of persons of color in local television news: Ethnic blame discourse or realistic group conflict. *Communication Research, 25,* 286–305.

Roslow, P., & Nicholls, J. A. F. (1996). Targeting the Hispanic market: Comparative persuasion of TV commercials in Spanish and English. *Journal of Advertising Research, 36,* 66–77.

Seggar, J., Hafen, J., & Hannonen-Gladden, H. (1981). Television's portrayals of minorities and women in drama and comedy drama, 1971–80. *Journal of Broadcasting, 25,* 277–288.

Sheley, J., & Ashkins, C. (1981). Crime, crime news, and crime views. *Public Opinion Quarterly, 45,* 492–506.

Signorielli, N. (1983). The demography of the television world. In G. Melischek, K. E. Rosengren, & J. Stappers (Eds.), *Cultural indicators: An international symposium* (pp. 553–573). Vienna, Austria: Austrian Academy of Sciences.

Signorielli, N. (1985). *Role portrayals and stereotyping on television: An annotated bibliography of studies relating to women, minorities, aging, sexual behavior, health, and handicaps.* Westport, CT: Greenwood Press.

Signorielli, N. (1991). *Role portrayals in the media: Images relating to sex roles, minorities, age-roles, religion, mental illness, and disabilities (1985–1991).* Prepared for U.S. Commission on Civil Rights. Washington, DC.

Smith, S. L., Wilson, B. J., Kunkel, D. Linz, D., Potter, W. J., Colvin, C., & Donnerstein, D. (1998).Violence in television programming overall: University of California, Santa Barbara. *National television violence study* (Vol. 3, pp. 5–220). Newbury Park, CA: Sage.

Stilling, E. (1997). The electronic melting pot hypothesis: The cultivation of acculturation among Hispanics through television viewing. *Howard Journal of Communication, 8,* 77–100.

Stone, V. (1988, July). *Pipelines and dead ends: Jobs held by minorities and women in broadcast news.* Paper presented to the Minorities and Communication Division of the Association for Education in Journalism and Mass Communication, Portland, OR.

Subervi-Velez, F. (1994). Mass communication and Hispanics. In F. Padilla (Ed.), *Handbook of Hispanic cultures in the United States: Sociology* (pp. 304–357). Houston, TX: Arte Publico Press.

Subervi-Velez, F., & Necochea, J. (1990). Television viewing and self-concept among Hispanic American children—A pilot study. *Howard Journal of Communication, 2,* 315–329.

Tamborini, R., Mastro, D., Chory-Assad, R., & Huang, R. (2000). The color of crime and the court: A content analysis of minority representation on television. *Journalism and Mass Communication Quarterly, 77,* 639–654.

Taylor, C., & Stern, B. (1997). Asian-Americans: Television advertising and the "model minority" stereotype. *Journal of Advertising, 26,* 47–61.

Tobenkin, D. (1997). Univision vs. Telemundo: Spanish language cable broadcasters compete for market share. *Broadcasting & Cable, 127,* 34–46.

U.S. Commission on Civil Rights. (1977). *Window dressing on the set: Women and minorities in television.* Washington, DC: U.S. Government Printing Office.

U.S. Commission on Civil Rights. (1979). *Window dressing on the set: An Update.* Washington, DC: U.S. Government Printing Office.

Weaver, D., Drew, D., & Wilhoit, G. (1985, August). *A profile of U.S. radio and television journalists.* Paper presented to the Radio and Television Division of the Association for Education in Journalism and Mass Communication, Memphis, TN.

Weigel, R., Kim, E., & Frost, J. (1995). Race relations on prime-time television reconsidered: Patterns of continuity and change. *Journal of Applied Social Psychology, 25,* 223–236.

Weigel, R., Loomis, J., & Soja, M. (1980). Race relations on prime time television. *Journal of Personality and Social Psychology, 39,* 884–893.

Weston, M. (1996). *Native Americans in the news: Images of Indians in the twentieth century press.* Westport, CT: Greenwood Press.

Wilkes, R. E., & Valencia, H. (1989). Hispanics and Blacks in television commercials. *Journal of Advertising, 18,* 19–25.

Wilson, C., & Gutierrez, F. (1995). *Race, multiculturalism, and the media: From mass to class communication* (pp. 61–105). Newbury Park, CA: Sage.

Whittler, T. (1991). The effects of actors' race in commercial advertising: Review and extension. *Journal of Advertising, 20,* 54–60.

Zuckerman, D., Singer, C., & Singer, J. (1980). Children's television viewing, racial and sex role attitudes. *Journal of Applied Social Psychology, 10,* 281–294.

Chapter 14

Media Influences on Marketing Communications

DAVID W. STEWART
PAULOS PAVLOU
University of Southern California

SCOTT WARD
University of Pennsylvania

In this chapter, we examine research and theory related to the characteristics of media, how these characteristics influence responses to marketing communications, and the processes by which this influence occurs. More specifically, we examine the unique and interactive effects of particular media types and vehicles on how marketing communication affects individual consumers and markets. An earlier review of this area (Stewart & Ward, 1994) examined relatively traditional effects of media in the context of advertising. It only briefly introduced the then nascent new media and the potential changes these new media suggested in both the characteristics of media and the influence of such media on advertising practice. Stewart and Ward (1994) also suggested that the continuing rapid evolution of media presented new opportunities for research, but that such research would require a change of focus from the stimulus—media characteristics—to the individual—the purposes and functions served by various media for individuals. Much that was suggested about the evolution of media has come to pass with the rise of the Internet, interactive television, and mobile communication. Thus, the present chapter will focus less on the effects of traditional media in advertising and more on the influences of the new media within the broader context of marketing communications.

The primary concern in this chapter is with media effects on individuals exposed to, interacting with, and responding to marketing communications, rather than with the effects of specific media characteristics on managerial decisions about marketing communications. That is, it is not unusual for the characteristics of particular media to influence managerial decisions: whether to advertise or not, how much to spend on it, what particular media types and/or vehicles to use. Nonetheless, it is necessary to address some issues related to the way in which perceptions of media effects influence marketing communications decisions, if only to distinguish these issues from the primary mission. In addition, the increasing interactivity of various media, ranging from the World Wide Web to mobile telephones and digital assistants, has tended to blur the boundaries among various types of marketing communication. Advertising, personal selling, service before and after a sale, distribution, and even the product being acquired have all become difficult to clearly and cleanly differentiate within the context of interactive media. Thus, this chapter will examine the broader topic of media influence on marketing communications, rather than focus only on media effects in advertising.

Most research on media effects within marketing has tended to focus on advertising effects, and this research has focused on traditional mass media: television, radio, and print. It is an empirical question whether or not results of past research applies to new media forms, and, in any case, the changing and more complex media environment requires that findings from earlier research be assessed in light of this new environment. Nevertheless, it is likely that much of what exists in the extant empirical and theoretical literature on media still holds within the context of traditional, noninteractive mass media. Interactivity and mobility have added new dimensions to media and the influence of media in marketing communications, however. We will examine these new dimensions in this chapter as well as summarize what is known about the influence of traditional media in a marketing context.

DEFINING MEDIA FOR MARKETING COMMUNICATIONS

At the most general level, a "medium" refers to any transmission vehicle or device through which communication may occur. In the context of marketing communication, the term *advertising* has traditionally been applied to mass communication media, to distinguish advertising from personal selling, which occurs through the medium of interpersonal communication, and from sales promotion activities, which can occur through various media forms. Advertising media have traditionally been characterized as "measured" media, to refer to the availability of quantitative information to assess the number of viewers or readers potentially exposed to advertising messages. In addition, advertising has traditionally been conceptualized as one-way communication from an advertiser to a recipient. Personal selling and direct response marketing have more typically been characterized as interactive.

Both the practice of marketing management—the organizational domain in which advertising decisions are generally made—and the technological environment have made traditional conceptions of advertising media open to discussion. Several scholars have argued that the increasing availability of information and the sophistication of the technology for obtaining, processing, and analyzing this information are blurring the boundaries of the several elements of the marketing mix (Glazer, 1989; Ray, 1985). There have also been calls for changes in the organization of both the marketing function and the firm itself to accommodate this blurring of the traditional functional lines within marketing and between marketing and other functional disciplines within and external to the firm (Glazer, 1989; Webster, 1989). Organizations are increasingly aware that there are more opportunities for controlled communications with consumers and other corporate stakeholders than advertising alone, and that many marketing communication decisions must be coordinated and rationalized within the context of the organization's objectives. For example, the choice of retail outlets represents a kind of "communications medium" decision. Whether a good is sold through Tiffany's or through discount merchandisers is an issue that is conceptually similar to whether an advertisement has the same impact in *The New Yorker* as it does in *Tennis* magazine. Similarly, a salesperson is a communications medium in the same sense as an ad in a weekly newsmagazine, although the characteristics of the medium are quite different.

In addition to the trend toward an expanded view of organizational communications media, trends and developments have extended the traditional definition of advertising and marketing communications media beyond the mass media. For example, sponsorships and place-based communication have become an important means for reaching consumers with marketing messages. The logos of well-known brands covered the bicycle and athletic wear of Lance Armstrong as he won the Tour de France. Such sponsorships, along with cable television, computer-based information services, facsimile machines, mobile telephones, and Web-enabled personal digital assistants now allow marketers to reach much more concentrated and focused audiences than with traditional mass media. Many of these communication technologies have also made it increasingly easy for the consumer to respond to the marketer's communications and even initiate communication with the marketer.

Consumers have accepted the Internet as a communication medium with marketers; hence, a new type of marketing communication, interactive advertising, has emerged, mainly as a result of traditional advertising embracing interactive technologies. Consistent with the view that the boundaries of the marketing mix are indeed blurring, interactive advertising shares some characteristics with personal selling, direct-response marketing, and even distribution channels. Expenditures for online advertising, only a single form of interactive communication, are estimated to have reached more than $5 billion in the year 2000 and are expected to exceed $45 billion by 2005 (Stone, 2000). Although this will still be only about 10% of all advertising expenditures, there is reason to believe that this figure will dramatically increase as both consumers and marketers recognize the benefits of interactive advertising.

The communication objectives associated with the use of nontraditional media tend to be similar to those for traditional mass media. For example, sponsorship of an athlete, such as Lance Armstrong, may influence attitude formation and change because an advertiser is associated with the athlete or a particular sporting event. At the very least, marketers hope for very high levels of brand-name exposure, as event audiences, as well as audiences that may witness the event on television, are repeatedly exposed to the sponsor's brand name, via messages during the event, billboards at the event, or attachment of the brand name to the object of the event (such as a sports clothing company's logo appearing on players' uniforms). On the other hand, interactive media greatly expand the potential objectives for marketing communication. For example, in contrast to traditional advertising, an interactive medium not only provides information, but it can also take the order and, in cases where products and services can be digitized, even deliver the product. As noted earlier, we believe that much of what is known about the influence of more-traditional media on response to marketing communication is generalizable to the "new media" under appropriate circumstances, although the new media will alter traditional uses of mass media by both the consumer and the marketer. Thus, we will consider the extant body of empirical and theoretical literature regarding more traditional media before turning to a discussion of the new media.

THE NATURE OF MEDIA EFFECTS ON MARKETING COMMUNICATIONS

It is probably safe to say that the early advertisers were less concerned with media choices and effects than they were with simply initiating communication. Mass communications historians tell us that the earliest models of communication effects posited that communications were very powerful: the early "bullet" or "hypodermic needle" models of mass communication (Katz & Lazarsfeld, 1955, p. 16) that gave rise to the earliest conception of communication effects: who says what to whom through what medium with what effects. Very quickly, marketers learned that advertising and other types of marketing communications are not so powerful. Virtually all advertising textbooks recall John Wanamaker's lament, after witnessing the failure of advertising to stimulate sales in his department store chain: "I know that half of my advertising budget is wasted; the trouble is, I don't know which half." The problem, of course, is that the effects of marketing communications are due to a myriad of factors, some related to the characteristics of the communication itself (and, therefore, under the control of the marketer) and some to relatively uncontrollable factors, such as consumer characteristics, marketing communications of competitors, and so forth. Further complicating the problem is the fact that the effects of marketing communications are not necessarily direct. That is, it is exceedingly difficult to separate the effects of media from message variables effects, both in the day-to-day practice of communications management and in empirical research on media effects. Communications and consumer characteristics also interact: it is difficult to partial out the unique effects of communication from the prior attitudes and experiences of consumers who see or hear it.

Managerial Approaches to Understanding Media Effects: Media Planning Models

With the advent of commercial television and printing technologies to make narrow, segment-specific magazines possible, advertisers have come to believe that individual media have unique capabilities and effects. Marketing communications managers evolved rules of thumb to account for these effects (e.g., print media are better to explain complex products, television is better because it can show product demonstrations). There was an evolving idea that there are "qualitative" media factors, but generally these were—and are today—relegated to the subjective judgment of media influences. Similarly, the advent of interactive technologies such as mobile telephones and the Internet has given rise to efforts to individualize communications or, at the very least, to customize marketing communications for very small but especially relevant audiences for the marketer's messages.

Early rules of thumb about media effects evolved into attempts to explicitly model these effects. This evolution was stimulated at least as much by the availability of large databases on the media habits of individuals and by computer technology as by communication or psychological theory. Generally, media models contain information concerning readership, viewership, listernership, Web browsing among households, and data about household purchasing behavior, among other things. Armed with such information, a planner can quickly identify the characteristics of heavy users of a brand or product category and determine the media habits of such buyers. Models employing such demographic and behavioral analysis merely offer insight into which media particular consumers use and, by implication, which media are most likely to reach the intended audience of the marketer.

The Advertising Response Function.   At the heart of most media planning models is an "advertising response function." This is the hypothesized relationship between the cumulative number of exposures of an individual (or aggregate of individuals) to communication for a product (within the same medium or across different media) and some dependent variable, such as purchase probability, product knowledge, and so forth. The specific form of this response function has been the subject of considerable debate. In general, however, one of two functions is thought to apply (Stewart, 1989): (a) a gentle S-curve indicating that advertising requires a few exposures to have any impact at all (hence a threshold for any effect at all), a few more exposures to reach its maximum impact, and then a declining marginal impact, and (b) a simple ogive function that also consists of a rapidly rising level of effectiveness with each additional exposure, followed by diminishing marginal impact of each subsequent exposure, but no threshold. Both functions have been documented extensively in the literature, which suggests that the specific form of the function may be contingent on other factors. Consistent with this contingency perspective is the suggestion by Burke and Srull (1988) that the threshold portion of the model is observed under conditions of competitive advertising. Their reasoning is consistent with a long tradition of research on interference effects in the learning literature. Simply put, Burke and Srull (1988) argue that the threshold effect represents the minimal advertising for a product to overcome the interference created by the advertising for competitive products. Thus, the threshold is likely to be most prominent in heavily advertised product categories and may disappear altogether when competitive advertising is relatively modest. This suggests that at least one dimension of the broader media context, the density of competing messages, may influence the very shape of the advertising response function.

Media Impact.   Finally, most media planning models include a capability for the media planner to specify "impact" factors. These are subjective weights that the planner can assign to certain factors, such as media types and vehicles, and types of consumers that will influence the model to select particular media types and/or vehicles that reach specified audience segments. There is a general consensus among advertisers and media planners that media do differentially impact the effectiveness of communications embedded within them (Stewart & Ward, 1994). General recognition that there exist qualitative differences among media that may influence response to advertising has not brought with it substantial skill in identifying and accommodating to these differences, however. Not only is there some debate about how to characterize different media across various dimensions, rather little is actually known about how people interact with different media. Media planners have tried to capture these effects through the use of subjective judgments. Unfortunately, subjective media judgments have not proven very reliable, even in simple cases (Haley, 1985).

This discussion of computer-based models actually used by media planners provides an overview of how advertisers estimate the nature of media effects and the knowledge advertisers use in accounting for variance in media effects. Variants of such models have been employed in making decisions about almost all media used in marketing communications, including such traditional media as television and magazines, nontraditional media such as event sponsorship, and newer forms of advertising such as banner ads on the Internet. Despite years of experience with such models, there is little empirical evidence to indicate with much precision the unique effects of media types and vehicles. Again, this is largely the result of media vehicle effects interacting with a variety of other effects and the difficulty of isolating unique media effects from the total "gestalt" of message characteristics, repetition effects, consumer characteristics, and the like on consumer responses. The models do require subjective judgments about *receivers* of advertising messages in different media. For example, media vehicle weights demand that the media planner weight characteristics of individuals who attend to particular media vehicles. However, these characteristics are normally only understood in terms of demographic characteristics or, in some cases, "psychographic" characteristics that attempt to characterize individuals in terms of attitudes, opinions, beliefs, and lifestyle habits. In contrast, academic research has focused on individual characteristics that may be correlated with demographics, but are oriented more toward processes by which individuals interact with communication media. We turn now to these research streams.

THEORETICAL AND EMPIRICAL APPROACHES TO UNDERSTANDING MEDIA EFFECTS

Marshall McLuhan is well known for his "Medium Is the Message" statement, implying that a medium communicates an image or generates effects independent of any single message it contains (McLuhan & Fiore, 1967). In fact, as the preceding discussion makes clear, media effects can only be understood in the context of consumer characteristics that influence the effectiveness of marketing communications in particular media. Although there are many such consumer characteristics, five factors have received considerable attention in empirical research and theory development:

1. Attitudes toward the medium
2. Uses of the medium
3. Involvement while using the medium
4. Mood states affecting media usage
5. Interactivity of the medium

In addition to these five factors, media effects are also conditional on media scheduling decisions, which result in differences in repetition of the same message and the frequency of exposure to marketing communication in the medium.

Attitudes Toward Media

The attitude of a consumer toward a specific medium can radically alter how that media affects the consumer and any marketing communications it carries. In an early landmark study, the Politz Research Organization compared the vehicle effects of *McCall's* with that of *Look* and *Life* magazines (Politz Research, Inc., 1962). Matched samples of readers were shown the same sets of advertisements, controlling for copy effects, but were told that they appeared in one magazine or the other. There were no differences in brand awareness and knowledge of brand claims, but there were significant differences in brand quality rating and in brand preference. For example, the gain attributed to one advertised brand as the "very highest quality" was 3.8% when the advertisement was said to run in *McCall's* magazine, but only 1.0% when the ad was said to run in the other two magazines. In a similar vein, Aaker and Brown (1972) examined the interaction of media vehicle types ("prestige" versus "expert" magazines) and copy appeals ("image" advertisements versus "reason-why" advertisements). The dependent variables were consumers' expected price, quality, and reliability. The results showed strong interaction effects among respondents who had not used the advertised products previously. Image advertisements performed better in prestige magazines than did reason-why advertisements. However, reason-why advertisements did not perform better in expert magazines than in prestige magazines in terms of the dependent variables. These studies provide some empirical basis for the notion that individual attitudes toward media vehicles condition their responses to marketing communications in those vehicles.

The Role of Relationship and Trust. One particularly important attitude toward a medium is related to its perceived credibility or trustworthiness (Shimp, 1990). There is considerable consistency with the conclusion that marketers' relationships with consumers play an important role in how consumers respond to marketing communications (Fontenot & Vlosky, 1998; Hoffman & Novak, 1996). Perhaps the most important element of a successful marketer–consumer relationship is the notion of trust. Research has shown that trust reduces transaction costs (Ganesan, 1994), lowers the risk of transacting (Mayer, Davis, & Schoorman, 1995), increases future interaction intentions (Doney & Cannon, 1997), and brings more favorable pricing terms (Pavlou & Ba, 2000). Moreover, Keen (2000) posited that the very foundation of electronic commerce rests on trust. Although consumers may decide to interact with the marketer in a variety of contexts, any collaboration will always be limited by the extent of mutual trust among consumers and marketers. Thus, for media that are interactive, the perceived trustworthiness of the medium is likely to play an especially important role in determining its influence on consumers.

Although trust has long been recognized as an extremely important element of every interaction (Dwyer, Schurr, & Oh, 1987), traditional advertising media provide the marketer with limited ability to raise the level of consumers' trust because one-way communication is unlikely to produce trust (Mayer et al., 1995). Reciprocal interaction, communication, and cooperation, however, facilitate trust building and commitment (Anderson & Weitz, 1989; Anderson & Narus, 1990). Hoffman, Novak, and Peralta (1999) noted that consumers do not trust most Internet marketers enough to engage in "relationship exchanges" involving money and personal information.

Trust is a subjective evaluation of another entity's characteristics based on limited information (Beccera & Gupta, 1999). In the context of marketing, limited information about products' attributes and the intent of the marketer to provide a fair transaction can give rise to the need for consumers either to trust the marketer, rely on third parties for additional information, or take other actions to reduce risk. Consumers' trust toward a marketer can be defined broadly as the subjective probability with which consumers believe that the marketer will perform a particular interaction in a manner consistent with their expectations. Although it is generally agreed that trust has an economic value (Hill, 1990) and can be a source of competitive advantage (Barney & Hansen, 1994), traditional advertising has not necessarily been focused on building trust, despite the fact that trust has an important influence on the behavior of consumers (Schurr & Ozanne, 1985). On the other hand, interactive media have the potential to promote consumers' trust toward the advertiser and product through reciprocal information exchange, customer support and technical assistance, reciprocal communication, operational linkages, and other specific adaptations by the marketer to the needs of the consumer (Forrest & Mizerski, 1996).

It is certainly clear that audiences have different perceptions of and attitudes toward different media. Knowing that consumers of various media perceive them differently and have different attitudes toward them still does not tell us how people interact with a given medium or how this interaction influences response. Chook (1983) made just this point when he stated that "the attitudinal approach is simple and relatively inexpensive, but at the same time is one that raises a number of critical questions. For one thing, measures of media interest, confidence, and enjoyment have no proven bearing on the performance of advertising. For another, such measures are too generalized for application to specific types of advertising" (p. 250).

Uses of Mass Media

In a broader sense, media effects may be considered in the context of the stream of research examining uses and gratifications individuals obtain from using mass media. This paradigm holds that social and psychological needs generate expectations of the mass media, which lead to differential patterns of exposure, need gratification, and other outcomes (Rubin, 1986; Atkin, 1985; Katz, Blumler, & Gurevitch, 1974). Although this research approach has been criticized on many grounds (see O'Guinn & Faber, 1991), the notion that people have uses for and obtain gratifications from exposure to marketing communications in different media is appealing. There is also some empirical support for the notion. For example, research has found that "social utility" motives influence the viewing of commercials on television. O'Guinn and Faber (1991) suggest that uses and gratification approaches may be most usefully applied to media such as special-interest magazine readership.

Evidence for different uses and gratifications from mass media is seen in studies of differential loyalty among consumers of media types and vehicles. In addition, there are selective patterns of exposure or preferential attitudinal dispositions toward certain kinds of media and vehicles within media that are not constant across all viewers (Gunter, 1985). How people think and feel about various vehicles or the extent to which the audience flows toward or across certain programs varies between demographic divisions of the population. More significant, however, are findings that indicate differences in viewing patterns or attitudinal preferences for programs associated with enduring psychological characteristics of viewers (Gunter, 1985).

The Role of Selective Exposure. There is also strong evidence that people selectively attend to information based on its relevance to them at a given point in time (Broadbent, 1977; Greenwald & Leavitt, 1984; Krugman, 1988; Pechmann & Stewart, 1988; Tolley, 1991). Research is rather clear on the point that characteristics of consumers directly influence media effects. For example, in her review of consumer processing of advertising, Thorson (1990) identifies such individual difference factors as motivation (involvement), ability, prior learning, and emotion, among others, that influence how, and even whether, consumers process advertising. The theoretical foundation for these effects is *selective exposure:* the proposition that consumers tend to see and hear communications that are favorable, congenial, or consistent with their predispositions and interests (Zillmann & Bryant, 1994).

For our purposes, the key issue is whether these findings are in some way related to the effectiveness of marketing communications in different media. It may be that the effects of commercial messages will differ substantially depending on the use a particular consumer is making of a given medium. For example, readers of certain publications and viewers of certain programs indicate that advertising content is an important reason for selecting a given vehicle, and in some cases is the sole reason for using a particular medium. On the other hand, it is likely that some commercial messages will not even gain an individual's attention, if they are inconsistent with the individual purpose in using a mass medium (i.e., they may spoil the mood, distract from the flow). Evidence on these hypotheses stems from research on the concept of "involvement," which we address next.

Involvement

The concept of involvement has become a key construct in a number of theories of attitude formation and change (see Chaiken, 1980; Chaiken, Liberman, Eagly, 1989; Greenwald & Leavitt, 1984; Petty & Cacioppo, 1986). Involvement has generally been conceptualized in terms of how consumers interact with a given medium or message. Messages and media are conceived of as more or less involving for a particular consumer, and such involvement is posited to influence the amount and type of information processing in which a consumer engages. Involvement has also been one of the more frequently researched and controversial constructs within the disciplines of social psychology, advertising, and communication (see Zaichowsky, 1985). One problem with an examination of the research on the effects of involvement is the lack of a generally accepted definition for the construct. Researchers have used the term to mean a number of distinctly different things. For example, Schwerin (1958) defined involving programs as "tense" programs. Kennedy (1971) defined involvement as interest in the program storyline, whereas Soldow and Principe (1981) interpreted involvement as suspense. More recently, Thorson et al. (1985) used liking for a television program and an assessment of cortical arousal as measures of involvement.

Related to these differences in the operationalization of the involvement construct is the issue of where to measure involvement. Marketing researchers have defined involvement in terms of the medium (or specific vehicle), in terms of the message, and in terms of the product that is the focus of the message. It is likely that the general inconsistency of research findings regarding involvement is due to differences in the way involvement has been defined and operationalized across studies (see Singh & Hitchon, 1989, for a review of this literature). With these caveats in mind, research in this area has yielded important findings on media effects.

In early work on the subject, Krugman (1965, 1966) posited the concept of involvement to counter the prevalent model of mass communications effects in the late 1950s and early 1960s, the so-called transactional model. In contrast to the earlier "hypodermic needle" or "bullet" model that posited strong communications effects, the essential notion of the transactional model is that mass media effects are quite limited. Individual characteristics, attitudes, experiences, and predispositions all mediate mass media effects. As some have put it, the conceptual shift was to change the focus from "what media do to people," to "what people do to mass media." Contemporary versions of the transactional model are still popular among attitude researchers today under the general rubric of cognitive response theory.

Cognitive response theory posits that the receivers of communications actively process information as it is received by generating thoughts (Greenwald, 1968). Cognitive response theory, of which there are a number of variations, suggests that people are not so much persuaded by communication as they persuade themselves through their own idiosyncratic thoughts in response to communications. The best-known cognitive response theory in advertising research is the elaboration likelihood model (ELM) associated with Petty and Cacioppo (1986). ELM posits a number of specific characteristics of receivers of communication that influence the likelihood of cognitive response (hence the name, elaboration likelihood). The two characteristics that have received the most attention from researchers are the ability of the receiver to use the information and the involvement of the receiver.

Krugman suggested that early transaction models were flaws because mass media "effects" are most often viewed as attitude changes regarding important issues—the focus of most empirical research in the area. Krugman argued that people are much less involved with content of marketing communications, especially in what he called "low-involvement" media, such as television. Cognitive response theory has not, by any means, ignored low-involvement situations. It suggests that there are differences between high-involvement and low-involvement situations. The underlying cognitive response mechanism is the same in both situations, however. What is hypothesized to differ is the content of the thoughts elicited by the communication. More-involving situations elicit more thoughts directly related to the message, whereas less-involving situations elicit more thoughts related to such nonmessage cues as source expertise, liking for the source, and so forth. In both high- and low-involvement circumstances the message recipient is viewed as an active information processor. What changes as a function of involvement is the nature of the information attended and processed.

Several studies have specifically examined the effect of various kinds of involvement on responses to marketing communication. Lloyd and Clancy (1989) and Audits and Surveys (1986) report large-scale studies that demonstrate that more highly involving media (i.e., print) are better vehicles for delivering product messages. This is true regardless of whether the measure of effectiveness of communication is recall, persuasion, or message credibility. Buchholz and Smith (1991) investigated the effect of the interaction of involvement and type of medium on a variety of measures. For these authors, involvement is a situational variable, which they induced by instructions that either directed respondents to pay careful attention to an ad or to pay attention to material surrounding the advertisement of interest. Their research demonstrated that in high-involvement situations message recipients were equally likely to process and remember advertising messages embedded in radio and television commercials. Under high-involvement situations, message recipients tended to generate more thoughts, and especially personally relevant thoughts, about the commercial message. In low-involvement situations, television, with its dual-channel input (audio and visual) was the superior medium. Cognitive responses and the number of personally relevant connections were substantially reduced in the low-involvement situation. Television was nonetheless superior to radio in low-involvement circumstances.

In sum, the involvement notion is an important one for the present topic because it has formed the basis for research that attempts to directly compare media effects. In general, findings show that media differ in the extent to which they invite different kinds of attentiveness and information processing of advertising. Additionally, despite the ambiguity of the construct, research has directly examined the complex interactions between effects of the medium itself, viewer characteristics, products, and, perhaps, the situation in which the communication occurs.

Mood

The term *mood* denotes specific subjective feeling states at the time of exposure to a marketing communication. A rather substantial body of research makes it quite clear that mood influences an array of psychological processes—attention, information processing, decision making, memory, and attitude formation. Srull (1990), Isen (1989), and Gardner (1985) provide reviews of much of this work and its implications for advertising and consumer behavior. Conceptually related to "uses and gratifications" research, discussed earlier, the concept of mood and the related construct of arousal focus on affective, rather than cognitive, factors that link individuals with media. The essential idea is that people use media to maintain or change feeling states (moods) or excitatory states (arousal). Self-report data suggest that people use television to both increase and decrease arousal (Condry, 1989), and physiological studies have shown that television viewing can alter blood pressure, heart rate, and other physiological states that presumably reflect arousal states (Klebber, 1985).

There is certainly evidence that moods induced by television programs interact with commercials embedded within these programs to produce differential responses among viewers. For example, Kennedy (1971) found viewers of suspense programs had poorer recall of a brand name in an embedded commercial than viewers of a comedy. However, attitudes toward the advertised brand were more positive among viewers of the suspense program than among viewers of a comedy. Similar results for recall are reported by Soldow and Principe (1981). Goldberg and Gorn (1987) found that, compared to commercials viewed in the context of a sad program, commercials viewed in the context of a happy television program resulted in happier moods during viewing of both the program and commercials, more positive cognitive responses about the commercials, and higher evaluations of commercial effectiveness. They also found that the mood induced by the program had a greater effect on commercials with a greater emotional appeal than commercials with more informational appeals. These investigators did not examine whether there was an interaction between the emotional tone of the commercials and the programs in which they were embedded.

The potential interaction of the emotional tone of commercials and programs was investigated by Kamins, Marks, and Skinner (1991). They find that a "sad" commercial embedded within a "sad" program was rated by viewers as more likeable and produced higher ratings of purchase intention than a humorous commercial embedded within a "sad" program. Conversely, a humorous commercial embedded within a humorous program performed better than a humorous commercial embedded within a "sad" program. The authors interpret these results in terms of consistency theory, which suggests that viewers seek to maintain a mood throughout a program. Because commercials represent interruptions, Kamins et al. (1991) suggest that commercials that are more consistent in emotional tone with the program will perform better than those that are inconsistent in tone.

In an earlier study, Krugman (1983) also examined the relationship between responses to advertising and the programming context. Although he did not explicitly address the question of mood, his hypotheses reflect processes that would seem to be conceptually related to the construct of mood: he tested the convention wisdom that "commercials are particularly objectionable when they interrupt interesting programs." Thus, some reasoned, "the more interesting the program, the less effective the commercial" (Soldow & Principe, 1981, p. 60). Krugman first distinguishes between viewer opinion and impact on viewers as separate phenomena. Then he examines the impact of advertising in 56 television programs that were determined to vary in interest level. He finds a pattern that is just the reverse of the conventional wisdom: commercials interrupting interesting programs are more effective. This is consistent with Krugman's earlier hypothesis that involvement with advertising tends to be consistent with interest in the editorial environment. Although this study does not make comparisons with other media and the notion of interest relates as much to message variables as it may relate to media effects, the finding is indicative of the importance of the media viewing context as a mediator of advertising effects.

Finally, a major field experiment (Yuspeh, 1977) examined the programming context as a determinant of responses to television advertising. This time, the programming context was manipulated by having viewers watch either situation comedies or action programs. No explanatory concepts are offered to suggest what it is about the different programming types that might account for different effects, but the implicit idea seems to be that linkage between programming stimuli and advertising responses is attributable to variations in mood or excitatory states experienced while watching (Yuspeh, 1977). Individuals were asked to watch particular programs (experimentally manipulated so that half watched three action programs and half watched three situation comedies). Commercials for six products were embedded in the programs, and effects were measured with multiple indicators, such as brand recall, attitudes and buying intention, and commercial element playback. Interestingly, there were only slight differences between the two types of programming contexts on commercial effectiveness. However, there were significant differences among specific episodes with each program type and across products and performance measures. It appears that different episodes of the same program may have different effects on the performance of commercials appearing in those programs. It is likely that such an effect is the outcome of a complex set of interactions between program type, advertising message, and viewer characteristics, especially programming-induced moods.

None of the studies that explore the relationship between programming context and advertising response clarify whether the effects of prior moods differ from programming-induced moods. Nor is it clear whether the types of mood effects that occur in a television context occur in other media, although it is certain that other media are capable of creating or changing moods (Gardner, 1985; Isen, 1989).

Interactivity

Within the last few years, a new form of marketing communications has emerged. This new form of communication is predominantly electronic, but it has many of the characteristics of other forms of communication: (a) it can be interactive, but without the human touch of personal selling, (b) it provides the opportunity for direct response from and to the consumer, (c) it allows mass communication among consumers without the marketer's intervention, and (d) it shares some of the characteristics of print and broadcast advertising, at least with respect to the more-traditional advertising that appears on it (banner ads, e-announcements). Cutler (1990) defined the "new media" as media that provide the capability to instantaneously advertise, execute a sale, and collect payment. With the advent of the Internet and other technologies (interactive Web technologies, streaming media, wireless devices, interactive TV, etc.), these new media go well beyond these basic capabilities to allow a more-comprehensive interaction between consumers and marketers and among consumers (Anderson, 1996). Therefore, perhaps the most interesting and novel attribute of the new media is their capability for *interactivity*, which is becoming increasingly more pronounced with the infusion of more-advanced communication media.

Using interactive media, consumers can collect and provide information by searching and navigating through commercial Web sites, interact with marketers through interactive Web-based software and mobile telephones, post and customize their preferences, communicate with other consumers and product and service providers, and conduct transactions anytime from anywhere. Similarly, marketers can use information obtained from consumers to customize their messages, segment their audiences, facilitate consumer search for selected types of information and products, and collect information about consumers' preferences to improve future products and services. Moreover, marketers can potentially provide consumers with a more enjoyable and informative experience by offering such services as personalized information, live messaging and entertainment, and quick customer service and technical support through e-mail, "smart" Web sites, live operators, streaming media, and videoconferencing. Thus, interactive media provide new capabilities (Burke, 1997) not found in more-traditional media.

The notion of interactivity has tended to be associated primarily with the Internet, but this is a limiting conceptualization in an era that is providing increasing opportunities for interactivity through a variety of different media ranging from interactive television to mobile telephones. Moreover, the concept of interactivity will strongly influence the conceptualization and practice of relationship marketing (Thirkwell, 1997) and change the way marketers think about communication. Leckenby and Li (2000) define interactive advertising as the presentation and promotion of products, services, and ideas by an identified sponsor through mediated means, involving mutual interaction between consumers and marketers.

The use of interactive media also draws attention to the theoretical differences between traditional conceptualizations on advertising and its applications to today's marketplace. Traditional approaches to advertising practice and research have implicitly assumed that advertising is something the marketer does *to* the consumer. In contrast, interactive advertising makes it clear that what advertising does to the consumer is only one limited dimension of advertising, highlighting the need to understand what consumers do to advertising (Cross & Smith, 1995) and how interactive media affect this two-way interaction. The reasons consumers seek, self-select, process, use, and respond to information are critical for understanding interactive marketing communication. Moreover, communication among multiple consumers over interactive media (e.g., portals, chat rooms) has the potential to alter the way consumers respond to marketers' communications. Interactive media of various types not only open new opportunities for communication with and among consumers (Spalter, 1996), they also create opportunities for creating new measures of consumer response to such communications, as well as to product offerings and other marketing initiatives. Interactive media highlight the importance of the consumer in marketing communication.

Benefits of Interactive Media. Interactive media will soon achieve the reach of television, the selectivity of direct marketing, and the richness of interaction rivaled only by an expert salesperson (Braunstein & Levine, 2000). Interactive media combine the dynamic delivery of broadcast media to send targeted streaming ad messages to consumers, while attracting new audiences that may not respond to traditional noninteractive media. Moreover, interactive media can offer communications that provide consumers with the ability to complete a transaction instantaneously (McKenna, 1997), while simultaneously monitoring results, analyzing consumer preferences, and adjusting the message and promotions to increase performance. This allows advertisers to target advertisements to consumers with different content type based on past online behavior, geographical location, and demographic information. Keeney (1999) has suggested a variety of ways in which the Internet might create value for consumers. These include minimizing errors in transactions, lowering costs of products and services, designing optimal products or product bundles, minimizing shopping time, and increasing the enjoyment of shopping, among others. These outcomes are undoubtedly valuable to consumers; nevertheless, the effects of interactive advertising go well beyond cost and convenience benefits to include satisfaction, customization, participation and involvement, better understanding and decision quality, and mutual confidence and trust.

By using interactive media, marketers can create profiles of consumers by either direct self-reporting or by tracking behavior. Consumers can also generate their own profile preferences, provided they see a benefit from doing this. For example, Mypoints.com (www.mypoints.com) promises to send personalized messages to consumers for products and services they care about if they reveal their preferences. In this sense, consumers receive value by learning about goods they are interested in on a timely manner. Apart from self-reporting, data mining is a powerful approach that allows marketers to learn about consumer preferences by tracking patterns of behavior such as the clickstream and purchase history data. For example, "cookies" are widely used software programs that keep track of consumers' Web behavior. Therefore, depending on the "expertise" of the system, Web tracking helps marketers learn more about their consumers and improve and target their messages and product offerings. Interactive advertising can also act as a "product simulator," providing a substitute for physical on-site selling. As bandwidth limitations become less restrictive, marketers can advertise their products by employing virtual showrooms where consumers can view products in 360-degree views. Furthermore, "live consultation" can also by employed by the power of interactive media that can help marketers respond to consumer inquiries in a manner similar to live consultation without employing human salespeople. In sum, interactive advertising offers a variety of benefits to both consumers and marketers, enabling a better and more fruitful interaction among consumers and marketers (Wikstrom, 1996).

Although interactive media may never achieve the human touch of personal interaction and might not translate the tone and body language of an expert salesperson, they can still offer an opportunity for a form of personal selling, one-to-one marketing (Burke, 1997). Because the interactive media can provide customized solutions to mass markets, they may enable marketing communication to enter areas where the "high touch" of a human salesperson is required. Indeed, Stewart, Frazier, and Martin (1996) argue that the Internet is merging traditional advertising and personal selling into a new integrated form of marketing communication. According to Lovelock (1996), interactive media can establish a channel of communication among consumers and marketers and give rise to better relationships. Customized and personalized media also have the potential to improve customer service after the sale (Berry, 1987, 1995; Peterson, Balasubramanian, & Bronnenberg, 1997).

The concept of "build-to-order" products is a possible consequence of employing interactive media. For example, Helper and MacDuffie (2000) proposed a hypothetical scenario where consumers can actively participate in a form of personal selling through interactive media to order custom-configured automobiles. In addition, *automatic replenishment* is a form of one-to-one marketing where the consumer is automatically notified about reordering new products. Automatic replenishment can be considered as another form of personal selling that adds value to the consumer experience, brings back existing customers, delivers new sales, and enhances customer relationships. Interactivity is a key element for the success of automatic replenishment because this form of advertising needs a customer-marketer relationship.

Despite such enormous possibilities arising from the use of interactive media in advertising, e-mail communication is still the most common form of personal selling using interactive media. For example, coolsavings.com (www.coolsavings.com) sends personalized e-mails to targeted consumers asking them to visit a site and purchase certain products. The ability to reach individual users immediately and reliably without significant costs makes e-mail communication more efficient than the traditional letter, telephone, or even broadcast medium. Consumers are also more likely to respond to e-mail offers that are personalized to their interests than to the mass media.

Interactive media can replace personal selling when the marketer knows enough about the consumer to provide knowledgeable and personalized ad messages. Although marketers could ideally use any information to benefit the consumer in terms of tailoring a message based on the consumers' preferences, collecting personal information could practically result in an invasion of the consumers' privacy. Online profiling is the practice of collecting information, often secretly, about consumers' Web-surfing habits and other personal purchasing preferences. One of the unique dimensions of the Internet is anonymity; hence, consumers are rightfully concerned over privacy of their personal information gathered by marketers during their Web surfing. Whereas Web tracking can have an enormous potential for marketers, concerns over loss of the consumer's privacy may hinder the marketers' efforts to understand consumers better. Similar to traditional forms of personal selling, interactive advertising can achieve a legitimate one-to-one communication when consumers are intentionally seeking such interaction.

Word-of-Mouth Communication in Interactive Media. Word-of-mouth (WOM) communication has long been regarded as the most credible, unbiased, and effective form of marketing communication (Cafferky, 1996; Hoyer & MacInnis, 2001; Kiely, 1993; Rosen, 2000). Many Internet portals allow consumers to actively communicate through e-mail group discussions, message boards, and chat rooms without marketer intervention, providing a viable form of mass WOM communication. Whereas consumers have always had the ability to spread information to other consumers (word of mouth), this "pass-it-on" phenomenon has become a prominent use of the new interactive media. For example, the term *viral marketing* describes the fact that consumers spread a marketers' message to other consumers with little or no effort by a marketer. For example, Web sites offering virtual greeting cards (e.g., www.bluemountain.com) spread information about the availability of such cards when consumers send each other greeting cards.

A new venue for third-party-driven forms of interactive communication has emerged among interactive media. Independent portals such as yahoo.com (www.yahoo.com) host virtual communities, message boards, chat rooms, and e-mail group discussion, which offer convenient ways to connect consumers who share the same interests and ideas. For example, eGroups.com (www.egroups.com) is an e-mail group service that allows consumers to easily create and join e-mail groups. This provides a form of dynamic WOM communication among millions of consumers. Although WOM communication is usually not marketer driven, advertisers can monitor and perhaps influence what information is communicated among consumers. Monitoring WOM communication in public venues not only does not violate consumer privacy, it can also provide valuable information about what information consumers find most important. Rather than copiously track consumer preferences, marketers can use publicly available information to understand how consumers form their preferences. Moreover, marketers can influence WOM communication by "seeding" sites (Rosen, 2000). In sum, consumer-to-consumer communication over interactive media can provide a form of dynamic WOM communication that can complement marketer-driven communications.

The availability of interactive media on a large scale is a very recent phenomenon. Thus, the full implications of these media in the context of marketing communications remain to be identified and explored. Nevertheless, interactivity fundamentally changes the nature of marketing communication. The traditional paradigm in marketing practice and research implicitly has assumed that communication is something the marketer does to the consumer. As we have pointed out, this is a very limited view. The traditional paradigm for research on marketing communication has served the profession well, but it is incomplete in an increasingly interactive context (Pavlou & Stewart, 2000). The future of interactive communication highlights the need for a new paradigm that focuses on what consumers do to marketing communications and how they respond to it. The focus of this new paradigm must also be the consumers' active participation in marketing communication, not merely their responses to it (Roehm & Haugtvedt, 1999).

This new paradigm requires that research on the influence and effects of marketing communications shift from a focus on outcomes to a focus on both processes and outcomes. The role of the consumer in selecting opportunities for communication, in choosing when and how to interact (if at all), and the goals and purposes of consumers involved in the interaction will be especially important dimensions of marketing communications that will require new measures and new conceptualizations of how communication works. It is also likely that as the marketing mix becomes increasingly integrated and the same vehicles assume multiple functions (communication, distribution, etc.), it will become increasingly difficult to conduct relevant research on marketing communications without consideration of the larger context of the full marketing mix. In addition, the consumers' use of other information sources, especially the consumers' interaction with other consumers, will be important for understanding how and why consumers respond as they do to marketing communications.

MEDIA CONTEXT AS A MEDIATOR OF THE INFLUENCE OF MARKETING COMMUNICATIONS

In the broadest sense, the five consumer characteristics discussed to this point form a complex context for media exposure. That is, attitudes toward media types and vehicles, uses and gratifications from media, involvement, mood states motivating and characterizing media use, and interactivity all form the context that influences consumers' decisions about whether or not to attend to particular media and consumers' cognitive and affective states while attending to media. However, a few studies focus more on media stimuli themselves than on consumer characteristics that determine communication effects in different media. We refer to these studies as focusing on the "media context." Studies in this area seek to explain relatively immediate outcomes of exposure to advertising, such as cognitive responses, attention behavior, and physiological responses, in terms of exposure to different media types. Other studies examine long-term responses to advertising as a function of frequency and timing of exposure, and these will be reviewed in the next section.

Krugman's involvement construct, discussed earlier, suggests that the inherent characteristics of media, in addition to consumer characteristics and product characteristics, interact in order to determine one's "involvement" with media. Terms such as *hot* (broadcast media) or *cool* (print media), however, do not tell us much about particular media characteristics that may be functionally related to different effects on individuals. A first question is whether the media context affects consumer responses to marketing communications, and, if so, what is the nature of these responses? Research that addresses these questions falls into several types: studies of cognitive response, observational studies, studies employing physiological measures, studies of "priming," and research on the mediating effects of various situational or environmental factors.

Cognitive Response.   A classic study by Wright (1973) examined the interaction of media and receiver involvement on a range of cognitive responses. Drawing heavily on previous research in psychology, Wright argued that individuals may experience an array of responses when exposed to marketing communications, and the nature and intensity of these responses is directly related to degree of involvement. These cognitive responses include counterarguments, source derogation, support arguments, and, in other research, "connections"—a construct very similar to Krugman's discussion of "bridging" that may occur, as individuals relate what they see in advertising to some aspect of their personal lives.

Wright was interested in the mediating role these cognitive response variables might play in determining consumer responses to marketing communications in different media, under different involvement conditions. Receiver involvement was manipulated by telling some subjects they would have to make a short-term decision after viewing advertising for a new soybean-based product (high involvement). Other subjects were not told of the impending decision (low involvement). Messages were transmitted by either audio means, similar to radio advertising, or by print means, similar to newspaper or magazine advertising. Wright found significantly more total cognitive responses, less source derogation, and more support arguments for a print version of an advertisement than for a radio version. Although acceptance of the ad message was not affected by the medium, buying intention was higher for the print condition than for the radio condition. In addition to the immediately measured cognitive response activity, delayed responses were elicited two days later; among the more highly involved subjects, supportive responses to the radio ad increased, but not for the print ad. Initially, the rapid transmission rate of broadcast media, compared to the more audience-controlled input of print, probably inhibits both the amount and variability of response activity. Over time, relatively more opportunity exists for increases in cognitive responses to broadcast media; the responses may, in turn, be related to different amounts of persistence of attitude change and behavior.

Observational Studies. Other studies also directly examine consumer responses while viewing marketing communications in different media contexts. Although Wright examined self-reports of cognitive responses while viewing marketing communications in different media, some researchers have examined actual behaviors while attending to media. For example, Ward, Levinson, and Wackman (1972) and Anderson and his colleagues (Bryant & Anderson, 1983), among others, examined actual behavior while watching television. Tolley (1991) used a unique lamplike device to unobtrusively track the eye movements of readers of newspapers. Rothschild and others (Rothschild & Hyun, 1990; Rothschild, Hyun, Reeves, Thorson, & Goldstein, 1988) have measured physiological responses among individuals exposed to television commercials. Unfortunately, most of these behavioral studies do not compare responses across media, unlike Wright's study, which compared responses to print and audio advertising.

In the Ward et al. research, mothers observed one of their children watching television and coded attention behavior. Results show a great deal of activity while watching television generally, ranging from not attending to the television set at all to full attention. During strings of commercials, children's attention initially increased when commercials interrupt programming but decreased steadily over the "pod" of commercials. Interestingly, there was some tendency for attention to increase later in commercial pods, apparently because children anticipate the return of programming. Bryant and Anderson's (1983) work has sought to identify those attributes of television programs that attract the attention of children. Attention was operationalized as visual selection, that is, the time the child's eyes were directed toward the television screen. Program characteristics most likely to draw attention to the television screen included movement, high levels of physical activity, and auditory changes in the program. Such findings have not been lost on the creators of children's advertising. Most such advertising routinely includes those elements that draw attention. Simply focusing on a television screen does not, however, assure that information is processed by the viewer.

Tolley (1991) found that readers of newspapers scan pages to decide whether and to what they will attend. Most individual newspaper pages received virtually no attention. Debriefings with readers suggested that they were using the quick scan as a means for identifying those items, editorial matter, ads, and so forth that were personally relevant. Such findings are consistent with research that suggests a preattentional process exists that acts to filter irrelevant information and helps the individual determine those environmental elements for which information processing is worth the effort (Broadbent, 1977; Greenwald & Leavitt, 1984). Tolley also observed that individuals appear to have consistent, but idiosyncratic, styles of reading.

Physiological Measures. Rothschild et al. examined physiological (EEG: electroencephalographic) responses of individuals watching television commercials and examined the relationship between EEG responses and memory for components of TV commercials (Rothschild & Hyun, 1990). They found significant EEG activity during commercial exposure and some differences in hypothesized directions for greater dominance by one brain hemisphere or the other. The latter is the topic of "hemispheric lateralization," referring to specialization of the right and left sides of the brain in information processing (Hellige, 1990). Some advance the idea that the right side of the brain is "better" at processing stimuli such as pictures and music, whereas the left side of the brain is better at processing words and numbers.

Priming. Another stream of research on the effects of media context has examined the degree to which media "prime" attention to specific elements of advertising and other types of marketing communications (Herr, 1989; Higgins & King, 1981; Wyer and Srull, 1981; Yi, 1990a, 1990b). Research in contexts other than advertising (Berkowitz & Rogers, 1986) suggests the presence of such an effect. The notion of priming suggests that the media context may predispose an individual to pay more attention to some elements of a communication message than others and may influence the interpretation that a viewer gives a complex or ambiguous stimulus. For example, the presence of an older model in an advertisement could be interpreted in terms of maturity, experience, conservatism, sophistication, steadfastness, or any of a number of other more- or less-positive attributes. Depending on the product, some of these interpretations would be more desirable to the marketer than others. For a perfume product, associations of experience and sophistication might be appropriate, whereas conservatism and steadfastness would be less appropriate (though they might be appropriate for a different "product" such as a bank). The media context might serve to prime one or more of these interpretations. For example, if the advertising were embedded in a program about a sensuous older woman, the associations elicited by an older female model in an ad might well include sophistication and experience.

On the other hand, if the program in which the advertising was embedded dealt with the struggle of an older woman to adjust to a near fatal illness, rather different associations might be elicited.

Several empirical studies demonstrate that such priming does occur. Further, this priming may occur for both cognitive and affective responses. For example, Yi (1990a) showed that a media context that emphasized one particular interpretation of an automobile attribute (size) resulted in greater salience for the primed interpretation. Similar effects have also been identified in other studies (Yi, 1990b; Herr, 1989) and are consistent with Wyer and Srull's (1981) model of cognitive accessibility and with recent research on framing effects (Bettman & Sujan, 1987). Yi (1990a) also demonstrated affective priming. Affective priming is a type of mood effect in that a mood is induced by the media context, in contrast to a mood that the individual brings to the medium. Yi found that the more positive the tone of the editorial matter, the more effective the ad (as measured by attitude toward the brand and purchase intention). He further demonstrated that this effect appeared to be mediated by more positive attitudes toward the ad.

Research on priming has generally assumed that priming is unidirectional, that is, that the effect is induced by media context in response to a message. This is probably not an unreasonable assumption under most circumstances, given the embeddedness of commercials within the more dominant media environment. It may be possible for the effect to work in the opposite direction, however, with a commercial (say prior to the beginning of a television program) serving to prime response to the medium. Another related question is the degree to which advertisements in the same medium or the same "pod" of commercials (or page in a magazine) might prime response to other advertisements. The role of priming in an interactive media context also poses an array of interesting questions. For example, the context in which a banner ad occurs on a Web site may influence both the propensity to respond to the ad as well as the nature of the response that follows.

EFFECTS OF MEDIA SCHEDULING

Evidence suggests that there are different effects of marketing communication in different media, depending on media scheduling, that is, how often individuals are exposed to advertising in a given time frame (frequency and repetition effects). Pechmann and Stewart (1988), after reviewing the substantial literature on advertising wearout, suggest that three "quality" exposures to a communication are probably sufficient for a message to have its effect, but note that it may take many exposure opportunities to produce the effect of three quality exposures. This is because potential message recipients may elect not to attend to a message even when it is present or may see or hear only a portion of the total message. It is also likely that marketing communications for competing products, as well as marketing communication in general, may interfere with the processing of a commercial message at any given point in time.

Several studies tend to support the view that there are rapidly diminishing returns to repeated exposures. Blair (1987/1988) and Blair and Rabuck (1998) report tests of television commercials that demonstrate that increased spending on advertising (with a concomitant increase in the average number of exposures and gross rating points) in a market increased sales in those cases where the commercial scored well on a measure of persuasion. Spending differences seemed to make no difference when persuasion was low. In other words, if an ad was not persuasive to begin with, even an infinite number of exposures was insufficient to produce a response. More relevant to the current discussion is the finding that the persuasive effect of advertising took place quickly, and this effect was in direct proportion to the number of gross rating points purchased for the commercial. Further, once commercials had reached their targeted consumers, there was no further effect of additional exposures. Once consumers were exposed to the advertising and had been persuaded or not, that was the end of the matter. Consumers did not become "more persuaded" with additional exposures.

Blair's studies examined television advertising, whereas a study carried out in the early 1980s by Time Inc. (1981) in collaboration with Joseph E. Seagram & Sons, Inc., examined repetition and frequency effects of print advertising. Although this study was restricted to one product category, liquor, and only two magazines, *Time* and *Sports Illustrated*, the study was well controlled and extended over a 48-week period. The results found that measures of brand awareness, brand attitude, and willingness to buy increased sharply after the very first "opportunity to see" the advertising. All measures tended to level off, then remain constant, in the latter weeks of the campaign for brands that had a high level of awareness at the beginning of the campaign. However, for brands that began with a low level of initial awareness, all measures tended to show a steady increase over the 48 weeks of the campaign. The influence of greater advertising frequency was greater for low-awareness brands than for high-awareness brands. These results are consistent with a learning view of marketing communication (Pechmann & Stewart, 1988). Thus, it is useful to compare processes of learning and forgetting marketing communication with basic research in memory processes.

Learning and Memory Effects. Most studies of media scheduling on advertising effects examine recall and other variables (especially attitude change) as a function of the frequency of exposure and/or repetition of advertising stimuli. This is quite similar to the methods of research on the psychology of learning. One of the pioneers of learning research, Ebbinghaus (1902), identified three basic memory processes:

1. *A negatively accelerating forgetting curve*. After 20 minutes, Ebbinghaus observed that subjects forgot one-third of what was learned: after six days, about one-fourth, and a full month later, about one-fifth.
2. *Serial position effects*. Items at the beginning or end of a series were most easily learned: items in the middle were learned most slowly and forgotten most rapidly.
3. *Overlearning*. Overlearning or repetition beyond the point of repetition made very long conscious memory possible (for example, "Things go better with _____").

The processes of learning and forgetting marketing communications and marketing-related stimuli are considerably more complex than learning simple stimuli in the laboratory, of course. Consumer characteristics, such as prior experiences, shape these processes, as well as such communications factors as message characteristics and media effects. Nevertheless, much of the laboratory research on verbal learning and forgetting appears to generalize well to a marketing communications context. Unlike the laboratory setting, the marketing communications context provides less control over the frequency of repetition. Media in which marketing communications appear are often defined by their frequency of appearance—nightly news, monthly magazine, daily newspaper, or regularly updated Web pages. These characteristics of media limit the advertiser's flexibility for scheduling repetitions. Further, as noted earlier in this chapter, an exposure opportunity (the placement of a communication in a particular medium) is not the same as an actual exposure. It is likely that there are many more exposure opportunities than actual exposures to any particular marketing communication. This fact, coupled with the temporal characteristics of various media, create problems for the marketer that are not present in the laboratory. Thus, a considerable body of research has addressed the issue of scheduling.

Advertising Scheduling.   Strong (1974, 1977) examined the scheduling and repetition effects of print advertising and found that greater advertising recognition occurred when consumers were exposed to weekly intervals of magazine advertising than to monthly or daily intervals. Another "classic" study used direct mail advertising. Zielske (1959) found that repetition was very effective in increasing advertising recall, both when repetitions occurred over a relatively short period of time and when repetitions occurred in a "pulsed" fashion over 1 year. Shortly after the 13th exposure, 63% of the people who had been mailed ads weekly recalled some of the content, as did 48% of those receiving monthly ads. After the monthly ads stopped, that group showed decay of recall, similar to the negatively accelerating forgetting curve observed by Ebbinghaus. In a later study, Zielske and Henry (1980) demonstrated similar effects for television advertising. Ray and Sawyer (1971) found that the percentages of subjects recalling an ad increased from 27 to 74% as the number of repetitions increased from one to six. Although recognition and recall increased as the number of repetitions increased, there were diminishing returns: additional repetitions resulted in decreasing magnitudes of gains in recall and recognition. Similar results have been found by a number of other researchers (see Pechmann & Stewart, 1988, for a review of this research).

There may be circumstances in which repetitions have a negative effect on recall and recognition. When consumers have negative attitudes toward a product, increased repetitions may result in more negative attitudes. Negative effects may also result from very high levels of repetition, regardless of consumer attitudes due to irritation (Pechmann & Stewart, 1988). As in many other areas of communication research, most studies of media scheduling effects do not compare effects across various media, and they do not isolate media effects from interactions. Few longitudinal studies have been conducted that would provide a basis for definitive statements about repetition and frequency effects of advertising in different media. In addition, scheduling and repetition factors cannot be separated from message variables. Particularly compelling or particularly dreary messages may accelerate or hamper the kinds of results found in studies reviewed here. Greenberg (1988), for example, suggests that "critical images" in television programming may have profound affects, in contrast to the view that television effects occur slowly and incrementally. He calls these strong effects the "drench" hypothesis:

> The drench hypothesis, in its current, primitive form, asserts that critical images may contribute more to impression-formation and image-building than does the sheer frequency of television and behaviors that are viewed. The hypothesis provides an alternative to the no-effects hypothesis and to the view that the slow accretion of impressions cumulate across an indefinite time period. Finally, it also suggests that striking new images can make a difference—that a single character or collection of characters may cause substantial changes in beliefs, perceptions, or expectations about a group or a role, particularly among young viewers. (pp. 100–101)

Finally, the advent of interactive media creates new and interesting issues with respect to media scheduling. Much of the work on media scheduling to date revolves around the question of how best to reach consumers who may not be actively seeking information, at least at the time of message exposure. Increasingly, consumers are becoming active users of interactive media in the quest for information, products, and services. The rapid growth of interactive media and specific vehicles within these media (e.g., Web sites) confront the consumer with the need for assistance in finding the information they need. Thus, there is increasing reliance on such tools as search engines, portals, and virtual communities to locate sites and sources of additional information. Assuring prominence for an organization, product, or service within these tools has become the latest challenge in scheduling media.

In addition, consumers are increasingly integrating different media, making the use of some media complementary rather than substitutes for other media. For example, consumers have already begun to provide evidence that they have integrated the Internet experience into their broader media use. Almost half of all personal computers are in the same room as the television set, and simultaneous viewing of television and access to the Internet are common (Cox, 1998). Web site addresses are now common in television and print advertising. Traditional media now routinely encourage consumers to seek out additional information on Web sites or via telephone. These traditional media are not simply offering advertising that is extended to another media environment. Entertainment programs on broadcast media and editorial content in print media may refer consumers to additional information about the program or editorial content. However, the site of this additional information may include marketing communications that were not present in the original broadcast or print medium. In addition, outdoor advertising or voice yellow pages may refer users of mobile telephones to Web sites or telephone numbers that provide information or opportunities for product or service purchase. As consumers integrate their own use of various media, it will become more difficult to separate passive media from interactive media. Such integration will also raise interesting issues with respect to the scheduling of marketing communications in complementary media.

MEDIA-RELATED OUTCOMES OF EXPOSURE TO MARKETING COMMUNICATIONS

To this point, we have related results from a number of studies, focusing more on independent variables than on dependent variables. Our focus has been on the independent and joint effects of marketing communications in various media types and vehicles on a variety of outcomes. Selection of dependent variables in many of these studies have been driven by the interests of marketing, consumer, and advertising researchers. Therefore, dependent variables usually pertain to effects having to do with consumption, such as "hierarchy of communication" effects (McGuire, 1969) thought to lead up to purchase behavior, cognitive processes mediating advertising effects, and learning outcomes (effects on long- and short-term memory). These variables include various recognition and recall measures, measures of product knowledge, interest and attitude, and purchase intention and brand choice (see Stewart, Furse, & Kozak, 1983, and Stewart, Pechmann, Ratneshwar, Stroud, & Bryant, 1985, for a review of the use of these measures for assessing the effectiveness of advertising). In addition, traditional measures of the effects and effectiveness of marketing communication have tended to focus on the response of a relatively passive consumer responding to an action by a marketer. Although there has been recognition of a reciprocal relationship between marketer-driven communications and actions and consumer responses, this reciprocity has generally been safely ignored because it has occurred over very long time periods. The advent of interactive media has changed all of this and produced a need to reconsider how the effects and effectiveness of marketing communications are measured.

Measuring the Effectiveness of Marketing Communication

The rise of interactive media poses new and difficult challenges related to the measurement of the success of marketing communication. Traditional measures of advertising effectiveness, such as recall, attitude change, and brand choice, although still useful, are only a subset of the potential measures of the effectiveness of marketing communications employing interactive media (Pavlou & Stewart, 2000). These traditional measures focus on the influence of communication on the consumer, offering limited insight into what the consumer does to and with advertising. This perspective views marketing communication as a causal independent variable and the consumer's response as the dependent variable. The typical research paradigm involves a forced exposure to some marketing message followed by some measure of consumer response. Assuming that consumers interact with marketing messages, the simple relationship between the independent and the dependent variables becomes obsolete. Therefore, in the interactive media environment this relationship becomes reciprocal and contingent on a host of other factors. When consumers actively decide to interact, their actions become powerful determinants of response to marketing communication.

Whereas advertising in the interactive media can take many forms, the most common method has been the *display banner ad* that occupies a small portion on a computer monitor and that through clicking redirects the consumer to the marketer's own Web site. Whereas many studies have examined where ad banners should be located to increase click-through (see a summary at webreference.com 2000), a universal measure of effectiveness for this popular advertising form has not yet been established. Click-through is only one of many proposed measures of the effectiveness interactive communications. Another proposed measure of online advertising is the *eyeball* method, or the number of unique visits into a given Web site. An additional measure of the quality of online relationships is the metric of *stickiness*, or the length of time viewers remain attached to a marketer's Web site. In general, these metrics, like the measures of traditional media that preceded them, measure the quantity of viewing, not the quality. None of these measures has been widely adopted.

Fundamental to any discussion of interactive marketing communications is the question of how different it is from marketing communications using more traditional media. Although interactive media have been touted as more powerful, responsive, and customizable than traditional media (Port, 1999; Hoffman & Novak, 1996), the empirical evidence suggests that consumers respond to interactive advertising in the same ways they respond to advertising in more traditional media, at least with respect to traditional measures of advertising effectiveness. For example, Drèze and Hussheer (1999) found response to advertising on the Internet to be similar to response to advertising in other media, except that advertising on the Internet appeared to be easier to ignore. Similarly, Lynch and Ariely (2000) found that consumers are less price sensitive when providers on the Internet offer different rather than identical products, a finding that directly parallels findings in more-traditional retail settings.

Despite the potential importance of interactive media in the future, very few studies have examined the interactivity of marketers, consumers, and ad messages (Oh, Cho, & Leckenby, 1999). Rodgers and Thorson (2000) have proposed a new model for conceptualizing the ways in which users perceive and process online advertising, but little empirical research exists to inform such a model. Interactive media place the consumer at the center of the study of marketing communication because effectiveness of marketing communications in such media hinges not only on how the marketer's message influences the consumer but also on how the consumer shapes and responds to the message. Therefore, research on interactive media will need to focus on the consumer and the marketer in order to maximize the reciprocal gains of interaction and collaboration (Pavlou & Stewart, 2000). This will give rise to the need for measures of the effectiveness of marketing communication that go beyond traditional measures. These new measures will focus on process as well as outcome and are likely to include measures of effectiveness that have previously been regarded as mediating variables.

Involvement.   Consumer involvement refers to a subjective psychological state of the consumer and defines the importance and personal relevance that consumers attach to an advertisement. Although involvement has long been considered an important variable mediating the influence of communication, it has been poorly defined and operationalized, as previously noted. It has long been possible to obtain self-reports of consumers' involvement, but interactive media have the potential to provide a direct measure of consumers' involvement through examination of the frequency and type of interaction with the marketer. Interactive media can involve the consumer in the communication process in a significant way. Indeed, enhanced consumer involvement can be an important benefit arising from the use of interactive media. For example, many commercial Web sites focus on involving consumers in the communication process by allowing them to actively search and collect information. The amount of time spent on a particular interactive medium, as well as the frequency of return to the medium, may be particularly useful measures of consumer involvement.

Comprehension. Comprehension refers to the recall of the message intended by the marketer in response to a product category and brand cue (Stewart & Furse, 1986; Stewart & Koslow, 1989). For marketing communication to be effective, both the marketer and the consumer must mutually agree that the consumer has understood the message (Clark & Wilkes-Gibbs, 1986; Clark & Brennan, 1991). Given the anonymous and ambiguous nature of much of the marketing communication on the Internet and interactive shopping (Alba et al., 1997), consumers may have difficulty comprehending the messages of marketers and may not fully understand the true characteristics of a product. Thus, comprehension is a vital part of interactive marketing communication, as it is with communication involving more traditional media. Interactive media have the potential advantage of providing a means for obtaining measures of comprehension on a real-time basis.

Feedback. Feedback from the consumer to the marketer plays an important role in marketing and in business more generally, as the consumer should understand what the marketer intends, and the marketer should, in turn, adjust the message so that it is clearly understood. To the extent that marketing communication fails to elicit feedback of some type, it is by definition not interactive regardless of the marketer's intent and the medium used. Feedback of some type is an objective of most marketing communication, as sales and customer satisfaction are almost always an ultimate objective. Both sales and customer satisfaction have always been measures of business success. Interactive media have the potential to provide such measures of success (feedback) instantaneously.

Persuasion. Persuasion implies an attempt to move, affect, or determine a purchasing decision (Schwerin & Newell, 1981). Interactive marketing communication may be a far more powerful persuasive tool than communication using traditional advertising media because it provides opportunities to personalize information presentation, promote trust, identify objections and points in need of further clarification, and modify the offering itself, much as is the case of personal selling. Therefore, interactive media should further enhance the ability of the marketer to persuade. Indeed, Zigurs, Poole, and DeSanctis (1988) have proposed that the pattern of persuasive behavior should be different depending on the degree to which communication is interactive. For example, resistance to the adoption of new products and services is an especially significant obstacle faced by marketers. Interactive communication may well have the effect of decreasing resistance to new products (Lucas, 1974), by reducing the communication of irrelevant or unimportant features of the product, and by improving the consumers' understanding of the product (Robey & Farrow, 1982; Stewart, 1986). On the other hand, interactive media are likely to make much more obvious those consumers who are impervious to the persuasive efforts of marketers. This may prove to be a benefit to both consumers and marketers. Consumers may be spared unwanted communications, and marketers may find their communication efforts more effective when focused on consumers who regard the marketer's message as relevant to their needs.

Quality of Decisions. Consumer satisfaction, loyalty, and trust are likely to be by-products of the quality of consumers' decision. Lam (1997) has demonstrated that the quality of decisions is better for complex tasks when interactive communication is involved. As noted earlier, interaction with consumers can provide significant information about the nature of consumers' preferences with respect to products and product features. Such information can provide marketers with the opportunity to modify and improve future products and make better decisions regarding product features that consumers find most useful. Moreover, interactive media can promote marketers' learning about consumers' characteristics and preferences, which should, in turn, improve customer support, technical assistance, and future promotions. Therefore, an important effect of interactivity should be a better quality of decisions for future marketing communications and products by the marketer, even as it also improves the quality of decisions by consumers. This is a very important and distinctive characteristic of interactive communication. In addition, the satisfaction of consumers with the *experience* of communication and the subsequent purchase decision (or decision not to purchase) will also be especially important measures of the effectiveness of marketing communication.

Decision Efficiency. Prior research suggests that effective communication reduces the time required to make decisions (Short, Williams, &
Christie, 1976). Dennis, George, Jessup, Nunamaker, and Vogel (1988)
concluded that an important outcome of interactive technologies is a
reduction in the time required to reach to a decision. As noted earlier,
interactive media have the potential to combine the processes of advertising, transacting the sale, and collecting payment (Cutler, 1990).
Because all of these actions can be performed nearly simultaneously via
interactive media, the total time and effort required to communicate a
message and sell a product should be substantially reduced. Stated
somewhat differently, measures of efficiency are likely to be more important and more useful in the context of interactive media than for more
traditional media.

EMERGING ISSUES IN THE USE OF INTERACTIVE MEDIA

The emergence of interactive media and its adoption as a means for marketing communications highlight a variety of issues related to the characteristics and use of these media that are rather different from the issues
associated with the use of traditional media for marketing communications. Insofar as traditional media continue to play an important role in
marketing communications, and they will, issues related to media context
and media scheduling will continue to be relevant to marketers. These
issues are also important in the use of interactive media, but by definition,
interactive media provide consumers with much more control over both
the media context and the schedule with which they are exposed (or not
exposed) to marketing communications. On the other hand, there are
issues that are relevant to all media used for marketing communications
that are especially salient in the context of interactive media.

The Necessity of Content Management

Although interactive media can bring wealth of information, most of this
information may be irrelevant and meaningless to consumers (Wurman
2000). Tillman (1995) has observed that "within the morass of networked
data are both valuable nuggets and an incredible amount of junk" (p. 1).
Given consumers' limited capacity to process information and the enormous amount of information available through the new media, content
management will be of fundamental importance. According to Simon
(1957), a wealth of information creates a poverty of attention. There is
already a realization that interactive media, such as the Internet and
mobile communication, have had the effect of increasing consumers'
search costs (Stewart & Zhao, 2000). Web sites are growing faster than

they can be cataloged, and a variety of techniques and economic incentives now operate to increase the likelihood that a site will be cataloged and occupy a coveted position near the beginning of a list of sites identified by a search engine or portal.

Content management will play an especially important role in interactive marketing communications. Marketers will need to assure that consumers can readily identify sources of information and will focus on what customers want and need to learn (assuming these things may be delivered at a profit), rather than provide an abundance of unnecessary information. Relevant and clear content can accelerate consumers' decision-making process and facilitate transactions. Although relevance and clarity have always been important elements of traditional advertising, these elements become essential in interactive advertising. Two content management tools, dynamic content and data mining combined with collaborative filtering, already play important roles in increasing the efficacy of interactive media in marketing communications.

Dynamic Content. Dynamic content involves changing information over time and in response to interaction with the consumer. The availability of relevant new information and new offerings serves to attract consumers and increase involvement with an interactive medium. Personalization engines and document management solutions will play an especially important role in dynamic content management. In addition, combinations of media will play an ever more important role in marketing communications. Thus, e-mail or voice mail may be used to inform consumers of new information and offerings that are available in some other medium (e.g., Web site, physical store location).

Information portals are electronic intermediaries that allow marketers to send their advertising messages and consumers to either respond to them or communicate among themselves. For example, yahoo.com (www.yahoo.com) is a popular Internet information portal that draws many marketers and consumers. Information portals can be separated into *vertical* ones that focus on specific information or *horizontal* portals that deal with a variety of issues. Whereas messages through horizontal portals have the ability to reach the masses, vertical portals reach a targeted audience, which can integrate community building. According to Meckler (2000), the future of content management favors vertical focus and original content as consumers seek greater customization and personalization.

Data Mining and Collaborative Filtering. Interactivity provides opportunities for gathering enormous amounts of information about the behavior of consumers. Although the collection and use of such data raise a variety of issues related to consumer privacy, these data also provide opportunities for marketers to provide more personalized information and more customized assortments of products and services. Data mining tools provide a means for identifying patterns in the behavior within individual consumers and across groups of consumers that are far more specific than even the most sophisticated segmentation approaches in use today. The results obtained from data mining exercises may be combined with collaborative filtering to improve content management. Collaborative filtering is essentially a "recommendation engine" that provides consumers with suggestions about products and services that consumers with similar preferences have purchased. For example, Amazon.com (www.amazon.com) uses collaborative filtering to offer consumers information about "Customers who bought this book also bought."

Mobile Commerce: Anytime, Anyplace

The advent of mobile telephone and small wireless digital assistants provides new opportunities for marketing communication and new opportunities for consumers to obtain information when and where they need it. For consumers, these new devices offer the ability to access information on demand, for example, a list of French restaurants in an unfamiliar city. For marketers, these new devices provide an opportunity to communicate with consumers wherever the consumer might be. For example, a real estate agent might provide information about a specific house a potential purchaser is passing or an automobile manufacturer might provide information about the make of an automobile that the consumer sees in a parking lot. Such communications will tend to be more under the control of the consumer but not always. Using permission marketing, a marketer might provide a consumer with the opportunity to identify types of information or types of products about which the consumer wished to receive information. The consumer would then receive a telephone call, e-mail, or voice mail message when such information or products are available.

Mobile commerce will place new demands on marketers in terms of responsiveness. Consumers will want to obtain information when they need it, not at the convenience of the marketer. Indeed, the immediate availability of information may be the difference between a customer making a purchase or not. Rather than focusing on the scheduling of media in particular vehicles or time slots, as is the case with traditional media scheduling in advertising, the marketer will need to assure that information is available whenever and wherever the customer needs it.

THE FUTURE OF RESEARCH ON MEDIA INFLUENCE IN MARKETING COMMUNICATIONS

The media landscape is undergoing profound changes that are creating a need to rethink how marketing communications are managed. These changes are also giving rise to the need for a new and different paradigm for theory and research on the role of media in marketing communications. The very rapid increase in the media options available to consumers and the greater selectivity exercised by individual consumers with respect to these options means, on the one hand, that it will be more difficult to reach target audiences through traditional mass media. On the other hand, the increase in the number of media vehicles available to consumers and consumers' selectivity in using these vehicles may also provide more opportunities to reach precisely defined audiences with the "optimal" message for the medium and the media use occasion. Realizing this possibility requires several things: (a) a better understanding of how and when people use and interact with various media, (b) a better understanding of how the mode of interaction with various media influences the processing of commercial messages, and (c) a better understanding of how to create commercial messages and distribution strategies that are appropriate in the context of specific media uses. Note that what is needed is not a better understanding of *media* but a better understanding of how people interact with various forms of media and embedded commercial messages. Indeed, the increasing use of interactive media by marketers and consumers makes it critical to place the consumer at the center of any theory of marketing communications.

The linking pins between channels of communication and marketing outcomes are the factors that influence the individual's self-selection process and the dimensions of interaction with media. The goals and purposes of the users of media are primary determinants of media effects when users have options. Unfortunately, this is an area that still has received rather little attention from researchers (Becker & Schoenbach, 1989; Pavlou & Stewart, 2000; Stewart & Ward, 1994). We do not believe that this is the result of lack of theory to guide such research. Rather, it appears to be an artifact of the fact that, until recently, there were relatively few genuinely different media options available. In such situations, the behavior of individuals is restricted and largely dwarfed by such differences in media as do exist.

In closing, we suggest that there are numerous candidate theories for guiding future research on the use of media and subsequent effects on advertising response. Control theory (Powers, 1973, 1978), with its origins in human factors research and its emphasis on purpose as the link between stimulus inputs and behavioral outcomes, may be particularly appropriate given its emphasis on how people get things done. Bandura's (1986) notion of self-efficacy and Ajzen and Madden's (1986) work on goal-directed behavior are also potential candidates. In any case, theoretical approaches to future studies of "media effects" should surely focus on individual characteristics that determine media usage patterns, factors that influence interactivity, and dependent measures that reflect the diversity of outcomes that may arise when consumers are in control of their information environment.

REFERENCES

Aaker, D. A., & Brown, P. K., (1972, August). Evaluating vehicle source effects, *Journal of Advertising Research, 12,* 11–16.

Ajzen, I. & Madden, J.T. (1986). Prediction of goal-directed: Attitudes, intentions and perceived behavioral. *Journal of Experimental Social Psychology, 22,* 453–474.

Alba, J., Lynch, J., Weitz, B., Janiszewski, C., Lutz, R., Sawyer, A., & Wood, S. (1997, July). Interactive home shopping: Consumer, retailer, and manufacturer incentives to participate in electronic marketplaces. *Journal of Marketing, 61,* 38–53.

Anderson, C. (1996). Computer as audience, mediated interactive messages. In E. Forrest & R. Mizerski (Eds.), *Interactive marketing: The future present.* Chicago: American Marketing Association, NTC Business Books.

Anderson, E., & Weitz, B. (1989). Determinants of continuity in conventional industrial channel dyads, *Marketing Science, 8*(4), 310–323.

Anderson, E., & Narus, J. A. (1990). A model of distributor firm and manufacturer firm working partnership. *Journal of Marketing, 54*(1), 42–58.

Atkin, C. K. (1985). Informational utility and selective exposure to entertainment media. In D. Zillmann, & J. Bryant (Eds.), *Selective exposure to communication* (pp. 63–92). Hillsdale, NJ: Lawrence Erlbaum Associates.

Audits and Surveys, Inc. (1986). *A study of media involvement,* New York: Audits and Surveys.

Bandura, A. (1986). *Social foundations of thought and action: A social cognitive theory.* Upper Saddle River, NJ: Prentice Hall.

Barney, J. B., & Hansen, M. H. (1994). Trustworthiness as a source of competitive advantage. *Strategic Management Journal, 15* (Special Issue), 175–190.

Beccera, M., & Gupta, A. K. (1999). Trust within the organization: Integrating the trust literature with agency theory and transaction cost economics. *Public Administration Quarterly, 23,* 177–203.

Becker, L. B., & Schoenbach, K. (1989). When media content diversifies: Anticipating audience behaviors. In L. B. Becker & K. Schoenbach (Eds.), *Audience response to media diversification: Coping with plenty* (pp. 1–28). (Hillsdale, NJ: Lawrence Erlbaum Associates).

Berkowitz, L., & Rogers. K. H. (1986). A priming effect analysis of media influences. In J. Bryant & D. Zillmann (Eds.), *Perspectives on media effects* (pp. 57–81). Hillsdale, NJ: Lawrence Erlbaum Associates.

Bettman, J. R., & Sujan, M. (1987, September). Effects of framing on evaluation of comparable and noncomparable alternatives by expert and novice consumers. *Journal of Consumer Research 14,* 141–154.

Berry, L. L. (1987). Big ideas in services marketing. *Journal of Services Marketing, 1*(1), 5–9.

Berry, L. L. (1995). Relationship marketing of services—growing interest, emerging perspectives. *Journal of the Academy of Marketing Science, 24*(4), 236–245.

Blair, M. H. (1987/88, December/January). An empirical investigation of advertising wearin and wearout. *Journal of Advertising Research,* 45–50.

Blair, M. H., & Rabuck, M. J. (1998, October). Advertising wearin and wearout: Ten years later—more empirical evidence and successful practice. *Journal of Advertising Research, 38,* 7–18.

Braunstein, M., & Levine, E. H. (2000). *Deep branding on the internet.* Roseville, CA: Prima Venture.

Broadbent, D. (1977). The hidden pre-attentive processes. *American Psychologist, 32*(2), 109–118.

Bryant, J., & Anderson, D. (1983). *Children's understanding of television: Research on attention and comprehension.* New York: Academic Press.

Buchholz, L. M., & Smith, R. E. (1991). The role of consumer involvement in determining cognitive response to broadcast advertising. *Journal of Advertising, 20*(1), 4–17.

Burke, R. R. (1997). Do you see what I see? The future of virtual shopping, *Journal of the Academy of Marketing Science, 25*(4), 352–360.

Burke, R. R., & Srull, T. K. (1988, June). Competitive interference and consumer memory for advertising. *Journal of Consumer Research, 15*, 55–68.

Cafferky, M. (1996). *Let your customers do the talking.* Chicago: Upstart.

Chaiken, S. (1980). Heuristic versus systematic information processing and the use of source versus message cues in persuasion. *Journal of Personality and Social Psychology, 29*(5), 751–766.

Chaiken, S., Liberman, A., & Eagly, A. H. (1989). Heuristic and systematic information processing within and beyond the persuasion context. In J. S. Uleman & J. A. Bargh. (Eds.), *Unintended thought: Limits of awareness, intention and control* (pp. 212–252) New York: Guilford.

Chook, P. H. (1983). *ARF model for evaluating media, making the promise a reality.* Advertising Research Foundation Transcript Proceedings of the Intermedia Comparisons Workshop. New York: Advertising Research Foundation.

Clark, H. H., & Brennan, S. E. (1991). Grounding in communication. In L. B. Resnick, J. M. Levine, & S. D. Teasley (Eds.), *Perspectives on socially shared cognition* (pp. 127–149). Washington, DC: American Psychological Association).

Clark, H. H., & Wilkes-Gibbs, D. (1986). Referring as a collaborative process. *Cognition, 22*, 1–39.

Condry, J. (1989). *The psychology of television.* Hillsdale, NJ: Lawrence Erlbaum Associates.

Cox, B. (1998, November 17). Report: TV, PC get equal time. *Advertising Report Archives.* Retrieved from http://www.internetnews.com/IAR/article/0,,12_13971,00.html

Cross, R., & Smith, J. (1995). Internet marketing that works for customers (Part 1). *Direct Marketing, 58*(4), 22–23.

Cutler, B. (1990, June). The fifth medium. *American Demographics,* 24–29.

Dennis, A. R., George, J. F., Jessup, L. M., Nunamaker, J. F., Jr., & Vogel, D. R. (1988, December). Information technology to support electronic meetings. *MIS Quarterly, 12*, 591–624.

Doney, P. M., & Cannon, J. P. (1997). An examination of the nature of trust in buyer-seller relationships. *Journal of Marketing, 61*(2), 35–52.

Drèze, X. & Hussherr, F. X. (1999). Internet advertising: Is anybody watching? Working paper, Department of Marketing, Marshall School of Business, University of Southern California.

Dwyer, F. R., Schurr, P. J., & Oh, S. (1987). Developing buyer-seller relationships. *Journal of Marketing, 52*(1), 21–34.

Herman Ebbinghaus, H. (1902). *Grundzuge der psychologie.* Leipzig: Viet.

Fontenot, R. J. Vlosky, R. P. (1998). Exploratory study of internet buyer-seller relationships. *American Marketing Association,* 169–170.

Forrest, E., & Mizerski, R. (1996). *Interactive marketing: The future present.* Chicago: American Marketing Association, NTC Business Books.

Ganesan, S. (1994). Determinants of long-term orientation in buyer-seller relationships. *Journal of Marketing, 58*, 1–19.

Gardner, M. P. (1985, December). Mood states and consumer behavior: A critical review. *Journal of Consumer Research, 12*, 281–300.

Glazer, R. (1989). Marketing and the changing information environment: Implications for strategy, structure, and the marketing mix. Report No. 89-108. Cambridge, MA: Marketing Science Institute.

Goldberg, M. E., & Gorn, G. J. (1987, December). Happy and sad TV programs: How they affect reactions to commercials. *Journal of Consumer Research, 14*, 387–403.

Greenberg, B. S. (1988). Some uncommon television images and the drench hypothesis. In S. Oskamp (Ed.), *Television as a social issue* (pp. 88–102). Newbury Park, CA: Sage.

Greenwald, A. C. (1968). Cognitive learning, cognitive response to persuasion, and attitude change. In A. G. Greenwald, T. C. Brock, & T. Ostrom (Eds.), *Psychological foundations of attitudes* (pp. 147–170). New York: Academic Press.

Greenwald, A. C., & Leavitt, C. (1984, June). Audience involvement in advertising: Four levels. *Journal of Consumer Research, 11,* 581–592.

Gunter, B. (1985). Determinants of television viewing preferences. In D. Zillmann & J. Bryant (Eds.), *Selective exposure to communication* (pp. 93–112). Hillsdale, NJ: Lawrence Erlbaum Associates.

Haley, R. I. (1985). *Developing effective communications strategy.* New York: John Wiley and Sons.

Helper, S. & MacDuffie, P. J. (2000). E-volving the auto industry: E-commerce effects on consumer and supplier relationships. In *E-business and the changing terms of competition: A view from within the sectors,* Working paper, Stanford University.

Hellige, J. B. (1990). Hemispheric asymmetry. *Annual Review of Psychology, 41,* 55–80.

Herr, Paul M. (1989, June). Priming price: Prior knowledge and context effects. *Journal of Consumer Research, 16,* 67–75.

Higgins, E. T., & King, G. (1981). Accessibility of social constructs: Information processing consequences of individual and contextual variability. In N. Cantor & J. Kihlstrom (Eds.), *Personality, cognition, and social interaction* (pp. 69–122). Hillsdale, NJ: Lawrence Erlbaum Associates.

Hill, C. W. L. (1990). Cooperation, opportunism, and the invisible hand: Implications for transaction cost theory. *Academy of Management Review, 15,* 500–513.

Hoffman, D. L., & Novak, T. P. (1996, July). Marketing in computer-mediated environments: Conceptual foundations. *Journal of Marketing, 60,* 50–68.

Hoffman, D. L., Novak, T. P., & Peralta, M. (1999). Building consumer trust online. *Communications of the ACM, 42*(4), 80–85.

Hoyer, W. D., & MacInnis, D. J. (2001). *Consumer behavior.* Boston: Houghton Mifflin.

Isen, A. M. (1989). Some ways in which affect influences cognitive processes: Implications for advertising and consumer behavior. In P. Cafferata and A. Tybout (Eds.), *Cognitive and Affective Responses to Advertising* (pp. 91–118). Lexington, MA: Lexington Books.

Kamins, M. A., Marks, L. J. & Skinner, D. (1991, June). Television commercial evaluation in the context of program induced mood: Congruency versus consistency effects. *Journal of Advertising, 20,* 1–14.

Katz, E., Blumler, J. G., & Gurevitch, M. (1974). Utilization of mass communication by the individual. In J. Blumler & E. Katz (Eds.), *The uses of mass communication* (pp. 19–32). Beverly Hills, CA: Sage.

Katz, E., & Lazarsfeld, P. F. (1955). *Personal influence: The part played by people in the flow of mass communications.* New York: Free Press.

Keen, P. G. W. (2000, March 13). Ensuring e-trust. *Computerworld, 34*(11), 46.

Keeney, R. L. (1999, April). The value of internet commerce to the customer. *Management Science, 45,* 533–542.

Kennedy, J. R. (1971). How program environment affects TV commercials. *Journal of Advertising Research, 11,* 33–38.

Kiely, M. (1993, September). Word-of-mouth marketing. *Marketing,* 6.

Klebber, J. M. (1985). Physiological measures of research: A review of brain activity, electrodermal response, pupil dilation, and voice analysis methods and studies. In J. H. Leigh & C. Martin, Jr. (Eds.), *Current issues and research in advertising* (pp. 53–76). Ann Arbor: University of Michigan.

Krugman, H. E. (1965). The impact of television advertising: Learning without involvement. *Public Opinion Quarterly, 29,* 349–356.

Krugman, H. E. (1966). The measurement of advertising involvement. *Public Opinion Quarterly, 30,* 583–596.

Krugman, H. E. (1983, February/March). Television program interest and commercial interruption: Are commercials on interesting programs less effective? *Journal of Advertising Research, 23,* 21–23.

Krugman, H. E. (1988, October/November). Point of view: Limits of attention to advertising. *Journal of Advertising Research, 28,* 47–50.

Lam, S. S. K. (1997). The effects of group decision support systems and task structures on group communication and decision quality. *Journal of Management Information Systems, 13*(4), 193–215.

Leckenby, J. D., and Li H. (2000, Fall). From the editors: Why we need the Journal of Interactive Advertising. *Journal of Interactive Advertising, 1,* (1). Retrieved from http://jiad.org/vol1/no1/editors/index.html

Lloyd, D. W., & Clancy, K. J. (1989). The effects of television program involvement on advertising response: Implications for media planning. *Transcript Proceedings of the First Annual Advertising Research Foundation Media Research Workshop.* New York: Advertising Research Foundation.

Lovelock, C. H. (1996). *Services Marketing,* (3rd ed.) Upper Saddle River, NJ: Prentice Hall.

Lucas, H. C., Jr. (1974). Systems quality, user reactions, and the use of information systems. *Management Informatics, 3*(4), 207–212.

Lynch, J. G., & Ariely, D. (2000). Wine online: Search costs and competition on price, quality, and distribution. *Marketing Science, 19*(1), 83–103.

Mayer, R. C., Davis, J. H., & Schoorman, F. D. (1995). An integrative model of organizational trust. *Academy of Management Review, 20*(3), 709–734.

McGuire, W. J. (1969). The nature of attitudes and attitude change. In G. Lindzey & E. Aronson (Eds.), *The handbook of social psychology* (2nd ed., Vol. 3, pp. 136–314). New York: Random House.

McKenna, R. (1997, July-August). Real-time marketing. *Harvard Business Review,* 87–98.

McLuhan, M., & Fiore, Q. (1967) *The Medium is the Message* New York: Bantam Books.

Meckler, A. (2000, September 26). I want my N-TV. *Business 2.0,* 124–126.

O'Guinn, T. C., & Faber, R. J. (1991). Mass communication and consumer behavior. In T. S. Robertson & H. Kassarjian (Eds.), *Handbook of consumer behavior* (pp. 349–400). Upper Saddle River, NJ: Prentice Hall.

Oh, K. W., Cho, C. H., & Leckenby, J. D. (1999). A comparative analysis of Korean and U.S. Web advertising. *Proceedings of the 1999 Conference of the American Academy of Advertising,* 73–86.

Pavlou, P. A., & Ba, S. (2000). Does online reputation matter? An empirical investigation of reputation and trust in online auction markets. *Proceedings of the 6th Americas Conference in Information Systems,* Long Beach, CA.

Pavlou, P. A., & Stewart, D. W. (2000). Measuring the effects and effectiveness of interactive advertising: A research agenda. *Journal of Interactive Advertising, 1,* 1. Retrieved from: http://jiad.org/vol1/no1/pavlou/index.html.

Pechmann, C., & Stewart, D. J. (1988). A critical review of wearin and wearout. *Current Issues and Research in Advertising, 11,* 285–330.

Peterson, R., Balasubramanian, S., & Bronnenberg, B. J. (1997). Exploring the implications of the Internet for consumer marketing. *Journal of the Academy of Marketing Science, 25*(4), 329–346.

Petty, R. E., & Cacioppo J. T. (1986). *Communication and persuasion: Central and peripheral routes to attitude change.* New York: Springer-Verlag.

Politz Research, Inc. (1962, November). *A measurement of advertising effectiveness: The influence of audience selectivity and editorial environment.*

Port, O. (1999, October 4). Customers move into the driver's seat. *Business Week,* 103–106.

Powers, W. T. (1973, January 26). Feedback: Beyond behaviorism. *Science, 179,* 351–356.

Powers, W. T. (1978). Quantitative analysis of purposive systems: Some spadework at the foundations of scientific psychology. *Psychological Review, 85,* 417–435.

Ray, M. L. (1985). An even more powerful consumer? In R. Buzzell (Ed.), *Marketing in an electronic age.* Cambridge, MA: Harvard University Press.

Ray, M. L., & Sawyer, A. G. (1971, February). Repetition in media models: A laboratory technique. *Journal of Marketing Research, 8,* 20–29.

Robey, D., & Farrow, D. L. (1982). User involvement in information system development: A conflict model and empirical test. *Management Science, 28*(1), 73–85.

Rodgers, S., & Thorson, E. (2000). The interactive advertising model: How users perceive and process online ads. *Journal of Interactive Advertising, 1,* 1. Retrieved from http://jiad.org/vol1/no1/pavlou/index.html

Roehm, H. A., & Haugtvedt, C. P. (1999). Understanding interactivity of cyberspace advertising. In D. W. Schumann & E. Thorson (Eds.), *Advertising and the World Wide Web* (pp. 27–39). Mahwah, NJ: Lawrence Erlbaum Associates.

Rosen, E. (2000). *The anatomy of buzz: How to create word of mouth marketing.* New York: Doubleday.

Rothschild, M. L., & Hyun, Y. J. (1990, March). Predicting memory for components of TV commercials from EEG. *Journal of Consumer Research, 16,* 472–479.

Rothschild, M. L., Hyun, Y. J., Reeves, B., Thorson, E., & Goldstein, R. (1988, September). Hemispherically lateralized EEG as a response to television commercials. *Journal of Consumer Research, 15,* 185–198.

Rubin, A. M. (1986). Uses, gratification, and media effects research. In J. Bryant and D. Zillman (Eds.), *Perspectives on Media Effects* (pp. 281–302). Hillsdale, NJ: Lawrence Erlbaum Associates.

Schurr, P. H., & Ozanne, J. L. (1985). Influences on exchange processes: Buyers' preconceptions of a seller's trustworthiness and bargaining toughness. *Journal of Consumer Research, 11*(4), 939–953.

Schwerin, H. (1958). Do today's programs provide the wrong commercial climate? *Television Magazine, 15*(8), 45–47, 90–91.

Schwerin, H., & Newell, H. H. (1981). *Persuasion in marketing.* New York: Wiley.

Shimp, T. A. (1990). *Promotion management and marketing communications* (2nd ed.). Hinsdale, IL: Dryden Press.

Short, J., Williams, E., & Christie, B. (1976). *The social psychology of telecommunications,* New York: John Wiley.

Simon, H. (1957). *Organizations.* New York: McGraw-Hill.

Singh, S. N., & Hitchon, J. C. (1989). The intensifying effects of exciting television programs on the reception of subsequent commercials. *Psychology and Marketing, 6,* 1–31.

Soldow, G. F. & Principe, V. (1981, Spring). Response to commercials as a function of program context. *Journal of Advertising Research, 21*(2), 59–65.

Spalter, M. (1996). Maintaining a customer focus in an interactive age, the seven I's to success. In E. Forrest & R. Mizerski (Eds.), *Interactive marketing: The future present.* Chicago: American Marketing Association, NTC Business Books.

Srull, T. K. (1990). Individual responses to advertising: Mood and its effects from an information processing perspective. In S. J. Agres, J. A. Edell, & T. M. Dubitsky (Eds.), *Emotion in advertising: Theoretical and practical explorations* (pp. 19–34). New York: Quorum Books.

Stewart, D. W. (1986). The moderating role of recall, comprehension, and brand differentiation on the persuasiveness of television advertising. *Journal of Advertising Research, 25,* 43–47.

Stewart, D. W. (1989, June/July). Measures, methods, and models of advertising response. *Journal of Advertising Research, 29,* 54–60.

Stewart, D. W., Frazier, G., & Martin, I. (1996). Integrated channel management: Merging the communication and distribution functions of the firm. In E. Thorson & J. Moore (Eds.), *Integrated Communication: Synergy of Persuasive Voices* (pp. 185–216). Hillsdale, NJ: Lawrence Erlbaum Associates.

Stewart, D. W,. & Furse, D. H. (1986). *Effective television advertising: A study of 1000 commercials.* Lexington, MA: Lexington Books.

Stewart, D. W., Furse, D. H. & Kozak, R. (1983). A descriptive analysis of commercial copytesting services. *Current Issues and Research in Advertising 6*, 1–44.

Stewart, D. W., & Koslow, S. (1989). Executional factors and advertising effectiveness: A replication. *Journal of Advertising, 18*(3), 21–32.

Stewart, D. W., Pechmann, C., Ratneshwar, S., Stroud, J. & Bryant, B. (1985). Methodological and theoretical foundations of advertising copy testing: A review. *Current Issues and Research in Advertising*, 1–74.

Stewart, D. W., & Ward, S. (1994). Media effects on advertising. In J. Bryant & D. Zillmann (Eds.), *Media effects: Advances in theory and research* (pp. 315–364). Hillsdale, NJ: Lawrence Erlbaum Associates.

Stewart, D. W., & Zhao, Q. (2000). Internet marketing, business models, and public policy. *Journal of Public Policy and Marketing, 19*, 287–296.

Stone, M. (2000, March 28). Web ad spending may outstrip broadcast by 2005. Retrieved from http://www.newsbytes.com/news/00/146437.html

Strong, E. C. (1974, November). The use of field experimental observations in estimating recall. *Journal of Marketing Research, 11*, 369–378.

Strong, E. C. (1977, December). The spacing and timing of advertising. *Journal of Advertising Research, 16*, 25–31.

Thirkwell, P. C. (1997). Caught by the Web: Implications of Internet technologies for the evolving relationship marketing paradigm. *Proceedings of the Third American Marketing Association Special Conference, New and Evolving Paradigms.* Dublin, Ireland, 334–348.

Thorson, E. B. (1990). Consumer processing of advertising. In J. H. Leigh & C. Martin, Jr. (Eds.), *Current Issues and Research in Advertising* (Vol. 12, pp. 197–230). Ann Arbor, University of Michigan.

Thorson, E., Reeves, B., Schleuder, J., Lang, A., & Rothschild, M. L. (1985). Effect of program context on the processing of television commercials. *Proceedings of the American Academy of Advertising*, R58–63.

Tillman, H. (1995). Evaluating the quality of information on the Internet or finding a needle in a haystack. Presentation delivered at the John F. Kennedy School of Government, Harvard University, Cambridge, MA, September 6, 1995.

Time Inc. (1981). *A study of the effectiveness of advertising frequency in magazines, the relationship between magazine advertising frequency and brand awareness, advertising recall, favorable brand rating, willingness to buy, and product use and purchase.* New York: Research Department, Magazine Group, Time Inc.

Tolley, B., & Bogart, L. (1994). "How readers process newspaper advertising." In E. Clark, T. Brock, & D. W. Stewart (Eds.), *Advertising and consumer psychology* (pp. 79–96). Hillsdale, NJ: Lawrence Erlbaum Associates.

Ward, S., Levinson, D., & Wackman, D. (1972). Children's attention to television advertising. In G. A. Comstock and J. P. Murray (Eds.), *Television and social behavior: Vol. IV. Television in day-to-day life.* Washington: Department of Health, Education and Welfare, HSM 70-9059.

Webster, F. E., Jr. (1989). It's 1990—do you know where your marketing is? *MSI White Paper.* Cambridge, MA: Marketing Science Institute.

Wikstrom, S. (1996). An integrated model of buyer-seller relationships. *Journal of the Academy of Marketing Science, 23*(4), 335–345.

Wright, P. L. (1973). The cognitive processes mediating acceptance of advertising. *Journal of Marketing Research, 10,* 53–62.

Wurman, R. S. (2000, November 28). Redesign the data pump. *Business 2.0,* 210–220.

Wyer, R. S., & Srull, T. K. (1981). Category accessibility: Some theoretical and empirical issues concerning the processing of social stimulus information. In E. T. Higgins, C. P. Herman, & M. P. Zanna (Eds.), *Social cognition: The Ontario symposium* (pp. 161–197). Hillsdale, NJ: Lawrence Erlbaum Associates.

Yi, Y. (1990a). Cognitive and affective priming effects of the context for print advertisements. *Journal of Advertising, 19*(2), 40–48.

Yi, Y. (1990b, September). The effects of contextual priming in print advertisements. *Journal of Consumer Research, 17,* 215–222.

Yuspeh, S. (1977, November). On-air: Are we testing the message or the medium? Paper delivered to J. Walter Thompson Research Conference, New York.

Zaichowsky, J. (1985). Measuring the involvement construct. *Journal of Consumer Research, 12,* 341–352.

Zielske, H. A. (1959). The remembering and forgetting of advertising. *Journal of Marketing,* 239–243.

Zielske, H. A., & Henry, W. (1980, April). Remembering and forgetting television ads. *Journal of Advertising Research, 20,* 7–13.

Zigurs I., Poole, M. S., & DeSanctis, G. L. (1988, December). A study of influence in computer-mediated group decision making. *MIS Quarterly, 12,* 625–644.

Zillman, D., & Bryant, J. (1994). Entertainment as media effect. In J. Bryant & D. Zillman (Eds.), *Media effects: Advances in theory and research* (pp. 437–462). Hillsdale, NJ: Lawrence Erlbaum Associates.

Chapter 15

Vast Wasteland or Vast Opportunity?

Effects of Educational Television on Children's Academic Knowledge, Skills, and Attitudes

SHALOM M. FISCH
MediaKidz Research and Consulting

> *"All television is educational, the only question is: what is it teaching?"*
> (Liebert & Schwartzberg, 1977, p. 170)

All too often, discussions of the effects of television on children focus solely on the negative. Some critics have argued—with little, if any, basis in empirical data—that exposure to television can lead to outcomes such as reduced attention spans, lack of interest in school, or children becoming passive "zombie viewers" (e.g., Healy, 1990; Postman, 1985; Winn, 1977). Although these claims have been refuted by research, other negative effects of television have found more support in the literature, such as the modeling of aggressive behavior (e.g., Wilson et al., 1997) or persuasive effects of advertising (e.g., John, 1999; Kunkel, 2001).

However, even those negative effects that are supported by data do not present the entire picture. Often, far less attention has been paid to the positive effects that educational television programs can hold. Yet, if we believe that children can learn negative lessons from television, then it stands to reason that they can learn positive lessons, too. The same medium through which children learn product information in commercials should also allow them to learn science concepts in an educational program. And the same medium that can influence children to act more aggressively should also be able to motivate them to engage in educational activities.

This chapter reviews research on the impact of educational television programs on children's knowledge, skills, and attitudes in academic areas such as literacy, science, and mathematics. The first section reviews key findings, and the second discusses theoretical mechanisms that have been proposed to explain effects. Due to space limitations, the focus will be on efforts designed for children rather than adults (e.g., Greenberg & Gantz, 1976; Singhal & Rogers, 1999; Winsten, 1994) and on unaided viewing by children, rather than viewing accompanied by adult-led follow-up discussions or activities (e.g., Block, Guth, & Austin, 1993; Cognition and Technology Group at Vanderbilt, 1997; Lampert, 1985; Sanders & Sonnad, 1980; Schauble & Peel, 1986).

Effects in the academic domain have been investigated in several subject areas, each of which is discussed in turn. First, research on the impact of preschool educational programming on young children's school readiness is reviewed. Next, effects of school-age programming in four areas— literacy, mathematics and problem solving, science and technology, and civics and social studies—are explored.

SCHOOL READINESS

Numerous educational television series have been created to promote school readiness among preschool children. Of course, the term *school readiness* encompasses not only academic skills, but also interpersonal skills and attitudes, such as self-confidence and cooperation with peers (Zero to Three/National Center for Clinical Infant Programs, 1992). This chapter reviews research on the impact of preschool television programs in the academic domain. Readers interested in the impact of prosocial programs on children's interpersonal skills are directed to a recent review by Mares and Woodard (2001).

Because of its particular prominence in this literature, the section will begin by reviewing several landmark studies on the impact of *Sesame Street*. (More detail on these studies may be found in Fisch & Truglio, 2001, and Fisch, Truglio, & Cole, 1999.) Next, research on the impact of other preschool series will be reviewed.

Sesame Street

The earliest indications of the educational power of *Sesame Street* emerged in a pair of experimental/control, pretest/posttest studies conducted by the Educational Testing Service (ETS) after the first and second seasons of production (Ball & Bogatz, 1970; Bogatz & Ball, 1971). Each study found that, among 3- to 5-year-olds, heavier viewers of *Sesame Street* showed significantly greater pretest-posttest gains on an assortment of academic skills related to the alphabet, numbers, body parts, shapes, relational terms, and sorting and classification. The areas that showed the greatest effects were the ones that had been emphasized the most in *Sesame Street* (e.g., letters). These effects held across age, sex, geographic location, socioeconomic status (SES) (with low-SES children showing greater gains than middle-SES children), native language (English or Spanish), and whether the children watched at home or in school. Indeed, even when Cook and his colleagues (1975) conducted a reanalysis of these data that controlled for other, potentially contributing factors such as mothers discussing *Sesame Street* with their child, the aforementioned effects were reduced, but many remained statistically significant.

These effects have found parallels in summative evaluations of several international coproductions of *Sesame Street* outside the United States. Significant differences in cognitive skills (often focused on literacy and mathematics) have been found between viewers and nonviewers of *Plaza Sésamo* in Mexico (Diaz-Guerreo & Holtzman, 1974; UNICEF, 1996), *Susam Sokagi* in Turkey (Sahin, 1990), *Rua Sésamo* in Portugal (Brederode-Santos, 1993), and *Ulitsa Sezam* in Russia (*Ulitsa Sezam* Department of Research and Content, 1998). Only one Mexican study failed to replicate this pattern of differences (Diaz-Guerrero, Reyes-Lagunes, Witzke, & Holtzman, 1976), but it turned that the control group had, in fact, been exposed to *Plaza Sésamo* as well. (See Cole, Richman, & McCann Brown, 2001, for a more detailed review of this research.)

Sesame Street has been found to hold long-term benefits for viewers as well. One component of the Bogatz and Ball (1971) study was a follow-up on a subset of the children who had participated in their earlier study (Ball & Bogatz, 1970). Teachers rated their students on several dimensions of school readiness (e.g., verbal readiness, quantitative readiness, attitude toward school, relationship with peers) without knowing their prior viewership of *Sesame Street*. Results indicated that those children who had been frequent *Sesame Street* viewers were rated as better prepared for school than their non- or low-viewing classmates.

More than 25 years later, the immediate and long-term effects of *Sesame Street* were confirmed by other data. A 3-year longitudinal study of low-SES preschoolers found that after controlling statistically for background variables such as parents' level of education, native language, and preschool attendance, preschool viewing of educational programs in general—and *Sesame Street* in particular—predicted time spent in reading and educational activities, letter–word knowledge, math skills, vocabulary size, and school readiness on age-appropriate standardized achievement tests. Also, as in the earlier Bogatz and Ball (1971) study, teachers more often rated *Sesame Street* viewers as well adjusted to school (Wright & Huston, 1995; Wright, Huston, Scantlin, & Kotler, 2001). A second study was a correlational analysis of data representing approximately 10,000 children from the U.S. Department of Education's National Household Education Survey in 1993. Although the data were correlational (and, thus, can suggest but not prove causality), results indicated that preschoolers who viewed *Sesame Street* were more likely to be able to recognize letters of the alphabet and tell connected stories when pretending to read; these effects were strongest among children from low-income families and held true even after the effects of other contributing factors (e.g., parental reading, preschool attendance, parental education) were removed statistically. In addition, first and second graders who had viewed *Sesame Street* as preschoolers were more likely to be reading storybooks on their own and less likely to require remedial reading instruction (Zill, 2001; Zill, Davies, & Daly, 1994).

Finally, the longest-term impact of *Sesame Street* was found in a "recontact" study that examined high school students who either had or had not watched educational television as preschoolers; the bulk of this viewing had consisted of watching *Sesame Street.* Results showed that high school students who had watched more educational television—and *Sesame Street* in particular—as preschoolers had significantly higher grades in English, mathematics, and science. They also used books more often, showed higher academic self-esteem, and placed a higher value on academic performance. These differences held true even after the students' early language skills and family background variables were factored out (Anderson, Huston, Wright, & Collins, 1998; Huston, Anderson, Wright, Linebarger, & Schmitt, 2001).

Other Preschool Series

To date, there has been little, if any, research to assess the long-term effects of preschool television series other than *Sesame Street* once children have entered school. However, research on several other preschool series has revealed similar types of immediate effects that, if sustained, also could contribute to later school readiness.

A series of studies by Jerome and Dorothy Singer and their colleagues assessed the educational effectiveness of *Barney & Friends* (see Singer & Singer, 1998, for a review). The popular series stars Barney, a purple dinosaur, and makes extensive use of songs set to familiar children's tunes (e.g., "I love you, you love me . . . " to the tune of "This Old Man"). Research with a largely white, middle-SES sample of 3- and 4-year-old children found that unaided viewing of 10 episodes resulted in viewers performing significantly better than nonviewers in counting skills, identifying colors, vocabulary, and knowledge of neighborhood, although not in identifying shapes or labeling emotions (Singer & Singer, 1994). However, a replication that included a greater representation of children from low-SES and minority families found that, for this population, viewing 10 episodes of the series without teacher follow-up produced only a small advantage over nonviewers (although effects were greater when *Barney & Friends* was combined with teacher-driven lessons; Singer & Singer, 1995). Additional studies found no significant effects for $5\frac{1}{2}$-year-old kindergartners, which was attributed to ceiling effects, but suggested that prosocial effects could exist for children as young as 2 years old (Singer & Singer, 1998; Singer, Singer, Miller, & Sells, 1994).

Outside public broadcasting, research also has assessed the impact of three preschool series in Nickelodeon's "Nick Jr." programming block: *Allegra's Window* (a live-action series featuring a little girl puppet named Allegra), *Gullah Gullah Island* (a live-action series about a black family set on a tropical island), and *Blue's Clues* (a popular, participatory series about an animated dog named Blue and her human friend Steve, who asks viewers directly for assistance in solving games and puzzles). Apart from a prominent prosocial component, each series also attempts to address cognitive, problem-solving-based goals that Nickelodeon has termed "flexible thinking."

One set of studies examined the combined effects of *Allegra's Window* and *Gullah Gullah Island* as preschool children either viewed or did not view the pair of series for two years (Bryant et al., 1997). The bulk of the data consisted of caregiver ratings, rather than direct assessments of children, so data must be interpreted cautiously. Still, over the course of the two years, caregivers perceived viewers as showing significantly greater increases than nonviewers on scales of flexible thinking (e.g., seeing things from multiple points of view, showing curiosity) and problem solving (e.g., trying different approaches to solve problems, concentrating well on activities, not giving up). The largest gains appeared within the first month of viewing and were sustained over the entire 2-year viewing period.

More direct support for these trends came from a study that compared viewers' and nonviewers' performance on three sets of hands-on problem-solving tasks (e.g., simplified versions of the classic Tower of Hanoi problem) after 2 years of viewing (Mulliken & Bryant, 1999). Data indicated that viewers produced significantly more correct answers in all three tasks. They also solved four of the six Tower of Hanoi problems in fewer moves than nonviewers, but no significant difference was found for response time in a Go-NoGo task (akin to signal detection) in which children distinguished between shapes and/or colors.

Subsequently, parallel research assessed the impact of *Blue's Clues* on preschool children's knowledge and cognitive development during a 2-year viewing period (Anderson et al., 2000; Bryant et al., 1999). On the most basic level, when presented with the same puzzles shown in individual episodes of *Blue's Clues* (incorporating skills such as matching, sequencing, and relational concepts, among others), viewers gave significantly more correct answers than nonviewers, suggesting recall of the material seen on television. More broadly, subscales from the Kaufman Assessment Battery for Children (K-ABC) and the Kaufman Brief Intelligence Test (K-BIT) revealed that viewers performed significantly better than nonviewers in solving nonhumorous riddles (e.g., "What is small, has two wings, and can fly?"), Gestalt closure of incomplete inkblot drawings, and a matrices task that tapped nonverbal problem solving; these effects were sustained throughout the 2-year viewing period. No effect was found for children's expressive vocabulary or self-esteem.

One unique feature of *Blue's Clues* is the degree to which it solicits viewer participation, with the aim of engaging viewers actively in its educational content. However, based on observations of children during viewing (Crawley, Anderson, Wilder, Williams, & Santomero, 1999), Anderson and his colleagues have hypothesized that (at least among preschoolers) viewer participation does not so much contribute to learning as reflect mastery *after* learning has occurred. As a result, they found participation to increase with repeated viewing of the same episode, as more children, presumably, learned the answers.

Language Development

One area of impact that has been examined across several different preschool television series is language development (see Naigles & Mayeux, 2001, for a review). A series of content analyses by Rice and her colleagues compared the spoken language used in television series such as *Sesame Street, Mister Rogers' Neighborhood,* and *The Electric Company* to the language parents use in child-directed speech for young children (Rice, 1984; Rice & Haight, 1986). In contrast to situation comedies such as *Gilligan's Island,* the researchers found that the language in the educational television series contained many of the same features that are believed to promote language development in child-directed speech: short length of utterance, repetition, language tied to immediate, concrete referents, and so on. Thus, the potential existed for such television series to contribute to language development.

However, subsequent research supported this hypothesis with regard to some aspects of language development but not others. Although not every study has found effects on children's vocabulary acquisition (e.g., Bryant et al., 1999), many studies have shown educational programs to contribute to lexical development. That is, preschool children can acquire new words from television (e.g., Rice, Huston, Truglio, & Wright, 1990; Rice & Woodsmall, 1988; Singer & Singer, 1994; cf. Naigles & Mayeux, 2001). By contrast, the few studies that have examined the role of television in grammatical development (i.e., the acquisition of syntax) provide little evidence for a significant effect of television in this area (e.g., Singer & Singer, 1981). Naigles and Mayeux (2001) hypothesize that grammatical development may require a socially based construction of meaning that the one-way communication of television does not provide.

Finally, it is worth noting that, under some conditions, educational television programs also may have unintended negative effects on language development. Naigles et al. (1995) found that, after watching 10 episodes of *Barney & Friends*, children demonstrated *decreased* understanding of the difference between the mental state verbs *know* (which reflects certainty) and *think* and *guess* (which are less certain). A subsequent examination of the 10 *Barney & Friends* episodes explained why: they included numerous uses of *know* or *think* in situations of certainty. Just as exposure to novel words in appropriate televised contexts can have positive effects on young children's vocabulary, it seemed that consistent misuses of words could have negative effects as well.

LITERACY

Many of the effects of preschool programming on school readiness have concerned literacy. These range from fairly immediate effects on letter recognition to long-term effects on subsequent reading performance.

Among school-age television series, too, many have been claimed as "literacy shows," but the term has been used quite broadly. Often, producers or broadcasters have labeled television series as serving literacy simply because their characters have been taken from books, regardless of whether the series is designed to model reading or writing skills. For example, *The New Adventures of Winnie the Pooh* was labeled as a literacy series, even though its storylines actually focused on socioemotional issues and were not adapted from books.

In fact, such claims are not without some merit. Anecdotal evidence suggests that the existence of television series based on books can stimulate greatly increased sales of the books on which they are based, a point that will be covered in discussing effects on motivation below. Nevertheless, this review focuses more narrowly on television series that explicitly attempt to promote reading and/or writing among children.

Basic Reading Skills

The first substantive research in this area was a pair of summative studies on *The Electric Company*, a magazine-format series in which each episode was comprised of a combination of comedy sketches, songs, and animations (e.g., the adventures of "Letterman," a super hero who solved problems by changing letters in words). *The Electric Company* targeted poor readers in the second grade, and, in keeping with leading educational practice of the time, much of its focus lay in demonstrating the correspondence between letters (or combinations of letters) and their associated sounds.

Ball and Bogatz (1973) assessed the impact of the first season of *The Electric Company* in an experimental/control, pretest-posttest study with more than 8,000 children in grades 1 through 4. Approximately one-half of the children were shown *The Electric Company* in school for 6 months, whereas the remaining children were not. Pretests and posttests included a paper-and-pencil battery of assessments that addressed all of *The Electric Company*'s 19 goal areas (e.g., the ability to read consonant blends, digraphs, sight words, and final E, among others); a subset of more than 1,000 children was also tested orally in one-on-one sessions with researchers.

The data showed significant gains among viewers of *The Electric Company* in almost all of the 19 goal areas, including a broad range of phonics-based skills, as well as their ability to read for meaning. These gains were greatest for first and second graders, presumably because they had shown the lowest initial performance in the pretest. (Recall also that *The Electric Company*'s target audience was poor readers in the second grade.) The effects held across sex, ethnicity, and native language (English or Spanish) and were confirmed by similar, though less-pronounced, effects in a subsequent study on the impact of the second season of *The Electric Company* (Ball, Bogatz, Karazow, & Rubin, 1974).

Parallel effects were found more than 25 years later for another PBS early literacy series, *Between the Lions*. Like *The Electric Company, Between the Lions* is a humorous, magazine-format series whose goals include promoting concepts of print, phonemic awareness, and letter–sound correspondences (plus other topics, such as whole language elements) among early readers. Linebarger (2000) presented 17 half-hour episodes to children in kindergarten and first grade over a period of 3 to 4 weeks. Using an experimental/control, pretest/posttest design, viewers' and nonviewers' reading performance was assessed on several levels: specific program content (e.g., ability to read words that had been shown in the program), three particular emergent literacy skills (i.e., letter naming, phonemic segmentation fluency, nonsense word fluency), and more generalized early reading ability as measured via a standardized test (including knowledge of the alphabet and its functions, and print conventions such as reading left to right). At the posttest, after controlling statistically for a variety of background variables, kindergarten viewers performed significantly better than nonviewers on three out of five measures of specific program content, all three measures of emergent literacy skill, and the test of early reading ability. However, apart from one significant effect in phonemic segmentation fluency, there were no significant differences among first graders. This appeared to be due largely to ceiling effects; first graders already possessed the bulk of the skills modeled in *Between the Lions*.

Reading Comprehension

Impact has been assessed on a somewhat broader level with regard to *Reading Rainbow* (Leitner, 1991). Aimed at 5- to 8-year-olds, each episode of *Reading Rainbow* presents a specific children's book that is read on air as the camera shows illustrations taken from the book; other segments in the episode deal with related topics in a variety of formats (e.g., songs, documentaries, interviews with children). In this study, fourth graders read a book about cacti in the desert after one of three treatments: (a) watching a 30-minute episode of *Reading Rainbow* that featured the book along with other segments about the desert and animals that live there, (b) a hands-on opportunity to touch and examine a potted cactus, or (c) a verbal pre-reading discussion in which groups of children were asked to imagine the kinds of things that might be in a book about the desert. Among the results of the study, children who viewed the relevant *Reading Rainbow* episode showed significantly greater comprehension than those who engaged in prereading discussions; no difference emerged between the prereading discussion and hands-on conditions. Leitner explained the data in terms of modality effects. However, her alternate explanation—that the effect was due to previewing the book through *Reading Rainbow*—seems at least as likely, since only the children in the *Reading Rainbow* condition heard the book read (via television) before they read it themselves. Thus, the crucial factor may not have been television per se, but, rather, an additional exposure to the book. Yet, although this may pose a confound for the research, it holds less serious implications in the real world. Indeed, this is much of the idea behind *Reading Rainbow*: to expose children to books with the intent of inspiring them to read these books subsequently on their own.

Motivation to Read and Write

As noted earlier, anecdotal evidence suggests that popular television series based on books can stimulate greatly increased sales of the books that inspired them, whether the television series are intended as educational (e.g., *Arthur*) or not (e.g., *Goosebumps*). More systematic research on *Reading Rainbow* has reported increases of 150% to 900% in the sales of books featured in the series, and a survey of librarians found that 82%

reported children asking for books they had seen on *Reading Rainbow* (Wood & Duke, 1997). However, it is not clear in these cases whether the television programs stimulated increased amounts of reading (i.e., reading that would not have occurred otherwise) or whether the television-related books merely displaced reading of other books by children who would have been reading anyway.

More direct assessments of impact on motivation to read and write were conducted in research on *Between the Lions* and *Ghostwriter.* Data on the motivational effects of *Between the Lions* have been mixed, with significant effects on parent and teacher ratings in some areas but not others. Among kindergartners, parents and teachers reported no difference in several measures (e.g., children looking at books or magazines alone, how often they asked people to read to them), but parents reported viewers going to libraries or bookstores more and writing significantly more than nonviewers. The only significant effects for first graders were in parents' ratings of how often children read books alone and teachers' reports of writing during free time (Linebarger, 2000).

Providing compelling opportunities to read and write was an explicit goal of *Ghostwriter,* a television series and multiple-media initiative for children ages 7 to 10. *Ghostwriter* featured a team of children who used literacy to solve mysteries with the aid of Ghostwriter, an invisible ghost who could communicate only via reading and writing. To date, there have been no experimental/control studies of the impact of *Ghostwriter.* However, findings from several pieces of research speak to the issue of providing children with compelling opportunities to engage in reading and writing.

On the most basic level, several studies have found that viewers typically chose to read the print that was shown on-screen in *Ghostwriter* (e.g., in the form of messages to and from Ghostwriter or characters recording information in their "casebooks"); one survey found that 83% of respondents said they read along, and an additional 8% "sometimes" did so (Nielsen New Media Services, 1993). Another study found that approximately 25% of the girls who viewed *Ghostwriter* kept casebooks of their own, and about 20% of the children said they regularly wrote in code (KRC Research & Consulting, 1994).

Perhaps the clearest evidence of *Ghostwriter*'s impact on children's pursuit of literacy activities lay in the large numbers of children who wrote letters to *Ghostwriter* and participated in mail-in contests that required them to engage in complex activities such as writing songs or creating their own original superheroes. Such activities were almost completely self-motivated on the part of children, and some reported that it was the first time they had written a letter. Children's participation required substantial effort—not only in writing the letters themselves, but also in learning how to address an envelope, obtaining the necessary postage, using zip codes, and so on. Despite all of these potential obstacles, more than 450,000 children wrote letters to *Ghostwriter* during its first two seasons (Children's Television Workshop, 1994)—direct evidence of *Ghostwriter*'s ability to motivate children to engage in reading and writing.

Long-Term Impact

As discussed in the section on school readiness, longitudinal studies of *Sesame Street* have found preschool viewing to carry long-term effects on children's literacy in first and second grade (Wright et al., 2001; Zill, 2001) and as late as high school (Anderson et al., 1998; Huston et al., 2001). Very little longitudinal research has assessed the long-term impact of school-age television programs on literacy, but summative research on the second season of *The Electric Company* suggests that such series also can hold long-term benefits (Ball et al., 1974). Participants in the study included a subsample of children who had participated in Ball and Bogatz's (1973) study of the first season of the series. Data from the pretest (i.e., before children saw any additional episodes of *The Electric Company*) indicated that the effect of viewers' initial exposure sustained itself, even though *The Electric Company* had not been broadcast during the several-month interval between studies. Interestingly, however, posttest data showed that the effect of viewing two seasons was not considerably greater than the effect of viewing one. Thus, the major impact of *The Electric Company* appeared to come from children's initial six-month exposure to the series, and this impact was sufficiently enduring to sustain itself several months after viewing.

MATHEMATICS AND PROBLEM SOLVING

The impact of school-age mathematics programs has been assessed on three types of outcome variables: knowledge of mathematics, mathematical problem-solving ability, and attitudes toward mathematics. Each is discussed below.

Knowledge of Mathematics

Effects on knowledge of mathematics have been found across studies and for two different school-age television series. Harvey, Quiroga, Crane, and Bottoms (1976) evaluated the impact of eight episodes of *Infinity Factory*, a magazine-format mathematics series for 8- to 11-year-old children, that had a particular focus on African-American and Latino children. The study found that viewers showed significant gains in mathematics performance at posttest, although white children showed greater gains than minority viewers.

Knowledge of mathematics was also the focus of an early summative study of *Square One TV*. Aimed at 8- to 12-year-olds, *Square One TV* employed a magazine format that included comedy sketches, game shows with real children, music videos, animation, and an ongoing mathematical detective serial, "Mathnet." The goals of the series were to promote positive attitudes toward mathematics, to promote the use and application of problem-solving processes, and to present sound mathematical content in an interesting, accessible, and meaningful manner. Peel, Rockwell, Esty, and Gonzer (1987) assessed children's comprehension of 10 mathematical problem-solving segments from the first season of *Square One TV*. Although limited by the absence of a pretest or nonviewing control group (because the study was intended to measure comprehension rather than learning), the study is notable for measuring comprehension on three different levels: *recall* of the problem and solution in each segment, *understanding* of the mathematics that underlay the segment, and *extension* of the mathematics content to new, related problems. As one might expect, comprehension at all levels varied somewhat across the segments tested, but a general trend emerged: The highest performance was found in recall, followed by understanding, which was followed in turn by extension. By drawing these distinctions explicitly, the study raises an important issue that must be considered in evaluating the effectiveness of educational television—namely, that researchers may find different results depending on the way they have defined "comprehension." This point will be discussed in the "Theoretical Mechanisms" section below.

Effects on Problem Solving

In keeping with an emerging reform movement in mathematics education that recommended embedding mathematics content in a context of problem solving (e.g., National Council of Teachers of Mathematics, 1989), *Square One TV* placed a heavy emphasis on mathematical problem solving. Hall, Esty, and Fisch (1990; Hall, Fisch, et al., 1990) assessed its impact in this area.

In this study, fifth graders in two elementary schools in Corpus Christi, Texas (where *Square One TV* had not been broadcast) were shown 30 episodes of *Square One TV*, whereas children in two other schools were not. A subsample of viewers and nonviewers were individually matched for sex, SES, ethnicity, and performance on a standardized mathematics test. At pretest and posttest, these children attempted several hands-on, nonroutine mathematical problem-solving activities (e.g., figuring out what was wrong with a mathematical game and fixing it), with interviewers and coders blind as to whether children were viewers or nonviewers. Results indicated that, from pretest to posttest, viewers showed significant gains in the number and variety of problem-solving heuristics they used to solve problems (e.g., looking for patterns, working backward), and they used significantly more than nonviewers at posttest. At the same time, viewers' solutions to two of the three problems became significantly more complete and sophisticated, whereas nonviewers showed no significant change. (Viewers showed no change on the third problem because of ceiling effects.) Thus, exposure to *Square One TV* affected both the ways in which children approached problems and the solutions they reached—effects that occurred regardless of the children's sex, ethnicity, SES, or performance on standardized mathematics tests.

Attitudes Toward Mathematics

The same study of *Square One TV* also assessed the series' effects on children's attitudes toward mathematics (Hall, Fisch, et al., 1990). In contrast to previous studies in mathematics education, which had assessed attitudes via fairly limited pencil-and-paper scales, attitudes in this study were assessed via in-depth interviews, which were then coded by blind coders. Pretest–posttest comparisons showed significant effects in several domains: Viewers showed a broader conception of "math" (i.e., beyond basic arithmetic) than nonviewers, a greater desire than nonviewers to pursue challenging mathematical tasks, and significantly greater gains than nonviewers in the number of times they spontaneously talked about enjoying mathematics and problem solving throughout the interview (i.e., without being asked directly about enjoyment). Again, there was no consistent effect of sex, ethnicity, or SES. Only one domain, children's conceptions of the usefulness of mathematics, produced no significant effect.

SCIENCE AND TECHNOLOGY

Television has a long tradition of broadcasting educational science series, from the debut of *Mr. Wizard* in 1951 through more recent efforts, such as *Beakman's World, Science Court,* and *Magic Schoolbus.* This section examines the impact of a few science-based series on children's knowledge of science, exploration and experimentation, and attitudes toward the subject. It is interesting to note that these series span several very different genres—presenter-based demonstrations, magazine-format documentary, and Saturday morning cartoon—but all have produced consistent patterns of significant effects.

Knowledge of Science

Numerous educational television series have been found to produce significant gains in children's knowledge of specific science content. Perhaps the greatest number of studies has concerned *3-2-1 Contact,* a daily magazine-format series targeting 8- to 12-year-olds. *3-2-1 Contact* relied heavily on live-action, mini-documentary segments with teenage hosts, but also included animations, songs, and a dramatized mystery serial called "The Bloodhound Gang." Each week of shows was built around a specific theme (e.g., electricity, outer space), with many of that week's segments corresponding to some aspect of that theme.

Research on the impact of *3-2-1 Contact* is somewhat limited by the methods used; almost all of the existing studies relied largely on paper-and-pencil (typically multiple-choice) quizzes to assess comprehension. Despite this limitation, however, a consistent pattern of effects has been observed with regard to comprehension. Studies have varied in the number of episodes presented to children (from 10 to more than 40). At all levels of exposure, these studies found that viewing *3-2-1 Contact* resulted in positive effects on children's comprehension of the science topics presented (Cambre & Fernie, 1985; Johnston, 1980; Johnston & Luker, 1983; Wagner, 1985). The effects were often strongest among girls, one of the populations that has often been found to demonstrate lower levels of science achievement (e.g., Levin, Sabar, & Libman, 1991).

Other studies have found parallel effects for the science content of other television series, such as *Bill Nye the Science Guy* (Rockman Et Al, 1996) and *Cro* (Fay, Teasley, Cheng, Bachman, & Schnakenberg, 1995; Goodman, Rylander, & Ross, 1993; cf. Fay, Yotive, et al., 1995; Fisch, Goodman, McCann, Rylander, & Ross, 1995) in the United States, the Australian series *Australia Naturally* (Noble & Creighton, 1981), and an assortment of individual episodes of *Owl TV, Know How, Tomorrow's World, Body Matters,* and *Erasmus Microman* in the United Kingdom (Clifford, Gunter, & McAleer, 1995).

Of course, comprehension of science content is dependent on the effectiveness of its presentation, as illustrated by research on *Cro. Cro* was a Saturday-morning animated series about a Cro-Magnon boy, designed to promote knowledge of and interest in science and technology among 6- to 11-year-old children. Summative research on the first season of *Cro* found that viewers demonstrated a significantly greater understanding of the technological principles presented in some episodes than nonviewers did. However, no differences were found in extension of these principles to new problems, and even on the level of understanding, differences were not significant for every episode tested (Goodman et al., 1993). Several factors distinguished between episodes that produced significant effects and those that did not: they focused on concrete devices rather than abstract principles, they embedded content in a context of problem solving in which characters continually refined solutions to make them more effective, and their educational content was central, rather than tangential, to the narrative plotline. The hypothesis was confirmed when these characteristics were subsequently built into all of the *Cro* episodes produced in Season II, and significant differences between viewers and nonviewers were found for comprehension of all of the episodes tested (Fay, Teasley, et al., 1995).

Exploration and Experimentation

Beyond comprehension of science concepts shown, Rockman Et Al (1996) assessed the impact of exposure to *Bill Nye the Science Guy* on children's hands-on science experimentation. Targeting children ages 8 to 10, each episode of *Bill Nye the Science Guy* featured real-life comedian/scientist Bill Nye conducting experiments and demonstrating scientific concepts (often with surprising effects) in a variety of settings. In this study, a series of hands-on science tasks (e.g., classifying animals, figuring out interesting ways in which tops might be used in *Bill Nye the Science Guy*) were presented to viewers and nonviewers before an extended viewing period in which viewers watched at least 12 episodes of the series in school or at home; the same problems were presented to a second group of viewers and nonviewers after the viewing period. Viewers' process of exploration showed significant improvement in the posttest (e.g., they made more observations and comparisons), as did the sophistication with which they classified animals (e.g., using categories such as "mammals" instead of number of legs). Although limited somewhat by the lack of within-subject controls, the data suggested that exposure to *Bill Nye the Science Guy* enhanced both the processes children used and the sophistication of their solutions—a finding consistent with mathematical problem-solving data on *Square One TV* (Hall, Esty, et al., 1990; Hall, Fisch, et al., 1990).

Attitudes Toward Science

Apart from conveying knowledge and modeling process, the goals of *3-2-1 Contact, Bill Nye the Science Guy,* and *Cro* also included stimulating positive attitudes toward science and/or technology. As in the research on knowledge, research on the impact of *3-2-1 Contact* on children's attitudes toward science is somewhat limited by its reliance on pencil-and-paper measures. Nevertheless, significant effects on children's interest in science and images of scientists have been found across these studies, although they have been moderate in size and less consistent than effects on knowledge (Cambre & Fernie, 1985; Johnston, 1980; Johnston & Luker, 1983; Wagner, 1985). It is not clear whether *3-2-1 Contact* had less impact in this area or whether the more moderate effects were due to the relatively limited measures used.

A wider array of measures was used to measure the impact of *Cro* on interest in science and technology, including pencil-and-paper measures, in-depth interviews, and behavioral observations of children as they chose to engage in technology-related vs. -unrelated activities (Fay, Teasley, et al., 1995; Fay, Yotive, et al., 1995). Under an experimental/ control, pretest/posttest design, children who viewed eight episodes of *Cro* were compared to nonviewers, who watched eight episodes of another animated educational series that did not concern science (*Where on Earth Is Carmen Sandiego?*). Results pointed to a variety of significant effects concerning interest: *Cro* viewers showed significantly greater pretest– posttest gains than nonviewers in their interest in doing technology activities related to episodes of *Cro* (e.g., making a catapult), exhibited greater interest in learning more about the technology content of particular episodes, and were significantly more likely to engage in hands-on activities connected to two episodes when given a choice among these activities and other, nontechnology activities (although parallel effects were not found for other episodes tested). However, gains were not significant for interest in technology activities that were not presented in *Cro,* perhaps because the children did not possess a mental construct of "technology" that was sufficiently broad to encompass all of these types of activities.

Finally, Rockman Et Al's (1996) evaluation of *Bill Nye the Science Guy* found little change in viewers' attitudes toward science as reflected in pencil-and-paper measures, but this was attributed to ceiling effects, as children scored highly even in the pretest. Some positive effects appeared in parents' reports: 61% believed their children's interest in science increased after watching *Bill Nye the Science Guy,* almost all believed their interest in participating in science activities increased, and 35% reported that their children talked with them about the content of specific episodes. Naturally, however, these data must be interpreted with caution because they reflect parent perceptions rather than direct assessments of children.

CIVICS AND SOCIAL STUDIES

Research in this domain has focused primarily on two areas: children's recall of current events content from television news, and the impact of televised *Schoolhouse Rock* songs on children's understanding of American history or the workings of government.

News and Current Events

Although Comstock and Paik (1991) observed that children get most of their news information from television, as opposed to newspapers, radio, or discussions with others, most research on television news has focused on adults rather than children. This is understandable, as the primary audience for news programming is typically adults, although Atkin and Gantz (1978) found that even elementary schoolchildren showed moderate increases in knowledge of political affairs and current events after watching adult news programs.

Issues concerning children's learning from television news take on greater significance when we consider news programs produced specifically for children. A series of studies in the Netherlands compared fourth and sixth graders' recall of news stories presented in one such program, *Jeugdjournaal* (*Children's News*), with print and audio versions of the same stories (Walma van der Molen & van der Voort, 1997, 1998, 2000). These studies consistently found immediate recall of news stories to be greater when presented on television than in any other form. However, the effect was greatest when the information in the televised visuals was redundant with (rather than complementary to) information in the audio track. This led the researchers to explain the advantages of the televised versions using Paivio's (1971) dual-coding hypothesis, which posits a greater likelihood of recall when the same material is presented in two modalities (audio and visual) than when it is presented in only one.

Perhaps the most prominent—and certainly the most controversial—example of American news programming for children is *Channel One,* a 10-minute news program (plus 2 minutes of commercials) that is broadcast, not to homes, but directly to middle and high schools. In exchange for delivering the program to students on at least 90% of school days, schools receive a satellite dish, two VCRs, and televisions in each classroom from Whittle Communications, the producer of *Channel One.* Several studies have measured learning from *Channel One* via forced-choice, paper-and-pencil assessments. Although one study found no effect (Knupfer & Hayes, 1994), most have found exposure to *Channel One* to result in viewers knowing more about the news topics covered in the broadcasts than nonviewers (Greenberg & Brand, 1993; Johnston & Brzezinski, 1994). However, even when effects were found, they were not always equal across viewers; some were not significant for children with grade point averages of C or D, or were stronger for students who were motivated or whose teachers discussed the news on a regular basis (Johnston & Brzezinski, 1994). Although some question how often teachers actually hold discussions to follow up on *Channel One* broadcasts (see Bachen, 1998, for a review), the latter finding raises a question as to the degree to which effects are attributable to the program per se or to the discussions it might stimulate.

Nevertheless, greater controversy has been provoked by data showing that viewers learn, not only from the news portion of the program, but also from its commercials. Children have been found to evaluate products more highly and express greater intent to buy products (although they were not significantly more likely to have bought them) if they had seen the products advertised on *Channel One* (Brand & Greenberg, 1994; Greenberg & Brand, 1993). The effectiveness of such in-school advertising, coupled with the increasing presence of advertising and commercial initiatives in schools, has led to debate over the propriety of such efforts (e.g., Richards, Wartella, Morton, & Thompson, 1998; Wartella & Jennings, 2001).

American History and Government

In the 1970s, a series of 3-minute educational interstitials, *Schoolhouse Rock,* aired between children's programs on ABC. Each animated interstitial presented a song about a topic in English, mathematics, science, or American history. At the time, no research was conducted to assess the educational effectiveness of *Schoolhouse Rock.* However, when *Schoolhouse Rock* was rebroadcast in the 1990s, a series of studies by Calvert and her colleagues (Calvert, 1995; Calvert & Pfordresher, 1994; Calvert, Rigaud, & Mazella, 1991; Calvert & Tart, 1993) tested children's and adults' comprehension of two *Schoolhouse Rock* interstitials: "I'm Just a Bill" (the steps through which a bill becomes a law) and "The Shot Heard 'Round the World" (the Revolutionary War). A third interstitial, "The Preamble" (verbatim text of the Preamble to the Constitution), was tested only with adults. Data from these studies suggested that the interstitials were less effective than alternate versions in which the audio track was spoken rather than sung. Repeated exposure to the original, musical versions improved verbatim recall, but was less effective than prose in promoting deeper comprehension of the educational content.

The researchers attributed this to modality effects (i.e., songs are better suited to verbatim recall) and/or a better match between the prose presentation and verbal recall measures. Yet, when others have found poor comprehension for individual songs in educational television programs, they have generally pointed to factors that were more specific to the particular songs involved; for example, Palmer attributed poor comprehension of one *Sesame Street* song to the rhyme scheme emphasizing the wrong words and drawing attention away from the educational content (Palmer & Fisch, 2001). Although one might hesitate, then, to conclude that songs *never* lend themselves to deep processing of content, it is clear that these three *Schoolhouse Rock* interstitials succeeded only on the level of verbatim recall.

Interest in News

Interest in and motivation to seek out news was assessed only in research on *Channel One*. Self-report data showed students and teachers reporting examples of having sought out information or contributing to dinnertime conversation because of *Channel One* (Ehman, 1995). However, quantitative comparisons of viewers and nonviewers found no significant difference in students' reports of talking about news stories outside class or using other media to learn about news stories (Johnston & Brzezinski, 1992; Johnston, Brzezinski, & Anderman, 1994). The latter findings, coupled with the issues that always surround self-report data, leave open the question of whether *Channel One* truly increased children's interest in seeking out news. To paraphrase Johnston et al. (1994): To the degree that *Channel One* held benefits for its viewers, it may have satisfied, rather than stimulated, their need to know.

THEORETICAL MECHANISMS

The applied nature of research on the impact of educational television has resulted in far more empirical studies gauging effects than theoretical models describing mechanisms responsible for those effects. This section reviews three such theoretical approaches, pertaining to comprehension of educational content on television, transfer of learning, and the long-term benefits of early viewing of educational television.

Comprehension of Educational Content:
The Capacity Model

Several studies have demonstrated that, as in the case of other complex stimuli, viewers' comprehension of television involves processing that draws on the limited capacity of working memory (Armstrong & Greenberg, 1990; Beentjes & van der Voort, 1993; Lang, Geiger, Strickwerda, & Sumner, 1993; Lorch & Castle, 1997; Meadowcroft & Reeves, 1989; Thorson, Reeves, & Schleuder, 1985). Viewers of educational television programs face even greater processing demands, because these programs typically present narrative content and educational content simultaneously, as in the example of a program about a boy who wants to join a band (narrative content) and learns how different musical instruments create sound through vibration (educational content). The *capacity model* (Fisch, 2000) proposes that comprehension of educational content depends not only on the cognitive demands of processing the educational content itself, but also on the demands presented by the narrative in which it is embedded. In addition, the model argues that comprehension is affected by *distance*, that is, the degree to which the educational content is integral or tangential to the narrative (Fig. 15.1). To best understand the notion of distance, imagine a television mystery in which the hero suddenly stops to give a lesson on mathematical rate-time-distance problems. If the mathematical content is not directly relevant to the mystery, it would be tangential to the narrative and distance would be large. Conversely, if the hero uses the rate-time-distance concept to prove that only one suspect was near enough to commit the crime (i.e., if it provides the key clue to solve the mystery), then the mathematical content is integral to the narrative and distance would be small.

According to the capacity model, if distance is large, the mental resources needed for comprehension are generally devoted primarily to the narrative; less resources are available for processing the educational content. However, if the educational content is integral to the narrative, then the two complement, rather than compete with, each other; the same processing that permits comprehension of the narrative simultaneously contributes to comprehension of the educational content. Thus, comprehension of educational content typically would be stronger under any of the following conditions: (a) when the processing demands of the narrative are relatively small (e.g., because few inferences are needed to understand the story or the viewer's language skills are sufficiently sophisticated to follow the narrative easily; see Fig. 15.1 and Fisch, 2000, for a full list of contributing factors), (b) when the processing demands of the educational content are small (e.g., because it is presented clearly or the viewer has some knowledge of the subject already), or (c) when distance is small. The model is consistent with a large body of existing literature on children's comprehension of television, but at the time of this writing, it has yet to be tested for predictive validity in new research.

Transfer of Learning

Comprehension—and even learning—of the educational content in a television program does not guarantee that viewers also will be able to apply the material successfully in new problems or situations. Recall, for example, Goodman et al.'s (1993) finding of significant differences between *Cro* viewers' and nonviewers' understanding of the science content presented,

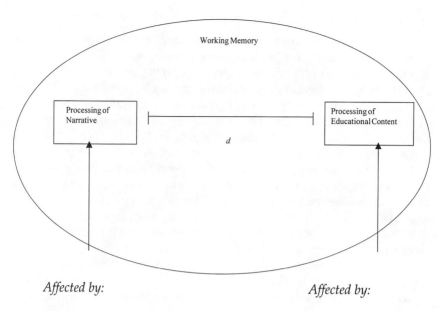

Affected by:

*Viewer
characteristics*
Prior knowledge: story/characters
Story schemas
Knowledge/schemas: formal features
Interest in subject matter
Verbal reasoning ability
Short-term memory

*Program
characteristics*
Complexity/coherence
   of story
Need for inferences
Fit to existing story
   schemas
Temporal organization
Advance organizers

Affected by:

*Viewer
characteristics*
Prior
   knowledge of
   content
Interest in
   content

*Program
characteristics*
Clarity of
   presentation
Explicitness of
   content
Advance
   organizers

FIG. 15.1.   Theoretical construct described by the capacity model, with factors that determine the resource demands for comprehending narrative and educational content (after Fisch, 2000).

but not in extension to new problems. Actually, this phenomenon is not exclusive to educational television; some researchers have noted that it is relatively rare to find transfer of learning for even classroom learning (e.g., Detterman & Sternberg, 1993). Yet, some studies have found evidence of transfer from educational television, such as significant effects on children's experimentation and problem solving in contexts different than those shown in the television programs (e.g., Hall, Esty, et al., 1990; Hall, Fisch, et al., 1990; Mulliken & Bryant, 1999; Rockman Et Al, 1996).

Why, then, has educational television been successful in producing transfer of learning in some studies but not in others? Speaking in terms of education more generally, Bransford, Brown, and Cocking (1999) have argued that successful transfer requires several key elements, including a rich understanding of the subject matter that has been presented, a representation of the knowledge that is abstracted beyond its original context, and a match between the representation of the knowledge and the new situation in which it might be applied. Yet, applying these principles to educational television would almost seem to produce a contradiction under the capacity model discussed above (Fisch, 2000): According to the capacity model, one of the chief ways to enrich comprehension of educational content (as is required for transfer) is to maintain a small distance between narrative and educational content. However, content that is overly tied to a narrative context may not be represented abstractly enough to transfer to new problems in different contexts (e.g., Cognition and Technology Group at Vanderbilt, 1997).

As I have proposed elsewhere (Fisch, 2001), the optimal solution may lie in not only maintaining a small distance between narrative and educational content, but also presenting the same educational content several times in several different narrative contexts (a principle demonstrated outside the realm of television by researchers such as Gick & Holyoak, 1983). Thus, for example, Goodman et al. (1993) found significant effects on understanding but not transfer for *Cro*, in which each discrete science concept was presented in only one episode and one narrative context. However, Hall, Esty, et al. (1990; Hall, Fisch, et al., 1990) found significant transfer of the problem-solving heuristics modeled in *Square One TV*, where the same heuristic (e.g., considering probability) was embedded in several different contexts (e.g., a game show in which contestants used probability to play strategically, a music video about choosing the right key to escape a haunted house). These multiple treatments of the same underlying content may have contributed toward a more abstract representation of the mathematical concepts involved and also may have encouraged a sense of these concepts as applicable in a broader variety of situations, thus encouraging transfer.

Long-Term Effects: The Early Learning Model

The preceding conceptions of comprehension and transfer are useful in considering the relatively immediate effects of educational television, but they are not sufficient to explain longer-term effects, particularly if the eventual outcomes bear little resemblance to the educational content that was presented on television. For example, when preschool viewing of *Sesame Street* was found to predict grade point averages in high school (Anderson et al., 1998; Huston et al., 2001), it was unlikely that students were applying the material they had learned from *Sesame Street* directly to their high school classes.

To explain such effects, Huston et al. proposed the *early learning model.* Under this model, three facets of early development are proposed as pathways by which long-term effects can result: (a) learning preacademic skills, particularly related to language and literacy; (b) developing motivation and interest; and (c) acquiring behavioral patterns of attentiveness, concentration, nonaggressiveness, and absence of restlessness or distractibility. (Note that the latter point runs directly counter to claims by Healy [1990] and others that *Sesame Street* reduces children's attention spans.) These factors contribute to early success in school, which then plays a significant role in determining children's long-term academic trajectories; children who demonstrate good skills early on are likely to be placed in higher ability groups, to be perceived as more competent by teachers, to receive more attention, to feel successful, and to be motivated to do well (Entwistle, Alexander, & Olson, 1997). In addition, these early successes may also affect the types of activities in which children choose to engage; for example, good readers may choose to read more on their own. Each of these outcomes can then result in further success over time. In this way, the model posits a cascading effect in which early exposure to educational television leads to early academic success, which in turn, contributes to a long-term trajectory of success that can endure for years.

CONCLUSION

Perhaps the broadest conclusion to be drawn from this review is that educational television works. Thoughtfully crafted television programs can hold many significant benefits for children of various ages. Moreover, the benefits of these programs can last for years.

This is not to say, of course, that all television programs are beneficial for children, any more than it would be reasonable to claim that all television is bad for them. Indeed, the 3-year longitudinal study of the impact of *Sesame Street* conducted by Wright et al. (2001) found not only that exposure to *Sesame Street* was associated with positive effects on literacy and school readiness, but also that preschool viewing of commercial entertainment cartoons sometimes had significant negative effects on the same outcome measures. Clearly, the critical factor is not the medium itself, but the content it carries.

Along with the content of television programs, we must also consider the context in which they are viewed and in which their effects are observed. Numerous studies have shown that children's learning from educational television can be increased through activities and follow-up discussion with parents or teachers (e.g., Reiser, Tessmer, & Phelps, 1984; Reiser, Williamson, & Suzuki, 1988; Salomon, 1977; Singer & Singer, 1995). Indeed, the early learning model proposed by Huston et al. (2001) highlights the point that nontelevision experiences play an important role, not only at the time of viewing, but also at the time when effects subsequently appear. Educational advantages provided by exposure to educational television can combine with other factors, such as positive feedback from teachers or engagement in other informal education activities, to result in effects that are stronger and more enduring than the effects of simple exposure to television.

Clearly, given the complex interactions at work among all of the relevant variables, we have a long way to go before the effects of educational television will be understood completely. However, even as we strive toward a distant goal of understanding effects, we must not lose sight of a more immediate point: Effective educational television programs already exist. The greatest value of research in this area does not lie in theoretical models, but in the concrete benefits that such programming has already been shown to hold for our children.

ACKNOWLEDGMENTS

Although my name appears as sole author, this review is built on the contributions of others. I gratefully acknowledge the many researchers who graciously provided me with copies of their work; one of the greatest challenges in creating this review was locating all of the (often unpublished) literature, and without their assistance, it would not have been possible. Roxanne Thomas Garcia performed numerous administrative support tasks. Most important, I must thank my wife, Susan, and children, Nachum and Chana, for their unflagging indulgence as I wrote the bulk of the text during what was ostensibly a 1-week vacation.

REFERENCES

Anderson, D. R., Bryant, J., Wilder, A., Santomero, A., Williams, M., & Crawley, A. M. (2000). Researching *Blue's Clues*: Viewing behavior and impact. *Media Psychology, 2,* 179–194.

Anderson, D. N., Huston, A. C., Wright, J. C., & Collins, P. A. (1998). *Sesame Street* and educational television for children. In R. G. Noll & M. E. Price (Eds.), *A communications cornucopia: Markle Foundation essays on information policy* (pp. 279–296). Washington, DC: Brookings Institution Press.

Armstrong, G. B., & Greenberg, B. S. (1990). Background television as an inhibitor of cognitive processing. *Human Communication Research, 16,* 355–386.

Atkin, C. K., & Gantz, W. (1978). Television news and the child audience. *Public Opinion Quarterly, 42,* 183–198.

Bachen, C. M. (1998). *Channel One* and the education of American youths. *Annals of the American Academy of Political and Social Science, 557,* 132–146.

Ball, S., & Bogatz, G. A. (1970). *The first year of Sesame Street: An evaluation.* Princeton, NJ: Educational Testing Service.

Ball, S., & Bogatz, G. A. (1973). *Reading with television: An evaluation of The Electric Company.* Princeton, NJ: Educational Testing Service.

Ball, S., Bogatz, G. A., Karazow, K. M., & Rubin, D. B. (1974). *Reading with television: A follow-up evaluation of The Electric Company.* Princeton, NJ: Educational Testing Service.

Beentjes, J. W. J., & van der Voort, T. H. A. (1993). Television viewing versus reading: Mental effort, retention, and inferential learning. *Communication Education, 42,* 191–205.

Block, C., Guth, G. J. A., & Austin, S. (1993). *Galaxy Classroom project evaluation: Language arts, grades 3–5, final report.* San Francisco, CA: Far West Laboratory for Educational Research and Development.

Bogatz, G. A., & Ball, S. (1971). *The second year of Sesame Street: A continuing evaluation.* Princeton, NJ: Educational Testing Service.

Brand, J. E., & Greenberg, B. S. (1994). Commercials in the classroom: The impact of *Channel One* advertising. *Journal of Advertising Research, 34,* 18–27.

Bransford, J. D., Brown, A. L., & Cocking, R. R. (Eds.). (1999). *How people learn: Brain, mind, experience, and school.* Washington, DC: National Academy Press.

Brederode-Santos, M. E. (1993). *Learning with television: The secret of* Rua Sésamo. [English translation of Portuguese, Brederode-Santos, M. E. (1991). *Com a Televiso o Segredo da* Rua Sésamo. Lison: TV Guia Editora.] Unpublished research report.

Bryant, J., McCollum, J., Ralstin, L., Raney, A., McGavin, L., Miron, D., Maxwell, M., Venugopalan, G., Thompson, S., DeWitt, D., & Lewis, K. (1997). *Effects of two years' viewing of Allegra's Window and Gullah Gullah Island.* Tuscaloosa: Institute for Communication Research, University of Alabama.

Bryant, J., Mulliken, L., Maxwell, M., Mundorf, N., Mundorf, J., Wilson, B., Smith, S., McCollum, J., & Owens, J. W. (1999). *Effects of two years' viewing of Blue's Clues.* Tuscaloosa: Institute for Communication Research, University of Alabama.

Calvert, S. L. (1995). *Impact of televised songs on children's and young adults' memory of verbally-presented content.* Unpublished manuscript, Department of Psychology, Georgetown University, Washington, DC.

Calvert, S. L., & Pfordresher, P. Q. (1994, August). *Impact of a televised song on students' memory of information.* Poster presented at the annual meeting of the American Psychological Association, Los Angeles, CA.

Calvert, S. L., Rigaud, E., & Mazella, J. (1991). *Presentational features for students' recall of televised educational content.* Poster presented at the biennial meeting of the Society for Research in Child Development, Seattle, WA.

Calvert, S. L., & Tart, M. (1993). Song versus verbal forms for very-long-term, long-term, and short-term verbatim recall. *Journal of Applied Developmental Psychology, 14,* 245–260.

Cambre, M. A., & Fernie, D. (1985). *Formative evaluation of Season IV, 3-2-1 Contact: Assessing the appeal of four weeks of educational television programs and their influence on children's science comprehension and science interest.* New York: Children's Television Workshop.

Children's Television Workshop. (1994). *Learning from* Ghostwriter: *Strategies and outcomes.* New York: Author.

Clifford, B. R., Gunter, B., & McAleer, J. (1995). *Television and children: Program evaluation, comprehension, and impact.* Hillsdale, NJ: Lawrence Erlbaum Associates.

Cognition and Technology Group at Vanderbilt. (1997). *The Jasper Project: Lessons in curriculum, instruction, assessment, and professional development.* Mahwah, NJ: Lawrence Erlbaum Associates.

Cole, C. F., Richman, B. A., & McCann Brown, S. K. (2001). The world of *Sesame Street* research. In S. M. Fisch & R. T. Truglio (Eds.), *"G" is for "growing": Thirty years of research on children and* Sesame Street (pp. 147–179). Mahwah, NJ: Lawrence Erlbaum Associates.

Comstock, G., & Paik, H. (1991). *Television and the American child.* New York: Academic Press.

Cook, T. D., Appleton, H., Conner, R. F., Shaffer, A., Tamkin, G., & Weber, S. (1975). *Sesame Street revisited.* New York: Russell Sage Foundation.

Crawley, A. M., Anderson, D. R., Wilder, A., Williams, M., & Santomero, A. (1999). Effects of repeated exposures to a single episode of the television program *Blue's Clues* on the viewing behaviors and comprehension of preschool children. *Journal of Educational Psychology, 91,* 630–637.

Detterman, D. K., & Sternberg, R. J. (Eds.). (1993). *Transfer on trial: Intelligence, cognition, and instruction.* Norwood, NJ: Ablex.

Diaz-Guerrero, R., and Holtzman, W. H. (1974). Learning by televised *Plaza Sésamo* in Mexico. *Journal of Educational Psychology, 66*(5), 632–643.

Diaz-Guerrero, R., Reyes-Lagunes, I., Witzke, D. B., and Holtzman, W. H. (1976). *Plaza Sésamo* in Mexico: An evaluation. *Journal of Communication, 26,* 145–154.

Ehman, L. (1995, April). *A case study of* Channel One *in the instruction and curriculum of a middle school.* Paper presented at the annual meeting of the American Education Research Association, San Francisco, CA.

Entwistle, D. R., Alexander, K. L., & Olson, L. S. (1997). *Children, schools, and inequality.* Boulder, CO: Westview Press.

Fay, A. L., Teasley, S. D., Cheng, B. H., Bachman, K. M., & Schnakenberg, J. H. (1995). *Children's interest in and their understanding of science and technology: A study of the effects of* Cro. Pittsburgh: University of Pittsburgh and New York: Children's Television Workshop.

Fay, A. L., Yotive, W. M., Fisch, S. M., Teasley, S. D., McCann, S. K., Garner, M. S., Ozaeta, M., Chen, L., & Lambert, M. H. (1995, August). The impact of *Cro* on children's interest in and understanding of technology. In S. M. Fisch (Chair), *Science on Saturday morning: The Children's Television Act and the role of* Cro. Symposium presented at the annual meeting of the American Psychological Association, New York.

Fisch, S. M. (2000). A capacity model of children's comprehension of educational content on television. *Media Psychology, 2*(1), 63–91.

Fisch, S. M. (2001). Transfer of learning from educational television: When and why does it occur? In S. M. Fisch (Chair), *Theoretical approaches to the long-term effects of television on children.* Symposium presented at the biennial meeting of the Society for Research in Child Development, Minneapolis, MN.

Fisch, S. M., Goodman, I. F., McCann, S. K., Rylander, K., & Ross, S. (1995, April). *The impact of informal science education: Cro and children's understanding of technology.* Poster presented at the 61st annual meeting of the Society for Research in Child Development, Indianapolis, IN.

Fisch, S. M., & Truglio, R. T. (Eds.). (2001). *"G" is for "growing": Thirty years of research on children and* Sesame Street (pp. 115–130). Mahwah, NJ: Lawrence Erlbaum Associates.

Fisch, S. M., Truglio, R. T., & Cole, C. F. (1999). The impact of *Sesame Street* on preschool children: A review and synthesis of thirty years' research. *Media Psychology, 1,* 165–190.

Gick, M. L., & Holyoak, K. J. (1983). Schema induction and analogical transfer. *Cognitive Psychology, 15,* 1–38.

Goodman, I. F., Rylander, K., & Ross, S. (1993). Cro *Season I summative evaluation.* Cambridge, MA: Sierra Research Associates.

Greenberg, B. S., & Brand, J. E. (1993). Television news and advertising in school: The *Channel One* controversy. *Journal of Communication, 43,* 143–151.

Greenberg, B. S., & Gantz, W. (1976). Public television and taboo topics: The impact of *VD Blues. Public Telecommunications Review, 4*(1), 56–59.

Hall, E. R., Esty, E. T., & Fisch, S. M. (1990). Television and children's problem-solving behavior: A synopsis of an evaluation of the effects of *Square One TV. Journal of Mathematical Behavior, 9,* 161–174.

Hall, E. R., Fisch, S. M., Esty, E. T., Debold, E., Miller, B. A., Bennett, D. T., & Solan, S. V. (1990). *Children's problem-solving behavior and their attitudes toward mathematics: A study of the effects of* Square One TV (Vols. 1–5). New York: Children's Television Workshop.

Harvey, F. A., Quiroga, B., Crane, V., & Bottoms, C. L. (1976). *Evaluation of eight* Infinity Factory *programs.* Newton, MA: Education Development Center.

Healy, J. M. (1990). *Endangered minds: Why our children don't think.* New York: Simon & Schuster.

Huston, A. C., Anderson, D. R., Wright, J. C., Linebarger, D. L., & Schmitt, K. L. (2001). *Sesame Street* viewers as adolescents: The recontact study. In S. M. Fisch & R. T. Truglio (Eds.), *"G" is for "growing": Thirty years of research on children and* Sesame Street (pp. 131–144). Mahwah, NJ: Lawrence Erlbaum Associates.

John, D. R. (1999). Consumer socialization of children: A retrospective look at 25 years of research. *Journal of Consumer Research, 26,* 183–213.

Johnston, J. (1980). *An exploratory study of the effects of viewing the first season of* 3-2-1 Contact. New York: Children's Television Workshop.

Johnston, J., & Brzezinski, E. (1992). *Taking the measure of* Channel One: *The first year.* Ann Arbor: Institute for Social Research, University of Michigan.

Johnston, J., & Brzezinski, E. (1994). *Executive summary,* Channel One: *A three year perspective.* Ann Arbo: Institute for Social Research, University of Michigan.

Johnston, J., Brzezinski, E., & Anderman, E. M. (1994). *Taking the measure of* Channel One: *A three year perspective.* Ann Arbor: Institute for Social Research, University of Michigan.

Johnston, J., & Luker, R. (1983). *The "Eriksson Study": An exploratory study of viewing two weeks of the second season of* 3-2-1 Contact. New York: Children's Television Workshop.

Knupfer, N., & Hayes, P. (1994). The effects of the *Channel One* broadcast on students' knowledge of current events. In A. DeVaney (Ed.), *Watching* Channel One: *The convergence of students, technology, and private business.* Albany: State University of New York Press.

KRC Research & Consulting. (1994). *An evaluative assessment of the* Ghostwriter *project.* New York: Author.

Kunkel, D. (2001). Children and television advertising. In D. G. Singer & J. L. Singer (Eds.), *Handbook of children and the media* (pp. 375–393). Thousand Oaks, CA: Sage.

Lampert, M. (1985). Mathematics learning in context: *The Voyage of the Mimi. Journal of Mathematical Behavior, 4,* 157–167.

Lang, A., Geiger, S., Strickwerda, M., & Sumner, J. (1993). The effects of related and unrelated cuts on television viewers' attention, processing capacity, and memory. *Communication Research, 20,* 4–29.

Leitner, R. K. (1991). *Comparing the effects on reading comprehension of educational video, direct experience, and print.* Unpublished doctoral thesis, University of San Francisco, CA.

Levin, T., Sabar, N., & Libman, Z. (1991). Achievements and attitudinal patterns of boys and girls in science. *Journal of Research in Science Teaching, 28,* 315–328.

Liebert, R., & Schwartzberg, N. (1977). Effects of mass media. *Annual Review of Psychology, 28,* 141–174.

Linebarger, D. L. (2000). *Summative evaluation of* Between the Lions: *A final report to WGBH Educational Foundation.* Kansas City: Juniper Gardens Children's Project, University of Kansas.

Lorch, E. P., & Castle, V. J. (1997). Preschool children's attention to television: Visual attention and probe response times. *Journal of Experimental Child Psychology, 66,* 111–127.

Mares, M. L., & Woodard, E. H. (2001). Prosocial effects on children's social interactions. In D. G. Singer & J. L. Singer (Eds.), *Handbook of children and the media* (pp. 183–205). Thousand Oaks, CA: Sage.

Meadowcroft, J. M., & Reeves, B. (1989). Influence of story schema development on children's attention to television. *Communication Research, 16,* 352–374.

Mulliken, L., & Bryant, J. A. (1999, May). *Effects of curriculum-based television programming on behavioral assessments of flexible thinking and structured and unstructured prosocial play behaviors.* Poster presented at the 49th annual conference of the International Communication Association, San Francisco, CA.

Naigles, L. R., & Mayeux, L. (2001). Television as incidental language teacher. In D. G. Singer & J. L. Singer (Eds.), *Handbook of children and the media* (pp. 135–152). Thousand Oaks, CA: Sage.

Naigles, L., Singer, D., Singer, J., Jean-Louis, B., Sells, D., & Rosen, C. (1995). *Watching "Barney" affects preschoolers' use of mental state verbs.* Paper presented at the annual meeting of the American Psychological Association, New York.

National Council of Teachers of Mathematics. (1989). *Curriculum and evaluation standards for school mathematics.* Reston, VA: Author.

Nielsen New Media Services. (1993). Ghostwriter *study, wave II: May, 1993.* Dunedin, FL: Author.

Noble, G., & Creighton, V. M. (1981). *Australia Naturally—Children's reactions.* Armidale, Australia: Author.

Paivio, A. (1971). *Imagery and verbal processes.* New York: Holt.

Palmer, E. L., & Fisch, S. M. (2001). The beginnings of *Sesame Street* research. In S. M. Fisch & R. T. Truglio (Eds.), *"G" is for "growing": Thirty years of research on children and Sesame Street* (pp. 3–23). Mahwah, NJ: Lawrence Erlbaum Associates.

Peel, T., Rockwell, A., Esty, E., & Gonzer, K. (1987). Square One Television: *The comprehension and problem solving study.* New York: Children's Television Workshop.

Postman, N. (1985). *Amusing ourselves to death.* New York: Penguin.

Reiser, R. A., Tessmer, M. A., & Phelps, P. C. (1984). Adult-child interaction in children's learning from *Sesame Street. Educational Communication and Technology Journal, 32,* 217–223.

Reiser, R. A., Williamson, N., & Suzuki, K. (1988). Using *Sesame Street* to facilitate children's recognition of letters and numbers. *Educational Communication and Technology Journal, 36,* 15–21.

Rice, M. L. (1984). The words of children's television. *Journal of Broadcasting, 28,* 445–461.

Rice, M. L., & Haight, P. L. (1986). "Motherese" of Mr. Rogers: A description of the dialogue of educational television programs. *Journal of Speech and Hearing Disorders, 51,* 282–287.

Rice, M. L., Huston, A. C., Truglio, R., & Wright, J. C. (1990). Words from *Sesame Street*: Learning vocabulary while viewing. *Developmental Psychology, 26,* 421–428.

Rice, M. L., & Woodsmall, L. (1988). Lessons from television: Children's word learning when viewing. *Child Development, 59,* 420–429.

Richards, J. I., Wartella, E. A., Morton, C. & Thompson, L. (1998). The growing commercialization of schools: Issues and practices. *Annals of the American Academy of Political and Social Science, 557,* 148–163.

Rockman Et Al. (1996). *Evaluation of* Bill Nye the Science Guy: *Television series and outreach.* San Francisco, CA: Author.

Sahin, N. (1990, September). *Preliminary report on the summative evaluation of the Turkish co-production of Sesame Street.* Paper presented at the International Conference on Adaptations of *Sesame Street,* Amsterdam, The Netherlands.

Salomon, G. (1977). Effects of encouraging Israeli mothers to co-observe *Sesame Street* with their five-year-olds. *Child Development, 48,* 1146–1151.

Sanders, J. R., & Sonnad, S. R. (1980). *Research on the introduction, use, and impact of* Thinkabout: *Executive summary.* Bloomington, IN: Agency for Instructional Television.

Schauble, L., & Peel. B. (1986). *The "Mathnet" format on* Square One: *Children's informal problem solving, understanding of mathematical concepts, and ideas and attitudes about mathematics.* New York: Children's Television Workshop.

Singer, D. G., Singer, J. L., Miller, R. H., & Sells, D. J. (1994). Barney and Friends *as education and entertainment: Phase 2, kindergarten sample—Can children learn through kindergarten exposure to* Barney and Friends? New Haven, CT: Yale University Family Television Research and Consultation Center.

Singer, J. L., & Singer, D. G. (1981). *Television, imagination, and aggression: A study of preschoolers.* Hillsdale, NJ: Lawrence Erlbaum Associates.

Singer, J. L., & Singer, D. G. (1994). Barney and Friends *as education and entertainment: Phase 2—Can children learn through preschool exposure to* Barney and Friends? New Haven, CT: Yale University Family Television Research and Consultation Center.

Singer, J. L., & Singer, D. G. (1995). Barney and Friends *as education and entertainment: Phase 3—A national study: Can children learn through preschool exposure to* Barney and Friends? New Haven, CT: Yale University Family Television Research and Consultation Center.

Singer, J. L., & Singer, D. G. (1998). *Barney & Friends* as entertainment and education: Evaluating the quality and effectiveness of a television series for preschool children. In J. K. Asamen & G. L. Berry (Eds.), *Research paradigms, television, and social behavior* (pp. 305–367). Thousand Oaks, CA: Sage.

Singhal, A., & Rogers, E. M. (1999). *Entertainment-education: A communication strategy for social change.* Mahwah, NJ: Lawrence Erlbaum Associates.

Thorson, E., Reeves, B., & Schleuder, J. (1985). Message complexity and attention to television. *Communication Research, 12,* 427–454.

Ulitsa Sezam Department of Research and Content. (1998, November). *Preliminary report of summative findings.* Report presented to the Children's Television Workshop, New York.

UNICEF (1996). *Executive summary: Summary assessment of* Plaza Sésamo IV—Mexico. [English translation of Spanish.] Unpublished research report. Mexico City, Mexico: Author.

Wagner, S. (1985). *Comprehensive evaluation of the fourth season of* 3-2-1 Contact. New York: Children's Television Workshop.

Walma van der Molen, J., & van der Voort, T. (1997). Children's recall of television and print news: A media comparison study. *Journal of Educational Psychology, 89,* 82–91.

Walma van der Molen, J., & van der Voort, T. (1998). Children's recall of the news: TV news stories compared with three print versions. *Educational Technology Research and Development, 46,* 39–52.

Walma van der Molen, J., & van der Voort, T. (2000). The impact of television, print, and audio on children's recall of the news: A study of three alternative explanations for the dual-coding hypothesis. *Human Communications Research, 26,* 3–26.

Wartella, E., & Jennings, N. (2001). Hazards and possibilities of commercial TV in the schools. In D. G. Singer & J. L. Singer (Eds.), *Handbook of children and the media* (pp. 557–570). Thousand Oaks, CA: Sage.

Wilson, B. J., Kunkel, D., Linz, D., Potter, J., Donnerstein, E., Smith, S. L., Blumenthal, E., & Gray, T. (1997). *National television violence study* (Vol. 1). Thousand Oaks, CA: Sage.

Winn, M. (1977). *The plug-in drug.* New York: Penguin.

Winsten, J. A. (1994). Promoting designated drivers: The Harvard Alcohol Project. *American Journal of Preventive Medicine, 10*(3), 11–14.

Wood, J. M., & Duke, N. K. (1997). Inside *Reading Rainbow:* A spectrum of strategies for promoting literacy. *Language Arts, 74,* 95–106.

Wright, J. C., & Huston, A. C. (1995). *Effects of educational TV viewing of lower income preschoolers on academic skills, school readiness, and school adjustment one to three years later: A report to the Children's Television Workshop.* Lawrence: Center for Research on the Influences of Television on Children, University of Kansas.

Wright, J. C., Huston, A. C., Scantlin, R., & Kotler, J. (2001). The Early Window project: *Sesame Street* prepares children for school. In S. M. Fisch & R. T. Truglio (Eds.), *"G" is for "growing": Thirty years of research on children and* Sesame Street (pp. 97–114). Mahwah, NJ: Lawrence Erlbaum Associates.

Zero to Three/National Center for Clinical Infant Programs.(1992). *Heart Start: The emotional foundations of school readiness.* Arlington, VA: Author.

Zill, N. (2001). Does *Sesame Street* enhance school readiness? Evidence from a national survey of children. In S. M. Fisch & R. T. Truglio (Eds.), *"G" is for "growing": Thirty years of research on children and* Sesame Street (pp. 115–130). Mahwah, NJ: Lawrence Erlbaum Associates.

Zill, N., Davies, E., & Daly, M. (1994). *Viewing of* Sesame Street *by preschool children and its relationship to school readiness: Report prepared for the Children's Television Workshop.* Rockville, MD: Westat, Inc.

Chapter 16

Communication Campaigns:

Theory, Design, Implementation, and Evaluation

RONALD E. RICE
Rutgers University

CHARLES K. ATKIN
Michigan State University

Public communication campaigns can be broadly defined as (a) purposive attempts; (b) to inform, persuade, or motivate behavior changes; (c) in a relatively well-defined and large audience; (d) generally for noncommercial benefits to the individuals and/or society at large; (e) typically within a given time period; (f) by means of organized communication activities involving mass media; and (g) often complemented by interpersonal support (adapted and expanded from Rogers & Storey, 1987).

Paisley (2001) distinguishes public service campaigns (where goals are generally supported by a broad array of stakeholders) from advocacy campaigns (where goals are controversial and challenged by significant stakeholders). Over time, some topics may shift from one type to another, such as gender equality or smoking. There are several other conceptual distinctions mentioned by Paisley (1998, 2001):

1. *Objectives or methods* (emphasizing campaigns as strategies of social control to achieve objectives, or campaigns as a genre of communication with associated methods, communication channels, and kinds of results)
2. *Strategies of change* (whether the campaign emphasizes education or providing information about how to change behaviors or attitudes, enforcement or negative consequences for not complying with accepted or desired behavior, or engineering or designing social systems to prevent unwanted behaviors or consequences)

3. *Individual or collective* benefits (whether campaigns emphasize individual or social changes and outcomes)
4. *First-party* and *second-party* entitlement (whether campaign sources pay the direct consequences and have a primary stake in the issue or whether they are not directly affected and represent other stakeholders who may not be able to present their case)
5. *Types of stakeholders* (whether the primary campaign sponsors and actors are associations, government agencies, foundations, trade unions, corporations, mass media, and social scientists, as they all differentially affect the public agenda, funding sources, campaign design, access to media, objectives, and audiences).

Although there has been extensive research and practice in campaign theorizing, design, implementation, evaluation, and critique over the past decade since our initial summary chapter (Rice & Atkin, 1994), many current campaigns still fall far below expectations, many theoretical aspects of campaigns are still only partially understood, and many (often unexpected or uncontrollable) factors may influence the direction, implementation, and outcomes of campaigns. Only when we understand underlying general principles of communication, persuasion, and social change and the relationships among the components of a campaign can we properly design and evaluate campaign efforts. This is especially true precisely for the reasons that social science is often criticized by practitioners: Reality is too complex to identify what really causes what and what is and is not effective, especially when perceptions are based solely on experience gained in a few campaigns.

The following 10 sections summarize general campaign components according to a framework derived from both Atkin (2001) and McGuire (2001). Additional sources for campaign summaries and reviews are provided in the appendix of Rice and Atkin (2001), as well as in Backer, Rogers, and Sopory (1992), who suggested 27 generalizations about successful health communication campaigns (pp. 30–32). We should note that one campaign activity underlying all the following components is ongoing evaluation. "Evaluation is the systematic application of research procedures to understand the conceptualization, design, implementation, and utility of interventions" (Valente, 2001, p. 106). Valente proposes that a comprehensive evaluation framework includes (a) assessing needs; (b) conducting formative research to design messages; (c) designing treatments, comparisons, instruments, and monitoring methods; (d) process research; (e) summative research; and (f) sharing results with stakeholders and other researchers. Developing an evaluation plan as an initial part of the campaign forces implementers and researchers to explicitly state the desired outcomes of the campaign and how the plan will be implemented to obtain those goals. The actual financial and time costs of evaluation are real, but are extremely valuable investments, both for the current campaign stakeholders as well as for stakeholders of subsequent campaigns.

UNDERSTAND HISTORICAL AND POLITICAL CONTEXT

There is a rich history of American communication campaigns before the era of federal government and social science involvement (Paisley, 2001). Early examples include the pamphleteers and individual reformers in the 18th century such as Cotton Mather and public inoculations, Benjamin Franklin and abolitionism, Thomas Paine and independence, and Dorethea Dix and treatment of the mentally ill. The 19th century saw the rise of associations using legislative testimony, mass communication, confrontation, and local organizing (Bracht, 2001) to promote slavery abolition, women's suffrage, temperance unions, and wilderness preservation. In the early 20th century, muckrakers harnessed the powerful reach of inexpensive newspapers to address issues such as child labor and adulterated food products. As the century progressed, the federal government played an increasingly central role with regulations concerning commerce, food and drugs, and the environment, as well as programs providing social services after the New Deal. By midcentury, campaigners were applying social science to the development and evaluation of campaigns; initial perspectives held that mass media campaigns had no direct effect, that audiences were largely uninterested or applied selective exposure and perception, and that most effects operated indirectly through opinion leaders, whereas more recent theories suggest that well-conceived campaigns can achieve moderate success by using appropriate mixes of social change, media advocacy, philosophical emphasis on participation, audience targeting, message design, channel usage, and time frames.

Also crucial to the success of campaigns is the ability to become an important and enduring part of the public agenda and to obtain first-party entitlement for significant stakeholders (Paisley, 2001). Some topics rise and fall over time, such as energy conservation, global warming, busing, endangered species, cancer, HIV/AIDS, tobacco, starvation due to famine, abortion, or civil rights. It seems that some periods are more "ideological," where issues are debated in the public agenda more extensively. One challenge in campaigns is to understand and try to shape these agenda items and to cut through the very cluttered set of public agenda items that compete for people's attention and understanding. Paisley (1998) concludes that campaigns must advise, inform, advocate, and reinforce rather than simply exhorting, because only the individual can grasp the various aspects of their social context.

REVIEW THE REALITIES, AND UNDERSTAND
THE SOCIOCULTURAL SITUATION

In undertaking campaigns, it's advisable to first review the realities (choose a significant problem for which there seems to be a cost-effective solution, and then identify available resources and determine the optimum apportionment) and to assess the campaign ethics (including direct and indirect consequences and the assumptions underlying campaign goal and audience identification).

This includes identifying the focal behaviors of the high-risk or goal audiences, their media usage patterns, social factors and institutional constraints, and what constitutes meaningful and acceptable change. It also involves identifying whether the campaign objectives are essentially creating awareness, instructing/educating, or persuading; among the "strategies of change" mentioned by Paisley, most campaigns emphasize the educational component rather than the enforcement or engineering aspects.

Part of this understanding is the philosophical foundation of the campaign. For example, the perspectives of sense-making, community, and two-way symmetric public relations campaigns have reconceptualized audience members (including publics, communities, and institutions) as peers and collaborators in the mutual and interactive development and implementation of a change effort (Bracht, 2001; Dervin & Frenette, 2001; Dozier, Grunig, & Grunig, 2001). These approaches differ from traditional campaigns by giving greater emphasis to audiences' social and cultural contexts, by replacing experts' goals with audience-derived goals, and by using audience networks as ways to generate, frame, and share messages (Dervin & Frenette, 2001).

UNDERSTAND THE AUDIENCE

One approach to improved understanding of the audience well enough to develop appropriate campaign efforts to that audience is segmentation— identifying subaudiences. Segmentation may involve analyses of demographics, media usage patterns, lifestyle, psychographics, ZIP code, uses and gratifications, and channel accessibility. This enables allocation of campaign efforts to the audience groups that are most in need of change and most receptive to the campaign and to design messages appropriate to the audience preferences, media usage, and abilities.

There are three major types of audiences. "Focal segments" are audiences grouped by levels of risk or illness, readiness, income and education, and other factors such as sensation seeking. "Interpersonal influencers" are opinion leaders, media advocates, and peer and role models who can mediate the campaign (positively or negatively) and help set the public agenda. "Societal policymakers" affect the legal, political, and resource infrastructure, such as through regulations on media messages, environmental conditions, or safety standards, and social action such as community-based campaigns, federal allocations (such as the gasoline or tobacco tax), and insurance and health care programs. Atkin (2001) argues that campaigns may want to develop a "product line" or continuum of intended outcomes, so that audiences with different levels of receptivity or resistance can find their comfortable location in the campaign mix.

One way of understanding the audience is the sense-making methodology, which aims to "ensure as far as possible that dialogue is encouraged in every aspect of communication campaign research, design, and implementation" (Dervin & Frenette, 2001, p. 72). This method helps participants communicate about their attempts to move through discontinuities (gaps in meaning across time, people, and space) in their life experiences by means of making sense, internally and externally, in the context of the intersection of past, present, and future. Cognitions, attitudes, beliefs, emotions, and narratives serve as bridges—or obstacles—across these gaps. The primary interviewing approach is called the micromoment time line, whereby participants are asked to describe a situation and how they experienced it through time, identifying both how they saw themselves as stopped or moving at a particular moment on the time line and how various utilities helped them move through time and space. Examples of campaigns using this approach include assessing antismoking messages from adolescents' perspectives (for example, showing how such messages did or did not acknowledge their needs, or unfairly portrayed young smokers in their social contexts), identifying the poor fit between traditional AIDS campaign issues and those mentioned by health care center patients, designing messages to encourage blood donors to donate again, and reducing stress in cancer clinic patients.

The concept of "two-way symmetrical campaigns" derived from public relations theory is, surprisingly, quite similar to some of the main goals of the sense-making approach (Dozier, Grunig, & Grunig, 2001). It emphasizes negotiating with an activist public, using conflict resolution in dealing with publics, helping management understand the opinions of particular publics, and determining how publics react to the organization. In particular, Dozier et al. highlight the significance of "invisible clients," those organizations that employ public relations activities to influence audiences without being explicitly identified as associated with the message. Examples include the tobacco industry, political ideologies (see Proctor, 2001), and the milk industry (through its "Got Milk?" campaigns—see Butler, 2001).

APPLY APPROPRIATE THEORY

After assessing the factors described, the campaign strategist should identify appropriate theoretical approaches. Although campaigns are typically
viewed as merely applied communication research, the most effective
campaigns carefully review and apply relevant theories; further, campaign
results can be used to extend and improve theories about media effects and
social change. Atkin (2001) advocates using informed diversification of
campaign approaches and channels rather than a single strategy.

Variants to the straightforward communication/persuasion matrix
(McGuire, 2001) include the following:

Elaboration likelihood model (Petty & Cacioppo, 1986): Messages have
greater or longer term effect or are more strongly rejected if the individual
is motivated to cognitively process (called elaboration) the message. This
is the "central" route to persuasion. Messages may also have modest
short-term attitudinal or behavioral effects without knowledge change if
the individual is not motivated to cognitively process the message. This is
the "peripheral" route.

Self-persuasion: Rather than relying solely on new, external messages,
persuasion attempts may also turn to activating information already
accepted, but perhaps without great salience. Thus, resistance to persuasion may be increased by providing prior exposure to threatening messages. Or, internal values may be changed by causing the individual to
confront those values, to inspect associated issues, or to evoke new arguments (McGuire, 1960).

Alternate causal chains: Rather than the simple sequence that knowledge
changes attitudes that in turn change behavior, it may well be that
changed behavior alters one's attitudes, which then causes one to seek out
supportive knowledge (Bem, 1970). Both cognitive dissonance and self-
perception theories support this altered causal path.

Theories most commonly invoked to guide successful campaigns
include the following:

Social learning (Bandura, 1977b; Flora, 2001): Individuals are likely to
exhibit behavior similar to that of role models who are credible, who
explicitly model intended behaviors, and who receive appropriate negative or positive reinforcements.

Social comparison (Festinger, 1954; Flora, 2001): People compare the
salience and outcomes of others' behavior, which, along with social
norms, attitudes, and intentions, influence one's subsequent behavior.

Reasoned action (Ajzen & Fishbein, 1980): A combination of one's personal attitudes, perceived norms of influential others, and motivation to
comply provides a parsimonious model of predictors of intended behavior. This model is derived from *expectancy-value* theory, which postulates

that one's beliefs about the likelihood that a given behavior leads to certain consequences, multiplied by one's evaluation of those consequences, is likely to predict attitudes and behavior.

Instrumental learning (Hovland, Janis, & Kelley, 1953): The classic model of persuasion combines characteristics of the source (such as attractiveness and credibility), incentives of the message appeal (such as fear, social acceptance, correct knowledge), and repetition and placement of the message to predict changes in knowledge, attitude, and behavior.

Self-efficacy (Bandura, 1977a): The extent to which one feels one has control over one's actions, or can in fact accomplish a task, affects the extent to which one engages in changing one's own attitudes and behaviors. Thus an intermediary goal of a campaign would be to improve the self-efficacy of the at-risk group, such as those attempting to stop smoking or adolescents attempting to learn and practice behaviors that reduce their risk of AIDS. Crucial to increasing self-efficacy is providing explicit strategies through role models (for children, peers are especially influential) and social comparisons to admired others.

The *extended parallel process model* (EPPM) (Stephenson & Witte, 2001): People both under- and overestimate their own health risks and overestimate risks to others relative to their own vulnerability, partially due to cognitive processing limits, denial, and attraction to risks (including sensation seeking; see Palmgreen, Donohew, & Harrington, 2001). Fear appeals, through arousal, perceived susceptibility and vulnerability, awareness of likelihood of a hazard, framing of messages in terms of potential gains or losses, and perceived threat, can be effective in changing risky attitudes and behaviors. However, there are two, parallel, responses to fear: a cognitive process involving ways to control or avert a danger, which may take advantage of the health message using a fear appeal, and an emotional process that attempts to control the fear, often by denial or coping, which will generally reject the message due to the fear appeal. (The third possible response is to ignore the message if it's deemed irrelevant or insignificant to the respondent.) The EPPM argues that perceived threat influences the strength of a danger or fear control response, whereas perceived efficacy influences whether danger or fear control responses are elicited. So a fear appeal must successfully convey both that the threat is salient and significant and that the audience member can do something about it, probably by emphasizing efficacy before threat.

Diffusion and influence through social networks (Piotrow & Kincaid, 2001; Rice, 1993; Rogers, 1981): Ideas, norms, and practices are diffused through—or rejected by—interpersonal networks because of the strong influence that evaluations and behavior of others—especially opinion leaders—have on network members. For example, students' estimates of their peers' drinking behaviors are typically significantly higher than the peers' actual behaviors; these inaccurate social projections encourage students to engage in excessive drinking until campaigns such as the RU Sure? Project (Lederman et al., 2001) provide accurate evidence from the individuals' own peer networks. Thus, perceived network influence is an important goal as well as a mechanism of campaigns taking social network theory seriously.

Integrative theory of behavior change (Cappella, Fishbein, Hornik, Ahern, & Sayeed, 2001): This model, developed to guide the evaluation of the National Youth Anti-Drug Media Campaign (NYADMC), integrates three major theories: Health Belief Model, social cognitive theory, and the theory of reasoned action. Outcome behaviors are influenced by skills, environmental constraints, and intentions. Intentions are influenced by attitudes, norms, and self-efficacy. Attitudes are influenced by behavioral beliefs and their evaluative aspects. Norms are influenced by normative beliefs and motivations to comply (such as with network members or opinion leaders or enforcement threats). Self-efficacy is influenced by efficacy beliefs. All the beliefs are influenced by a variety of external variables (situational, institutional, and infrastructural), demographics, attitudes, personality traits, and other individual differences, such as gender, race, and culture). This model highlights several crucial aspects, such as whether a given behavioral intention is more influenced by attitudinal, normative, or self-efficacy control. For example, fear appeal messages received by people with high perceived vulnerability but low self-efficacy are likely to avoid, deny, or displace the promoted healthy behaviors. Further, identifying what audience segments hold what beliefs or what social groupings are more influenced by social norms helps campaign implementers focus their efforts.

A particular use of this model is to determine how messages about some behaviors may be used to *prime* or cue other behaviors by affecting "the relative weights for criteria used in determining an attitude, opinion, or behavior induced by a message" (Cappella et al., 2001, p. 222), which is different than traditional persuasion through the message itself, as its main effect is achieved through increasing cognitive processing and accessibility of the message. At the social level, raising an issue's location on the public agenda, as Paisley (2001) discussed, is one way to prime related campaign messages.

The *transtheoretical model* (Buller et al., 2001; Prochaska, DiClemente, & Norcross, 1992): This model identifies subaudiences on the basis of their stage in the process of behavior change. The five stages, with respect to a specific health behavior, are precontemplation, contemplation, preparation, action, or maintenance. Progression along these stages is influenced by a variety of processes: consciousness raising, dramatic relief, self-reevaluation, environmental reevaluation, self-liberation, helping relationships, counterconditioning, contingency management, stimulus, control, and social liberation. Thus, based on the audience's stage, a campaign should emphasize different processes, behaviors, and messages. This is an ideal challenge for interactive Web sites, as users can first assess their own stage and then be provided material and activities appropriate for that stage and the associated processes, such as in the Consider This Web-based smoking cessation and prevention program for children (Buller et al., 2001), or children's interactive CD-ROMs and video games (Lieberman, 2001).

The *Health Communication-Behavior Change Model* (CBC), the basis of the Stanford Three-Community Campaign to reduce cardiovascular disease through integrated community-wide projects, outlines three major project components: communication inputs (media, face-to-face, and community programs), communication functions for the receiver (attention, information, incentives, models, training, cues to action, support, self-management) and behavior objectives for the receiver (awareness, knowledge, motivation, skills, action, practice self-management skills, social network members) (Flora, 2001).

APPLY THE COMMUNICATION/PERSUASION MATRIX TO MESSAGE DESIGN

It is important to understand the role of and interaction among communication input variables and output variables. Communication *input variables* include source, message, channel, audience, and outcomes. Campaign *output variables* include the 13 possibly sequential persuasion steps of exposure, attention, liking, comprehension, generating related cognitions, acquiring skills, attitude change, storing, retrieving, decision to act in accord with retrieved position, action, cognitive integration of behavior, and encouraging others to behave similarly (McGuire, 2001).

Typical source (or messenger) variables include credibility, attractiveness, and power. However, their effect may covary with other factors, such as attractiveness with formality of dress and credibility with sameness of gender or ethnicity between source and audience. Interesting message variables include credibility, attractiveness, relevance, understandability, argument structure, evidence, one-sided vs. two-sided content, types of arguments, types of appeals, style (humor, clarity), and amount. More effective appeals associate (a) some valued (positive/negative) incentive(s) with (b) a sufficient probability of (c) the (healthy/unhealthy) goal behaviors. Typical incentives relate to health, time/effort, economics, aspirations, social acceptance, and status. For example, well-designed fear appeals can increase the perceived probability of social rejection by continued smoking even though they may not bring the distant likelihood of lung cancer to salient levels. Atkin (2001) feels that probability is more effective than valence when both cannot be achieved, and that multiple appeals are a more efficient as well as effective strategy. Evidence is more important for forming beliefs when the source lacks complete credibility or when the audience is more involved. Other message variables include stylistic, modality, and production factors, which should be appropriately matched to the nature of the argument, audience, and desired outcomes.

Channel variables include different media's reach, specialization, informativeness, interactivity (receiver involvement), modalities, decodability (cognitive effort), effect on agenda setting, accessibility, homogeneity of audience, efficiency of production and dissemination, and context in which the audience uses the medium (Atkin, 2001; McGuire, 2001). Challenging audience variables include risk, cognitive development, education, and susceptibility to social influence (affected by anxiety, peer norms and behaviors, self-efficacy, and compensatory mechanisms such as threat-avoiding coping habits). Central outcomes include beliefs, attitudes, behavior, persistence of outcome, and resistance to persuasion. McGuire (2001) discusses how each of these may be moderated by, or interact with, other factors.

Potentially valuable output or persuasion variables to consider include audience choices and social settings of media use; whether there may be different paths to persuasion; the actual sequence of these 13 steps for different people or settings; the role that liking, comprehension, and recall play in affecting behavioral outcomes; and whether the goal is to promote positive behaviors and attitudes or reduce or prevent negative ones. This latter issue, for example, raises questions of whether fear appeals, counterarguing, or social benefits from alternative behaviors are most appropriate.

Atkin (2001) points out that depending on the nature of the campaign goal and type of message—awareness, instruction, or persuasion—different input and output variables would be emphasized. For example, messages intended to create awareness need to stimulate and facilitate audience members to seek additional information or sensitize or prime them to note particular kinds of messages. Some messages are designed to instruction or educate, such as procedures to use to resist peer pressure to engage in unhealthy behaviors, or to inoculate audiences against misleading advertisements. Finally, persuasion messages create or change attitudes through the promise, or association, of positive or negative incentives, located in the present or the future, in one's person or one's social interactions. Crucial to successful persuasion messages is activating or creating the salience and likelihood of positive outcomes.

The communication inputs and the output response steps—creating what is typically called the communication/persuasion matrix—interact to mediate the persuasive response, so all the stages must work together to identify the appropriate campaign components and timing. This matrix helps to identify some common campaign fallacies (McGuire, 1989):

1. Overestimating the likelihood of achieving the final outcomes (*attenuated effects*): because each of the outcome steps is likely to be only partially attained, the net multiplicative effect is likely to be quite low.
2. Not clarifying the temporal nature of the outcome (*distal measure*): is it immediate exposure, liking the message, short-term knowledge change, moderate-term attitude change, or long-term behavioral change?
3. Ignoring interactions among communication inputs (*neglected-mediator*): For example, production standards may predominate in making the source credible and familiar (such as Smokey Bear), but submerge the message content (as Smokey really doesn't tell us how to prevent forest fires; Rice, 2001).
4. Overlooking contrasting effects (*compensatory principle*): Different variables may affect behavior outcome in opposite directions; for example, if the audience is aware of the persuasive intent of the source, perceived trustworthiness may decrease, but clarification of the message may increase.
5. Overemphasizing communication inputs: Because of some of the other principles and interactions among stages, the eventual outcome may be highest at middle levels of several inputs (*golden mean*).

CONDUCT FORMATIVE EVALUATION

As part of campaign management, information and feedback systems should be implemented because campaigns are complex and longitudinal projects. They must be monitored for ongoing administration, scheduling, delivery of materials, effectiveness, diagnosis, and improvement.

An important part of this campaign planning and design is *formative evaluation*, which provides data and perspectives to improve messages during the course of creation (Atkin & Freimuth, 2001; Flora, 2001) and helps avoid unintended outcomes such as boomerang effects or shifting unhealthy behaviors to other domains.

A general goal of formative evaluation is to understand what McGuire calls the "sociocultural situation," the situational circumstances, whether economic, cultural, political, or psychological, that instigate and maintain the undesirable target behavior or that sustain the desired target behavior. This understanding is obtained through *preproduction research.* Messages are then revised based on *production testing* (pretesting).

Atkin and Freimuth (2001) identified these stages in preproduction research:

1. *Identify the target audiences:* Who is at risk, who is accessible through communication channels, who can influence others at risk, and who is most and least persuasible? The Stanford project also involved community stakeholders such as health agencies, commercial organizations (restaurants and workplaces), and community leaders, so its formative evaluation included an *organizational needs analysis* (Flora, 2001).

2. *Specify the target behavior:* Insofar as most global behaviors consist of component behaviors that are influenced by contextual factors, campaign messages should focus on specific effective component behaviors. For example, formative evaluation of weight-loss messages in the Stanford Community Studies found that whereas women were aware of their weight problems and motivated to change, men greatly underestimated their weight problem, were not generally motivated to change, and had low self-efficacy about their ability to lose weight (Flora, 2001).

3. *Elaborate intermediate responses:* As the hierarchy-of-effects model suggests, there is a long causal chain between exposure and integrated behavior. Formative evaluation can identify how these steps are linked and what intermediate steps are most amenable to campaign efforts. Some of the intermediate responses include knowledge and lexicon, beliefs and images, attitudes and values, salience priorities, and efficacy and skills. For example, Cialdini (2001) argued that campaigns must avoid unintentionally providing persuasive models of undesirable but popular norms while explicitly concentrating on desirable but unpopular prescriptive norms.

4. *Ascertain channel use:* Using any kind of media without knowing which media the target audience uses, at what times, for how long or how many times, and in what combination is an ineffective use of campaign resources. Formative evaluation can identify media exposure and attitudes toward the different media.

There are many useful database resources for preproduction, such as Prizm Lifestyle Segmentation data, American Healthstyles data, American Youthstyles data, Nielsen Media Research, and Simmons Teenage Research Study data.

The Stanford project (Flora, 2001) used extensive preproduction research, involving data sources such as community media analysis, audience use information, baseline population measures of cognitions, attitudes and health behaviors, and unstructured interviews.

Then these stages of production testing or pretesting research can be applied:

1. *Develop the concept:* Test audiences can suggest and amplify more-appropriate message ideas or more-relevant message sources (e.g., Should the source be a doctor or a celebrity?). Words, phrases, or descriptions used by target audiences in their discussions about the campaign topic can also be incorporated into message content.

2. *Create the test message:* Rough, preliminary versions of messages can be tested for the following attributes: attention, comprehensibility, strong and weak points, relevance, or controversial aspects.

Several methods are useful in pretesting messages, including focus group interviews, in-depth interviews, central-location intercept interviews, self-administered questionnaires, theater testing, day-after recall, media gatekeeper review, and physiological response analysis.

ENGAGE THE MEDIA

Campaigns must make their messages available through a variety of communication channels that are appropriate for the target audience. The message must also communicate specific information, understandings, and behaviors that are actually accessible, feasible, and culturally acceptable (Rice & Atkin, 1989).

We have seen that the communication/persuasion matrix, along with formative evaluation, can be used to design or identify persuasive and informational attributes of source, message, and channel. A social marketing perspective also emphasizes the need to understand the competition, particularly alternative messages and behaviors. Any mass media message competes with hundreds of other messages. Any concept competes with dozens of related mental concepts. So there is a need to identify the "competitive advantage" of the particular campaign objective. For example, exercising as a means of preventing heart disease can also be advertised as a social activity.

Approaches to Media Use: Placement, Data, Services

Alcalay and Taplin (1989) highlighted the importance and utility of *public relations* ("news about an issue, service, client, or product," p. 116) and *public affairs* ("lobbying and working on regulatory or legislative issues with administrators and legislators," p. 122). Because it has "third-party" credibility, public relations can be very useful in not only increasing public awareness of a campaign, but also in deterring opposition to an otherwise controversial issue, such as family planning. Public affairs is important not only in shaping legislation that may affect campaign objectives, but also in gaining support for resources and spokespeople. Editorials, press releases, and hard news coverage may be powerful media modes when managed properly.

It is common practice to request local and sometimes national media to place *public service announcements* (PSAs). The practice of broadcasting PSAs was in large part an outgrowth of Federal Communication Commission requirements that stations using the broadcasting frequencies serve the public interest and necessity. With the increase in media outlets and the movement toward deregulation of the media, opportunities to broadcast PSAs have declined. It can be argued that PSAs are typically of limited value anyway, because they cannot be scheduled for times when the specific target audience is most likely to be watching or listening or in known amounts of exposure. Nevertheless, PSAs can be placed in specialized outlets such as local radio stations or print media that are more likely to reach a target audience, such as teenagers or retired people.

Commercial *broadcast rating* services such as Nielsen can help identify the most-effective and efficient channels. Similar data are available for newspapers, magazines, billboards, mailing lists, and even bus posters. By providing figures to calculate the percentage of the target audience exposed to the program or channel at specific time periods, as well as the extent to which audiences change across time periods or are consistent, campaign implementers can determine the *reach* (number of different individuals in the audience) or *frequency* (number of times any individual may be exposed). Different campaign objectives would be achieved through increased reach or increased frequency. For example, increasing awareness about a common issue by the public at large could be achieved more cost effectively through using a specific time/channel combination to maximize reach. However, achieving and maintaining learning or attitude change in a specific at-risk audience would require increased frequency, which may involve a different time/channel mix. A jazz or classical music station, for example, may have high frequency but low reach.

The Advertising Council provides in-kind creative and agency services to support approximately 36 public communication campaigns a year in the United States. Further, in-place commercial distribution channels can be used to support delivery of campaign messages and materials. For example, getting 7–Eleven or Sears stores involved in a campaign would provide immediate delivery channels across the United States.

Education-Entertainment Approaches

Some campaigns have engaged in cooperative efforts with the entertainment industry to produce attractive music videos and PSAs, to insert themes in popular TV programs, or to create prosocial television series such as *Freestyle* in the United States (LaRose, 1989), *Sun City* in South Africa (Singhal & Rogers, 2001), and the seatbelt campaign in television programs (Winsten & DeJong, 2001). This form of campaign, sometimes called *infotainment* or *eduentertainment*, consciously mixes theories of social modeling (providing role models for behavior and attitudes), parasocial interaction (getting the audience personally involved in the characters and content), and expectancy value (combining perceived social norms with beliefs about the source's normative expectations concerning those norms) with commercial entertainment values, media personalities, and wide-scale distribution. Celebrities often provide credible and influential sources, especially for certain at-risk populations who distrust or are not otherwise exposed to traditional authority figures. This campaign approach also generates revenues through successful programming that allows sustainability, improvement, and expansion over time.

However, Singhal and Rogers (2001) note a variety of ethical issues in such campaigns, including (a) how well the social change goals match the moral and values guidelines of the campaign, (b) who establishes just exactly what is or is not "prosocial," (c) the extent to which all audience segments receive the positive and helpful messages equally or eventually, (d) whether the entertaining message is somehow indirect or even subliminal rather than an explicit communication campaign, (e) how sociocultural equality—inclusion of all relevant voices—can be achieved through entertainment-education, and (f) how to avoid unintended negative effects.

New Media

Researchers are examining the potential roles of *new communication media*, such as electronic mail, voice response systems, interactive video, DVD and CD-ROM, and computer games, in reaching particular at-risk populations and in influencing learning, attitudes, and behaviors (Buller et al., 2001; Lieberman, 2001; Piotrow & Kincaid, 2001; Rice and associates, 1984; Rice & Katz, 2001). Lieberman (2001) recommends that campaign designers take advantage of the interactive, multimedia, networked, personalized, and portable aspects of these new media. This allows computer-mediated campaigns to apply young people's media and genres, use characters that appeal to that age group, support information seeking, incorporate challenges and goals, use learning-by-doing, create functional learning environments, facilitate social interaction, allow user anonymity when appropriate, and involve young people in product design and testing.

Media Advocacy

Finally, a different and complementary approach to campaign implementation is *media advocacy* (Piotrow & Kincaid, 2001; Wallack & Dorfman, 2001). In line with the critique that most campaigns emphasize individual blame and responsibility, this approach emphasizes the wide range of social forces that influence public health, particularly the salient and consequential policy issues that are ignored by most communication campaigns.

Although the media are key vehicles for communication campaigns, certain types of media content can also produce a wide variety of contradictions for public communication campaigns (Wallack, 1989). A wide variety of unhealthy behaviors and antisocial attitudes is shown in both programs and commercials on television. Stereotypes of gender roles, race relations, age-specific behaviors, behavior by medical personnel, and treatments of physical and mental problems are all developed and reinforced through media portrayals that overwhelm attempts by other messages to reduce such stereotypes. It is difficult for family planning or AIDS prevention campaigns to compete with regular program and advertising content that portrays and glamorizes irresponsible or promiscuous sexual behaviors. In the media, health and social problems are also seen as individually caused and individually solved, avoiding discussion of the social and economic causes.

Instead, successful campaigns must be linked to broader community action (see Bracht, 2001; Dervin & Frenette, 2001; Dozier et al., 2001; Flora, 2001). As the systems model proposed by Rice and Foote (2001) indicates, there are many broad and pervasive prestate conditions that can overwhelm or prevent any campaign intentions or messages. Thus, populations, policy, and public agendas should be the primary targets of health campaigns—the salient audiences are the stakeholders and potential participants in any social change process.

This requires a media advocacy approach—"the strategic use of mass media in combination with community organizing to advance healthy public policies" (Wallack & Dorfman, 2001, p. 393). It explicitly attempts to associate social problems with social structures and inequities, change public policy rather than individual behavior, reach opinion leaders and policymakers, work with groups to increase involvement in the communication process, and reduce the power gap instead of simply providing more information. (Note the overlap in philosophy and actions between the media advocacy, sense-making, and two-symmetric public relations approaches.) The four primary activities involved in media advocacy include (a) develop an overall strategy that involves formulating policy options, identifying the stakeholders that have power to create relevant change and apply pressure to foster change, and developing messages for these stakeholders; (b) set the agenda, including gaining access to the news media through stories, news events, and editorials; (c) shape the debate, including framing the public health problems as policy issues salient to significant audiences, emphasizing social accountability, and providing evidence for the broader claims; and (d) advance the policy, including maintaining interest, pressure, and coverage over time. According to Wallack and Dorfman, "Media advocacy approaches designed to change policy must be integrated into public health interventions" (2001, p. 398).

ENGAGE THE COMMUNITY

A related means of integrating media and interpersonal communication is to conduct and involve campaign activities at and by the community level (Bracht, 2001). Indeed, many funding agencies now require community involvement as part of the design and implementation protocol. Bracht (2001) outlines five key stages in organizing community campaigns.

1. Conduct a community analysis, including identifying the community's assets and history; defining the community according to geographic, population, and political jurisdiction; collecting data with community participation; and assessing community capacity and readiness for change.
2. Design and initiate the campaign, including developing an organizational structure for collaboration, increasing community participation and membership in the organization, and developing an initial intervention plan.
3. Implement the campaign, including clarifying the roles and responsibilities of all partners, providing orientation and training to citizens and volunteers, refining the intervention plan to accommodate local contexts, and generating broad citizen participation.
4. Consolidate program maintenance, including maintaining high levels of volunteer effort and continuing to integrate intervention activities into community networks.

5. Disseminate results and foster sustainability of the community campaign, including reassessing campaign activities and outcomes, refining the sustainability plan, and updating the community analysis.

Community-level approaches were emphasized in the Stanford heart disease prevention programs (Flora, 2001). Three models of community mobilization were applied as appropriate: (a) *consensus development*, or participation by diverse community members; (b) *social action*, or mobilizing the community to create new social structures and engage in the political process; and (c) *social planning*, or using expert data to propose and plan systemwide change. Campaign messages, resources, and activities were developed and implemented through media, training instructors, workplace contests and workshops, schools, restaurants and grocery stores, health professionals, and contests or lotteries.

The exceptional success of HIV/AIDS prevention campaigns in San Francisco is largely attributable to the *social ecology* approach taken there. Dearing (2001, p. 305) observes that "social change occurs because of complementary and reinforcing information circulating through social and organized systems that constitute a community . . . [by means of] multiple positively related interventions at multiple levels of impact with a given geographic area." Note that although we list community engagement late in the list of campaign components, a truly community-based campaign would engage stakeholders right from the start.

CONDUCT SUMMATIVE EVALUATION

Proper summative evaluation can distinguish between *theory failure*, the extent to which underlying causal chains are rejected by the evaluation results, and *process or program failure*, the extent to which the implementation of the campaign was inadequate or incorrect, thus allocating blame, credit, and lessons for future campaigns accordingly. Note that theory drives the design of messages and interventions, as theory is required to specify the causal processes and temporal sequence of inputs and outcomes. *Summative evaluation* consists of identifying and measuring answers to question about six campaign aspects: the *audience* (e.g., size, characteristics), *implementation* of the planned campaign components (e.g., as exposure of the audience to messages and/or services), *effectiveness* (e.g., influence on attitudes, behaviors, and health conditions), *impacts* or effects on larger aggregations (e.g., families or government agencies), *cost* (e.g., total expenditures, and cost effectiveness), and *causal processes* (e.g., isolating the reasons why effects occurred or not) (Flay & Cook, 1989).

A Systems Perspective

Rice and Foote (2001) suggested a *systems-theoretical* approach to planning campaign evaluation, with particular application to health communication campaigns in developing countries. The approach includes these stages: (a) specifying the goals and underlying assumptions of the project; (b) specifying the model at the project level; (c) specifying prior states, system phases, and system constraints; (d) specifying immediate as well as long-term intended post states, and guarding against unintended outcomes (boomerang effects), such as normalizing the unhealthy behavior, psychological reactance, and generating anxiety through fear appeals to those with low self-efficacy (Atkin, 2001); (e) specifying the model at the individual and the social (e.g., community network) levels; (f) choosing among research approaches appropriate to the system; and (g) assessing implications for design.

Concerning research design, Valente (2001) summarizes classical study designs that help reduce threats to validity due to selectivity, testing, history and maturation, and sensitization. Levels and timing of interventions and outcomes influence whether cross-sectional, cohort, panel, time-series, or event-history designs are most appropriate and whether interventions occur at the individual, group, or community level. Other factors to consider are the roles of self-selection, treatment diffusion across communities, and communication and influence through interpersonal and mediated networks.

The basic assumption underlying this systems approach is that campaign inputs intended to alter prior states are mediated by a set of system constraints and enter into a process whereby some inputs are converted into outputs, thus evolving into a new poststate and altering system constraints. Further, this dynamic system occurs at the global project level, the community level, and the individual level of analysis. Campaign evaluation planning must match the timing and nature of inputs (such as media channels, messages, and material resources) and measurements with relevant phases of the system. As a part of a process evaluation, Rice and Foote (2001) distinguished between *planned*, *real*, and *engaged* inputs. For example, only 75% of planned radio spots may actually be broadcast on a particular station, only 40% of the audience may have the radio turned on during the day, and only 60% of those listeners may be able to recall any campaign messages. Informed campaign evaluations should measure and analyze these kinds of inputs separately. For example, Synder's (2001) meta-analysis of 48 U.S. health campaigns found that an average of only 40% of people in intervention communities reported being exposed to their particular campaign. The Stanford Five-Community Study collected extensive data on message objectives, content, reach, and exposure so it could explicitly evaluate the quantity of programming, broadcasting and interpersonal delivery, and engagement of a broad range of communication interventions.

Similarly comprehensive programs of systems planning and integrated campaigns have been applied to complex problems such as rat control in grain-producing countries and communitywide issues such as adolescent drinking (Adhikarya, 2001; Bracht, 2001).

Assessing Effectiveness and Effects

Assessing campaign effectiveness is not easily achieved, even with sophisticated summative evaluation designs. This is because "effects" are not the same as "effectiveness," and what constitutes "effectiveness" itself is controversial and often ambiguous (Salmon & Murray-Johnson, 2001). There are at least six kinds of "effectiveness" that determine what are considered to be the central measures of effectiveness.

1. *Definitional* effectiveness is somewhat political: it is the extent to which various stakeholders attain success in having a social phenomenon defined as a social problem. As noted previously, Paisley (2001) considered this problem in terms of getting the problem on the public agenda— just how important *is* this health problem, anyway?—and defining campaign interests as first-party or second-party advocacy. For example, Butler (2001) shows how the "Got Milk?" campaign was fraught with issues of industry sponsorship and lack of evaluation in spite of federal regulations and counterindicative research.

2. *Ideological* effectiveness concerns whether the problem is defined as primarily individual or social; that is, should alcohol abuse be seen, and treated as, primarily an issue of individual responsibility (as in the "designated driver" television campaign—see Winsten & DeJong, 2001), or should it be considered as embedded in extensive advertising and mediated portrayals of drinking?

3. *Political* effectiveness is the extent to which a campaign creates visibility or symbolic value for some stakeholder, regardless of other outcome measures.

4. *Contextual* effectiveness assesses the extent to which the intervention achieved its goals within a particular context. For example, education, enforcement, or engineering approaches are differently appropriate for different problems (Paisley, 2001), so it would be unfair to evaluate (and probably unwise to implement) an attitude-change campaign if engineering approaches are the most suitable (such as reducing automobile exhaust).

5. *Cost-effectiveness* concerns the trade-offs between different inputs and outputs over time. For example, prevention campaigns may in fact

save much more money over time than treatment campaigns, but the outcomes are harder to measure and occur over different time spans. Further, treating some problems (such as those with low prevalence or those that generate widespread fear) may generate increased costs in other areas, thus lowering health effectiveness overall.

6. Finally, *programmatic* effectiveness is probably the most familiar approach, whereby campaign performance is assessed relative to its stated goals and objectives.

As discussed elsewhere in this chapter, this form of effectiveness requires an explicit statement of measurable goals and outcomes and explicit distinctions between theory and process evaluation. In the end, Salmon and Murray-Johnson (2001) show that campaigns should be assessed on two dimensions: whether or not there were effects and whether or not the campaign was effective. The resulting four conditions lead to very different overall evaluations. Public service announcements for local health agencies are a good example of a highly effective campaign (high and measurable exposure) with no effect (no measurable evidence of increased referrals or visits or reduced illness).

Regarding degree of effects, a meta-analysis of 48 mediated health campaigns (Snyder, 2001) showed 7 to 10% more overall behavior change by people in intervention communities than in control communities, representing a correlation of .09. Promoting new behaviors seems more effective than stopping old behaviors or preventing new behaviors (12% compared to 5% and 4%), and enforcement strategies and provision of new information both noticeably increased outcomes (17% and 14% change).

CONSIDER ONGOING CHALLENGES

We would like to end simply by noting that a variety of theoretical and practical challenges and tensions continue to exist in the design, implementation, and evaluation of public communication campaigns. Here are some issues to consider:

- Many important social problems involve *collective benefits* (such as reducing littering), yet most campaigns have succeeded only when they promote *individual benefits*. How can campaigns increase the salience of collective benefits (see Liu, 2001, for experiences with China's large-scale collective benefit campaigns)?
- What is the proper mix of *education* and *entertainment?* Will or should new "infotainment" campaigns be embedded in the commercial media mainstream (Singhal & Rogers, 2001)?

- How can campaigns, which generally use the mass media, overcome the *simultaneous pervasive negative influence of the mass media* on the campaign issue (such as alcoholism or violence) (Wallack & Dorfman, 2001)?
- Few theories or campaign designs explicitly distinguish *short-term* from *long-term* effects and objectives. What should be the relative emphasis on each, and how can campaigns achieve longer-term outcomes (McGuire, 2001; Valente, 2001)?
- What is the proper mix of *interpersonal, mass media* and *new, more interactive media* communication for specific campaign goals (Cappella et al., 2001; Rice & Foote, 2001; Rice & Katz, 2001)?
- How can campaigns successfully promote a *prevention* approach in order to avoid the generally more expensive and less-effective *treatment* approach typically favored by organizations, government agencies, and the electorate (Dervin & Frenette, 2001; Rice, 2001; Wallack & Dorfman, 2001)?
- What are the relative influences of *individual differences* versus *social structure* on the problems targeted by communication campaigns (Piotrow & Kincaid, 2001; Rice & Foote, 2001)?
- How can campaigns *communicate effectively with young people*, who have fundamentally different evaluations of risk and future consequences, who are using radically different interactive and personal media, and who are deeply embedded in peer networks (Piotrow & Kincaid, 2001)?

REFERENCES

Adhikarya, R. (2001). The strategic extension campaigns on rat control in Bangladesh. In R. E. Rice & C. K. Atkin (Eds.), *Public communication campaigns* (3rd ed., pp. 283–285). Thousand Oaks, CA: Sage.

Ajzen, I., & Fishbein, M. (1980). *Understanding attitudes and predicting social behavior.* Upper Saddle River, NJ: Prentice Hall.

Alcalay, R., & Taplin, S. (1989). Community health campaigns: From theory to action. In R. E. Rice & C. Atkin (Eds.), *Public communication campaigns* (2nd ed., pp. 105–130). Newbury Park, CA: Sage.

Atkin, C. K. (2001). Theory and principles of media health campaigns. In R. E. Rice & C. K. Atkin (Eds.), *Public communication campaigns* (3rd ed., pp. 49–68). Thousand Oaks, CA: Sage.

Atkin, C. K., & Freimuth, V. (2001). Formative evaluation research in campaign design. In R. E. Rice & C. K. Atkin (Eds.), *Public communication campaigns* (3rd ed., pp. 125–145). Thousand Oaks, CA: Sage.

Backer, T., Rogers, E. M., & Sopory, P. (1992). *Designing health communication campaigns: What works?* Newbury Park, CA: Sage.

Bandura, A. (1977a). Self-efficacy: Toward a unifying theory of behavioral change. *Psychological Review, 84*(2), 191–215.

Bandura, A. (1977b). *Social learning theory.* Upper Saddle River, NJ: Prentice Hall.

Bem, D. (1970). *Beliefs, attitudes and human affairs.* Belmont, CA: Brooks/Cole.

Bracht, N. (2001). Community partnership strategies in health campaigns. In R. E. Rice & C. K. Atkin (Eds.), *Public communication campaigns* (3rd ed., pp. 323–342). Thousand Oaks, CA: Sage.

Buller, D., Woodall, W. G., Hall, J., Borland, R., Ax, B., Brown, M., & Hines, J. M. (2001). A web-based smoking cessation and prevention program for children aged 12–15. In R. E. Rice & C. K. Atkin (Eds.), *Public communication campaigns* (3rd ed., pp. 357–372). Thousand Oaks, CA: Sage.

Butler, M. (2001). America's sacred cow. In R. E. Rice & C. K. Atkin (Eds.), *Public communication campaigns* (3rd ed., pp. 309–314). Thousand Oaks, CA: Sage.

Cappella, J., Fishbein, M., Hornik, R., Ahern, R. K., & Sayeed, S. (2001). Using theory to select messages in anti-drug media campaigns: Reasoned action and media priming. In R. E. Rice & C. K. Atkin (Eds.), *Public communication campaigns* (3rd ed., pp. 214–230). Thousand Oaks, CA: Sage.

Cialdini, R. (2001). Littering: When every litter bit hurts. In R. E. Rice & C. K. Atkin (Eds.), *Public communication campaigns* (3rd ed., pp. 280–282). Thousand Oaks, CA: Sage.

Dearing, J. (2001). The cumulative community response to AIDS in San Francisco. In R. E. Rice & C. K. Atkin (Eds.), *Public communication campaigns* (3rd ed., pp. 305–308). Thousand Oaks, CA: Sage.

Dervin, B., & Frenette, M. (2001). Applying sense-making methodology: Communicating communicatively with audiences as listeners, learners, teachers, confidantes. In R. E. Rice & C. K. Atkin (Eds.), *Public communication campaigns* (3rd ed., pp. 69–87). Thousand Oaks, CA: Sage.

Dozier, D., Grunig, L., & Grunig, J. (2001). Public relations as communication campaign. In R. E. Rice & C. K. Atkin (Eds.), *Public communication campaigns* (3rd ed., pp. 231–248). Thousand Oaks, CA: Sage.

Festinger, L. (1954). A theory of social comparison processes. *Human Relations, 7,* 117–140.

Flay, B., & Cook, T. (1989). Three models for summative evaluation of prevention campaigns with a mass media component. In R. E. Rice & C. K. Atkin (Eds.), *Public communication campaigns* (2nd ed., pp. 175–196). Newbury Park, CA: Sage.

Flora, J. (2001). The Stanford community studies: Campaigns to reduce cardiovascular disease. In R. E. Rice & C. K. Atkin (Eds.), *Public communication campaigns* (3rd ed., pp. 193–213). Thousand Oaks, CA: Sage.

Hovland, C., Janis, I., & Kelley, H. (1953). *Communication and persuasion.* New Haven, CT: Yale University Press.

LaRose, R. (1989). Freestyle, revisited. In R. E. Rice & C. K. Atkin (Eds.), *Public communication campaigns* (2nd ed., pp. 206–209). Newbury Park, CA: Sage.

Lederman, L. C., Stewart, L., Barr, S., Powell, R., Laitman, L., & Goodhart, F. W. (2001). RU sure? Using communication theory to reduce dangerous drinking on a college campus. In R. E. Rice & C. K. Atkin (Eds.), *Public communication campaigns* (3rd ed., pp. 295–299). Thousand Oaks, CA: Sage.

Lieberman, D. (2001). Using interactive media in communication campaigns for children and adolescents. In R. E. Rice & C. K. Atkin (Eds.), *Public communication campaigns* (3rd ed., pp. 373–38). Thousand Oaks, CA: Sage.

Liu, A. P. (2001). Mass campaigns in the People's Republic of China during the Mao era. In R. E. Rice & C. K. Atkin (Eds.), *Public communication campaigns* (3rd ed., pp. 286–289). Thousand Oaks, CA: Sage.

McGuire, W. J. (1960). A syllogistic analysis of congnitive relationships. In M. J. Rosenberg & C. I. Hovland (Eds.), *Attitute organization and change* (pp. 65–111). New Haven, CT: Yale University Press.

McGuire, W. J. (1989). Theoretical foundations of campaigns. In R. E. Rice & C. K. Atkins (Eds.), *Public communication campaigns* (2nd ed., pp. 43–65). Newbury Park, CA: Sage.

McGuire, W. (2001). Input and output variables currently promising for constructing persuasive communications. In R. E. Rice & C. K. Atkin (Eds.), *Public communication campaigns* (3rd ed., pp. 22–48). Thousand Oaks, CA: Sage.

Paisley, W. (1998). Scientific literacy and the competition for public attention and understanding. *Science Communication, 20,* 70–80.

Paisley, W. (2001). Public communication campaigns: The American experience. In R. E. Rice & C. K. Atkin (Eds.), *Public communication campaigns* (3rd ed., pp. 3–21). Thousand Oaks, CA: Sage.

Palmgreen, P., Donohew, L., & Harrington, N. (2001). Sensation seeking in anti-drug campaign and message design. In R. E. Rice & C. K. Atkin (Eds.), *Public communication campaigns* (3rd ed., pp. 300–304). Thousand Oaks, CA: Sage.

Petty, R., & Cacioppo, J. (1986). *Communication and persuasion: Central and peripheral routes to attitude change.* New York: Springer-Verlag.

Piotrow, P., & Kincaid, L. (2001). Strategic communication for international health programs. In R. E. Rice & C. K. Atkin (Eds.), *Public communication campaigns* (3rd ed., pp. 249–266). Thousand Oaks, CA: Sage.

Prochaska, J. O., DiClemente, C. C., & Norcross, J. C. (1992). In search of how people change: Applications to addictive behaviors. *American Psychologist, 47,* 1102–1114.

Proctor, R. (2001). The Nazi anti-tobacco campaign. In R. E. Rice & C. K. Atkin (Eds.), *Public communication campaigns* (3rd ed., pp. 315–319). Thousand Oaks, CA: Sage.

Rice, R. E. (1993). Using network concepts to clarify sources and mechanisms of social influence. In W. Richards, Jr., & G. Barnett (Eds.), *Progress in communication sciences: Vol. 12. Advances in communication network analysis* (pp. 43–52). Norwood, NJ: Ablex.

Rice, R. E. (2001). Smokey Bear. In R. E. Rice & C. K. Atkin (Eds.), *Public communication campaigns* (3rd ed., pp. 276–279). Thousand Oaks, CA: Sage.

Rice, R. E., and Associates. (1984). *The new media: Communication, research and technology.* Newbury Park, CA: Sage.

Rice, R. E., & Atkin, C. K. (Eds.). (1989). *Public communication campaigns* (2nd ed.). Newbury Park, CA: Sage.

Rice, R. E., & Atkin, C. (1994). Principles of successful communication campaigns: A summary from recent research. In J. Bryant & D. Zillmann (Eds.), *Media effects: Advances in theory and research* (pp. 365–387). Hillsdale, NJ: Lawrence Erlbaum Associates.

Rice, R. E., & Foote, D. (2001). A systems-based evaluation planning model for health communication campaigns in developing countries. In R. E. Rice & C. K. Atkin (Eds.), *Public communication campaigns* (3rd ed., pp. 146–167). Thousand Oaks, CA: Sage.

Rice, R. E., & Katz, J. K. (Eds.) (2001). *The Internet and health communication.* Thousand Oaks, CA: Sage.

Rogers, E. M. (1981). *Communication networks: A new paradigm for research.* New York: Free Press.

Rogers, E. M., & Storey, D. (1987). Communication campaigns. In C. Berger & S. Chaffee (Eds.), *Handbook of communication science* (pp. 817–846). Newbury Park, CA: Sage.

Salmon, C., & Murray-Johnson, L. (2001). Communication campaign effectiveness: Some critical distinctions. In R. E. Rice & C. K. Atkin (Eds.), *Public communication campaigns* (3rd ed., pp. 168–180). Thousand Oaks, CA: Sage.

Singhal, A., & Rogers, E. M. (2001). The entertainment-education strategy in communication campaigns. In R. E. Rice & C. K. Atkin (Eds.), *Public communication campaigns* (3rd ed., pp. 343–356). Thousand Oaks, CA: Sage.

Snyder, L. (2001). How effective are mediated health campaigns? In R. E. Rice & C. K. Atkin (Eds.), *Public communication campaigns* (3rd ed., pp. 181–190). Thousand Oaks, CA: Sage.

Stephenson, M., & Witte, K. (2001). Creating fear in a risky world: Generating effective health risk messages. In R. E. Rice & C. K. Atkin (Eds.), *Public communication campaigns* (3rd ed., pp. 88–102). Thousand Oaks, CA: Sage.

Valente, T. (2001). Evaluating communication campaigns. In R. E. Rice & C. K. Atkin (Eds.), *Public communication campaigns* (3rd ed., pp. 105–124). Thousand Oaks, CA: Sage.

Wallack, L. (1989). Mass media and health promotion: A critical perspective. In R. E. Rice & C. K. Atkin (Eds.), *Public communication campaigns* (2nd ed., pp. 353–368). Newbury Park, CA: Sage.

Wallack, L., & Dorfman, L. (2001). Putting policy into health communication: The role of media advocacy. In R. E. Rice & C. K. Atkin (Eds.), *Public communication campaigns* (3rd ed., pp. 389–401). Thousand Oaks, CA: Sage.

Winsten, J., & DeJong, W. (2001). The designated driver campaign. In R. E. Rice & C. K. Atkin (Eds.), *Public communication campaigns* (3rd ed., pp. 290–294). Thousand Oaks, CA: Sage.

Chapter 17

Effects of Media on Personal and Public Health

JANE D. BROWN
University of North Carolina—Chapel Hill

KIM WALSH-CHILDERS
University of Florida

The mass media are full of images and messages that may have an impact on a wide array of physical and mental health issues: advertising pushes "heart-healthy" breakfast cereal, women's magazines sell the latest way to lose those 10 extra pounds; the news tells of the latest breakthrough in cancer research; teens on prime-time TV discuss whether to have sex or not; and the Internet provides all of these and more.

Interest in the effect of such content has increased over the past decade, as it has become clearer that the media do shape how individuals make decisions about their own and others' health behaviors. Studies typically have focused on the negative effects of advertising (e.g., for cigarettes, alcohol) and entertainment (e.g., unprotected sex) on individuals. In chapter 16, Rice and Atkin examined how the intentional use of media also can result in positive health attitudes and behaviors. Although negative effects and public health campaigns have received the most research attention, there are other important domains that have been studied and/or deserve more study.

This chapter organizes the research on the health effects of the mass media along three dimensions: (a) level of influence (personal/public), (b) intention of the message producer (intended/unintended), and (c) outcome (positive/negative). As health policy expert Milio (1986) has pointed out, the mass media can influence health at both a personal and public level. At the *personal level*, the mass media may provide information and models that stimulate changes—either positive or negative—in health-related attitudes and behaviors. At the *public level*, the mass media

453

also may raise awareness of health issues among policymakers and, thus, may contribute to changing the context in which people make choices about their health. The effects of the media may be *intended* by the message producer, as is the case when health educators develop public information campaigns, or may be *unintended*, as is the case when viewers adopt unhealthy behaviors that are portrayed only for entertainment value on television programs. The outcome may be either *positive* or *negative* from a public health point of view. A typology of the kinds of effects generated by these three dimensions and some examples that are discussed in this chapter are presented in Table 17.1.[1]

TABLE 17.1

Examples of the potential effects of the mass media on personal and public health

Personal-level health effects		
Intended	Positive	*Entertainment-Education:* More people know about emergency contraceptives after seeing it used on *ER*
	Negative	*Marketing* unhealthy products: Cigarette, alcohol ads directed at young people increases smoking, drinking
Unintended	Positive	*Risk perception:* News increases awareness of environmental hazards
		Agenda-setting: News of medical breakthroughs informs consumers
	Negative	*Displacement:* More media use, less physical activity, greater body weight
		Modeling: Adolescent girls try to attain media's thin-body standard

Public-level health effects		
Intended	Positive	*Media advocacy* campaign: Gets sexist alcohol billboards removed from urban neighborhoods
	Negative	*Advertising leverage:* Cigarette industry's advertising clout reduces editorial content re: cancer risk
Unintended	Positive	*Agenda-setting/framing:* Positive news coverage of the war on drugs leads to Congressional approval for more funding
	Negative	*Budget priorities:* Media coverage increases funding for war on drugs at expense of other health and social issues

---

[1]In this chapter we define health broadly, adopting the World Health Organization's definition, "Health is a state of complete physical, mental, and social well-being and not merely the absence of disease or infirmity." We do not consider the media's effects on violence, one of the most intensively studied health-related topics, or public health campaigns because those topics are covered elsewhere in this volume (chaps. 10, 11, and 16).

THE INTERNET AND HEALTH

Without a doubt, one of the most important changes in the media industry in the past 10 years has been the growth of the Internet and the World
Wide Web. Already, it is clear that this new media form will have tremendous implications for individual health and probably for health policy as
well. Even in the early days of the Internet, people were using it for a variety of health-related purposes: to find information, to communicate with
health care providers and with other consumers about their illnesses or
health problems, to buy both prescription and nonprescription drugs, and
even to receive medical consultation or care.

Use of the Internet for health apparently differs according to the user's
health status. In one survey, more than half of the people searching for
health information online were well and were searching primarily for preventive medicine and wellness information. People newly diagnosed
with a medical condition made up about 5% of online health consumers,
and they typically expended considerable amounts of time searching
online for information about their condition, often with the help of family
and friends, within the first few weeks after the diagnosis. Other users
were the chronically ill and their caregivers, who used the Internet as part
of their active daily management of the illness (Cain, Mittman, Sarasohn-
Kahn, & Wayne, 2000). Almost all of the respondents to an online survey
said they had found useful medical/health information on the Internet,
and 88% reported having found the information they were seeking. Use of
the Web for information about prescription drugs also was common
(Health on the Net, 1999).[2]

Internet as Sex Educator

Given the inability of many schools to offer comprehensive sexuality information to young people, the Internet may also be an important resource for
teens who want to learn more about their sexuality. The Network for Family Life Education at Rutgers University, for example, developed a Web site
devoted to sexuality education and promoted its availability through a
newsletter written primarily by teens sent to high school teachers and students across the country. They also write a monthly feature in *Teen People*

---

[2]The HON surveys use nonprobability samples, soliciting participation by posting the
questionnaire on the HON Web site and in other locations where it is likely to be seen by
individuals who use the Web for health-related purposes in the United States and Europe.
For the October/November 1999 survey, 58% of the respondents were from North America,
and 54% were consumers, that is, individuals not in the health professions.

magazine (circulation 1.6 million in 2000) called "The Sex Files" that references the site. In 2000, the Internet site averaged 3,400 users per day who stayed an average of 8 minutes. More than 1,000 visitors per month sent e-mail questions that were answered by a panel of experts —sexuality educators, physicians, and other health professionals (Wilson, 2000).

Three attributes of the Internet make it especially appealing for obtaining sexual information. The Internet is anonymous, accessible, and affordable (Cooper, 1998). These same attributes have made sexually explicit material the driving force of the development of the Internet. "Sex" has been the number one search term used on the Internet. Sites offering sexually explicit material were those most likely to be turning a profit in the early days of the commercial Internet (Cooper, 1998). It is not clear whether young people will continue to have access to such sites, however, as a number of school systems have imposed mandatory blocking programs to minimize the likelihood of students seeing sexually explicit material, and often the sites providing less-explicit sexual information are blocked at the same time.

Privacy and security concerns are other commonly cited reasons for not using the Internet for health information, and surveys have found that these concerns are most common among individuals in poorer health. Regardless of health status, more than half of Internet users say they would be concerned about their insurance company finding out about their health-related activities online, and about half expressed worry that their employers could find out about their online health activities (Grimes-Gruczka & Gratzer, 2000).

Quality and Use of Internet Health Information

Despite these concerns, it is clear the Internet is being used for health information.[3] It is less clear how good that information is and what people are doing with or because of the information they find online. A search on almost any health topic reveals that the quality of information available online varies dramatically. In an attempt to help consumers assess the quality of online health information, a number of rating systems have been developed. Jadad and Gagliardi (1998) identified 47 ratings instruments, but concluded that "it is unclear whether they should exist in the first place, whether they measure what they claim to measure, or whether they lead to more harm than good" (p. 614).

---

[3]Online health-related activities also include participating in support groups related to specific health conditions as well as communicating with health care providers and maintaining and transmitting personal medical records. These kinds of activities are not discussed here because they fall more under the rubric of interpersonal rather than mass media effects.

We also know relatively little about how consumers use the health care information they find online, regardless of its quality. Among North American respondents to the Health on the Net (1999) survey, more than three fourths said they had discussed drug and other information they found online with their health care providers, and 18% reported that they buy drugs via the Internet. In another survey, about half of the respondents who had sought health information online reported that they had encouraged a family member or friend to see a doctor, made a decision about treatment for a medical condition, or changed their diet or exercise routines as a result of the information (Cyber Dialogue, 2000). Some also join online support groups focused on their medical condition (Kassirer, 2000).

Access to the wealth of health information online certainly has the potential to empower consumers, increase their understandings of their own health problems, and improve their ability to avoid or to manage and cope with disease or other health problems. Individuals might find information online that encourages them to seek health care they need and to ask their health care providers better questions when they do seek care. It is obvious, however, that there are individual health risks related to using inaccurate health information or of inappropriately interpreting the accurate information found online. Thus far, there is no study that would tell us how often people fall victim to online "snake oil" cures that may damage their health.

Some critics argue that consumers' desire to discuss online information with their health care providers may have negative consequences at the health system level. Kleinke (2000), for example, argued that because the Internet gives patients virtually unlimited access to information about treatment alternatives, comparative cost and quality data on providers, and knowledge about what care other patients are receiving, patients' use of the Internet is most likely to drive up demand for new products, additional services, alternative therapies, and the most expensive providers. Kleinke (2000) points out that when people are comparing alternative providers for a major health service such as heart bypass surgery, they are unlikely to choose the lowest bidder; instead choosing the most expensive provider, "presuming (usually correctly) that higher cost connotes higher quality, just like in the rest of our economy" (p. 67).

INTENDED PERSONAL-LEVEL HEALTH EFFECTS

Entertainment-Education

One of the most promising intentional ways of reaching the public with positive health messages is to develop entertaining programming for radio, television, movies, or music. Known as "entertainment-education" (also called "enter-educate," "pro-social entertainment," or "edu-tainment"), the strategy has been used throughout the world, often in concert with other kinds of public health information campaigns (see chap. 16). Building on Bandura's (1986) social learning theory, this approach presents an idea, such as family planning, through drama and provides lessons on the rewards of a new behavior and disadvantages of an old one in an entertaining context.

In one of the earliest uses of the strategy, two popular singers, Tatiana and Johnny, sang entertainment-education songs and appeared on a video that aired in 12 Latin American countries. One of the songs, "Cuando Estemos Juntos" ("When We Are Together") hit the top of the musical charts in Mexico and Peru. Evaluators found that half of the male audience said they talked to their female friends about the songs in the campaign, and one third of the female audience reported discussing the songs with male friends. The key messages of "postponing sex" and "waiting to be together [with a partner]" were correctly interpreted by one third to two thirds of the audience (Kincaid, Jara, Coleman, & Segura, 1988). In India, Africa, and Latin America, popular soap operas that include plots about family planning and HIV prevention have had pro-found effects on cultural norms and health behaviors (Singhal & Rogers, 1999).

Embedded Health Messages

In the United States, however, due to the private ownership of the media system and First Amendment concerns, it typically is more difficult to dis-seminate long-running pro-social messages or shows that are produced by the government or nonprofit agencies. Rather than producing whole shows, U.S. advocates have been working with the commercial media to embed subtle health messages into existing entertainment programming. AIDS awareness messages have appeared on soap operas such as *General Hospital*, and pro-condom messages on the prime-time situation comedy *Friends*. A number of organizations maintain Hollywood offices to encour-age media producers to include their point of view in entertainment pro-gramming (Montgomery, 1989).

Although most of the efforts have not been evaluated systematically, there is some evidence that these embedded messages can have an effect. The Harvard School of Public Health's campaign against drunk driving in the 1980s generated more than 80 television episodes that mentioned or showed designated drivers and has been credited with increasing aware-ness and use of designated drivers (DeJong & Winsten, 1989). In the late 1990s, a rape hotline number presented at the end of a prime-time two-part *Felicity* episode on date rape received more than 1,000 calls. Viewers' knowledge of emergency contraception increased 17% after *ER* showed a date rape victim being treated with a morning-after pill (Folb, 2000).

The insertion of socially responsible messages in entertainment media is a potentially powerful way of affecting sexual behavior because the "selling" of a particular behavior isn't as obvious as it may be in a public service advertisement, and thus, audiences may not be as likely to resist the message. These messages also are more likely to reach and attract attention, compared to PSAs that rarely are shown at strategic times and are not aired frequently enough. The primary drawback to such a strategy in the United States, however, is that the media are unlikely to run messages they may think are controversial, such as condom use as a contraceptive, because the controversy may upset advertisers (Wallack, Dorfman, Jernigan, & Themba, 1993). Such efforts also have to be continued and monitored because awareness and effects may not last, and the intended lessons may be re- or misinterpreted. For example, a follow-up survey of those who had seen the *ER* episode showed a significant decrease in awareness of the emergency contraceptive (Kaiser Family Foundation, 1997). In the late 1990s, a survey of 16- to 19-year-olds found that a large majority thought it was acceptable to drink if there was a designated driver and more than half thought that it was OK for the designated driver to drink, too (Tanner, 1998, cited in Strasburger, 2001).

Commercial Product Advertising

Advertising is ubiquitous in all forms of the media in the United States and increasingly in other countries. Some of the most frequently advertised products, such as cigarettes and alcohol, have severe negative personal and public-level health effects.

Tobacco Advertising

Cigarette smoking continues to be the major preventable cause of death in the United States and increasingly around the world. Despite a relatively steady decline in cigarette smoking since the early 1970s, more than one in five American adults smokes, and more than one third of high school students currently smoke (Ozer, Brindis, Millstein, Knopf, & Irwin, 1997).

Recognition of the harmful effects of smoking has led many countries to restrict tobacco advertising. In some, such as New Zealand and Norway, cigarette consumption decreased significantly after the bans (Vickers, 1992). In the United States, cigarette advertising was banned on television and radio in 1971, but flourished in other kinds of media, especially newspapers, magazines, billboards, and event promotion, such as the Winston Cup stock car races. In the 1990s, as states became more aware of the heavy burden in health care they were assuming as smokers became ill and as evidence increased that the tobacco companies had been deceptive in promoting the use of a deadly product, an agreement between the state attorneys general and the tobacco companies put further restrictions on the promotion of tobacco products. Among other stipulations, the Master Settlement Agreement (MSA) banned billboards larger than 14 square feet; prohibited the use of cartoons in ads, merchandise with brand-name logos, and other ways of targeting youth; and forbid payment to TV and movie producers for tobacco product placements (Master Settlement Agreement, 1998). However, the Supreme Court ruled that the Food and Drug Administration (FDA) had overstepped its authority when it tried to impose black-and-white, text-only advertisements and forbid self-service displays in retail outlets (*Food and Drug Administration et al. v. Brown & Williamson Tobacco Corp.*, 2000).[4]

Effects on Editorial Content. An alarming indirect effect of tobacco advertising has been the stifling of news coverage of tobacco-related health risks. Magazines, dependent on advertising for at least 50% of their revenue, are especially vulnerable to pressure from advertisers who want their messages in an advertising-friendly atmosphere. In both the United States and in Europe studies have shown that magazines that accept cigarette advertising are less likely to print articles discussing the harmful effects of tobacco than magazines that do not run cigarette advertising (European Union Commission, 1998; Hesterman, 1987). Such lack of information about the risks of smoking may contribute to the public's still remarkably low awareness of the hazards of smoking. In one study, nearly half of the eighth graders interviewed did not believe that smoking a pack of cigarettes a day was a health risk (Johnston, O'Malley, & Bachman, 1994). Fortunately, most magazines targeted at teen girls do not accept tobacco ads, and some, including *Teen* and *Seventeen* magazine, in the late 1990s pledged to increase coverage of the dangers of smoking and tips on how to quit (Bound, 1999).

---

[4]Many tobacco control advocates were critical of the Master Settlement Agreement, arguing that it did not go far enough, that a number of the restrictions, such as no product placement in movies, were already in place, and that there was no "look back" provision in case the tobacco industry violated the agreement (Tobacco Control Resource Center, Inc., 2000). The primary benefit may be that the MSA increased the price of cigarettes 40 to 50 cents per pack. Increased prices are known to reduce smoking rates. A number of states also earmarked some of the settlement money for tobacco control efforts. The MSA also established the American Legacy Foundation that began running a hard-hitting antismoking public communication campaign and a Web site called Truth.com. The Foundation also commissions research to monitor the industry's compliance with the MSA.

Effects of Tobacco Marketing.   Restrictions on tobacco advertising have been based to a large extent on research that has shown that all but about 10% of smokers begin during adolescence (U.S. Dept. of Health and Human Services, 1994), and that even young children are influenced by the allure of cigarette smoking aggressively promulgated by the tobacco industry. Studies of the use of the cartoon character Joe Camel to promote Camel cigarettes showed, for example, that one third of 3-year-olds could make the association between the image of Old Joe the Camel and a pack of cigarettes. In the 3 years after the introduction of the cartoon camel, preference for Camel cigarettes increased from 0.5 to 32% among adolescent smokers (DiFranza et al., 1991). Studies in both the United States and England consistently have shown that the most popular brands among young people are the most heavily advertised (Pierce et al., 1991; Vickers, 1992). Historical analysis of gender-specific cigarette advertising campaigns showed that smoking initiation among young women increased abruptly when campaigns targeting women such as the Virginia Slims' "You've come a long way, baby" were introduced (Pierce, Lee, & Gilpin, 1994).

Increasing cross-sectional and longitudinal evidence has shown that receptivity and exposure to cigarette advertising, and ownership of promotional materials (e.g., caps, lighters with cigarette brand logos) is related to tobacco use among young people. A few studies have found that awareness of and involvement with tobacco promotions even exceeds the influence of family members and peers who smoke (Altman, Levine, Coeytaux, Slade, & Jaffe, 1996; Biener & Siegel, 2000; Pierce, Choi, Gilpin, Farkas, & Berry, 1998). Experimental studies suggest that advertising promotions increase the perception among young people that smoking is normative, glamorous, and risk-free (Pechmann & Ratneshwar, 1994).

Point-of-Purchase Marketing.   As restrictions on tobacco advertising have tightened, tobacco companies in the United States have shifted their marketing strategies to spend more money on point-of-purchase marketing ($2.7 billion in 1997) than on all other forms of promotion (newspaper, magazine, billboard, and transit advertising) combined (Federal Trade Commission [FTC], 1999). Much of this promotion is in convenience stores that young people visit frequently. Studies have shown that tobacco ads are more numerous and in children's line of sight (near candy and below the height of 3 feet) in stores located near schools (Woodruff, Agro, Wildey, & Conway, 1995) and in neighborhoods with a higher proportion of residents under age 18 (Pucci, Joseph, & Siegel, 1998). It would be hard for a customer to miss the cigarette promotions. Studies have found on average 14 to 27 tobacco ads inside the stores and 3.6 to 7.5 ads outside (DiFranza,

Coleman, & Cyr, 1999; Feighery, Ribisl, Achabal, & Tyebjee, 1999). Some of the first experimental research on the effects of such promotions suggest that in-store promotions affect adolescents' perceptions of the availability, use, and popularity of cigarettes, all factors that contribute to the likelihood that an adolescent will begin smoking (Henriksen & Flora, 2001).

Future Research. In the future, research on the media's effects on young people's use of tobacco probably will focus on alternative marketing strategies such as in-store and Internet promotion as the tobacco industry continues to look for ways to recruit new users and keep current smokers. A few studies of the currently unregulated Internet suggest that it may be an important new venue for tobacco promotion. One content analysis found many easily accessible pro-tobacco Web sites from which tobacco products could be ordered. Only 11% contained health warnings and instead associated smoking with glamorous lifestyles and included images of young males and (thin, attractive) females smoking recognizable brands (Hong & Cody, 2001).

Alcohol Advertising

Misuse of alcohol exacts a psychological, physical, and financial toll on individuals and families. Alcohol use is linked to family violence toward spouses and children, sexual assault, and homicide. Underage drinking is now normative, with a majority of high school seniors saying they currently drink alcohol, and one fourth report binge drinking (five or more drinks consumed on one occasion). Drinking and driving are a primary cause of the high incidence of car crashes and fatalities among adolescents. Almost one third of adolescents who use alcohol and are of driving age (16 to 21) report driving after drinking and riding in a car with a driver who has used alcohol (Ozer et al., 1997).

Unlike cigarette advertising, beer and wine ads appear frequently on television as well as in other media. In these ads, drinking, similar to cigarette smoking, is portrayed as normative and fun, with no negative consequences (Grube, 1993). In one study, more than one third of the ads showed people driving or engaging in water sports while drinking (Madden & Grube, 1994). Beer and wine ads are most frequent on sports-related programming. About one alcohol commercial appears every four hours on prime time as compared to 2.4 ads in every hour of sports programming (Grube, 1995).

Effects of Advertising. Studies have found consistent relationships between awareness of alcohol advertising and positive beliefs about drinking and intentions to drink (Grube, 1999). In a study of third, sixth, and ninth graders, Austin and Knaus (1998) found that exposure to advertising and promotional merchandise at a young age was predictive of drinking behavior during adolescence. Austin and her colleagues' research is important because it also shows that a number of factors intervene in the relationship between exposure to alcohol portrayals and ads and subsequent drinking behavior. Taking an active audience approach, they have found that teens' perception of the realism of TV as a source of teen trends, their identification with characters in TV shows and ads, and their positive expectations of drinking alcohol are more strongly related to actual drinking behavior than sheer amount of time spent with TV. Parents' comments may reinforce or counter the typically positive portrayal of alcohol on TV (Austin, Pinkleton, & Fujioka, 2000). More research like this that puts media exposure in the context of the individual will move us closer to understanding often subtle and indirect media effects.

Health Warning Labels. The U.S. government has mandated warning labels on container labels for beer, wine, and liquor since 1989, but as yet, has not required warnings on advertising. Studies of both cigarette warnings and the newer alcohol warnings suggest that such warnings have little positive effect and may, with some audiences, actually boomerang, increasing the perception of benefits and decreasing the perception of risks (Fox, Krugman, Fletcher, & Fischer, 1998; Snyder & Blood, 1992).

Over-the-Counter and Prescription Drug Advertising

Another type of advertising that is likely to affect individuals' health is advertising for prescription and nonprescription (over-the-counter) drugs. How to classify these effects within our matrix may depend somewhat on the specific effects that occur and on one's willingness to accept the pharmaceutical manufacturers' claims of concern about improving health. When the advertising encourages consumers to obtain and correctly use medications that are effective in treating health problems or in preventing more serious problems or influences them to seek needed medical attention, then the effects on individuals are intended and positive. However, drug advertising also may have unintended and negative consequences if it encourages individuals to buy and use medications they may not actually need or that are less effective and/or more costly than other drugs or treatments for the same health problem.

Americans have access to about 300,000 over-the-counter (OTC) medications (Schulz, 1998). In 1999, Americans bought $30 billion worth of OTC drugs, as well as vitamins, nutritional supplements, and herbal therapies. The average American spends $100 a year on nonprescription drugs, and

40% of Americans use at least one OTC medication every 2 days (Knapp, 2000). One survey found that most Americans take OTC medications before consulting a health professional for treatment of headaches (80%), stomach upset (76%), coughs and colds (73%), and fevers (71%). One in three respondents said they had at times taken more than the recommended dose of an OTC medication because they believed the higher dosage would treat their problem more effectively (Navigating the Medication Marketplace, 1997).

Health experts say over-the-counter drugs generally are safe—if used correctly. But "correct" use can be complicated because it not only means taking the correct dosage of a medicine and choosing the right medicine but also avoiding the use of OTCs that may interact adversely with other prescription or nonprescription drugs or with alcohol. For instance, people who are taking blood-thinning agents and then use painkillers such as Advil and Motrin can develop stomach ulcers leading to excessive bleeding. For people who have three or more alcoholic drinks a day, taking acetaminophen (Tylenol) can lead to liver damage (*Drug & Therapy Perspectives*, 2000). Older people are at increased risk because they, in general, take more medications, increasing the likelihood of drug interactions (Schultz, 2000).

Effects of OTC Drug Advertising.   Schultz (2000) argued that advertising may increase the likelihood that consumers will overuse and/or misuse OTC drugs because ads for brand-name drugs "can lead consumers to expect quick and safe 'fixes' from the use of these products" (p. 5). Content analyses of OTC drug ads suggest that they do portray these medicines as fast, safe solutions to minor health problems and encourage a casual attitude toward drug use (Byrd-Bredbenner & Grasso, 1999, 2000).

Unfortunately, little empirical research on consumers' responses to OTC drug advertising exists. Some early critics of OTC drug ads on television charged that such ads promoted drug use generally, creating "a model of drug-taking behavior that children may emulate" (Craig, 1992, p. 303). One former Federal Communications Commission (FCC) commissioner, Nicholas Johnson, even proposed a ban on TV commercials for OTC medications, and other critics have argued that OTC ads may contribute to children overdosing on OTC medicines (Choate & Debevoise, 1976). Donohue, Meyer, and Henke (1978) found that children who watched substantial amounts of television believed that taking the medicines and vitamins they saw advertised made people healthier. However, Martin and Duncan's (1984) review of the quantitative research on the effects of drug ads concluded that there was no substantive support for a causal link between exposure to OTC ads and drug abuse or other negative effects. Updated research, particularly focusing on how OTC drug ads affect children and the elderly, is needed.

Prescription Drug Advertising. One possible explanation for the dearth of recent research on OTC drug ads is that these ads have been overshadowed by the phenomenal growth of direct-to-consumer (DTC) marketing of prescription drugs. Expenditures for consumer-direct advertising of prescription drugs has exploded since 1997, when the Food and Drug Administration clarified the regulations on such advertising and made it easier for pharmaceutical companies to market their products directly to consumers via the mass media (National Institute for Health Care Management [NIHCM], 2000). In the first six months of 2000, U.S. pharmaceutical manufacturers had spent $1.3 billion on DTC advertising, matching the total *annual* expenditure two years earlier (*IMS HEALTH news release,* 2000). The pharmaceuticals appear to be getting their money's worth. For the 25 best-selling drugs marketed directly to consumers, overall sales growth for 1999 was 43.2%, compared to a growth rate of 13.3% for all other drugs that year (NIHCM, 2000).

Effects of DTC Advertising. Even before the increase in DTC drug advertising, research indicated the ads not only were increasing consumers' awareness of drug brands but also were influencing their decisions about medications. One survey found that about one third (35%) of respondents had asked their doctor for more information about a prescription drug they had seen advertised, and almost one in five had requested a prescription for an advertised drug (Bell, Kravitz, & Wilkes, 1999). However, another survey found that the majority of respondents who had seen magazine or newspaper ads for prescription drugs read very little of the required detailed information, and only 15% had read all of it (Food and Drug Administration, 2000).

Wilkes, Bell, and Kravitz (2000) argue that "DTC advertising clearly increases the volume of prescribed drugs. The question is whether these additional prescriptions are appropriate" (p. 120). Many physicians believe that DTC ads may promote inaccurate beliefs among consumers and may "encourage patients to pressure their physicians to switch them from well-studied treatments to new drugs, for which knowledge about benefits and risks is more limited" (p. 120).

Food and Nutrition

The mass media also have unintended, primarily negative effects on consumers' knowledge and behaviors regarding food and nutrition.

Beliefs About Nutrition and Food Consumption. The majority of commercials during children's programming promote foods with low nutritional value, including candy, soft drinks, sugared cereals, potato chips, and other high-salt, high-fat snacks (Kotz & Story, 1994; Taras & Gage, 1995). Even when healthier foods are being sold, the commercials focus on themes of fun and happiness rather than health. A study of the commercials in prime-time programs most often watched by 2- to 11-year-olds found that 89% of food and beverage ads (almost one fourth of all ads) focused on taste, convenience, and low cost; only 10% of the ads used nutrition or health factors alone to sell the products (Byrd-Bredbenner and Grasso, 1999). Lank, Vickery, Cotugna, & Shade (1992) found that food and beverage commercials during highly rated daytime serials generally promoted foods that were low in sugar, fat, and sodium, although they also were low in dietary fiber. However, three fourths of the foods advertised as "low cholesterol" or "low saturated fat" actually were high in fat. Of the commercials using a nutrition message to sell the product (e.g., "sugar-free"), 43% were for low-nutrient flavored drinks. Analyses of food and nutrition messages during TV programs have found that characters eat more between-meal snacks than regular meals and food consumption satisfies social and emotional needs more often than hunger (Story & Faulkner, 1990).

Effects on Nutrition Beliefs. There is ample evidence that watching TV commercials and programming is related to children's beliefs about food and nutrition. Positive relationships between heavy TV viewing and poorer nutrition knowledge have been found, even controlling for other factors that might be related to either heavy viewing or low knowledge, such as parent education, child's reading level, and socioeconomic status. Heavy TV viewing and/or more-frequent exposure to low-nutrition foods also is related to children's preference for unhealthy foods and to poor eating habits including frequent consumption of presweetened breakfast cereals, fast food, sugared or high-fat, high-salt snacks, and soft drinks (Signorielli & Lears, 1992; Signorielli & Staples, 1997). Taras, Sallis, Patterson, Nader, and Nelson (1989) found a positive relationship between TV viewing and children's requests for their parents to buy foods advertised on TV and on children's overall caloric intake. Children who watch TV while eating meals consume fewer fruits, vegetables, and juices and more pizzas, snack foods, and soft drinks than children who do not watch TV while eating (Coon, Goldberg, Rogers, & Tucker, 2001).

Physical Inactivity and Obesity. A second area of concern related to media's effect on physical fitness stems not so much from the content itself but rather from the sedentary nature of media use in general. With the exception of listening to the radio or other music formats, most mass media use occurs while people are sitting or lying down and relatively inactive. A substantial amount of research has investigated the links between television viewing and computer use and physical inactivity among both children and adults.

Adult men and women in the United States who watch more than 3 hours of television per day are twice as likely to be obese as men and women who watch less than 1 hour per day, even after controlling for a variety of other potentially related factors (Tucker & Bagwell, 1991; Tucker & Friedman, 1989). Another study found that among high-income women, frequent TV viewing was significantly associated with an increase in body mass index over time (Jeffery & French, 1998). Similar patterns have been found among Australian adults (Salmon, Bauman, Crawford, Timperio, & Owen, 2000). Frequent TV viewing also has been related to obesity and physical inactivity among elementary school students and young adults (Armstrong et al., 1998; Tucker, 1990).

In a study of adolescents, McMurray et al. (2000) found that a significant positive relationship between TV viewing on nonschool days and being overweight became nonsignificant after controlling for ethnicity and socioeconomic status, but time spent playing video games remained significantly positively related to being overweight. Berkey et al. (2000) also found significant positive relationships between time spent with television and video games and increases in body mass index over a year for 9- to 14-year-old boys and girls. Although the magnitude of the estimated effect for 1 year was small, the cumulative effects throughout adolescence could be considerable, suggesting that reducing the amount of time children and teenagers spent watching TV and playing video games could help to prevent the current epidemic of obesity in the United States. One experimental study did find that children who reduced the amount of time they spent watching TV and videotapes and playing video games had significant reductions in body fat and waist–hip measures (Robinson, 1997).

Thin-Body Ideal and Eating Disorders. The third area of concern regarding media effects on food and nutrition habits stems from a substantial body of research linking exposure to thin-ideal body images in the mass media to individuals' dissatisfaction with their bodies and disordered eating behaviors. Research over the past 20 years has shown that the women who appear in the media are substantially thinner than the average American woman (Fouts & Burggraf, 1999; Silverstein, Perdue, Peterson, & Kelly, 1986; Wiseman, Gray, Mosimann, & Ahrens, 1990). The average model 20 years ago weighed 8% less than the average American woman; today, the disparity is 23% (The Media and Eating Disorders, 2001). Analyses of body measurement statistics from 500 models listed on modeling agency Web sites and from *Playboy* centerfolds from 1985 to 1997 showed that nearly all the centerfolds and three-fourths of the models had body mass indexes of 17.5 or below—the American Psychological Association's criteria for anorexia nervosa (Owen & Laurel-Seller, 2000). A similar study suggests that the media now promote an equally unattainable ideal image for men: Leit, Pope, and Gray (2001), comparing the male centerfold models in *Playgirl* magazine from 1973 to 1997, found that over time, the men were significantly more muscular.

When the first version of this chapter was written 10 years ago, we noted that research had yet to establish a link between exposure to these thin images and the development of eating disorders. That statement is no longer accurate; numerous studies have demonstrated that exposure to thin-ideal media images is related to internalization of the thin-ideal, body dissatisfaction, and eating disorder symptoms (Botta, 1999, 2000; Field et al., 2001; Harrison, 1997, 2000; Hofshire & Greenberg, 2002; Stice & Shaw, 1994).

Entertainment Media (TV, Movies, Music)

Substance Use and Abuse

The frequency and kind of portrayals of alcohol, tobacco, and illicit drugs differ within and across entertainment media (see Table 17.2). The rela-

TABLE 17.2
Frequency of depiction and consequences to user of alcohol, tobacco, and illicit drugs in movies, entertainment TV, and popular songs

	% referring or depicting substance / % depicting consequences to user		
	Movies	TV	Popular Songs
Alcohol	93% / 43%	75% / 23%	17% / 9%
Tobacco	89% / 13%	22% / 1%	3% / –
Illicit Drugs	22% / 48%	20% / 67%	18% / 19%

Note: Proportions are based on 200 most-popular movie rentals and 1,000 most-popular songs from 1996 and 1997 (Roberts, Henricksen, & Christenson, 1999), and four consecutive episodes of the 42 top-rated prime-time series of the 1998–1999 season (Christenson, Henriksen, & Roberts, 2000) as summarized in Roberts and Christenson (2000). There were so few references to tobacco in the songs analyzed that the frequency of consequences was not calculated.

tively few studies of the effects of the portrayals of alcohol and tobacco in entertainment programming suggest that young people may learn norms about drinking and may find cigarette smoking more appealing when media characters they identify with smoke.

Alcohol. References to alcohol use—either visual and/or verbal—occur several times during an average hour of prime-time television programming. An analysis of four episodes of the top 20 teen and top 20 adult shows from the fall 1998–1999 TV season found that more than three fourths of the episodes included references to alcohol. Although earlier studies had found that alcohol was consumed more frequently than any other beverage on TV, this study found that alcohol was the drink of choice only on the adult shows. On teen shows alcohol still appears frequently (one or more major characters are shown drinking on average 1.6 minutes per hour) (Christenson, Henriksen, & Roberts, 2000).

Alcohol use is more prevalent in the movies. Two content analyses found that 80 to more than 90 percent of all kinds of films showed at least one major character drinking (Everett, Schnuth, & Tribble, 1998; Roberts, Henriksen, & Christenson, 1999). On television and in the movies positive references outnumbered negative ones by more than a 10 to 1 margin. The typical alcohol user is an adult, white, higher-status male, the kind of character likely to be identified with and perhaps imitated, at least by young males. In the study of the 200 most popular movie rentals in 1996 and 1997, when alcohol was por-trayed, no consequences of drinking were depicted in more than half. One in five of the movies that depicted drinking included at least one statement that suggested that drinking was a good thing to do; fewer than 1 in 10 contained an antiuse statement (Roberts, Henriksen, & Christenson, 1999).

Although popular music has often been the subject of criticism for its antisocial and unhealthy themes, little systematic research has been done on substance use in music or music videos. It is clear, though, that por-trayals differ dramatically by musical genre. Early analyses of country music showed that about 10% mentioned alcohol use and that portrayals were ambivalent. Although most characterized drinking as morally wrong or problematic in some way, the same songs often presented alco-hol consumption as normal and functional, a typical way of escaping problems, getting over a lost love, and so forth (discussed in Roberts & Christensen, 2000). Analysis of more than 500 music videos showed that rap and rock videos were the most likely to portray alcohol use (about one-fourth showed one or more characters drinking) (DuRant et al.,

1997). Across all music genres, no consequences were mentioned in 91% of the lyrics that included references to drinking (Roberts, Henriksen, & Christenson, 1999).

Effects of Alcohol Portrayals.   Young people are likely to be affected by such portrayals because they have less conflicting real-world experience and typically are seeking information about how they might become part of the adult world. A few studies have begun to establish a link between amount of time spent viewing these portrayals and actual drinking behavior. Robinson, Chen, & Killen (1998), for example, found in a longitudinal study of 14- and 15-year-olds that for every extra hour per day spent watching music videos, the adolescents were 31% more likely to begin drinking alcohol during the next 18 months. An extra hour of regular television viewing increased their chances of drinking by nearly 10%. These data also are indicative of a pattern that some have called "delinquent media use" (Roe, 1995). Young people who already are leaning toward riskier behavior, such as drinking, may select media genres such as music videos that portray and sometimes glamorize such behavior and in the process have their emerging attitudes and behaviors reinforced.

Tobacco

From the haze of smoke that sometimes threatened to obscure early TV newscasters, to the cigarette draped on the lips of movie idol James Dean, tobacco has been a staple prop of television programs and in the movies. Although in the 1980s depictions declined from the pervasive portrayals of the early days, the gap between the prevalence of tobacco use in the movies and in actual life steadily widened in the 1990s (Stockwell & Glantz, 1997). Young adults were shown smoking in about 75% of music videos (DuRant et al., 1997).

A number of studies of the movies, a medium that attracts a large youth audience, have found that tobacco use is frequent and rarely depicted as potentially dangerous to the health of the user or others. Almost all (95%) of the 250 highest-grossing movies released from 1988 to 1997 depicted characters using tobacco. Even though the tobacco industry agreed to ban paid product placement in movies in 1990, one study found that cigarette brands appeared as frequently after the ban as they did before. The major difference was that after the ban, brands were more likely depicted while being handled or used by an actor rather than only in the background (e.g., the Marlboro truck in "Superman") (Sargent et al., 2001).

In the movies, tobacco use is associated with other high-risk behaviors—major women characters who smoke are more likely to have sexual affairs, engage in illegal activities, and drive recklessly. Male characters who smoke are more violent and dangerous. Thus, tobacco may be used as a kind of character cue for "bad" women and "tough" men (Sargent, Dalton, Tickle, Ahrens, & Heatherton, 2000). An analysis of 50 G-rated, animated feature films released between 1937 and 1997, however, found that "good" characters were shown using tobacco and alcohol as frequently as "bad" characters (Goldstein, Sobel, & Newman, 1999).

Although there is little evidence linking these portrayals to young people's perceptions of or initiation of smoking or drinking, some intriguing analyses of movie stars suggests that it matters that attractive people are shown using tobacco as if it were normal and risk-free. One study found that adolescent smokers were more likely than nonsmokers to name actors who smoked either on or off screen as their favorite stars (Distefan, Gilpin, Sargent, & Pierce, 1999). Another study of 50 movies featuring adolescents' favorite female stars found that tobacco use was depicted in more than one fourth of the length of the movies. The rare negative messages regarding tobacco product use (e.g., coughing, grimacing at the smell of smoke) were even less likely in PG/PG-13 films than in those rated R (Escamilla, Cradock, & Kawachi, 2000).

Social learning theory predicts that behaviors that are shown frequently and without negative consequence are more likely imitated, and that behaviors of attractive characters are more likely modeled by observers (Bandura, 1986). We know that adolescents who overestimate smoking prevalence are more likely to become smokers themselves. Thus, it appears reasonable to think that the unrealistic picture of tobacco use presented in the movies may be contributing to the continued high levels of smoking among young people and may be undermining the extensive antismoking media campaigns underway across the country.

Illicit Drugs

Illicit drugs appear less frequently and are more likely negatively portrayed than either alcohol or tobacco. Marijuana and cocaine are portrayed most frequently, although some popular movies, such as *Traffic*, have depicted heroin use. Roberts et al. (1999) found that illicit drugs appeared in about one fifth of movies and popular song lyrics. Illicit drug users are more likely to suffer negative consequences than alcohol or cigarette users, although drug addiction is rarely shown, and addicts usually are portrayed as evil rather than ill. Music video viewers are most likely to see illicit drug use. One content analysis estimated that the average MTV viewer sees illicit drugs every 40 minutes compared with every 100 minutes in the movies and every 112 minutes on prime-time TV (Gerbner & Ozyegin, 1997).

No studies have tied these portrayals directly to beliefs, attitudes, or behaviors. Illicit drug use among adolescents declined significantly from the early 1980s through the early 1990s, but began to increase in the late 1990s, just as there seemed to be a comeback of marijuana in Hollywood movies such as *There's Something About Mary* (Ozer et al., 1997; Strasburger, 2001). Research is needed on how the frequency of positive or negative portrayals contributes to youths' attitudes toward illicit drug use.

Sexuality

American youth have the highest rates of teen pregnancy and one of the highest rates of sexually transmitted diseases (gonorrhea, syphilis, chlamydia, HIV) in the industrialized world. Some of these STDs are deadly, and others can result in infertility and long-term reproductive and health problems. American teens are at high risk for STDs and pregnancy because nearly half of all high school students have had sexual intercourse, often without protection, and almost one in five has had four or more partners (Ozer et al., 1997).

Sexual talk and displays are frequent and increasingly explicit in the mediated world in which children are growing up. In 45 episodes of the top prime-time television shows that teens watched most frequently in 1996 (including *Friends* and *Married with Children*), the primarily young adult characters talked about sex and engaged in sexual behavior in two thirds of the shows (Cope & Kunkel, 2002). One fifth to one half of music videos, depending on the music genre, portray sexuality or eroticism (DuRant et al., 1997). Two thirds of Hollywood movies made each year are R-rated, and most young people have seen these movies long before they are the required 16 years old (Greenberg et al., 1993). Although teen girls' and women's magazines, such as *Seventeen* and *Glamour,* have increased their coverage of sexual health issues, the majority of advertising and editorial content remains focused on what girls and women should do to get and keep their man (Walsh-Childers, Gotthoffer, & Lepre, 2002). The Internet also has increased the availability of sexually explicit content. According to a national survey of young people (10–17 years old) who regularly use the Internet, one out of four encountered unwanted pornography in the past year, and one out of five was exposed to unwanted sexual solicitations or approaches (Finkelhor, Mitchell, & Wolak, 2000).

Despite increasing public concern about the potential health risks of early, unprotected sexual activity, the media rarely depict three Cs of responsible sexual behavior: commitment, contraceptives, and consequences. Although more than half of the couples who engage in sexual intercourse on television are in an established relationship, 1 in 10 are couples who have met only recently; more than one-fourth do not maintain a relationship after having sex. Only about 1 in 11 of the programs on television that include sexual content mentions possible risks or responsibilities associated with sexual activity. Sexually transmitted diseases other than HIV/AIDS are almost never discussed, and unintended pregnancies are rarely shown as the outcomes of unprotected sex (Kunkel et al., 1999). Abortion is a taboo topic, too controversial for commercial television and magazines (Walsh-Childers et al., 2002), and homosexual and transgendered people rarely are portrayed positively (Wolf & Kielwasser, 1991).

Effects of Sexual Content. Do media consumers learn about sex from this array of sexual information and portrayals? The perceived sensitivity of sex as a research topic and a focus on television to the exclusion of other media has restricted the kind of research that has been done.[5] Much of the empirical work has been analyses of content that allow only speculation about what effects the content might have on audiences. However, an emerging set of studies that go beyond content to address how audiences select, interpret, and apply sexual content suggests that the media do play an important role in sexual socialization (Steele, 1999).

When asked where they have learned the most about sex, younger adolescents (13 to 15 years old) rank the mass media fourth behind parents, friends, and schools. Older adolescents (16 to 17 years old) put friends first, then parents, and then the media (Yankelovich Partners, 1993). The media are used as sources of information about sexuality at some times more than others. One qualitative study suggested that sexual portrayals in the media are attended to more when girls are interested personally in learning about relationship norms, strategies for establishing relationships, and tips on how to become sexually attractive (Brown, White, & Nikopoulou, 1993). All members of an audience also do not see or interpret the same sexual message in the same way. Ward, Gorvine, and Cytron (2002) showed college students portions of situation comedies such as *Roseanne* and *Martin*. They found that young women were more likely than young men to think the sexual scenes they saw were realistic, and the women were more approving than the men of behaviors that were relationship-maintaining (e.g., jealous husband protecting wife) and less approving of relationship threats (e.g., man contemplating cheating).

Does the sexual content in the media influence how adolescents behave sexually? The relatively few correlational and still fewer experimental

---

[5]Much of the research on sexual media content has focused on the effects of pornography and sexually explicit material on adults. For a thorough review of that literature see chapter 12 in this volume. In this chapter, we focus on mainstream media, what most would consider nonpornographic content, and effects on adolescents' sexuality.

studies of the relationship between exposure to sexual media content and effects suggest that the media do have an impact in at least three ways: (a) by keeping sexual behavior on public and personal agendas, (b) by reinforcing a relatively consistent set of sexual and relationship norms, and (c) by rarely including sexually responsible models. Tests of the cultivation hypothesis have found, for example, that junior and senior high school students who frequently viewed daytime soap operas were more likely than those who watched less often to believe that single mothers have relatively easy lives, have good jobs, and do not live in poverty (Larson, 1996). Exposure to stereotypical images of gender and sexuality in music videos has been found to increase older adolescents' acceptance of nonmarital sexual behavior and interpersonal violence (Kalof, 1999).

Two studies found relationships between the frequency of television viewing and initiation of intercourse in samples of high school students. However, because these were only cross-sectional analyses, it was not possible to say with certainty which came first—the TV viewing or the sexual behavior (Brown & Newcomer, 1991; Peterson, Moore, & Furstenberg, 1991). It is possible that teens who were becoming interested in sex had turned to sexual content in the media because it was now salient in their lives. It also is possible that the teens saw the ubiquitous and typically risk-free sexual media content as encouragement for them to engage in sexual behavior sooner than they might have otherwise. It is likely that both causal sequences are operating, but longitudinal studies are needed to conclude that with more certainty.

Mental Health

We know relatively little about the effects of the media on mental health at either the personal or public levels. One issue that has been studied is the extent to which some kinds of music are related to psychosocial problems among adolescents. A number of studies suggest that being a heavy metal fan may be a marker for mental health problems. For instance, Scheel and Westefeld (1999) found that, in comparison to fans of other music genres, high school students (especially boys) who preferred heavy metal music scored lower on a Reasons for Living inventory and reported having more frequent thoughts of suicide (especially girls). Stack, Gundlach, and Reeves (1994) found that youth suicide rates were highest in states that also had the highest penetration of heavy metal magazine subscriptions. They suggested that listening to heavy metal music and being involved in the heavy metal subculture nurtures preexisting suicidal tendencies. In a small study of teens who were in-patients in a hospital psychiatric unit, Weidinger and Demi (1993) found that a history of dysfunctional psychosocial behaviors was more common among teens who mostly listened to music with negative lyrics and themes than among teens who preferred other types of music. Based on these and other studies, the American Academy of Pediatrics concluded, "It is in children's best interest to listen to lyrics that are not violent, sexist, drug-oriented or antisocial" (American Academy of Pediatrics, 1996, p. 2).

An intriguing couple of studies suggest that the preference for heavy metal music and similar genres may be neurologically driven. In a study of Australian adolescents, Martin, Clarke, and Pearce (1993) found significant relationships between a preference for heavy metal rock music and suicidal thoughts, deliberate self-injury, depression, delinquent behavior, drug use, and family dysfunction, particularly among girls. They also found that the most disturbed teens reported feeling sadder after listening to their preferred music. Roberts, Dimsdale, East, and Friedman (1998) similarly found significant positive associations between strong emotional responses to music and engaging in health-risk behaviors—whether the emotional response was positive or negative. The two studies together suggest that the teens at greatest risk are those who listen to music to engender negative emotions. Longitudinal study is needed to sort out whether listening to heavy metal or other types of music causes an increased risk of mental health problems or serves primarily as a marker for other, perhaps more biologically rooted, problems.

Stigmatization.   A second, more general, effect the mass media may have on mental health is the stigmatizing effect of media portrayals of people with mental illnesses. Signorielli (1989) found, for instance, that 72% of the mentally ill characters portrayed in prime-time television dramas are violent, and more than one in five are portrayed as killers (compared to about 9% of major nonmentally ill adult characters). Images of murderous mental patients also are common in movies such as *Silence of the Lambs* and the *Scream* series. These portrayals may be dangerous because the public reports that mass media are their primary source of information about people with mental illnesses (Robert Wood Johnson Foundation, 1990).

Exposure to mass media depictions of people with mental illnesses is related to more negative attitudes toward the mentally ill (Granello, Pauley, & Carmichael, 1999; Thornton & Wahl, 1996). The media's contribution to stigmatizing the mentally ill has the potential to affect both individuals and public health policy. March (1999) argues that distorted media images may discourage people from seeking care for a mental illness. In addition, she suggests, these images may discourage employers from being willing to hire people with mental illnesses. Even health care professionals are likely to be influenced by these media depictions, leading them to respond to the mentally ill patients in accord with the stereotypes they have learned from the mass media (Matisoff-Li, 1999). These negative attitudes also may result in the public and policymakers being less willing to support publicly funded services for people with mental illnesses.

UNINTENDED PERSONAL-LEVEL HEALTH EFFECTS

News about Health Issues

Health is an important and popular topic in the news media. The media have played a crucial role in informing the public about HIV/AIDS and a number of other important health issues. Singer and Endreny (1994) assert that most of the public's information about environmental health risks comes from the mass media, particularly "news and feature stories about accidents, illnesses, natural disasters, and scientific breakthroughs" (p. 1).

News coverage of celebrities' health problems has substantial impact on individuals' behavior related to those same health problems. Magic Johnson's announcement that he was HIV-positive increased perception of HIV risk and intentions to change sexual behaviors or get an HIV blood test (Basil, 1996). News coverage of former First Lady Nancy Reagan's decision to undergo a mastectomy influenced the behavior of women diagnosed with breast cancer (Nattinger, Hoffmann, Howell-Pelz, & Goodwin, 1998).

News coverage of environmental risks also can affect perceptions of personal risk. One experimental study showed that the hazard level described in stories about a hypothetical chemical spill had the greatest effect on readers' perceptions of their own risk, followed by the level of outrage attributed to people living near the spill. The amount of technical risk information in the story was not related to readers' risk perceptions (Sandman, 1994). The public also tends to perceive risks as more dangerous when there is someone to blame, which is something the media frequently do, rather than when the risk is naturally occurring, even though scientific evaluation of the relative risks may not differ (i.e., radon from natural deposits of radioactive rock versus radon from industrial waste) (Singer & Endreny, 1994).

UNINTENDED PUBLIC-LEVEL HEALTH EFFECTS

News and Health Policy

The news media also can help set the health policy agenda for citizens and policymakers by focusing attention on certain issues or diseases and ignoring others. Agenda-setting theory suggests that this may lead to public concern about frequently covered issues that overestimates the actual public health impact of those issues, and this (perhaps unfounded) public concern may lead to policy action. The framing of health issues (e.g., focusing on health problems as problems of individual behavior rather than a lack of access to healthy environments) also can affect the *types* of policy solutions the public and policymakers consider (Wallack & Dorfman, 1996).

Although news influences on policy development can be positive, effects also can be negative if media pressure spurs legislators to approve policies that have not been carefully considered or evaluated (Danielian & Reese, 1989). Shoemaker, Wanta, and Leggett (1989) found that coverage of drug abuse in the national news media accounted for half the variance in public concern about drugs expressed in Gallup Polls from 1972 through 1986. They argued that the media's intense coverage of the drug problem during the summer of 1986 likely influenced Congress's rapid passage of a $1.7 billion antidrug legislation package.

Case studies of newspaper coverage of specific health issues suggests that news coverage is most likely to influence public health policy development when health experts agree on the solutions to a problem, when the change can occur at the local or state policy level, and when there are private citizen groups and/or public officials working toward specific policy changes supported by the news content (Walsh-Childers, 1994a, 1994b). For the most part, news influences on public health policy must be considered unintended effects. News organizations rarely acknowledge publishing or broadcasting stories with the intent to influence public policy. In some circumstances, however, news organizations or individual journalists may develop stories designed to spur policy action and may publish follow-up stories and/or editorials intended to pressure policymakers into taking action (Walsh-Childers, Chance, & Swain, 1999). Given the current trend of "public journalism projects"—in which news organizations take an active role in initiating and/or promoting civic action within their communities—health reporting intended to affect public policy change may become increasingly common.

INTENDED PUBLIC-LEVEL HEALTH EFFECTS

Media Advocacy and the Public Health Environment

Traditionally, public health promotion efforts have focused on changing individuals' behaviors from risky or unhealthy practices to those that either improve individuals' health or at least do not endanger or undermine their health. From this perspective, "public health" is defined as the absence of disease, injury, or other health-compromising conditions, and poor health is defined primarily as an information gap problem: "(I)f people just had the right information, then they would behave in a healthy manner" (Wallack & Dorfman, 1996, p. 297). However, proponents of what is known as the "new public health" argue that health encompasses more than simply the absence of disease or other characteristics of poor health; rather, "health is the presence of physical, social and economic well-being" (Wallack & Dorfman, 1996, p. 295). This view acknowledges that even when individuals have received and accepted messages promoting healthier behaviors, their physical, financial, and social environments do not necessarily enable them to adopt those behaviors.

One mechanism public health activists have used in efforts to create healthier environments is media advocacy, defined as the strategic use of mass media for advancing social or public policy initiatives (Pertschuk, 1988). Media advocacy campaigns make use of the power of the media, particularly news media, to influence both public and policymaker agendas and to determine which characteristics of the issues on those agendas will receive emphasis. Public health advocates attempt to gain media attention for an issue while simultaneously influencing the framing of that issue in news coverage to focus on policy change rather than individual behavior change as a solution to health problems.

Media advocacy has been used in numerous campaigns aimed at influencing both governmental and business policies for a wide range of health issues. Case studies have indicated that media advocacy campaigns can influence news coverage and increase public awareness of an issue as well as public recognition of and support for public policy solutions. Holder and Treno (1997) reported, for instance, that a media advocacy campaign designed to increase a community's support for local regulations on drinking and driving resulted in a significant increase in news coverage of the issue and greater public awareness of the issues. Schooler, Sundar, and Flora (1996) concluded that in one of two cities in which a media advocacy campaign was conducted in concert with the Stanford Five-City Project to reduce cardiovascular disease (CVD), the local newspaper published more CVD-related articles and staff-written CVD articles, made those articles more prominent, and increased the stories' emphasis on prevention.

Similarly, Woodruff's (1996) case study of the California-based "Dangerous Promises" campaign suggests that media advocacy efforts were successful in influencing news media in California to print or broadcast stories about a coalition's efforts to discourage alcohol manufacturers from using sexist advertising to promote their products. Perhaps more importantly, those stories generally covered the controversy from the public health perspective, emphasizing the campaign's message that "sexist alcohol ads reinforce myths that contribute to violence against women" (p. 338). Coalition advocates believed the year's worth of media attention to the controversy in San Diego County led to the removal of all alcohol billboards featuring women and to the beer and distilled spirits trade associations' revision of their codes of ethics to include provisions discouraging sexist advertising messages.

CONCLUSIONS

Over the past 10 years, since the first edition of this book, we have seen a dramatic increase in interest in the effects of the media on health. Much of this interest has been supported by federal agencies and states that have begun to realize that significant shifts in cultural norms are necessary if individuals are to be expected to behave in healthy ways. For example, initial funds from a few states' settlements with the tobacco companies generated excellent new research on the effects of cigarette advertising on youth that ultimately affected the content of the Master Settlement Agreement and increased restrictions on the promotion of tobacco products.

Another trend obvious here is that the research on the media's impact on health beliefs and behaviors at both the personal and public level is becoming increasingly sophisticated and theoretically based, moving away from only content analyses to more complicated longitudinal designs that put media exposure into the context of individual's lives. Austin's program of research on the effects of alcohol advertisements on children's beliefs about alcohol and subsequent drinking behavior is a good example of theory-based research that helps explain as well as describe the process of media effects (Austin, Pinkleton, & Fujioka, 2000). Similar research is needed to understand the effectiveness of media advocacy efforts designed to have an effect at the public policy level.

Another important development is the Internet as a source of health information. We know relatively little about this hybrid medium that combines attributes of both interpersonal communication and mass media. Over the next decade, we expect to see a great deal of research focused on how the Internet is used for obtaining health information and the extent to which the increased potential for individual choice undermines the notion of "mass" media. It may well be that in the future, as some predict, all forms of media will be available on demand in one delivery system. Will this be beneficial to our health?

Finally, given the overriding theme in much of the existing research that the media have the greatest impact on children and young people who are developing their own health beliefs and behaviors, we expect to see more work on the effectiveness of media literacy programs. Media literacy is an educational effort to give people (usually schoolchildren) the tools to critically analyze media messages and to develop messages they would rather see and hear about. Media educators believe that understanding how "reality" is constructed through the mass media means understanding the production process (including technological, economic, bureaucratic, and legal constraints), the text, and the audience/receiver/end user. By gaining critical analysis and viewing skills and participating in media production, media literacy is believed to lead not only to a greater understanding of the stories (e.g., sexual scripts) that media tell and their sources, but also may result in personal changes, such as improvements in self-esteem (e.g., the ability to say "no" to cigarettes, alcohol), taking responsibility for one's life (e.g., always designating a driver), sharing experiences with others (e.g., negotiating condom use), and learning the ability to express oneself.

In the 1990s, a number of health-related institutions in the United States began media literacy initiatives. The American Academy of Pediatrics (AAP) launched "Media Matters," an educational campaign complete with a kit that encouraged pediatricians to talk with their young patients about the potentially harmful health effects of various kinds of media. The AAP also teamed up with the U.S. Centers for Disease Control and the Center for Substance Abuse Prevention to create a short curriculum called "Media Sharp" that was designed to help young people analyze tobacco and alcohol messages. So far, few media literacy curricula have been evaluated systematically. However, some emerging current work suggests that such efforts have value. In one experimental study, Austin and Johnson (1997) found that media literacy training on alcohol advertising increased third graders' understanding of the persuasive intent in alcohol advertising and social norms for alcohol use. This is a promising direction that may have a significant impact on the role the media play in personal and public health in the future.

REFERENCES

Altman, D. G., Levine, D. W., Coeytaux, R., Slade, J., & Jaffe, R. (1996). Tobacco promotion and susceptibility to tobacco use among adolescents aged 12 through 17 years in a nationally representative sample. *American Journal of Public Health, 86*(11), 1590–1593.

American Academy of Pediatrics. (1996). Impact of music lyrics and music videos on children and youth: Policy statement. *Pediatrics, 98*(6), 1219–1221.

Armstrong, C. A., Sallis, J. F., Alcaraz, J. E., Kolody, B., McKenzie, T. L., & Hovell, M. F. (1998). Children's television viewing, body fat and physical fitness. *American Journal of Health Promotion, 12*(6), 363–368.

Austin, E. W., & Johnson, K. K. (1997). Immediate and delayed effects of media literacy training on third graders' decision making for alcohol. *Health Communication, 9*(4), 323–349.

Austin, E. W., & Knaus, C. (1998, August). *Predicting future risky behavior among those "too young" to drink as the result of advertising desirability.* Paper presented at the meeting of the Association for Education in Journalism and Mass Communication, Baltimore, MD.

Austin, E. W., Pinkleton, B. E., & Fujioka, Y. (2000). The role of interpretation processes and parental discussion in the media's effects on adolescents' use of alcohol. *Pediatrics, 105*(2), 343–349.

Bandura, A. (1986). *Social foundations of thought and action: A social cognitive theory.* Upper Saddle River, NJ: Prentice Hall.

Basil, M. D. (1996). Identification as a mediator of celebrity effects. *Journal of Broadcasting and Electronic Media, 40,* 478–495.

Bell, R. A., Kravitz, R. L., & Wilkes, M. S. (1999). Direct-to-consumer prescription drug advertising and the public. *Journal of General Internal Medicine, 14*(11), 651–657.

Berkey, C. S. Rockett, H. R. H., Field, A. E., Gillman, M. W., Frazier, A. L., Camargo, C. A., Jr., & Colditz, G. A. (2000). Activity, dietary intake, and weight changes in a longitudinal study of preadolescent and adolescent boys and girls. *Pediatrics, 105*(4), p. e56. Retrieved January 15, 2001, from http://www.pediatrics.org/cgi/content/full/105/4/e56

Biener, L., & Siegel, M. (2000). Tobacco marketing and adolescent smoking: More support for a causal inference. *American Journal of Public Health, 90*(3), 407–411.

Botta, R. (1999). Television images and adolescent girls' body image disturbance. *Journal of Communication, 49*(2), 22–41.

Botta, R. (2000). The mirror of television: A comparison of black and white adolescents' body image. *Journal of Communication, 50*(3), 144–159.

Bound, W. (1999, May 6). Keeping teens from smoking, with style. *Wall Street Journal,* p. B6.

Brown, J. D., & Newcomer, S. (1991). Television viewing and adolescents' sexual behavior. *Journal of Homosexuality, 21*(1/2), 77–91.

Brown, J. D., White A. B., & Nikopoulou, L. (1993). Disinterest, intrigue, resistance: Early adolescents' girls' use of sexual media content. In B. S. Greenberg, J. D. Brown, & N. Buerkel-Rothfuss (Eds.), *Media, Sex and the Adolescent* (pp. 177–195). Cresskill, NJ: Hampton Press.

Byrd-Bredbenner, C., & Grasso, D. (1999). Prime-time health: An analysis of health content in television commercials broadcast during programs viewed heavily by children. *International Electronic Journal of Health Education, 2*(4), 159–169.

Byrd-Bredbenner, C., & Grasso, D. (2000). Health, medicine, and food messages in television commercials in 1992 and 1998. *Journal of School Health, 70*(2), 61–65.

Cain, M. M., Mittman, R., Sarasohn-Kahn, J., and Wayne, J. C. (2000, August). *Health e-People: The Online Consumer Experience, 5-Year Forecast.* Oakland, CA: California HealthCare Foundation. Retrieved January 17, 2001, from http://admin.chcf.org/documents/ehealth/HealthEPeople.pdf

Choate, R., & Debevoise, N. (1976). Caution! Keep this commercial out of reach of children! *Journal of Drug Issues, 6*(1), 91–98.

Christenson, P. G., Henricksen, L., & Roberts, D. F. (2000). *Substance use in popular prime-time television.* Washington, DC: Office of National Drug Control Policy.

Coon, K. A., Goldberg, J. G., Rogers, B. L., & Tucker, K. L. (2001). Relationships between use of television during meals and children's food consumption patterns. *Pediatrics, 107*(1), 1–9.

Cooper, A. (1998). Sexuality and the Internet: Surfing into the new millennium. *CyberPsychology & Behavior, 1*(2), 187–193.

Cope, K. M. & Kunkel, D. (2002). Sexual messages in teens' favorite prime-time TV programs. In J. D. Brown, J. R. Steele, & K. Walsh-Childers (Eds.), *Sexual teens, sexual media* (pp. 59–78). Mahwah, NJ: Lawrence Erlbaum Associates.

Craig, R. S. (1992). Women as home care givers: Gender portrayal in OTC drug commercials. *Journal of Drug Education, 22*(4), 303–312.

Cyber Dialogue. (2000). Cybercitizen health 2000. Cited in Kassirer, J. P. (2000). Patients, physicians, and the Internet. *Health Affairs, 19*(6), 115–123.

Danielian, L. H., & Reese, S. D. (1989). A closer look at the intermedia influences on agenda setting: The cocaine issue of 1986. In P. J. Shoemaker (Ed.), *Communication Campaigns About Drugs: Government, Media and the Public* (pp. 47–66). Hillsdale, NJ: Lawrence Erlbaum Associates.

DeJong, W., & Winsten, J. A. (1989). *Recommendations for future mass media campaigns to prevent preteen and adolescent substance abuse.* (Special Report). Cambridge, MA: Harvard School of Public Health Center for Health Communication.

DiFranza, J. R., Richards, J. W., Paulman, P. M., Wolf-Gillespie, N., Fletcher, C., Jaffe, R. D., & Murray, D. (1991). RJR Nabisco's cartoon camel promotes Camel cigarettes to children. *Journal of the American Medical Association, 266,* 3149–3153.

DiFranza, J. R., Coleman, M., & Cyr, D. S. (1999). A comparison of the advertising and accessibility of cigars, cigarettes, chewing tobacco, and loose tobacco. *Preventive Medicine, 29,* 321–326.

Distefan, J. M., Gilpin, E. A., Sargent, J. D., & Pierce, J. P. (1999). Do movie stars encourage adolescents to start smoking? Evidence from California. *Preventive Medicine, 28*(1), 1–11.

Donohue, T., Meyer, T., & Henke, L. (1978). Black and white children's perceptions of television commercials. *Journal of Marketing, 42,* 34–40.

Drug and Therapy Perspectives. (2000). OTC drugs can be harmful to the unborn child. *16*(3), 12-1. Retrieved January 3, 2001, from http://www.medscape.com/adis/DTP/2000/v16.n03/dtp1603.04/pnt-dtp1603.04.html

DuRant, R. H., Rome, E. S., Rich, M., Allred, E., Emans, S. J., & Woods, E. R. (1997). Tobacco and alcohol use behaviors portrayed in music videos: A content analysis. *American Journal of Public Health, 87,* 1131–1135.

Escamilla, G., Cradock, A. L., & Kawachi, I. (2000). Women and smoking in Hollywood movies: A content analysis. *American Journal of Public Health, 90*(3), 412–414.

European Union Commission. (1998). Women's magazines and tobacco in Europe. *The Lancet, 352,* 786.

Everett, S. A., Schnuth, R. L., & Tribble, J. L. (1998). Tobacco and alcohol use in top-grossing American films. *Journal of Community Health, 23*(4), 317–324.

Federal Trade Commission. (1999). *Report to Congress for 1997 pursuant to the federal cigarette labeling and advertising act.* Washington, DC: U.S. Federal Trade Commisssion.

Feighery, E. C., Ribisl, K. M., Achabal, D. D., & Tyebjee, T. (1999). Retail trade incentives: How tobacco industry practices compare with those of other industries. *American Journal of Public Health, 89*(10), 1564–1566.

Field, A. E., Camargo, C.A., Jr., Taylor, C. B., Berkey, C. S., Roberts, S. B., & Colditz, G. A. (2001, January). Peer, parent and media influences on the development of weight concerns and frequent dieting among preadolescent and adolescent girls and boys. *Pediatrics, 107*(1), 54–60.

Finkelhor, D., Mitchell, K., & Wolak, J. (2000). *Online victimization: A report on the nation's youth.* Washington, DC: National Center for Missing and Exploited Children.

Folb, K. (2000). "Don't touch that dial!" TV as a—What!?—positive influence. *SIECUS Report, 28*(5), 16–18.

Food and Drug Administration et al. v. Brown & Williamson Tobacco Corp., 120 S. Ct. 1291, 1316 (2000).

Food and Drug Administration. (2000). Attitudes and behaviors associated with direct-to-consumer (DTC) promotion of prescription drugs: Preliminary survey results. Retrieved January 10, 2001, from http://www.fda.gov/cder/ddmac/DTCtitle.htm

Fouts, G., & Burggraf, K. (1999). Television situation comedies: Female body image and verbal reinforcements. *Sex Roles, 40,* 473–481.

Fox, R. J., Krugman, D. M., Fletcher, J. E., & Fischer, P. M. (1998). Adolescents' attention to beer and cigarette print ads and associated product warnings. *Journal of Advertising, 27*(3), 57–68.

Gerbner, G., & Ozyegin, N. (1997, March 20). *Alcohol, tobacco, and illicit drugs in entertainment television, commericals, news, "reality shows," movies, and music channels.* Princeton, NJ: Robert Wood Johnson Foundation.

Goldstein, A. O., Sobel, R. A. & Newman, G. R. (1999). Tobacco and alcohol use in G-rated children's animated films. *Journal of the American Medical Association, 281,* 1131–1136.

Granello, D. H., Pauley, P. S., & Carmichael, A. (1999). Relationship of the media to attitudes toward people with mental illness. *Journal of Humanistic Counseling, Education and Development, 38*(2), 98–110.

Greenberg, B. S., Siemicki, M., Dorfman, S., Heeter, C., Stanley, C., Soderman, A., & Linsangan, R. (1993). Sex content in R-rated films viewed by adolescents. In B. S. Greenberg, J. D. Brown, & N. Buerkel-Rothfuss (Eds.), *Media, Sex and the Adolescent* (pp. 45–58). Cresskill, NJ: Hampton Press.

Grimes-Gruczka, T., & Gratzer, C. (2000). *Ethics Survey of Consumer Attitudes about Health Web Sites.* California HealthCare Foundation and Internet Healthcare Coalition. Retrieved January 17, 2001, from http://admin.chcf.org/documents/ehealth/Ethics2ndEdition.pdf

Grube, J. W. (1993). Alcohol portrayals and alcohol advertising on television. *Alcohol Health & Research World, 17,* 61–66.

Grube, J. W. (1995). Television alcohol portrayals, alcohol advertising, and alcohol expectancies among children and adolescents. In S. E. Martin (Ed.), *The effects of the mass media on use and abuse of alcohol* (pp. 105–121). Bethesda, MD: National Institute on Alcohol Abuse and Alcoholism.

Grube, J. W. (1999). Alchohol advertising and alcohol consumption: A review of recent research. *NIAA tenth special report to Congress on alcohol and health.* Bethesda, MD: National Institute on Alcohol Abuse and Alcoholism.

Harrison, K. (1997). Does interpersonal attraction to thin media personalities promote eating disorders? *Journal of Broadcasting and Electronic Media, 41,* 478–500.

Harrison, K. (2000). The body electric: Thin-ideal media and eating disorders in adolescents. *Journal of Communication, 50*(3), 119–143.

Health on the Net Foundation. (1999, October-November). 5th HON Survey on the Evolution of Internet Use for Health Purposes. Retrived January 17, 2001 from http://222.hon.ch/Survey/ResultsSummary_oct_nov99.html

Henriksen, L., & Flora, J. A. (2001, May). *Effects of adolescents' exposure to retail tobacco advertising.* Paper presented at the meeting of the International Communication Association, Washington, D.C.

Hesterman, V. (1987, August). *You've come a long way, baby—or have you?* Paper presented at the meeting of the Association for Education in Journalism and Mass Communication, San Antonio, TX.

Hofshire, L. J., & Greenberg, B. S. (2002). Media's impact on adolescents' body dissatisfaction. In J. D. Brown, J. R. Steele, & K. Walsh-Childers (Eds.), *Sexual Teens, Sexual Media.* Mahwah, NJ: Lawrence Erlbaum Associates.

Holder, H. D., & Treno, A. J. (1997). Media advocacy in community prevention: News as a means to advance policy change. *Addiction, 92,* supplement 2, S189–S199.

Hong, T., & Cody, M. J. (2001, May). *Presence of pro-tobacco messages on the Web.* Paper presented at the meeting of the International Communication Association, Washington, DC.

IMS Health News Release. (2000). IMS HEALTH reports pharmaceutical direct-to-consumer advertising investment in U.S. reaches $1.3 billion in first-half 2000. Retrieved January 4, 2001, from http://www.imshealth.com/public/structure/dispcontent/1,2779,1009-1009-8228,00.html

Jadad, A. R., & Gagliardi, A. (1998). Rating health information on the Internet: Navigating to knowledge or to Babel? *Journal of the American Medical Association, 279*(8), 611–614.

Jeffery, R. W., & French, S. A. (1998). Epidemic obesity in the United States: Are fast foods and television viewing contributing? *American Journal of Public Health, 88*(2), 277–280.

Johnston, L. D., O'Malley, P. M., & Bachman, J. G. (1994). *National survey results on drug use from the Monitoring the Future Study, 1975–1993.* Washington, DC: National Institute on Drug Abuse.

Kaiser Family Foundation. (1997). *Survey of ER Viewers, April 1997.* Menlo, Park, CA: The Henry J. Kaiser Family Foundation.

Kalof, L. (1999). The effects of gender and music video imagery on sexual attitudes. *Journal of Social Psychology, 139*(3), 378–386.

Kassirer, J. P. (2000). Patients, physicians, and the Internet. *Health Affairs, 19*(6), 115–123.

Kincaid, D. L., Jara, R., Coleman, P., & Segura, F. (1988). *Getting the message: The communication for young people project.* Washington, DC: U.S. Agency for International Development, AID Evaluation Special Study 56.

Kleinke, J. D. (2000, November/December). Vaporware.com: The failed promise of the health care Internet. *Health Affairs, 19*(6), 57–71.

Knapp, K. K. (2000). The OTC movement. Paper presented at the American Pharmaceutical Association Annual Meeting, Washington, DC, March 10–14, 2000. Retrieved January 3, 2001, from http://www.medscape.com/medscape/CNO/2000/APHA/APHA-10.html

Kotz, K., & Story, M. (1994). Food advertisements during children's Saturday morning television programming: Are they consistent with dietary recommendations? *Journal of the American Dietetic Association, 94*(11), 1296–1300.

Kunkel, D., Cope, K., Farinola, W., Biely, E., Rollin, E., & Donnerstein, E. (1999). *Sex on TV: A biennial report to the Kaiser Family Foundation.* Menlo Park, CA: The Henry J. Kaiser Family Foundation.

Lank, N. H., Vickery, C. E., Cotugna, N., & Shade, D. D. (1992). Food commercials during television soap operas: What is the nutrition message? *Journal of Community Health, 17*(6), 377–384.

Larson, M. (1996). Sex roles and soap operas: What adolescents learn about single motherhood. *Sex Roles: A Journal of Research, 35*(1/2), 97–121.

Leit, R. A., Pope, H. G., Jr., & Gray, J. J. (2001). Cultural expectations of muscularity in men: The evolution of *Playgirl* centerfolds. *International Journal of Eating Disorders, 29*(1), 90–93.

Madden, P. A., & Grube, J. W. (1994). The frequency and nature of alcohol and tobacco advertising in televised sports, 1990 through 1992. *American Journal of Public Health, 84,* 297–299.

March, P. A. (1999). Ethical responses to media depictions of mental illness: An advocacy approach. *Journal of Humanistic Counseling, Education and Development, 38*(2), 70–79.

Master Settlement Agreement. (1998). National Association of Attorneys General. Retrieved December 10, 2000, from http://www.naag.org/tobaccopublic/library.cfm

Martin, C., & Duncan, D. (1984). Televised OTC drug ads as surrogate dope pushers among young people: Fact or fiction. *Journal of Alcohol and Drug Education, 2913,* 19–30.

Martin, G., Clarke, M., & Pearce, C. (1993, May). Adolescent suicide: Music preference as an indicator of vulnerability. *Journal of the American Academy of Child and Adolescent Psychiatry, 32*(3), 530–535.

Matisoff-Li, A. (1999, March 25). Media madness: Negative portrayals of mental illness. *Nurseweek/Healthweek.* Retrived January 15, 2001, from http://www.nurseweek.com/features/99-3/mhealth.html

McMurray, R. G., Harrell, J. S., Deng, S., Bradley, C. B., Cox, L. M., & Bangdiwala, S. I. (2000). The influence of physical activity, socioeconomic status, and ethnicity on the weight status of adolescents. *Obesity Research, 8*(2), 130–139.

Milio, N. (1986). Health and the media in Australia—An uneasy relationship. *Community Health Studies, 10*(4), 419–422.

Montgomery, K. (1989). *Target: Prime time: Advocacy groups and the struggle over entertainment television.* New York: Oxford University Press.

National Institute for Health Care Management. (2000). Prescription drugs and mass media advertising. *NIHCM Foundation Research Brief,* September.

Nattinger, A. B., Hoffmann, R. G., Howell-Pelz, A., & Goodwin, J. S. (1998). Effect of Nancy Reagan's mastectomy on choice of surgery for breast cancer by U.S. women. *Journal of the American Medical Association, 279*(10), 762–767.

Navigating the medication marketplace: How consumers choose. (1997). Washington, DC: Prevention/American Pharmaceutical Association.

Nelkin, D. (1994). Reporting risk: The case of silicone breast implants. *Risk, 5.* Retrieved January 17, 2001, from http://www.fplc.edu/RISK/vol5/winter/trauth.htm

Owen, P. R., & Laurel-Seller, E. (2000). Weight and shape ideals: Thin is dangerously in. *Journal of Applied Social Psychology, 30*(5), 979–990.

Ozer, E. M., Brindis, C. D., Millstein, S. G., Knopf, D. K., & Irwin, C. E., Jr. (1997). *America's adolescents: Are they healthy?* San Francisco: University of California–San Francisco, National Adolescent Health Information Center.

Pechmann, C., & Ratneshwar, S. (1994). The effects of antismoking and cigarette advertising on young adolescents' perceptions of peers who smoke. *Journal of Consumer Research, 21*(2), 236–251.

Pertschuk, M. (1988). *Smoking control: Media advocacy guidelines.* Washington, DC: Advocacy Institute for the National Cancer Institute, National Institutes of Health.

Peterson, J., Moore, K., & Furstenberg, F. (1991). Television viewing and early initiation of sexual intercourse. Is there a link? *Journal of Homosexuality, 21*(1/2), 93–118.

Pierce, J. P., Choi, W. S., Gilpin, E. A., Farkas, A. J., & Berry, C. (1998). Industry promotion of cigarettes and adolescent smoking. *Journal of the American Medical Association, 279,* 511–515.

Pierce, J. P., Gilpin, E. A., Burns, D. M., Whalen, E., Rosbrook, B., Shopland, D., & Johnson, M. (1991). Does tobacco advertising target young people to start smoking? *Journal of the American Medical Association, 266,* 3154–3158.

Pierce, J. P., Lee, L., & Gilpin, E. A. (1994). Smoking initiation by adolescent girls, 1944 though 1988: An association with targeted advertising. *Journal of the American Medical Association, 271*(8), 608–611.

Pucci, L. G., Joseph, H. M., Jr., & Siegel, M. (1998). Outdoor tobacco advertising in six Boston neighborhoods: Evaluating youth exposure. *American Journal of Preventive Medicine, 15*(2), 155–159.

Robert Wood Johnson Foundation. (1990). *Public attitudes toward people with chronic mental illnesses.* Boston: Robert Wood Johnson Program on Chronic Mental Illnesses.

Roberts, D., & Christenson, P. G. (2000). *"Here's looking at you, kid": Alcohol, drugs and tobacco in entertainment media.* New York: National Center on Addiction and Substance Abuse at Columbia University.

Roberts, D. F., Henriksen, L., & Christenson, P. G. (1999). *Substance use in popular movies and music.* Washington, DC: Office of National Drug Control Policy.

Roberts, K. R., Dimsdale, J., East, P., & Friedman, L. (1998, July). Adolescent emotional response to music and its relationship to risk-taking behaviors. *Journal of Adolescent Health, 23*(1), 49–54.

Robinson, T. N. (1997). Reducing children's television viewing to prevent obesity: A randomized controlled trial. *Journal of the American Medical Association, 282*(16), 1561–1567.

Robinson, T. N., Chen, H. L., & Killen, J. D. (1998). Television and music video exposure and risk of adolescent alcohol use. *Pediatrics, 102*(5), E54.

Roe, K. (1995). Adolescents' use of socially disvalued media: Towards a theory of media delinquency. *Journal of Youth and Adolescence, 24*(5), 617–631.

Salmon, J., Bauman, A., Crawford, D., Timpenio, A., & Owen, N. (2000). The association between television viewing and overweight among Australian adults participating in varying levels of leisure-time physical activity. *International Journal of Obesity, 24,* 600–606.

Sandman, P. M. (1994). Mass media and environmental risk: Seven principles. *Risk, 5.* Retrieved January 17, 2001, from http://www.fplc.edu/RISK/vol5/winter/trauth.htm

Sargent, J. D., Dalton, M. A., Tickle, J. J., Ahrens, M. B., & Heatherton, T. F. (2000). *Tobacco use in motion pictures: Is Hollywood addicted?* Paper presented to Pediatric Academic Societies, Boston, MA.

Sargent, J. D., Tickle, J. J., Beach, M. L., Dalton, M. A., Ahrens, M. B., & Heatherton, T. F. (2001). Brand appearances in contemporary cinema films and contribution to global marketing of cigarettes. *The Lancet, 357,* 29–32.

Scheel, K. R., & Westefeld, J. S. (1999). Heavy metal music and adolescent suicidality: An empirical investigation. *Adolescence, 34,* 253–273.

Schooler, C., Sundar, S. S., & Flora, J. (1996). Effects of the Stanford Five-City Project Media Advocacy Program. *Health Education Quarterly, 23*(3), 346–364.

Schulz, A. T. (1998). Over-the-counter drugs: Safe if used wisely. *Women & Aging Letter,* 2(6). Retrieved October 4, 2001, from http://www.aoa.dhhs.gov/elderpage/walotc-drugs.html

Shoemaker, P. J., Wanta, W., & Leggett, D. (1989). Drug coverage and public opinion, 1972–1986. In P. J. Shoemaker (Ed.), *Communication Campaigns About Drugs: Government, Media and the Public* (pp. 67-80). Hillsdale, NJ: Lawrence Erlbaum Associates.

Signorielli, N. (1989). The stigma of mental illness on television. *Journal of Broadcasting & Electronic Media, 33,* 325–331.

Signorielli, N., & Lears, M. (1992). Television and children's conceptions of nutrition: Unhealthy messages. *Health Communication, 4*(4), 245–257.

Signorielli, N., & Staples, J. (1997). Television and children's conceptions of nutrition. *Health Communication, 9*(4), 289–301.

Silverstein, B., Perdue, L., Peterson, B., & Kelly, E. (1986). The role of the mass media in promoting a thin standard of attractiveness for women. *Sex Roles, 14,* 519–532.

Singer, E., & Endreny, P. J. (1994). Reporting on risk: How the mass media portray accidents, diseases, disasters and other hazards. *Risk, 5.* Retrieved January 17, 2001, from http://www.fplc.edu/RISK/vol5/winter/trauth.htm

Singhal, A., & Rogers, E. M. (1999). *Entertainment-education: A communication strategy for social change.* Mahwah, NJ: Lawrence Erlbaum Associates.

Snyder, L. B., & Blood, D. J. (1992). Caution: Alcohol advertising and the Surgeon General's alcohol warnings may have adverse effects on young adults. *Journal of Applied Communication Research, 20*(1), 37–53.

Stack, S., Gundlach, J., & Reeves, J. L. (1994). The heavy metal subculture and suicide. *Suicide and Life Threatening Behavior, 24*(1), 15–23.

Steele, J. R. (1999). Teenage sexuality and media practice: Factoring in the influences of family, friends and school. *Journal of Sex Research, 36*(4), 331–341.

Stice, E., & Shaw, H. E. (1994). Adverse effects of the media portrayed thin-ideal on women and linkages to bulimic symptomatology. *Journal of Social and Clinical Psychology, 13,* 288–308.

Stockwell, T. F., & Glantz, S. A. (1997). Tobacco use is increasing in popular films. *Tobacco Control, 6,* 282–284.

Story, M., & Faulkner, P. (1990). The prime time diet: A content analysis of eating behavior and food messages in television program content and commercials. *American Journal of Public Health, 80*(6), 738–740.

Strasburger, V. (2001). Children, adolescents, drugs, and the media. In D. G. Singer & J. L. Singer (Eds.), *Handbook of children and the media* (pp. 415–445). Thousand Oaks, CA: Sage.

Taras, H. L., & Gage, M. (1995). Advertised foods on children's television. *Archives of Pediatric and Adolescent Medicine, 149*(6), 649–652.

Taras, H. L., Sallis, J. F., Patterson, T. L., Nader, P. R., & Nelson, J. A. (1989). Television's influence on children's diet and physical activity. *Journal of Developmental and Behavioral Pediatrics, 10*(4), 176–180.

The Media and Eating Disorders. (2001). Rader Programs. Retrieved September 21, 2001, from http://www.raderprograms.com/media/htm

Thornton, J. A., & Wahl, O. (1996). Impact of a newspaper article on attitudes toward mental illness. *Journal of Community Psychology, 24*, 17–25.

Tobacco Control Resource Center, Inc. (2000). *The emperor's fig leaf: Draft summary of AG tobacco deal contains few new public health provisions and lacks many critical industry concessions.* Retrieved December 1, 2000, from http://www.tobacco.neu.edu/Extra/analysis_of_draft.htm

Tucker, L. A. (1990). Television viewing and physical fitness in adults. *Research Quarterly in Exercise and Sport, 61*(4), 315–320.

Tucker, L. A., & Bagwell, M. (1991). Television viewing and obesity in adult females. *American Journal of Public Health, 81*(7), 908–911.

Tucker, L. A., & Friedman, G. M. (1989). Television viewing and obesity in adult males. *American Journal of Public Health, 79*(4), 516–518.

U.S. Dept. of Health and Human Services. (1994). *Preventing tobacco use among young people: Report of the Surgeon General.* Washington, DC: U.S. Government Printing Office.

Vickers, A. (1992). Why cigarette advertising should be banned. *British Medical Journal, 304*, 1195–1196.

Wallack, L., & Dorfman, L. (1996). Media advocacy: A strategy for advancing policy and promoting health. *Health Education Quarterly, 23*(3), 293–317.

Wallack, L., Dorfman, L., Jernigan, D., & Themba, M. (1993). *Media advocacy and public health: Power for prevention.* Newbury Park, CA: Sage.

Walsh-Childers, K. (1994a). "A Death in the Family": A case study of newspaper influence on health policy development. *Journalism Quarterly, 71*(4), 820–829.

Walsh-Childers, K. (1994b). Newspaper influences on health policy development. *Newspaper Research Journal, 15*(3), 89–104.

Walsh-Childers, K., Chance, J., & Swain, K. A. (1999). Daily newspaper coverage of the organization, delivery and financing of health care. *Newspaper Research Journal, 20*(2), 2–22.

Walsh-Childers, K., Gotthoffer, A., & Lepre, C. R. (2002). From "Just the Facts" to "Downright Salacious": Teen's and women's magazines' coverage of sex and sexual health. In J. D. Brown, J. R. Steele, & K.Walsh-Childers (Eds.), *Sexual teens, sexual media* (pp. 153–172). Mahwah, NJ: Lawrence Erlbaum Associates.

Ward, L. M., Gorvine, B., & Cytron, A. (2001). Would that really happen? Adolescents' perceptions of sexuality according to television. In J. D. Brown, J. R. Steele, & K. Walsh-Childers (Eds.). *Sexual teens, sexual media* (pp. 95–124). Mahwah, NJ: Lawrence Erlbaum Associates.

Weidinger, C. K., & Demi, A. S. (1993). Music listening preferences and preadmission dysfunctional psychosocial behaviors of adolescents hospitalized on an in-patient psychiatric unit. *Journal of the American Academy of Child and Adolescent Psychiatry, 32*(3), 530–535.

Wilkes, M. S., Bell, R. A., & Kravitz, R. L. (2000). Direct-to-consumer prescription drug advertising: Trends, impact, and implications. *Health Affairs, 19*(2), 110–128.

Wilson, S. N. (2000). Raising the voices of teens to change sex education. *SIECUS Report, 28*(6), 20–24.

Wiseman, C. V., Gray, J. J., Mosimann, J. E., & Ahrens, A. H. (1990). Cultural expectations of thinness in women: An update. *International Journal of Eating Disorders, 11,* 85–89.

Wolf, M. A., & Kielwasser, A. P. (1991). *Gay people, sex, and the media.* New York: Harrington Park Press.

Woodruff, K. (1996). Alcohol ads and violence against women: A media advocacy case study. *Health Education Quarterly, 23*(3), 330–345.

Woodruff, S., Agro, A., Wildey, M., & Conway, T. (1995). Point-of-purchase tobacco advertising: Prevalence, correlates, and brief intervention. *Health Values, 19,* 56–62.

Yankelovich Partners, Inc. (1993, May 24). How should we teach our children about sex? *Time,* 60–66.

Chapter 18

The Third-Person Effect

RICHARD M. PERLOFF
Cleveland State University

What effect do the media have on you? Does news change your mind about issues? Do commercials sway you? Does television violence make you more aggressive? Not really, you say. You make up your own mind, form your own ideas about politics and products, and you're not much fazed by TV crime shows, though goodness knows, you've watched your share of them over the years. Okay—Do me this favor, estimate the impact that news, commercials, and television violence have on other people. That is, guess how they influence other individuals who tune them in. Say what? You think that news, advertising, and TV violence have a strong effect on other people? That others buy into what they see on the tube?

Do we have a problem, Houston? Is there an inconsistency here?

According to the third-person effect hypothesis, there is. If you are right that other people are influenced by media, then it certainly stands to reason that you too should be affected. On the other hand, if you are correct that you're not affected and everyone else presumably claims the same lack of media influence, then you exaggerate the impact of media on others. "In either case," as James Tiedge and his colleagues (1991) note, "most people appear to be willing to subscribe to the logical inconsistency inherent in maintaining that the mass media influence others considerably more than themselves" (Tiedge, Silverblatt, Havice, & Rosenfeld, p. 152).[1]

Welcome to the domain of the third-person effect—a complex, labyrinthlike area in which perceptions become reality, reality is enshrouded by perceptions, and perceptions hinge on the very important factor of whether you are considering the media's impact on other people or on yourself. As uses and gratifications did in the 1970s, the third-person effect hypothesis turns conventional media effects theorizing on its head. Instead of looking at media effects on beliefs, it examines beliefs

[1]On the individual level of analysis, it is theoretically possible for an individual (e.g., a prescient person from a foreign land) to *correctly* assert that a particular media message will have a strong effect on native citizens, but not on himself. The problem occurs on the aggregate level, where large numbers of people engage in the self-other discrepancy; it is on this level of analysis that third-person effects are more difficult to defend on logical grounds.

about media effects. Rather than assuming that media affect perceptions, it assumes that perceptions can shape media.

For this reason, the third-person effect (TPE) has generated substantial research interest in recent years—approximately 100 journal articles and convention papers and in 1998 a CBS News poll that probed whether respondents believed that other people were more interested in news reports of President Clinton's sex life than they were. Only 7% of respondents indicated that they were fascinated by news stories on Clinton's sex life; 37% confessed they were mildly curious; and 50% claimed that they were not interested at all. Yet when asked to judge most people's interest in the stories, respondents reacted much differently. Twenty-five percent of the same sample said most people were fascinated, 49% claimed most people were mildly curious, and only 18% believed that most people harbored no interest at all (Berke, 1998).

The third-person effect is a relatively new concept, as social science constructs go. It was invented in 1983 by sociologist W. Phillips Davison in a clever article that drew on intuition and public opinion theory. The third-person effect is an individual's perception that a message will exert a stronger impact on others than on the self. The "third-person" term derives from the expectation that a message will not have its greatest influence on "me" (the grammatical first person), or "you" (the second person), but on "them"—the third persons. Individuals may overestimate the impact that mass media exert on others, underestimate media effects on the self, or both.

The TPE hypothesis has two parts. The perceptual hypothesis asserts that people assume that communications influence others more than the self. The behavioral component suggests that people's expectations of media impact on others leads them to take action, perhaps because they want to thwart the predicted effects. There is intuitive appeal to the third-person effect. It resonates with everyday experience in which people attribute powerful, typically negative, effects to "the media" (frequently pronounced as one word and thought to be a singular entity). At the same time, people deny that the media have affected them personally or have difficulty locating a single instance in which the same mass media have altered their ways of seeing the world. The behavioral component of the hypothesis comports with a flurry of contemporary events, such as activists' concerns about the effects of controversial movies (*The Siege*'s portrayal of Muslim terrorists), provocative art (a Brooklyn museum portrait of the Virgin Mary adorned with elephant dung), and rap music (hip-hopper Eminem's hate-filled lyrics). Convinced that such art will profoundly influence third persons, partisans have sought to restrict access to the messages.

This raises a question. Is the third-person effect a new phenomenon, coming into its own in the age of mass media and taking new form with the development of interactive media? Or does it date back thousands of years to ancient Greece, when Socrates was accused of corrupting the youth of Athens through his creative use of the spoken word (de Botton, 2000)? Can one not see glimmerings of the effect in Plato's fear that great harm would be caused by the "ascendency of the written word over the spoken word" (Starker, 1989, p. 7)? Do third-person effects lurk behind 19th-century critics' fears that reading novels will occasion "the entire destruction of the powers of the mind" (Starker, p. 8) and that all manner of media—newspapers, movies, television violence, and Internet pornography—will have harmful effects on a vulnerable public that somehow excludes the perceiver (Baughman, 1989; Wartella & Reeves, 1985)?

Although third-person biases undoubtedly operated throughout human history, they are of greater consequence today than in the pre–mass society era. When people's experiences of the world were limited by the contours of their communities and their life-space was restricted to the little towns in which they grew up, there was no possibility for opinions to spiral out and influence the world at large. Life is different today. Public opinion exerts a significant impact on political and social behavior and affects mass and elite decisions. Consequently, perceptions of public opinion can have direct and indirect, "ripple" effects, particularly when these perceptions are widely reported in the mass media (Mutz, 1998).

Although the third-person effect is more hypothesis than full-blown theory, it has roots firmly planted in venerable communication concepts and respected research traditions. It is one of a family of concepts that bridges sociology and psychology, focuses on perceptions of social reality, and centers on beliefs *about* public opinion (Glynn, Ostman, & McDonald, 1995). Like such constructs as pluralistic ignorance, it emphasizes that people harbor illusions—mistaken beliefs about others' opinions. Yet it contrasts sharply with such concepts as looking-glass perception (Fields & Schuman, 1976) or its psychological counterpart, false consensus. According to looking-glass self or false consensus, people perceive that others share their views of the world. The third-person effect view is different. It claims that people are prone to assume that media have different—invariably stronger—influences on others than on themselves.

On a psychological level, the third-person effect links up with the social psychology of risk, particularly the tendency to separate out judgments of risk for oneself and society at large (Tyler & Cook, 1984). The most direct linkage is with theories of unrealistic optimism (Weinstein, 1980) and self-serving biases, notably people's self-serving tendency to assume that they are better than average (Alicke, Klotz, Breitenbecher, Yurak, & Vredenburg, 1995) and less susceptible to personal harm than everyone else. Theorists argue that optimistic biases help people maintain a sense of control over unpredictable life events, but critics worry that illusions of invulnerability can lead to "maladaptive complacency" regarding health (and perhaps media?) risks (Smith, Gerrard, & Gibbons, 1997, p. 144).

The centerpiece of the third-person effect is perception and the implicit assumption that perceptions are not fixed at some final Archimedean point, but vary as a function of the gaze of the perceiver (toward others or self). Decidedly Western in its bifurcation of the subject (self) and the object (the world outside), the third-person effect hypothesis distinctively departs from other related public opinion concepts in its emphasis on the message or more precisely, the perceived effects of the message.

RESEARCH FINDINGS

The third-person effect has been studied in a variety of ways, but typically survey respondents are asked to estimate effects of researcher-described messages on others and self. In some cases, people read or view a communication; subsequently, they indicate their beliefs about the message's impact on third persons and themselves. Wording and question order vary with the study, a point to be discussed later in this chapter. In any case, when one reviews the research, it becomes abundantly clear that third-person effects have been ripe for the picking, emerging in virtually every published study on the topic. What's more, third-person effects have occurred in a variety of contexts, spanning news, advertising, health, and entertainment. Consider the following findings:

- A national sample of U.S. respondents estimated that the news media had a greater impact on others' opinions of the 1996 presidential candidates than on their own views (Salwen, 1998). In a study of the third-person effect and press coverage of the O. J. Simpson trial, Salwen and Driscoll (1997) found that survey respondents perceived that news reports exerted a greater influence on others' opinions about Simpson's guilt or innocence than on their own.
- Third-person perceptions also emerge in the commercial and public service advertising (PSA) domains. Individuals perceived that other people were more influenced than themselves by commercials for household products and by liquor and beer ads (Gunther & Thorson, 1992; Shah, Faber, & Youn, 1999). Self-other discrepancies also emerge for televised safer sex PSAs (Chapin, 2000), particularly when the advertisements are of low professional quality (Duck, Terry, & Hogg, 1995). Even children exhibit third-person perceptions. Elementary and middle school students perceived that cigarette ads have a significantly greater impact on others than on themselves (Henriksen & Flora, 1999).

- Extending the perceptual hypothesis to entertainment media, Gunther (1995) found that over 60% of U.S. adults believe that others are more negatively influenced by pornography than themselves. Similar findings emerged for antisocial rap music lyrics and television violence (McLeod, Eveland, & Nathanson, 1997; Salwen & Dupagne, 1999). In addition, female college students who viewed horror movie segments (e.g., *Friday the 13th, Part III*) estimated the fright responses of other females to be significantly higher than their own (Mundorf, Weaver, & Zillmann, 1989).
- Extrapolating the third-person effect from perceived media effects to perceptions of media uses, Peiser and Peter (2000) reported that German adults believe others are more likely than they are to gravitate to undesirable television viewing behaviors, such as escape and habit. By contrast, respondents perceived that they were more inclined to desirable TV viewing behaviors, like information seeking.

Even stronger support for the pervasiveness of the third-person effect is provided by a meta-analysis of 32 published and unpublished studies of the perceptual hypothesis. Using meta-analytic techniques to determine the strength of the perceptual effect, Paul, Salwen, and Dupagne (2000) found substantial support for the third-person perception. The effect size, or magnitude of difference between estimated media effects on self and others, was $r = .50$, considerably larger than that reported for the effect of TV violence on antisocial behavior ($r = .31$) and pornography on aggression ($r = .13$; cf. Paul et al., 2000).

WHY THEE (AND THEM) MORE THAN ME?

At the heart of every political philosophy is an appraisal of human nature (Oreskes, 2000). The same is true of social scientific theories. What makes the TPE hypothesis intriguing is that explanatory mechanisms stake out different appraisals of human motivation and cognition.

The prevailing interpretation is that the third-person effect is a subset of a universal human tendency to perceive the self in ways that make us look good or at least better than other people. Admitting that one has been influenced by media may be tantamount to acknowledging gullibility or that one possesses socially undesirable traits. By assuming the self is invulnerable to communication effects while others are naively susceptible, individuals preserve a positive sense of self and reaffirm their belief that they are superior to others.

A second interpretation is that people are motivated by a need to control unpredictable life events. If we believed that every media program or stimulus had strong effects on us, we'd be basket cases. By assuming that the self is not influenced by mass media, individuals can go about their days in a media-dominated world, using media, deriving gratifications, and sensibly integrating media into their lives.

A third, related, explanation invokes projection, a psychodynamic process. According to this view, people are *actually* influenced by media, but cannot consciously acknowledge media influence. Admitting to media effects would threaten individuals' valued sense of self or reduce their perception of control over external events. As a result, people project media effects onto others, perhaps to defensively distance themselves from undesirable components of self that they would rather not acknowledge (Schimel, Greenberg, Pyszczynski, O'Mahen, & Arndt, 2000).[2]

Other interpretations of the third-person effect emphasize cognitive, rather than motivational, mechanisms. An attributional approach assumes that people attribute their own actions to situational factors, but believe that others' behavior is governed by personality dispositions. Applying this to the third-person effect, Gunther (1991) suggested that when estimating media effects on themselves, people take into account the role played by external factors like persuasive intent. But when judging message effects on third persons, observers assume that others' dispositional shortcomings (e.g., gullibility) render them incapable of factoring in situational factors like persuasive intent. This logically leads observers to the conclusion that others will yield to messages that they see through (Lasorsa, 1992).

A fifth interpretation, also cognitively based, emphasizes media schemas. According to this view, people possess simple schemas of media effects—the time-honored hypodermic needle model, coupled with a "passive sheep" view of audience behavior. When asked to estimate media effects, respondents activate these beliefs and apply them to survey questions.

---

[2]The projection interpretation leads some observers to conclude that the third-person effect is a trivial phenomenon, one that obviously follows from people's tendency to project negative effects onto others. There are several problems with this view. Problems include the following: (a) there is little evidence to suggest that projection is the only explanation for the third-person effect; (b) projection is notoriously difficult to prove, given its neo-Freudian orientation; (c) projection emphasizes that people underestimate communication effects on themselves, thereby understating the theoretically interesting flip side (people overestimate effects on others); (d) whatever the explanation (and even if projection), the self-other disparity emphasized by the third-person effect sheds light on the complexity of social perception and public opinion; (e) the third-person effect offers a distinctive, receiver-focused approach to media effects; (f) even if people merely project effects onto others, these effects can have important effects on behaviors ranging from censorship to decisions leaders make based on inferences about media effects; and (g) third-person perceptions offer clues for how to design persuasive messages that overcome illusions of vulnerability, thereby building theory and helping solve practical problems.

A sixth view, focusing on why individuals do not acknowledge media effects on themselves, notes that people lack access to their own mental processes (Nisbett & Wilson, 1977) or do not have detailed episodic memory for previous behavior (Schwarz, 1999). If people employ audience prototypes to estimate media effects on others (Explanation 5) and engage in automatic thinking when it comes to their own media behavior (Interpretation 6), it is easy to understand why they might assume that others are more affected by mass communications than they are themselves.

Pluralists will say that all explanations are true, and they may be right. At present, though, self-enhancement has the most evidence in its behalf. Some scholars have gone so far as to argue that the third-person effect is a subset of the human tendency to perceive oneself in a favorable light (Peiser & Peter, 2000). However, self-enhancement cannot explain all the variance in third-person perceptions (Paul et al., 2000; Perloff, 1999), which suggests we should remain open to diverse explanations.

WHAT CONDITIONS INFLUENCE THE STRENGTH OF THE TPE?

Early research on the third-person effect suggested that it was a universal phenomenon, one that emerged every time individuals were asked to estimate media effects on others and the self. With more research and inevitable dampening of panglossian perceptions has come the realization that, like most things in science, the effect is more likely to occur under particular conditions. Indeed, a careful look at third-person research reveals that some respondents are more prone to third-person perceptions than others; for some messages, people do not discriminate between self and others; and for still other communications, people are prone to do something that might bedevil Davison himself: they acknowledge they are susceptible to media effects. What are the major factors that delimit third-person perceptions? The next sections address this question.

Desirability of the Message

Self-enhancement theories tell us that people should be loathe to admit that they are influenced by messages when such admission reflects negatively on the self. Third-person effects should be particularly pronounced when the message is perceived as undesirable—that is, when people infer that "this message may not be so good for me" or "it's not cool to admit you're influenced by this media program." In line with these predictions, research finds that people perceive content that is typically thought to be antisocial to have a larger impact on others than on themselves (e.g., television violence, pornography, antisocial rap; see Perloff, 1999).

The flip side to these findings is more interesting. According to a self-enhancement view, if the third-person effect is driven by a desire to preserve self-esteem, people should be willing to acknowledge effects for communications that are regarded as socially desirable, healthy, or otherwise good for the self. "Being influenced by such messages," Hoorens and Ruiter (1996) note, "may indeed be seen as an indicator of highly valued characteristics such as openness to innovation, flexibility, or humanity, or of particularly good luck" (p. 601).

Research substantiates these predictions. People say they are more influenced than others by advertisements with positive emotional content, but not by neutral ads (Gunther & Thorson, 1992). They acknowledge greater personal influence for a persuasive message with strong, but not weak, arguments (White, 1997). When AIDS prevention ads are of high professional quality, students estimate they will be influenced more than others, but revert to a third-person effect for ads of low quality (Duck, Terry, & Hogg, 1995). Children believe that cigarette ads have greater influence on others than themselves, but perceive that antismoking PSAs have a greater impact on the self than others (Henriksen & Flora, 1999).

Useful as the construct is, message desirability is multifaceted and ambiguous, encompassing perceived message benefits to self, impression management concerns, and perceived congruence with existing attitudes. Conceptual clarifications are sorely needed. Nonetheless, research in this area has usefully revised the conventional wisdom by pinpointing conditions under which first-person effects are obtained.

One additional note: The horrific bombings of the World Trade Center and Pentagon force us (one wishes it were otherwise) to look at message desirability in light of perceptions of media coverage of these events. One suspects that Americans were probably more than willing to acknowledge that mass media affected them in myriad emotional ways, after nonstop television coverage of the events. Many Americans might have been proud to say that media coverage made them feel particularly sad or moved. For the present purposes, such coverage falls under the category of a socially desirable message, and probable first-person effects follow from research on this concept.

Social Distance

Up to this point, I have implicitly treated the "third persons" in the third-person effect as a singular whole, making no effort to break the term down into smaller parts. But this oversimplifies matters. The magnitude of the third-person effect hinges on the particular others that observers have in mind when they estimate media effects. This is the heart of the *social dis-*

tance corollary, the notion that self-other disparities grow in magnitude with increases in perceived distance between self and comparison others. Consistent with this notion, Cohen, Mutz, Price, and Gunther (1988) reported larger perceived effects on others as the "other" increased in generality from "other Stanford students" to "other Californians" to "public opinion at large." Nearly all of the studies that have tested the social distance corollary have confirmed it. Apparently, the greater the perceived distance between self and others, the easier it is to assume that others will fall prey to effects that "I" see through. It is easier to assume that the mass, faceless audience will be susceptible to media effects than individuated others, who readily conjure up identities in observers' minds.

A number of explanations for social distance findings have been advanced, including an assumption that distant others are part of a negatively valued peer group, prototypical beliefs about distant others' susceptibility to persuasion, and perception that distant others have more exposure to mass media messages (Eveland, Nathanson, Detenber, & McLeod, 1999; Perloff, 1999). Adding an even more subjective tinge to the third-person effect, social distance research suggests that the ways in which perceivers construct the audience influences the magnitude of self-other disparities.

Individual and Group Differences

One of the perennial questions in third-person research is whether the effect is more likely to emerge among highly educated people. Educated people, the argument goes, are predisposed to see themselves as mentally superior to others and therefore should perceive that they are more resistant to persuasive communications. Consistent with this argument, Paul et al.'s (2000) meta-analysis found that the third-person perception is significantly larger in college student samples than in random and nonstudent samples. (On the other hand, it could be that college students simply are more apt to catch onto the research hypothesis and parrot back third-person findings à la demand characteristics.) More generally, education has a mixed record in predicting third-person effects, and in any event does not provide an explanatory mechanism for whatever effects are found. For this reason, researchers have argued that psychological processes may be more crucial than exogenous factors like education in explaining third-person effects.

Consistent with this view, self-perceived knowledge (perceiving that you have expertise on the topic in question) and believing that one is better educated than others handsomely predict the third-person effect (Driscoll & Salwen, 1997; Lasorsa, 1989; Peiser & Peter, 2000; Salwen & Dupagne, 2000). These findings, coupled with evidence that self-esteem magnifies third-person perceptions (David & Johnson, 1998), are consistent with the view that self-enhancement underlies the third-person effect.

Another individual-level factor that enhances third-person perceptions is *ego-involvement*, defined as identification with a social group and possession of extreme attitudes on an issue relevant to the group. If you believe the media are biased against your side of a social issue, if you have heard liberals accuse the media of toeing a conservative line, or if you have listened to Republicans charge that the news has a left-liberal bias, you can appreciate the role that ego-involvement plays in the third-person effect. People with strong attitudes and group identifications frequently charge that the media intentionally slant stories against their side, a phenomenon that falls under the rubric of *hostile media bias* (Vallone, Ross, & Lepper, 1985).

In studies of news coverage of the Middle East, an area teeming with ego-involved partisans, researchers have found that pro-Israeli and pro-Arab partisans perceive that news is biased against their side (Giner-Sorolla & Chaiken, 1994; Vallone et al., 1985) and further believe that television news coverage will cause neutral viewers to become more unfavorable toward their side and more favorable toward their antagonists (Perloff, 1989; for related findings, see Driscoll & Salwen, 1997; Duck, Hogg, & Terry, 1995; Price, Tewksbury, & Huang, 1998). Involvement influences perceptions of media effects through several mechanisms, including simplistic lay theories of media impact, assumption that the audience constitutes a political outgroup susceptible to communication effects, prior beliefs about overall media bias that color perceptions of a specific message, and perceived imperviousness of self to influence. In any case, when people are highly involved in an issue, they rush to judgments about media effects that are exaggerated and extreme. These judgments can polarize attitudes, possibly leading to increased fragmentation of social groups and greater intolerance.

Summary.   The search for individual differences in third-person perceptions has identified self-perceived knowledge, ego-involvement, and self-esteem as potential moderators of the third-person effect. Does this mean that social-structural factors have no bearing on self-other disparities? Is there no sociology or cultural anthropology of third-person perceptions? Empirically, there has been limited evidence that demographic factors such as age and gender influence perceived effects on others or the self (e.g., Salwen & Dupagne, 2000). What's more, the third-person effect has emerged across different nationality groups (Gunther & Hwa, 1996; Paul et al., 2000), including Asian cultures, which supposedly stress interrelatedness of persons to the social environment. Nonetheless, it seems likely that there are subcultural differences in third-person perceptions. Poor people, particularly minorities, are exposed to so many risks that they may have no choice but to acknowledge vulnerability to danger (Mays & Cochran, 1988).

CONSEQUENCES OF THE THIRD-PERSON EFFECT

Thus far I have emphasized the perceptual dimension of the third-person effect. But what energizes practitioners and intrigues us all is the behavioral hypothesis, which suggests that perceptions can influence behavior. The hypothesis is vague and terribly simplistic; it ignores the many processes that mediate the perception-behavior relationship. Nonetheless, when you consider recent efforts of (Voldemort) activist groups to ban books like *Harry Potter* in the United States,[3] and government attempts to restrict access to the Internet across the globe (Margolis & Resnick, 2000), you can appreciate the possibility that perceptions of harmful effects on third persons propel people to action.

Research finds that the third-person effect predicts support for restricting pornography (Gunther, 1995), television violence (Rojas, Shah, & Faber, 1996; Salwen & Dupagne, 1999), particularly when behavioral (rather than perceptual) effects are considered (Hoffner et al., 1999), as well as antisocial rap music (McLeod et al., 1997) and liquor and gambling advertising (Shah, Faber, & Youn, 1999). However, third-person perceptions are not as likely to forecast support for restricting news, perhaps because (a) news is seen as a more legitimate message, (b) First Amendment beliefs trump paternalistic fears of effects, and (c) effects are seen as less pernicious (e.g., Price, Tewksbury, & Huang, 1998; Salwen & Driscoll, 1997). Note that although the behavioral hypothesis has been tested rigorously, there is ambiguity about the direction of causal impact, and actual censorship behavior has never been tapped. Effects of third-person perceptions on censorship are further complicated by evidence that perceived effects on self, as well as perceived effects on others, forecast support for censorship (Hoffner et al., 1999; Price et al., 1998).

As provocative as censorship is, it is not the only likely consequence of third-person perceptions. Scholars have speculated that perceived media effects on others may influence perceptions of public opinion, perhaps inducing agenda-setting, spiral of silence, or social behavioral effects (Mutz & Soss, 1997; Tewksbury, Moy, & Weis, 2000). Such effects may be consequential when they influence elites, as when the media and other elite groups concluded that Ronald Reagan's skills as a television communicator

---

[3]Voldemort is a villain in the *Harry Potter* books; he tries to kill Harry.

molded public opinion, an inference that may have led risk-averse journalists to steer clear of criticizing the Gipper, at least until Iran-Contra (Schudson, 1995; see also Schoenbach & Becker, 1995).

A more recent application, consistent with Gunther's (1998) persuasive press inference, occurred shortly after the 2000 presidential election. Conservative talk radio hosts, understandably upset about television networks' early call that Al Gore had won the state of Florida, argued without evidence that the networks had led thousands of dispirited Bush supporters to decide not to vote for the Texas governor. The talk shows hosts' pronouncements of media effects on third persons may, in turn, have shaped public opinion by reinforcing the opinion propensities of partisans and offering a perspective that some news media felt obligated to cover. Note that these ripple effects are the result of ideologues' interpretations of mass media and their efforts to use such interpretations to shape public opinion. Third-person effects do not occur in a vacuum or neutral cocoon. Political elites promote third-person perceptions to advance agendas, adding a perceptual layer to political marketing efforts. This dimension is frequently overlooked, especially by busy citizens who take public actors' statements of media effects at face value.

IS IT REAL OR ARTIFACT?

Third-person effects have emerged with such regularity that it is only natural for skeptics to wonder if the effect is real or in some sense artificial. Have researchers unwittingly encouraged respondents to make third-person perceptions by asking biased questions or framing the questions in such a way so as to lead respondents to exaggerate media effects on others? Do the constraints of participating in research subtly push respondents into making judgments they do not ordinarily make?

Brosius and Engel (1996), hypothesizing that grammar is everything, argued that participants might be unwilling to acknowledge effects on self simply because the question, "What impact does advertising have on you?" treats the respondent as the object of effects, an acknowledgment that people would rather not make. Reasoning that people might be more willing to acknowledge effects when the phrasing makes the respondent the active subject ("I let myself be influenced by advertising when I go shopping") than when it refers to the respondent in the typically passive fashion, Brosius and Engel varied the phrasing of questions, only to find that the third-person effect emerged regardless of how the question was worded.

If question wording does not attenuate the third-person effect, perhaps the order of questions does. Critics have speculated that the practice of asking self-other questions in a back-to-back format encourages individuals to *contrast* responses to a media-effects-on-self question with that of a media-effects-on-others query (Price & Tewksbury, 1996). The first question can serve as an anchor for the second, leading respondents to interpret the second in light of the orientation of the first. For example, answering the media-impact-on-others question first might lead respondents to estimate large effects on others and then to adjust the impact on self downward to preserve self-esteem. Such a contrast might not happen if respondents were asked to estimate effects on self first or if they were asked to make only a single estimate of media impact (either on themselves or others) rather than doing both.

A number of studies have examined whether the third-person effect disappears when question order is counterbalanced or experimentally manipulated. The answer that emerges from the overwhelming number of studies is: No, the effect persists, regardless of question order or format (e.g., Gunther, 1995; Price & Tewksbury, 1996; Salwen & Driscoll, 1997).[4]

We are not home free yet. There is a final, nettlesome possibility that the third-person effect may subtly be influenced by the survey research environment. This is, after all, a context in which individuals must answer questions bearing on their view of themselves, questions that are designed by people they do not know. It is a formal setting, which probably makes it more difficult for individuals to acknowledge unique vulnerability. Might the context itself goad people into projecting effects onto others? Perhaps individuals would be more likely to acknowledge media effects if questions were posed in a nonthreatening environment, such as in the privacy of their homes by a friend who permitted them to acknowledge that an undesirable message (e.g., TV violence) might affect them in one domain (e.g., elicit fear about going out at night) but not another (cause them to become physically aggressive). Such a method would not eliminate third-person effects—they seem too robust for that—but they might diminish them or open up new perceptual vistas.

CYBERSPACE AND BEYOND

The third-person effect was conceptualized to explain divergent perceptions of communication effects, particularly those of mass media. What happens when mass media become amalgamated with a host of new media, particularly the Internet? At first blush, it might seem as if the third-person effect would wither away. The Internet is not a mass

---

[4]Although question order does not explain away third-person effects, it would be surprising if it had no influence whatsoever, given the role that perceptual contrasts play in third-person perceptions. A minority of studies have found question-order effects (David & Johnson, 1998; Dupagne, Salwen, & Paul, 1999; Price & Tewksbury, 1996), suggesting that third-person perceptions may be more sensitive to situational variations than Davison suspected, a point that contemporary theorists have come to accept.

medium in the traditional sense. There are not always mass audiences, and effects may be limited to audience segments who tune into various Web sites. Under such circumstances, observers may be less likely to adhere to hypodermic needle models of effects or to stereotypic views of the mass audience. What's more, when people are simultaneously message transmitters and receivers, they may view communication effects through more complex lenses.

Third-person perceptions will change to fit new media, but they are unlikely to disappear. Given the psychological functions that third-person perceptions serve and the ability they have shown to adapt to diverse communication situations over time, the more likely scenario is that we will continue to find discrepancies in beliefs about cyberspace message effects on self and others. It is commonplace to read that parents want to restrict adolescents' interactive computer services or access to cyberporn sites. Yet it is ironic and noteworthy from a theoretical perspective that teenagers who regularly use the Internet and are approached for "cybersex" typically "give such solicitors the brush-off, believing them to be in their own age group" (Thomas, 2000, p. 1A). Perhaps parents underestimate the ability of their children to stave off harmful media effects. More generally, as this example suggests, the Internet is rife with implications for third-person effects. Issues include (a) perceptions of the impact of racy chat room discussions on vulnerable audiences, (b) employers' (possibly exaggerated) beliefs that employees' on-the-job use of entertaining Web sites will reduce their productivity, and (c) interfaces between third-person perceptions of defamatory communications and 21st-century libel law, which probably will revise rigid distinctions between private citizens and public officials (Rosen, 2000).

In sum, nearly two decades after Davison published his pioneering paper, the third-person effect continues to intrigue scholars and engage practitioners. Yet if the area is to advance scientific knowledge in the years to come, researchers must elucidate the contexts in which third-person perceptions are most likely to operate and conduct studies that are less artificial or more ecologically valid. What's more, if the third-person effect is to fully emerge "as a major media-effects approach" (Salwen & Driscoll, 1997, p. 61), we researchers must do a better job of linking perceptions with actual media effects. We need to build third-person theory into the design of campaign messages.

Conventional approaches to communication campaigns—arouse fear and convince people they can cope with danger—need to be revised to take into account what we know about individuals' propensity to deny that bad things will happen to them. In the area of AIDS prevention, communications frequently run up against people's illusions of invulnerability. Consequently, practitioners might have better luck if they focused on the third-person angle—correcting adolescents' misimpressions that peers believe safer sex is a bad thing. Similarly, campaigns aimed at reducing binge drinking on campus might be more successful if they focused on changing beliefs about how much other students drink than on arousing fear (e.g., Zernike, 2000). Anti-binge drinking messages are likely to run up against standard defense mechanisms, notably students' illusory conviction that "bad things won't happen to me if I regularly get drunk." Accordingly, practitioners might be more likely to change attitudes if they emphasized that students overestimate how much their peers drink than that they underestimate their own personal dangers of binge drinking (Perloff, 2000). Given that students who overestimate how much peers drink are more likely to drink heavily (Zernike, 2000), the emphasis on social norms might resonate with student audiences.

A final agenda for TPE research is the linkage between third-person perceptions and larger societal issues. The third-person effect is typically viewed as an individual-level factor; yet it can be seen as operating on a social level as well. Communities and cultures vary along third-person effect lines, with some cultures probably exhibiting stronger self-other disparities than others. In communities where risks are ubiquitous and there is little time for introspection about personal vulnerability to danger, third-person effects may be diminished. At the same time, third-person effects should be augmented by certain social factors and curtailed by others. For instance, when opinions are polarized and group identities salient, third-person effects should be more likely to emerge. But when intergroup tolerance is encouraged or social norms encourage acknowledgment of personal influence, third-person effects should be diminished.

In the final analysis, society benefits when people gain insight into their own third-person perceptions. Social life is strengthened when individuals recognize that their perceptions of other people are not always accurate and that their fellow citizens are more capable of separating out the political wheat from the chaff than they typically assume. In a fragmented era, it is particularly important to reduce people's inclination to psychologically separate themselves from others and to encourage individuals to view others and the self through the same sets of lenses.

REFERENCES

Alicke, M. D., Klotz, M. L., Breitenbecher, D. L., Yurak, T. J., & Vredenburg, D. S. (1995). Personal contact, individuation, and the better-than-average effect. *Journal of Personality and Social Psychology, 68*, 804–825.

Baughman, J. L. (1989). The world is ruled by those who holler the loudest: The third-person effect in American journalism history. *Journalism History, 16,* 12–19.

Berke, R. L. (1998, February 15). Clinton's O.K. in the polls, right? *New York Times*, pp. 4-1, 4-5.

Brosius, H. B., & Engel, D. (1996). The causes of third-person effects: Unrealistic optimism, impersonal impact, or generalized negative attitudes towards media influence? *International Journal of Public Opinion Research, 8*, 142–162.

Chapin, J. R. (2000). Third-person perception and optimistic bias among urban minority at-risk youth. *Communication Research, 27*, 51–81.

Cohen, J., Mutz, D., Price, V., & Gunther, A. (1988). Perceived impact of defamation: An experiment on third-person effects. *Public Opinion Quarterly, 52*, 161–173.

David, P., & Johnson, M. A. (1998). The role of self in third-person effects about body image. *Journal of Communication, 48*(4), 37–58.

Davison, W. P. (1983). The third-person effect in communication. *Public Opinion Quarterly, 47*, 1–15.

de Botton, A. (2000). *The consolations of philosophy*. New York: Pantheon.

Driscoll, P. D., & Salwen, M. B. (1997). Self-perceived knowledge of the O. J. Simpson trial: Third-person perception and perceptions of guilt. *Journalism & Mass Communication Quarterly, 74*, 541–556.

Duck, J. M., Hogg, M. A., & Terry, D. J. (1995). Me, us and them: Political identification and the third-person effect in the 1993 Australian federal election. *European Journal of Social Psychology, 25*, 195–215.

Duck, J. M., Terry, D. J., & Hogg, M. A. (1995). The perceived influence of AIDS advertising: Third-person effects in the context of positive media content. *Basic and Applied Social Psychology, 17*, 305–325.

Dupagne, M., Salwen, M. B., & Paul, B. (1999). Impact of question order on the third-person effect. *International Journal of Public Opinion Research, 11*, 334–345.

Eveland, W. P., Jr., Nathanson, A. I., Detenber, B. H., & McLeod, D. M. (1999). Rethinking the social distance corollary: Perceived likelihood of exposure and the third-person perception. *Communication Research, 26*, 275–302.

Fields, J., & Schuman, H. (1976). Public beliefs about the beliefs of the public. *Public Opinion Quarterly, 40*, 427–448.

Giner-Sorolla, R., & Chaiken, S. (1994).The causes of hostile media judgments. *Journal of Experimental Social Psychology, 30*, 165–180.

Glynn, C. J., Ostman, R. E., & McDonald, D. G. (1995). Opinions, perception, and social reality. In T. L. Glasser & C. T. Salmon (Eds.), *Public opinion and the communication of consent* (pp. 249–277). New York: Guilford.

Gunther, A. C. (1991). What we think others think: Cause and consequence in the third-person effect. *Communication Research, 18*, 355–372.

Gunther, A. C. (1995). Overrating the X-rating: The third-person perception and support for censorship of pornography. *Journal of Communication, 45*(1), 27–38.

Gunther, A. C. (1998). The persuasive press inference: Effects of mass media on perceived public opinion. *Communication Research, 25*, 486–504.

Gunther, A. C., & Hwa, A. P. (1996). Public perceptions of television influence and opinions about censorship in Singapore. *International Journal of Public Opinion Research, 8*, 248–265.

Gunther, A. C., & Thorson, E. (1992). Perceived persuasive effects of product commercials and public service announcements: Third-person effects in new domains. *Communication Research, 19*, 574–596.

Henriksen, L., & Flora, J. A. (1999). Third-person perception and children: Perceived impact of pro- and anti-smoking ads. *Communication Research, 26*, 643–665.

Hoffner, C., Buchanan, M., Anderson, J. D., Hubbs, L. A., Kamigaki, S. K., Kowalczyk, L., Pastorek, A., Plotkin, R. S., & Silberg, K. J. (1999). Support for censorship of television violence: The role of the third-person effect and news exposure. *Communication Research, 26,* 726–742.

Hoorens, V., & Ruiter, S. (1996). The optimal impact phenomenon: Beyond the third person effect. *European Journal of Social Psychology, 26,* 599–610.

Lasorsa, D. L. (1989). Real and perceived effects of "Amerika." *Journalism Quarterly, 66,* 373–378, 529.

Lasorsa, D. L. (1992). Policymakers and the third-person effect. In J. D. Kennamer (Ed.), *Public opinion, the press, and public policy* (pp. 163–175). Westport, CT: Praeger.

McLeod, D. M., Eveland, W. P., Jr., & Nathanson, A. I. (1997). Support for censorship of violent and misogynic rap lyrics: An analysis of the third-person effect. *Communication Research, 24,* 153–174.

Margolis, M., & Resnick, D. (2000). *Politics as usual: The cyberspace "revolution."* Thousand Oaks, CA: Sage.

Mays, V. M., & Cochran, S. D. (1988). Issues in the perception of AIDS risk and risk reduction activities by Black and Hispanic/Latina women. *American Psychologist, 43,* 949–957.

Mundorf, N., Weaver, J., & Zillmann, D. (1989). Effects of gender roles and self perceptions on affective reactions to horror films. *Sex Roles, 20,* 655–673.

Mutz, D. C. (1998). *Impersonal influence: How perceptions of mass collectives affect political attitudes.* New York: Cambridge University Press.

Mutz, D. C., & Soss, J. (1997). Reading public opinion: The influence of news coverage on perceptions of public sentiment. *Public Opinion Quarterly, 61,* 431–451.

Nisbett, R. E., & Wilson, T. D. (1977). Telling more than we can know: Verbal reports on mental processes. *Psychological Review, 84,* 231–259.

Oreskes, M. (2000, June 4). Troubling the waters of nuclear deterrence. *New York Times,* Week in Review, p. 3.

Paul, B., Salwen, M. B., & Dupagne, M. (2000). The third-person effect: A meta-analysis of the perceptual hypothesis. *Mass Communication & Society, 3,* 57–85.

Peiser, W., & Peter, J. (2000). Third-person perception of television-viewing behavior. *Journal of Communication,* 25–45.

Perloff, R. M. (1989). Ego-involvement and the third person effect of televised news coverage. *Communication Research, 16,* 236–262.

Perloff, R. M. (1999). The third-person effect: A critical review and synthesis. *Media Psychology, 1,* 353–378.

Perloff, R. M. (2000, October 9). Do students drink too much? [Letter to the Editor]. *New York Times,* p. A26

Price, V., & Tewksbury, D. (1996). Measuring the third-person effect of news: The impact of question order, contrast and knowledge. *International Journal of Public Opinion Research, 8,* 120–141.

Price, V., Tewksbury, D., & Huang, L. N. (1998). Third-person effects on publication of a Holocaust-denial advertisement. *Journal of Communication, 48(2),* 3–26.

Rojas, H., Shah, D. V., & Faber, R. J. (1996). For the good of others: Censorship and the third-person effect. *International Journal of Public Opinion Research, 8,* 163–186.

Rosen, J. (2000). *The unwanted gaze: The destruction of privacy in America.* New York: Random House.

Salwen, M. B. (1998). Perceptions of media influence and support for censorship: The third-person effect in the 1996 presidential election. *Communication Research, 25,* 259–285.

Salwen, M. B., & Driscoll, P. D. (1997). Consequences of third-person perception in support of press restrictions in the O. J. Simpson trial. *Journal of Communication, 47(2),* 60–75.

Salwen, M. B., & Dupagne, M. (1999). The third-person effect: Perceptions of the media's influence and immoral consequences. *Communication Research, 26,* 523–549.

Salwen, M. B., & Dupagne, M. (2000, June). *Self-perceived knowledge of television violence and the third-person effect: Predicting media influence on self and others.* Paper presented to the annual convention of the International Communication Association, Acapulco, Mexico.

Schimel, J., Greenberg, J., Pyszczynski, T., O'Mahen, H., & Arndt, J. (2000). Running from the shadow: Psychological distancing from others to deny characteristics people fear in themselves. *Journal of Personality and Social Psychology, 78,* 446–462.

Schoenbach, K. & Becker, L. B. (1995). Origins and consequences of mediated public opinion. In T. L. Glasser & C. T. Salmon (Eds.), *Public opinion and the communication of consent* (pp. 323–347). New York: Guilford.

Schudson, M. (1995). *The power of news.* Cambridge, MA: Harvard University Press.

Schwarz, N. (1999). Self-reports: How the questions shape the answers. *American Psychologist, 54,* 93–105.

Shah, D. V., Faber, R. J., & Youn, S. (1999). Susceptibility and severity: Perceptual dimensions underlying the third-person effect. *Communication Research, 26,* 240–267.

Smith, G. E., Gerrard, M., & Gibbons, F. X. (1997). Self-esteem and the relation between risk behavior and perceptions of vulnerability to unplanned pregnancy in college women. *Health Psychology, 16,* 137–146.

Starker, S. (1989). *Evil influences: Crusades against the mass media.* New Brunswick, NJ: Transaction.

Tewksbury, D., Moy, P., & Weis, D. (2000, November). *Preparations for the millennium bug: Extending the behavioral component of the third-person effect.* Paper presented to the annual convention of the Midwest Association for Public Opinion Research, Chicago.

Thomas, K. (2000, June 8). Kids run a 20% risk of "cybersex" advances. *USA Today,* p. 1A.

Tiedge, J. T., Silverblatt, A., Havice, M. J., & Rosenfeld, R. (1991). Discrepancy between perceived first-person and perceived third-person mass media effects. *Journalism Quarterly, 68,* 141–154.

Tyler, T. R., & Cook, F. L. (1984). The mass media and judgments of risk: Distinguishing impact on personal and societal level judgments. *Journal of Personality and Social Psychology, 47,* 693–708.

Vallone, R., Ross, L., & Lepper, M. (1985). The hostile media phenomenon: Biased perception and perceptions of media bias in coverage of the Beirut massacre. *Journal of Personality and Social Psychology, 49,* 577–585.

Wartella, E., & Reeves, B. (1985). Historical trends in research on children and the media: 1900–1960. *Journal of Communication, 35,* 118–133.

Weinstein, N. D. (1980). Unrealistic optimism about future life events. *Journal of Personality and Social Psychology, 39,* 806–820.

White, H. A. (1997). Considering interacting factors in the third-person effect: Argument strength and social distance. *Journalism & Mass Communication Quarterly, 74,* 557–564.

Zernike, K. (2000, October 3). New tactic on college drinking: Play it down. *New York Times,* pp. A1, A21.

Chapter 19

Individual Differences in Media Effects

MARY BETH OLIVER
Pennsylvania State University

The idea that media have a direct or uniform effect on viewers is a position that is generally understood to be a simplification of the way that researchers in the discipline conceptualize media influences. Not only are media effects models generally more subtle in recognizing the conditions under which effects are most likely to occur, they are also quite ready to acknowledge the importance of viewers' selection, interpretation, and memory. As with most scholarship in the social sciences, though, media effects research often reports small to moderate effect sizes—a situation that has allowed some critics to suggest that the media have no effect or that the effects of media are completely overwhelmed by other social forces. This chapter acknowledges the importance of unexplained variance and, like some critics, sees it as an issue deserving of attention. However, this chapter takes the position that unexplained variance represents the very thing that makes human beings interesting, unique, and infinitely worthy of our research attention: individual differences.

The topic of individual differences is inherently a messy one. Not only can it be difficult to identify the differences or set of differences that are important moderators in any given situation, but the list of possible differences and the ways in which they operate are seemingly infinite. Indeed, the use of random assignment in most experimental studies is illustrative of the idea that it is virtually impossible to account for the limitless ways that people may vary. This chapter acknowledges the diversity that exists among media audiences, but narrows the focus to those differences that represent enduring dispositions, attitudes, or cognitions. Although these types of individual differences are undoubtedly the result of a combination of heredity and environment and are therefore interrelated and most certainly associated with characteristics such as gender, race, age, class, or experience, the focus of this examination lies in those differences that may vary among individuals who may nevertheless share some demographically based social group. Given this definition, this chapter first reviews how individual differences function in enjoyment of and emotional responses to media. Subsequently, the role of individual differences in viewers' selective exposure, interpretation, and recall of media content are explored. The final section of this chapter considers how individual differences may function in the process of the effects that media messages have on viewers' attitudes and behaviors.

ENJOYMENT AND EMOTIONAL RESPONSE

Given that media use clearly varies between individuals, it follows that many individual difference indictors successfully predict motivations for using media and general media consumption patterns such as television viewing or Internet use (Dittmar, 1994; Finn, 1997; McIlwraith, 1998; McKenna & Bargh, 2000; Rubin, Perse, & Powell, 1985; Weaver, 2000). Aside from individual variations in general media use, though, the diversity that exists in media *content* is also evidence of the importance of individual variations in preferences for, enjoyment of, and responses to specific *types* of media fare. Although many preferences likely reflect habitual use or more transitory states such as mood (Zillmann, 1988), other preferences such as affinities for certain types of genres or appreciation of specific types of portrayals appear to be more enduring and stable. Why might one person consistently report great enjoyment for action and suspense, while the next person reports high levels of distaste for the same fare? Research exploring a variety of individual difference measures suggests that more enduring traits and dispositions likely play important roles in predicting audience reactions.

Individual Differences as "Needs"

Because many individual difference measures can be conceptualized as "needs" or "affinities," it follows that stimuli that address or fulfill needs should be more frequently sought after and enjoyed. For example, the need for cognition is conceptualized as a personality trait characterized by the enjoyment of cognitive activities and the propensity to engage in such activities when given the chance (Cacioppo, Petty, Feinstein, & Jarvis, 1996). Consistent with this definition, Perse (1992) reported that need for cognition scores were positively associated with greater attention to news reports and with greater tendencies to watch local television news for purposes of utility (e.g., information gain) as opposed to simply passing the time.

Similarly, sensation seeking is an additional individual difference that can be thought of as representing a need or affinity. This trait is conceptualized as the biologically based need to seek out experiences or stimuli that have the potential to elicit high levels of arousal (Zuckerman, 1979, 1994). Consistent with this definition, studies generally support the idea that higher levels of different aspects of sensation seeking are associated with greater viewing and enjoyment of arousing or action-packed media entertainment such as horror films, action adventures, violent programming, or pornography (Aluja-Fabregat & Torrubia-Beltri, 1998; Perse, 1996; Tamborini & Stiff, 1987; Zuckerman, 1996; Zuckerman & Litle, 1986).

Individual Differences as "Readiness to Respond"

Although individual differences conceptualized as "needs" make predictive sense in studies of viewers' enjoyment, other individual differences imply stronger or more intense emotional responses to media portrayals. For example, numerous researchers have explored the role of empathy in viewers' reactions to entertainment. Although empathic responses have been conceptualized in many ways, dispositional empathy is generally understood as the caring and concern for the well-being of others and the propensity to experience emotional responses that either reflect others' affective reactions or that reflect concern for others' situations (Eisenberg, 2000; Hoffner & Cantor, 1991; Zillmann, 1991). Given this definition, it follows that individuals who are highly empathic should experience more intense emotional responses to media portrayals that feature others' misfortunes or suffering (Tamborini, 1996). Consistent with this reasoning, Tamborini, Stiff, and Heidel (1990) reported that higher levels of empathy were positively associated with arousal and coping behaviors (e.g., turning away, covering one's eyes) in response to a frightening film and were negatively associated with enjoyment. Similar findings have also been reported for viewers' responses to sad or tragic portrayals, with higher levels of empathy associated with greater self-reported crying and sadness (Choti, Marston, Holston, & Hart, 1987). However, in contrast to studies of frightening films, research on sad films also tends to report that higher levels of empathy are associated with greater rather than lesser enjoyment (Oliver, 1993). The fact that distress would be associated with greater enjoyment in one instance (e.g., sad films) but with lesser enjoyment in another (e.g., horror) implies that future research may benefit from not only exploring how individual differences predict emotional responses per se, but also how individual differences predict viewers' *experience of* the emotional responses that are elicited (cf. Mills, 1993; Oliver, 1993).

In addition to showing that individual differences may play a role in predicting more-intense emotional responses to entertainment, recent research also suggests that individual differences may serve to obscure intense responses, at least as traditionally assessed through self-report measures. Specifically, Sparks, Pellechia, and Irvine (1999) examined the role of repressive coping styles on individuals' physiological responses and self-reported levels of fear in reaction to a scary movie. Repressive copers were identified as individuals who are likely to experience intense levels of distress or anxiety (i.e., high on manifest anxiety), but who cope with their reactions by suppressing them (i.e., high on social desirability). Consistent with predictions, repressors and nonrepressors reported equal levels of negative affect in responses to the frightening film, though physiological indicators revealed significantly higher levels of arousal among repressors than nonrepressors. Although the results of this study cannot clarify the nature of repressors' experience while viewing, this research clearly illustrates that the inclusion of individual difference indicators can allow for the examination of audience responses that would have otherwise gone undetected.

Individual Differences as "Traits"

Although many individual differences imply needs or states of emotional readiness, additional differences can perhaps be best described as enduring traits or dispositions. This sort of conceptualization of individual differences is likely best illustrated in terms of research related to personality. Included here would be traits such as shyness, aggressiveness, Machiavellianism, deceit, loyalty, optimism, or permissiveness, among hundreds of others, or constellations of traits such as neuroticism, extraversion, and psychoticism (Eysenck, 1990).

In this regard, viewers' reactions to media violence have likely received the greatest share of attention, with research generally suggesting that affinity for this type of media fare is highest among individuals who would seem most likely to be aggressive themselves. That is, studies generally support the notion that enjoyment of violent entertainment and curiosity about witnessing aggression or harm is associated with traits such as aggression, masculinity, psychoticism, and Machiavellianism, among others (Aluja-Fabregat, 2000; Aluja-Fabregat & Torrubia-Beltri, 1998; Bushman, 1995; Oliver, Sargent, & Weaver, 1998; Tamborini, Stiff, & Zillmann, 1987; Weaver, 1991). These patterns of enjoyment of violent entertainment are also mirrored in studies concerning the enjoyment of different types of musical genres. For example, Robinson, Weaver, and Zillmann (1996) reported that participants scoring higher on measures of psychoticism and vindictive, malicious rebelliousness reported greater enjoyment of music videos featuring hard rock/rebellious music (e.g., Guns N'Roses) and lesser enjoyment of music videos featuring soft rock/nonrebellious music (e.g., Chicago) than did participants scoring low on these indicators (see also Bleich, Zillmann, & Weaver 1991). Similarly, Hansen and Hansen's (2000) review of research on personality and musical tastes reported that fans of hard rock and heavy metal tend to score higher on Machiavellianism, toughmindedness, and machismo, whereas fans of punk rock tend to score lower on acceptance of authority (see also Hansen & Hansen, 1991).

Of course, individual differences in enjoyment are also observed for other types of entertainment, including genres that fall at the opposite end of the violent or rebellious continuum. For example, studies of sad films report that although femininity is associated with greater sadness or distress in response to this form of entertainment, it is also associated with greater enjoyment and more-frequent viewing (Oliver, 1993; Oliver et al., 1998). In addition, Oliver, Weaver, and Sargent (2000) reported that femininity was particularly associated with greater anticipated enjoyment of sad films when the films were described as focused on relational issues (e.g., friendship) rather than more instrumental problems (e.g., physical impairment).

Individual Differences as "Evaluative Dispositions"

In addition to examining enjoyment of genres or portrayals per se, other researchers have explored enjoyment as a function of viewers' responses to characters. In particular, disposition theory suggests that enjoyment of entertainment is largely a reflection of both viewers' dispositions toward the characters in the presentation, and the outcomes that the characters experience (Zillmann, 1985, 1991, 2000; Zillmann & Cantor, 1977). Enjoyment is highest when characters who are perceived as "good" experience positive outcomes, and when characters who are perceived as "bad" experience negative outcomes. The importance that individual differences may play in dispositional models is in terms of viewers' evaluation of characters. Specifically, whereas a great deal of entertainment fare explicitly identifies the "good" and "bad" characters as heroes and villains respectively, disposition theory acknowledges that perceptions of "good" and "bad" can vary between individuals. This variation implies, then, that individual differences associated with more extreme dispositional evaluations can lead to greater and lesser enjoyment of dramatic presentations, depending on the outcome experienced by the character (Zillmann, 2000).

This line of reasoning has been employed in studies exploring a variety of different genres, including suspense, comedy, crime drama, and sports, among others. For example, Zillmann, Taylor, and Lewis (1999) reported that negative dispositions toward groups or issues featured in news stories (e.g., pro-life/pro-choice agenda) were associated with greater enjoyment of the stories when the group was characterized as being defeated or ridiculed. In contrast, positive dispositions toward the groups or issues were associated with lesser enjoyment when the groups or issues were defeated or ridiculed (see also Zillmann, Taylor, and Lewis, 1998). Although Zillmann et al. (1998, 1999) assessed affective dispositions toward the issues presented in the news stories directly, other researchers have examined the ways in which individual differences may indirectly imply variations in dispositional evaluations. For example, Oliver (1996) reasoned that because authoritarianism is associated with deference to authority, contempt for lawbreakers, and higher levels of racial prejudice, higher levels of authoritarianism should be associated with greater enjoyment of entertainment featuring criminals being punished by authority figures and, particularly, African-American criminals. As dispositions theory would predict, authoritarianism was positively associated with enjoyment of a reality-based police program featuring police aggression toward a suspect, but only if the suspect was African American rather than Caucasian.

One implication of disposition theory is that viewers should experience little gratification from viewing media portrayals featuring undeserved bad fortunes or the suffering of liked characters. Although much entertainment fare likely avoids these types of negative portrayals, there are several notable exceptions to this rule. For example, sad films or tragedies prominently feature problems such as heartache and death, and mournful love songs bemoan broken relationships and lost loves. Paradoxically, some research suggests that enjoyment of these types of misfortunes may be highest among those individuals who would intuitively seem to be the ones least likely to experience gratification. For example, Mares and Cantor (1992) found that older viewers who scored high on loneliness reported more positive affect after viewing a media portrayal of a lonely, depressed man, but reported more negative affect after viewing a happy, integrated man. These authors interpreted their findings as suggesting that lonely participants engaged in downward social comparison and consequently felt better about their own circumstances after seeing a person who was worse off.

Summary

To summarize, enjoyment of media entertainment is highly variable, but numerous studies demonstrate that many stable and enduring traits and dispositions successfully predict a variety of emotional reactions to media portrayals, gratification included. It is important to keep in mind that this discussion of individual differences does not imply exhaustiveness, nor does it imply mutual exclusivity. Indeed, the consistency of patterns related to viewers' responses and enjoyment likely reflects the fact that many individual differences are related, if not redundant. In addition, it is also important to keep in mind that no single explanation for the manner in which individual differences function likely captures the complexity of the process. Although individual differences may function as needs, emotionally responsive states, or evaluative dispositions, there are undoubtedly many additional roles that individual differences may play. Consequently, the challenge for researchers now lies in exploring more fully the theoretical mechanisms that underlie the relationships between individual differences and viewers' enjoyment and emotional responses.

SELECTIVE EXPOSURE, INTERPRETATION, AND MEMORY

Variations in enjoyment of media offerings clearly imply similar variations in media consumption patterns. However, exposure to media messages can obviously reflect more than the extent to which the content succeeds in generating pleasing emotional states. Rather, many patterns in media selection are likely a reflection of the extent to which the viewer perceives the messages as useful in achieving goals, as informative, or as consistent with or confirming of attitudes or beliefs. This section focuses specifically on individual differences related to attitudes and beliefs and the role they play in selective exposure, interpretation, and memory.

Selection and Avoidance

The idea that individuals select information that is consistent with attitudes and beliefs and ignore or avoid information that is discrepant is largely understood in terms of theories of cognitive dissonance (Festinger, 1957). In essence, cognitive dissonance theory and similar theories such as balance theory (Heider, 1958) and congruity theory (Osgood & Tannenbaum, 1955) maintain that individuals seek consistency in their cognitions. Cognitive dissonance theory further argues that when inconsistent cognitions exist, people experience cognitive dissonance—an aversive psychological state that motives the alleviation of the dissonance. One implication of this theory is that once a person has established an attitude or belief, that person should be more likely to expose him or herself to congruent information and to avoid incongruent information that would give rise to dissonance. Many scholars have studied the application of dissonance theory to mass communication. For example, Klapper's (1960) argument that the media serve to reinforce beliefs was largely based on the phenomena of selective exposure to information.

The importance of individual differences to theories of selective exposure seems somewhat self-evident. That is, if individuals select and avoid media messages as a function of their attitudes, beliefs, or cognitions, then individual variations in this regard should be predictive of media use patterns. For example, Sweeney and Gruber (1984) reported that interest in and attention to the Watergate hearings was highest among McGovern supporters, lowest among Nixon supporters, and moderate among undecided citizens. Cappella, Turow, and Jamieson (1996) found similar results in terms of listening to political talk shows on the radio. In their sample, 70% of the individuals who listened to Rush Limbaugh were politically conservative, compared to 19% of the individuals who listened to liberal/moderate radio talk shows. These types of exposure patterns have been reported for a variety of different types of media content, including health-related messages and persuasive appeals, among others.

Despite studies such as these that show support for the basic processes of selective exposure, the larger body of research employing dissonance models has not gone without criticism. For example, Freedman and Sears (1965) argued that exposure to attitudinally consistent information may not necessarily reflect preferences for or selection of congruent information, but may rather be an artifact of the availability of information or the usefulness of information in attaining goals. Similarly, Frey's (1986) review of dissonance research suggested that, in some cases, individuals might actually choose to expose themselves to inconsistent information, especially if the information is easily refutable. Finally, other researchers have suggested that additional work needs to more closely examine the moderating variables involved in the selective exposure process. Cotton's (1985) review of cognitive dissonance and selective exposure pointed out that research has yet to identify clearly the role that individual differences play in predicting who is most likely to select and avoid media messages to avoid dissonance. In sum, then, though the basic phenomenon of cognitive dissonance and the implications that it has for individual differences in selective exposure are generally supported in the literature, additional research is needed to further examine the individual differences associated with greater and lesser tolerance of dissonance and the manner in which these variations successfully predict selective exposure to and avoidance of media content.

Selective Perception

Although the seemingly most obvious way that viewers may confirm their beliefs is through exposure to congruent messages, selective exposure is not always necessarily desired, nor is it always an option. Rather, the central role that media play in the typical day of the average person likely means that a wide variety of opinions and attitudes are encountered, many of which likely conflict with the beliefs of the viewer.

Although inconsistent information may ultimately serve to create dissonance or to *change* viewers' attitudes or beliefs, research on selective perception suggests that individual differences play important roles in viewers' interpretations of media content in a way that may serve to maintain or reinforce existing beliefs (Klapper, 1960).

One role that individual differences play in selective perception is in terms of viewers' interpretations and judgments of the characters and issues portrayed. In this regard, research generally supports the idea that individuals more favorably perceive characters and issues that are similar to the self (Hoffner & Cantor, 1991), and that perceptions typically reflect or confirm preexisting attitudes or beliefs. In a classic demonstration of selective perception, Vidmar and Rokeach (1974) assessed enjoyment and interpretations of *All in the Family* among high- and low-prejudiced individuals. Although both groups reported approximately equal viewing and enjoyment of the program, high-prejudiced individuals tended to interpret the program as sympathetic to the bigoted main character, whereas low-prejudiced individuals tended to interpret the program as sympathetic to the politically liberal main character (see also Cooks & Orbe, 1993). The importance of viewers' racial attitudes on evaluative judgments was also demonstrated in an experimental study of viewers' perceptions of crime news (Peffley, Shields, & Williams, 1996). Specifically, higher levels of racial prejudice were associated with more negative evaluations of a criminal suspect when the suspect was African American, but more positive evaluations when the suspect was Caucasian. Of course, racial attitudes are simply one example of the hundreds of individual differences associated with evaluative perceptions and judgments. For example, numerous studies have also reported similar findings in terms of political attitudes, with individuals tending to perceive their own political candidates more favorably than the opponents (e.g., Apple, 1976; Bothwell & Brigham, 1983; Kraus, 1962).

In addition to affecting perceptions of characters and issues, a sizable body of research also suggests that individual differences play a role in viewers' perceptions of media sources themselves, with sources judged as less credible or more biased when reporting attitudinally inconsistent information. For example, Oliver, Mares, and Cantor (1993) had participants rate their perceptions of the credibility of a news story that was either critical about U.S. propaganda in the Gulf War or critical about Iraqi propaganda. Individuals with more favorable attitudes about U.S. involvement in the war rated the story as more credible when it was critical of Iraq and less credible when it was critical of the United States. Although this study showed that information that is obviously incongruent can affect individuals' perceptions of media sources, additional research has also shown that media content that shows no apparent bias can result in similar patterns of judgments. In particular, research concerning the hostile media phenomenon reports that individuals who are partisan on a given issue are more likely to perceive negative bias in media coverage of that issue than are individuals who are nonpartisan (Giner-Sorolla & Chaiken, 1994; Vallone, Ross, & Lepper, 1985).

Selective Memory

In addition to showing that individual differences play important moderating roles in viewers' exposure and interpretation, a sizable amount of research also suggests that viewers' prior expectations and attitudes can influence what is remembered. In their review of the literature concerning attitudes and selective memory, Eagly and Chaiken (1993) pointed out that prior beliefs and cognitions can affect memory by influencing attention and elaboration at the time of encoding and by influencing retrieval and reconstruction of information subsequent to exposure. Overall, these researchers concluded that although individuals may be likely to attend to and store both attitudinally consistent and inconsistent information, retrieval and reconstruction of stored information tends to favor congruency.

Applied to media contexts, research on the role of prior cognitions on viewers' memory of media messages implies that information that is accurately recalled or inaccurately reconstructed should tend to reflect the viewers' existing attitudes or beliefs. Consistent with this reasoning, several studies have demonstrated that media portrayals featuring counterstereotypical content are often misremembered by the viewer as having shown stereotypical content instead. As illustration of this type of phenomenon, many people point to Allport and Postman's (1947/1965) classic demonstration of the role that rumor plays on information distortion. In over half of the trials in their study, participants' descriptions of a picture incorrectly identified an African-American man as holding a weapon, whereas the actual picture showed the weapon in the hands of a Caucasian man. Similar types of findings have also been reported in terms of television-related stimuli. For example, Drabman et al. (1981) showed children a videotape featuring a female physician (Dr. Mary Nancy) and a male nurse (Nurse David Gregory). Immediately after viewing, more than 95% of the first and second graders in the sample incorrectly identified the physician as male and the nurse as female. One week after viewing, almost half of the seventh graders made the same mistake.

Although these types of studies imply that the viewers' cognitions or attitudes played a role in their recall of the media messages, some research has directly assessed viewers' attitudes in explorations of memory. For example, Oliver (1999) showed Caucasian individuals a newscast that featured either an African-American or a Caucasian criminal suspect.

Identification measures of the criminal suspects taken approximately 3 months later showed that anti-Black attitudes were associated with an increased tendency to misidentify African-American photographs and a decreased tendency to misidentify Caucasian photographs as the person who was featured as the criminal.

Summary

To summarize, research on viewers' selective exposure, perception, and memory highlight the importance that individual differences play in the experience of media content. In general, this body of research shows a tendency for viewers to select, interpret, and remember portrayals that are consistent with or confirming of their existing attitudes and beliefs. In this regard, research in this area appears to support a limited-effects perspective. Nevertheless, it is important to remember that viewers do not always have control over their media exposure, and that media content is not always sufficiently ambiguous as to allow for multiple interpretations or selective memory. In addition, individual differences may well play a role in reinforcement in some circumstances, but in other instances they can serve to allow for or can intensify media influences.

EFFECTS ON VIEWERS

Examinations of individual differences in more traditional media effects research has received much less attention than in studies of viewer selection, response, and interpretation of media content. This is understandable given the typical way that research from these perspectives conceptualize the independent variable of interest. That is, in studies of viewer selection and enjoyment, the independent variable is often some characteristic of the viewer that predicts how media content is received. In contrast, in studies of media effects, the independent variable is typically an exposure to some aspect of media content. In these latter instances, individual differences are often treated as "noise" or error variance, with researchers typically accounting for these variations either through random assignment to experimental conditions or through the treatment of individual difference variables as covariates. However, some models of media effects that explicitly employ individual difference variables as factors in their analyses demonstrate that individual variations can serve as important moderating variables.

One notable area of research that routinely employs individual difference variables is the study of persuasion. For example, dual-process theories generally suggest that attitude change resulting from exposure to a persuasive message can result from systematic elaboration of the merits of the arguments presented, from heuristic or peripheral processing, or from some combination of both of these processes (see Petty, chap. 7; see also Eagly & Chaiken, 1993; Chaiken, Wood, & Eagly, 1996). Although the primary persuasive route that is employed and the reaction that individuals have to various aspects of persuasive messages depends on a large number of variables, Petty and Wegener's (1998) review of the literature in this area highlighted numerous individual difference variables that have been shown to play a role in attitude change, including intelligence, self-esteem, self-monitoring, and need for cognition. These authors pointed out that in some instances, individual differences predict variations in the types of appeals that are influential. For example, their review of research on self-monitoring suggested that high self-monitors (i.e., individuals sensitive to social approval) are more influenced by message appeals focused on status or image, whereas low self-monitors are more influenced by message appeals focused on quality or values. In other instances, individual differences predict the extent to which receivers tend to engage in message scrutiny. For example, individuals scoring high on the need for cognition tend to engage in greater elaboration than do individuals low on the need for cognition and are therefore more influenced by argument strength than by peripheral cues (e.g., source attractiveness). Recently, Fabrigar, Priester, Petty, and Wegener (1998) also revealed similar findings in terms of the role that attitude accessibility plays on elaboration likelihood. Specifically, these authors found that greater accessibility of attitudes pertaining to the topic of a persuasive message increased elaboration, thereby resulting in positive attitude change for strong arguments, and negative attitude change for weak arguments.

In addition to showing that individual differences can play an important role in moderating the direction and nature of media influence, additional research also suggests that in some instances, the existence of certain individual characteristics may heighten or intensify media influences or may even provide a necessary condition for media influences to occur. One model of media effects that is illustrative of this role of individual differences is Berkowitz' research on priming, derived from research on cognitive neoassociation theory (Berkowitz, 1984; Jo & Berkowitz, 1994). Briefly, associative priming theory suggests that semantically related cognitions, feelings, and action tendencies are connected through associative pathways. When a stimulus activates or primes one of the nodes within a cognitive framework, that activation radiates out and primes related thoughts and feelings and thereby heightens the probability that the activated cognitions will be employed in subsequent behaviors and interpretations of new stimuli. As Bushman (1995) pointed out, the importance of individual differences to this model rests on the central role of cognitive networks that allow for the priming of related thoughts. Although it is certainly the case that many cognitive associations are culturally shared (e.g., stereotypes), it is also likely that variations exist in both the strength of cognitive associations and the frequency with which they are activated. Consequently, individual differences associated with variations in cognitive networks should predict the extent to which media stimuli serve to prime related thoughts and, as a consequence, influence behavior.

Bushman (1995) employed this line of reasoning in a series of studies pertaining to media violence. Specifically, exposure to violent films was shown to increase both aggressive affect (Study 2) and aggressive behaviors (Study 3), but particularly among individuals who scored high on measures of trait aggressiveness. Additional research has reported similar results, both in terms of responses to media violence and in terms of responses to sexually explicit materials. For example, Scharrer (2001) found that males' exposure to a violent television program resulted in increases in self-reported aggression/hostility, but only among the participants who scored high on measures of hypermasculinity. Likewise, McKenzie-Mohr and Zanna (1990) reported that gender-schematic males (i.e., males scoring high on masculinity and low on femininity) who had viewed pornography were more likely to display sexually suggestive mannerisms in a subsequent interaction with a woman, whereas aschematic males were largely unaffected by the pornography exposure.

Taken together, the results of these studies suggest that individual differences can play a crucial moderating role in the way that media can prime semantically related cognitions. However, an alternate interpretation of these results could be that individual difference variables indicating the presence of a given trait (e.g., hostility) lead to greater viewer acceptance of media portrayals featuring behaviorally consistent portrayals (e.g., violence). Zillmann and Weaver (1997) employed a similar interpretation in their study examining the effects of long-term exposure to film violence on the acceptance of violence as a means of conflict resolution. Their research showed that exposure to films featuring gratuitous violence (e.g., *Death Warrant*, *Total Recall*) resulted in greater acceptance and perceived effectiveness of violent conflict resolution, but only among male respondents who scored high on psychoticism. Clearly, this interpretation is not necessarily inconsistent with interpretations based on priming theory, though it does suggest that individual difference variables likely play multiple roles in moderating the influence that media may have. Certainly, future research would benefit from more extensive explorations of the way that individual differences can be incorporated into established models of media influence, and the way that individual variations may call for modifications of existing theories.

CONCLUDING COMMENTS

This chapter began with the argument that unexplained variance can be appreciated as representing the opportunity for researchers to explore the importance of individual differences in the media effects process. Although research shows that viewers' selection and enjoyment of much media content reflects variations in enduring traits or dispositions, this should not be interpreted as suggesting that individual differences imply only limited or trivial effects. In contrast, it is important to note that the presence of certain traits or dispositions can play a role in predicting not only the *type* of influence that media may have, but also the *strength* of influence that can be expected. That is, if individual differences are *not* acknowledged, some programs of research run the risk of incorrectly concluding that media have no effects or inconsequentially small effects on viewers.

This cautionary note is not to suggest that individual difference variables become part of every research design. In fact, the measurement of individual differences without theoretical motivation may lead to inflated estimates of the importance of those differences. For example, the ease with which gender is measured in most studies likely creates a scenario in which gender differences are routinely examined—even if not called for by theory, but are reported only if significance is obtained (Hyde, 1994). In contrast, what this reasoning does suggest is that media effects research could certainly benefit from the inclusion of individual differences in a way that is motivated by theory and in a way that extends our understanding of how individual variations serve as important predictors of media use and moderators of media influence. By acknowledging the importance of what the audience brings *to* the viewing situation, media effects research stands to move beyond seeing unexplained variance as only a nuisance and move toward celebrating diversity in a way that is both methodologically productive and theoretically enriching.

REFERENCES

Allport, G. W., & Postman, L. (1965). *The psychology of rumour.* New York: Russell & Russell. (Original work published 1947.)

Aluja-Fabregat, A. (2000). Personality and curiosity about TV and films violence in adolescents. *Personality and Individual Differences, 29,* 379–392.

Aluja-Fabregat, A., & Torrubia-Beltri, R. (1998). Viewing of mass media violence, perception of violence, personality and academic achievement. *Personality and Individual Differences, 25,* 973–989.

Apple, R. W. (1976, September 27). Voter poll finds debate aided Ford and cut Carter lead. *New York Times,* p. 1.

Berkowitz, L. (1984). Some effects of thoughts on anti-social and prosocial influences of media effects: A cognitive-neoassociation analysis. *Psychological Bulletin, 95,* 410–427.

Bleich, S., Zillmann, D., & Weaver, J. B. (1991). Enjoyment and consumption of defiant rock music as a function of adolescent rebelliousness. *Journal of Broadcasting & Electronic Media, 35,* 351–366.

Bothwell, R. K., & Brigham, J. C. (1983). Selective evaluation and recall during the 1980 Reagan-Carter debate. *Journal of Applied Social Psychology, 13,* 427–442.

Bushman, B. J. (1995). Moderating role of trait aggressiveness in the effects of violent media on aggression. *Journal of Personality and Social Psychology, 69,* 950–960.

Cacioppo, J. T., Petty, R. E., Feinstein, J., & Jarvis, B. (1996). Individual differences in cognitive motivation: The life and times of people varying in need for cognition. *Psychological Bulletin, 119,* 197–253.

Cappella, J. N., Turow, J., & Jamieson, K. H. (1996). Call-in political talk radio: Background, content, audiences, portrayal in mainstream media. (Report Series No. 5). Philadelphia: University of Pennsylvania, Annenberg Public Policy Center.

Chaiken, S., Wood, W., & Eagly, A. H. (1996). Principles of persuasion. In E. T. Higgins & A. W. Kruglanski (Eds.), *Social psychology: Handbook of basic principles* (pp. 702–742). New York: Guilford.

Choti, S., Marston, A. R., Holston, S. G., & Hart, J. T. (1987). Gender and personality variables in film-induced sadness and crying. *Journal of Social and Clinical Psychology, 5,* 535–544.

Cooks, L. M., & Orbe, M. P. (1993). Beyond the satire: Selective exposure and selective perception in "In Living Color." *Howard Journal of Communications, 4,* 217–233.

Cotton, J. L. (1985). Cognitive dissonance in selective exposure. In D. Zillmann & J. Bryant (Eds.), *Selective exposure to communication* (pp. 11–33). Hillsdale, NJ: Lawrence Erlbaum Associates.

Dittmar, M. L. (1994). Relations among depression, gender, and television viewing of college students. *Journal of Social Behavior and Personality, 9,* 317–328.

Drabman, R. S., Robertson, S. J., Patterson, J. N., Jarvie, G. J., Hammer, D., & Cordua, G. (1981). Children's perception of media-portrayed sex roles. *Sex Roles, 7,* 379–389.

Eagly, A. H., & Chaiken, S. (1993). *The psychology of attitudes.* Fort Worth, TX: Harcourt Brace Jovanovich.

Eisenberg, N. (2000). Empathy and sympathy. In M. Lewis & L. M. Haviland-Jones (Eds.), *Handbook of emotions* (2nd ed., pp. 677–691). New York: Guilford Press.

Eysenck, H. J. (1990). Biological dimensions of personality. In L. A. Pervin (Ed.), *Handbook of personality and research* (pp. 244–276). New York: Guilford.

Fabrigar, L. R., Priester, J. R., Petty, R. E., & Wegener, D. T. (1998). The impact of attitude accessibility on elaboration of persuasive messages. *Personality and Social Psychology Bulletin, 24,* 339–353.

Festinger, L. (1957). *A theory of cognitive dissonance.* Evanston, IL: Row, Peterson.

Finn, S. (1997). Origins of media exposure: Linking personality traits to TV, radio, print, and film use. *Communication Research, 24,* 507–529.

Freedman, J. L., & Sears, D. O. (1965). Selective exposure. In L. Berkowitz (Ed.), *Advances in experimental social psychology* (Vol. 2, pp. 57–97). San Diego, CA: Academic Press.

Frey, D. (1986). Recent research on selective exposure to information. In L. Berkowitz (Ed.), *Advances in experimental social psychology* (Vol. 19, pp. 41–80). San Diego, CA: Academic Press.

Giner-Sorolla, R., & Chaiken, S. (1994). The causes of hostile media judgments. *Journal of Experimental Social Psychology, 30,* 165–180.

Hansen, C. H., & Hansen, R. D. (1991). Constructing personality and social reality through music: Individual differences among fans of punk and heavy metal music. *Journal of Broadcasting & Electronic Media, 35,* 335–350.

Hansen, C. H., & Hansen, R. D. (2000). Music and music videos. In D. Zillmann & P. Vorderer (Eds.), *Media entertainment: The psychology of its appeal* (pp. 175–213). Mahwah, NJ: Lawrence Erlbaum Associates.

Heider, F. (1958). *The psychology of interpersonal relations.* New York: Wiley.

Hoffner, C., & Cantor, J. (1991). Perceiving and responding to mass media characters. In J. Bryant & D. Zillmann (Eds.), *Responding to the screen: Reception and reaction processes* (pp. 63–101). Hillsdale, NJ: Lawrence Erlbaum Associates.

Hyde, J. S. (1994). Should psychologists study gender differences? Yes, with some guidelines. *Feminism & Psychology, 4,* 507–512.

Jo, E., & Berkowitz, L. (1994). A priming effect analysis of media influences: An update. In J. Bryant & D. Zillmann (Eds.), *Media effects: Advances in theory and research* (pp. 43–60). Hillsdale, NJ: Lawrence Erlbaum Associates.

Klapper, J. T. (1960). *The effects of mass communication.* New York: Free Press.

Kraus, S. (1962). *The great debates: Background, perspective, effects.* Bloomington: Indiana University Press.

Mares, M. L., & Cantor, J. (1992). Elderly viewers' responses to televised portrayals of old age: Empathy and mood management versus social comparison. *Communication Research, 19,* 459–478.

McIlwraith, R. D. (1998). "I'm addicted to television": The personality, imagination, and TV watching patterns of self-identified TV addicts. *Journal of Broadcasting & Electronic Media, 42,* 371–386.

McKenna, K. Y. A., & Bargh, J. A. (2000). Plan 9 from cyberspace: The implications of the Internet for personality and social psychology. *Personality and Social Psychology Review, 4,* 57–75.

McKenzie-Mohr, D., & Zanna, M. P. (1990). Treating women as sexual objects: Look to the (gender schematic) male who has viewed pornography. *Personality and Social Psychology Bulletin, 16,* 296–308.

Mills, J. (1993). The appeal of tragedy: An attitude interpretation. *Basic and Applied Social Psychology, 14,* 255–271.

Oliver, M. B. (1993). Exploring the paradox of the enjoyment of sad films. *Human Communication Research, 19,* 315–342.

Oliver, M. B. (1996). Influences of authoritarianism and portrayals of race on Caucasian viewers' responses to reality-based crime dramas. *Communication Reports, 9,* 141–150.

Oliver, M. B. (1999). Caucasian viewers' memory of Black and White criminal suspects in the news. *Journal of Communication 49*(3), 46–60.

Oliver, M. B., Mares, M. L., & Cantor, J. (1993). News viewing, authoritarianism, and attitudes toward the Gulf War. In R. E. Denton, Jr. (Ed.), *The Media and the Persian Gulf War* (pp. 145–164). New York: Praeger.

Oliver, M. B., Sargent, S., & Weaver, J. B. (1998). The impact of sex and gender-role self-perception on affective reactions to different types of film. *Sex Roles, 38,* 45–62.

Oliver, M. B., Weaver, J. B., & Sargent, S. (2000). An examination of factors related to sex differences in enjoyment of sad films. *Journal of Broadcasting & Electronic Media, 44,* 282–300.

Osgood, C. E., & Tannenbaum, P. H. (1955). The principle of congruity in the prediction of attitude change. *Psychological Review, 62,* 42–55.

Peffley, M., Shields, T., & Williams, B. (1996). The intersection of race and crime in television news stories: An experimental study. *Political Communication, 13,* 309–327.

Perse, E. M. (1992). Predicting attention to local television news: Need for cognition and motives for viewing. *Communication Reports, 5,* 40–49.

Perse, E. M. (1996). Sensation seeking and the use of television for arousal. *Communication Reports, 9,* 37–48.

Petty, R. E., & Wegener, D. T. (1998). Attitude change: Multiple roles for persuasion variables. In D. Gilbert, S. T. Fiske, & G. Lindzey (Eds.), *The handbook of social psychology* (4th ed., Vol. 1, pp. 323–390). Boston: McGraw-Hill.

Robinson, T. O., Weaver, J. B., & Zillmann, D. (1996). Exploring the relation between personality and the appreciation of rock music. *Psychological Reports, 78,* 259–269.

Rubin, A. M., Perse, E. M., & Powell, R. A. (1985). Loneliness, parasocial interaction, and local television news viewing. *Human Communication Research, 12,* 155–180.

Scharrer, E. (2001). Men, muscles, and machismo: The relationship between television exposure and aggression in the presence of hypermasculinity. *Media Psychology, 3,* 159–188.

Sparks, G. G., Pellechia, M., & Irvine, C. (1999). The repressive coping style and fright reactions to mass media. *Communication Research, 26,* 176–192.

Sweeney, P. D., & Gruber, K. L. (1984). Selective exposure: Voter information preferences and the Watergate affair. *Journal of Personality and Social Psychology, 46,* 1208–1221.

Tamborini, R. (1996). A model of empathy and emotional reactions to horror. In J. B. Weaver & R. Tamborini (Eds.), *Horror films: Current research on audience preferences and reactions* (pp. 103–123). Mahwah, NJ: Lawrence Erlbaum Associates.

Tamborini, R., & Stiff, J. (1987). Predictors of horror film attendance and appeal: An analysis of the audience for frightening films. *Communication Research, 14,* 415–436.

Tamborini, R., Stiff, J., & Heidel, C. (1990). Reacting to graphic horror: A model of empathy and emotional behavior. *Communication Research, 17,* 616–640.

Tamborini, R., Stiff, J., & Zillmann, D. (1987). Preference for graphic horror featuring male versus female victimization: Personality and past film viewing experiences. *Human Communication Research, 13,* 529–552.

Vallone, R. P., Ross, L., & Lepper, M. R. (1985). The hostile media phenomenon: Biased perception and perceptions of media bias in coverage of the Beirut Massacre. *Journal of Personality and Social Psychology, 49,* 577–585.

Vidmar, N., & Rokeach, M. (1974). Archie Bunker's bigotry: A study in selective perception and exposure. *Journal of Communication, 24*(1), 36–47.

Weaver, J. B. (1991). Exploring the links between personality and media preferences. *Personality and Individual Differences, 12,* 1293–1299.

Weaver, J. B. (2000). Personality and entertainment preferences. In D. Zillmann & P. Vorderer (Eds.), *Media entertainment: The psychology of its appeal* (pp. 235–248). Mahwah, NJ: Lawrence Erlbaum Associates.

Zillmann, D. (1985). The experimental exploration of gratifications from media entertainment. In K. E. Rosengren, L. A. Wenner, & P. Palmgreen (Eds.), *Media gratifications research: Current perspectives* (pp. 225–239). Beverly Hills, CA: Sage.

Zillmann, D. (1988). Mood management: Using entertainment to full advantage. In L. Donohew, H. E. Sypher, & E. T. Higgins (Eds.), *Communication, social cognition, and affect* (pp. 147–171). Hillsdale, NJ: Lawrence Erlbaum Associates.

Zillmann, D. (1991). Empathy: Affect from bearing witness to the emotions of others. In J. Bryant & D. Zillmann (Eds.), *Responding to the screen: Reception and reaction processes* (pp. 135–167). Hillsdale, NJ: Lawrence Erlbaum Associates.

Zillmann, D. (2000). Humor and comedy. In D. Zillmann & P. Vorderer (Eds.), *Media entertainment: The psychology of its appeal* (pp. 37–57). Mahwah, NJ: Lawrence Erlbaum Associates.

Zillmann, D., & Cantor, J. R. (1977). Affective responses to the emotions of a protagonist. *Journal of Experimental Social Psychology, 13,* 155–165.

Zillmann, D., Taylor, K., & Lewis, K. (1998). News as nonfiction theater: How dispositions toward the public cast of characters affect reactions. *Journal of Broadcasting & Electronic Media, 42,* 153–169.

Zillmann, D., Taylor, K., & Lewis, K. (1999). Dispositions toward public issues as determinants of reactions to bad and good news. *Medienpsychologie, 11,* 231–243.

Zillmann, D., & Weaver, J. B. (1997). Psychoticism in the effect of prolonged exposure to gratuitous media violence on the acceptance of violence as a preferred means of conflict resolution. *Personality and Individual Differences, 22,* 613–627.

Zuckerman, M. (1979). *Sensation seeking: Beyond the optimal level of arousal.* Hillsdale, NJ: Lawrence Erlbaum Associates.

Zuckerman, M. (1994). *Behavioral expressions of biosocial bases of sensation seeking.* Cambridge: Cambridge University Press.

Zuckerman, M. (1996). Sensation seeking and the taste for vicarious horror. In J. B. Weaver & R. Tamborini (Eds.), *Horror films: Current research on audience preferences and reactions* (pp. 147–160). Mahwah, NJ: Lawrence Erlbaum Associates.

Zuckerman, M., & Litle, P. (1986). Personality and curiosity about morbid and sexual events. *Personality and Individual Differences, 7,* 49–56.

Chapter 20

The Uses-and-Gratifications Perspective of Media Effects

ALAN M. RUBIN
Kent State University

Media effects researchers seek to isolate communicator, channel, or message elements that explain the impact of messages on receivers. One view of this process emanates from a mechanistic perspective and assumes direct influence on message recipients. Primary components of mechanistic effects research are: seeing audience members as passive and reactive; focusing on short-term, immediate, and measurable changes in thoughts, attitudes, or behaviors; and assuming direct influence on audiences.

Some have suggested that other elements intervene between media messages and effects. Over 40 years ago, Klapper (1960) questioned the validity of mechanistic approaches. In his phenomenistic approach he proposed that several elements intercede between a message and one's response so that, in most instances, media messages that are intended to persuade actually reinforce existing attitudes. These mediating factors include: individual predispositions and selective perception processes, group norms, message dissemination via interpersonal channels, opinion leadership, and the free-enterprise nature of the media in some societies. Accordingly, we could argue that (a) by themselves, mass media typically are not necessary or sufficient causes of audience effects, and (b) a medium or message is only a single source of influence in the social and psychological environment, although it is an important and crucial one.

A PSYCHOLOGICAL PERSPECTIVE

Uses and gratifications sees a medium or message as a source of influence within the context of other possible influences. It sees media audiences as variably active communicators, rather than passive recipients of messages. Uses and gratifications underscores the role of social and psychological elements in mitigating mechanistic effects and sees mediated communication as being socially and psychologically constrained. Rosengren (1974) wrote that uses and gratifications rests on a mediated view of communication influence, which stresses how individual differences constrain direct media effects. Therefore, to explain media effects, we must first understand the characteristics, motivation, selectivity, and involvement of audience members.

Uses and gratifications, then, is a psychological communication perspective. It shifts the focus of inquiry from a mechanistic perspective's interest in direct effects of media on receivers to assessing how people use the media: "that is, what purposes or functions the media serve for a body of active receivers" (Fisher, 1978, p. 159). The psychological perspective stresses individual use and choice. As such, researchers seek to explain media effects "in terms of the purposes, functions or uses (that is, uses and gratifications) as controlled by the choice patterns of receivers" (Fisher, p. 159).

In contrast to mechanistic views, writers have suggested functional and psychological views of media influence. This chapter will consider the psychological and functional roots of uses and gratifications, the objectives and functions of the paradigm, and the evolution of uses-and-gratifications research. Then, it addresses the links between media uses and effects, focusing on audience activity and media orientations, dependency and functional alternatives, and social and psychological circumstances. Lastly, it considers some directions, especially as linked to personal involvement and parasocial interaction.

FUNCTIONAL APPROACHES TO MEDIA

A few early works exemplify a functional approach. Lasswell (1948), for example, suggested that by performing certain activities—surveillance of the environment, correlation of environmental parts, and transmission of social heritage—media content has common effects on those in a society. Wright (1960) added entertainment as a fourth activity and assessed manifest and latent functions and dysfunctions of the media when performing surveillance, correlation, transmission, and entertainment activities. More specifically, Lazarsfeld and Merton (1948) proposed that the media perform status-conferral and ethicizing functions and a narcotizing dysfunction.

Other researchers suggested that the media serve many functions for people and societies. Horton and Wohl (1956), for example, proposed that television provides viewers with a sense of parasocial relationship with media personalities. Pearlin (1959) argued that television watching allows viewers to escape from unpleasant life experiences. Mendelsohn (1963) noted that media entertainment reduces anxiety that is created by media news. Stephenson (1967) argued that television provides people the opportunity for play. And, McCombs and Shaw (1972) hypothesized that the media set the agenda in election campaigns.

Research focusing on audience motivation for using the media surrounded these functional studies. The belief that an object is best defined by its *use* guided such research. Klapper (1963) argued that mass communication research "too frequently and too long focused on determining whether some particular effect does or does not occur" (p. 517). He noted that media researchers had found few clear-cut answers to questions about the effects of the mass media. Consistent with Katz (1959), who suggested that a media message ordinarily could not influence a person who had no use for it, Klapper called for an expansion of uses-and-gratifications inquiry.

THE USES-AND-GRATIFICATIONS PARADIGM

The principal elements of uses and gratifications include our psychological and social environment, our needs and motives to communicate, the media, our attitudes and expectations about the media, functional alternatives to using the media, our communication behavior, and the outcomes or consequences of our behavior. In 1974, Katz, Blumler, and Gurevitch outlined the principal objectives of uses and gratifications inquiry: (a) to explain how people use media to gratify their needs, (b) to understand motives for media behavior, and (c) to identify functions or consequences that follow from needs, motives, and behavior. Uses and gratifications focuses on: "(1) the social and psychological origins of (2) needs, which generate (3) expectations of (4) the mass media or other sources, which lead to (5) differential patterns of media exposure (or engagement in other activities), resulting in (6) need gratifications and (7) other consequences, perhaps mostly unintended ones" (Katz et al., p. 20).

Rosengren (1974) and Katz and his colleagues (1974) sketched the initial tenets of uses and gratifications. These assumptions have been revised since then to reflect what we have learned about media audiences (see Palmgreen, 1984; Palmgreen, Wenner, & Rosengren, 1985; A. M. Rubin, 1986, 1993, 1994). A contemporary view of uses and gratifications is grounded in five assumptions:

1. Communication behavior, including the selection and use of the media, is goal-directed, purposive, and motivated. People choose media or media content. That behavior is functional and has consequences for individuals and societies.

2. People initiate the selection and use of communication vehicles. Instead of being used by the media, people select and use media to satisfy their felt needs or desires (Katz, Gurevitch, & Haas, 1973). Media audiences, then, are variably active communicators. Media use may respond to needs, but also satisfies wants or interests such as seeking information to solve a personal dilemma.

3. A host of social and psychological factors guide, filter, or mediate communication behavior. Our predispositions, the environment in which we live, and our interpersonal interactions shape our expectations about the media and media content. Communication behavior responds to media and their messages as they are filtered through our personalities, social categories and relationships, potential for interpersonal interaction, and communication channel availability.

4. The media compete with other forms of communication—or, functional alternatives—such as interpersonal interaction for selection, attention, and use so that we can seek to gratify our needs or wants. There are definite relationships between personal and mediated channels in this process. How well the media satisfy our needs, motives, or desires varies among individuals based on their social and psychological circumstances.

5. People are typically more influential than the media in this process, but not always. Our own initiative mediates the patterns and consequences of media use. Through this process, media may affect individual characteristics or social, political, cultural, or economic structures of society and how people may come to rely on certain communication media (Rosengren, 1974; A. M. Rubin & Windahl, 1986).

Katz and his colleagues (1974) listed two other early assumptions. First, methodologically, we can articulate our own motives to communicate. In other words, self-reports provide accurate data about media use. Second, value judgments about the cultural significance of media content or of using media content should be suspended until we fully understand motives and gratifications. Self-reports are still typically used, but so are other modes of inquiry. In addition, we now have a clearer understanding of the role of motives and gratifications, so that inquiry can include questions of cultural significance. Some have even advocated a shift in audience-based research toward examining cultural interaction of individuals with the media (e.g., Massey, 1995).

The assumptions of uses and gratifications underscore the role of audience initiative and activity. Communication behavior is largely goal directed and purposive. People typically choose to participate and select media or messages from a variety of communication alternatives in response to their expectations and desires. These expectations and desires emanate from and are constrained by personal traits, social context, and interaction. A person has the capacity for subjective choice and interpretation and initiates such behavior as media or message selection. This initiative affects the outcomes of media use. Our degree of initiative or activity, though, has been seen as more variable than absolute over the past two decades (e.g., Blumler, 1979; Levy & Windahl, 1984, 1985; A. M. Rubin & Perse, 1987a, 1987b).

THE EVOLUTION OF USES-AND-GRATIFICATIONS RESEARCH

Uses-and-gratifications research has focused on audience motivation and consumption. It has been guided by revised research questions shifting our focus to what people do with the media, instead of what the media do to people (Klapper, 1963). Research was descriptive and unsystematic in its early development, mostly identifying motives rather than explaining the processes or effects of media use. The early work was a precursor to research depicting typologies of media motives. For the most part, subsequent research became more systematic, and some investigators began to ask about the consequences of media use.

Media-Use Typologies

Early gratifications investigators sought to learn why people used certain media content. Lazarsfeld (1940), for example, considered the appeals of radio programs. Such studies preceded formal conceptualization of a uses-and-gratifications perspective. The early studies described audience motives rather than media effects. Examples include (a) the competitive, educational, self-rating, and sporting appeals of a radio quiz program, *Professor Quiz,* for its listeners (Herzog, 1940); (b) the emotional-release, wishful-thinking, and advice-seeking gratifications women listeners received from radio daytime serials (Herzog, 1944); and (c) the reasons why people read the newspaper—to interpret public affairs, as a daily tool for living, for social prestige, and to escape (Berelson, 1949). Such early descriptive research was largely abandoned in favor of studies of personal influence and media functions during the 1950s and 1960s.

In the early 1970s uses-and-gratifications researchers sought to identify the motives of audience members for using the media by developing typologies of how people used the media to gratify social and psychological needs (Katz et al., 1973). Needs were related to social roles and psychological dispositions and often took the form of strengthening or weakening a connection with self, family, or society. Katz et al., for example, developed a typology of the helpfulness of the media in satisfying important needs: strengthening understanding of self, friends, others, or society; strengthening the status of self or society; and strengthening contact with family, friends, society, or culture.

In addressing links between personal and mediated communication, Lull (1980) observed the behavior of families when watching television and developed a typology of the social uses of television. He suggested that television could be used *structurally*—as an environmental resource (e.g., for companionship) or as a behavioral regulator (e.g., punctuating time)—or *relationally*—to facilitate communication (e.g., an agenda for conversation), for affiliation or avoidance (e.g., conflict resolution), for social learning (e.g., behavioral modeling), or for competence or dominance (e.g., role reinforcement).

Researchers used such typologies to describe and explain media consumption. The typologies speak to connections between goals and outcomes and suggest the complexities of media uses and effects. McQuail, Blumler, and Brown (1972), for example, categorized the types of gratifications people seek from viewing television content. They linked people's background and social circumstances with the gratifications sought and formulated a typology of media-person interactions. McQuail and associates observed that people are motivated to watch television for: diversion—to escape and for emotional release; personal relationships—for companionship and social utility; personal identity—for personal reference, reality exploration, and value reinforcement; and surveillance—to acquire news and information.

Rosengren and Windahl (1972) also considered the links among audience involvement, reality proximity, and media dependency. They noted that people might seek media as functional alternatives to personal interaction—as a supplement, complement, or substitute—for such reasons as compensation, change, escape, or vicarious experience. They suggested that needs for interaction and identification can result in different degrees of media involvement: detachment, parasocial interaction, solitary identification, or capture. Rosengren and Windahl argued that, by merging the traditions of media effects and media uses, it is possible "to ask what effect a given use made of the mass media, or a given gratification obtained from them, may have" (p. 176).

Criticisms

During this period, some criticized uses and gratifications for several reasons. Many of the criticisms reflected the state of affairs at that time and were directed at initial assumptions and research. These criticisms included (a) the compartmentalized nature of typologies, making it difficult to predict beyond those studied or to consider the societal or cultural implications of media use; (b) the lack of clarity of central constructs and how researchers attached different meanings to concepts such as motives, uses, gratifications, and functional alternatives; (c) the nature of the audience and whether the audience was treated as being too active or rational in its behavior; and (d) the methodological reliance on self-report data (e.g., Anderson & Meyer, 1975; Carey & Kreiling, 1974; Elliott, 1974; Swanson, 1977).

Most of the criticisms have been addressed in the many studies of the past 25 to 30 years. For one thing, researchers adapted and extended the use of consistent media-use measures across different contexts. Greenberg (1974) developed the scales with British children and adolescents and observed links among media behavior, television attitudes, aggressive attitudes, and viewing motives. A partial replication of that work in the United States identified six reasons why children and adolescents watched television: for learning, habit/pass time, companionship, escape, arousal, and relaxation (A. M. Rubin, 1979). Habitual viewing related negatively to watching news and positively to TV affinity and watching comedies. Viewing to learn related positively to perceived TV realism. Arousal motivation was linked to watching action/adventure programs, and companionship motivation was linked to watching comedy programs. These results were similar to Greenberg's, presenting a consistent portrait across cultures.

The research also supported stability and consistency of responses via test-retest reliability of viewing-motive items and convergent validity of the motive scales with responses to open-ended queries of viewing reasons (A. M. Rubin, 1979). Respondents were able to verbalize their reasons for using media. A similar technique in a later study supported convergent validity for a wider sample, ranging from children to older adults, and continued programmatic development and synthesis (A. M. Rubin, 1981a).

Besides supporting the consistency and accuracy of self-report motive scales, researchers also used experimental (e.g., Bryant & Zillmann, 1984), ethnographic (e.g., Lemish, 1985; Lull, 1980), and diary/narrative (e.g., Massey, 1995) methods. Investigators also sought to develop and extend conceptual, focused, and systematic lines of inquiry. They came to regard the audience to be less than universally active and treated audience activity as a variable rather than an absolute (e.g., Blumler, 1979; Levy & Windahl, 1984, 1985; A. M. Rubin & Perse, 1987a, 1987b).

Contemporary Studies

Uses-and-gratifications research has demonstrated systematic progression during the past 30 years. Research has helped explain media behavior and has furthered our understanding of media uses and effects. Researchers have provided a systematic analysis of media use by adapting similar motivation measures (e.g., Bantz, 1982; Eastman, 1979; Greenberg, 1974; Palmgreen & Rayburn, 1979; A. M. Rubin, 1979, 1981a, 1981b). Studies within and across these research programs have included replication and secondary analysis. Six research directions and connections to media effects research are drawn in the following sections:

- One direction has been the links among media-use motives and their associations with media attitudes and behaviors. This has led to the development of typologies of communication motives. Research has suggested consistent patterns of media use such as meeting cognitive and affective needs, gratifying utilitarian and diversionary motivations, and fostering instrumental and ritualized orientations (e.g., Perse, 1986, 1990a; A. M. Rubin, 1983, 1984, 1985; A. M. Rubin & Bantz, 1989; A. M. Rubin & Rubin, 1982b). Lometti, Reeves, and Bybee (1977), for example, identified surveillance/entertainment, affective guidance, and behavioral guidance media-use gratification dimensions.
- A second direction has been to compare motives across media. This has produced comparative analyses of the appropriateness and effectiveness of channels—including evolving communication technologies such as the VCR, the Internet, and the World Wide Web—to meet people's needs and wants (e.g., Bantz, 1982; Cohen, Levy, & Golden, 1988; Dobos, 1992; Ferguson, 1992; Ferguson & Perse, 2000; Katz et al., 1973; Lichtenstein & Rosenfeld, 1983, 1984; Lin, 1999; Westmyer, DiCioccio, & Rubin, 1998). Elliott and Quattlebaum (1979), for example, reported that various media serve similar needs, namely to maintain societal contact or to satisfy personal needs. Cowles (1989) found that interactive media were felt to have more personal characteristics than noninteractive media. And, Perse and Courtright (1993) observed that interpersonal channels (i.e., conversation and telephone) had more social presence and better met personal needs, when compared with channels such as the computer.
- A third direction has been to examine the different social and psychological circumstances of media use. Researchers have addressed how various factors influence media behavior (e.g., Adoni, 1979; Dimmick, McCain, & Bolton, 1979; Finn & Gorr, 1988; Hamilton & Rubin, 1992; Lull, 1980; Perse & Rubin, 1990; A. M. Rubin, Perse & Powell, 1985; A. M. Rubin & Rubin, 1982a, 1989; R. B. Rubin & Rubin, 1982; Windahl, Hojerback, & Hedinsson, 1986). Researchers have examined the role of life position, lifestyle, personality, loneliness, isolation, need for cognition, religiosity, media deprivation, family-viewing environment, and the like.

- A fourth direction has been the links between gratifications sought and obtained when using media or their content. This research has addressed how people's motives for using media are satisfied. These authors have proposed transactional, discrepancy, and expectancy-value models of media uses and gratifications (e.g., Babrow, 1989; Babrow & Swanson, 1988; Donohew, Palmgreen, & Rayburn, 1987; Galloway & Meek, 1981; Palmgreen & Rayburn, 1979, 1982, 1985; Palmgreen, Wenner, & Rayburn, 1980, 1981; Rayburn & Palmgreen, 1984; Wenner, 1982, 1986). For example, expectancy-value models predict gratification seeking from communication channels based on an expected outcome. They stress the consideration of expectancy and evaluative thresholds for behaviors and comparisons of the congruence of expectation and outcome.
- A fifth direction has assessed how variations in background variables, motives, and exposure affect outcomes such as perceptions of relationship, cultivation, involvement, parasocial interaction, satisfaction, and political knowledge (e.g., Alexander, 1985; Carveth & Alexander, 1985; Garramone, 1984; Perse, 1990a; Perse & Rubin, 1988; A. M. Rubin, 1985; R. B. Rubin & McHugh, 1987). Haridakis (2001), for example, observed that experience with crime and motivation for watching violent television content have been underemphasized in research and policy when considering viewer aggression.
- A sixth direction has considered the method, reliability, and validity for measuring motivation (e.g., Babrow, 1988; Dobos & Dimmick, 1988; McDonald & Glynn, 1984).

MEDIA USES AND EFFECTS

Some have proposed a synthesis of uses-and-gratifications and media-effects research (e.g., Rosengren & Windahl, 1972; A. M. Rubin & Windahl, 1986; Windahl, 1981). The primary difference between the two traditions is that a media-effects researcher "most often looks at the mass communication process from the communicator's end," whereas a uses researcher begins with the audience member (Windahl, 1981, p. 176). Windahl argued that it is more beneficial to stress the similarities rather than the differences of the two traditions. One such similarity is that both uses and effects seek to explain the outcomes or consequences of mass communication such as attitude or perception formation (e.g., cultivation), behavioral changes (e.g., dependency), and societal effects (e.g., knowledge gaps). Uses and gratifications does so, however, recognizing the greater potential for audience initiative, choice, and activity.

Audience Activity and Media Orientations

Audience activity is the core concept in uses and gratifications. Audience activity refers to the utility, intentionality, selectivity, and involvement of the audience with the media (Blumler, 1979). Uses-and-gratifications researchers regard audience members to be variably—not universally—active; they are not equally active at all times. According to Windahl (1981), depicting the audience "as superational and very selective . . . invites criticism" (p. 176). A valid view of audience activeness lies on a continuum between being passive (and expected to be directly influenced by messages) and being active (and expected to make rational decisions about accepting or rejecting messages; A. M. Rubin, 1993).

Levy and Windahl (1984) tested the proposition about the variable nature of activity and identified three activity periods for Swedish television viewers: previewing, during viewing, and postviewing. Although they found preactivity or intention to watch to be weakly related to entertainment media use, it was strongly related to surveillance use. They argued that viewers actively seek news to gain information, but may not actively seek diversion. Lin (1993) noted that strongly motivated viewers engage in more activities and experience greater satisfaction when watching television as compared with weakly motivated viewers. She also found that the diversification of the home-media environment affects activity levels (Lin, 1994). Because they present more options, more diversified media households (e.g., greater cable, satellite, and computer opportunities) enable greater audience choice and selectivity.

Some researchers have approached motives as interrelated structures—or complex viewing orientations—rather than isolated entities (e.g., Abelman, 1987; Perse, 1986, 1990a; Perse & Rubin, 1988; A. M. Rubin, 1981b, 1983, 1984; A. M. Rubin & Perse, 1987a; A. M. Rubin & Rubin, 1982b). As such, Finn (1992) suggested proactive (mood management) and passive (social compensation) dimensions of media use. McDonald (1990) noted that two orientations—surveillance (i.e., needing to know about the community and world) and communication utility (i.e., using information in social interaction)—explained much of the variance in news-seeking behavior. Abelman and Atkin (1997) also supported interrelated patterns of television use by identifying three viewer archetypes: medium-, station-, and network-oriented viewers. Some of these approaches stem from work that suggested that media use could be described as primarily ritualized (diversionary) or instrumental (utilitarian) in nature (e.g., A. M. Rubin, 1984).

Ritualized and instrumental media orientations tell us about the amount and type of media use and about one's media attitudes and expectations. These orientations reflect the complexity of audience activity. *Ritualized* use is using a medium more habitually to consume time and for diversion. It entails greater exposure to and affinity with the *medium.* Ritualized use suggests utility but an otherwise less-active or less-goal-directed state. *Instrumental* use is seeking certain media *content* for informational reasons. It entails greater exposure to news and informational content and perceiving that content to be realistic. Instrumental use is active and purposive. It suggests utility, intention, selectivity, and involvement.

To a large extent, activity depends on the social context, potential for interaction, and attitudes. Elements such as mobility and loneliness are important. Reduced mobility and greater loneliness, for example, result in ritualized media orientations and greater reliance on the media (Perse & Rubin, 1990; A. M. Rubin & Rubin, 1982a). Attitudinal dispositions such as affinity and perceived realism also are important. Attitudes affect our media expectations and how we perceive and interpret messages. They filter media and message selection and use. This is consistent with Swanson's (1979) notion of the importance of "the perceptual activity of interpreting or creating meaning for messages" (p. 42). Potter (1986) and others have argued that such outcomes as cultivation are mediated by the differential perceptions people have about how realistic the media content is. For example, one study found that watching action/adventure programs predicted a cultivation effect of feeling less safe, whereas watching television, in general, led to perceptions of greater safety (A. M. Rubin, Perse, & Taylor, 1988). Stronger cultivation effects were evident when media content was seen as being realistic.

Blumler (1979) argued that activity means imperviousness to influence. In other words, activity is a deterrent to media effects. This conclusion, though, is questionable. Activity plays an important intervening role in the effects process. Because activity denotes a more selective, attentive, and involved state of media use, it may actually be a catalyst to message effects. In two studies we found that more active, instrumental television use led to cognitive (i.e., thinking about content), affective (i.e., parasocially interacting with media personalities), and behavioral (i.e., discussing content with others) involvement with news and soap opera programs (A. M. Rubin & Perse, 1987a, 1987b). Later, we observed that different activities could be catalysts or deterrents to media effects (Kim & Rubin, 1997). Activities—such as selectivity, attention, and involvement—facilitate such outcomes as parasocial interaction, cultivation, and communication satisfaction. Other activities—such as avoiding messages, being distracted, and being skeptical—inhibit these outcomes because they reduce our awareness and comprehension of messages.

Therefore, it is reasonable to suggest that differences in audience activity—as evidenced in ritualized and instrumental orientations—

have important implications for media effects. In other words, as Windahl (1981) argued, using a medium instrumentally or ritualistically leads to different outcomes. He saw *effects* as the outcome of using media content and *consequences* as the outcome of using a medium. Instrumental orientations may produce stronger attitudinal and behavioral effects than ritualized orientations because instrumental orientations incorporate greater motivation to use and involvement with messages. Involvement suggests a state of readiness to select, interpret, and respond to messages.

Dependency and Functional Alternatives

According to McIlwraith, Jacobvitz, Kubey, and Alexander (1991), watching television can relax and distract viewers and decrease negative affect, and some viewers may excessively depend on television because they anticipate this effect. The notion of media dependency is grounded in the availability and utilization of functional alternatives (Rosengren & Windahl, 1972). Dependency on a particular medium results from the motives we have to communicate, the strategies we use to obtain gratifications, and the restricted availability of functional alternatives. It mediates how we use the media and the potential impact of the media (e.g., Lindlof, 1986; Windahl et al., 1986).

On one hand, dependency results from an environment that restricts the availability of functional alternatives and produces a certain pattern of media use. Dotan and Cohen (1976), for example, found that fulfilling cognitive needs was most important and fulfilling escapist and affective needs was least important when using television, radio, and newspapers during and following the October 1973 Middle East war. People turned to television and radio in wartime to fulfill most needs, especially surveillance needs.

In addition, individual life-position attributes—such as health, mobility, interaction, activity, life satisfaction, and economic security—affect the availability and choice of communication alternatives, our motives to communicate, our strategies for seeking information and diversion, and dependency on a medium. In two studies of a life-position construct we called *contextual age*, for example, we found a negative link between one's degree of self-reliance and television dependency; that is, the less healthy and less mobile depended more on television than did the more healthy and more mobile (A. M. Rubin & Rubin, 1982a; R. B. Rubin & Rubin, 1982). As Miller and Reese (1982) argued, "dependency on a medium appears to enhance the opportunity for that medium to have predicted effects" (p. 245). They observed that certain political effects (i.e., activity and efficacy) were more evident from exposure to a relied-upon medium.

We also proposed a model to highlight the links among media uses and effects. The Uses and Dependency Model depicts links between one's needs and motives to communicate, strategies for seeking information, uses of media and functional alternatives, and media dependency (A. M. Rubin & Windahl, 1986). According to the model, needs and motives that produce narrow information-seeking strategies might lead to dependency on certain channels. In turn, dependency leads to other effects such as attitude change or behavior and feeds back to alter other relationships in the society. Different outcomes would result from ritualized use of a medium and instrumental use of media content.

In one application of the Uses and Dependency Model to development communication in Sierra Leone, Taylor (1992) found that those who were dependent on radio for information about development used that medium instrumentally—they planned to acquire information and sought stimulating information from the radio. Those who were dependent on newspapers for information about development also used that medium instrumentally—they intentionally sought and selected stimulating information from the newspapers. Taylor observed that, as compared with the less dependent, those who were more dependent on radio showed greater interest and participation in national development.

Social and Psychological Circumstances

The concept of media dependency highlights the interface of personal and mediated communication, including the importance of social and psychological circumstances—that is, individual differences—in media effects. Resourceful communicators have "a wider availability of alternative channels, a broader conception of the potential channels, and the capacity for using more diversified message- and interaction-seeking strategies" (A. M. Rubin & Rubin, 1985, p. 39). They might, for example, use several available channels—including e-mail—to maintain their interpersonal relationships (Stafford, Kline, & Dimmick, 1999). Resourceful communicators are less likely to be dependent on any given person or communication channel. Effects should be more pronounced for those who come to depend on the messages of a particular medium such as talk radio or the Internet.

For example, telephoning a talk-radio host to express one's views is an accessible and nonthreatening alternative to interpersonal communication for those talk-radio listeners with restricted mobility, who are apprehensive about face-to-face interaction, and who feel others do not value what they have to say in interpersonal encounters (Armstrong & Rubin, 1989; also see Avery, Ellis, & Glover, 1978; Turow, 1974). Similarly, the Internet is a functional alternative to face-to-face communication for those who are anxious about interpersonal interaction and do not find such interaction to be rewarding (Papacharissi & Rubin, 2000; cf. Flaherty, Pearce, & Rubin, 1998). On the other hand, those who are extroverted and agreeable seem to prefer nonmedia activities such as conversation with others (Finn, 1997). Such individual differences contribute to communication preferences and to the opportunity for certain sources to influence people.

Media uses and effects, then, depend on the potential for and the context of interaction. This is heavily influenced by people's social and psychological circumstances, including lifestyle, life position, and personality (e.g., Finn & Gorr, 1988; A. M. Rubin & Rubin, 1982a). Life satisfaction, mobility, loneliness, and mood, to name a few factors, are determinants of media behavior. For example, reduced life satisfaction and anxiety contribute to escapist television viewing (Conway & Rubin, 1991; A. M. Rubin, 1985), and restricted mobility and greater loneliness result in ritualized media behavior and reliance on television (Perse & Rubin, 1990; A. M. Rubin & Rubin, 1982a). Those who are heavily reliant on television—that is, self-reported television addicts—have been found to be neurotic, introverted, and easily bored, watching television to forget unpleasant thoughts, to regulate moods, and to fill time (McIlwraith, 1998). In addition, mood influences media choice so that boredom leads to selecting exciting content and stress to selecting relaxing content (Bryant & Zillmann, 1984).

Differences in personality, cognition, social affiliation, and motivation affect exposure, cultivation, satisfaction, parasocial interaction, identification, and news attention and elaboration (e.g., Carveth & Alexander, 1985; Perse, 1990b, 1992; R. B. Rubin & McHugh, 1987). Krcmar and Greene (1999), for example, found that disinhibited adolescents tended to watch violent television programs, but sensation seekers who exhibited risky behavior were unlike those who watched violent content. Johnson (1995) noted that four motivations—gore, thrill, independence, and problem watching—affected adolescents' cognitive and affective responses to viewing graphic horror films. And, Harwood (1999) found that, by selecting programs that featured young characters, young adults increased age-group identification.

CONCLUSIONS AND DIRECTIONS

Uses and gratifications sees communication influence as being socially and psychologically constrained and affected by individual differences and choice. Variations in expectations, attitudes, activity, and involvement lead to different communication behaviors and outcomes. Personality, social context, motivation, and availability—based on culture and economic, political, and social structure—all impact the possible influence of media and their messages.

In 1974 Katz and his colleagues argued, "hardly any substantive or empirical effort has been devoted to connecting gratifications and effects" (p. 28). Five years later, Blumler (1979) echoed those sentiments: "We lack a well-formed perspective about which gratifications sought from which forms of content are likely to facilitate which effects" (p. 16). Although some precision has been lacking, this state of affairs has changed during the past 25 to 30 years as investigators have sought to link social and psychological antecedents, communication motivation, attitudes, audience activity and involvement, behavior, and outcomes. More focused consideration of media orientations and audience activity has produced renewed interest in examining the place of motivation in explaining communication processes and outcomes. Yet, we still need increased specificity, especially as attention turns to newer communication media.

Blumler (1979) summarized cognitive, diversionary, and personal identity uses of the media. He proposed three hypotheses about media effects based on these uses: (a) cognitive motivation will facilitate information gain, (b) diversion or escape motivation will facilitate audience perceptions of the accuracy of social portrayals in entertainment media, and (c) personal identity motivation will promote reinforcement effects.

Such hypotheses have received some attention to date. For example, we have learned that cognitive or instrumental motivation leads to seeking information and to cognitive involvement (Perse, 1990a; A. M. Rubin, 1983, 1984; A. M. Rubin & Perse, 1987b; A. M. Rubin & Rubin, 1982b). Levy and Windahl (1984), for example, found that increased planning and intention to watch television were strongly related to surveillance use. Vincent and Basil (1997) found that increased surveillance needs resulted in greater use of all news media among a college-student sample. In addition, researchers have observed links between cognitive or instrumental information-seeking motivation and information gain during a political campaign (McLeod & Becker, 1974), about political candidates (Atkin & Heald, 1976), and about candidates' stands on issues. They have found that public affairs media use and interest lead to increased political knowledge (Pettey, 1988).

The second hypothesis about diversionary motivation and acceptance of role portrayals, though, must recognize the mediating role of attitudes and experiences in media effects. We have learned that attitudes and experience affect audience perceptions. Some studies support cultivation effects contingent on the perceived reality of content (Potter, 1986; A. M. Rubin et al., 1988), audience members' personal experiences with crime (Weaver & Wakshlag, 1986), and media utility and selectivity (Perse,

1986). There is much room for researchers to expand attention to links between attitudes, motivation, and involvement, on one hand, and perceptions of media content and role portrayals, on the other.

As to the third hypothesis, we have seen that media function as alternatives to personal interaction for the immobile, dissatisfied, and apprehensive (Armstrong & Rubin, 1989; Papacharissi & Rubin, 2000; Perse & Rubin, 1990; A. M. Rubin & Rubin, 1982a). We also have found that social utility motivation might lead to a reduced sense of parasocial interaction with television personalities (A. M. Rubin & Perse, 1987a).

One fruitful path has been the study of personal involvement in the media uses and effects process. Involvement influences information acquisition and processing. It signifies attention, participation, cognitive processing, affect, and emotion. It also has led to the study of *parasocial interaction,* emphasizing the role of media personalities in real and perceived relationships with audience members. The concept also reinforces the relevance of interpersonal concepts such as attraction, similarity, homophily, impression management, and empathy to understanding the role and influence of media and newer technologies. Harrison (1997), for example, argued that interpersonal attraction to thin media characters promoted eating disorders in women college students. And, O'Sullivan (2000) considered the role of mediated communication channels (e.g., telephone, answering machine, electronic mail) for managing impressions in relationships.

In 1956 Horton and Wohl proposed that television and radio personalities foster an illusionary parasocial relationship with viewers and listeners. Parasocial interaction is a sense of friendship with these media personae. It suggests an audience member's felt affective or emotional relationship with the media personality (Rosengren & Windahl, 1972; A. M. Rubin & Perse, 1987a), which may be experienced as "seeking guidance from a media persona, seeing media personalities as friends, imagining being part of a favorite program's social world, and desiring to meet media performers" (A. M. Rubin et al., 1985, pp. 156–157). Audience members often see particular media personalities in a manner parallel to their interpersonal friends—as natural, down-to-earth folks who are attractive and similar to them. Media formats and techniques encourage and promote the development of parasocial relationships. As with other media, audience members, though, must choose to participate or interact.

We have looked at parasocial interaction with television newscasters and soap-opera characters (A. M. Rubin & Perse, 1987a, 1987b), with talk-radio hosts (A. M. Rubin & Step, 2000), and with favorite television personalities (Conway & Rubin, 1991; R. B. Rubin & McHugh, 1987). We developed a measure to attempt to gauge the extent of the relationships (A. M. Rubin et al., 1985; A. M. Rubin & Perse, 1987a). Basically, involved viewers, not necessarily heavy viewers, appear to form parasocial relationships.

Parasocial interaction suggests involved and instrumental media use, that is, a more active orientation to media use (e.g., Kim & Rubin, 1997; Perse, 1990b; A. M. Rubin & Perse, 1987a). It has been positively related to being socially and task-attracted to a favorite television personality (R. B. Rubin & McHugh, 1987), to reducing uncertainty in relationships (Perse & Rubin, 1989), and to attitude homophily with television news and entertainment personalities (Turner, 1993). As affective and emotional involvement, parasocial interaction affects media attitudes, behaviors, and expectations and should accentuate potential effects. For example, in an analysis of critical responses of British viewers, Livingstone (1988) suggested that the personally involving nature of soap operas has important implications for media effects. In addition, Brown and Basil (1995) found that emotional involvement with a media celebrity mediated persuasive communication and increased personal concern about health messages and risky sexual behavior. Also, we found that parasocially interacting with a public-affairs talk-radio host predicted planned and frequent listening, treating the host as an important source of information, and feeling the host influenced how listeners felt about and acted upon societal issues (A. M. Rubin & Step, 2000).

Windahl (1981) argued that a synthesis would help overcome limitations and criticisms of both media uses and media effects traditions. Such a synthesis recognizes that: media perceptions and expectations guide people's behavior; motivation is derived from needs, interests, and externally imposed constraints; there are functional alternatives to media consumption; there are important interpersonal dimensions to the media experience; and audience activity, involvement, and attitudes about media content play an important role in media effects.

Since the early days of media-use typologies, researchers have sought to address theoretical links among media uses and effects. We have learned more about audience members as variably active and involved communicators. We have seen the contributions of interpersonal communication for understanding media uses and effects. The media uses and effects process remains complex, requiring careful attention to antecedent, mediating, and consequent conditions. Single-variable explanations continue to have appeal to some researchers and policymakers. However, such explanations distract us from the conceptual complexity of media effects. As Ruggiero (2000) argued, uses and gratifications has been "a cutting-edge theoretical approach" in the early stages of new communication media. Uses and gratifications will be especially valuable as we seek to understand the newer, interactive media environment.

ACKNOWLEDGMENT

This chapter is based on two earlier essays: "Uses, Gratifications, and Media Effects Research," in J. Bryant and D. Zillmann (1986), *Perspectives on Media Effects,* and "Media Uses and Effects: A Uses-and-Gratifications Perspective," in J. Bryant & D. Zillmann (1994), *Media Effects: Advances in Theory and Research,* both published by Lawrence Erlbaum Associates.

REFERENCES

Abelman, R. (1987). Religious television uses and gratifications. *Journal of Broadcasting & Electronic Media, 31,* 293–307.

Abelman, R., & Atkin, D. (1997). What viewers watch when they watch TV: Affiliation change as case study. *Journal of Broadcasting & Electronic Media, 41,* 360–379.

Adoni, H. (1979). The functions of mass media in the political socialization of adolescents. *Communication Research, 6,* 84–106.

Alexander, A. (1985). Adolescents' soap opera viewing and relational perceptions. *Journal of Broadcasting & Electronic Media, 29,* 295–308.

Anderson, J. A., & Meyer, T. P. (1975). Functionalism and the mass media. *Journal of Broadcasting, 19,* 11–22.

Armstrong, C. B., & Rubin, A. M. (1989). Talk radio as interpersonal communication. *Journal of Communication, 39*(2), 84–94.

Atkin, C. K., & Heald, G. (1976). Effects of political advertising. *Public Opinion Quarterly, 40,* 216–228.

Avery, R. K., Ellis, D. G., & Glover, T. W. (1978). Patterns of communication on talk radio. *Journal of Broadcasting, 22,* 5–17.

Babrow, A. S. (1988). Theory and method in research on audience motives. *Journal of Broadcasting & Electronic Media, 32,* 471–487.

Babrow, A. S. (1989). An expectancy-value analysis of the student soap opera audience. *Communication Research, 16,* 155–178.

Babrow, A. S., & Swanson, D. L. (1988). Disentangling antecedents of audience exposure levels: Extending expectancy-value analyses of gratifications sought from television news. *Communication Monographs, 55,* 1–21.

Bantz, C. R. (1982). Exploring uses and gratifications: A comparison of reported uses of television and reported uses of favorite program type. *Communication Research, 9,* 352–379.

Berelson, B. (1949). What "missing the newspaper" means. In P. F. Lazarsfeld & F. N. Stanton (Eds.), *Communications research 1948–1949* (pp. 111–129). New York: Harper.

Blumler, J. G. (1979). The role of theory in uses and gratifications studies. *Communication Research, 6,* 9–36.

Brown, W. J., & Basil, M. D. (1995). Media celebrities and public health: Responses to "Magic" Johnson's HIV disclosure and its impact on AIDS risk and high-risk behaviors. *Health Communication, 7,* 345–370.

Bryant, J., & Zillmann, D. (1984). Using television to alleviate boredom and stress: Selective exposure as a function of induced excitational states. *Journal of Broadcasting, 28,* 1–20.

Carey, J. W., & Kreiling, A. L. (1974). Popular culture and uses and gratifications: Notes toward an accommodation. In J. G. Blumler & E. Katz (Eds.), *The uses of mass communications: Current perspectives on gratifications research* (pp. 225–248). Beverly Hills, CA: Sage.

Carveth, R., & Alexander, A. (1985). Soap opera viewing motivations and the cultivation process. *Journal of Broadcasting & Electronic Media, 29,* 259–273.

Cohen, A. A., Levy, M. R., & Golden, K. (1988). Children's uses and gratifications of home VCRs: Evolution or revolution. *Communication Research, 15,* 772–780.

Conway, J. C., & Rubin, A. M. (1991). Psychological predictors of television viewing motivation. *Communication Research, 18,* 443–464.

Cowles, D. L. (1989). Consumer perceptions of interactive media. *Journal of Broadcasting & Electronic Media, 33,* 83–89.

Dimmick, J. W., McCain, T. A., & Bolton, W. T. (1979). Media use and the life span. *American Behavioral Scientist, 23*(1), 7–31.

Dobos, J. (1992). Gratification models of satisfaction and choice of communication channels in organizations. *Communication Research, 19,* 29–51.

Dobos, J., & Dimmick, J. (1988). Factor analysis and gratification constructs. *Journal of Broadcasting & Electronic Media, 32,* 335–350.

Donohew, L., Palmgreen, P., & Rayburn, J. D., II. (1987). Social and psychological origins of media use: A lifestyle analysis. *Journal of Broadcasting & Electronic Media, 31,* 255–278.

Dotan, J., & Cohen, A. A. (1976). Mass media use in the family during war and peace: Israel 1973–1974. *Communication Research, 3,* 393–402.

Eastman, S. T. (1979). Uses of television viewing and consumer life styles: A multivariate analysis. *Journal of Broadcasting, 23,* 491–500.

Elliott, P. (1974). Uses and gratifications research: A critique and a sociological alternative. In J. G. Blumler & E. Katz (Eds.), *The uses of mass communications: Current perspectives on gratifications research* (pp. 249–268). Beverly Hills, CA: Sage.

Elliott, W. R., & Quattlebaum, C. P. (1979). Similarities in patterns of media use: A cluster analysis of media gratifications. *Western Journal of Speech Communication, 43,* 61–72.

Ferguson, D. A. (1992). Channel repertoire in the presence of remote control devices, VCRs, and cable television. *Journal of Broadcasting & Electronic Media, 36,* 83–91.

Ferguson, D. A., & Perse, E. M. (2000). The World Wide Web as a functional alternative to television. *Journal of Broadcasting & Electronic Media, 44,* 155–174.

Finn, S. (1992). Television addiction? An evaluation of four competing media-use models. *Journalism Quarterly, 69,* 422–435.

Finn, S. (1997). Origins of media exposure: Linking personality traits to TV, radio, print, and film use. *Communication Research, 24,* 507–529.

Finn, S., & Gorr, M. B. (1988). Social isolation and social support as correlates of television viewing motivations. *Communication Research, 15,* 135–158.

Fisher, B. A. (1978). *Perspectives on human communication.* New York: Macmillan.

Flaherty, L. M., Pearce, K. J., & Rubin, R. B. (1998). Internet and face-to-face communication: Not functional alternatives. *Communication Quarterly, 46,* 250–268.

Galloway, J. J., & Meek, F. L. (1981). Audience uses and gratifications: An expectancy model. *Communication Research, 8,* 435–449.

Garramone, G. M. (1984). Audience motivation effect: More evidence. *Communication Research, 11,* 79–96.

Greenberg, B. S. (1974). Gratifications of television viewing and their correlates for British children. In J. G. Blumler & E. Katz (Eds.), *The uses of mass communications: Current perspectives on gratifications research* (pp. 71–92). Beverly Hills, CA: Sage.

Hamilton, N. F., & Rubin, A. M. (1992). The influence of religiosity on television use. *Journalism Quarterly, 69,* 667–678.

Haridakis, P. M. (2001). The role of motivation in policy considerations addressing television violence (Doctoral dissertation, Kent State University, 2000). *Dissertation Abstracts International, A61/07,* 2505.

Harrison, K. (1997). Does interpersonal attraction to thin media personalities promote eating disorders? *Journal of Broadcasting & Electronic Media, 41,* 478–500.

Harwood, J. (1999). Age identification, social identity gratifications, and television viewing. *Journal of Broadcasting & Electronic Media, 43,* 123–136.

Herzog, H. (1940). Professor quiz: A gratification study. In P. F. Lazarsfeld, *Radio and the printed page* (pp. 64–93). New York: Duell, Sloan & Pearce.

Herzog, H. (1944). What do we really know about daytime serial listeners? In P. F. Lazarsfeld & F. N. Stanton (Eds.), *Radio research 1942–1943* (pp. 3–33). New York: Duell, Sloan & Pearce.

Horton, D., & Wohl, R. R. (1956). Mass communication and para-social interaction. *Psychiatry, 19*, 215–229.

Johnson, D. D. (1995). Adolescents' motivations for viewing graphic horror. *Human Communication Research, 21*, 522–552.

Katz, E. (1959). Mass communication research and the study of popular culture. *Studies in Public Communication, 2*, 1–6.

Katz, E., Blumler, J. G., & Gurevitch, M. (1974). Utilization of mass communication by the individual. In J. G. Blumler & E. Katz (Eds.), *The uses of mass communications: Current perspectives on gratifications research* (pp. 19–32). Beverly Hills, CA: Sage.

Katz, E., Gurevitch, M., & Haas, H. (1973). On the use of the mass media for important things. *American Sociological Review, 38*, 164–181.

Kim, J., & Rubin, A. M. (1997). The variable influence of audience activity on media effects. *Communication Research, 24*, 107–135.

Klapper, J. T. (1960). *The effects of mass communication.* New York: Free Press.

Klapper, J. T. (1963). Mass communication research: An old road resurveyed. *Public Opinion Quarterly, 27*, 515–527.

Krcmar, M., & Greene, K. (1999). Predicting exposure to and uses of television violence. *Journal of Communication, 49*(3), 24–45.

Lasswell, H. D. (1948). The structure and function of communication in society. In L. Bryson (Ed.), *The communication of ideas* (pp. 37–51). New York: Harper.

Lazarsfeld, P. F. (1940). *Radio and the printed page.* New York: Duell, Sloan & Pearce.

Lazarsfeld, P. F., & Merton, R. K. (1948). Mass communication, popular taste and organized social action. In L. Bryson (Ed.), *The communication of ideas* (pp. 95–118). New York: Harper.

Lemish, D. (1985). Soap opera viewing in college: A naturalistic inquiry. *Journal of Broadcasting & Electronic Media, 29*, 275–293.

Levy, M. R., & Windahl, S. (1984). Audience activity and gratifications: A conceptual clarification and exploration. *Communication Research, 11*, 51–78.

Levy, M. R., & Windahl, S. (1985). The concept of audience activity. In K. E. Rosengren, L. A. Wenner, & P. Palmgreen (Eds.), *Media gratifications research: Current perspectives* (pp. 109–122). Beverly Hills, CA: Sage.

Lichtenstein, A., & Rosenfeld, L. B. (1983). Uses and misuses of gratifications research: An explication of media functions. *Communication Research, 10*, 97–109.

Lichtenstein, A., & Rosenfeld, L. (1984). Normative expectations and individual decisions concerning media gratification choices. *Communication Research, 11*, 393–413.

Lin, C. A. (1993). Modeling the gratification-seeking process of television viewing. *Human Communication Research, 20*, 224–244.

Lin, C. A. (1994). Audience fragmentation in a competitive video marketplace. *Journal of Advertising Research, 34*(6), 30–38.

Lin, C. A. (1999). Online-service adoption likelihood. *Journal of Advertising Research, 39*(2), 79–89.

Lindlof, T. R. (1986). Social and structural constraints on media use in incarceration. *Journal of Broadcasting & Electronic Media, 30*, 341–355.

Livingstone, S. M. (1988). Why people watch soap operas: An analysis of the explanations of British viewers. *European Journal of Communication, 3*, 55–80.

Lometti, G., Reeves, B., & Bybee, C. R. (1977). Investigating the assumptions of uses and gratifications research. *Communication Research, 4*, 321–338.

Lull, J. (1980). The social uses of television. *Human Communication Research, 6*, 197–209.

Massey, K. B. (1995). Analyzing the uses and gratifications concept of audience activity with a qualitative approach: Media encounters during the 1989 Loma Prieta earthquake disaster. *Journal of Broadcasting & Electronic Media, 39*, 328–349.

McCombs, M. E., & Shaw, D. L. (1972). The agenda-setting function of mass media. *Public Opinion Quarterly, 36*, 176–187.

McDonald, D. G. (1990). Media orientation and television news viewing. *Journalism and Mass Communication Quarterly, 67*, 11–20.

McDonald, D. G., & Glynn, C. J. (1984). The stability of media gratifications. *Journalism Quarterly, 61*, 542–549, 741.

McIlwraith, R. D. (1998). "I'm addicted to television": The personality, imagination, and TV watching patterns of self-identified TV addicts. *Journal of Broadcasting & Electronic Media, 42*, 371–386.

McIlwraith, R., Jacobvitz, R. S., Kubey, R., & Alexander, A. (1991). Television addiction: Theories and data behind the ubiquitous metaphor. *American Behavioral Scientist, 35*(2), 104–121.

McLeod, J. M., & Becker, L. B. (1974). Testing the validity of gratification measures through political effects analysis. In J. G. Blumler & E. Katz (Eds.), *The uses of mass communications: Current perspectives on gratifications research* (pp. 137–164). Beverly Hills, CA: Sage.

McQuail, D., Blumler, J. G., & Brown, J. R. (1972). The television audience: A revised perspective. In D. McQuail (Ed.), *Sociology of mass communications* (pp. 135–165). Middlesex, England: Penguin.

Mendelsohn, H. (1963). Socio-psychological perspectives on the mass media and public anxiety. *Journalism Quarterly, 40*, 511–516.

Miller, M. M., & Reese, S. D. (1982). Media dependency as interaction: Effects of exposure and reliance on political activity and efficacy. *Communication Research, 9*, 227–248.

O'Sullivan, P. B. (2000). What you don't know won't hurt me: Impression management functions of communication channels in relationships. *Human Communication Research, 26*, 403–431.

Palmgreen, P. (1984). Uses and gratifications: A theoretical perspective. *Communication Yearbook, 8*, 20–55.

Palmgreen, P., & Rayburn, J. D., II. (1979). Uses and gratifications and exposure to public television: A discrepancy approach. *Communication Research, 6*, 155–179.

Palmgreen, P., & Rayburn, J. D., II. (1982). Gratifications sought and media exposure: An expectancy value model. *Communication Research, 9*, 561–580.

Palmgreen, P., & Rayburn, J. D., II. (1985). A comparison of gratification models of media satisfaction. *Communication Monographs, 52*, 334–346.

Palmgreen, P., Wenner, L. A., & Rayburn, J. D., II. (1980). Relations between gratifications sought and obtained: A study of television news. *Communication Research, 7*, 161–192.

Palmgreen, P., Wenner, L. A., & Rayburn, J. D., II. (1981). Gratification discrepancies and news program choice. *Communication Research, 8*, 451–478.

Palmgreen, P., Wenner, L. A., & Rosengren, K. E. (1985). Uses and gratifications research: The past ten years. In K. E. Rosengren, L. A. Wenner, & P. Palmgreen (Eds.), *Media gratifications research: Current perspectives* (pp. 11–37). Beverly Hills, CA: Sage.

Papacharissi, Z., & Rubin, A. M. (2000). Predictors of Internet use. *Journal of Broadcasting & Electronic Media, 44*, 175–196.

Pearlin, L. I. (1959). Social and personal stress and escape television viewing. *Public Opinion Quarterly, 23*, 255–259.

Perse, E. M. (1986). Soap opera viewing patterns of college students and cultivation. *Journal of Broadcasting & Electronic Media, 30*, 175–193.

Perse, E. M. (1990a). Involvement with local television news: Cognitive and emotional dimensions. *Human Communication Research, 16,* 556–581.

Perse, E. M. (1990b). Media involvement and local news effects. *Journal of Broadcasting & Electronic Media, 34,* 17–36.

Perse, E. M. (1992). Predicting attention to local television news: Need for cognition and motives for viewing. *Communication Reports, 5,* 40–49.

Perse, E. M., & Courtright, J. A. (1993). Normative images of communication media: Mass and interpersonal channels in the new media environment. *Human Communication Research, 19,* 485–503.

Perse, E. M., & Rubin, A. M. (1988). Audience activity and satisfaction with favorite television soap opera. *Journalism Quarterly, 65,* 368–375.

Perse, E. M., & Rubin, A. M. (1990). Chronic loneliness and television use. *Journal of Broadcasting & Electronic Media, 34,* 37–53.

Perse, E. M., & Rubin, R. B. (1989). Attribution in social and parasocial relationships. *Communication Research, 16,* 59–77.

Pettey, G. R. (1988). The interaction of the individual's social environment, attention and interest, and public affairs media use on political knowledge holding. *Communication Research, 15,* 265–281.

Potter, W. J. (1986). Perceived reality and the cultivation hypothesis. *Journal of Broadcasting & Electronic Media, 30,* 159–174.

Rayburn, J. D., II, & Palmgreen, P. (1984). Merging uses and gratifications and expectancy-value theory. *Communication Research, 11,* 537–562.

Rosengren, K. E. (1974). Uses and gratifications: A paradigm outlined. In J. G. Blumler & E. Katz (Eds.), *The uses of mass communications: Current perspectives on gratifications research* (pp. 269–286). Beverly Hills, CA: Sage.

Rosengren, K. E., & Windahl, S. (1972). Mass media consumption as a functional alternative. In D. McQuail (Ed.), *Sociology of mass communications* (pp. 166–194). Middlesex, England: Penguin.

Rubin, A. M. (1979). Television use by children and adolescents. *Human Communication Research, 5,* 109–120.

Rubin, A. M. (1981a). An examination of television viewing motivations. *Communication Research, 8,* 141–165.

Rubin, A. M. (1981b). A multivariate analysis of *60 Minutes* viewing motivations. *Journalism Quarterly, 58,* 529–534.

Rubin, A. M. (1983). Television uses and gratifications: The interactions of viewing patterns and motivations. *Journal of Broadcasting, 27,* 37–51.

Rubin, A. M. (1984). Ritualized and instrumental television viewing. *Journal of Communication, 34*(3), 67–77.

Rubin, A. M. (1985). Uses of daytime television soap opera by college students. *Journal of Broadcasting & Electronic Media, 29,* 241–258.

Rubin, A. M. (1986). Uses, gratifications, and media effects research. In J. Bryant & D. Zillmann (Eds.), *Perspectives on media effects* (pp. 281–301). Hillsdale, NJ: Lawrence Erlbaum Associates.

Rubin, A. M. (1993). Audience activity and media use. *Communication Monographs, 60,* 98–105.

Rubin, A. M. (1994). Media uses and effects: A uses-and-gratifications perspective. In J. Bryant & D. Zillmann (Eds.), *Media effects: Advances in theory and research* (pp. 417–436). Hillsdale, NJ: Lawrence Erlbaum Associates.

Rubin, A. M., & Bantz, C. R. (1989). Uses and gratifications of videocassette recorders. In J. Salvaggio & J. Bryant (Eds.), *Media use in the information age: Emerging patterns of adoption and consumer use* (pp. 181–195). Hillsdale, NJ: Lawrence Erlbaum Associates.

Rubin, A. M., & Perse, E. M. (1987a). Audience activity and soap opera involvement: A uses and effects investigation. *Human Communication Research, 14,* 246–268.

Rubin, A. M., & Perse, E. M. (1987b). Audience activity and television news gratifications. *Communication Research, 14,* 58–84.

Rubin, A. M., Perse, E. M., & Powell, R. A. (1985). Loneliness, parasocial interaction, and local television news viewing. *Human Communication Research, 12,* 155–180.

Rubin, A. M., Perse, E. M., & Taylor, D. S. (1988). A methodological examination of cultivation. *Communication Research, 15,* 107–134.

Rubin, A. M., & Rubin, R. B. (1982a). Contextual age and television use. *Human Communication Research, 8,* 228–244.

Rubin, A. M., & Rubin, R. B. (1982b). Older persons' TV viewing patterns and motivations. *Communication Research, 9,* 287–313.

Rubin, A. M., & Rubin, R. B. (1985). Interface of personal and mediated communication: A research agenda. *Critical Studies in Mass Communication, 2,* 36–53.

Rubin, A. M., & Rubin, R. B. (1989). Social and psychological antecedents of VCR use. In M. R. Levy (Ed.), *The VCR age: Home video and mass communication* (pp. 92–111). Newbury Park, CA: Sage.

Rubin, A. M., & Step, M. M. (2000). Impact of motivation, attraction, and parasocial interaction on talk radio listening. *Journal of Broadcasting & Electronic Media, 44,* 635–654.

Rubin, A. M., & Windahl, S. (1986). The uses and dependency model of mass communication. *Critical Studies in Mass Communication, 3,* 184–199.

Rubin, R. B., & McHugh, M. P. (1987). Development of parasocial interaction relationships. *Journal of Broadcasting & Electronic Media, 31,* 279–292.

Rubin, R. B., & Rubin, A. M. (1982). Contextual age and television use: Reexamining a life-position indicator. *Communication Yearbook, 6,* 583–604.

Ruggiero, T. E. (2000). Uses and gratifications theory in the 21st century. *Mass Communication & Society, 3*(1), 3–37.

Stafford, L., Kline, S. L., & Dimmick, J. (1999). Home e-mail: Relational maintenance and gratification opportunities. *Journal of Broadcasting & Electronic Media, 43,* 659–669.

Stephenson, W. (1967). *The play theory of mass communication.* Chicago: University of Chicago Press.

Swanson, D. L. (1977). The uses and misuses of uses and gratifications. *Human Communication Research, 3,* 214–221.

Swanson, D. L. (1979). Political communication research and the uses and gratifications model: A critique. *Communication Research, 6,* 37–53.

Taylor, D. S. (1992). Application of the uses and dependency model of mass communication to development communication in the western area of Sierra Leone (Doctoral dissertation, Kent State University, 1991). *Dissertation Abstracts International, A52/12,* 4134.

Turner, J. R. (1993). Interpersonal and psychological predictors of parasocial interaction with different television performers. *Communication Quarterly, 41,* 443–453.

Turow, J. (1974). Talk-show radio as interpersonal communication. *Journal of Broadcasting, 18,* 171–179.

Vincent, R. C., & Basil, M. D. (1997). College students' news gratifications, media use and current events knowledge. *Journal of Broadcasting & Electronic Media, 41,* 380–392.

Weaver, J., & Wakshlag, J. (1986). Perceived vulnerability to crime, criminal victimization experience, and television viewing. *Journal of Broadcasting & Electronic Media, 30,* 141–158.

Wenner, L. A. (1982). Gratifications sought and obtained in program dependency: A study of network evening news programs and *60 Minutes. Communication Research, 9,* 539–560.

Wenner, L. A. (1986). Model specification and theoretical development in gratifications sought and obtained research: A comparison of discrepancy and transactional approaches. *Communication Monographs, 53*, 160–179.

Westmyer, S. A., DiCioccio, R. L., & Rubin, R. B. (1998). Appropriateness and effectiveness of communication channels in competent interpersonal communication. *Journal of Communication, 48*(3), 27–48.

Windahl, S. (1981). Uses and gratifications at the crossroads. *Mass Communication Review Yearbook, 2*, 174–185.

Windahl, S., Hojerback, I., & Hedinsson, E. (1986). Adolescents without television: A study in media deprivation. *Journal of Broadcasting & Electronic Media, 30*, 47–63.

Wright, C. R. (1960). Functional analysis and mass communication. *Public Opinion Quarterly, 24*, 605–620.

Chapter 21

Entertainment as Media Effect

JENNINGS BRYANT
University of Alabama

DORINA MIRON
University of Alabama

Many of the chapters in this volume examine effects of media messages that are not intended by producers of these messages (e.g., distorted perceptions of reality, aggression, obesity, sexual dispositions) and that are the by-product of trying to attract and maintain large audiences for entertaining, informational, and commercial messages. Other chapters consider the intended effects of messages with primarily persuasive intent (e.g., public communication campaigns, political advertising). Although these types of media effects clearly are important and worthy of the rich research traditions they represent, when considered in terms of normative patterns of media influence, these frequently studied effects are not the primary intended effects of most of today's media messages. From the perspective of producers, the primary purpose of the preponderance of today's electronic media messages is *entertainment.*

CONCEPTUALIZATION OF ENTERTAINMENT

Entertainment is a ubiquitous phenomenon. No culture of which we have an adequate accounting has been entirely without it. As soon as the struggle for survival left human groups with sufficient time for relaxation, some form of communicative activity in which dangers and threats and their mastery and elimination were represented seems to have come into being (e.g., Hauser, 1953; Kuhn, 1962–1963; Malinowski, 1948). By the time permanent records were left for posterity, cultures had developed well-defined rites. These rites, to be sure, served the maintenance of social structure and postmortem welfare. In large measure, however, they also served the cause of amusement, merriment, gaiety, fun, and joyous enlightenment. In other words, they served the cause of entertainment. If entertainment is crudely defined as any activity designed to delight and, to a smaller degree, enlighten through the exhibition of the fortunes or misfortunes of others, but also through the display of special skills by others and/or self, it becomes clear that the concept encompasses more than comedy, drama, and tragedy. It engulfs any kind of game or play, athletic or not, competitive or not, whether witnessed only, taken part in, or performed alone. It subsumes, for instance, musical performances by self for self or others, of others for self, or with others; similarly, it subsumes dancing by self, of others, or with others.

Given such a broad conceptualization, entertainment happenings must have been obtrusive enough to catch the attention of those inclined to understand social phenomena. And they did.

The Ancients

Aristotle on Pleasure.   In his *Poetics* (1999), Aristotle (384–322 B.C.) distinguished between bodily pleasures and pleasures of the soul (e.g., righteousness or justice). The former were associated with sense perceptions, the latter with the exercise of moral judgment. Aristotle believed that an activity was promoted by its enjoyment, which also inhibited alternative activities (Urmson, 1968). This observation is a precursor of the modern displacement concept, as well as a precursor of the concept of addiction.

Epicurus' Philosophy of Pleasure.   Epicurus (341?–270 B.C.) defined pleasure as the opposite of pain or as the complete absence of pain or discomfort, as an end-state toward which we can work by removing troubles or sources of pain (e.g., hunger, thirst, sexual pressure) (Epicurus, 1993). Epicurus warned that if pursuits (eating, drinking, sexual activities) were confounded with the end state (pleasure/happiness), anxieties and addictions would develop (Anderson, 2001). Although Epicurus' concept of end state was rendered obsolete by psychological science, which demonstrated the simultaneity of sensorial stimulation and pleasure, the pain-pleasure dichotomy persisted in modern hedonic science.

Modern Views of Pleasure

Great thinkers' interest in the issue of pleasure continued for two millennia but was confined to speculations until experimental psychology developed and started to clarify how pleasure really "works." For example, Campbell (1973) redefined pleasure in neurophysiological terms as "activation of the limbic areas" (p. 70). "In normal animals, including man, the pleasure areas deep inside the brain are activated when the sense organs on the periphery of the body are stimulated" (Campbell, 1973, pp. 40–41). It is no coincidence that we speak of *"feeling* pleasure" (Campbell, 1973, p. 65). Neurophysiological science thus confirmed Aristotle's bodily pleasures.

Bousfield (1926/1999) refined the Epicurean model. He proposed that pain is not a true antithesis of pleasure. "Pleasure appears to be in some measure proportional to the rate of fall of tension" (p. 28) and is therefore "a factor of time, as well as of tension" (p. 29)—which supports Freud's (1920/1989) theory that pain and pleasure depend on the quantity of excitation present in the psychic life and the amount of diminution or increase of tension in a given time. Bousfield (1926/1999) concurred that "the degree of unpleasant affect is relatively proportional to the degree of tension present" (p. 26) and further observed that "there is no loss of tension without tension having first being produced, and so there can be no pleasure without pain or potential pain having first being present, so finally, it may be there can be no love unless hate or potential hate has first existed" (pp. 88–89).

Other contemporary theorists question the concept of pleasure as tension reduction based on findings that pleasure and pain appear to be mediated by different neurotransmitters and approach and avoidance tendencies can occur simultaneously or in rapid alternation, generating internal conflict (Kahneman, Diener, & Schwarz, 1999). The model proposed as an alternative posits that affective evaluation is bivalent rather than bipolar (Cacioppo & Berntson, 1994; Ito & Cacioppo, 1999). In an effort at reconciliation, Lang (1995) argued that the two models are not necessarily exclusive, and a bivalent system can yield a bipolar structure if the separate mechanisms that mediate "good" and "bad" are reciprocally innervated and mutually inhibitory or if the relevant output of the system is the difference between the levels of activity of the two mechanisms. Davidson (1992) suggested that the brain may compute both the sum and the difference of the levels of activity in the separate systems that mediate positive and negative affect and proposed that the good/bad value corresponds to the difference and the emotional arousal corresponds to the summed activity in the two systems—which would account for forms of entertainment that are felt to be exciting without being perceived as "good."

The concomitance of pain and pleasure is particularly important in the discussion of media-related pleasure, because media content can simultaneously effect bottom-up sensorial stimulation—a capacity greatly enhanced by technological progress in the area of telepresence (Tamborini, 2000)—and trigger top-down cortical activity that reaches the pleasure areas. This possibility of activating neural networks that may include various pains *and* pleasures poses an acute problem of hedonic management.

Old Wine in New Bottles with New Labels

The history of entertainment may be disappointing if we consider content: the same old attractions—sex and violence—for thousands of years. Nevertheless, a few examples of perennial pleasure-related problems will illustrate the development, albeit sometimes slow and convoluted, of pleasure and entertainment theories.

Circus and Acculturation.   In the ancient Mediterranean world, warfare was the main business and engaged a large part of the male population. Some exhilaration intrinsic to the process seems to have kept the warriors involved in destruction: the pleasure of extreme physical exercise and eventually the enjoyment of winning, that is, killing and robbing others, as well as appropriating goods and pleasures that belonged to the enemies. Physical abilities and weapon handling (killing skills) came to be associated with wealth, status, and sexual desirability. Their value thus expanded into peacetime activities. When not engaged in wars, the ancient Greek and Roman males would enjoy physical training and competitions (e.g., the Olympic Games, which started in Greece in 776 B.C., and three other famous sporting festivals held at Delphy, Nemea, and Corinth) and gladiatorial games (circus spectacles). The popularity of games in ancient times is hard for us to imagine. Suffice it to say that Circus Maximus in Rome was rebuilt in the time of Julius Caesar (first century B.C.) to seat 150,000 spectators, and it reached a seating capacity of 250,000 under Constantine I. In the middle of the fourth century A.D., the Roman Empire had 175 days a year dedicated to state-supported entertainments, mostly games (Zillmann, 2000b).

The stoics (fifth century B.C.), and later on Cicero (106–43 B.C.), appreciated circus spectacles as visual apprenticeship of pain and death and as a means of developing in the audience endurance to those widespread and unpleasant realities (Frau-Meigs & Jehel, 1997). Their view reflects a schema shared by rites of passage across societies and time, which also underlies the current use of cinematic horror by adolescents (Zillmann, 1998b; Zillmann & Gibson, 1996; Zillmann & Weaver, 1996). Bok (1998) went even further, contending that in ancient Rome circus was an official policy: "Violent spectacles kept the citizenry distracted, engaged, and entertained" and "provided the continuing acculturation to violence needed by a warrior state" (p. 16).

Tragedy, Catharsis, and Ethics.   Another form of violent entertainment in the classical Mediterranean world was tragedy. Early philosophers expressed concern about people's willingness to expose themselves to theatrical events that would naturally elicit strong negative feelings.

Plato (427–347 B.C.) was mostly concerned about effects. He believed that "empathic distress would render respondents vulnerable to self-pity on encountering misfortunes of their own. He deemed such sensitivity inappropriate—that is, antagonistic to his notion of virtue—and favored the banishment of the genre altogether" (Zillmann, 1998a, p. 5). Plato's view corresponds to the modern notions of repeated exposure, rehearsal of empathic distress, and chronic accessibility of fear and pity schemata. Such schemata obviously posed a threat to the fighter mind-set needed to maintain the ancient warrior states and empires.

Aristotle (384–322 B.C.) disagreed with Plato and proposed the catharsis hypothesis. He presumed that a tragedy could get the audience to experience fear and pity, which would thus be purged. The notion of catharsis challenged thinkers for more than 2,000 years before the development of psychology allowed for empirical testing and subsequent widespread refutation of the theory of catharsis in the canons of media effects. Although Aristotle's catharsis has largely failed to receive empirical support (e.g., Geen & Quanty, 1977; Zillmann, 1998a), the concept has nevertheless endured as a "legend" (Harris & Scott, in press).

Zillmann (1998b) offered alternative explanations to account for the attraction of drama. He pointed out that the concept of witness identification with actors, running from Aristotle's catharsis theory to Freud's ego confusion theory, failed to explain a spectator's enjoyment of someone else's distress (Zillmann, 1998b). What Zillmann suggested instead was that we witness drama as third parties (Zillmann, 1991a) and voluntarily rather than automatically identify with characters (Zillmann, 1998b): We pick the characters we want to identify with, and we choose the degree and duration of identification in such a way as to maximize our personal pleasure. Zillmann's disposition theory (e.g., Zillmann, 1985, 1994; Zillmann & Cantor, 1977), or theory of dispositional alignments (Zillmann, 1998b), posited that disposition toward characters (liking or disliking) mediates moral judgment and renders enjoyable the harms suffered by enemies, who are deemed to deserve punishment (Zillmann & Bryant, 1975). Although refuting catharsis, Zillmann's dispositional alignment theory confirmed Aristotle's intuition that humans derive pleasures not only from sensorial (bottom-up) stimulation but also from exercising moral judgment (Zillmann, 2000a), which means involvement of top-down cortical activity in pleasure processes.

Zillmann's disposition theory accounted for enjoyment of spectacle violence based on endorsement of social norms. To round out the picture, Zillmann also proposed a norm violation theory of violence enjoyment hinged on some people's "desire to violate the norms of socially acceptable behavior, or to see them violated by others" (Tamborini, Stiff, & Zillmann, 1987, p. 584). Zillmann's norm violation theory is tangent to Nietzsche's

(1886/1966, 1887/1956) celebration of cruelty as "liberating and exhilarating" (Bok, 1998, p. 27). Nietzsche's and Zillmann's joy of transgression makes perfect sense under a system of norms perceived by individuals as oppressive. It provides an appealing alternative to Freud's (1933) mysterious death instinct that allegedly drives people toward the destruction of self and others. Zillmann's norm violation theory can be applied to explain the enormous popularity in the United States of hard rock, heavy metal, gangsta, and other similarly violent music, whose lyrics create a coherent universe of "satanism, drug abuse, sexual assaults and murder" (Jipping, 2001, p. 65). The American youth may experience a power crisis and may use such music as a vehicle for power trips of violence, sexism, and greed (Davis, 1990).

Our Times, Our Pleasure Problems

Our hopping back and forth in history in search of footholds for a pleasure theory has hopefully given the reader a flavor of hedonic problematizing and theorizing. A legitimate question at this point would be: Have thinkers of the media age raised any new issues?

Lacan and Barthes: The Ephemeral Jouissance. Lacan (1979) contested Freud's (1920/1989) conservative, homeostatic, pleasure principle and proposed a different concept of jouissance or desire, an insatiable drive toward unattainable limits. Barthes (1973/1990) argued that the conservative homeostatic pleasure dwells on culture, and he endorsed bliss or jouissance, which he believed to be self-generated crisis associated with unsettling historical, cultural, and psychological assumptions. According to Barthes, "the extreme *guarantees* [emphasis added] bliss: an average perversion quickly loads itself up with a play of subordinate finalities: prestige, ostentation, rivalry . . ." (pp. 51–52). Beside intervening subordinate finalities that tended to extend pleasure, Barthes' bliss involved a seemingly paradoxical feature of evanescent momentariness: Bliss was defined as the final and most intense stage of pleasure, the state between pleasure and its transcendence in anxiety and death, between the consolidation of the ego and its dissolution, "the site of loss, the seam, the cut, the deflation . . . , an edge" (p. 7). The intensity of the moment was obviously due to experiencing pleasure together *with* the enhancing/arousing anticipation of its imminent loss. The loss/termination of pleasure became *the* most important ingredient for maximizing pleasure. Thus we got to the point of knowingly, willingly, deliberately pleasuring ourselves with death. Barthes' theory of bliss can finally account for the gladiator's and the matador's "romance with death" (Guttmann, 1998, p. 24) and for the macabre thrills of snuff pornography that depicts the killing of women through sexual torture (Jacob, 2000).

Lyotard: The Greater Joy of Ideas. Lyotard (1988), in his postmodern aesthetic, redefined the sublime as the melancholy and despair "of never being able to present something within reality on the scale of the Idea" that "overrides the joy of being nonetheless called upon to do so" (p. 179). Prior to him, from antiquity till modern times, pleasure had been a challenge for intelligence, which had to harness and exploit the senses in order to beat the level of natural, spontaneous, pleasure. The new spin Lyotard put on hedonism—designing one's pleasure(s) and assuming leadership and authorship—brought with it a new problem: the gap between experience and ideation. Lyotard's grand Idea is, metaphorically speaking, spurring for a pleasure ride a beaten up plough horse and feeding it fire to make it fly. Certainly, the pleasure achieved will be inferior to the pleasure imagined. As the enactment of pleasure in real life is bound to be disappointing, we are left mostly with our minds and "virtual" reality to enjoy.

Now that Barthes more or less prescribed the killing of pleasures (for better enjoyment) and Lyotard has shifted the responsibility (leadership) of pleasure making to cortical activities, the question is, can the cortex fulfill these tasks? Are these tasks realistic?

A Glimpse at the Current State of Hedonic Theory

According to Campbell (1973), "to be an animal is to be a pleasure seeker" (p. 110)! This bold claim is based on the discovery that nerve fibers serving pleasure seeking are inextricably interwoven with fibers that control physiological functions that are indispensable for individual and species survival, such as heartbeats, breathing, blood pressures, and sexual excitation. Those functions activate pleasure networks and are in turn activated by neural constellations in the pleasure areas. Thus, the limbic system (pleasure headquarters) emerged as a coordinator of the basic survival functions.

The fact that the limbic system is the highest part of the brain in the earliest vertebrates suggests "it evolved as a more efficient organizer of pleasure seeking than our closest invertebrate ancestor possessed" (Campbell, 1973, p. 67). Efficiency comes from centralized control: "Other parts of the brain exist and carry out their tasks solely to contribute to the proper activation of the limbic system" (p. 67). Even the neocortex, which supports advanced operations such as logic or time and space referencing, "survived and evolved because its intricate neuronal organization is superlatively efficient at keeping the limbic system active" (p. 68). In ordinary life, "when activation [of the pleasure areas] decreases, nerve impulses are sent to the motor centers that control the muscles involved in exploratory behavior, until the animal finds a new source of sensory stimulation and a new source of temporary pleasure. This scheme is to be regarded as the most fundamental and basic neural mechanism of behavior" (Campbell, 1973, pp. 76–77).

What happens when pleasure more intense than that naturally provided by ordinary life experiences becomes available? Experiments with intracranial self-stimulation revealed compulsive pleasure-seeking behavior that preempts other activity. The findings led brain scientists to the conclusion that everything animals (including humans) do in their normal life, their entire behavior, "is directed at evoking electrical activity in the pleasure areas of the brain" (Campbell, 1973, p. 66). It is preposterous, then, not only to blame people for making pleasures their main occupation in life, but also to decry their natural tendency to pursue more and more intense pleasures.

Defying the Genetic Tyranny.   The fact that we are naturally equipped for survival/pleasure does not mean that we can exploit our bodies for pleasure without limits. Nature also built in barriers that humans have constantly tried to beat. We appear to be engaged in a *race for pleasure against nature.* Greenfield (2000) believes that this race diversifies and personalizes individual pleasures, making us more human (less animal): "Our more sophisticated brains will liberate us from single-minded genetic tyranny and allow us to develop individual, ontogenetic agendas as we interact with the environment" (p. 43). Her thesis invites an examination of the pleasure race.

Hardwired for Pleasure: The Autonomic System.   The five senses, which are the main providers of limbic stimulation, are the interface between the environment and an individual's autonomic system, which is the part of the human brain that looks after basic survival and reproduction processes and ensures that these functions are performed "automatically" (unconsciously). The pleasure provided by the autonomic activity has survival value because it motivates us to stay connected to the world and adjust (respond in ways that minimize discomfort and maximize pleasure) (Greenfield, 2000).

The autonomic system energizes and monitors two types of functions: maintenance (routine) processes, for which resource deployment is minimized, and processes that support emergency activities, for which resource deployment needs to be maximized (fight-or-flight response, sexual intercourse).

Autonomic activities surface in consciousness typically in relation to deprivation (pain in case of deficiency and pleasure in case of remedied deficiency—e.g., pleasure of movement after immobility, pleasure of breathing fresh air after stifling in a crowded room). But it is also possible to consciously experience pleasure during energy-intensive activities. Examples mentioned in literature are, among others, "the ebullience of Battle of Britain pilots and of members of the German Luftwaffe" (Campbell, 1973, p. 198) and the "runner's high" (Kahneman, Diener, & Schwarz, 1999, p. xi). The role of pleasure in such situations is to supplement resource investment beyond the "automatic" deployment encoded for the base level of that function.

Taking Control: Your Self/Memory Is There to Pleasure You. The common denominator in the default hedonic choice built in our bodies is pleasure. Each activity has a hedonic component (Bargh, 1997; Zajonc, 1980, 1997), which means that the neural constellation activated during the experience of that activity includes neurons located in the pleasure areas. Neurons have the property of being irreversibly changed by any single activation. Their plasticity serves to store patterns of activation corresponding to an individual's successive experiences. Repeated activation through similar experiences builds meaning into our experience of the world by means of quasi-permanent connections among neurons (preferred pathways) that personalize our brain (Greenfield, 2000). This cell circuitry configured by personal experiences "is constantly updated as we live out each moment" (p. 13).

The prefrontal cortex that individualizes a brain by means of time and space referencing, which is essential for an individual's history, supports the most sophisticated part of memory. The human prefrontal cortex is twice as large as that of a primate of our weight, although our "DNA is only 1 percent different" from a chimpanzee's (Greenfield, 2000, p. 45)—which points to the heavy use and importance of this part of the human brain. The contextualization of experiences makes possible the recognition and choice of situations (rather than isolated stimuli), which provide similar pleasures. Theoretically, this can serve both hedonic optimization and homeostasis. Practically, this linkage makes us prisoners of our gradually stabilizing (closing) universe of pleasures. Responsible for this unfortunate tendency is the natural decay of our memory (i.e., deactivation of unused links), which is an efficiency bias that pushes us toward extreme and easy (sensorial) sources of pleasure and makes us disregard other activities that have either lower hedonic potential or have higher hedonic potential but are more difficult to derive pleasure from (involve more pain). Once a child has developed the habit of listening to heavy metal, he/she will have less desire to learn how to play the flute, and once a teenager has become hooked on hard porn, he/she will have less interest in books on gender psychology.

The Pleasure Race Against Nature

Autonomic Activity.   The pleasure seeker's advantages in using autonomic sources of stimulation are the "surefire" (automatically generated response/pleasure) and the simple strategy for heightening such stimulations to the level of consciousness. Autonomic pleasure (associated with the five senses and basic activities such as eating, drinking, physical activity, or sexual activity) can be enhanced by sequencing *deprivation and excess,* repeating the sequence, simultaneously applying the schema to several autonomic processes, and further synergizing by means of combinations with other nonautonomic activities/stimulations.

The additional pleasure does not come without costs, however: Both deprivation and excesses throw out of balance the neatly coordinated autonomic system and reduce its functional efficiency and/or effectiveness (cause resource dissipation/waste). If practiced long term, they may lead to physical exhaustion and illnesses. Fortunately, some natural protection mechanisms have evolved to balance human greed for pleasure and to promote homeostasis (system stability).

Adaptation.   The most basic safety mechanism is adaptation, the decay of excitation at the level of peripheral receptors (Campbell, 1973). The pleasure seeker's strategies for circumventing adaptation are *changing the sources* of stimulation and searching for *new sources.* Each novel stimulus triggers fewer associations and is more readily displaced. The turnover rate of processing novel stimuli is faster, and that keeps a pleasure seeker bombarded by his/her senses, experiencing intense pleasure (Greenfield, 2000).

Hedonic Reversal.   A second natural protection against stimulation excesses is hedonic reversal. At excessive speeds of change and at too high a stimulus density, the processing capacity is overwhelmed, and the hedonic quality of the experience is spontaneously reversed from pleasure to displeasure. "Pleasure shades into fear when the stimulation is just *too* fast and *too* novel" (Greenfield, 2000, p. 113).

One strategy for dealing with this problem is choosing sources of stimulation in such a way as to optimize arousal and thus maximize the hedonic balance. Zillmann's (1988; Bryant & Zillmann, 1984) mood *management* theory and Apter's (1994) reversal theory of enjoyment of violence endorse the notion that pleasure is a curvilinear function of arousal, with displeasure occurring at too high or too low levels of stimulation.

Another strategy for avoiding hedonic reversal is "sustaining pure pleasure" (Greenfield, 2000) by adding a *"protective frame"* (Apter, 1994, p. 9) so that the pleasure seeker does not feel in immediate unavoidable personal danger. Examples of "protected" experiences are sports, which exploit environmental dangers and control risk primarily through equipment (e.g., skydiving with a parachute); games, which exploit dangers associated with personal interactions and control risk primarily through rules and equipment; and spectacles, which exploit all possible dangers and limit risk through environment artificiality (controllability) and the indirect (vicarious) nature of the experience that gives the spectator a choice between empathy and detachment.

Habituation.   A third natural protection against excessive stimulation is habituation, a "safety cognition" that develops through repeated stimulation experiences. If an unpleasant (potentially dangerous) stimulus has not involved aggravation (in terms of harmful effects) in prior experiences, then the brain will decide "not to pay attention" simply "because there is nothing to worry about" (Campbell, 1973, p. 73).

The pleasure seeker's strategy to overcome this natural protection is beating memory on its own ground by *increasing stimulus intensity* (which heightens arousal and strengthens the memory trace) and by *repetition* (which develops chronic accessibility). A typical example is that of a teenager playing the same music over and over again and turning up the volume higher and higher: This keeps giving him/her pleasure, but it also prevents the neighbors from habituating.

RESEARCH APPROACHES TO ENTERTAINMENT

In addition to the significant contributions of philosophers and psychologists, communication researchers probed the uses and gratifications of what the mass media offered (e.g., Blumler & Katz, 1974; Katz, Gurevitch, & Haas, 1973; Palmgreen & Rayburn, 1982). Although the realization that radio and television are primarily media of entertainment was slow in coming (cf. Tannenbaum, 1980) and the acknowledgment of this *fact* continues to disillusion numerous irrepressible media idealists, the specifics of what is being consumed for what reason started to be investigated. The assessments were exploratory and largely nontheoretical. The technique was the interview, and the instrument was mainly the questionnaire. Media users reported their perceptions of why they consumed what they consumed, and they did so in unstructured or moderately to highly structured interviews (e.g., Blumler & Katz, 1974).

Assessments of this sort provided valuable insight into the entertainment consumers' beliefs about their motives for choosing this and that, as well as about their distaste for some material. The consumers' perceptions are not necessarily veridical, however, in the sense of reflecting correctly the actual motives that govern their entertainment choices. Consumers may be unaware of the actual determinants of their choices, and should they have reliable introspections of these determinants, they may be unable to articulate them. In addition, they may have cause to distort in efforts at projecting a favorable image of themselves—whatever they know and can articulate. For these reasons, it would seem prudent to consider many of the survey findings concerning people's motives for consuming entertaining fare as suggestive rather than conclusive. The motives projected on the basis of consumers' introspections could be treated as hypotheses that are yet to be subjected to testing that is capable of circumventing the problems and limitations associated with introspective assessments. Such testing is known, of course, as behavioral research.

In the study of communication phenomena, psychologists and communication researchers alike have successfully employed the behavioral approach for decades. Research has concentrated on persuasion (e.g., Rosnow & Robinson, 1967), interpersonal communication (e.g., Berscheid & Waister, 1969; Miller, 1966), nonverbal communication (e.g., Harper, Wiens, & Matarazzo, 1978; Knapp, 1978), and on the impact of asocial (e.g., Donnerstein, 1980; Geen, 1976) and prosocial messages (e.g., Rushton, 1979). Oddly enough, until recently nobody saw fit to apply the behavioral approach to the study of why people enjoy whatever they enjoy by way of entertainment. Only recently has research been published that probes the determinants of enjoyment and enlightenment in a behavioral fashion and is designed to test proposals deriving from survey research on motives as well as from motivation and emotion theory generally.

In this chapter, we attempt to provide an overview of what has been accomplished in this behavioral exploration of entertainment consumption and its immediate affective effects. The reader who is interested specifically in the perceptions of what makes consumers choose whatever they choose is referred to up-to-date reviews of the pertinent research by Atkin (1985) and Rubin (chap. 20). We briefly inspect the exploration of entertainment choices and then turn to theory and research concerning the enjoyment of entertaining messages.

SELECTIVE EXPOSURE TO ENTERTAINMENT

In making entertainment choices, people can be very deliberate. A particular program might have attracted their attention, they may have decided to watch it, and they may be determined to turn to it once it becomes available. Such deliberate choices appear to be the exception, however. The choice of entertainment is usually made "on impulse." The program that holds the greatest appeal at a given time and under given circumstances, for whatever particular reasons, is likely to be picked. The factors that determine this appeal tend to be unclear to many if not most respondents. When using traditional, noninteractive media, it would be the rare exception for respondents to engage in formal and explicit evaluative comparisons of the choices before them. It is more likely that they make these choices rather "mindlessly," without using reliable and never-changing criteria in their appeal assessments and ultimately in their choices. Once the proposal is accepted that most entertainment choices are made spontaneously, rather than calculated like business deals, it can be projected that these choices are situationally variable and serve ends of which respondents need not be and probably are not aware.

These arguments have resulted in two theories that have received substantial empirical support: selective-exposure theory (e.g., Zillmann & Bryant, 1985) and mood-management theory (e.g., Zillmann, 1988, 2000c). Mood-management theory often resides on the methodological shoulders of selective-exposure theory and posits, "Persons tend to arrange their stimulus environments so as to increase the likelihood that bad moods are short lived and their experiential intensity is reduced, that good moods are prolonged and their experiential intensity is enhanced, and that bad moods are terminated and superseded by good moods of the highest possible experiential intensity" (Zillmann, 2000c, pp. 103–104).

Excitement Versus Relaxation as Ends

Entertaining fare can produce considerable excitement in respondents (cf. Zillmann, 1982). Such excitement manifests itself in obtrusive sympathetic dominance in the autonomic nervous system, among other things, and it produces intense affective reactions. Hedonically speaking, these reactions can be positive or negative, depending on the respondents' idiosyncratic appraisals of what transpired. Television's capacity to produce excitement is obviously greater for persons experiencing low levels of excitation than for persons already experiencing high levels. To the extent that this capacity might influence entertainment choices, it should do so more strongly for people who suffered through a hapless day characterized by monotonous and boring chores than for people who were confronted with uncertainty, competition, and other pressures—in short, people who suffer from overstimulation and stress. Under the assumption that levels of excitation that vary within a normal range constitute a necessary, though not sufficient, condition for an individual's feelings of well-being, it has been proposed (Zillmann & Bryant, 1985) that entertainment from television or elsewhere might be employed to regulate excitation. Understimulated, bored persons should be eager to expose themselves to exciting television fare. Even if the material is not intrinsically pleasant, such exposure should be pleasantly experienced because it brings these persons back to levels of excitation that are more closely linked to feeling good. If the materials are intrinsically enjoyable, all the better. Thus, for understimulated, bored persons, exposure to exciting television programs can be seen as having the benefit of returning them conveniently (i.e., with minimal effort and safely) to a hedonically superior and, hence, desirable state. Put bluntly, entertainment consumers of this kind should be appreciative of each and every arousal kick that television or any other medium provides (Tannenbaum, 1980).

But entertainment not only has the capacity to excite. It can soothe and calm as well (cf. Zillmann, 1982). This capacity may benefit those who are uptight, upset, annoyed, angry, mad, or otherwise disturbed. All these experiences are associated with sympathetic hyperactivity, and those who experience such hyperactivity obviously would profit from exposure to nonexciting, relaxing entertainment fare because this exposure would lower these persons' excitation and return it to more desirable levels. Stressed persons, then, would do well to avoid exciting fare and to seek out materials capable of calming them down.

Intuitive Grounds

Television's excitation- and mood-altering effects are not in doubt. But can it be assumed that, in selecting programs for viewing, people make choices that serve excitatory homeostasis? Do people do what is good for them spontaneously and without reflection? Can it be assumed that bored persons prefer exciting materials over relaxing ones and that stressed persons display the opposite preference? It can, indeed, based on the premise that bored persons experience relief when watching exciting programs, that stressed people experience relief when watching relaxing programs, and that the experience of relief constitutes negative reinforcement that shapes initially random choice patterns into mood-specific entertainment preferences (cf. Zillmann & Bryant, 1985). The proposal that people form mood-specific preferences (i.e., behave as if they had a tacit understanding of what is good for them under particular affective circumstances) has been supported by experimental research (Bryant & Zillmann, 1984). Research participants were placed into states of boredom versus stress and then, ostensibly in a waiting period, allowed to watch television as they pleased. Their choice was among three exciting and three relaxing programs. Time of program consumption was unobtrusively recorded. The data revealed that exciting programs attracted bored participants significantly more than stressed participants and that relaxing programs attracted stressed participants significantly more than bored participants.

Effects of self-determined exposure on excitation were assessed as well, and it was found that almost all participants had chosen materials that helped them to escape effectively from undesirable excitatory states. In fact, almost all participants overcorrected; that is, bored participants ended up above base levels and stressed ones below base levels of excitation. The few bored participants that failed to behave in line with expectations elected to watch relaxing fare and, as a result, remained in a state of subnormal excitation.

Affective Relief as an End

The tacit understanding of the benefits that accrue to consuming entertainment fare is not limited to exciting and calming materials but extends to other message characteristics. Experimental research has provided evidence that people select programs that are involving to different degrees as a function of their affective states. Choices are such that persons who would affectively benefit from distraction (i.e., rid themselves of a bad mood) tend to select highly absorbing fare. Those with less need for distraction show less appetite for this kind of material (cf. Zillmann & Bryant, 1985). And those confronted with acute problems from which distraction through entertainment cannot offer any escape or prompt relief (e.g., anger from provocation that demands corrective action) tend to stay away from entertainment altogether, at least temporarily (Christ & Medoff, 1984).

In seeking mood changes for the better (i.e., in terminating bad moods, in switching over into good moods, or in facilitating and extending good moods), humor and comedy appear to play a special role. To those in acute need of some cheering up, merriment and laughter must be assumed to hold considerable appeal. Generally speaking, entertainment that seems capable of stimulating positive affect immediately and frequently should be the pick of those suffering from the blahs. These people should be strongly inclined to choose comedy and its kin over alternative, competing offerings.

An investigation that makes this point most compellingly has been conducted with women at different stages in the menstrual cycle (Meadowcroft & Zillmann, 1984). On the premise that the premenstrual syndrome is created mainly by the rapid withdrawal of progesterone and estrogen that afforded anesthetizing protection earlier, it was argued that premenstrual and menstrual women should suffer from bad moods, *if* not from feelings of depression. As a result, these women should experience the greatest need for relief through merriment and laughter. Midway through the cycle, when estrogen levels are elevated and progesterone levels rise, this need should be less pronounced, if existent at all. As there is little that premenstrual and menstrual women can do about their misery, comedy of any kind offers a most convenient way out and, consequently, should become highly attractive.

To test this proposition, women were asked to select programs they would enjoy watching. They chose from among known situation comedies, action dramas, and game shows. Their position in the cycle was ascertained afterward. On the basis of the latter information, the women were placed into 4-day phase groups throughout the cycle, thus allowing the tracing of programs chosen for consumption as a function of hormonal conditions. In confirmation of the hypothesis, it was found that premenstrual and menstrual women are indeed significantly more eager to expose themselves to comedy than are women in other phases of the cycle. At midcycle, the women exhibited comparatively little interest in comedy and showed appetite for drama instead. On gloomy days, then, comedy becomes hyperattractive. If the behavior of the premenstrual and menstrual women is any indication, all people who are down on their luck may be expected to seek, and obtain, mood lifts from comedy.

The findings concerning cycle position and comedy choice were recently extended by Helregel and Weaver (1989). These investigators addressed the variation in progesterone and estrogen during and after pregnancy and observed that low concentrations of these hormones were associated with depressive moods. More importantly, however, they observed that during these depressed mood states the women exhibited a strong preference for comedy.

But comedy is not by necessity a mood improver. Television comedy, in particular, is laden with teasing and demeaning happenings, even with considerable hostility (Zillmann, 1977). Material of this sort is unlikely to amuse persons who have recently been targets of similarly debasing actions because exposure to the material will tend to reinstate the unpleasantness and the annoyance from the treatments in question. Acutely angry persons, for example, cannot expect favorable mood changes from comedy that dwells on hostile actions. Angry persons thus would be well advised to refrain from exposure to such comedy, though not from other *forms* of comedy. Experimental research again shows that people behave as if they had tacit knowledge of these effects. Provoked, angry persons were found to refrain from watching hostile comedy and to turn to alternative offerings (Zillmann, Hezel, & Medoff, 1980).

Research by O'Neal and Taylor (1989) revealed an interesting exception to the indicated relief-seeking. It was found that angry men who believe they will get a chance to retaliate against their tormentor selected violent material over alternative, potentially calming choices. This was in contrast to equally angry men who believed they would not encounter their annoyer again. These men preferred calming material. It appears, then, that when the maintenance of a noxious emotion, such as anger, has utility, persons refrain from seeking relief and rather choose material likely to keep their emotion going.

Interestingly, children as young as 4 and 5 years of age are already capable of using television fare to improve their mood states. In an experiment by Masters, Ford, and Arend (1983), boys and girls of this age were placed into a nurturant, neutral, or hostile social environment and then provided with an opportunity to watch children's television programs. In the neutral condition, the participants received the same treatment from an adult supervisor as did a same-gender peer. In the nurturant or good-mood condition, the supervisor repeatedly criticized and belittled the peer; by implication the participant was doing fine. In the hostile or bad-mood condition, the supervisor continually and obtrusively admired and praised the participant's companion. Participants in this condition were thus made to feel unimportant, disliked, and rejected. Once the different affective states had been induced, the participants were allowed to watch television for as long as they pleased. They were free to shut off the monitor on which only one program could be received. This program was either nurturant or neutral. The nurturant one was composed of segments from *Mister Rogers' Neighborhood*. Mr. Rogers was highly supportive at all times, making nurturant comments like "I really like you," and "You know, you are a nice person." The neutral program consisted of new shows for children that presented world events devoid of emotional content. The time the children elected to watch one or the other program served as a measure of exposure.

The effects were clear-cut and as expected for boys. Boys treated in a hostile manner stayed with the nurturant program more than twice as long as boys treated in a nurturant manner. Boys in a good mood exhibited the least need for exposure to nurturant fare. In contrast, the mood treatment had no appreciable effect on exposure to the neutral program. For girls, the mood treatment had apparently failed. Girls confronted with the supervisor who treated them nonnurturantly coped with this situation by paying minimal attention to the discriminating treatment, and reliable exposure effects could not be observed.

Recent research has revealed that popular music can aid in mood management. Knobloch and Zillmann (in press) selected popular music from Billboard Top-30 charts and pretested it for energy level and joyfulness. In an experiment, respondents were placed in states of bad versus neutral versus good moods and given an opportunity to select music to which they listened via a computerized "jukebox." Consistent with predictions from mood-management theory, respondents in bad moods chose to listen to highly energetic–joyful music for longer periods than did respondents in good moods. Moreover, the energetic–joyful music they selected was quite effective in restoring respondents to good moods.

Avoiding Discomfort

The boys in the study by Masters et al. (1983) may have found relief in the exposure experience and tried to extend that experience because it felt so good. The information that was offered in the television program was apparently comforting to those in acute need of being comforted. However, the program that proved comforting might be classified as education rather than entertainment. The question thus arises: Can pure entertainment provide comfort? Is it used to obtain comfort or, at least, to minimize and avert discomfort? The research-based answer is, Surely!

How exposure to entertaining fare can provide comfort and help avoid discomfort in adult respondents has been discussed elsewhere (e.g., Zillmann, 1982; Zillmann & Bryant, 1985). Here we concentrate on the spontaneous selection of entertaining programs and on the tendency in this selection to choose programs that are likely to minimize discomfort through avoidance of disturbing events and, at the same time, maximize comfort through the provision of pacifying information.

An experiment conducted by Wakshlag, Vial, and Tamborini (1983) shows these selection tendencies most clearly. Male and female adults were placed in a state of apprehension about becoming victims of crime, especially violent crime, and later given an opportunity to select entertaining drama for consumption. The differently apprehensive participants chose from a list of film synopses, which had been pretested and received scores for the degree to which a film was perceived as featuring violent victimization and/or the punitive restoration of justice. Measures of the appeal of violence and justice were obtained by summing the scores across the films that were selected.

The findings revealed strong gender differences in the appeal of both violent victimization and justice restoration. Females responded less favorably to violence than did males. At the same time, they were attracted more strongly than males to justice restoration as a salient theme of drama. Irrespective of these overall gender differences, both crime-apprehensive males and crime-apprehensive females proved equally sensitive to the drama dimensions under consideration. Acutely apprehensive persons selected drama that was lower in violent victimization and higher in justice restoration than did their nonapprehensive counterparts. Apprehensive persons thus exhibited the proposed tendency to minimize exposure to disturbing events. Moreover, they exhibited the proposed tendency to expose themselves to information capable of diminishing their apprehensions. The main message of television crime drama—namely, that criminals are being caught and put away, which should make the streets safer—apparently holds great appeal for those who worry about crime (cf. Zillmann, 1980).

The reader who is interested in a more complete accounting of the research on selective exposure is referred to a recent collection of exposés on that topic (Zillmann & Bryant, 1985). The purpose of the discussion here is only to highlight recent behavioral research into selective exposure to entertainment and to indicate the emerging choice-controlling variables.

ENJOYMENT OF ENTERTAINMENT

Quite obviously, mass media entertainment does not merely serve the regulation of arousal and associated affect or produce a contagion with merriment for persons in need of overcoming the blahs. Entertaining messages are capable of gratifying respondents because of unique intrinsic properties, along with the respondents' idiosyncratic appraisals of these properties. But what are these properties? What are the ingredients of good entertainment? And what properties spoil enjoyment?

The enjoyment of drama, comedy, and sports is influenced by a multitude of variables, many of which have received considerable attention (e.g., Goldstein, 1979; Jauss, 1982). But none seem to control enjoyment as strongly and as universally as do affective dispositions toward interacting parties, especially parties confronted with problems, conflict, and aversive conditions. The exhibition of human conflict in the raw has often been singled out as the stuff of which all good drama is made (e.g., Smiley, 1971). The focus on conflict constitutes only a starting point, however. The dramatic portrayal of intense conflict, in and of itself, does not with any degree of regularity, certainly not by necessity, lead to enjoyment reactions in the audience. Enjoyment depends not so much on conflict as on its resolution and on what the resolution means to the parties involved. It depends on how much those who come out on top are liked and loved and on how much those who come out on the short end are disliked and hated. Good drama, then, relies on positive and negative sentiments toward the parties in conflict and on the extent to which the audience can accept a resolution. Indifference toward protagonists and antagonists is the antidote to good drama. Positive and negative affective dispositions toward the agents in drama are vital and must be created if drama is to evoke strong emotions, enjoyment included. There need be beloved heroes (regardless of how their definition might change over the years), and there need be villains whom the audience can love to hate.

Dispositions and Affective Reactions

The response side of what is commonly referred to as "character development" is affect. The portrayal of goodness in protagonists is to make them likable and lovable. Analogously, the portrayal of evil in antagonists is to make them dislikable and hateable. To the extent that any intended character development works, it produces positive and negative dispositions toward the agents of a play.

Character development is effective, generally speaking, because respondents bring empathy and, more important, moral considerations to the screen. What the agents in a play do matters the most. It is the basis for the audience's approval or disapproval of conduct. Such approval or disapproval is a moral verdict, of course. The fact that this is not generally recognized by respondents (and those who study their behavior) does not alter that circumstance. Approval of conduct is assumed to promote liking; disapproval is assumed to promote disliking. Affective dispositions toward protagonists and antagonists derive in large measure from moral considerations (cf. Zillmann, 1991c).

Once an audience has thus placed its sentiments pro and con particular characters, enjoyment of conflict and its resolution in drama depends on the ultimate outcome for the loved and hated parties. Positive affective dispositions inspire hopes of positive outcomes and fears of negative ones. Protagonists are deemed deserving of good fortunes and utterly undeserving of bad ones. Negative affective dispositions, on the other hand, activate the opposite inclinations: fear of positive outcomes and hopes for negative ones. Antagonists are deemed utterly undeserving of good fortunes and deserving of bad ones. Such hopes and fears are obviously mediated by moral considerations.

These hopes and fears lead respondents to empathize with the emotions displayed by protagonists. The joys as well as the suffering of liked characters tend to evoke concordant affect in the audience. Positive and negative affect is said to be "shared." In contrast, these hopes and fears prompt counterempathetic reactions to the emotions experienced by antagonists. The villains' joy is the audience's distress, and their suffering, their being brought to justice, and their getting their comeuppance is the audience's delight (cf. Zillmann, 1983, 1991a). These basic dynamics of affect in spectators are summarized in Fig. 21.1.

Although these dynamics of affect have been outlined in dichotomous terms, they should not be construed as merely dichotomous. They should be thought of as a dichotomous system underneath which continuous variables exist. Liking and disliking of characters are clearly matters of degree, and the projection of consequences for the enjoyment of events and final outcomes must take this into account. In more formal terms, the following predictions can be stated (cf. Zillmann, 1980):

1. Enjoyment deriving from witnessing the debasement, failure, or defeat of a party, agent, or object increases with the intensity of negative sentiment and decreases with the intensity of positive sentiment toward these entities.

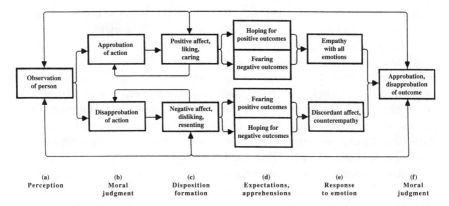

FIG. 21.1. A model of disposition formation, affective expectations, and emotional responding to benefited and punished characters in drama (from Zillmann, 1991a; reprinted with permission).

2. Enjoyment deriving from witnessing the enhancement, success, or victory of a party, agent, or object decreases with the intensity of negative sentiment and increases with the intensity of positive sentiment toward these entities.
3. Annoyance deriving from witnessing the debasement, failure, or defeat of a party, agent, or object decreases with the intensity of negative sentiment and increases with the intensity of positive sentiment toward these entities.
4. Annoyance deriving from witnessing the enhancement, success, or victory of a party, agent, or object increases with the intensity of negative sentiment and decreases with the intensity of positive sentiment toward these entities.
5. Propositions 1 through 4 apply jointly. Consequently, all contributions to enjoyment and/or annoyance combine in total enjoyment or annoyance. In this integration of contributions, annoyance is conceived of as negative enjoyment, and contributions to enjoyment and to annoyance are assumed to combine in an additive fashion.

Predictions from this disposition model have been confirmed not only for the enjoyment of drama, but also for humor appreciation and the enjoyment of sports (Zillmann & Bryant, 1991; Zillmann, Bryant, & Sapolsky, 1979; Zillmann & Cantor, 1976). Comedy can, of course, be construed as a form of drama that differs from drama proper only in that cues abound that signal that things are not to be taken too seriously (McGhee, 1979). Most tendentious jokes (i.e., hostile and/or sexual ones in which somebody is victimized) can also be construed as dramatic episodes—

miniaturized ones, to be sure—in which there is conflict that is resolved in favor of a deserving party and to the detriment of a victim who had it coming. Setting someone up for the punch line is nothing other than making him or her deserving of the humorous knockdown.

The dispositional mechanics of enjoyment are most obvious in sports spectatorship. Sports fans have favorite players and teams. They also have players and teams that they detest with considerable intensity. Seeing a beloved competing party humble and humiliate a resented one obviously constitutes the ultimate in sports enjoyment. And the reverse outcome is the kind of event that can make grown men cry. It is clear, in addition, that indifference toward persons or teams in a contest is the kind of condition under which excitement and intense enjoyment cannot materialize. Hirt, Zillmann, Erickson, and Kennedy (1992) provided compelling evidence for these mechanics and showed that the projected emotions transcend enjoyment or despair proper. Enjoyment from seeing a beloved team win was found to elevate the fans' self-esteem and enhance confidence in their physical, mental, and social abilities and skills. Despair from seeing their beloved team defeated, in contrast, deflated self-esteem and diminished confidence in their own talents. Surely, in the enjoyment of athletic events, there are many other factors that must be considered (Zillmann et al., 1979). But the dispositional mechanics seem of overriding significance in the enjoyment of dramatic confrontations of any kind.

On Thrills and Suspense

After cursory inspection, the enjoyment of suspenseful drama may strike one as being contradictory, even paradoxical. Such drama tends to be enjoyed despite the fact that for most of its duration the protagonist or protagonists (i.e., those dear to the audience) are seen in duress and in peril; they appear to be doomed (Zillmann, 1980, 1991c). Over considerable periods of time, the heroes are tormented and about to be overpowered and destroyed by evil forces or extraordinary dangers. Dreaded, disastrous happenings are imminent—repeatedly, frequently, and in the latest action-packed raids on the audience, almost continually. How can anybody, under these circumstances, enjoy drama? The dominant affective experience should be one of empathetic distress. Surely, such distress is relieved at times when the feared and seemingly imminent events fail to materialize and, especially in the resolution, when in the grandest of fashions and usually against all odds, the protagonists overcome the dangers that threatened them and destroy the evil forces manifesting these dangers, too. At times, of course, the resolution is less full fledged, and the protagonists merely get away with dear life (e.g., the survivors of typical disaster movies). Contemporary horror movies tend to take that format also, as tormented ladies barely escape the chain saws, and the villains are spared for the sequel. But even in these resolutions that do not feature the annihilation of evil forces, there is cause for jubilation, and the resolution can be deemed satisfying.

Generally speaking, then, suspenseful drama exhibits much of the condition describable as "hero in peril," but it also offers a resolution that is satisfying, if only minimally so. The indicated paradox consists of the fact that such drama should evoke more empathetic distress than euphoria, at least in terms of time. It should be suffered more—or more accurately, longer—than it should be enjoyed. How can this formula work for non-masochistic audiences?

One explanation is that the persons attracted to such drama are sufficiently understimulated and bored to appreciate any shake-up of their excitatory state (Tannenbaum, 1980; Zillmann, 1991b; Zuckerman, 1979). If arousal levels are subnormal, excitatory reactions—even those derived from distress—can help return arousal to more pleasantly experienced levels. The safety and convenience of the exposure situation make it unlikely that levels rise to uncomfortable heights. Still, the immediate affective experience associated with any arousal kicks tends to be construed as negative in valence, and this seems to favor a more elaborate explanation.

According to the alternative account, residues of excitation from empathetic distress and/or from the response to the threatening stimuli persist through resolutions and intensify the euphoric experience that is evoked by these resolutions. Because the magnitude of residual excitation is greater the more intense the distressful experience, it follows that the enjoyment of satisfying resolutions will be the more intensified the greater (and more immediate) the preceding distress reaction. The simple consequence of this is that suspenseful drama will be the more enjoyable, the more the audience is initially made to suffer, through empathy with the endangered protagonists and/or any duress induced by those dangers with which the protagonists struggled. Great enjoyment rides the back of great distress. Evidence for this relationship has been provided by numerous experimental investigations of suspenseful drama (Zillmann, 1980, 1991c).

The intensification of the enjoyment of favorable final outcomes by residual excitation from preceding uncertainty and distress should apply to the appreciation of athletic performances, too. A liked team's victory after a close, tense game should be more enjoyable than a similar victory that was decided early in the contest (Sapolsky, 1980). An investigation by Bryant, Rockwell, and Owens (1994) supported this contention experimentally. A high school football game was videotaped with multiple cameras, edited, and embellished with different versions of play-by-play and color commentary. Conditions were created under which viewers of the various versions of the game saw play in which the outcome was decided either early in the game or on the very last play of the game—a field goal. Enjoyment of the game was more pronounced when the outcome was decided as the clock expired.

Gan, Tuggle, Mitrook, Coussement, and Zillmann (1997) found substantial gender differences in the enjoyment of suspenseful televised sports contests. For men, the higher the level of suspense, the more they enjoyed the game. In marked contrast, when watching extremely suspenseful games, women's enjoyment dropped to the same level as for minimally suspenseful games. Additional research yielded a "gender gap" in the enjoyment of a wide variety of televised sporting events (Sargent, Zillmann, & Weaver, 1998).

Tragic Events and Bad News

The phenomenon that is most puzzling in the projection of enjoyment from the discussed disposition model is the apparent appeal of tragedy and news reports about disasters and the like. The persons who are witnessed suffering misfortunes and grievous occurrences are, as a rule, not resented and not considered deserving of tragic happenings. However, despite the fact that fiction often entails circumstances that make a tragic outcome more acceptable (e.g., the hero's so-called tragic flaw), it need not be assumed that the immediate affective reactions to the portrayal of tragic events are in any way positive. In all probability, these immediate reactions are negative, even intensely so. Tearjerkers are, after all, known to jerk tears, and negative affect in response to newscasts on tragic events is not in doubt (Veitch & Griffitt, 1976). This makes the fascination with seeing the victimization of parties that are neither disliked nor deemed deserving of what happens to them all the more bewildering. Granted that tragic drama is not exactly the main course of popular drama, it does enjoy a considerable following that needs to be explained. The same applies, outside fiction, to the appeal of bad news in print and broadcast journalism, which is said to be ubiquitous and growing in popularity (Haskins, 1981). Even acutely annoyed men, who would emotionally benefit from exposure to good or affectively neutral news, cannot resist the lure of bad news about misfortunes, mayhem, and disasters (Biswas, Riffe, & Zillmann, 1994). What needs might be satisfied by exposure to tragic happenings? And how can such exposure be gratifying, if it is gratifying in some way?

Some have postulated that the fascination with tragic events reflects morbid curiosity (Haskins, 1981). Others have suggested that responding sadly to the sadness of suffering people affords respondents an opportunity to celebrate their own emotional sensitivity (Smith, 1759/1971). Sobbing through a tearjerker is proof to oneself that a valued social skill is abundantly present. Yet others have emphasized that exposure to tragic events invites social comparison, that respondents contrast their own situation with that of the suffering parties they witness, and that this contrasting eventually produces a form of satisfaction (Aust, 1984). Seeing misfortunes befall others and seeing them suffering from it thus may make viewers cognizant and appreciative of how good they have it. And as such positive feelings accrue to seeing tragedy strike, in reality or in fiction, tragedy becomes appealing despite the negative affect that is initially associated with it.

All these explanatory efforts remain conjecture at present. Research has failed to elucidate the response to the exhibition of tragedy in people's lives. Not only does it remain unclear why respondents are initially drawn to watching truly tragic events, but it remains particularly puzzling why exposure is sought repeatedly, as it seems likely that immediate responses were noxious and noxious experiences are generally avoided. Understanding tragedy and, in particular, the popularity of bad news thus poses a formidable challenge to entertainment research.

Audience Influences

Much of the consumption of entertaining messages occurs in particular social situations. Going to the movies is an event that usually involves friends or that happens in the context of dating (Mendelsohn, 1966). Going to see an athletic contest similarly tends to involve well-known others. Television fare is also consumed in the company of such others, but with one big difference: The television audience is limited to comparatively small numbers, in contrast to the backdrop of large audiences composed of unknown others at the movies or, especially, at athletic events.

Given these social circumstances, it should not be surprising to find that a considerable amount of speculation exists that deals with the consequences of specific social conditions for the enjoyment of the entertaining event, even with the consequences of the entertaining event for cohesion in the audience and for affective inclinations among members of that audience. Regarding the latter effect, Ovid (*Artis amatoriae*) was one of the first to propose that audience members' romantic passions might be enhanced by arousing, potentially violent, and bloody entertaining events. His intuition has actually received experimental support in recent years (e.g., White, Fishbein, & Rutstein, 1981). But many other socially relevant effects on the audience have remained unexplored, in spite of the fact that they are highly obtrusive on occasion. For instance, winning an Olympic hockey match against a powerful nation, especially when the victory comes unexpectedly, seems to have the capacity for uniting—for a limited period—a nation in some not so tangible way. In a similar vein, entire communities become high-spirited cities of champions when they have a winning team or fall into gloom if their athletic entertainers fail to defeat the out-of-towners. Effects of this kind have received little attention by researchers. Rigorous exploration is difficult and, presumably for this reason, virtually nonexistent (Schwarz, Strack, Kommer, & Wagner, 1987; Schweitzer, Zillmann, Weaver, & Luttrell, 1992).

The exploration of the effects of social conditions of consumption on the enjoyment of entertaining events has met with greater success but is quite incomplete nonetheless. The best-documented phenomenon of this kind is the facilitative influence of others' laughter on the laughter of respondents (e.g., Chapman, 1973b; Chapman & Wright, 1976; Fuller & Sheehy-Skeffington, 1974; Smyth & Fuller, 1972). Even the canned laughter that accompanies comedy and humorous situations has been found to enhance laughter in child and adult audiences; moreover, it has been found to increase enjoyment in many, though not in all, instances (e.g., Chapman, 1973a; Cupchik & Leventhal, 1974; Leventhal & Cupchik, 1975; Leventhal & Mace, 1970). Persons responding to humor appear to take the reactions of others as a cue that signals the extent to which the events before them are laughable and, ultimately, enjoyable. The facilitative effect of others' laughter on laughter and enjoyment, then, seems to derive from the informational utility of the reactions of others rather than from a mechanical contagion that produces laughter, which, through self-monitoring, eventually leads to a distorted appraisal of enjoyment. Such an interpretation is suggested by the finding that a model's laughter in response to particular stimuli tends to enhance an observer's laughter to these stimuli at a later time; that is, laughter is enhanced in the absence of the laughter of others that could function as an immediate stimulus for laughter in observers and thus serve contagion (Brown, Brown, & Ramos, 1981; Brown, Wheeler, & Cash, 1980).

Applause in response to musical performances functions analogously. As others' laughter makes humor appear funnier, others' applause makes music seem better. Hocking, Margreiter, and Hylton (1977), for instance, succeeded in planting numerous confederates into a nightclub, and members of the audience later evaluated the quality of the band and its music. This quality was deemed higher on nights when the confederates showed delight by applauding enthusiastically than on nights when they failed to do so.

Oddly enough, where the social facilitation of enjoyment is thought to be least in doubt—namely, in the cheering, quasi-hysterical crowds at athletic events—research has failed us, and we must continue to trust journalistic assertions (Hocking, 1982). Research on the effects of the social conditions under which athletic contests are watched on television has proven similarly uninformative. Audience size, for instance, could not be shown to exert an appreciable degree of influence on the enjoyment of a game (Sapolsky & Zillmann, 1978).

Audience size, in and of itself, may not have the impact that many feel it has. What people in the audience do, in contrast, seems to matter greatly. In many instances, the expression of particular emotions may well affect similar emotions in those amidst an expressive audience. The effects can be far more complicated, however, than any model of empathetic contagion and escalation would suggest.

A specific kind of influence of a companion's behavior on the enjoyment of drama has been demonstrated for horror movies. In an investigation by Zillmann, Weaver, Mundorf, and Aust (1986), participants saw terrifying events from the latest horror flicks in the presence of an opposite-gender confederate who gave ample indication of being terrified in a distress condition, gave no indication of affective responsiveness in a neutral condition, or gave clear signs of taking things with the greatest of ease in a mastery condition. Following exposure to the materials, participants reported their enjoyment.

Could their enjoyment be affected by these audience conditions and, if so, in what way? Those who believe in affective contagion might expect the terrified companion to enhance similar reactions in the participants and, because the object of horror movies is to terrify the audience, the film is deemed scarier and, hence, better and more enjoyable, at least in retrospect. It could also be conjectured that seeing horror with a terrified companion enhances enjoyment in those who enjoy being scared and/or seeing others scared and that it diminishes enjoyment in those who detest being scared and/or seeing others scared. But the findings are consistent with another model that is somewhat more elaborate yet also more obvious.

On the premise that in our own and in most other societies young men are expected to master fear-arousing situations and, if scared, to deny such a response, whereas young women are allowed, if not encouraged, to express their distress freely, it can be argued that horror films, for better or worse, are a significant socializing institution. The horror genre provides a forum in which persons can confront terrifying happenings such as gruesome maimings and killings, and they can do so safely (i.e., without suffering bodily harm). Respondents can gauge their emotional reactions, and in case these reactions should become overly intense, they can curb them by discounting the disturbing events as mere fiction. The reactions are thus always bearable, and thanks to excitatory habituation (cf. Zillmann, 1982), they should grow smaller with repeated exposure to similar stimuli.

Boys and young men apparently benefit most from such habituation. As their distress reactions diminish, they can more readily pretend not to be distressed at all. In fact, they should become proficient in denying any distress by expressing amusement or by similarly belittling the terrifying events before them. How better to exhibit mastery of terror than by waving it off with a smile? And what better companion for showing off this mastery than an apparently terrified female? The presence of such a female, compared to a less-expressive one or, worst of all, one that exhibits mastery herself, should make the male feel great because (a) the movie is obviously scary, and (b) he is so cool about it that he could virtually comfort his disturbed companion. Young women, on the other hand, are not burdened with acculturation pressures toward callousness. They can live through and express their dismay. But as they do, an equally frightened male companion renders little comfort. He who effectively pretends not to be disturbed about the terrifying happenings is the one who radiates security, and a terrified female should feel inclined to seek comfort with him rather than with his more sensitive (or less callous) counterparts. The frightened maiden's desire to snuggle up on the macho companion is a cliché for horror movies. If there is any truth to it, we can see why boys want to master, why girls want to scream, and why both parties want to go to such movies in the first place. We can see the implications of entertainment consumption for falling in love. But what about enjoyment of the movies themselves? Here it may be assumed that persons do not fully comprehend what it is that gives them pleasure. They do not neatly identify the sources of their enjoyment and trace different contributions. Rather, they are likely to come to a global assessment of how much they enjoyed a particular movie. Enjoyment that derives from the social circumstances of consumption tends to go unrecognized and is usually misattributed to the entertaining message.

According to this, young men should enjoy horror more in the company of an apparently frightened female companion than in the company of an unexpressive or mastering female. Young women, on the other hand, should enjoy horror more in the company of a mastering male companion than in the company of an unexpressive or distressed male. The experimental investigation (Zillmann et al., 1986) confirmed just that very strongly.

CONCLUDING REMARKS

This brief introduction to research into the entertainment experience is necessarily incomplete. The interested reader is referred to the various cited summaries of research in particular domains (i.e., the exploration of enjoyment from suspense, comedy, horror, or sports). But granted incompleteness, this exposition should make the point that it is most meaningful to treat the entertainment experience as an effect. It is, in fact, *the* effect of entertainment consumption. It is the primary effect that is sought out and pursued for the benefits that it entails—benefits such as being distracted from acute grievances, having boredom removed, being cheered up, being given great excitement, being helped to calm down, or being fed pacifying messages. Surely, many media analysts might be inclined to label the attainment of these benefits *escapism*. Heavy consumption of entertainment is indeed likely to be maladaptive in the sense that problems that could be resolved by appropriate action remain unresolved and may grow to calamity levels. The consumption of much entertainment does not fit such an account, however. Consumption is often not just not maladaptive; it can be highly adaptive. This is the case when consumption serves to improve on prevailing moods, affects, and emotions, shifting them from bad to good or from good to better, under conditions in which undesirable states cannot be eliminated and altered through well-targeted action. What should an individual who comes home exhausted from a long day's work in a steel mill or, for that matter, in an executive office do about this undesirable situation? And what can a woman with premenstrual pains do about the pain-inducing conditions? If entertainment consumption manages to calm them down, cheer them up, and get them ready for the next similarly trying day, is it fair to condemn such benefit as escapism? Would it not be more reasonable to accept such effects on mood and emotional well-being as recreational success?

But regardless of how media analysts might elect to characterize the effects in question, the fact remains that much entertainment is consumed to alter moods, affects, and emotions in the specified fashion; moreover, the fact remains that the desired effects come about with considerable regularity. De facto, then, the consumption of much entertainment has beneficial consequences. It is adaptive, recreational, restorative, and in this sense, therapeutic. This is not to say that all of entertainment necessarily has these effects or that massive consumption has benefits. Quite obviously, numerous highly undesirable side effects exist. This volume gives ample testimony to that. It is to say, however, that entertainment provided by the so-called mass media can provide highly beneficial emotional experiences that are truly recreational and that may be uplifting. These effects of entertainment, presumably because of the ready condemnation of entertainment as cheap escapism, have received very little attention from researchers. We feel that some reevaluation is in order, and we hope that the exploration of the entertainment experience with its consequences for the emotional welfare of the consumers of entertaining fare will receive the attention that it deserves.

REFERENCES

Anderson, E. (2001). *Hedonism and the happy life: The Epicurean theory of pleasure.* Retrieved March 13, 2001, from http://www.epicureans.org/intro.htm.

Apter, M. J. (1994, October). *Why we enjoy media violence: A reversal theory approach.* Paper presented at the International Conference on Violence in the Media, St. John's University, New York, NY.

Atkin, C. (1985). Informational utility and selective exposure to entertainment media. In D. Zillmann & J. Bryant (Eds.), *Selective exposure to communication* (pp. 63–82). Hillsdale, NJ: Lawrence Erlbaum Associates.

Aristotle (1999). *Poetics.* Cambridge, MA: Harvard University Press.

Aust, C. F. (1984). *The effect of bad news on respondents' satisfaction with their own situation.* Unpublished master's thesis, Indiana University, Bloomington.

Bargh, J. A. (1997). The automaticity of everyday life. In R. S. Wyer, Jr. (Ed.), *Advances in social cognition* (Vol. 10, pp. 1–61). Mahwah, NJ: Lawrence Erlbaum Associates.

Berscheid, E., & Waister, E. (1969). *Interpersonal attraction.* Reading, MA: Addison-Wesley.

Biswas, R., Riffe, D., & Zillmann, D. (1994). Mood influence on the appeal of bad news. *Journalism Quarterly, 71,* 689–696.

Blumler, J. C., & Katz, E. (Eds.). (1974). *The uses of mass communication: Current perspectives on gratifications research.* Beverly Hills, CA: Sage.

Bok, S. (1998). *Mayhem: Violence as public entertainment.* Reading, MA: Merloyd Lawrence & Addison-Wesley.

Bousfield, P. (1999). *Pleasure and pain: A theory of the energic foundation of feeling.* London: Routledge. (Original work published 1926.)

Brown, C. E., Brown, D., & Ramos, J. (1981). Effects of a laughing versus a nonlaughing model on humor responses in college students. *Psychological Reports, 48,* 35–40.

Brown, C. E., Wheeler, K. J., & Cash, M. (1980). The effects of a laughing versus a nonlaughing model on humor responses in preschool children. *Journal of Experimental Child Psychology, 29,* 334–339.

Bryant, J., Rockwell, S. C., & Owens, J. W. (1994). "Buzzer beaters" and "barn burners": The effects on enjoyment of watching the game go "down to the wire." *Journal of Sport and Social Issues, 18,* 326–339.

Bryant, J., & Zillmann, D. (1984). Using television to alleviate boredom and stress: Selective exposure as a function of induced excitational states. *Journal of Broadcasting, 28*(1), 1–20.

Cacioppo, J. T., & Berntson, G. G. (1994). Relationships between attitudes and evaluative space: A critical review with emphasis on the separability of positive and negative substrates. *Psychological Bulletin, 115,* 401–423.

Campbell, H. J. (1973). *The pleasure areas: A new theory of behavior.* New York: Delacorte.

Chapman, A. J. (1973a). Funniness of jokes, canned laughter and recall performance. *Sociometry, 36,* 569–578.

Chapman, A. J. (1973b). Social facilitation of laughter in children. *Journal of Experimental Social Psychology, 9,* 528–541.

Chapman, A. J., & Wright, D. S. (1976). Social enhancement of laughter: An experimental analysis of some companion variables. *Journal of Experimental Child Psychology, 21,* 201–218.

Christ, W. C., & Medoff, N. J. (1984). Affective state and selective exposure to and use of television. *Journal of Broadcasting, 28,* 51–63.

Cupchik, G. C., & Leventhal, H. (1974). Consistency between expressive behavior and the evaluation of humorous stimuli: The role of sex and self-observation. *Journal of Personality and Social Psychology, 30,* 429–442.

Davidson, R. J. (1992). Anterior cerebral asymmetry and the nature of emotion. *Brain and Cognition, 6,* 245–268.

Davis, M. (1990). *City of quartz: Excavating the future of Los Angeles.* New York: Verso.

Donnerstein, E. (1980). Pornography and violence against women: Experimental studies. *Annals of the New York Academy of Sciences, 347,* 277–288.

Epicurus. (1993). *The essential Epicurus: Letters, principal doctrines, Vatican sayings, and fragments* (E. O'Connor, Trans.). Buffalo, NY: Prometheus.

Frau-Meigs, D., & Jehel, S. (1997). *Les ecrans de la violence: Enjeux economiques et responsabilites sociales* [The screens of violence: Economic interests and social responsibilities]. Paris: Economica.

Freud, S. (1933). *New introductory lectures on psycho-analysis.* New York: Norton.

Freud, S. (1989). *Beyond the pleasure principle.* New York: Norton. (Original work published 1920.)

Fuller, R. C. C., & Sheehy-Skeffington, A. (1974). Effects of group laughter on response to humorous material: A replication and extension. *Psychological Reports, 35,* 531–534.

Gan, S., Tuggle, C. A., Mitrook, M. A., Coussement, S. H., & Zillmann, D. (1987). The thrill of a close game: Who enjoys it and who doesn't? *Journal of Sport & Social Issues, 21,* 53–64.

Geen, R. C. (1976). Observing violence in the mass media: Implications of basic research. In R. C. Geen & E. C. O'Neal (Eds.), *Perspectives on aggression* (pp. 193–234). New York: Academic.

Geen, R. G., & Quanty, M. B. (1977). The catharsis of aggression: An evaluation of a hypothesis. In L. Berkowitz (Ed.), *Advances in experimental social psychology* (Vol. 10, pp. 1–37). New York: Academic.

Greenfield, S. (2000). *The private life of the brain: Emotions, consciousness, and the secret of the self.* New York: Wiley.

Goldstein, J. H. (Ed.). (1979). *Sports, games, and play: Social and psychological viewpoints.* Hillsdale, NJ: Lawrence Erlbaum Associates.

Guttmann, A. (1998). The appeal of violent sports. In J. Goldstein (Ed.), *Why we watch: The attractions of violent entertainment* (pp. 179–211). New York: Oxford University Press.

Harper, R. G., Wiens, A. N., & Matarazzo, J. D. (1978). *Nonverbal communication: The state of the art.* New York: Wiley.

Harris, R. J., & Scott, C. L. (in press). Effects of sex in the media. In J. Bryant & D. Zillmann (Eds.), *Media effects: Advances in theory and research* (2nd ed.). Mahwah, NJ: Lawrence Erlbaum Associates.

Haskins, J. B. (1981). The trouble with bad news. *Newspaper Research Journal, 2(2),* 3–16.

Hauser, A. (1953). *Sozialgeschichte der Kunst und Literatur* (Vols. 1 & 2). Munchen: C. H. Beck'sche Verlagsbuchhandlung.

Helregel, B. K., & Weaver, J. B. (1989). Mood-management during pregnancy through selective exposure to television. *Journal of Broadcasting & Electronic Media, 33,* 15–33.

Hirt, E. R., Zillmann, D., Erickson, G. A., & Kennedy, C. (1992). Costs and benefits of allegiance: Changes in fans' self-ascribed competencies after team victory versus defeat. *Journal of Personality and Social Psychology, 63(5),* 724–738.

Hocking, J. E. (1982). Sports and spectators: Intra-audience effects. *Journal of Communication, 32(1),* 100–108.

Hocking, J. E., Margreiter, D. G., & Hylton, C. (1977). Intra-audience effects: A field text. *Human Communication Research, 3(3),* 243–249.

Ito, T. A., & Cacioppo, J. T. (1999). The psychophysiology of utility appraisals. In D. Kahneman, E. Diener, & H. Schwarz (Eds.), *Well-being: The foundations of hedonic psychology* (pp. 470–488). New York: Russell Sage Foundation.

Jacob, K. K. (2000). Crime without punishment: Pornography in a rape culture. In J. Gold

& S. Villari (Eds.), *Just sex: Students rewrite the rules on sex, violence, activism, and equality* (pp. 105–120). Lanham, MD: Rowman & Littlefield.

Jauss, H. R. (1982). *Aesthetic experience and literary hermeneutics: Vol. 3. Theory and history of literature* (M. Shaw, Trans.). Minneapolis: University of Minnesota Press.

Jipping, T. L. (2001). Popular music contributes to teenage violence. In J. D. Torr (Ed.), *Violence in the media* (Current Controversies Series) (pp. 61–66). San Diego, CA: Greenhaven.

Kahneman, D., Diener, E., & Schwarz, H. (Eds.). (1999). *Well-being: The foundations of hedonic psychology* (pp. 355–373). New York: Russell Sage Foundation.

Katz, E., Gurevitch, M., & Haas, H. (1973). On the use of the mass media for important things. *American Sociological Review, 38,* 164–181.

Knapp, M. (1978). *Nonverbal communication in human interaction.* New York: Holt, Rinehart & Winston.

Knobloch, S., & Zillmann, D. (in press). Mood management via the digital jukebox. *Journal of Communication.*

Kuhn, H. (1962–1963). *Vorgeschichte der Menschheit* (Vols. 1 & 2). Köln, Germany: Verlag M. DuMont Schauberg.

Lacan, J. (1979). *The four fundamental concepts of psycho-analysis* (A. Sheridan, Trans.). Harmondsworth, England: Penguin.

Lang, P. (1995). The emotion probe: Studies of motivation and attention. *American Psychologist, 50,* 372–385.

Leventhal, H., & Cupchik, C. C. (1975). The informational and facilitative effects of an audience upon expression and evaluation of humorous stimuli. *Journal of Experimental Social Psychology, 11,* 363–380.

Leventhal, H., & Mace, W. (1970). The effect of laughter on evaluation of a slapstick movie. *Journal of Personality, 38,* 16–30.

Lyotard, J.-F. (1988). *The differend: Phrases in dispute* (Georges Van Den Abbeele, Trans.). Manchester, UK: Manchester University Press.

Malinowski, B. (1948). *Magic, science and religion.* Garden City, NY: Doubleday Anchor Books.

Masters, J. C., Ford, M. E., & Arend, R. A. (1983). Children's strategies for controlling affective responses to aversive social experience. *Motivation and Emotion, 7,* 103–116.

McGhee, P. E. (1979). *Humor: It's origin and development.* San Francisco: Freeman.

Meadowcroft, J., & Zillmann, D. (1984, August). *The influence of hormonal fluctuations on women's selection and enjoyment of television programs.* Paper presented at the meeting of the Association for Education in Journalism and Mass Communication, Gainesville, FL.

Mendelsohn, H. (1966). *Mass entertainment.* New Haven, CT: College & University Press.

Miller, G. R. (1966). *Speech communication: A behavioral approach.* Indianapolis, IN: Bobbs-Merrill.

Nietzsche, F. (1956). *The birth of tragedy: The genealogy of morals* (F. Golffing, Trans.). Garden City, NY: Doubleday. (Original work published 1887.)

Nietzsche, F. (1966). *Beyond good and evil: Prelude to a philosophy of the future* (W. Kaufmann, Trans.). New York: Vintage. (Original work published 1886.)

O'Neal, E. C., & Taylor, S. L. (1989). Status of the provoker, opportunity to retaliate, and interest in video violence. *Aggressive Behavior, 15,* 171–180.

Palmgreen, P., & Rayburn, J. O. (1982). Gratifications sought and media exposure: An expectancy model. *Communication Research, 9,* 561–580.

Rosnow, R. L., & Robinson, E. J. (Eds.). (1967). *Experiments in persuasion.* New York: Academic.

Rushton, J. P. (1979). Effects of prosocial television and film material on the behavior of viewers. In L. Berkowitz (Ed.), *Advances in experimental social psychology* (Vol. 12, pp. 321–351). New York: Academic.

Sapolsky, B. S. (1980). The effect of spectator disposition and suspense on the enjoyment of sport contests. *International Journal of Sport Psychology, 11*(1), 1–10.

Sapolsky, B. S., & Zillmann, D. (1978). Enjoyment of a televised sport contest under different social conditions of viewing. *Perceptual and Motor Skills, 46,* 29–30.

Sargent, S. L., Zillmann, D., & Weaver, J. B. (1998). The gender gap in the enjoyment of televised sports. *Journal of Sport & Social Issues, 22,* 46–64.

Schwarz, N., Strack, F., Kommer, D., & Wagner, D. (1987). Soccer, rooms, and the quality of your life: Mood effects on judgments of satisfaction with life in general and with specific domains. *European Journal of Social Psychology, 17,* 69–79.

Schweitzer, K., Zillmann, D., Weaver, J. B., & Luttrell, E. S. (1992). Perception of threatening events in the emotional aftermath of a televised college football game. *Journal of Broadcasting and Electronic Media, 36,* 75–82.

Smiley, S. (1971). *Playwriting: The structure of action.* Upper Saddle River, NJ: Prentice Hall.

Smith, A. (1971). *The theory of moral sentiments.* New York: Garland. (Original work published 1759.)

Smyth, M. M., & Fuller, R. G. C. (1972). Effects of group laughter on responses to humorous material. *Psychological Reports, 30,* 132–134.

Tamborini, R. (2000, November). *The experience of telepresence in violent video games.* Paper presented at the 8th annual convention of the National Communication Association, Seattle, WA.

Tamborini, R., Stiff, J., & Zillmann, D. (1987). Preference for graphic horror featuring male versus female victimization: Personality and past film viewing experiences. *Human Communication Research, 13,* 529–552.

Tannenbaum, P. H. (1980). An unstructured introduction to an amorphous area. In P. H. Tannenbaum (Ed.), *The entertainment functions of television* (pp. 1–12). Hillsdale, NJ: Lawrence Erlbaum Associates.

Veitch, R., & Griffitt, W. (1976). Good news-bad news: Affective and interpersonal effects. *Journal of Applied Social Psychology, 6,* 69–75.

Wakshlag, J., Vial, V., & Tamborini, R. (1983). Selecting crime drama and apprehension about crime. *Human Communication Research, 10,* 227–242.

White, C. L., Fishbein, S., & Rutstein, J. (1981). Passionate love and the misattribution of arousal. *Journal of Personality and Social Psychology, 41,* 56–62.

Zajonc, R. B. (1980). Feeling and thinking: Preferences need no inferences. *American Psychologist, 35,* 151–175.

Zajonc, R. B. (1997). Emotions. In D. T. Gilbert, S. T. Fiske, & G. Lindzey (Eds.), *Handbook of social psychology* (4th ed., pp. 591–632). New York: Oxford University Press.

Zillmann, D. (1977). Humor and communication. In A. J. Chapman & H. C. Foot (Eds.), *It's a funny thing, humor* (pp. 291–301). Oxford: Pergammon.

Zillmann, D. (1980). Anatomy of suspense. In P. H. Tannenbaum (Ed.), *The entertainment functions of television* (pp. 133–163). Hillsdale, NJ: Lawrence Erlbaum Associates.

Zillmann, D. (1982). Television viewing and arousal. In D. Pearl, L. Bouthilet, & J. Lazar (Eds.), *Television and behavior: Ten years of scientific progress and implications for the eighties: Vol 2. Technical reviews* (pp. 53–67). Washington, DC: U.S. Government Printing Office.

Zillmann, D. (1983). Cognition-excitation interdependencies in aggressive behavior. *Aggressive Behavior, 14,* 51–64.

Zillmann, D. (1985). The experimental exploration of gratifications from media entertainment. In K. E. Rosengren, L. A. Wener, & P. Palmgreen (Eds.), *Media gratifications research: Current perspectives* (pp. 225–239). Beverly Hills, CA: Sage.

Zillmann, D. (1988). Mood management: Using entertainment to full advantage. In L. Donohew, H. E. Sypher, & E. T. Higgins (Eds.) *Communication, social cognition, and affect* (pp. 147–171). Hillsdale, NJ: Lawrence Erlbaum Associates.

Zillmann, D. (1991a). Empathy: Affect from bearing witness to the emotions of others. In

J. Bryant & D. Zillmann (Eds.), *Responding to the screen: Reception and reaction processes* (pp. 135–167). Hillsdale, NJ: Lawrence Erlbaum Associates.

Zillmann, D. (1991b). Television viewing and physiological arousal. In J. Bryant & D. Zillmann (Eds.), *Responding to the screen: Reception and reaction processes* (pp. 103–133). Hillsdale, NJ: Lawrence Erlbaum Associates.

Zillmann, D. (1991c). The logic of suspense and mystery. In J. Bryant & D. Zillmann (Eds.), *Responding to the screen: Reception and reaction processes* (pp. 281–303). Hillsdale, NJ: Lawrence Erlbaum Associates.

Zillmann, D. (1994). Mechanisms of emotional involvement with drama. *Poetics, 23*, 33–51.

Zillmann, D. (1998a). Does the tragic drama have redeeming value? *Spiel, 17*, 1, 4–14.

Zillmann, D. (1998b). The psychology of the appeal of portrayals of violence. In J. Goldstein (Ed.), *Why we watch: The attractions of violent entertainment* (pp. 179–211). New York: Oxford University Press.

Zillmann, D. (2000a). Basal morality in drama appreciation. In I. Bondebjerg (Ed.), *Moving images, culture and the mind* (pp. 53–63). Luton, England: University of Luton Press.

Zillmann, D. (2000b). The coming of media entertainment. In D. Zillmann & P. Vorderer (Eds.), *Media entertainment: The psychology of its appeal* (pp. 1–20). Mahwah, NJ: Lawrence Erlbaum Associates.

Zillmann, D. (2000c). Mood management in the context of selective exposure theory. In M. E. Roloff (Ed.), *Communication Yearbook 23* (pp. 103–123). Thousand Oaks, CA: Sage.

Zillmann, D., & Bryant, J. (1975). Viewer's moral sanction of retribution in the appreciation of dramatic representations. *Journal of Experimental Social Psychology, 11*, 572–582.

Zillmann, D., & Bryant, J. (1985). Affect, mood, and emotion as determinants of selective exposure. In D. Zillmann & J. Bryant (Eds.), *Selective exposure to communication* (pp. 157–190). Hillsdale, NJ: Lawrence Erlbaum Associates.

Zillmann, D., & Bryant, J. (1991). Responding to comedy: The sense and nonsense of humor. In J. Bryant & D. Zillmann (Eds.), *Responding to the screen: Reception and reaction processes* (pp. 261–279). Hillsdale, NJ: Lawrence Erlbaum Associates.

Zillmann, D., Bryant, J., & Sapolsky, B. S. (1979). The enjoyment of watching sport contests. In J. H. Goldstein (Ed.), *Sports, games, and play: Social and psychological viewpoints* (pp. 297–335). Hillsdale, NJ: Lawrence Erlbaum Associates.

Zillmann, D., & Cantor, J. R. (1976). A disposition theory of humour and mirth. In A. J. Chapman & H. C. Foot (Eds.), *Humour and laughter: Theory, research, and applications* (pp. 93–115). London: Wiley.

Zillmann, D., & Cantor, J. R. (1977). Affective responses to the emotions of a protagonist. *Journal of Experimental Social Psychology, 13*, 155–165.

Zillmann, D., & Gibson, R. (1996). Evolution of the horror genre. In J. Weaver & R. Tamborini (Eds.), *Horror films: Current research in audience preferences and reactions* (pp. 15–31). Mahweh, NJ: Lawrence Erlbaum Associates.

Zillmann, D., Hezel, R. T., & Medoff, N. J. (1980). The effect of affective states on selective exposure to televised entertainment fare. *Journal of Applied Social Psychology, 10*, 323–339.

Zillmann, D., & Weaver, J. B. (1996). Gender socialization theory of horror. In J. B. Weaver & R. Tamborini (Eds.), *Horror films: Current research in audience preferences and reactions* (pp. 81–101). Mahwah, NJ: Lawrence Erlbaum Associates.

Zillmann, D., Weaver, J. B., Mundorf, N., & Aust, C. F. (1986). Effects of an opposite-gender companion's affect to horror on distress, delight, and attraction. *Journal of Personality and Social Psychology, 51*, 586–594.

Zuckerman, M. (1979). *Sensation seeking: Beyond the optimal level of arousal.* Hillsdale, NJ: Lawrence Erlbaum Associates.

Chapter 22

Social and Psychological Effects of Information Technologies and Other Interactive Media

NORBERT MUNDORF
University of Rhode Island

KENNETH R. LAIRD
Southern Connecticut State University

Significant advances in converging information technologies of computers, telecommunications, and consumer electronics have created a wide spectrum of new opportunities for both individuals and organizations to become more productive and effective in their daily activities. In the 1980s, technologies such as decision support systems (DSS), electronic mail (e-mail), videoconferencing, expert systems, voice messaging, and voice mail began to impact our day-to-day activities (Daft, 1989). In the 1990s, the Internet provided a number of low-cost and mass market accessible applications that continue to create numerous benefits not only to organizations but also to individuals and how they connect and communicate with each other. The impact of information technologies on organizations is well documented. However, research is just beginning to focus on the impact of such technologies on the social and psychological effects on individuals. This chapter will provide a review of these effects. We will then discuss some managerial implications of these trends.

FACTORS CONTRIBUTING TO GROWTH AND ACCEPTANCE OF INFORMATION TECHNOLOGY AND INTERACTIVE MEDIA

Expanded Technological Capability

Convergence of technologies has a critical impact on home computing as well as information and entertainment. Whereas analog technologies generally coincide with a one-on-one relationship of applications and appliances, digital technologies have made it possible to perform multiple functions with the same piece of equipment. This has lead to an increasing overlap between the telecommunications, television, and consumer electronics industries. For the user, it means that the same appliance can be used for work at home, chat, children's entertainment, and online shopping or banking. Apart from technological innovation and cooperation among industry sectors, adoption of interactive media consumption patterns by the users is the third dimension of convergence. There is continuing debate as to how rapidly convergence will take place. Even though convergence is technically feasible, it has been limited due to lifestyle preferences and other factors (Stipp, 1998).

Responding to digital satellite competition, cable companies offer digital services, which enhance the existing fiber/coax physical plant of the cable system with digital set-top boxes and digital distribution technology. Besides digital picture, this technology offers an on-screen program guide and several dozen pay-per-view (PPV) channels, as well as multiplexed premium cable channels and digital music channels. In a typical digital cable offering, interactivity is limited to two levels of information, which can be retrieved while watching a program or perusing the on-screen program guide, PPV ordering, as well as selection, programming, and recording of future programs through the on-screen guide.

Several providers have experimented with interactive applications that give the viewer options beyond simply choosing a program. These include game show participation, choice of camera angles at sports games, access to background information for products advertised in commercials, and choice of plot lines and endings in movies. Other interactive uses of television are calling up additional information on news and sports or television/personal computer (TV/PC) multitasking.

Access, Content, and User Interface

Much discussion on information technology (IT) effects appropriately focuses on the Internet. However, innovations associated with traditional media also offer considerable potential, in part because all electronic media are evolving rapidly, converging with other media, and becoming increasingly interactive. These hybrid media often reach the majority of the population (in some countries, a vast majority) that lacks regular, adequate Internet access. It affords them participation in activities that have considerable potential to increase their economic well-being and quality of life (Cairncross, 1997; Schonfeld, 2000).

Worldwide, television consumption is still the prevalent leisure activity, mainly because of its universal, low-cost accessibility and its ability to afford hours of entertainment and information with minimal effort. Although usage patterns are changing rapidly, for some time consumers may continue to choose television for news and entertainment and PCs for other sources of information and electronic commerce. Video delivery will increasingly involve home computing devices, such as combination TV/PC or Web-TV and digital recording technology such as TiVo (Schonfeld, 2000).

INTERACTIVE MEDIA IN THE PRIVATE HOME

Prior to the 1990s, home information technology was either entirely separate or adapted from business technology. Increasingly, IT developments for the home affect business uses. The diffusion and use of interactive media in the home is a complex phenomenon that warrants increasing attention. However, our understanding of the impact of interactivity and related attributes is still very limited (Bryant & Love, 1996; Mundorf & Westin, 1996; Vorderer, 2000).

Interactive Entertainment

Content is the key to adoption of advanced interactive services. Because of the high visibility of movies, the great public interest in this type of content, and their easy availability, Movies-on-Demand was the offering of choice for early interactive trials. Music, sports, and special-interest programming also have received their share of attention by the programmers of interactive cable systems. Interactive game channels are added to some systems. In-home gambling has strong economic appeal; regulatory barriers prevail, however. Anecdotal evidence suggests that participants in interactive trials enjoyed watching regular television programs they missed during the week, newscasts tailored to individual preferences (Time Warner is pulling the plug, 1997), as well as erotica.

Several television providers have experimented with interactive applications that give the viewer options beyond simply choosing a program. These include participation in game shows such as *Wheel of Fortune* and *Jeopardy*, "pick-the-play" games for *Monday Night Football*, ordering pizza using Web-TV during a *Star Trek* marathon (Bloom, 2000), access to background information for products advertised in commercials, and choice of plot lines and endings in movies. Compared to the massive number of traditional movies available, interactive movies are few and far between. They are difficult to produce and require considerable technology. Even most sites for Internet video provide mainly repackaged, conventional programming. Audience demand for interactivity is not yet understood. Many children and teens feel comfortable with it due to exposure to video and computer games; in fact, a considerable number of toys now include interactive components and interface with the World Wide Web (Lockwood Tooher, 2000).

Television Versus Internet

Stipp (1998) points out that most people still look to the television for relaxation and entertainment, whereas the PC is a source of information (and increasingly commerce and service). It appears that most PC users have not significantly reduced their television viewing. Recent adopters tend to use the PC less than early adopters. Differentials during daytime could be due to employment patterns. Stipp stresses that the market for television and PC consumption is highly segmented and heterogeneous. Convergence takes place in certain populations and at certain times. But it is far from becoming a populationwide phenomenon. However, for some demographic and psychographic segments, surfing or chatting on the Web may be more absorbing than watching television and help take their mind off the stress of work and personal life.

Stipp (1998) also argues that interactive features, unlike a larger television screen, which is seen as an important characteristic by many, will not dramatically enhance the experience of watching a movie or sitcom. By contrast, sports, news, and commercials may benefit from interactivity. These are content areas that have prospered on the Internet, often as supplements to television offerings (e.g., ESPN SportsZone or MSNBC). However, Vorderer (2000) has argued that even fictional events could benefit from greater interactivity. He gives an example of a movie where a person has to cut one of several wires to prevent a terrible explosion. This is obviously a highly involving scenario. But one might argue also that if the viewer is in a position to make this decision, the involvement is potentially much greater. However, the viewer would also lose the safety associated with the typical Hollywood "happy ending." A wrong decision might provide negative feedback and thus reduce that enjoyment of the experience for many viewers. This issue is far from settled. Video game players experience this feedback cycle and seem to enjoy the challenge of constant improvement.

Traditional media consumption also lends itself more to a group setting. Television provides a sense of "virtual community," when viewers can discuss a tragic plane crash or the latest episode of a popular sitcom. Whereas Internet consumption in a group is still problematic, the network has produced virtual communities and substitutes for discussions around the watercooler.

The interaction of televisions and PCs is underscored by the observation that television promotion often drives Web traffic. Traditional media promote Web sites, thus achieving considerable crossover (e.g., ESPN viewers may seek out the Web site during the workday). This type of interactivity, then, is not the traditional model of interactivity within one piece of technology, but a crossover phenomenon between technologies.

ADOPTION AND USES OF INFORMATION TECHNOLOGY AND ELECTRONIC SERVICES BY CONSUMERS

Carey (2000) recently reported the results of a longitudinal study of adoption and uses of broadband services by consumers. The study involved in-depth interviews with broadband users (all had cable modem access) in their homes and observations of how they interacted with Web content as well as with other household media. The people in the study had broadband service for an average of just over 1 year. About half of the respondents were classic early adopters: they wanted to be the first to have such services. An equal number of the respondents had only moderate interest in technology and did not have a home filled with electronics. The primary reason for adopting broadband services was to get faster connections to regular Web content.

The study concluded that there is a latent appetite for video delivered over the Web based on the evolving behavior of broadband Web users. However, in order for this to become active demand by a mass audience, Web video will have to meet a higher standard than is currently delivered under most conditions. Most broadband users are currently located in work environments, and many are located in universities, although the home broadband market is growing at a rapid pace. Most current users adopt the service for high-speed access to regular Web sites, not expanded broadband services. What about interactivity, customization, and other features that broadband services could provide? Do people want these added features? The study suggests that there is no simple answer. Some broadband services have fared poorly in the past, and they may still face obstacles. However, the study concludes that some new variations of broadband services may prove to be popular.

Interactivity and Its Effects

Interactivity has been discussed during the past two decades, both as a function of computer activities, especially games, and enhanced forms of television. Originating as feedback in Wiener's Cybernetics around 1950, it received little attention until the 1980s, when Rogers (1986) and his coworkers identified it as a key function of new media. But interactivity is not a simple, one-dimensional concept. Fortin (1997) cites close to 20 researchers that have identified underlying dimensions of interactivity. He concludes that interactivity implies the shift from one-way communication prevalent in traditional media to interchangeable roles of senders and receivers (which can be human or machines). The end user has a high level of control over access, timing, and sequencing of information, entertainment, or services. Interactive communication may be either synchronous or asynchronous. Bryant and Love (1996) identify several dimensions that may differentiate interactive media from traditional counterparts. Their typology includes the dimensions of selectivity, diet, interactivity, agency, personalization, and dimensionality. Cable or satellite television (in combination with the videocassette recorder, VCR) primarily provide increased selectivity. The tremendous success of home video and multichannel cable in the 1980s clearly indicates that viewers like to expand their viewing choices, even though much of the interest is in early availability of blockbuster material. Recent developments in digital cable and satellite have mainly catered to this trend: more channels are available; starting times vary; and viewers have more immediate control through onscreen program/recording features.

Other researchers have attempted to identify the underlying dimensions of interactivity. One example is Goertz' (1995) distinction, which includes (1) the degree of selectivity, (2) the degree to which a given content may be modified by the viewer, (3) the quantity of different content that can be selected and modified, (4) the degree of linearity/nonlinearity, and (5) the number of different senses that are activated while using the media.

Video games respond to several of Goertz' (1995) criteria: Content can be modified (e.g., the player can take on the identity of different participants in a race, different levels of difficulty can be selected). Some games also provide tactile feedback in addition to the traditional video and audio. Steuer (1992) points to *speed* (response time to input), *range* (the extent to which attributes can be manipulated), and *mapping* (match with the real environment) as key factors in interactivity. For video games, in particular, Tamborini et al. (2000) utilize the concept of telepresence, the (perceived) ability to alter the form and content of the environment. "Real-time interaction where the user performs natural actions that instantaneously alter a wide variety of characteristics in the mediated environment should create a heightened level of telepresence" (p. 12). Telepresence is both an attribute created by technology and an individual difference variable determined by the extent to which subjects perceive their "presence" in a virtual environment.

Computer and, in particular, Internet-based technologies tend to maximize selectivity, nonlinearity, and available modification. However, one may argue that much Internet activity is based on an extremely high level of selectivity, whereas modification of content or interaction is limited. A notable exception is e-mail, which is low on appeal to different senses (even though it has become a vehicle for infidelity) but has generated a new wave of social and parasocial interactions. McKenna and Bargh (1999) point out that interpersonal communication is the number one use of the Internet at home. Besides conventional e-mail, they point to chat rooms, bulletin boards, and electronic "communities." Their research correlates personality traits and individual differences with preference for the Internet as a social vehicle, focusing on stigmatized and constrained identities and/or social anxiety, loneliness, hectic lifestyle, and safety issues.

Rockwell and Bryant (1999) explored how different levels of interactivity and affective dispositions toward characters influence responses to interactive media. Increased interactivity fostered enjoyment of the program and tended to enhance the children's involvement with the entertainment experience. Surprisingly, children who had more chances to interact with the program also reported liking the characters more compared to the low-interactivity condition.

Fortin's (1997) review of research found some tentative positive effects of interactivity on learning and attitude change, even though most studies were inconclusive or failed to adequately operationalize interactivity. Fortin's study found that the effect of interactivity on "social presence" leveled off at intermediate exposure, whereas the impact of vividness appeared linear.

Effects of Video Games

Tamborini (2000) points out that video games are higher not only in interactivity and vividness but also in that users need to pay careful attention, to make mental maps for future use, and to coordinate visual attention with motor behavior. The user needs to act in order for the game to proceed, leading to "a strong sense of involvement" (p. 12). Moreover, many games involve vicarious aggressive action, priming aggressive scripts (Anderson & Dill, 2000) suggesting aggressive environments, and violent problem solving strategies. Video games with enhanced virtual reality

(VR) capabilities are expected to lead to a higher level of immersion because involvement in the games is greater and distractions from the "real world" are minimized.

Tamborini et al. (2000) tested the impact of different game conditions on players' hostile thoughts and surprisingly found that level of hostile thought was highest when subjects *observed* a violent game being played. The authors attribute this unexpected finding either to the high level of frustration among those excluded from playing themselves or to the involvement of those learning to play the game, which may then distract them from hostile thoughts. Further analysis showed that in the standard (violent, non-VR) game condition those subjects high on presence unexpectedly had a much lower level of hostile thought compared to those low on presence. Immersive tendencies in general were also associated with lower hostile thought. These findings also may indicate that being involved in the game may serve to deflect hostile thought or lead to greater enjoyment and thus reduced hostility.

SOCIAL AND PSYCHOLOGICAL EFFECTS OF INFORMATION TECHNOLOGY ON INDIVIDUALS

Uses and Gratifications of Internet Use

Papacharissi and Rubin (2000) identified motives of computer-mediated communication (CMC) use. Interpersonal utility emerged as the first factor, explaining 18.1% of the variance. The other factors were information seeking (8.3% of variance), pass time (7.5%), convenience (6.2%), and entertainment (4.2%). As far as reasons for using the Internet, information seeking and entertainment ranked highest, followed by convenience. The were no significant differences between males and females. Those who found interpersonal communication to be less rewarding and experienced anxiety resulting from face-to-face communication tended to use the Internet for interpersonal utility. Even though one could conclude that the Internet is a substitute, even a crutch, for those who find face-to-face communication less rewarding, it could also be seen as a benefit in that it offers an opportunity for those who are "interpersonally challenged" to build and maintain relationships. The authors also found life satisfaction to be negatively related to Internet affinity. Again, chances are that those who are less happy with their life are drawn to the Internet for interpersonal utility, although there is insufficient evidence to support the claim that the Internet causes negative life or interpersonal satisfaction.

Effects on Social Interactions

Oravec (2000) reports that family counselors now encounter the Internet as a vehicle for family issues and problems. However, she points out that often the Internet is used as a scapegoat for more deep-seated issues. On the other hand, Internet access in the home can actually be the cause of family conflict (e.g., in terms of control over access to information and entertainment, e.g., pornography, by adolescents in the home). Also, online acquaintances are often more difficult to control than friends who live in the neighborhood. The invasion of privacy through online data collection as well as the potential for fraud present additional sources of concern for families. Time allocation is also affected by increased family members' time spent online.

Kraut et al. (1998) conducted a longitudinal study of 1st- and 2nd-year Internet users. Although Internet use for communication prevailed, heavy use coincides with increasing loneliness and anxiety. One possible explanation is the displacement of social time with time used online (analogously to similar effects found for television viewing in earlier studies). However, the authors concede that the Internet has turned out to be much more social than television, even though these social interactions differ significantly from conventional interpersonal relations, especially as far as newly formed relationships are concerned.

The findings of the study imply that greater use of the Internet was associated with subsequent decline in the size of the local social circle. There was also indication of a decline in the size of the distant social circle. The negative association between Internet use and subsequent social support failed to achieve significance. Internet use was, however, associated with subsequent increases in loneliness. The increase in stressors was not significant. In spite of a negative association between Internet use and depression, the authors claim that it is consistent with the interpretation that use of the Internet causes an increase in depression. Although the evidence in this study was rather limited, it generated considerable public discussion, including significant criticism of its methodology.

A number of other studies have focused on the negative effects of the Internet, in particular social isolation and Internet "addiction." Nie and Ebring (2000) reported significant changes in their life for the 36% of their sample of households that use the Internet for more than 5 hours a week, and even stronger effects for the 15% that spend 10 or more hours. A subsample of those respondents reported reduced time with friends or family and attending events outside the home.

In contrast to the widely discussed study by Kraut et al. (1998), McKenna and Bargh (1999) applied a more rigorous methodology and discovered largely beneficial effects resulting from interpersonal Internet use. These include increased self-disclosure, decreased feelings of estrangement and isolation, decreased depression, and greater liking and acceptance by others, as well as a widening social circle.

McKenna and Bargh (1999) underscore people's need to "present their 'true' or inner self to the outside world" (p. 254); for many, the Internet has become the vehicle for this self-presentation. People try on different personas on the Internet that are closed to them as options in the real world. Even though this ability of the Internet has been abused for criminal or undesirable activities (such as child pornography), several studies have shown beneficial effects for those who are shy, socially anxious, lonely, or stigmatized (e.g., through their sexual identity). Also, hectic lifestyle and safety concerns are predictors of Internet use. Several studies have shown self-disclosure, a key determinant of evolving intimacy in relationships, to be associated with Internet friendships. McKenna and Bargh (1999) even found that relationships form more quickly on the Internet than they do in face-to-face situations and that a greater liking resulted if two interaction partners met on the Internet before meeting face-to-face.

McKenna and Bargh (1999) also take issue with the Kraut et al. (1998) conclusion that Internet use is associated with increased levels of loneliness, based on methodological and other considerations. In the Kraut (1998) study, the correlation between Internet use and loneliness was small, and the sample consisted of participants who already had a fairly large social circle. One of the more surprising findings in McKenna and Bargh's (1999) research was that participants who had met each other online before meeting face-to-face reported greater mutual liking compared to those who met face-to-face both times. Even more compelling was the finding that participants reported liking the same person more during an encounter in an Internet chat room compared to meeting the same person face-to-face (subjects actually thought they met two different people).

Recent research by Jeffrey Cole (2000) on the social and psychological effects of technology (particularly the Internet) has found that nearly two thirds of all Americans have ventured online, and the majority of the respondents deny that Internet creates social isolation. For instance, more than 75% said they do not feel as if they are being ignored by relatives and friends as a result of chat room activity. More respondents feel ignored because of television compared to Internet use. In fact, the majority of Internet users said e-mail, Web sites, and chat rooms have a "modestly positive impact" on their abilities to make new friends and communicate more with family. Almost half of the respondents report "spending at least some time each week using the Internet with other household members" (p. 29). Parents report a neutral, if not positive effect (26.2%) on children's grades. However, concerns about privacy were cited by a majority of users and even more nonusers of the Internet. The study concludes that the Web will have profound long-term effects that most users can't yet detect which range from values to communication patterns and consumer behavior.

Internet Addiction

Another area of negative Internet effects is the potential for addiction. Although it is unclear if Internet addiction is actually a meaningful concept, it describes a group of less-than-desirable behaviors that are associated with heavy Internet use. Male teenagers were initially thought to be the typical "addicts," but some research has found different demographic characteristics. Petrie and Gunn (1998) point out that older females are more likely to volunteer for research studies and may thus overrepresent themselves as Internet addicts. In addition, the proportion of female Internet users is growing rapidly. One problem is that many of these studies rely on self-defined addiction. However, Petrie and Gunn found a significant relationship between high Internet use and both depression and introversion. An early survey by Katz and Aspden (1997) failed to produce evidence of a reduction in time spent communicating with family and friends, and other studies also point to social relationships formed online (Parks & Floyd, 1995).

Direction of causality is a key issue, as with many other media effects studies. It might be that those who are social to begin with use online media to keep in touch with friends and family. On the other hand, those who are socially challenged might also resort to chat rooms and newsgroups as a way to avoid face-to-face interactions, while at the same time creating a feeling of social involvement. In fact, because Internet users tend to be younger, more educated, and somewhat better off economically, these variables per se might coincide with a higher level of social activity, which creates an additional source of confounding.

Individual Differences

Vorderer (2000) has raised the question of to what extent interactivity is desirable for different populations. Many argue that people enjoy the "couch potato" existence of minimal activity in front of the set: ". . . everybody has the right and need to be lazy" (p. 9). Whereas this is still true, there are apparent demographic and other individual differences that help determine the appeal of interactive features. Age and other sociodemographic differences in adoption of new technology are well established. But Vorderer and his coworkers have also found support for greater enjoyment of suspense presented in an interactive mode for those who are more intellectually active (as indicated by response time to on-screen questions) and those with a higher level of education. Some research indicates that these patterns even hold true for more futuristic, three-dimensional, multiperson settings. For example, Hanisch (1999) found that enjoyment of "Immersion Studios" (also called "voomies") is also greater among those with higher education levels and cognitive capabilities.

Effects of Age and Gender

The Internet was initially seen as the realm of young, often upscale, tech-nologically savvy males. Many older workers felt uncomfortable with the technology and did not catch on until later. One resulting dilemma was that junior colleagues often had more control over technology and net-works than senior executives.

However, the increasing diffusion of Internet access has led to consid-erable diversity in its user groups. Although business and academic use of the network is still predominant, home access gained considerable momentum, especially because it became increasingly cheaper with flat fee and even free services. Recently, high-speed access via cable modem and digital subscriber line (DSL) has become available to private homes in many locations.

For the elderly, the Internet is emerging as a relatively low-cost and convenient tool for social support (White, McConnell, Clipp, & Bynum, 1999). Many elderly are being cut off from their social support network and are increasingly isolated (Mundorf, Bryant, & Brownell, 1997). In spite of the prevailing myth of computer aversion among older people, computer ownership is fairly high among the elderly, and many are active online. White et al. (1999) point out that slower cognitive processing capa-bilities may impair the speed of acquiring computer skills. But because most elderly computer use is for private purposes, this difference is of lit-tle importance. Many communities provide computer access through libraries and community centers, and inexpensive access technologies such as Web-TV permit even those on fixed incomes to use the Internet. However, education and other socioeconomic variables are significant predictors of Internet use, and issues related to the "digital divide" apply to older citizens in particular.

White et al. (1999) conducted a study of the effects of providing access to computers and teaching Internet skills in a retirement community. One of the notable effects measured in this study was the decrease in loneli-ness, as measured by the UCLA Loneliness Scale, for most of the partici-pants, even though for a small group loneliness actually increased.

It does, however, affect training strategies for different age groups. Several studies have shown considerable benefits to promote rehabilitation, self-sufficiency, and lifelong learning (see White et al., 1999, for a review).

WORKING AND LEARNING IN
AN INTERACTIVE ENVIRONMENT

Interactive entertainment is only one subset of applications made possible through an advanced electronic infrastructure. Telework, telebanking, teleshopping, telemedicine, and distance learning have gained importance. The same "pipe" can be used to transmit different types of content, adding to return on investment. Research on the effects of these settings is even more limited as the focus tends to be on business and economics.

EFFECTS OF ELECTRONICALLY MEDIATED
TRAINING AND DEVELOPMENT

Distance Learning

In order to make distance learning work, it needs to have some of the key features of interactivity—notably selectivity, ability to modify and individualize content, and a high degree of nonlinearity, as well as activation of different senses. The widespread availability of computers in schools and homes and of satellite and videoconferencing technology have led to the prospect of interactive distance learning that is accessible to considerable parts of the population (Levy, 1999).

Information technologies can provide students with far greater involvement in and control over the process of learning. Rather than replacing the current educational system, distance learning is expected to complement it (Goldberg, 1998). Using the Web for training purposes decreases the restrictions of location, seat limitations, and travel costs (Mottl, 2000). Concerns about distance learning are the technical problems with speed and bandwidth, the decreased quality of education, and the issue of cheating.

Hecht and Klass (1999) successfully combined asynchronous Web-based materials with synchronous audio and video transmission and real-time chat and discussion even in highly technical, research-oriented courses. Some students still report a sense of disconnection, besides technical issues.

Hodge-Hardin (1997) found that interactive television was an adequate method of providing developmental algebra instruction beyond the confines of the campus as measured by the student's final numerical grades. Cavanaugh (1999) found that distance learning by itself showed only a small positive effect for K–12 academic achievement. A group that received classroom instruction coupled with off-campus learning via various telecommunication methods boasted the highest positive effects. Apparently, the face-to-face complement added to the quality of the classroom experience. Cohn (2000) is one of the skeptics, who points out that distance learning cannot provide the things that all combine to truly give a student a well-rounded education, such as "beer, pizza, and more beer."

Dholakia, Mundorf, Dholakia, and Xiao (2000) investigated distance learning and its potential impact on college student transportation behavior. The study found considerable traffic substitution potential of interactive technology. Students' interest in Internet use for travel substitution was greater among those who use the Internet for obtaining information and who perceive the money-saving potential of traffic substitution.

EFFECTS OF VIRTUAL WORK ENVIRONMENTS

Information Technology Impact in Business Settings

Simon (1977) was one of the first to advance in a major work the idea that the new IT would have a significant economic impact on organizations. Whisler (1970), in an early work, found that a number of significant changes resulted from the implementation of IT systems through integration and consolidation of previously separate decision systems. This integration had a significant effect on the pattern of departmentalization and usually resulted in a consolidation of departments and a decrease in the number of levels in an organization.

Gerrity (1971) contends that IT impacted more structured tasks within organizations but not complex and unstructured decision-making tasks. A decade later, Sprague and Carlson (1982) point to management information systems and DSS focusing on information relevant to middle and upper management. Otway and Peltu (1984) contend that the new office technology cannot be regarded as just another step in a long history of automation of work but rather as a giant stride, having radical implications for managers, both for their personal development and for the changes it will cause in how organizations function. Stallard, Smith, and Reese (1983) suggest that the use of electronic information systems in an office environment creates a new environment and impacts the traditional organizational structure. It can increase speed, geographic distribution, and structure of organizational relationship (Hammer & Mangurian, 1987).

The Virtual Organization

Most findings regarding virtual organizations are speculative, in spite of numerous articles in the popular press and in trade books. Virtual teams have obvious advantages through lower cost, greater flexibility, and better resource utilization. Limited research findings seem to indicate that, compared to teams meeting face to face, virtual teams report less trust, reduced team cohesion, and less communication satisfaction.

Such deficiencies may be of concern, as they may have a negative impact on team performance and productivity. Teams meeting face-to-face are reported to have greater team identification compared to those meeting remotely using IT methods.

The IT impact on the individual has been viewed as its effects on social capital or social structure of social units. Putnam (2000) describes social capital as social networks that create norms of reciprocity and trustworthiness. They merit the name *capital* in his view and that of other social scientists (Rosen and Astley, 1988), because they have value, specifically in improving the productivity of individuals and groups.

Traditional organizations depended heavily on hierarchies to optimize information flow. People higher up in the hierarchy typically knew more than those in the lower ranks. This pattern is shifting because organizations rely more and more on "knowledge workers," even in the lower ranks of the organization. A virtual organization, then, will move away from the hierarchical model toward a "flat" model, with temporary teams that are based on projects and team member expertise. This is sometimes referred to as "Adhocracy" or "Hyperarchy." Needless to say, these teams often work over long distances and thus rely heavily on IT (Ostroff, 1999).

This change leads to an increase of "richness" and "reach" (i.e. customized, interactive information can be sent to more customers or colleagues without having to rely on personal selling channels). The organization has a far wider reach, taking advantage of telecommunications and multimedia and thus becoming increasingly independent of traditional channels. Traditionally, the hierarchy of channel richness implied more immediate and thus effective communication for face-to-face, compared to telephone, e-mail, and personal and formal written communication. Most writers found CMC suitable for task-oriented communication, not for relationship building (e.g., Rice, 1984). However, several researchers found that e-mail users in an organization were more committed and better informed compared to those preferring the traditional channels. Also, computer-mediated groups were found to use less attacking and more supportive communication, while at the same time being less cohesive and satisfied about group outcomes (Straus, 1997). Walther (1997) and Parks and Floyd (1996) found evidence for the development of interpersonal relationships and failed to find an intrinsic advantage of face-to-face or telephone communication. However, online users often added audiovisual means and moved on to add telephone and face-to-face communication. Interaction patterns were not necessarily distinctly different between online and face-to-face groups, where status might be a stronger predictor in decision making.

Effects on Telecommuting and Office Automation

Telecommuting, also referred to as telework or work-at-home, has experienced considerable growth in the United States as a result of technological and social changes. Quite a few companies (e.g., AT&T) offer telecommuting options often to midlevel, nonunionized workers. Most telework is not done in a context of a formal company telecommuting setup; it is either complementary to a conventional office job, or part of a part-time, contract-work, or small home-business arrangement. Increasingly, knowledge workers who leave their companies set up a small home-based business and frequently work for their former employer. There are approximately 35 million home offices in the United States (Clark, 1997). Diffusion of Internet access and ownership of PCs in private homes along with increased computer literacy and lack of qualified workers in key areas is likely to increase the proportion of telework. The impact of this trend on family life and culture is yet to be determined (Garhammer & Mundorf, 1997).

Watad and DiSanzo (2000) contend that despite considerable research, many managers remain ambivalent about introducing telecommuting as a business strategy. In a recent publication, they describe in detail the organizational and individual impacts of a successful telecommuting program implemented in a 150-person company that provides interactive marketing and sample-distribution services for the pharmaceutical industry. The study found that the program benefited the organization by increasing revenue in at least three different ways. It streamlined internal operations and sales force field time and improved customer relationships. The impact on work life was realized in the quality of life of the field force. The study also identified some unintended outcomes of the project: informal telecommuting, where other executives chose to operate out of the office; the adoption of a common technology platform across the organization; and enhanced knowledge management.

CONCLUSION

With the effects of the Internet and related technologies, we are analyzing a moving target: the rapid move from the relatively small, text-based and mainly academic network of the early 1990s to the multimedia, multiuser, private, public, and business network, and beyond, maybe to a world of multisensory mobile connectivity. Compared to other media effects discussed in this book, the Internet represents a multidimensional range of content, user types, and applications. It is used not only for entertainment and information like typical video or film but also for business transactions and in particular as an interpersonal communication medium. In addition, we are increasingly witnessing a combination of the Internet with existing, older media, especially TV, but also radio (real audio) and newspaper (barcode scanners for related Web sites). In the future, we may see the Internet as the primary vehicle for all mediated communication, which can be accessed via a range of interface devices.

The Internet has had a tremendous impact on organizational environments and the workplace. Both global connectivity and virtual work environments have lead to increased productivity. Although employee satisfaction has by and large increased, many lament the vanishing separation of work and private life, and the "24/7" lifestyle associated with it. Also the idea that the Internet adds to information overload, the excessive amount of messages encountered by the individual in the Information Age, deserves exploring.

Apart from business and organizational uses, the primary focus of Internet effects studies has been on intra- and interpersonal implications. The effects are ambivalent: They are both beneficial and detrimental. The Internet helps to connect those who are isolated or mobility challenged, but it may also serve as a catalyst for further withdrawal to those who are already socially challenged. We only have anecdotal evidence about the impact of the Internet on "vices" such as pornography use. One can, however, assume that it is yet another channel for access and thus might lead to similar, if not amplified, effects as exposure to sexually explicit media through other channels. For adolescents, in particular, the increased realism of sexually explicit chat and "Webcam" type sites may lead to further confusion of reality and fiction in intimate relationships.

REFERENCES

Anderson, C. A., & Dill, K. E. (2000). Video games and aggressive thoughts, feelings, and behavior in the laboratory and in life. *Journal of Personality and Social Psychology, 78,* 772–790.

Bryant, J., & Love, C. (1996). Entertainment as the driver of New Information Technology. In R. R. Dholakia, N. Mundorf, & N. Dholakia (Eds.), *New infotainment technologies in the home: Demand-side perspectives* (pp. 35–58). Mahwah, NJ: Lawrence Erlbaum Associates.

Cairncross, F. (1997). *The Death of Distance (DOD).* Boston, MA: Harvard Business School Press.

Carey, J. (2000, November 10). *AudienceDemand for TV over the internet.* New York: Columbia University, CITI Conference, "TV over the Internet."

Cavanaugh, C. (1999). *The effectiveness of interactive distance education technologies in K–12 learning: A meta-analysis.* Research report intended for practitioners and teachers (ERIC Document Reproduction Service No. ED 430 547).

Clark, K. (1997, November 24). Home is where the work is. *Fortune,* 219.

Cohn, M. (2000). Internet U. *Spring House, 13*(1), 46–59.

Cole, J. (2000). *Surveying the digital future.* Los Angeles: UCLA Center for Communication Policy.

Daft, R. (1989). *Organization theory and design.* (3rd ed.). St. Paul, MN: West.

Dholakia, N., Mundorf, N., Dholakia, R. R., & Xiao, J. (2000, October). *Interactions of transportation and telecommunications behaviors in relations to RIIR: Modeling the user perspective.* 13th Rhode Island Transportation Forum, Kingston.

Garhammer, M., & Mundorf, N. (1997). *Teleheimarbeit und Telecommuting: Ein deutschamerikanischer Vergleich.* [Telework and telecommuting: A German-American comparison]. *Zeitschrift fuer Arbeitswissenschaft,* 232–239.

Fortin, D. (1997). *The impact of interactivity on advertising effectiveness.* Doctoral Dissertation, University of Rhode Island, Kingston.

Gerrity, T. P. (1971). Design of man-machine decision systems: An application to portfolio management. *Sloan Management Review, 12,* 59–75.

Goertz. (1995). Wie interaktiv sind die neuen Medien? Auf dem Weg zu einer Definition von Interaktivität. [How interactive are the new media? On the way towards a definition of interactivity]. *Rundfunk und Fernsehen, 43,* 477–493.

Goldberg, D. (1998, April). Learning from a distance. *Washington Post,* R04–R08.

Hammer, M., & Mangurian, G. E. (1987, Winter). The changing value of communications technology. *Sloan Management Review, 29,* 65–71.

Hanisch, S. (1999). *Let's go to the voomies. Der Einfluss von Persoenlichkeitsmerkmalen auf die Affinitaet zu Neuen Medien* [The influence of personality traits on the affinity to the new media]. Unpublished diploma thesis, University of Music and Theater, Hannover, Germany.

Hecht, J., & Klass, P. (1999). *The evolution of qualitative and quantitative research classes when delivered via distance education.* Paper presented at the annual meeting of the American Educational Research Association, Ontario, Canada. (ERIC Document Reproduction Service No. ED 430 480).

Hodge-Hardin, S. (1997). *Interactive television vs. a traditional classroom setting: A comparison of student math achievement.* Mid-South Instructional Technology Conference Proceedings, Murfreesboro, TN. (ERIC Document Reproduction Service No. ED 430 521).

Katz, J. E., & Aspden, P. (1997). A nation of strangers? *Communications of the AMC, 40,* 81–86.

Kraut, R., Patterson, M., Lundmark, V., Kiesler, S., Mukopadhyay, T., & Scherlis, W. (1998). Internet paradox: A social technology that reduces social involvement and psychological well-being? *American Psychologist, 53,* 1017–1031.

Levy, S. (1999, May 31). The new digital galaxy. *Newsweek,* 57–63.

Lockwood Tooher, N. (2000, February 14). The next big thing: Interactivity. *Providence Journal,* A1, A7.

McKenna, K. Y. A., & Bargh, J. A. (1999). Causes and consequences of social interaction on the Internet: A conceptual framework. *Media Psychology, 1,* 249–269.

Mottl, J. (2000). Learn at a distance. *Information Week, 767,* 75–78.

Mundorf, N., Bryant, J., & Brownell, W. (1997). Information Technology and the Elderly. In N. Al-Deen (Ed.), *Cross-cultural communication and aging in the United States* (pp. 43–62). Hillsdale, NJ: Lawrence Erlbaum Associates.

Mundorf, N., & Westin, S. (1996). Adoption of information technology: Contributing factors. In R. R. Dholakia, N. Mundorf, & N. Dholakia (Eds.), *New infotainment technolo-*

gies in the home: Demand-side perspectives (pp. 157–172). Mahwah, NJ: Lawrence Erlbaum Associates.

Nie, N. H., & Ebring, L. (2000). Internet and society: A preliminary report. Stanford, CA: Institute for the Quantitative Study of Society.

Ostroff, F. (1999). The horizontal organization. New York: Oxford Press.

Oravec, J. A. (2000). Internet and computer technology hazards: Perspectives for family counselling. British Journal of Guidance and Counselling, 28, 309–324.

Ottway, H., & Peltu, M. (1984). New office technology: The managerial challenge. Norwood, NJ: Ablex.

Papacharissi, Z., & Rubin, A. (2000). Predictors of Internet use. Journal of Broadcasting and Electronic Media, 175–196.

Parks, M. R., & Floyd, K. (1996). Making friends in cyberspace. Journal of Communication, 46, 80–97.

Petrie, H., & Gunn, D. (1998, December). Internet "addiction": The effects of sex, age, depression, and introversion. Paper presented at the British Psychological Society, London.

Putnam, R. (2000). Bowling alone: The collapse and revival of American community. New York: Simon & Schuster.

Rice, R. E. (1984). Mediated group communication. In R. E. Rice & Associates (Ed.), The new media: Communication, research and technology (pp. 129–154). Beverly Hills, CA: Sage.

Rogers, E. (1986). Communication technology: The new media in society. New York: Free Press.

Rockwell, S. C., & Bryant, J. (1999). Enjoyment of interactivity in an entertainment program for children. Medien-Psychologie, 244–259.

Rosen, M., & Astley, G. (1988). Christmas time and control: An exploration in the social structure of formal organizations. Research in the Sociology of Organizations, 6, 159–182.

Schonfeld, E. (2000, November). Don't just sit there, do something. E-company, 155–164.

Simon, H. A. (1977). The new science of management decision (rev. ed.). Upper Saddle River, NJ: Prentice Hall.

Sprague, R. H., & Carlson, E. D. (1982). Building effective decision support systems. Upper Saddle River, NJ: Prentice Hall.

Stallard J. J., Smith, E. R., & Reese, D. (1983). The electronic office: A guide for managers. Homewood, IL: Dow Jones Irwin.

Steuer, J. (1992). Defining virtual reality: Dimensions determining telepresence. Journal of Communication, 42(4), 73–93.

Stipp, H. (1998, July). Should TV marry PC? American Demographics, 20, 16–21.

Straus, S. G. (1997). Technology, group processes, and group outcomes: Testing the connections in performance in computer-mediated and face-to-face groups. Human-Computer Interaction, 12, 227–266.

Tamborini, R. (2000). The experience of telepresence in violent video games. Paper presented at the National Communication Association, Seattle, WA.

Tamborini, R., Eastin, M., Lachlan, K., Fediuk, T. Brady, R., & Skalski, P. (2000, November). The effects of violent virtual video games on aggressive thoughts and behaviors. Paper presented at the 86th annual convention of the National Communication Association, Seattle, WA.

Time Warner is pulling the plug on a visionary foray into interactive TV. (1997, May 11). Providence Journal, A17.

Venkatesh, A. (1996). Computers and other interactive technologies for the home. Communications of the ACM, 39, 47–54.

Vorderer, P. (2000). Interactive entertainment and beyond. In D. Zillmann & P. Vorderer. (Eds.), Media entertainment: The psychology of its appeal (pp. 21–36). Mahwah, NJ: Lawrence Erlbaum Associates.

Walther, J. B. (1997). Group and interpersonal effects in international computer-mediated collaboration: A meta-analysis of social and anti-social communication. *Human Communication Research, 23,* 342–369.

Watad, M., & DiSanzo, F. J. (2000, Winter). Case study: The synergism of telecommuting and office automation *Sloan Management Review, 41*(2), 85–96.

Whisler, T. L. (1970). *The impact of computers on organization.* New York: Praeger.

White, H., McConnell, E., Clipp, E., & Bynum, L. (1999). Surfing the net in later life: A review of the literature and pilot study of computer use and quality of life. *Journal of Applied Gerontology, 18,* 358–378.

Author Index

Page numbers in italics denote full bibliographic information.

A

Aaker, D.A., *179, 189, 360, 390*
Aakewr, J.L., *176, 189*
Abel, G.G., *319, 326*
Abelman, R., *534, 542*
Abelson, R.P., *73, 94*
Abramson, P.R., *311, 316, 326*
Achabal, D.D., *462, 482*
Adams, C., *157, 189*
Adams, S.M., *321, 329*
Adams, W.C., *224, 255*
Adhikarya, R., *446, 448*
Adoni, H., *137, 149, 532, 542*
Agro, A., *461, 488*
Ahern, R.K., *434, 448, 449*
Ahrens, A.H., *467, 487*
Ahrens, M.B., *470, 471, 486*
Aidman, A.J., *308, 331*
Ajzen, I., *74, 92, 186, 189, 191, 226, 258, 389, 390, 432, 448*
Akhavan-Majid, R., *223, 256*
Alario, A., *289, 305*
Alba, J., *384, 390*
Alba, J.W., *176, 179,189*
Albert, S.M., *164, 192*
Alcalay, R., *439, 448*
Alcaraz, J.E., *467, 480*
Alessi, C., *169, 192*
Alessis, C., *29, 40,*
Alexander, A., *533, 536, 538, 542, 545*
Alexander, K.L., *419, 422*
Alicke, M.D., *491, 503*
Alioto, J.T., *274, 282*
Allen, M., *315, 320, 325, 326*
Allen, S.G., *223, 230, 231, 240, 251, 262*

Allport, G.W., *516, 520*
Allred, E., *469, 470, 472, 482*
Alpers, P., *276, 282*
Altheide, D.L, *221, 256*
Altman, D.G., *461, 480*
Aluja-Fabregat, A., *281, 282, 509, 510, 520*
Alvarez, R.M., *248, 256*
Amor, D.L., *235, 240, 241, 256, 260, 262*
Amundson, D., *335, 349*
Anderman, E.M., *415, 423*
Anderson, C., *282, 368, 390*
Anderson, C.A., *99, 102, 106, 107, 109, 110, 111, 116, 279, 280, 282, 589, 599*
Anderson, D., *375, 391*
Anderson, D.N., *400, 419, 421*
Anderson, D.R., *400, 402, 407, 420, 421, 422, 423*
Anderson, E., *361, 390, 550, 578*
Anderson, J., *103, 116*
Anderson, J.A., *531, 542*
Anderson, J.D., *499, 504*
Anderson, K.B., *102, 107, 116*
Anderson, R.L., *310, 325, 329*
Andsager, J., *12, 17, 103,*
Ansolabehere, S., *226, 246, 256*
Apple, R.W., *515, 520*
Appleton, H., *399, 422*
Apter, M.J., *558, 578*
Arend, R.A., *565, 566, 580*
Ariely, D., *383, 393*
Armstrong, C.A., *467, 480*
Armstrong, C.B., *537, 540, 542*
Armstrong, G., *343, 344, 347*
Armstrong, G.B., *415, 421*
Arndt, J., *494, 506*
Arpan-Ralstin, L.A., *112, 119*

Subject Index